LONELY PLANET PUBLICATIONS

KT-539-743

ANDREW BURKE
AUSTIN BUSH

BANGKOK
CITY GUIDE

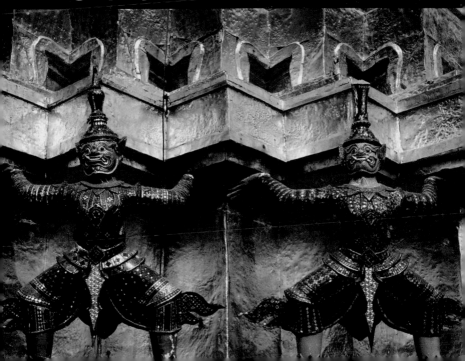

INTRODUCING BANGKOK

The mesmerising spires of Wat Pho (p57)

Same same, but different. It's Thailish T-shirt philosophy that neatly sums up Bangkok, a city combining the tastes of many places into a unique and often-spicy dish that is never, ever boring.

Such contradictions give the City of Angels its rich, multi-faceted personality. Delve just a little deeper and you'll find a city of climate-controlled mega-malls and international brand names just minutes from 200-year-old village homes; of gold-spired Buddhist temples sharing space with neon-lit strips of sleaze; of slow-moving rivers of cars bypassed by long-tail boats plying the royal river; and of streets lined with food carts selling Thai classics for next to nothing, overlooked by restaurants on top of skyscrapers serving international cuisine.

If all this sounds dizzying, rest assured that despite its international flavour, Bangkok remains resolutely Thai. The capital's cultural underpinnings are evident in virtually all facets of everyday life, and most enjoyably through the Thai sense of *sànùk*, loosely translated as 'fun'. In Thailand anything worth doing – even work – should have an element of *sànùk*. Whether you're ordering food, changing money or haggling at the vast Chatuchak Market, it will usually involve a sense of playfulness – a dash of flirtation, perhaps – and a smile.

In fairness, there are times in Bangkok that are more fun than others. The city's three seasons (cool, hot and wet) are all pretty warm, but November to February is the most enjoyable – not that the rest of the year is impossible – and the tropical storms of the wet season bring a dramatic relief.

BANGKOK LIFE

With almost half of Thailand's urban population squeezed into the capital, it's understandable that most change in the land of smiles begins here. Change doesn't come much more sweeping than a *coup d'etat*. Bangkokians, who have a tendency towards great swings between political apathy and extraordinary groundswells of activism, were integral in creating the conditions for the coup that ousted former prime minister Thaksin Shinawatra. Yet after everybody went home, the City of Angels settled into an uncharacteristic slump.

Ironically, after 15 months where few major decisions were made and investment, major public works and a whole lot of political careers were on hold, the rest of the country voted the pro-Thaksin People's Power Party into power. Talk about a slap in the face. The election result underlined yet again the huge gulf that exists between the people of Bangkok and the rest of the country, even though most Bangkokians are originally from somewhere else.

Whether its citizens like it or not, new prime minister, Samak Sundaravej, has resurrected a range of Thaksin-era policies that don't appeal to the more free-spirited souls. A second 'war on drugs' has been declared, to the outrage of organisations such as Human Rights Watch that fears another round of extrajudicial killings. Meanwhile a renewed effort to impose 'social order' means the 1am curfew on bars is again being vigorously enforced.

The future for Thaksin's drive to promote Thai arts is uncertain, but that hasn't stopped hundreds of galleries opening in recent years. The movie business is booming and Thai and foreign critics alike speak of a Thai 'new wave', which is almost entirely focused on Bangkok. On the small screen the controversial *War of Angels* – about short-skirted flight attendants battling each other for hunky pilots – has become a major topic of conversation around the water cooler.

Earthbound traffic remains a time-consuming hassle for most Bangkokians. The city has too many cars for the available roads and during peak hours the Thai idea of *jai yen* (cool heart) – remaining unperturbed even in the most trying of situations – is tested to the full.

What these movements towards the city's future, whether in art, mass transport or urban planning, signal is that the turbulent politics and relative economic slowdown have done little to blunt Bangkok's almost urgent rush forward. Jump on.

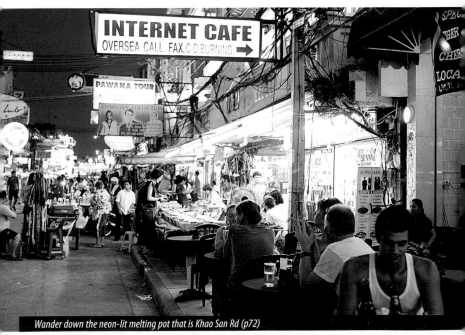

Wander down the neon-lit melting pot that is Khao San Rd (p72)

3

HIGHLIGHTS

BANGKOK BY DAY

Bangkok by day is about gold-topped temples, unfeasibly large Buddha images, royal palaces and, ahm, traffic. Less touristy but just as memorable are the heaving markets, the vibrantly green parks and the serene chaos of the river.

 **Jim Thompson's House**
Walk through the legendary silk merchant's jungle-clad teak home (p97).

2 **Amulet Market**
Buy yourself some holy protection (p129).

3 **Wat Arun**
Cross the river to this landmark stupa with its mosaic decorations (p65).

4 **Wat Pho**
Gaze at the 46m-long Reclining Buddha (p57), then get rubbed in the massage school (p57).

5 **Lumphini Park**
Escape the urban jungle in this oasis of relaxation (p106).

6 **Chatuchak Weekend Market**
Get lost in the mother of all outdoor markets (p140).

7 **Dusit Park**
Witness the Victorian sense and Thai sensibilities merge in this royal enclave (p80).

BANGKOK BY NIGHT

The City of Angels is possibly most famous (or infamous) for its after hours action, but there's more than just skin shows. Think sunset cocktails atop skyscrapers, romantic dinners in fine restaurants, rocking alternative bars and...muay thai fight nights.

① Banglamphu Bars
Follow your ears around Bangkok's hip alternative music scene (p176).

② Soi 11 Clubs
Dance down Bangkok's premier clubbing *soi* to Bed Supperclub (p183) and Q Bar (p182).

③ Spring
Eat modern Asian seafood while relaxing on a beanbag in the garden (p167).

④ Food
Taste delicious food from a swish restaurant or roadside stall (p153).

⑤ Lumphini Stadium
Soak up the action and atmosphere in this Bangkok institution (p199).

⑥ Moon Bar at Vertigo
Drink in the sunset from the roof of a skyscraper (p177).

⑦ Face
Eat sumptuous Thai food amid teak, jungle and ponds (p166).

① Songkran
Celebrate New Year, or perhaps it's really just the world's biggest water fight (p13).

② Ayuthaya
Cycle around the monumental remains of the old Siamese kingdom (p226).

③ Loi Krathong
Float your bad luck down the river with the rest of Bangkok (p14).

④ Kanchanaburi
Take the train across the bridge over the River Kwai (p242).

FESTIVALS & EXCURSIONS

Most of Bangkok's festivals combine a spiritual or serious element with an unashamed pursuit of sanuk, aka 'fun' – where else can you have a bucket of water thrown over you by laughing locals to celebrate the new year? Excursions are also fun, be it to an old royal capital, forested national park, beaches or sleepy riverside towns.

CONTENTS

INTRODUCING BANGKOK 2

HIGHLIGHTS 4

THE AUTHORS 11

GETTING STARTED 12
When to Go 12
Costs & Money 14
Internet Resources 15

BACKGROUND 16
History 16
Arts 26
Architecture 37
Environment & Planning 40
Culture & Identity 42
Government & Politics 44
Media 45
Fashion 46

NEIGHBOURHOODS 47
Itinerary Builder 50
Ko Ratanakosin & Thonburi 54
Banglamphu 67
Thewet & Dusit 78
Chinatown 82
Local Voices 89
Siam Square, Pratunam, Ploenchit & Ratchathewi 97
Riverside, Silom & Lumphini 106
Thanon Sukhumvit 116
Greater Bangkok 123

SHOPPING 127
Ko Ratanakosin & Thonburi 128
Banglamphu 130
Chinatown 131

Siam Square, Pratunam & Ploenchit 132
Riverside, Silom & Lumphini 136
Thanon Sukhumvit 138
Greater Bangkok 139

EATING 143
Ko Ratanakosin & Thonburi 154
Banglamphu 155
Thewet & Dusit 157
Chinatown 158
Siam Square, Pratunam & Ploenchit 160
Riverside, Silom & Lumphini 160
Thanon Sukhumvit 165
Greater Bangkok 170

DRINKING & NIGHTLIFE 173
Drinks 174
Drinking 175
Gay & Lesbian Bangkok 178
Live Music 180
Clubbing 182
Go-Go Bars 185

ENTERTAINMENT & THE ARTS 187
Theatre & Dance 188
Dinner Theatre 189
Kàthoey Cabaret 190
Cinemas 190
Galleries 191

SPORTS & ACTIVITIES 195
Health & Fitness 196
Activities 198
Spectator Sports 198

Continued from previous page.

SLEEPING　　　　**201**

Ko Ratanakosin &
Thonburi　　　　202
Banglamphu　　　　203
Thewet & Dusit　　　　207
Chinatown　　　　207
Siam Square & Pratunam　　209
Riverside & Silom　　　211
Lumphini & East Sathon　　215
Thanon Sukhumvit　　　216
Greater Bangkok　　　220

EXCURSIONS　　　**223**

TRANSPORT　　　**250**

DIRECTORY　　　**256**

LANGUAGE　　　**272**

BEHIND THE SCENES　**277**

INDEX　　　　**286**

WORLD TIME ZONES　**295**

MAP LEGEND　　　**296**

THE AUTHORS

Andrew Burke

Andrew has been coming to Bangkok long enough to remember Th Khao San with barely any neon and Sukhumvit traffic before the Skytrain (not a good memory). Since then he's spent 15 years travelling through, photographing and writing about Asia, the Middle East and Africa, and the last eight living in Hong Kong, Phnom Penh and now the manic megalopolis that is Bangkok. Andrew has written or contributed to more than 15 books for Lonely Planet, including *Thailand's Islands & Beaches*, *Laos*, *Iran* and *The Asia Book*.

ANDREW'S TOP BANGKOK DAY

This morning, I'll take the Chao Phraya Express (p253) up to Th Saphan Phut and start on a Chinatown walking tour (p86). I'll eat breakfast at any street stall that takes my fancy and continue south to Talat Noi. I'll take a river ferry ride up to Wang Lang, then the cross-river ferry to Tha Hua Chang. Time for lunch at one of the restaurants overhanging the river before getting the camera out and delving into the amulet market (p129). Then I'll head to Wat Pho (p57) for a massage. It's now time for a drink at the Deck (p154) to enjoy the views over Wat Arun (p65). Friends join me for dinner here before we head to Banglamphu for more drinks.

Austin Bush

After graduating from the University of Oregon with a degree in linguistics, Austin received a scholarship to study Thai at Chiang Mai University and has remained in Thailand ever since. After working several years at a stable job, he made the questionable decision to pursue a career as a freelance photographer/writer. This choice has since taken him as far as northern Pakistan, and as near as Bangkok's Or Tor Kor Market. He enjoys writing and taking photos about food most of all because it's a great way to connect with people.

LONELY PLANET AUTHORS

Why is our travel information the best in the world? It's simple: our authors are independent, dedicated travellers. They don't research using just the internet or phone, and they don't take freebies, so you can rely on their advice being well researched and impartial. They travel widely, to all the popular spots and off the beaten track. They personally visit thousands of hotels, restaurants, cafés, bars, galleries, palaces, museums and more – and they take great pride in getting all the details right and telling it like it is. Think you can do it? Find out how at lonelyplanet.com

The legendary traffic notwithstanding, Bangkok is an easy place to travel and one of the safest cities in Asia. Transport is cheap and fairly efficient, enough people speak English to help you out and there are hundreds of hotels (p202) and restaurants (p144) catering to any budget. Bangkok is well-wired so it's easy to research most lodgings and events online.

WHEN TO GO

The 'City of Angels' has three distinct seasons: the hot season runs from March to May or June, followed by the rainy season until November, and the cool season from November until the end of February. With its low humidity, relatively low temperatures and clear skies, the cool season is the best time to visit, though regular days of high 20s and low 30s might leave you wondering just who came up with the term 'cool'. The hot season vivifies the famous Noel Coward verse: 'In Bangkok at twelve o'clock they foam at the mouth and run, But mad dogs and Englishmen go out in the midday sun.' The fresh winds from February to April are a relief, but May is deadly. The monsoon season brings rain almost daily, but it's rare that it will rain all day and it's often limited to a short, refreshing afternoon downpour.

Not surprisingly, Bangkok's peak tourist season is during the cool season, with a secondary peak during July and August. If your main objective is to avoid crowds and to take advantage of discounted rooms and low-season rates, come during April to June and September and October.

FESTIVALS

Bangkok hosts an ever-more-eclectic mix of festivals, from Buddhist celebrations to celebrations of hefty women. Dates and venues often vary from year to year, either because the festival adheres to the lunar calendar or local authorities change festival days. Either way, pinning down exact dates is difficult. The Tourism Authority of Thailand (www.tourismthailand.org) features some festivals, but many others have no or long out-of-date websites. Good luck. On Buddhist holidays it's illegal to sell alcohol so bars stay closed. For a list of public holidays, see p260. For a lunar calendar, see http://kalender-365.de/lunar-calendar.php.

January & February

CHINESE NEW YEAR

From late January to late February, Bangkok's large Thai-Chinese population celebrate their lunar new year, called *trùt jiin* in Thai, with a week full of house cleaning, lion dances and fireworks. The most impressive festivities, unsurprisingly, take place in Chinatown.

MAKHA BUCHA

Makha Bucha is held on the full moon of the third lunar month (late February to early March) to commemorate the Buddha preaching to 1250 enlightened monks who came to hear him 'without prior summons'. The festival culminates with a candle-lit walk around the main chapel at every *wat*.

March

BANGKOK INTERNATIONAL FASHION WEEK

www.thaicatwalk.com
Thai designers show their work in this trade fair that is busy with catwalk shows and parties, usually in mid-March. If you want a seat but don't have a ticket, be sure to look the part. In 2008 the rival Elle Bangkok Fashion Week (try www.thailandfashion.net) held its spring/summer show at the same time.

KITE-FLYING SEASON

During the windy season from mid-February to early April colourful kites battle it out over the skies of Sanam Luang and Lumphini Park. The Thailand International Kite Festival is held at this time every second year; next in 2010.

WORLD THAI MARTIAL ARTS FESTIVAL

Ayuthaya World Heritage Site
Week-long Muay Thai festival in mid-March with a spiritual aspect, the ancient Waikru Muay Thai ceremony.

April

SONGKRAN FESTIVAL
Songkran is the celebration of the Thai New Year on 13 to 15 April. Those Bangkokians who don't head home for the holiday observe traditional rites such as Buddha images being 'bathed' and monks and elders receiving the respect of younger Thais through the sprinkling of water over their hands. Travellers tend to become thoroughly immersed in one mega-waterfight or another. The biggest are organised shows at Th Khao San (p130) and Patpong (p137), where you can arm yourself with a high-calibre water gun and go beserk. Don't carry anything you don't want to get wet.

MISS JUMBO QUEEN CONTEST
With fat trends creeping across the globe, Thailand hosts a beauty pageant for extra-large (over 80kg) women who display the grace of an elephant at Nakhon Pathom's Samphran Elephant Park.

May

ROYAL PLOUGHING CEREMONY
Sanam Luang (Map p56)
To kick off the official rice-planting season in early May, either the king or the crown prince participates in this ancient Brahman ritual that culminates in sacred white oxen ploughing the earth. Thousands gather to watch, including farmers from across Thailand.

VISAKHA BUCHA
Full moon of 6th lunar month
Visakha Bucha is considered the date of the Buddha's birth, enlightenment and *parinibbana* (passing away). Activities are centred on the local wat, with candle-lit processions, chanting and sermonising, while a larger festival is held at Sanam Luang.

July

ASANHA BUCHA & KHAO PHANSA
Full moon of 8th lunar month
This Buddhist festival commemorates the day the Buddha preached his first sermon after attaining enlightenment and is marked at Theravada Buddhist temples with a candle-lit procession at night. The following day is *khao phansǎa*, the beginning of the Buddhist rains retreat when young men traditionally enter the monkhood for the rainy season, and all monks sequest themselves in a monastery for three months. It's a good time to observe a Buddhist ordination.

BANGKOK INTERNATIONAL FILM FESTIVAL
www.bangkokfilm.org
Dates and venues are notoriously fickle for Bangkok's two film festivals, but this one usually runs for 10 days and most recently was held at SF Cinema (p191) in late July. About 150 films are shown, with an emphasis on Asian cinema. Events end with the awarding of the festival's Golden Kinnaree in a range of categories. For popular films, book ahead.

September

WORLD GOURMET FESTIVAL
The Four Seasons hotel (p209) hosts Bangkok's premier food event, bringing together international chefs for a 10-day feast.

INTERNATIONAL FESTIVAL OF MUSIC & DANCE
www.bangkokfestivals.com
Usually held at the Thailand Cultural Centre (p189), this month-long festival presents international and local orchestral music, jazz, ballet, opera and world music.

THAILAND INTERNATIONAL SWAN BOAT RACES
www.thailandgrandfestival.com
More than 20 international teams race traditional Thai-style long boats in various classes (the largest has 55 paddlers) along Mae Nam Chao Phraya in Ayuthaya.

October

NAVARATREE HINDU FESTIVAL
Centred around the Sri Mariamman Temple (p111) on Th Silom, this Hindu temple festival sees Th Silom pedestrianised as men worship shrines and pierce themselves before smashing coconuts on the sidewalks. Attendees should wear white.

VEGETARIAN FESTIVAL
A 10-day Chinese-Buddhist festival, *thêhtsàkaan kin jeh* wheels out streetside

vendors serving meatless meals to help cleanse the body, all announced with yellow banners. Most of the action is in Chinatown.

KING CHULALONGKORN DAY

Rama V is honoured on the anniversary of his death (23 October) at his revered Royal Plaza statue. Crowds of devotees come to make merit with incense and flower garlands.

WORLD FILM FESTIVAL

www.worldfilmbkk.com
Bangkok's other, less commercial, film festival, usually held late October to early November. In 2007 it combined with the EU Film Festival.

November

LOI KRATHONG

www.bangkoktourist.com
On the night of the full moon of the 12th lunar month, small lotus-shaped *krathong* (baskets or boats made of a section of banana trunk for flotation – don't use the Styrofoam versions – banana leaves containing flowers, incense, candles and a coin) are floated on the Mae Nam Chao Phraya and other rivers, lakes and canals across Thailand. The ceremony, which originated in Sukhothai, is both an offering to the water spirits and a symbolic cleansing of bad luck.

WAT SAKET FAIR

The grandest of Bangkok's temple fairs *(ngan wat)* is held at Wat Saket and the Golden Mount around Loi Krathong. The temple grounds turn into a colourful, noisy fair selling flowers, incense, bells and saffron cloth and tonnes of Thai food. The highlight is a candlelit circumambulation on the mount.

BANGKOK PRIDE WEEK

www.pridefestival.org
This week-long festival of parades, parties, awards, sequins and feather boas is organised by city businesses and organisations for Bangkok's gay, lesbian, bisexual and transgender community. Usually in early November. Don't miss the opening 'Pink in the Park' fair in Lumphini Park (p106).

FAT FESTIVAL

Sponsored by FAT 104.5FM radio, Bangkok's premier indie music festival has grown to include everything from pop to thrash via hip-hop, plus nonmusic alternative arts. It's usually on the first or second weekend in November; venues alternate.

December

KING'S BIRTHDAY

Celebrating King Bhumibol's birthday on 5 December, the city is festooned with lights and large portraits of the king (especially on Th Ratchadamnoen). In the afternoon, Sanam Luang is packed for a fireworks display that segues appropriately into a noisy concert with popular Thai musicians.

BANGKOK JAZZ FESTIVAL

www.bangkokjazzfestival.com
Started in 2003, the three-night jazz fest kicks off at Sanam Suea Pa at Dusit in commemoration of His Majesty the King's love of jazz. The line-up usually includes internationally known artists such as Larry Carlton, Earl Klugh and Bob James – focusing on the lighter side of jazz, per Thai public taste.

CONCERT IN THE PARK

www.bangkoksymphony.net
Playing every Sunday evening (from 5.30pm to 7.30pm) between mid-December and mid-February at Lumphini Park.

PHRA NAKHON SI AYUTHAYA WORLD HERITAGE FAIR

Ayuthaya
A series of cultural performances and evening sound-and-light shows among the ruins of the World Heritage site in the former Thai capital.

COSTS & MONEY

Bangkok is inexpensive by Western standards but you can still burn through a lot of baht if you choose. On the tightest of budgets you could scrape by on about 700B a day, staying in the simplest guesthouse accommodation, eating mainly street food, seeing a sight or two, taking local transport and buying horrible Chang beer at 7-Elevens. With closer to 2000B you can creep into the comforts of the mid-range, and with 3000B you can find a dash of style, a decent restaurant meal and

HOW MUCH?

Skytrain ride 15–40B

Chao Phraya Express boat ride 10–34B

3km taxi ride 50–100B, depending on traffic

640ml Singha beer from bar 60–120B

1L petrol 33B

500ml/1.5L bottle water 7/15B

Phat thai 25–40B

Cup of coffee 40–70B

Two-hour traditional Thai massage 400–4000B

Souvenir T-shirt 160–250B

perhaps a rooftop cocktail or two. If you plan on frequenting the city's best hotels, restaurants and clubs you're looking at more than 5000B a day. See p209 for detailed accommodation costs and p154 for meal costs. These numbers are for solo travellers, and per person costs fall if you're travelling as a couple.

Getting your hands on Thai baht is easy enough through the city's thousands of ATMs. Credit cards are widely accepted; see p263.

INTERNET RESOURCES

Take a look at these websites to help plan your trip.

Bangkok Recorder (www.bangkokrecorder.com) For what's on, mainly in bars and clubs.

Bangkok Scam (www.bangkokscam.com) Forewarned is forearmed.

Bangkok Tourist (www.bangkoktourist.com) Enough Bangkok sights to fill a lifetime of sightseeing.

Lonely Planet (www.lonelyplanet.com) Country-specific information as well as reader information exchange on the Thorn Tree forum.

Thai Students Online (www.thaistudents.com) Sriwittayapaknam School in Samut Prakan maintains one of Thailand's most informative websites.

Thailand Daily (www.thailanddaily.com) Part of World News Network, offering a thorough digest of Thailand-related news in English.

Tourism Authority of Thailand (www.tourismthailand .org) Handy planning hints and events guide.

BACKGROUND

HISTORY

Since the late 18th century, the history of Bangkok has essentially been the history of Thailand. Many of the country's defining events have unfolded here, and today the language, culture and food of the city have come to represent those of the entire country. This role is unlikely, given the city's origins as little more than an obscure Chinese trading port, but today boasting a population of 10 million, it is certain that Bangkok will be shaping Thailand's history for some time to come.

FROM THE BEGINNING – AYUTHAYA & THONBURI

Before it became the capital of Thailand in 1782, the tiny settlement known as Baang Màkàwk was merely a backwater village opposite the larger Thonburi Si Mahasamut on the banks of Mae Nam Chao Phraya, not far from the Gulf of Siam.

Thonburi Si Mahasamut itself had been founded on the right bank of the Chao Phraya River by a group of wealthy Thais during the reign of King Chakkaphat (1548–68) as an important relay point for sea and riverborne trade between the Gulf of Siam and Ayuthaya, 86km upriver. Ayuthaya served as the royal capital of Siam – as Thailand was then known – from 1350 to 1767. Encircled by rivers with access to the gulf, Ayuthaya flourished as a river port courted by Dutch, Portuguese, French, English, Chinese and Japanese merchants. By the end of the 17th century the city's population had reached one million and Ayuthaya was one of the wealthiest and most powerful cities in Asia. Virtually all foreign visitors claimed it to be the most illustrious city they had ever seen, beside which London and Paris paled in comparison.

Throughout four centuries of Ayuthaya reign, European powers tried without success to colonise the kingdom of Siam. An Asian power finally subdued the capital when the Burmese sacked Ayuthaya in 1767, destroying most of its Buddhist temples and royal edifices.

Many Siamese were marched off to Pegu (Bago, Myanmar today), where they were forced to serve the Burmese court. However, the remaining Siamese regrouped under Phaya Taksin, a half-Chinese, half-Thai general who decided to move the capital further south along Chao Phraya River, closer to the Gulf of Siam. Thonburi Si Mahasamut was a logical choice.

Succumbing to mental illness, Taksin came to regard himself as the next Buddha, and his behaviour became increasingly violent and bizarre. Monks who wouldn't worship him as the Maitreya (the future Buddha) would be flogged, for example. Disapproving of his religious fantasies and fearing the king had lost his mind, his ministers deposed Taksin and then executed him in the custom reserved for royalty – by sealing him inside a velvet sack (so that no royal blood touched the ground) and beating him to death with a scented sandalwood club in 1782.

The Chakri Dynasty & the Birth of Bangkok

One of Taksin's key generals, Phraya Chakri, came to power and was crowned in 1782 as Phra Yot Fa. Fearing Thonburi to be vulnerable to Burmese attack from the west, Chakri moved the

1548–68	1768	1782
Thonburi Si Mahasamut, at the time little more than a Chinese trading post on the right bank of Mae Nam Chao Phraya, is founded.	King Taksin the Great moves the Thai capital from Ayuthaya to Thonburi Si Mahasamut, a location he regarded as beneficial for both trade and defence.	Phutthayotfa Chulalok, known today as King Rama I, re-establishes the Siamese court across the river from Thonburi, resulting in the creation of both the current Thai capital and the Chakri Dynasty.

Siamese capital across the river to Baang Màkàwk (Olive Plum riverbank), named for the trees that grew there in abundance. As the first monarch of the new Chakri royal dynasty – which continues to this day – Phraya Chakri was posthumously dubbed King Rama I.

The first task set before the planners of the new city was to create hallowed ground for royal palaces and Buddhist monasteries. Astrologers divined that construction of the new royal palace should begin on 6 May 1782, and ceremonies consecrated Rama I's transfer to a temporary new residence a month later.

Construction of permanent throne halls, residence halls and palace temples followed.

The plan of the original buildings, their position relative to the river and the royal chapel, and the royal parade and cremation grounds to the north of the palace (today's Sanam Luang) exactly copied the royal compound at Ayuthaya. Master craftsmen who had survived the sacking of Ayuthaya created the designs for several of the more magnificent temples and royal administrative buildings in the new capital.

Upon completion of the royal district in 1785, at a three-day consecration ceremony attended by tens of thousands of Siamese, the city was given a new name: 'Krungthep mahanakhon amon-ratanakosin mahintara ayuthaya mahadilok popnopparat ratchathani burirom udomratchaniwet mahasathan amonpiman avatansathit sakkathattiya witsanukamprasit'. This lexical gymnastic feat translates roughly as: 'Great City of Angels, the Repository of Divine Gems, the Great Land Unconquerable, the Grand and Prominent Realm, the Royal and Delightful Capital City full of Nine Noble Gems, the Highest Royal Dwelling and Grand Palace, the Divine Shelter and Living Place of Reincarnated Spirits'.

Foreign traders continued to call the capital Bang Makok, which eventually truncated itself to 'Bangkok', the name most commonly known to the outside world. The Thais, meanwhile, commonly use a shortened version of the name, Krung Thep (City of Angels) or, when refer-ring to the city and burgeoning metropolitan area surrounding it, Krung Thep Mahanakhon (Metropolis of the City of Angels).

In time, Ayuthaya's control of tribute states in Laos and western Cambodia (including Angkor, ruled by the Siamese from 1432 to 1859) was transferred to Bangkok, and thousands of prisoners of war were brought to the capital to work as coolie labour. Bangkok also had ample access to free Thai labour via the *phrâi lǔang* (commoner/noble) system, under which all commoners were required to provide labour to the state in lieu of taxes.

Using this immense pool of labour, Rama I augmented Bangkok's natural canal-and-river system with hundreds of artificial waterways feeding into Thailand's hydraulic lifeline, the broad Mae Nam Chao Phraya. Chakri also ordered the construction of 10km of city walls and *khlawng râwp krung* (canals around the city), to create a royal 'island' – Ko Ratanakosin – be-tween Mae Nam Chao Phraya and the canal loop. Sections of the 4.5m-thick walls still stand in Wat Saket and the Golden Mount, and water still flows, albeit sluggishly, in the canals of the original royal district.

The break with Ayuthaya was ideological as well as temporal. As Chakri shared no bloodline with earlier royalty, he garnered loyalty by modelling himself as a Dhammaraja (dhamma king) supporting Buddhist law rather than a Devaraja (god king) linked to the divine.

Under the second and third reigns of the Chakri dynasty, more temples were built and the system of rivers, streams and natural canals surrounding the capital was augmented by the excavation of additional waterways. Waterborne traffic dominated the city, supplemented by a meagre network of footpaths, well into the middle of the 19th century.

1783	1785	1779
Chinese residents of the present-day Ko Ratanakosin area of Bangkok are relocated upriver along the Mae Nam Chao Phraya to today's Yaowarat district, resulting in the city's Chinatown.	The majority of the construction of Ko Ratanakosin, Bangkok's royal district, including famous landmarks such as the Grand Palace and Wat Phra Kaew, is finished.	After a brutal war of territorial expan-sion, the Emerald Buddha, Thailand's most sacred Buddha image, is brought to Bangkok from Laos, along with hundreds of Lao slaves.

ALL THE KINGS' WOMEN

Until polygamy was outlawed by Rama VI, it was expected of Thai monarchs to maintain a harem consisting of numerous 'major' and 'minor' wives, and the children of these relationships. This led to some truly 'extended' families: Rama I had 42 children by 28 mothers; Rama II, 73 children by 40 mothers; Rama III, 51 children by 37 mothers (he would eventually accumulate a total of 242 wives and consorts); Rama IV, 82 children by 35 mothers; and Rama V, 77 children by 40 mothers. In the case of Rama V, his seven 'major' wives were all half-sisters or first cousins, a conscious effort to maintain the purity of the bloodline of the Chakri Dynasty. Other consorts or 'minor' wives were often the daughters of families wishing to gain greater ties with the royal family.

In contrast to the precedence set by his predecessors, Rama VI had one wife and one child, a girl born only a few hours before his death. As a result, his brother, Prajadhipok, Rama VII, was appointed as his successor. Rama VII also had only one wife and failed to produce any heirs. After abdicating in 1935, he did not exercise his right to appoint a successor, and once again, lines were drawn back to Rama V, and the grandson of one of his remaining 'major' wives, nine-year-old Ananda Mahidol, was chosen to be the next king.

Temple construction remained the highlight of early development in Bangkok until the reign of Rama III (1824–51), when attention turned to upgrading the port for international sea trade. The city soon became a regional centre for Chinese trading ships, slowly surpassing even the British port at Singapore.

By the mid-19th century Western naval shipping technology had eclipsed the Chinese junk fleets. Bangkok's rulers began to feel threatened as the British and French made colonial inroads into Cambodia, Laos and Burma. This prompted the suspension of a great iron chain across Mae Nam Chao Phraya to guard against the entry of unauthorised ships.

Waterways & Roadways

During the reign of the first five Chakri kings, canal building constituted the lion's share of public works projects, changing the natural geography of the city, and city planners added two lengthy canals to one of the river's largest natural curves. The canals Khlong Rop Krung (today's Khlong Banglamphu) and Khlong Ong Ang were constructed to create Ko Ratanakosin. The island quickly accumulated an impressive architectural portfolio centred on the Grand Palace, political hub of the new Siamese capital, and the adjacent royal monastery of Wat Phra Kaew.

Throughout the early history of the Chakri Dynasty, royal administrations added to the system. Khlong Mahawawat was excavated during the reign of King Rama IV to link Mae Nam Chao Phraya with Mae Nam Tha Chin, thus expanding the canal-and-river system by hundreds of kilometres. Lined with fruit orchards and stilted houses draped with fishing nets, Khlong Mahawawat remains one of the most traditional and least visited of the Bangkok canals.

Khlong Saen Saep was built to shorten travel between Mae Nam Chao Phraya and Mae Nam Bang Pakong, and today is heavily used by boat-taxi commuters moving across the city. Likewise Khlong Sunak Hon and Khlong Damoen Saduak link up the Tha Chin and Mae Klong. Khlong Prem Prachakon was dug purely to facilitate travel for Rama V between Bangkok and Ayuthaya, while Khlong Prawet Burirom shortened the distance between Samut Prakan and Chachoengsao provinces.

1821	1851	1855
A boatload of opium marks the visit of the first Western trader to Bangkok; the trade of this substance is eventually banned nearly 20 years later.	King Mongkut, the fourth king of the Chakri Dynasty, comes to power, courts relations with the West and encourages the study of modern science in Thailand.	Bangkok, now Siam's major trading centre, begins to feel pressure from colonial influences; King Rama IV signs the Bowring Treaty, which liberalises foreign trade in Thailand.

When King Rama IV loosened Thai trade restrictions, many Western powers signed trade agreements with the monarch. He also sponsored Siam's second printing press and instituted educational reforms, developing a school system along European lines. Although the king courted the West, he did so with caution and warned his subjects: 'Whatever they have invented or done which we should know of and do, we can imitate and learn from them, but do not wholeheartedly believe in them.' Rama IV was the first monarch to show his face to the Thai public.

In 1861 Bangkok's European diplomats and merchants delivered a petition to Rama IV requesting roadways so that they could enjoy horseback riding for physical fitness and pleasure. The royal government acquiesced, and established a handful of roads suitable for horse-drawn carriages and rickshaws. The first – and the most ambitious road project for nearly a century to come – was Th Charoen Krung (also known by its English name, New Rd), which extended 10km south from Wat Pho along the east bank of Mae Nam Chao Phraya. This swath of hand-laid cobblestone, which took nearly four years to finish, eventually accommodated a tramway as well as early automobiles.

Shortly thereafter, Rama IV ordered the construction of the much shorter Bamrung Meuang (a former elephant path) and Feuang Nakhon roads to provide access to royal temples from Charoen Krung. His successor Rama V (King Chulalongkorn; 1868–1910) added the much wider Th Ratchadamnoen Klang to provide a suitably royal promenade – modelled after the Champs Elysées and lined with ornamental gardens – between the Grand Palace and the expanding commercial centre to the east of Ko Ratanakosin.

THE AGE OF POLITICS
European Influence & the 1932 Revolution

Towards the end of the 19th century, Bangkok's city limits encompassed no more than a dozen square kilometres, with a population of about half a million. Despite its modest size, the capital successfully administered the much larger kingdom of Siam – which then extended into what today are Laos, western Cambodia and northern Malaysia. Even more impressively, Siamese rulers were able to stave off intense pressure from the Portuguese, the Dutch, the French and the English, all of whom at one time or another harboured desires to add Siam to their colonial portfolios. By the end of the century, France and England had established a strong presence in every one of Siam's neighbouring countries – the French in Laos and Cambodia, and the British in Burma and Malaya.

Facing increasing pressure from British colonies in neighbouring Burma and Malaya, Rama IV signed the 1855 Bowring Treaty with Britain. This agreement marked Siam's break from an exclusive economic involvement with China, a relationship that had dominated the previous century.

The signing of this document, and the subsequent ascension of Rama V's son, King Chulalongkorn, led to the largest period of European influence on Thailand. Wishing to head off any potential invasion plans, Rama V ceded Laos and Cambodia to the French and northern Malaya to the British between 1893 and 1910. The two European powers, for their part, were happy to use Thailand as a buffer state between their respective colonial domains.

Rama V gave Bangkok 120 new roads during his reign, inspired by street plans from Batavia (the Dutch colonial centre now known as Jakarta), Calcutta, Penang and Singapore. Germans

1868	1893	1910
At the age of 15, King Chulalongkorn, the oldest son of Rama IV, becomes the fifth king of the Chakri Dynasty upon the death of his father.	After minor territory dispute, France sends gunboats to threaten Bangkok, forcing Siam to give up most of its territory east of the Mekong River; Siam gains much of its modern boundaries.	Vajiravudh becomes the sixth king of the Chakri Dynasty after the death of his older brother; he fails to produce a male heir during his reign.

were hired to design and build railways emanating from the capital, while the Dutch contributed the design of Bangkok's Hualamphong Railway Station, today considered a minor masterpiece of civic Art Deco.

In 1893 Bangkok opened its first railway line, extending 22km from Bangkok to Pak Nam, where Mae Nam Chao Phraya enters the Gulf of Thailand; at that time it cost just 1B to travel in 1st class. A 20km electric tramway opened the following year, paralleling the left bank of Mae Nam Chao Phraya. By 1904 three more rail lines out of Bangkok had been added: northeast to Khorat (306km), with a branch line to Lopburi (42km); south-southwest to Phetburi (151km); and south to Tha Chin (34km).

Italian sculptor Corrado Feroci contributed several national monuments to the city and helped found the country's first fine-arts university. Americans established Siam's first printing press along with the kingdom's first newspaper in 1864. The first Thai-language newspaper, *Darunovadha*, came along in 1874, and by 1900 Bangkok boasted three daily English-language newspapers: the *Bangkok Times*, *Siam Observer* and *Siam Free Press*.

As Bangkok prospered, many wealthy merchant families sent their children to study in Europe. Students of humbler socioeconomic status who excelled at school had access to government scholarships for overseas study as well. In 1924 a handful of Thai students in Paris formed the Promoters of Political Change, a group that met to discuss ideas for a future Siamese government modelled on Western democracy.

After finishing their studies and returning to Bangkok, three of the 'Promoters', lawyer Pridi Banomyong and military officers Phibul Songkhram and Prayoon Phamonmontri, organised an underground 'People's Party' dedicated to the overthrow of the Siamese system of government. The People's Party found a willing accomplice in Rama VII, and a bloodless revolution in 1932 transformed Thailand from an absolute monarchy into a constitutional one. Bangkok thus found itself the nerve centre of a vast new civil service, which, coupled with its growing success as a world port, transformed the city into a mecca for Thais seeking economic opportunities.

WWII & the Struggle for Democracy

Phibul Songkhram, appointed prime minister by the People's Party in December 1938, changed the country's name from Siam to Thailand and introduced the Western solar calendar. When the Japanese invaded Southeast Asia in 1941, outflanking Allied troops in Malaya and Burma, Phibul allowed Japanese regiments access to the Gulf of Thailand. Japanese troops bombed and briefly occupied parts of Bangkok on their way to the Thai–Burmese border to fight the British in Burma and, as a result of public insecurity, the Thai economy stagnated.

Phibul resigned in 1944 under pressure from the Thai underground resistance, and after V-J Day in 1945 was exiled to Japan. Bangkok resumed its pace towards modernisation, even after Phibul returned to Thailand in 1948 and took over the leadership again via a military coup. Over the next 15 years, bridges were built over Mae Nam Chao Phraya, canals were filled in to provide space for new roads, and multistorey buildings began crowding out traditional teak structures.

Another coup installed Field Marshal Sarit Thanarat in 1957, and Phibul Songkhram once again found himself exiled to Japan, where he died in 1964. From 1964 to 1973 – the peak years of the 1962–75 Indochina War – Thai army officers Thanom Kittikachorn and Praphat Charusathien ruled Thailand and allowed the US to establish several army bases within Thai borders to support the US campaign in Indochina. During this time Bangkok gained notoriety as a 'rest and recreation' (R&R) spot for foreign troops stationed in Southeast Asia.

1914	1917	1932
Official opening of Don Muang, Thailand's first international airport; the airport remained the country's main domestic and international airport until the opening of Suvarnabhumi in 2006.	Founding of Bangkok's Chulalongkorn University, the country's first Western-style institute of higher education; today the university is still regarded as the most prestigious in the country.	A bloodless coup transforms Siam from an absolute to a constitutional monarchy; the deposed king, Prajadhipok, continued to remained on the throne until his resignation three years later.

In October 1973 the Thai military brutally suppressed a large pro-democracy student demonstration at Thammasat University in Bangkok, but King Bhumiphol and General Krit Sivara, who sympathised with the students, refused to support further bloodshed, forcing Thanom and Praphat to leave Thailand. Oxford-educated Kukrit Pramoj took charge of a 14-party coalition government and steered a leftist agenda past the conservative parliament. Among Kukrit's lasting achievements were a national minimum wage, the repeal of anticommunist laws and the ejection of US military forces from Thailand.

The military regained control in 1976 after right-wing, paramilitary civilian groups assaulted a group of 2000 students holding a sit-in at Thammasat, killing hundreds. Many students fled Bangkok and joined the People's Liberation Army of Thailand (PLAT), an armed communist insurgency based in the hills, which had been active in Thailand since the 1930s.

Bangkok continued to seesaw between civilian and military rule for the next 15 years. Although a general amnesty in 1982 brought an end to the PLAT, and students, workers and farmers returned to their homes, a new era of political tolerance exposed the military once again to civilian fire.

In May 1992 several huge demonstrations demanding the resignation of the next in a long line of military dictators, General Suchinda Kraprayoon, rocked Bangkok and the large provincial capitals. Charismatic Bangkok governor Chamlong Srimuang, winner of the 1992 Magsaysay Award (a humanitarian service award issued in the Philippines) for his role in galvanising the public to reject Suchinda, led the protests. After confrontations between the protesters and the military near the Democracy Monument resulted in nearly 50 deaths and hundreds of injuries, King Bhumibol summoned both Suchinda and Chamlong for a rare public scolding. Suchinda resigned, having been in power for less than six weeks, and Chamlong's career was all but finished.

During the 20th century Bangkok grew from a mere 13 sq km in 1900 to an astounding metropolitan area of more than 330 sq km by the turn of the century. Today the city encompasses not only Bangkok proper, but also the former capital of Thonburi, across Mae Nam Chao Phraya to the west, along with the densely populated 'suburb' provinces, Samut Prakan to the east and Nonthaburi to the north. More than half of Thailand's urban population lives in Bangkok.

THE RECENT PAST
The People's Constitution & the Emergence of Thaksin

Bangkok started the new millennium riding a tide of events that set new ways of governing and living in the capital. The most defining moment occurred in July 1997 when – after several months of warning signs that nearly everyone in Thailand and the international community ignored – the Thai currency fell into a deflationary tailspin and the national economy screeched to a virtual halt. Bangkok, which rode at the forefront of the 1980s double-digit economic boom, suffered more than elsewhere in the country in terms of job losses and massive income erosion.

Two months after the crash, the Thai parliament voted in a new constitution that guaranteed – at least on paper – more human and civil rights than had ever been granted in Thailand previously. The so-called 'people's constitution' fostered great hope in a population left emotionally battered by the 1997 economic crisis.

1935–46	1946	1951–63
Ananda Mahidol, a grandson of one of Rama V's 'major' wives, is appointed king; most of his reign is spent abroad and ends abruptly when he is found shot in his room under mysterious circumstances.	Pridi Phanomyong, one of the architects of the 1932 coup, becomes Thailand's first democratically elected prime minister; after a military coup, Pridi is forced to flee Thailand, returning only briefly one more time.	Field Marshal Sarit Thanarat wrests power from Phibul Songkhram, abolishes the constitution and embarks on one of most repressive and authoritarian regimes in Thai history.

THE KING

If you see a yellow Rolls Royce flashing by along city avenues, accompanied by a police escort, you've just caught a glimpse of Thailand's longest-reigning monarch – and the longest-reigning living monarch in the world – King Bhumibol Adulyadej. Also known in English as Rama IX (the ninth king of the Chakri dynasty), Bhumibol was born in the USA in 1927, while his father Prince Mahidol was studying medicine at Harvard University.

Fluent in English, French, German and Thai, His Majesty ascended the throne in 1946 following the death of his brother Rama VIII (King Ananda Mahidol), who reigned for only one year before dying under mysterious circumstances.

An ardent jazz composer and saxophonist when he was younger, King Bhumibol has hosted jam sessions with the likes of jazz greats Woody Herman and Benny Goodman. His compositions are often played on Thai radio.

His Majesty administers royal duties from Chitralada Palace in the city's Dusit precinct, north of Ko Ratanakosin. As protector of both nation and religion, King Bhumibol traditionally presides over several important Buddhist and Brahmanist ceremonies during the year. Among the more colourful are the seasonal robe-changing of the jade Buddha in Wat Phra Kaew and the annual Royal Ploughing Ceremony, in which ceremonial rice is sowed to insure a robust economy for the coming year, at Sanam Luang.

The king and Queen Sirikit have four children: Princess Ubol Ratana (born 1951), Crown Prince Maha Vajiralongkorn (1952), Princess Mahachakri Sirindhorn (1955) and Princess Chulabhorn (1957).

After 60 years in power, and having recently reached his 80th birthday, the king is preparing for his succession. For the last few years the Crown Prince has performed most of the royal ceremonies the king would normally perform, such as presiding over the Royal Ploughing Ceremony (see p13), changing the attire on the Emerald Buddha (see p58) and handing out academic degrees at university commencements.

Along with nation and religion, the monarchy is very highly regarded in Thai society – negative comment about the king or any member of the royal family is a social as well as legal taboo.

Prime Minister Chavalit Yongchaiyudh, whose move to float the baht effectively triggered the economic crisis, was forced to resign. Former Prime Minister Chuan Leekpai was then re-elected, and proceeded to implement tough economic reforms suggested by the International Monetary Fund (IMF). During the next few years, Bangkok's economy began to show signs of recovery.

In January 2001, billionaire and former police colonel Thaksin Shinawatra became prime minister after winning a landslide victory in nationwide elections – the first in Thailand under the strict guidelines established in the 1997 constitution. Thaksin's new party called Thai Rak Thai (TRT; Thais Love Thailand) swept into power on a populist agenda that seemed at odds with the man's enormous wealth and influence.

The sixth-richest ruler in the world as of late 2003, Thaksin owned the country's only private TV station through his family-owned Shin Corporation, the country's largest telecommunications company. Shin Corp also owned Asia's first privately owned satellite company, Shin Satellite, and a large stake in Thai AirAsia, a subsidiary of the Malaysia-based Air Asia.

Mistakes, Missteps & Stumbling Blocks

Days before he became prime minister, Thaksin transferred his shares in Shin Corp to his siblings, chauffeur and even household servants in an apparent attempt to conceal his true assets.

1962	1973	1981
America's involvement in the Indochina War leads to massive economic and infrastructural expansion of Bangkok; dissatisfaction with the authoritarian Thai government leads to a period of Communist insurgency.	Large-scale student protests in Bangkok lead to violent military suppression; 1971 coup leader Thanom Kittikachorn is ordered into exile by King Bumiphol; Kukrit Pramoj's civilian government takes charge.	General Prem Tinsulanonda is appointed prime minister after a military coup and is largely able to stabilise Thai politics over the next eight years.

Eventually the country's constitutional court cleared him of all fraud charges connected with the shares transfer in a controversial eight-to-seven vote.

Thaksin publicly stated his ambition to keep his party in office for four consecutive terms, a total of 16 years. Before he had even finished his first four-year term, however, some Thais became annoyed with the government's perceived slowness to react to problems in the countryside, leading to regular demonstrations in Bangkok.

In 2003, Thaksin announced a 'War on drugs' that he claimed would free the country of illicit drug use within 90 days. Lists of alleged drug dealers and users were compiled in every province. The police were given arrest quotas to fulfil, and could lose their jobs if they didn't follow orders. Within two months, more than 2000 Thais on the government blacklist had been killed. The Thaksin administration denied accusations by the UN, the US State Department, Amnesty International and Thailand's own human rights commission that the deaths were extra-judicial killings by Thai police.

Meanwhile, in the south, a decades-old Muslim nationalist movement began to reheat after the Thaksin administration dismantled a key intelligence operation. Sporadic attacks on police stations, schools, military installations and other government institutions resulted in a string of Thai deaths. Tensions took a turn for the worse when Thai police gunned down 112 machete-wielding Muslim militants inside an historic mosque in Pattani in April 2004. Five months later, police broke up a large demonstration in southern Thailand. After around 1300 detainees were stuffed into overcrowded trucks, 78 died of suffocation or from being crushed under the weight of other arrestees.

Several other crises in public confidence shook Bangkok and the nation that same year. Firstly, avian influenza turned up in Thailand's bird population. When it became known that the administration had been aware of the infections since November 2003, the EU and Japan banned all imports of Thai chicken. Avian flu claimed the lives of eight Thais – all of whom were infected while handling live poultry – before authorities got a handle on the crisis. By mid-2004 the epidemic had cost the Thai economy 19 billion baht.

Just as the bird flu came under control, the Interior Ministry said that in March 2004, all entertainment establishments in Thailand would be required to close at midnight. In Bangkok the government exempted three districts – Patpong, Ratchada and Royal City Avenue (RCA) – in an all-too-apparent attempt to appease the city's most powerful mafia dons. Public reaction against this decision was so strong (mafia figures who control other areas of the city reportedly announced a billion-baht price on the prime minister's head) that the government back-pedalled, allowing nightspots to stay open till 1am, regardless of zoning.

Immediately on the heels of the uproar over new closing hours came the government's announcement that the Electricity Generating Authority of Thailand (EGAT) and other state enterprises would be put on an accelerated schedule for privatisation. Tens of thousands of government employees demonstrated in Bangkok, and once again the government backtracked, putting privatisation plans on hold.

In the 2004 Bangkok gubernatorial race, Democrat Apirak Kosayodhin scored an upset victory over Paveena Hongsakul, an independent candidate with the unofficial support of the ruling TRT, capturing 40% of the vote. Apirak won on promises to upgrade city services and mass transit, and to make city government more transparent – a direct challenge to Thaksin's self-dubbed CEO leadership style.

1985	1992	1997
Chamlong Srimuang is elected mayor of Bangkok; three years later, after forming his own largely Buddhist-based political group, the Palang Dharma Party, he is elected mayor again.	Street protests led by Chamlong Srimuang against 1991 coup leader Suchinda Krapprayoon lead to violent confrontations; both Chamlong and Suchinda are publicly scolded by the king, leading to Suchinda's resignation.	Thailand devalues its currency, the baht, triggering the Asian economic crisis; massive unemployment and personal debt, and a significant crash of the Thai stock market, follow.

Thaksin's Surprise Comeback & the Final Straw

During the February 2005 general elections, the Thaksin administration scored a second four-year mandate in a landslide victory with a record 19 million votes, surprising academic critics who expected the bird flu crisis, drug war deaths, early bar closing and privatisation protests to dent the party's images. Armchair observers speculated that the blame lay with the opposition's lack of a positive platform to deal with these same problems. Thaksin thus became the first Thai leader in history to be re-elected to a consecutive second term.

However, time was running short for Thaksin and party. The final straw came in January 2006, when Thaksin announced that his family had sold off its controlling interest in Shin Corp to a Singapore investment firm. Since deals made through the Stock Exchange of Thailand (SET) were exempt from capital gains tax, Thaksin's family paid no tax on the US$1.9 billion sale, which enraged Bangkok's middle class.

Many of the PM's most highly placed supporters had also turned against him. Most prominently, media mogul and former friend, Sondhi Limthongkul organised a series of massive anti-Thaksin rallies in Bangkok, culminating in a rally at Bangkok's Royal Plaza on 4 and 5 February that drew tens of thousands of protestors.

Retired major general Chamlong Srimuang, a former Bangkok governor and one of Thaksin's earliest and strongest supporters, also turned against him and joined Sondhi in leading the protests, which strengthened throughout February. Two of Thaksin's ministers resigned from the cabinet and from the TRT, adding to the mounting pressure on the embattled premier.

Thaksin's ministers responded by dissolving the national assembly and scheduling snap elections for 2 April 2006, three years ahead of schedule. The opposition was aghast, claiming that Thaksin called the election to whitewash allegations of impropriety over the Shin Corp sale.

After Thaksin refused to sign a pledge to commit to constitutional reform, the Democrats and two other major opposition parties announced that they would boycott the 2 April election. Regardless, the results gave the TRT another resounding victory, with 66% of the popular vote. However, in the Democrat-controlled south, 38 TRT candidates failed to gain the 20% of the vote required to win an uncontested national assembly seat. This led to fears of a constitutional crisis, as the government would not have enough parliamentarians to open the national assembly.

During the campaign, TRT was accused of 'hiring' smaller parties to run in the election to ensure their victory. Thaksin initially claimed victory, but after a conference with the king, announced that he would take a break from politics. Thaksin designated himself caretaker prime minister before another round of elections was scheduled for later that year.

Then on 25 April, the king gave a speech urging the judiciary to solve the deadlock. This gave the Constitutional Court a green light to nullify the elections, ostensibly due to questionable positioning of voting booths. Elections were set again for 15 October, but postponed until late November after several election commissioners were convicted of illegally aiding Mr Thaksin in the April polls.

During this time, tensions rose between Thaksin and the palace after Thaksin claimed a 'highly influential individual' planned to overthrow him. Many suspected he was speaking about Privy Council President Prem Tinsulanonda, or even the king himself.

1999	2001	2004
The BTS Skytrain, Bangkok's first expansive metro system, opens in commemoration of King Rama IX's 6th cycle (72nd) birthday; the system is currently in the process of being expanded.	Thaksin Shinawatra, Thailand's richest man, is elected prime minister on a populist platform in what some have called the most open, corruption-free election in Thai history.	The MRT, Bangkok's first underground public transport system, is opened; an accident the next year injures 140 and causes the system to shut down for two weeks.

The Bloodless Coup

On the evening of 19 September 2006, while Thaksin was attending a UN conference in New York, the Thai military led by General Sonthi Boonyaratglin took power in a bloodless coup. Calling themselves the Council for Democratic Reform under the Constitutional Monarch, the junta cited the TRT government's alleged les-majesty, corruption, interference with state agencies and creation of social divisions as justification for the coup. The public initially overwhelmingly supported the coup, and scenes of smiling tourists and Thai families posing in front of tanks remain the defining images of the event. Thaksin quickly flew to London, where he has more or less remained in exile.

On 1 October 2006, the junta appointed Surayud Chulanont, a retired army general, as interim prime minister before elections scheduled for the following October. The choice of Surayud was seen as a strategic one by many, as he is widely respected among both military personnel and civilians. The Surayud administration enjoyed a honeymoon period until late December, when it imposed stringent capital controls and a series of bombings rocked Bangkok during New Year's Eve, killing three people.

In January 2007, an Assets Examination Committee put together by the junta found Thaksin guilty of concealing assets to avoid paying taxes. Two months later, Thaksin's wife and brother-in-law were also charged with conspiracy to evade taxes. In late May, a court established by the military government found TRT guilty of breaking election laws. The court dissolved the party and banned its executive members from public service for five years.

In July, growing dissatisfaction with the junta's slow progress towards elections reached a peak when a large group of antigovernment protesters known as the Democratic Alliance Against Dictatorship lay siege to the residence of Prem Tinsulanonda, who they accused of masterminding the coup. Several protesters and police were injured. Nine of the group's leaders were sent to jail, the largest crackdown yet by the junta, which had previously tolerated small-scale protests.

Two months later the Supreme Court issued warrants for Thaksin and his wife, citing 'misconduct of a government official and violation of a ban on state officials being party to transactions involving public interests' in reference to an allegedly unfair land purchase in 2003. Thaksin's assets, some 73 billion baht, were frozen by a graft-busting agency set up after the coup. However, despite his apparent financial troubles, in July 2007 Thaksin fulfilled a long-held dream when he purchased Manchester City Football Club.

In a nationwide referendum held on 19 August, Thais approved a military-drafted constitution. Although the document includes a number of undemocratic provisions, including one that mandates a Senate not entirely comprised of elected politicians, its passage was largely regarded as a message that the Thai people want to see elections and progress.

Under the new constitution, long-awaited elections were finally conducted on 23 December. The newly formed People Power Party, of which Thaksin has an advisory role, won a significant number of seats in parliament, but failed to win an outright majority. After forming a loose coalition with several other parties, parliament chose the veteran politician and close Thaksin ally, Samak Sundaravej as prime minister. This, and Thaksin's return to Thailand in March 2008, has ushered in what is certainly yet another period of uncertainty in Thailand politics.

2006	2007	23 December 2007
A bloodless coup sees the Thai military take power from Thaksin while he is at a UN meeting in New York; he remains in exile in London. Official opening of Suvarnabhumi Airport.	In a nationwide referendum, voters agree to approve a military-drafted constitution, Thailand's 17th, despite the constitution being regarded by many Thais and international observers as deeply flawed.	A general election sees the Thaksin-allied People's Power Party gain a significant number of seats in parliament. A coalition, led by veteran politician Samak Sundaravej, is formed.

AN ELEPHANT'S MEMORY

One of the more clichéd tourist images of Bangkok is that of elaborately dressed classical Thai dancers performing at the Hindu shrine in front of the Grand Hyatt Erawan Hotel. As with many things in Thailand, there is a great deal hidden behind the serene façade.

The shrine was originally built in 1956 as something of a last-ditch effort to end a string of misfortunes that occurred during the construction of the hotel, at that time known as the Erawan Hotel. After several incidents ranging from injured construction workers to the sinking of a ship carrying marble for the hotel, a Brahmin priest was consulted. Since the hotel was to be named after the elephant escort of Indra in Hindu mythology, the priest determined that Erawan required a passenger, and suggested it be that of Lord Brahma (Phra Phrom in Thai). A statue was built, and lo and behold, the misfortunes miraculously ended.

Although the original Erawan Hotel was demolished in 1987, the shrine still exists, and today remains an important place of pilgrimage for Thais, particularly those in need of some material assistance. Those granting a wish from the statue should ideally come between 7am and 8am, or 7pm and 8pm, and should offer a specific list of items that includes candles, incense, sugar cane and bananas, all of which are almost exclusively given in multiples of seven. Particularly popular are teak elephants, the money gained through the purchase of which is donated to a charity run by the hotel. And as the tourist brochures depict, it is also possible to charter a classical Thai dance, often done as a way of giving thanks if a wish was granted.

After 40 years of largely benign existence, the Erawan shrine became a point of focus when just after midnight on 21 March 2006, 27-year-old Thanakorn Pakdeepol destroyed the gilded plaster image of Brahma with a hammer. Pakdeepol, who had a history of mental illness and depression, was almost immediately attacked and beaten to death by two Thai rubbish collectors in the vicinity.

Although the government ordered a swift restoration of the statue, the incident became a galvanising omen for the anti-Thaksin movement, which was in full swing at the time. At a political rally the following day, protest leader Sondhi Limthongkul suggested that the prime minister had masterminded the Brahma image's destruction in order to replace the deity with a 'dark force' allied to Thaksin. Rumours spreading through the capital claimed that Thaksin had hired Cambodian shamans to put spells on Pakdeepol so that he would perform the unspeakable deed. In response, Pakdeepol's father was quoted as saying that Sondhi was 'the biggest liar I have ever seen'. Thaksin, when asked to comment on Sondhi's accusations, simply replied, 'That's insane.' A new statue, built using bits of the previous one, was installed a month later, and at the time of writing, Thaksin has yet to return to Thailand.

ARTS

Despite the utterly utilitarian face of the modern city, Bangkok is among Southeast Asia's contemporary art capitals. This tradition stems back to the founding of the city in the late 18th century, when the early Chakri kings weren't satisfied to merely invite artists and artisans from previous Thai royal capitals such as Ayuthaya, Sukhothai and Chiang Mai. Whether via political coercion of neighbouring countries or seductive promises of wealth and position, Bangkok's rulers also had access to the artistic cream of Cambodia, Laos and Myanmar. Mon and Khmer peoples native to the Thai kingdom also contributed much to the visual arts scene. The great artistic traditions of India and China, the subtle renderings of Indo- and Sino-influenced art in neighbouring countries, and the colonial and postcolonial cultural influx from Europe have also played huge roles in the development of art in Bangkok. Likewise the decades surrounding the two world wars, Thailand's military dictatorships of the '50s, '60s and '70s, followed by the protest-fuelled democracy movement brought a healthy dose of politics and social conscience to the city's art scene. Today, influences from just about every corner of the globe now find free play in the capital.

VISUAL ARTS
Divine Inspiration

The wát served as a locus for the highest expressions of Thai art for roughly 800 years, from the Lanna to Ratanakosin eras. Accordingly, Bangkok's 400-plus Buddhist temples are brimming with the figuratively imaginative if thematically formulaic art of Thailand's foremost muralists. Always instructional in intent, such painted images range from the depiction of the *jataka* (stories of the Buddha's past lives) and scenes from the Indian Hindu epic *Ramayana*, to elaborate scenes detailing daily life in Thailand. Artists traditionally applied natural pigments to plastered temple walls, creating a fragile medium of which very few examples remain.

Today the study and application of mural painting remains very much alive. Modern temple projects are undertaken somewhere within the capital virtually every day of the year, often using improved techniques and paints that promise to hold fast much longer than the temple murals of old. A privileged few in Bangkok's art community receive handsome sums for painting the interior walls of well-endowed ordination halls.

In sculpture the Thai artists have long been masters, using wood, stone, ivory, clay and metal and a variety of techniques – including carving, modelling, construction and casting – to achieve their designs. Bangkok's most famous sculptural output has been bronze Buddha images, coveted the world over for their originality and grace. Nowadays, historic bronzes have all but disappeared from the art market in Thailand and are zealously protected by temples, museums or private collectors.

The Modern Era

In 1913 the Thai government opened the School of Arts and Crafts in order to train teachers of art and design as well as to codify the teaching of silversmithing, nielloware, lacquerwork, and wood carving in traditional Thai styles. It was an effort that was badly timed, as interest in Thai classicism began to weaken in the aftermath of WWI, perhaps the first event in world history to inspire rank-and-file urban Thais to ponder global issues.

The beginnings of Thailand's modern visual-arts movement are usually attributed to Italian artist Corrado Feroci, who was invited to Thailand by King Rama VI in 1924. In 1933 Feroci founded the country's first School of Fine Arts (SOFA).

Public monuments sponsored during the Phibun Songkhram government (1938–44) led the government to expand the SOFA's status in 1943 so that it became part of newly founded Silpakorn University (p192), Thailand's premier training ground for artists and art historians. Feroci continued

COBRA SWAMP

If you arrive in Bangkok by air, bear in mind that the sleek glass and steel terminal you will most likely pull into was nearly 40 years in the making. Suvarnabhumi (pronounced *sù wanná phoom*), Sanskrit for 'Golden Land', could hardly be a more apt name for Thailand's new airport, particularly for the politicians and investors involved.

Originally begun in 1973, the location chosen for Thailand's new international airport was an unremarkable marshy area with the slightly less illustrious working title of Nong Ngu Hao, Thai for 'Cobra Swamp'. Despite the seemingly disadvantageous setting, over the years the flat marshland was eagerly bought and sold by politicians and developers hoping to make a quick profit.

It wasn't until the self-styled CEO administration of Thaksin Shinawatra that work on the airport began in earnest. Thaksin harboured desires to make Bangkok a 'transportation hub' to rival Hong Kong and Singapore, and went on a spending spree, commissioning construction of the world's tallest flight control tower, as well as the world's largest terminal building.

Not surprisingly, the construction of Suvarnabhumi was rife with allegations of corruption, including the use of faulty building materials, and a substandard runway. At one point Thaksin suggested making the area around the airport into an entirely new province, an idea that appeared to have no benefit other than to enrich area landowners, primarily his friends and associates. Undoubtedly the most embarrassing scandal associated with the airport was the corruption-laden purchase of 20 CTX security scanners from a US company.

On 29 September 2005, Thaksin presided over a much-criticised 'soft' opening. The ceremony was essentially little more than a face-saving measure considering that the airport was still far from operational. Suvarnabhumi eventually began flights a year later, on 28 September 2006. In an ironic twist of fate, Thaksin, the main catalyst behind the project, was in exile in England, having been ousted in a military coup the week before, the junta citing corruption and shoddy construction of the airport among their justifications for the takeover.

Despite being the largest airport in Southeast Asia, and among the largest in the world, in March 2007 many domestic flights were relocated back to the old Don Muang Airport, officials citing overcrowding of runways and safety concerns as reasons for the move. With fantastically little foresight, a train link to the distant airport was only begun after its opening, and was not expected to be finished until early 2008. For details on arriving at Suvarnabhumi, see p252.

lonelyplanet.com

as dean of the university, and in gratitude for his contributions, the government gave Feroci the Thai name Silpa Bhirasri.

In 1944 Bhirasri established the National Art Exhibition, which became an important catalyst for the evolution of Thai contemporary art. The first juried art event in Thai history, the annual exhibition created new standards and formed part of a heretofore nonexistent national art agenda. In the absence of galleries in this era, the competition served as the only venue in Bangkok – in all of Thailand, for that matter – where young artists could display their work publicly. Among the most celebrated art of the period were works of realism painted by Chamras Khietkong, Piman Moolpramook, Sweang Songmangmee and Silpa Bhirasri himself.

Other artists involved in this blossoming of modern art, including Jitr Buabusaya, Fua Haripitak, Misiem Yipintsoi, Tawee Nandakhwang and Sawasdi Tantisuk, drew on European movements such as Impressionism, Post-Impressionism, Expressionism and Cubism. For the first time in the Thai modern art movement, there was also a move towards the fusion of indigenous artistic sources with modern modes of expression, as seen in the paintings by Prasong Patamanuj and sculptures of Khien Yimsiri and Chit Rienpracha.

Meanwhile, while writing and lecturing against the iron rule of Field Marshal Sarit Thanarat (1957–59), Thai Marxist academic Jit Phumisak founded the Art for Life *(sǐnlápà phêua chiiwít)* movement, which had many parallels with the famous Mexican School in its belief that only art with social or political content was worth creating. This movement gained considerable ground during the 1973 democracy movement, when students, farmers and workers joined hands with Bangkok urbanites to resist General Thanom Kittikachorn's right-wing military dictatorship. Much of the art (and music) produced at this time carried content commenting on poverty, urban-rural inequities and political repression, and were typically boldly and quickly executed. Painters Sompote Upa-In and Chang Saetang became the most famous Art for Life exponents.

A contrasting but equally important movement in Thai art later in the same decade eschewed politics and instead updated Buddhist themes and temple art. Initiated by painters Pichai

top picks

BANGKOK ART EXPERIENCES

- 100 Tonson (p191)
- Bangkok University Art Gallery (p191)
- Jim Thompson's House (p192)
- National Museum (p60)
- Wat Suthat (p71)

BACKGROUND ARTS

TEMPLE MURALS

Because of the relative wealth of Bangkok, as well as its role as the country's artistic and cultural centre, the artists commissioned to paint the walls of the city's various temples were among the most talented around, and Bangkok's temple paintings are regarded as the finest in Thailand. Some particularly exceptional works include:

Wat Bowonniwet (Map pp68–9) Painted by an artist called In Kong during the reign of Rama II, the murals in the panels of the *ubosot* (chapel) of this temple show Thai depictions of Western life during the early 19th century.

Wat Chong Nonsi (Map pp124–5) Dating back to the late Ayuthaya period, Bangkok's earliest surviving temple paintings are faded and missing in parts, but the depictions of everyday Thai life, including bawdy illustrations of a sexual manner, are well worth visiting.

Phra Thii Nang Phutthaisawan (Buddhaisawan Chapel; Map p56) Although construction of this temple located in the National Museum began in 1795, the paintings were probably finished during the reign of Rama III (1824–51). Among other scenes, the murals depict the conception, birth and early life of the Buddha – common topics among Thai temple murals.

Wat Suthat (Map pp68–9) Almost as impressive in their vast scale as much as their quality, the murals at Wat Suthat are among the most awe-inspiring in the country. Gory depictions of Buddhist hell can be found on a pillar directly behind the Buddha statue.

Wat Suwannaram (Map pp124–5) These paintings inside a late Ayuthaya-era temple in Thonburi contain skilled and vivid depictions of battle scenes and foreigners, including Chinese and Muslim warriors.

Wat Tritosathep Mahaworawihan (Map pp68–9) Although still a work in progress, Chakrabhand Posayakrit's postmodern murals at this temple in Banglamphu have already been recognised as masterworks of Thai Buddhist art.

Nirand, Thawan Duchanee and Prateung Emjaroen, the movement combined modern Western schemata with Thai motifs, moving from painting to sculpture and then to mixed media. Artists associated with this neo-Thai, neo-Buddhist school include Surasit Saokong, Songdej Thipthong, Monchai Kaosamang, Tawatchai Somkong and the late Montien Boonma. All are frequently exhibited and collected outside Thailand.

Since the 1980s boom years secular sculpture and painting in Bangkok have enjoyed more international recognition, with Impressionism-inspired Jitr (Prakit) Buabusaya and Sriwan Janehuttakarnkit among the very few to have reached this vaunted status. On Thailand's art stage, famous names include artists of the 'Fireball' school such as Vasan Sitthiket and Manit Sriwanichpoom, who specialise in politically motivated, mixed-media art installations. These artists delight in breaking Thai social codes and means of expression. Even when their purported message is Thai nationalism and self-sufficiency, they are sometimes considered 'anti-Thai'.

In recent years the emphasis is moving away from traditional influences and political commentary and more towards contemporary art. Works such as Yuree Kensaku's cartoon-like paintings, or Porntaweesak Rimsakul's mechanised installations are gaining attention, both in Thailand and abroad.

Modern painting and sculpture are exhibited at dozens of galleries around Bangkok, from the delicately lit darlings of Thai high society to industrially decorated spaces in empty warehouses. Other venues and sources of support for modern Thai art include the rotating displays at Bangkok's luxury hotels, particularly the Grand Hyatt Erawan (p210), the Sukhothai (p215) and the Metropolitan (p215).

LITERATURE
Classical
The written word has a long history in Thailand, dating back to the 11th or 12th centuries when the first Thai script was fashioned from an older Mon alphabet. Sukhothai king Phaya Lithai is thought to have composed the first work of Thai literature in 1345. This was *Traiphum Phra Ruang*, a treatise that described the three realms of existence according to Hindu-Buddhist cosmology. According to contemporary scholars, this work and its symbolism continues to have considerable influence on Thailand's art and culture.

Of all classical Thai literature, however, the *Ramakian* is the most pervasive and influential. Its Indian precursor – the Ramayana – came to Thailand with the Khmers 900 years ago, first appearing as stone reliefs on Prasat Hin Phimai and other Angkor temples in the northeast. Eventually, Thailand developed its own version of the epic, which was first written during the reign of Rama I. This version contains 60,000 stanzas and is a quarter again longer than the Sanskrit original.

The 30,000-line *Phra Aphaimani*, composed by poet Sunthorn Phu in the late 18th century, is Thailand's most famous classical literary work. Like many of its epic predecessors around the world, it tells the story of an exiled prince who must triumph in an odyssey of love and war before returning to his kingdom.

During the Ayuthaya period, Thailand developed a classical poetic tradition based on five types of verse – *chân, kàap, khlong, klawn* and *râi*. Each form uses a complex set of rules to regulate metre, rhyming patterns and number of syllables. During the political upheavals of the 1970s, several Thai newspaper editors, most notably Kukrit Pramoj, composed lightly disguised political commentary in *klawn* verse. Modern Thai poets seldom use the classical forms, preferring to compose in blank verse or with song-style rhyming.

Contemporary
The first Thai-language novel appeared only about 70 years ago, in direct imitation of Western models. Thus far, no more than 10 have been translated into English.

The first Thai novel of substance, *The Circus of Life* (Thai 1929; English 1994) by

top picks

NOVELS
- *A Woman of Bangkok*, Jack Reynolds (1956)
- *Bangkok 8*, John Burdett (2003)
- *Four Reigns*, Kukrit Pramoj (Si Phaendin; 1953, translated 1981)
- *Jasmine Nights*, SP Somtow (1995)
- *Sightseeing*, Rattawut Lapcharoensap (2004)

BACKGROUND ARTS

BANGKOK FICTION

First-time visitors to virtually any of Bangkok's English-language bookstores will notice an abundance of novels with titles such as *The Butterfly Trap, Confessions of a Bangkok Private Eye, Even Thai Girls Cry, Fast Eddie's Lucky 7 A Go Go, Lady of Pattaya, The Go Go Dancer Who Stole My Viagra, My Name Lon You Like Me?, The Pole Dancer,* and *Thai Touch.* Welcome to the Bangkok school of fiction, a genre, as the titles suggest, defined by its obsession with crime, exoticism, and Thai women.

The birth of this genre can be traced back to Jack Reynolds' 1956 novel, *A Woman of Bangkok.* Although long out of print, the book is still an acknowledged influence for many Bangkok-based writers, and Reynolds' formula of Western-man-meets-beautiful-but-dangerous-Thai-woman – occasionally spiced up with a dose of crime – is a staple of the modern genre.

Standouts include John Burdett's *Bangkok 8* (2003), a page-turner in which a half-Thai, half-*faràng* (Westerner) police detective investigates the python-and-cobras murder of a US Marine in Bangkok. Along the way we're treated to vivid portraits of Bangkok's gritty nightlife scene and insights into Thai Buddhism. A film version of the novel is in the early stages of production, and its sequels, *Bangkok Tattoo* and *Bangkok Haunts,* have sold well in the US.

Christopher G Moore, a Canadian who has lived in Bangkok for the last two decades, has authored 19 mostly Bangkok-based crime novels to positive praise both in Thailand and abroad. His description of Bangkok's sleazy Thermae Coffee House (called 'Zeno' in *A Killing Smile*) is the closest literature comes to evoking the perpetual male adolescence to which such places cater.

Private Dancer, by popular English thriller author Stephen Leather, is another classic example of Bangkok fiction, despite having only been available via download until recently. One of the book's main characters, Big Ron, is based on the real-life owner of Jool's Bar & Restaurant (p176), a Nana-area nightlife staple.

Jake Needham's 1999 thriller *The Big Mango* provides tongue-in-cheek references to the Bangkok bargirl scene and later became the first expat novel to be translated into Thai.

Arkartdamkeung Rapheephat, follows a young, upper class Thai as he travels to London, Paris, the USA and China in the 1920s. The novel's existentialist tone created quite a stir in Thailand when it was released and became an instant bestseller. The fact that the author, himself a Thai prince, took his own life at the age of 26 only added to the mystique surrounding this work.

The late Kukrit Pramoj, former ambassador and Thai prime minister, novelised Bangkok court life from the late 19th century through to the 1940s in *Four Reigns* (Thai 1953; English 1981), the longest novel ever published in Thai. *The Story of Jan Dara* (Thai 1966; English 1994), by journalist and short-story writer Utsana Phleungtham, traces the sexual obsessions of a Thai aristocrat as they are passed to his son. In 2001, director/producer Nonzee Nimibutr turned the remarkable novel into a rather melodramatic film (see p35). Praphatsorn Seiwikun's rapid-paced *Time in a Bottle* (Thai 1984; English 1996) turned the dilemmas of a fictional middle-class Bangkok family into a bestseller.

Many Thai authors, including the notable Khamphoon Boonthawi *(Luk Isan)* and Chart Kobjitt *(Time),* have been honoured with the SEA Write Award, an annual prize presented to fiction writers from countries in the Association of South East Asian Nations (Asean). A one-stop collection of fiction thus awarded can be found in *The SEA Write Anthology of Thai Short Stories and Poems* (1996).

When it comes to novels written in English, Thai wunderkind SP Somtow has written and published more titles than any other Thai writer. Born in Bangkok, educated at Eton and Cambridge, and now a commuter between two 'cities of angels' – Los Angeles and Bangkok – Somtow's prodigious output includes a string of well-reviewed science fiction/fantasy/horror stories, including *Moon Dance, Darker Angels* and *The Vampire's Beautiful Daughter.* The Somtow novel most evocative of Thailand and Thai culture is *Jasmine Nights* (1995), which also happens to be one of his most accessible reads. Following a 12-year-old Thai boy's friendship with an African-American boy in Bangkok in the 1960s, this semiautobiographical work blends Thai, Greek and African myths, American Civil War lore and a dollop of magic realism into a seamless whole.

All Soul's Day (1997), by Bill Morris is a sharp, well-researched historical novel set in Bangkok circa 1963. The story, which involves vintage Buicks and the pre-Second Indochina War American military build-up, would do Graham Greene proud.

Thai-American Rattawut Lapcharoensap's *Sightseeing* (2004), a collection of short stories set in present-day Thailand, has been widely lauded for its deft portrayal of the intersection between Thai and foreign cultures, both tourist and expat.

MUSIC
Classical Thai

Classical central-Thai music *(phleng thai doem)* features a dazzling array of textures and subtleties, hair-raising tempos and pastoral melodies. The classical orchestra or *pìi-phâat* can include as few as five players or more than 20. Leading the band is *pìi*, a straight-lined woodwind instrument with a reed mouthpiece and an oboe-like tone; you'll hear it most at *muay thai* (Thai boxing) matches. The four-stringed *phin*, plucked like a guitar, lends subtle counterpoint, while *ránâat èhk*, a bamboo-keyed percussion instrument resembling the xylophone, carries the main melodies. The slender *saw*, a bowed instrument with a coconut-shell soundbox, provides soaring embellishments, as does the *khlùi* or wooden Thai flute.

One of the more noticeable *pìiphâat* instruments, *kháwng wong yài*, consists of tuned gongs arranged in a semicircle and played in simple rhythmic lines to provide the music's underlying fabric. Several types of drums, some played with the hands, some with sticks, carry the beat, often through several tempo changes in a single song. The most important type of drum is the *tàphon* (or *thon*), a double-headed hand-drum that sets the tempo for the entire ensemble. Prior to a performance, the players offer incense and flowers to *tàphon*, considered to be the conductor of the music's spiritual content.

The *pìi-phâat* ensemble was originally developed to accompany classical dance-drama and shadow theatre but is also commonly heard in straightforward concert performances. Classical Thai music may sound strange to Western visitors due to the use of the standard Thai scale, which divides the octave into seven full-tone intervals with no semitones. Thai scales were first transcribed by the Thai-German composer Peter Feit (whose Thai name was Phra Chen Duriyanga), who also composed Thailand's national anthem in 1932.

Thai Pop & Rock

Popular Thai music has borrowed much from Western music, particularly in instrumentation, but retains a distinct flavour of its own. The bestselling of all modern musical genres in Thailand remains *lûuk thûng*. Literally 'children of the fields', *lûuk thûng* dates back to the 1940s, is analogous to country and western in the USA, and is a genre that tends to appeal most to working-class Thais. Subject matter almost always cleaves to tales of lost love, tragic early death and the dire circumstances of farmers who work day in and day out and, at the end of the year, still owe money to the bank.

Lûuk thûng song structures tend to be formulaic as well. There are two basic styles, the original Suphanburi style, with lyrics in standard Thai, and an Ubon style sung in Isan (northeastern) dialect. Thailand's most famous *lûuk thûng* singer, Pumpuang Duangjan, rated a royally sponsored cremation when she died in 1992, and a major shrine at Suphanburi's Wat Thapkradan, which receives a steady stream of worshippers.

Chai Muang Sing and Siriporn Amphaipong have been the most beloved *lûuk thûng* superstars for several years, with lesser lights coming and going. Other more recent stars include God Chakraband (a former soap opera star whose nickname is taken from *The Godfather*, and who is known as the Prince of Lûuk Thûng), and Mike Piromporn, whose working class ballads have proved enormously popular. One of the more surprising acts of recent years is Jonas-Kristy, a blonde-haired, blue-eyed Swede and his Dutch-English partner, who have been among the hottest-selling *lûuk thûng* acts in the country.

Another genre more firmly rooted in northeastern Thailand, and nearly as popular in Bangkok, is *mǎw lam*. Based on the songs played on the Lao-Isan *khaen*, a wind instrument devised of a double row of bamboo-like reeds fitted into a hardwood soundbox, *mǎw lam* features a simple but insistent bass beat and plaintive vocal melodies. If *lûuk thûng* is Thailand's country and western, then *mǎw lam* is its blues. Jintara Poonlap and Pornsak Songsaeng continue to reign as queen and king of *mǎw lam*. Tune into Bangkok radio station Luk Thung FM (FM 95.0) for large doses of *lûuk thûng* and *mǎw lam*.

BACKGROUND VISUAL ARTS

The 1970s ushered in a new style inspired by the politically conscious folk rock of the US and Europe, which the Thais dubbed *phleng phêua chiiwít* (literally 'music for life') after Marxist Jit Phumisak's earlier Art for Life movement. Closely identified with the Thai band Caravan – which still performs regularly – the introduction of this style was the most significant musical shift in Thailand since *lûuk thûng* arose in the 1940s.

Phleng phêua chiiwít has political and environmental topics rather than the usual love themes. During the authoritarian dictatorships of the '70s many of Caravan's songs were banned. Following the massacre of student demonstrators in 1976, some members of the band fled to the hills to take up with armed communist groups. Another proponent of this style, Carabao, took *phleng phêua chiiwít*, fused it with *lûuk thûng*, rock and heavy metal to become one of the biggest bands Thailand has seen (see the boxed text, below).

In recent years, Thailand has also developed a thriving teen-pop industry – sometimes referred to as T-Pop – centred on artists who have been chosen for their good looks, and then matched with syrupy song arrangements. Labels GMM Grammy and RS Productions are the heavyweights of this genre, and their rivalry has resulted in a flood of copycat acts. For example, after RS released Parn, an artist meant to appeal to 30-somehing female listeners, Grammy countered with the nearly identical Beau Sunita. Likewise with Grammy's Golf-Mike and RS's Dan-Beam – two nearly indistinguishable boy bands.

One pop artist seemingly able to subvert genres altogether, not to mention being one of the most popular Thai stars of the last two decades, is Thongchai 'Bird' McIntyre. Born to a half-Scottish father in a musical family, *Phîi Bóed* (big-brother Bird), as he is affectionately known, is one of the country's few genuine musical superstars. Many of Bird's songs have become modern Thai pop classics, and in recent years he has expanded his repertoire, working with the likes of *măw lam* legend, Jintara Poonlap.

In an effort to bring in more listeners, many of the big labels have also formed smaller imprints. The most influential of these was Bakery Music, a subsidiary of Sony BMG, and a platform for several quasi-alternative, lite-rock and easy listening acts such as Bo, Groove Riders, PRU and Boyd. Many of these artists later went on to form Love Is, currently the 'in' independent label.

In the rock arena, late '90s crowd pleaser Loso (from 'low society') reinvented Carabao's Thai folk melodies and rhythms with indie guitar rock. Grammy responded with a rash of similar Thai headbangers designed to fill stadiums and outsell the indies (independent labels), and popular post-Loso rock acts include Big Ass, Potato and Bodyslam.

Yet another movement in modern Thai music has been the fusion of international jazz with Thai classical and folk styles. Fong Nam, a Thai orchestra led by US composer Bruce Gaston,

MADE IN THAILAND

You've undoubtedly seen his lanky frame on billboards, enthusiastically sporting his band's forked-finger salute to promote their eponymous energy drink. You may also have caught him on TV, singing a rallying anthem to sell Chang Beer. And you've probably even heard taxi drivers make passing references to his hit song, 'Made in Thailand'. All these sightings probably have you thinking, who is this guy?

The guy is Yuengyong Ophakun, better known as Aed Carabao, lead singer of Carabao, a Thai band many consider to be the Rolling Stones of Asia.

The name Carabao comes from the Tagalog word for buffalo, and implies diligence and patience (ironically contrasting with the Thai word for buffalo, which is synonymous with stupidity or dim-wittedness). Not unlike the Ramones, the founding members of Carabao, Aed and Khiao (Kirati Promsakha Na Sakon Nakhorn), adopted the word as a surrogate surname after forming the band as students in the Philippines in the early 1980s. Their style of music was inspired by the Thai protest music of the era known as *phleng phêua chiiwít*, Filipino music, as well as a healthy dose of Western-style rock and roll. Since their first album, Chut Khii Mao ('Drunkard's Album'), and in the 24 that have followed, Carabao's lyrics have remained political and occasionally controversial. Ganchaa (marijuana), a song from their second album, was promptly banned from Thai radio – the first of many. In 2001 Carabao dedicated an album in support of Shan rebels in Burma, a source of consternation for the Thai government. When not generating controversy they are almost constantly performing, and have also played in most Southeast Asian countries, as well as Europe and the US.

Through the years, the band has inspired countless copycat acts, but it's unlikely that few acts of any genre will ever equal the influence and popularity of the brothers Carabao.

performs a blend of Western and Thai classical motifs, which has become a favourite for movie soundtracks, TV commercials and tourism promotions. Fong Nam plays regularly at Tawan Daeng German Brewhouse (p182). Another leading exponent of this genre is the composer and instrumentalist Tewan Sapsanyakorn (also known as Tong Tewan), who plays soprano and alto sax, violin and *khlùi* with equal virtuosity. Other groups fusing international jazz and indigenous Thai music include Kangsadarn and Boy Thai; the latter adds Brazilian samba and reggae to the mix.

Thai Alt/Indie/Hip-Hop

In the 1990s an alternative pop scene – known as *klawng sehrii* or 'free drum' in Thailand, also *phleng tâi din*, 'underground music' – grew in Bangkok. Modern Dog, a Britpop-inspired band of four Chulalongkorn University graduates, is generally credited with bringing independent Thai music into the mainstream, and their success prompted an explosion of similar bands and indie recording labels. Other major alternative acts in Thailand include the rock outfit Day Tripper, punk metal band Ebola, and the electronica/underground group Futon, which is made up of British and Thai band members. Truly independent labels to look for include Small Room, Panda Records and Spicy Disc.

The indie stuff is almost always reserved for concert performances or one-off club appearances. One spot with regular weekend concerts is the outdoor stage at Centrepoint, Siam Sq. The biggest indie event of the year is Fat Radio–organised, Heineken-sponsored Fat Festival, a three-day outdoor music festival held annually in November. For the latest indie Thai, tune into Fat Radio on 104.5 FM (www.thisisclick.com/1045).

Hip-hop is huge in Thailand in terms of radio play and CD sales, but few Thai groups are proficient in performing this genre. Hip-hop/ska artist Joey Boy not only paved the way for others, but released lyrics that the Department of Culture banned. One song, for example, included the Thai euphemism for male masturbation, *chák wâo* (fly a kite). Another hip-hop act that has gained attention is Thaitanium, an all-Thai group that does all its recording in New York and distributes its music independently in Thailand.

CINEMA
Birth of an Industry

Bangkok Film launched Thailand's film industry with the first Thai-directed silent movie, *Chok Sorng Chan*, in 1927. Silent films proved to be more popular than talkies right into the 1960s, and as late as 1969 Thai studios were still producing them from 16mm stock. Perhaps partially influenced by India's famed masala (curry mix) movies – which enjoyed a strong following in post-WWII Bangkok – film companies blended romance, comedy, melodrama and adventure to give Thai audiences a little bit of everything.

The first Thai director to film in the 35mm format was Ratana Pestonji, whose films such as *Rong Raem Narok* (*Country Hotel*: 1957) still influence modern Thai filmmakers. The arrival of 35mm movies in Thailand sparked a proliferation of modern cinema halls and a surge in movie making, and Thai films attracted more cinema-goers than *năng faràng* (movies from Europe and America). Many today consider the '60s to be a golden age of Thai cinema. More than half of the approximately 75 films produced annually during this period starred the much-admired onscreen duo Mit Chaibancha and Petchara Chaowaraj.

Despite the founding of a government committee in 1970 to promote Thai cinema, Thai film production in the '70s and early '80s was mostly limited to inexpensive action or romance

top picks
THAI CDS

Most of these CDs are available from Tower Records in the Emporium (Map pp118–19) and at Central World Plaza (Map pp98–9). You can also order online at www.nongtaprachan.com or www.ethaicd.com.

- *Lust for Live* (Bakery Music) Collection of live alt-rock performances by Modern Dog, Chou Chou, Yokee Playboy, P.O.P. and Rudklao Amraticha.
- *Made in Thailand* (Carabao) Carabao's classic and internationally popular album.
- *Maw Lam Sa-On 1 - 12* (Jintara Poonlap) Good introduction to *măw lam*.
- *The Best of Loso* (Loso) Thai anthems of teen angst.
- *Best* (Pumpuang Duangjan) Compilation of the late *lûuk thûng* diva's most famous tunes.

BACKGROUND ARTS

HALF CHILD

Leaf through any Thai fashion magazine and you'll come across at least two or three *lûuk khrêung* faces. Turn on the TV to watch Thai soap operas, commercials or music videos and you're even more likely to see the offspring of *faràng*/Thai couplings.

Literally 'half child', the *lûuk khrêung* wasn't always a mainstay of Thai media. In the 1970s and '80s most *lûuk khrêung* were the children of male American servicemen stationed at one of the seven US military bases scattered around Thailand during the Indochina War. Their mothers may have been Thai women associated only briefly with their fathers; some were *mia châo* ('rental wives' – a euphemism for prostitute). The resulting Amerasian children of these alliances were typically looked down upon by other Thais.

That perception began to change following Thailand's economic boom in the '80s and '90s, when *lûuk khrêung* who were schooled abroad or educated at bilingual international schools in Thailand became adults. A new wave of *lûuk khrêung* who were the children of expats with more permanent ties to Thailand was also born during this time, in circumstances deemed more 'respectable' within Thai society.

Coupled with the fading public memory of the Indochina War births, the stigma formerly attached to *lûuk khrêung* almost overnight became positive rather than negative. Fluency in English and whiter skin tones – apparently a Thai preference long before Europeans arrived in Thailand – lend *lûuk khrêung* a significant advantage as media figures. Today a high proportion of models, actors, VJs, beauty queens and pop music stars are *lûuk khrêung*.

Among the most well known *lûuk khrêung* in Thailand are Tata Young (music), Paula Taylor (music/film/VJ), Sonya Couling (modelling), Nat Myria (music), Peter Corp Dyrendal (music), Ananda Everingham (TV/film), Sunny Suwanmethanon (film), and of course 'Bird' McIntyre (music/film).

The *lûuk khrêung* phenomenon has become so topical in Thailand nowadays that a 2006 TV soap opera, *Lady Mahachon*, revolved around a *lûuk khrêung* pop star (played by real-life *lûuk khrêung* pop star Paula Taylor) looking for her American father (Erich Fleshman, a bilingual American actor), whom she hadn't seen since early childhood.

stories. An exception could be found in the films of Prince Chatrichalerm Yukol, in particular *Theptida Rongram* (The Angel: 1974) and *Thongpoon Khokpo Rasadorn Temkan* (The Citizen: 1977), which introduced substantial doses of dark realism to the Thai film scene. In the same genre was *Luk Isan* (Child of the North-East; 1983) which, based on a Thai novel of the same name, follows the ups and downs of a farming family living in drought-ridden Isan. *Luk Isan* became one of the first popular films to offer urban Thais an understanding of the hardships endured by many northeasterners.

Modern Thai Film

The Thai movie industry almost died during the '80s and '90s, swamped by Hollywood extravaganzas and the boom era's taste for anything imported. From a 1970s peak of about 200 releases per year, the Thai output shrank to an average of only 10 films a year by 1997. The Southeast Asian economic crisis that year threatened to further bludgeon the ailing industry, but the lack of funding coupled with foreign competition brought about a new emphasis on quality rather than quantity. The current era boasts a new generation of seriously good Thai directors, several of whom studied film abroad during Thailand's '80s and early '90s boom period.

Recent efforts have been so encouraging that Thai and foreign critics alike speak of a current Thai 'new wave'. Avoiding the soap operatics of the past, the current crop of directors favour gritty realism, artistic innovation and a strengthened Thai identity. Pen-Ek Ratanaruang's *Fun Bar Karaoke* is a 1997 satire of Bangkok life in which the main characters are an ageing Thai playboy and his daughter; the film received critical acclaim for its true-to-life depiction of modern urban living blended with sage humour. It was the first feature-length outing by a young Thai who is fast becoming one of the kingdom's most internationally noted directors. The film played well to international audiences but achieved only limited box-office success at home. Similarly, Nonzee Nimibutr's *2499 Antaphan Krong Meuang* (Dang Bireley's Young Gangsters) was hailed abroad – winning first prize at the 1997 Brussels International Film Festival – but was only modestly successful in Thailand.

A harbinger for the Thai film industry was Nonzee Nimibutr's 1998 release of *Nang Nak*, an exquisite retelling of the Mae Nak Phrakhanong legend, in which the spirit of a woman who died during childbirth haunts the home of her husband. This story has had no fewer than 20 previous cinematic renderings. *Nang Nak* not only features excellent acting and period detailing, but manages to transform Nak into a sympathetic character rather than a horrific ghost. The film earned awards for best director, best art director and best sound at the 1999 Asia-Pacific Film Festival.

In 1999 director Pen-Ek Ratanaruang came out with his second feature, a finely crafted thriller set in Bangkok called *Ruang Talok 69* (6ixtynin9). Like his first film, it was a critical success that saw relatively little screen time in Thailand.

The 2000 film *Satree Lex* (Iron Ladies) humorously dramatises the real-life exploits of a Lampang volleyball team made up almost entirely of transvestites and transsexuals. At home, this Yongyoot Thongkongtoon–directed film became one of Thai cinema's biggest-grossing films to date, and was the first Thai film ever to reach the art-house cinemas of Europe and the US on general release.

Fah Talai Jone (2000), directed by Wisit Sasanatieng, presents a campy and colourful parody of quasi-cowboy Thai melodramas of the '50s and '60s. The film received an honourable mention at Cannes (where it was quickly dubbed a 'cult hit') and took an award at the Vancouver Film Festival. When Miramax distributed the film in the USA, it was called *Tears of the Black Tiger*.

The next Thai film to garner international attention was 2001's *Suriyothai*, an historic epic directed by Prince Chatrichalerm Yukol. Almost 3½ years and US$20 million in the making, the three-hour film lavishly narrates a well-known episode in Thai history in which an Ayuthaya queen sacrifices herself at the 1548 Battle of Hanthawaddy to save her king's life. *Suriyothai* went on to become the highest-grossing film in Thai history, earning more than 600 million baht, but flopped overseas and was widely criticised for being ponderous and overly long.

In 2001 Nonzee Nimibutr returned with *Jan Dara*, a cinematic rendition of Utsana Pleungtham's controversially erotic 1966 novel of the same name. Filmed almost entirely on sound stages save for outdoor scenes shot in Luang Prabang, Laos, the film was critically compared with Vietnam's famous *Scent of Green Papaya*.

For evidence that Thailand's role in world cinema will continue to expand, you don't need to look any further than Pen-Ek's *Mon Rak Transistor*. This acclaimed film broke ground by seizing a thoroughly Thai theme – the tragicomic odyssey of a young villager who tries to crack the big-time *lûuk thûng* music scene in Bangkok – and upgrading production values to international standards. The 2001 release was honoured with a special Directors' Fortnight showing at Cannes 2002, and went on to earn Best Asian Film at the Seattle International Film Festival '02 and the Audience Award at the Vienna International Film Festival '02.

One of Thai cinema's finest moments arrived when Cannes 2002 chose *Sud Sanaeha* (Blissfully Yours) for the coveted Un Certain Regard (Of Special Consideration) screening, an event that showcases notable work by new directors. Directed by 31-year-old Apichatpong Weerasethakul, the film dramatises a budding romance between a Thai woman and an illegal Burmese immigrant, and went on to win a prize in the category.

Another favourite on the 2002 festival circuit, and a blockbuster in Thailand as well, was Jira Malikul's film *15 Kham Deuan 11* (Mekhong Full Moon Party). The storyline juxtaposes folk beliefs about mysterious 'dragon lights' emanating from the Mekong River with the scepticism of Bangkok scientists and news media, and also with Thai Buddhism. As with *Mon Rak Transistor*, the film affectionately evokes everyday Thai culture for the whole world to enjoy. It's also the first Thai feature film where most of the script is written in the Isan dialect, necessitating Thai subtitles.

The year 2003 saw *Faen Chan* (My Girl), a nostalgic but well-directed-and-acted drama/comedy about childhood friends who become re-acquainted as adults when one of them is about to marry. Directed by a team of six young Thais, the film was hugely successful in Thailand and garnered attention abroad as well.

A further watershed occurred when the 2004 Cannes Film Festival awarded Apichatpong's dream-like *Sud Pralad* (Tropical Malady) the Jury Prize. None of the young

top picks

THAI FILMS

- *Mon Rak Transistor*, Pen-Ek Ratanaruang (2001)
- *Faen Chan* (My Girl), Komkrit Treewimol et al (2003)
- *Nang Nak*, Nonzee Nimibutr (1998)
- *Ong Bak*, Prachya Pinkaew (2004)
- *Sud Pralad* (Tropical Malady), Apichatpong Weerasethakul (2004)

lonelyplanet.com

director's films has generated much interest in Thailand, however, where they are seen as too Western in tone. Much more well received, box office-wise, both in Thailand and abroad, was Prachya Pinkaew's *Ong Bak* (2004), widely hailed around the world as one of the finest 'old-school' martial arts films of all time. The film also set the stage for action star Tony Jaa (Thai name: Panom Yeerum), currently Thailand's hottest big-screen export.

Apichatpong's most recent release, *Syndromes and a Century* (2006), gained somewhat more attention when the director was ordered by the Thai censorship board to cut four seemingly innocuous scenes. This led Apichatpong to cancel the local release of the film in protest, and sparked a subsequent campaign by industry people, critics and audience to demand that the government do away with the country's antiquated 1930 Film Act and introduce a rating system.

In 2007 Prince Chatrichalerm Yukol followed up 2001's massively popular *Suriyothai* with a duo of historical dramas, *The Legend of King Naresuan*, parts I and II. The epics are a semi-sequel to *Suriyothai*, and tell the story of the 16th century Thai king who was taken hostage by the Burmese after Ayuthaya was sacked, and who later reclaimed the kingdom's independence. A third part, starring Tony Jaa, is due for release in late 2008.

Today Thailand plays host to two large film festivals, the Bangkok International Film Festival (BKKIFF), and the World Film Festival of Bangkok, further evidence that the country lies at the epicentre of a growing film industry.

THEATRE & DANCE

Traditional Thai theatre consists of five dramatic forms. *Khŏn* is a formal, masked dance-drama depicting scenes from the *Ramakian* (the Thai version of India's Ramayana), and originally performed only for the royal court. *Lákhawn* is a general term that covers several types of dance-drama (usually for nonroyal occasions), including *mánohraa*, the southern Thai version based on a 2000-year-old Indian story, and Western theatre. *Líkeh* (likay) is a partly improvised, often bawdy folk play featuring dancing, comedy, melodrama and music. *Lákhawn lék* or *hùn lŭang* is puppet theatre, and *lákhawn phûut* is modern spoken theatre.

Khŏn

In all *khŏn* performances, four types of characters are represented – male humans, female humans, monkeys and demons. Monkey and demon figures are always masked with the elaborate head coverings often seen in tourist promo material. Behind the masks and make-up, all actors are male. Traditional *khŏn* is very expensive to produce – Ravana's retinue alone (Ravana is the Ramakian's principal villain) consists of more than 100 demons, each with a distinctive mask.

Perhaps because it was once limited to royal venues and hence never gained a popular following, the *khŏn* or Ramakian dance-drama tradition nearly died out in Thailand. Bangkok's National Theatre (p188) was once the only place where *khŏn* was regularly performed for the public; the renovated Chalermkrung Royal Theatre (p188) now hosts occasional *khŏn* performances, enhanced by laser graphics and hi-tech audio.

Scenes performed in traditional *khŏn* (and *lákhawn* performances – see the following section) come from the 'epic journey' tale of the Ramayana, with parallels in the Greek Odyssey and the myth of Jason and the Argonauts.

Lákhawn

The more formal *lákhawn nai* (inner *lákhawn*, which means that it is performed inside the palace) was originally performed for lower nobility by all-female ensembles. Today it's a dying art, even more so than royal *khŏn*. In addition to scenes from the *Ramakian*, *lákhawn nai* performances may include traditional Thai folk tales; whatever the story, text is always sung. *Lákhawn nâwt* (outer *lákhawn*, performed outside the palace) deals exclusively with folk tales and features a mix of sung and spoken text, sometimes with improvisation. Male and female performers are permitted. Like *khŏn* and *lákhawn nai*, performances are increasingly rare.

Much more common these days is the less refined *lákhawn chaatrii*, a fast-paced, costumed dance-drama usually performed at upcountry temple festivals. *Chaatrii* stories are often influenced by the older *mánohraa* theatre of southern Thailand.

A variation on *chaatrii* that has evolved specifically for shrine worship, *lákhawn kâe bon*, involves an ensemble of about 20, including musicians. At an important shrine such as Bangkok's Lak Meuang, four *kâe bon* troupes may alternate, each for a week at a time, as each performance lasts from 9am to 3pm and there is usually a long list of worshippers waiting to hire them.

Líkeh

In outlying working-class neighbourhoods of Bangkok you may be lucky enough to come across the gaudy, raucous *líkeh*. This theatrical art form is thought to have descended from drama-rituals brought to southern Thailand by Arab and Malay traders. The first native public performance in central Thailand came about when a group of Thai Muslims staged *líkeh* for Rama V in Bangkok during the funeral commemoration of Queen Sunantha. *Líkeh* grew very popular under Rama VI, peaked in the early 20th century and has been fading slowly since the 1960s.

Most often performed at Buddhist festivals by troupes of travelling performers, *líkeh* is a colourful mixture of folk and classical music, outrageous costumes, melodrama, slapstick comedy, sexual innuendo and commentary on Thai politics and society. *Faràng* – even those who speak fluent Thai – are often left behind by the highly idiomatic language and gestures. Most *líkeh* performances begin with the *àwk khàek*, a prelude in which an actor dressed in Malay costume takes the stage to pay homage to the troupe's teacher and to narrate a brief summary of the play to the audience. For true *líkeh* aficionados, the visit of a renowned troupe is a bigger occasion than the release of an international blockbuster at the local cinema.

Lákhawn Lék

Lákhawn lék (little theatre; also known as *hùn lùang*, or royal puppets), like *khŏn*, was once reserved for court performances. Metre-high marionettes made of *khòi* paper and wire, wearing elaborate costumes modelled on those of the *khŏn*, were used to convey similar themes, music and dance movements.

Two to three puppet masters were required to manipulate each *hùn lùang* – including arms, legs, hands, even fingers and eyes – by means of wires attached to long poles. Stories were drawn from Thai folk tales, particularly *Phra Aphaimani* (a classical Thai literary work), and occasionally from the *Ramakian*. *Hùn lùang* is no longer performed, as the performance techniques and puppet-making skills have been lost. The *hùn lùang* puppets themselves are highly collectable; the Bangkok National Museum has only one example in its collection. Surviving examples of a smaller, 30cm court version called *hùn lék* (little puppets) are occasionally used in live performances; only one puppeteer is required for each marionette in *hùn lék*.

Another form of Thai puppet theatre, *hùn kràbàwk* (cylinder puppets), is based on popular Hainanese puppet shows. It uses 30cm hand puppets carved from wood and viewed only from the waist up. *Hùn kràbàwk* marionettes are still crafted and used in performances today, most notably at the Traditional Thai Puppet Theatre (see p189).

Lákhawn Phûut

Lákhawn phûut – 'speaking theatre', or live contemporary theatre as known in the West – is enjoyed by a small elite audience in Bangkok. Virtually the entire scene, such as it is, centres on two venues, Patravadi Theatre (p188) and Bangkok Playhouse (p188).

ARCHITECTURE

TEMPLES, FORTS & SHOPHOUSES

When Bangkok became the capital of the kingdom of Siam in 1782, the first task set before designers of the new city was to create hallowed ground for royal palaces and Buddhist monasteries. Indian astrologers and high-ranking Buddhist monks conferred to select and consecrate the most auspicious riverside locations, marking them off with small carved stone pillars. Siam's most talented architects and artisans then weighed in, creating majestic and ornate edifices designed to astound all who ventured into the new capital.

The temples and palaces along the riverbanks of Mae Nam Chao Phraya transformed humble Bang Makok into the glitter and glory of Ko Ratanakosin (Ratanakosin Island), and their scale and intricacy continue to make a lasting impression on new arrivals. Whether approaching by river or by road, from a distance your eye is instantly caught by the sunlight refracting off the multitude of gilded spires peeking over the huge walls of Wat Phra Kaew (p55), the Temple of the Emerald Buddha. Inside the brick-and-stucco walls, you can easily lose yourself amid the million-sq-metre grounds, which bring together more than 100 buildings and about two centuries of royal history and architectural experimentation.

Early Bangkok was both a citadel and a city of temples and palaces. Today the massive white-washed walls of Phra Sumen (p74), punctured by tiny windows and topped with neat crenulations, still loom over the northern end of trendy Th Phra Athit, facing Mae Nam Chao Phraya. On the other side of the battlements, Khlong Banglamphu (Banglamphu Canal) cuts away from the river at a sharp angle, creating the northern tip of Ko Ratanakosin, a man-made 'island' out of the left bank of the river. Erected in 1783 and named for the mythical Mt Meru (Phra Sumen in Thai) of Hindu-Buddhist cosmology, the octagonal brick-and-stucco bunker was one of 14 city fortresses built along Khlong Banglamphu. Of the 4m-high, 3m-thick ramparts that once lined the entire canal, only Phra Sumen and Mahakan have been preserved to show what 18th-century Bangkok was really about – keeping foreign armies at bay.

Open trade with the Portuguese, Dutch, English, French and Chinese made the fortifications obsolete by the mid-19th century, and most of the original city wall was demolished to make way for sealed roadways. By 1900 these roadways were lined with two-storey Sino-Gothic shophouses inspired by King Rama V's visits to Singapore and Penang.

Bangkok's oldest residential and business district fans out along the Chao Phraya River between Phra Pin Klao bridge and Hualamphong station. Largely inhabited by the descendants of Chinese residents who moved out of Ko Ratanakosin to make way for royal temples and palaces in the early 19th century, Thais refer to the neighbourhood as Yaowarat (for the major avenue bisecting the neighbourhood) or by the English term 'Chinatown'. One of the most atmospheric streets in this area is Th Plaeng Naam, where several Chinese shophouses, some nearly a century old, can be found.

In the 19th century, Chinese architecture began exerting a strong influence on the city. In Talat Noi (Little Market), a riverside neighbourhood just south of the older Yaowarat, Chinese entrepreneur Chao Sua Son founded a market where larger riverboats could offload wholesale goods to city merchants. Chao Sua Son's house still stands (Map p84), a rare example of traditional Chinese architecture in Thailand.

Talat Noi serves as a cultural and geographic bridge between the almost exclusively Chinese ambience of Yaowarat to the immediate north and the almost exclusively Western – historically speaking, if not in present-day Bangkok – district of European trading houses and embassies to the immediate south. A portion of Talat Noi was given over to Portuguese residents of Bangkok, who in 1787 built the Holy Rosary Church (Map p84), the capital's oldest place of Christian worship. Originally assembled of wood, after an 1890 fire it was replaced with brick and stucco in the Neo-Gothic stucco style. Today the interior is graced by Romanesque stained-glass windows, gilded ceilings and a very old, life-sized Jesus effigy carried in the streets during Easter processions.

South of Talat Noi at least two or more miles of the Chao Phraya riverside was once given over to such international mercantile enterprises as the East Asiatic Co, Chartered Bank, British Dispensary, Bombay Burmah Trading Co, Banque de l'Indochine, Messrs Howarth Erskine, as well as the Portuguese, French, Russian, British, American, German and Italian embassies. For the era, the well-financed architecture for this area – known then, as today, as Bang Rak – was Bangkok's most flamboyant, a mixture of grand neo-classical fronts, shuttered Victorian windows and Beaux Arts ornamentation. Some of these old buildings have survived to the present. All have been obscured by more modern structures along Charoen Krung Rd, and hence the best way to appreciate them as a group is from the river itself, by boat.

Thais began mixing traditional Thai with European forms in the late 19th and early 20th centuries, as exemplified by Bangkok's Vimanmek Teak Mansion (p80), the Author's Wing of the Oriental Hotel (p212), the Chakri Mahaprasat (p57) next to Wat Phra Kaew, and any number of older residences and shophouses in Bangkok. This style is usually referred to as 'old Bangkok' or 'Ratanakosin'. The Old Siam Plaza shopping centre (p159), adjacent to Bangkok's Sala Chalermkrung (p188), is an attempt to revive the old Bangkok school.

ARCHITECTURAL ETHICS

Thailand has made numerous admirable efforts to preserve historic religious architecture, from venerable old stupas to ancient temple compounds. The Department of Fine Arts in fact enforces various legislation that makes it a crime to destroy or modify such monuments, and even structures found on private lands are protected.

On the other hand, Thailand has less to be proud of in terms of preserving secular civil architecture such as old government offices and shophouses. Only a few of Bangkok's Ratanakosin and Asian Deco buildings have been preserved, along with a handful of private mansions and shophouses, but typically only because the owners of these buildings took the initiative to do so. Thailand has little legislation in place to protect historic buildings or neighbourhoods, and distinctive early Bangkok architecture is disappearing fast, often to be replaced by plain cement, steel and glass structures of little historic or artistic value. For an illustrated list of buildings in Thailand that have received government protection, seek out the coffee-table book *174 Architectural Heritage in Thailand* (Saowalak Phongsatha Posayanan/Siam Architect Society, 2004).

Many other countries around the world have regulations that allow the registration of historic homes and whole neighbourhoods can be designated as national monuments. In neighbouring Laos, Unesco has helped to preserve the charming Lao-French architecture of Luang Prabang by designating the city as a World Heritage Site.

While Bangkok has gone so far in the direction of modern development that it will never recover much of the charm of its 18th- to early 20th-century architecture, if the city or nation doesn't take steps soon to preserve historic secular architecture, there will nothing left but an internationally homogenous hodge-podge of styles.

Disembark at the Mae Nam Chao Phraya pier of Tha Tien (Map p56), weave your way through the vendor carts selling grilled squid and rice noodles, and you'll find yourself standing between two rows of shophouses of the sort once found along all the streets near the river. Inside, the ground floors display multi-hued tiles of French, Italian or Dutch design, while upper floors are planked with polished teak. Similar shophouses can be found along Th Tanao in Banglamphu.

In the early 20th century, architects left the Victorian era behind, blended European Art Deco with functionalist restraint and created Thai Art Deco. Built just before WWI, an early and outstanding example of this style is Hualamphong Railway Station (p83). The station's vaulted iron roof and neoclassical portico are a testament to state-of-the-art engineering, while the patterned, two-toned skylights exemplify Dutch modernism.

Fully realised examples of Thai Deco from the 1920s and '30s can be found along Chinatown's main streets, particularly Th Yaowarat. Whimsical Deco-style sculptures – the Eiffel Tower, a lion, an elephant, a Moorish dome – surmount vertical towers over doorways. Atop one commercial building on Th Songwat perches a rusting model of a WWII Japanese Zero warplane. Placed there by the Japanese during their brief occupation of Bangkok in 1941, it coordinates perfectly with the surrounding Thai Deco elements. Other examples are the Sala Chalermkrung (p188), the Royal Hotel (p206) and Ratchadamnoen Boxing Stadium (p199).

OFFICE TOWERS, HOTELS & SHOPPING CENTRES

During most of the post-WWII era, the trend in modern Thai architecture – inspired by the German Bauhaus movement – was towards a boring International Style functionalism, and the average building looked like a giant egg carton turned on its side. The Thai aesthetic, so vibrant in pre-war eras, almost disappeared in this characterless style of architecture.

The city has been moving skywards almost as quickly as it has expanded outwards. When the Dusit Thani Hotel (p213) opened in 1970 it was the capital's tallest building, and even by the end of that decade fewer than 25 buildings stood taller than six floors. By the year 2000, nearly 1000 buildings could claim that distinction, with at least 20 of them towering higher than 45 floors.

On Th Sathon Tai is the Bank of Asia headquarters (p113), known locally as the 'Robot Building'. Thai architect Sumet Jumsai combined nut-and-bolt motifs at various elevations with a pair of lightning rods on the roof (arranged to resemble sci-fi robot-like antennae) and two metallic-lidded 'eyes' staring out from the upper façade. Another equally whimsical example can be seen in the Elephant Building (Map pp124–5) on Th Phaholyothin in northern Bangkok. Taking influence from Thailand's national symbol, every aspect of the building, from its external shape down to the door handles, is reminiscent of a pachyderm. Both of these buildings represent the

top picks

BANGKOK BUILDINGS

- Bangkok Bank (Map p84; cnr Soi Wanit 1 & Th Mangkon, Chinatown)
- Chalermkrung Royal Theatre (Map p84; 66 Th Charoen Krung, Chinatown)
- Chao Sua Son's House (Map p84; Talat Noi, Chinatown)
- Thai Wah II (Map p112; Th Sathon Tai, Sathon)
- Sukhothai Hotel (Map p112; Th Sathon Tai, Sathon)

last examples of architectural modernism in Bangkok, a trend that had all but concluded by the mid-1980s.

Almost every monumental project constructed in Bangkok now falls squarely in the postmodernist camp, combining rationalism with decorative elements from the past. Proclaiming its monumental verticality like a colossal exclamation point, the 60-storey Thai Wah II building (Map p112), also on Th Sathon Tai, combines rectangles and squares to create a geometric mosaic updating Egyptian Deco. At 305m, the cloud-stabbing Baiyoke Tower II (p104) is currently the second-tallest structure in Southeast Asia after Kuala Lumpur's towering Petronas Twin Towers. Stylistically it shows the inspiration of American post-Deco.

Pure verticality is now giving way to tiered skyscrapers in accordance with the city's setback regulations for allowing light into city streets. The tiered Bangkok City Tower (Map pp108–9) stacks marble, glass and granite around recessed entryways and window lines to create a stunning Mesopotamia-meets-Madison Ave effect. Everything 'neo' is in, including neo-Thai. The Four Seasons (p209), Sukhothai (p215) and Grand Hyatt Erawan (p210) are all examples of hotels that make extensive use of Thai classical motifs in layout and ornamentation.

ENVIRONMENT & PLANNING

THE LAND

Located halfway along Thailand's 1860km north–south axis, Bangkok lies approximately 14° north of the equator, putting it on a latitudinal level with Madras, Manila, Guatemala and Khartoum. The rivers and tributaries of northern and central Thailand drain into Mae Nam Chao Phraya, which in turn disgorges into the Gulf of Thailand, a large cul-de-sac of the South China Sea. Bangkok is partly surrounded by a huge, wet, flat and extremely fertile area known as 'the rice bowl of Asia' – more rice is grown here than in any other area of comparable size in all of Asia. Thailand has, in fact, been the world's top exporter of rice for at least the last 30 years.

Metropolitan Bangkok covers 1569 sq km, and may contain as many as 15 million people, making it one of the largest and most densely populated cities in the world. Built on swampland in the midst of one of Southeast Asia's most significant river deltas, the city is only 2m above sea level and sinking 5cm to 10cm a year, which means with rising sea levels it won't be long until the city lies below sea level. Hundreds of kilometres of natural and artificial canals crisscross the region, although many have been filled to create land for new roads and buildings. These canals, or khlong, were once Thailand's hydraulic lifeline, but are now seriously degraded by pollution and neglect.

GREEN BANGKOK

So extensive are the developments around Bangkok that you'd hardly realise the city is built on one of the world's great river deltas. Even the vast network of canals that once earned Bangkok the nickname 'Venice of the east' are largely lost, and few people remember the vast natural resources and fisheries now submerged by a sea of buildings and pollution. With the world's fastest-growing economy in the 1990s, Thailand in general, and Bangkok in particular, sacrificed environmental concerns in the face of massive profiteering. Bangkok boosts 1000 registered skyscrapers, with hundreds more planned in the ongoing construction boom, leaving little room for unprofitable concepts like city parks, green spaces, or healthy ecosystems.

All of the city's canals, as well as the lower reaches of Mae Nam Chao Phraya itself, are considered highly polluted, although plenty of Bangkok residents make daily use of these waterways for bathing, laundry, recreation and even drinking water (after treating it, of course). The worst water quality is found in the black-water canals on the Bangkok side of the river. On average, bacterial contamination of the city's waterways exceeds permissible limits by 75 to 400 times, and contact exposes you to the life-threatening infections that torment the lives of river residents.

The city has undertaken efforts to clean up the canals over the last couple of decades, but with one million cubic metres of liquid waste pouring into the waters each day, there is limited hope for measurable success. It is estimated that 98% of the region's households dump sewage directly into the rivers and canals and this isn't likely to change anytime soon. Efforts to 'clean' the canals includes planting water hyacinths and pumping polluted waters out of canals and pouring it into the river where it flows away into the ocean (out of sight, out of mind).

Roughly 50% of Bangkok's water supply is drawn directly from groundwater siphoned out of significantly depleted aquifers, leaving this water-laden city facing an impending water shortage. Since 1950 the government has constructed about 3000 dams in the Chao Phraya Basin, diverting water for flood control and irrigation, but leaving the lower reaches of the river increasingly contaminated by salt water that surges upstream as fresh water flows diminish.

On a more positive note, Bangkok's notoriously toxic air quality has improved dramatically over the past 15 years. With blue skies now the norm, Bangkok has emerged as a role model for other pollution-choked cities in Asia, and placed it on par with air quality found in North America. This is particularly impressive given that traffic has increased 40% in the past decade.

This isn't to say that the city doesn't suffer air quality issues found in other major cities. In 1999, Bangkok introduced the Skytrain, an elevated light-rail system that runs above the city's vehicle-clogged avenues. This public transit system provides welcome relief from the interminable traffic jams and takes cars off the road, but ironically air pollution gets trapped under the train's elevated concrete platforms and creates some of the worst air quality problems in the city.

Bangkok is constructing five new or extended light-rail lines, in a spoke-and-wheel configuration around the city, to persuade more Bangkokians to leave their cars and motorcycles at home. Also in the works are plans for a network of dedicated bus lanes on highways as a way of encouraging more people to use public transport. On a more practical level, every motorcycle sold in Thailand is now required to have a clean-burning four-stroke engine. This is a complete reversal from 10 years ago when all motorcycles were polluting two-stroke models. Air quality in Bangkok is expected to continue improving as old motorcycles and derelict buses are decommissioned and replaced with newer models that adhere to strict European emission standards.

In addition to several large city parks filled with trees and other vegetation, Bangkok relies on immense green areas to the west of the city as a means of detoxifying the air. One of the greatest threats to the environment is continued development, not only in the city centre, but also in outlying areas and neighbouring provinces. Realising the importance of maintaining green 'lungs' for the city, the Thai government attempts to maintain strict control on development in these areas. It has had less success controlling development in the inner city, and almost no success controlling vehicle circulation, one of the most obvious problem areas.

The public rubbish collection system in Bangkok works fairly smoothly, with the city managing to dispose of around 90% of all solid waste produced, an average of 9000 tonnes per day. The piles of street rubbish commonly seen in some South and Southeast Asian capitals are noticeably fewer in Bangkok. Where the rubbish goes is another question altogether. Although some serious attempts to separate and recycle paper, glass and plastic are under way, an estimated 80% of all solid waste ends up at sanitary landfill sites outside Bangkok.

URBAN PLANNING & DEVELOPMENT

When Bangkok became the new royal capital in 1782, the city was originally laid out in a traditional Buddhist mandala (*monthon* in Thai) plan, inspired by earlier capitals at Ayuthaya, Sukhothai and Chiang Mai. The Lak Meuang (City Pillar), palaces and royal monasteries stood at the centre, while Khlong Rop Krung was dug around the immediate perimeters to create an island called Ko Ratanakosin. Those nobles and merchants of value to the royal court were encouraged to settle just outside Ko Ratanakosin, and other canals were dug to circumscribe this next layer out from the centre. This rough plan of inner and outer rings – land alternating

lonelyplanet.com

with water – was a conscious attempt to pay homage to sacred Mt Meru (Phra Sumen in Thai) of Hindu-Buddhist mythology.

Early Bangkok was as much a citadel as a city. Today the massive whitewashed walls of Phra Sumen Fort still loom over one end of trendy Th Phra Athit, thrusting out towards Mae Nam Chao Phraya. This brick-and-stucco bunker was one of 14 city *pom* (fortresses) built along Khlong Banglamphu, which forms a bow-shaped arc carving an 'island' out of Mae Nam Chao Phraya's left bank.

On the other side of the battlements, Khlong Banglamphu cuts away from the river at a sharp angle, creating the northern tip of Ko Ratanakosin, the royal island that once was the whole of Bangkok. Although often neglected by residents and visitors alike, here stands one of the capital's pivotal points in understanding the city's original plan.

In the other direction, the 7km-long canal curves gently inland towards another wall-and-bunker cluster, Mahakan Fort, marking the southern reach of Ko Ratanakosin. Of the 4m-high, 3m-thick ramparts that once lined the entire canal, only Phra Sumen and Mahakan have been preserved to remind us what 18th-century Bangkok really was about – keeping foreign armies at bay.

Beginning in the early 19th century, Thai kings relinquished the mandala concept and began refashioning the city following European and American models, a process that has continued to this day. Open trade with the Portuguese, Dutch, English, French and Chinese had made the fortifications obsolete by the mid-19th century, and most of the original wall was demolished to make way for sealed roadways. By 1900 these roadways were lined with two-storey, brick-and-stucco Sino-Gothic shophouses inspired by Rama V's visits to Singapore and Penang.

Following WWII, when the Japanese briefly occupied parts of the city, Thai engineers built bridges over Mae Nam Chao Phraya and began filling in canals to provide space for new roads and shophouses. Although many residents continued to occupy stilted houses along the *khlong* and to move about their neighbourhoods by boat, a future of cars and asphalt was inevitable. In the 1960s and '70s the capital's area doubled in size, yet scant attention was paid to managing growth. Well into the 1980s, as adjacent provinces began filling with factories, housing estates, shopping malls, amusement parks and golf courses, urban planning was virtually nonexistent.

Bangkok's first official city plan was issued in 1992, and nowadays the Bangkok Metropolitan Administration (BMA) employs engineers and urban-planning experts to tackle growth and make plans for the future. So far most planning remains confined to paper – noble ideas without supporting actions, or with actions thwarted by infighting and profiteering. In theory city authorities have the power to regulate construction by zones, and to monitor land use, but in practice most new developments follow capital, with little thought given to such issues as parking, drainage, or social and environmental impact. For the most part city planners seem preoccupied with the immediate exigencies of maintaining basic city services.

CULTURE & IDENTITY

Whether native or newcomer, virtually every Bangkokian you meet has a story. Although the majority no doubt find themselves in Bangkok owing to the simple fact that they were born in the city, a healthy percentage of the population hails from other parts of Thailand and from around the world. Some have followed the promise of work, while others have simply sought out one of the world's most vibrant social climates.

Climb into one of the capital's ubiquitous yellow-and-green taxis and the music issuing from your driver's radio or cassette player will often suggest where he's (virtually all Bangkok taxi drivers are male) from. If it's *măw lam*, with the churning sound of Thai-Lao bamboo panpipes *(khaen)* pounding out zydeco-like chord figures over a strong, simple rhythm, then chances are he moved to Bangkok from one of Thailand's distant northeastern provinces, such as Roi Et or Sakon Nakhon. Switch to *lûuk thûng*, a unique hybrid of Thai, Indian and Latin musical influences popular with rural audiences, and the driver almost certainly comes from a province closer to Bangkok, perhaps Suphanburi or Saraburi. And if it's syrupy Thai pop or an older, crooning Bangkok style called *lûuk krung*, then you've most likely hitched a ride with a city native.

Only a little more than half of the city's inhabitants are in fact true Bangkok Thais, that is, those born of Thai parentage who speak Bangkok Thai as their first language. Although Thais are found in all walks of life, they are the backbone of the city's blue-collar workforce, construction, automotive repair and river transport.

Although Chinese Thais live in every quarter of the sprawling city, their presence is most noticeable in a densely populated core of multistorey shophouses along Th Charoen Krung and Th Yaowarat near Mae Nam Chao Phraya, a precinct known as Yaowarat, Sampeng or 'Chinatown'. Chinese in these areas tend to be engaged in all manner of commerce, from wholesale trade in auto parts to the manufacture of high-end kitchen utensils. In other parts of the city they dominate higher education, international trade, banking and white-collar employment in general. Both immigrant and Thailand-born Chinese residents probably enjoy better relations with the majority population here than in any other country in Southeast Asia.

One in 10 Thai citizens lives and works in Bangkok. Roughly 60% of the country's wealth is concentrated here, and per-capita income runs well above the average for the rest of the country – second only to Phuket, an island province in the south. The legal minimum daily wage in Bangkok and the adjacent provinces of Samut Prakan, Samut Sakhon, Pathum Thani, Nonthaburi and Nakhon Pathom amounted to 184B (US$4.85) in 2006, roughly 40B higher than in the rest of Thailand.

A typical civil servant in an entry-level government job earns around 7500B a month, but with promotions and extra job training may earn up to 15,000B. In the private sector an office worker starts at about the same level but will receive pay rises more quickly than those in government positions. Of course Bangkok thrives on private enterprise, from Talat Noi junk auto-parts shops eking out a profit of less than 500B a day, to huge multinational corporations whose upper-level employees drive the latest BMW sedans.

Bangkok women typically control the family finances, and are more likely than men to inherit real estate. Women constitute close to half of the city's workforce, outranking many world capitals. In fields such as economics, academia and health services, women hold a majority of the professional positions – 80% of all Thai dentists, for example, are female.

All of Bangkok's diverse cultures pay respect to the Thai king. The monarchy is considered one of the most important stabilising influences in modern Thai political and cultural life, and on Coronation Day and the King's Birthday the city is festooned with strings of lights and portraits of the king.

Another cultural constant is Theravada Buddhism, the world's oldest and most traditional Buddhist sect. Around 90% of Bangkokians are Buddhists, who believe that individuals work out their own paths to *nibbana* (nirvana) through a combination of good works, meditation and study of the *dhamma* or Buddhist philosophy. The social and administrative centre for Thai Buddhism is the wát or monastery, a walled compound containing several buildings constructed

THE CHINESE INFLUENCE

In many ways Bangkok is a Chinese, as much as a Thai, city. The presence of the Chinese in Bangkok dates back to before the founding of the city, when Thonburi Si Mahasamut was little more than a Chinese trading outpost on the Chao Phraya River. In the 1780s, during the construction of the new capital under Rama I, Hokkien, Teochiew and Hakka Chinese were hired as coolies and labourers. The Chinese already living in the area were relocated to the districts of Yaowarat and Sampeng, today known as Bangkok's Chinatown.

During the reign of King Rama I many Chinese began to move up in status and wealth. They controlled many of Bangkok's shops and businesses, and because of increased trading ties with China, were responsible for an immense expansion in Thailand's market economy. Visiting Europeans during the 1820s were astonished by the number of Chinese trading ships in the Chao Phraya River, and some assumed that the Chinese formed the majority of Bangkok's population.

The newfound wealth of certain Chinese trading families created one of Thailand's first elite classes that was not directly related to royalty. Known as *jâo sǔa*, these 'merchant lords' eventually obtained additional status by accepting official posts and royal titles, as well as offering their daughters to the royal family. At one point, King Rama V took a Chinese consort. Today it is believed that more than half of the people in Bangkok can claim some Chinese ancestry. The current Thai king is also believed to have partial Chinese ancestry.

During the reign of King Rama III, the Thai capital began to absorb many elements of Chinese food, design, fashion and literature. This growing ubiquity of Chinese culture, coupled with the tendency of the Chinese men to marry Thai women and assimilate into Thai culture had, by the beginning of the 20th century, resulted in relatively little difference between the Chinese and their Siamese counterparts.

in the traditional Thai style with steep, swooping roof lines and colourful interior murals; the most important structures contain solemn Buddha statues cast in bronze. The sheer number of wats scattered around the city – more than 300 – serves as a constant reminder that Buddhism retains a certain dominance even in increasingly secular Bangkok.

Walk the streets of Bangkok early in the morning and you'll catch the flash of shaved heads bobbing above bright ochre robes, as monks all over the city engage in *binthabàat*, the daily house-to-house alms food-gathering. Thai men are expected to shave their heads and don monastic robes temporarily at least once in their lives. Some enter the monkhood twice, first as 10-vow novices in their preteen years and again as fully ordained, 227-vow monks sometime after the age of 20. Monks depend on the faithful for their daily meals, permitted only before noon and collected in large, black-lacquered bowls from lay devotees.

Green-hued onion domes looming over rooftops belong to mosques and mark the immediate neighbourhood as Muslim, while brightly painted and ornately carved cement spires indicate a Hindu temple. Wander down congested Th Chakraphet in the Phahurat district to find Sri Gurusingh Sabha, a Sikh temple where visitors are very welcome. A handful of steepled Christian churches, including a few historic ones, have taken root over the centuries and can be found near the banks of Mae Nam Chao Phraya. In Chinatown large, round doorways topped with heavily inscribed Chinese characters and flanked by red paper lanterns mark the location of *sǎan jâo*, Chinese temples dedicated to the worship of Buddhist, Taoist and Confucian deities.

Thai royal ceremony remains almost exclusively the domain of one of the most ancient religious traditions still functioning in the kingdom, Brahmanism. White-robed, topknotted priests of Indian descent keep alive an arcane collection of rituals that, it is generally believed, must be performed at regular intervals to sustain the three pillars of Thai nationhood: sovereignty, religion and the monarchy. Such rituals are performed regularly at a complex of shrines near Wat Suthat in the centre of the city. Devasathan (Abode of Gods) contains shrines to Shiva and Ganesha and thus hosts priestly ceremonies in the Shaiva tradition, while the smaller Sathan Phra Narai (Abode of Vishnu) is reserved for Vaishnava ritual.

Animism predates the arrival of all other religions in Bangkok, and it still plays an important role in the everyday life of most city residents. Believing that *phrá phuum* or guardian spirits inhabit rivers, canals, trees and other natural features, and that these spirits must be placated whenever humans trespass upon or make use of these features, the Thais build spirit shrines to house the displaced spirits. These doll house-like structures perch on wood or cement pillars next to their homes and receive daily offerings of rice, fruit, flowers and water. Peek inside the smaller, more modest spirit homes and you'll typically see a collection of ceramic or plastic figurines representing the property's guardian spirits.

Larger and more elaborate spirit shrines stand alongside hotels and office buildings, and may contain elaborate bronze images of Brahma or Shiva. At virtually all times of the day and night, you'll see Thais kneeling before such shrines to offer stacks of flowers, incense and candles, and to pray for favours from these Indian 'spirit kings'.

The Thais may bestow Thai royal spirits with similar guardian qualities. The spirit of King Rama V, who ruled over Siam from 1868 to 1910 and who is particularly venerated for having successfully resisted colonialism, is thought to remain active and powerful in Bangkok today. Every Tuesday evening thousands of Bangkokians throng a bronze equestrian statue of Rama V standing opposite Abhisek Dusit Throne Hall, offering candles, pink roses, incense and liquor to the royal demigod.

GOVERNMENT & POLITICS

The Bangkok Metropolitan Administration (BMA) administers the capital, which is segmented into 50 districts covering 1569 sq km. Since 1985 metropolitan Bangkok has boasted the country's only elected governors (provincial governors are appointed), and perhaps the most charismatic of these was former army major general, Chamlong Srimuang.

A devout Buddhist, Chamlong is also a self-confessed celibate and a strict vegetarian. In 1985, Chamlong ran for governor as an independent, supported by an organisation calling itself Ruam Phalang (United Force), made up mostly of volunteers from the Santi Asoke Buddhist sect, of which he is a member. Despite facing a much more politically experienced and well-funded competitor, Chamlong won the election by a large margin.

As Governor of Bangkok, Chamlong had a large impact on making the city a more liveable place. He persuaded city street sweepers to sweep streets for the entire day, rather than just during the morning, and encouraged roadside hawkers, technically illegal, to stop selling their wares on Wednesdays. His anti-poverty projects included paving footpaths in squatter communities and establishing thrift stores for the poor. He even established a chain of vegetarian restaurants throughout the city.

In 1988, Chamlong established the Palang Dharma (Moral Force) Party (PDP), a largely Buddhist-based political entity, to contest nationwide parliamentary elections. The party went on to lose these, but Chamlong was able to hold on as Governor of Bangkok. Two years later, Chamlong was again voted governor, and his PDP won 49 out of 55 seats in the election for Bangkok City Council. It was during this term of office that Chamlong became the key opponent and protest leader of the 1991 military government led by army chief Suchinda Kraprayoon. Resigning as governor, Suchinda led massive protests, underwent a hunger strike and was even fired upon by the military before being publicly scolded along with Suchinda by the king on national television.

Many thought that Chamlong's political career was over after the incidents of 1991. However, in 2006 Chamlong once again gained the political spotlight in Bangkok when he became a key leader of the People's Alliance for Democracy, a coalition of protesters against the government of Thaksin Shinawatra. Although to Chamlong's chagrin it was the military that eventually took his former protégée out of office, he was instrumental in leading protests in downtown Bangkok that quite possibly led to Thaksin's demise.

In 2004, Bangkok gubernatorial candidate Apirak Kosayothin won a hotly contested race against a candidate backed by the ruling party, Thai Rak Thai. His victory was widely seen as a major loss of face for then Prime Minister Thaksin Shinawatra, leader of Thai Rak Thai. Governor Apirak named the reduction of corruption and traffic congestion as his main objectives, and has already embarked on plans to expand the BTS, the city's mass-transit system. However, some of his policies, including 'smart' taxi and bus stops, flopped, and his proposed Bus Rapid Transit (BRT) project has seen little progress.

In March 2008 Apirak voluntarily stepped down as governor so as not to influence an investigation into a fire truck procurement scandal that allegedly involved him and prime minister Samak Sundaravej.

MEDIA

Bangkok – and Thailand's – first printed periodical was the *Bangkok Recorder*, a monthly newspaper founded in 1844 by American missionary Dr Dan Beach Bradley. Today Thailand has 38 newspapers, four political weekly magazines, four political monthly magazines, two Chinese newspapers, one newspaper for Muslims, and two English-language newspapers: the *Bangkok Post* and *The Nation*.

In 1955 Thailand became the first country in Southeast Asia to broadcast television programmes. Today there are six free channels and a variety of subscription channels. Thailand also has 523 radio stations, most of which are run by the Public Relations Department, which supervises Radio Thailand, the central government station responsible for broadcasting local and daily news.

The country's previous constitution ensured freedom of the press, although the Royal Police Department reserved the power to suspend publishing licences for national security reasons. Editors generally exercise self-censorship in certain realms, especially with regard to the monarchy.

Thai press freedom reached its high-water mark in the mid-1990s, while Chuan Leekpai's Democrat Party was in power. Following the ascension of Thaksin Shinawatra's Thai Rak Thai Party in 2001, Thailand's domestic media found itself increasingly subject to interference by political and financial interests. The country's international reputation for press freedom took a serious dent in 2002 when two Western journalists were nearly expelled for reporting on a public address presented by the Thai king on his birthday, a portion of which was highly critical of PM Thaksin. In 2004 Veera Prateepchaikul, editor in chief of the *Bangkok Post*, lost his job due to direct pressure from board members with ties to Thaksin and Thai Rak Thai. Allegedly the latter were upset with *Post* criticism of the way in which the PM handled the 2003–04 bird flu crisis.

DRESSED TO THE NINES

Don't be fooled by the fashion aesthetics promoted by the tourist brochures and hotel lobbies. Within Bangkok's city limits, modern, not traditional, costumes rule the streetside runways that would make Milan feel underdressed. European labels are hotly pursued by fashionistas, but local labels are turning heads both here and abroad.

Local fashion houses, like Fly Now, Senada Theory and Greyhound, are frequent attendees to London and Paris fashion weeks. Fly Now started as a ladies boutique in 1983 and has expanded across the city with wearable art. Greyhound raced onto the scene in 1980 as a men's wear line and has since expanded to suit the fairer sex. The various lines are urban hip and amorphically Asian. The addition of a café in the Emporium shopping mall helped define Greyhound's lifestyle image with the global elite. Of the maturing new-wave designers, Senada Theory flirts most closely with ethnic chic, but succeeds in producing couture.

Established designers have stores in Gaysorn and the Emporium, while younger ready-to-wear designers open little boutiques in Siam Sq or Chatuchak Market. Even Th Khao San is beginning to show more home-grown design. The government is keen to promote Bangkok's garment industry and the city now hosts two fashion weeks: Bangkok Fashion Week in August and Elle Fashion Week in November. More ambitious plans have yet to materialise and critics point out that Thailand still lacks skilled craftspeople and high-end fabrics. But for now the raw enthusiasm makes stunning window dressing.

Observers agree that by 2005 Thai press freedom had reached it lowest ebb since the 1970s era of Thai military dictatorship. However, as popular opinion turned against Thaksin in late 2005 and early 2006, virtually all media (save for military-run TV channel 11) shook off the cloak of self-censorship and joined the public clamour that eventually resulted in Thaksin's deposition from power.

FASHION

Unsurprisingly, Bangkok is Thailand's fashion hub, and in fact in all of Southeast Asia only Singapore is a serious rival. Bangkokians not only dabble in the latest American, European and Japanese designer trends, but they have an up-and-coming couture all their own. Shops run by modern Thai designers are particularly easy to find at the Emporium, Gaysorn Plaza, Siam Paragon and Siam Center shopping centres, and in the small lanes of Siam Sq. Siam Sq focuses on inexpensive 'underground' Thai fashions favoured by university students and young office workers, while Emporium and Siam Center are much more upmarket. Local labels to look for include anr, Good Mixer, Fly Now, Greyhound, Jaspal and Senada Theory. Chatuchak Weekend Market is another place to seek out Bangkok designs at bargain prices.

Take a stroll through Siam Sq or Central World Plaza, especially on a weekend, and the explosion of styles and colours can't fail to impress. On weekends the middle *soi* (lane) of Siam Sq – an area known as Centrepoint – is filled with young Thais wearing the most outrageous clothing experiments they can create. It may not be on par with Tokyo's famous Harajuku district, but in a few years who knows what it may become?

Fashion shows grace the lobbies of various shopping centres around the city practically every weekend of the year. Since 1999 one of the biggest annual events has been Bangkok Fashion Week, a string of fashion shows in various venues around the city, including the new Fashion Dome, an air dome constructed over the middle of the lake at Benjakitti Park, adjacent to the Queen Sirikit National Convention Center. The Bangkok International Fashion Fair, held in September, is mostly a trade event but weekend days are usually open to the public.

The Thai government's clumsily named Office of the Bangkok Fashion City promotes fashion events and aims to turn Bangkok into a world-class – rather than simply regional – fashion centre by 2012. The office, however, has clashed more than once with Thailand's culture minister, who regularly chastises the organisers of Bangkok Fashion Week for the skimpiness of some of the outfits displayed on the catwalks. Coupled with the conservative night-time entertainment venue closing times, such Puritanism leads many in Bangkok's fashion community to question whether the city can attain world-class status with such government interference.

NEIGHBOURHOODS

top picks

- **Wat Pho** (p57) Stare up at the serene Reclining Buddha, then get a massage
- **River ferries** (p253) Discover the Mae Nam Chao Phraya and Thonburi by longtail or slow ferry
- **Wat Suthat** (p71) The way to see temples: a fine Buddha, sky-high murals and no tourists
- **Sampeng Lane** (p131) Commerce on steroids in a narrow lane that's seen trading for 230 years
- **Jim Thompson's House** (p97) The teak mansion that made Thai style cool
- **Baan Krua** (p100) The Muslim village where Jim Thompson discovered silk
- **Rooftop cocktails** Where else can you sip cocktails in an open-air, skyscraping rooftop bar? Moon Bar at Vertigo (p177) and Sirocco (p177).

NEIGHBOURHOODS

Bangkok sprawls across the rice-paddy–flat Chao Phraya plain, hugging both the snaking river itself and a spaghetti of newer concrete arteries. At first it can be hard to get your head around, with concrete towers seemingly spread as far as the eye can see and no discernible centre. But delve into the rivers of flowing metal and sprouting concrete and you'll find a megalopolis that's much more diverse that it first appears, and easier to navigate than you might think.

Along the banks of Mae Nam Chao Phraya (Chao Phraya River) the ancient monuments of king, country and religion marked the first shoots of the new capital to grow out of the flood plains. Straddling the river the ancient and relatively skyscraper-free districts of Ko Ratanakosin (Ratanakosin Island, p54) and Thonburi (p64) retain their historic charm. Ko Ratanakosin's relics of the old royal capital and the country's most revered Buddhist wats (temples) make it the most visited neighbourhood in the city.

The grand boulevard of Th Ratchadamnoen leads north to Banglamphu (p67), whose small villages of yellow-and-green shophouses once supplied the royal palace with its many ornate necessities. The regal enclave of Dusit (p78) sits like a crown on the northern apex of Banglamphu, fashioned after the capitals of Europe with wide boulevards and palaces set in manicured parks. It is flanked by the contrasting lower middle-class riverside neighbourhood of Thewet, which has an altogether less pretentious feel.

South of Ko Ratanakosin is the cramped and chaotic district of Chinatown (p82), where deals have been done since the city was founded and continue apace today. Chinatown is the most congested, hot and noisy part of town. South along the Mae Nam Chao Phraya the historic Riverside (p106) centre of international trade leads east into the business high-rise neighbourhoods of Silom and Sathon, and the relief and relative sanity of Lumphini Park.

To the north and east, the city pours forward like an endless concrete spill. Skyscrapers, shopping centres and expressway flyovers dominate the skyline in place of temples. Th Phra Ram I feeds into Siam Sq (p97), a thriving and heaving shopping district that has, for lack of a more obvious candidate, become the unofficial 'centre' of Bangkok. Further east is Th Sukhumvit (p116), a busy commercial neighbourhood where the internationals and cosmopolitans congregate.

GET LOST

Think of the 'sights' described in this chapter not as the only things to see in Bangkok, but rather as an excuse for exploring some of the city's most colourful neighbourhoods. These are your destinations but much of the most interesting travel is what happens in between, who you meet and what you see – especially if you get lost.

Every block will reveal something you've never seen before – blind troubadours with portable karaoke machines, *soi* dogs wearing T-shirts (who does dress these stray dogs?), vendors selling fresh pineapple, grilled meat, everything plus the kitchen sink. And, let's be honest, there'll be some things that are all too familiar – most likely another 7-Eleven store. To add to the excitement, you have to deal with Bangkok's notoriously dodgy pavements, which can be as traffic-clogged as its roads. Look forward to sidestepping a mass of humanity while ducking under huge umbrellas and canvas awnings pitched right at the level of your forehead, before having to squeeze through a bottleneck at a stall selling desserts that look like tacos. It's fun, really, as long as you take the occasional air-conditioned breather.

Most neighbourhoods have a walking tour and these are designed to be followed as strictly or loosely as you like. Or just invent your own, remembering that getting lost is the best gift Bangkok gives to visitors.

Bangkok's best neighbourhoods for getting lost in are its oldest districts. The maze of narrow streets, hidden temples and unconstrained commerce in Chinatown (p82) is a good start. Banglamphu boasts several village-like areas where modest communities live much as they have for decades. Those alongside Khlong Lawt (p67), Khlong Saen Saeb (p67) and Khlong Ong Ang (p82) are a hive of old-style activity and the *khlong*-side paths are often shaded and usually free of motorised transport. The columns and ornate façades of the warehouses and shops near Tha Tien (p54) show off the success of wealthier businesses, while the suburbs along the other side of the river in Thonburi (p64) are perhaps the best of the lot – as local as you like and barely a tourist anywhere. So go on, liberate yourself from the constraints of trying to follow a map, and go forth and wander.

GREATER BANGKOK
(p123)

2 km
1 miles
0
0

THANON
SUKHUMVIT
(p116)

SIAM SQUARE, PRATUNAM,
PLOENCHIT & RATCHATHEWI
(p97)

RIVERSIDE,
SILOM & LUMPHINI
(p106)

THEWET &
DUSIT
(p78)

CHINATOWN
(p82)

BANGLAMPHU
(p67)

KO RATANAKOSIN
& THONBURI
(p54)

ITINERARY BUILDER

Bangkok's big-ticket sights are concentrated in the older part of town around Ko Ratanakosin, Thonburi, Dusit and Banglamphu. However, the city's shopping, eating, galleries, bars and places to get a good massage are widespread. For late-night entertainment, the Sukhumvit and Silom areas are probably best.

AREA	ACTIVITIES	Sights	Outdoors	Shopping
	Ko Ratanakosin & Thonburi	Wat Pho (p57) Wat Phra Kaew and Grand Palace (p55) Royal Barges National Museum (p65)	Wat Arun (p65) Chao Phraya Express Boat (p253)	Amulet Market (p129) Traditional Medicine Shops (p128)
	Banglamphu & Dusit	Wat Suthat (p71) Wat Saket and Golden Mount (p67) Dusit Park (p80)	Dusit Park (p80) Monk's Bowl Village (p71) Th Khao San (p72)	It's Happened To Be A Closet (p130) Taekee Taekon (p130) Nittaya Curry Shop (p130)
	Chinatown	Wat Mangkon Kamalawat (p83) Wat Traimit (p85) Hualamphong Railway Station (p83)	Talat Noi (p83) Saphan Phut Night Bazaar (p132)	Sampeng Lane (p131) Pak Khlong Market (p132) Johnny's Gems p131)
	Siam Sq & Around	Jim Thompson's House (p97) Siam Ocean World (p101) Wang Suan Phakkat (p104)	Baan Krua (p100) Erawan Shrine (p102) Lingam Shrine (p101)	Siam Center & Siam Discovery Center (p135) Mahboonkrong (MBK, p134) Promenade Arcade (p134)
	Riverside, Silom & Lumphini	Queen Saovabha Memorial Institute (Snake Farm, p107) Oriental Hotel (p212) Bangkokian Museum (p107)	Lumphini Park (p106) Hotel ferries (p113) Haroon Village (p113)	Thai Home Industries (p136) Suan Lum Night Bazaar (p137) Patpong Night Market (p137)
	Th Sukhumvit	Ban Kamthieng (p116)	Benjakiti Park (p116) Soi 38 Night Market (p169) Skytrain (p254)	Thanon Sukhumvit Market (p138) L'Arcadia (p138) Nandakwang (p138)
	Greater Bangkok		Ko Kret (p230) Khlong Toey Market (p117) Rama IX Park (p123)	Chatuchak Weekend Market (p140) Vespa Market (p141)

HOW TO USE THIS TABLE

The table below allows you to plan a day's worth of activities in any area of the city. Simply select which area you wish to explore, and then mix and match from the corresponding listings to build your day. The first item in each cell represents a well-known highlight of the area, while the other items are more off-the-beaten-track gems.

Activities & the Arts	Eating	Drinking & Nightlife
Wat Pho Thai Traditional Massage School (p197) Patravardi Theatre (p188) National Theatre (p188)	Deck (p154) Rachanawi Samosawn (Navy Club Restaurant; p154) Wang Lang Market (p154)	Amorosa (p154)
Ratchadamnoen Stadium (p199) Num Thong Gallery (p192) Queen's Gallery (p192)	Chote Chitr (p155) Hemlock (p155) May Kaidee (p157)	Taksura (p177) Phranakorn Bar (p177) Brick Bar (p181)
Sala Chalermkrung (p188) About Café/About Studio (p191)	Tang Jai Yuu (p158) Chiang Kii (p159) Royal India (p159)	Nang Nual Riverside Pub (p177) River View Guest House (p208)
100 Tonson Gallery (p191) Bangkok Art & Cultural Centre (p191)	Kuaytiaw Reua Tha Siam (p160) Gianni Ristorante (p160) Sanguan Sri (p160)	Café Trio (p175) To-Sit (p178) Club Culture (p183)
H Gallery (p192) Lumphini Stadium (p199) Ruen-Nuad Massage (p197)	Cy'An (p161) Le Bouchon (p162) Khrua Aroy Aroy (p163)	Moon Bar at Vertigo (p177) Ad Makers (p181) DJ Station (p179)
Rasayana Retreat (p197) Buathip Thai Massage (p196) Gallery F-Stop (p192)	Face (p166) Spring (p167) Nasser Elmassry Restaurant (p168)	Bed Supperclub (p183) Tuba (p178) Living Room (p181)
Skills Development Centre for the Blind (p197) Bangkok University Art Gallery (BUG; p191) Thailand Cultural Centre (p189)	River Bar Café (p170) Yusup (p171) Baan Klang Nam 1 (p170)	Parking Toys (p181) Saxophone Pub & Restaurant (p181) Slim/Fix (p184)

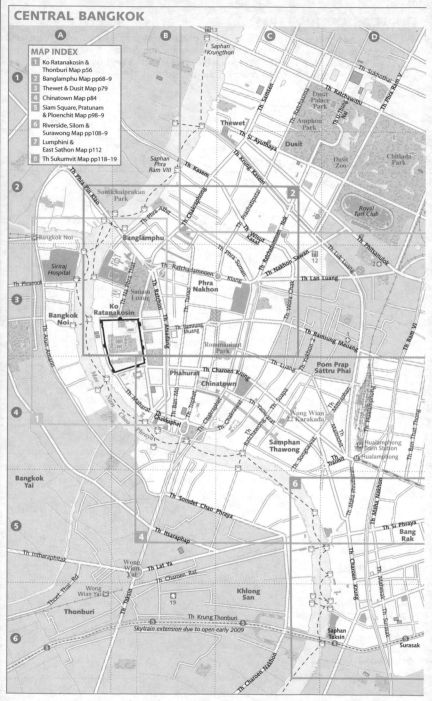

MAP INDEX

1 Ko Ratanakosin & Thonburi Map p56
2 Banglamphu Map pp68–9
3 Thewet & Dusit Map p79
4 Chinatown Map p84
5 Siam Square, Pratunam & Ploenchit Map p98–9
6 Riverside, Silom & Surawong Map pp108–9
7 Lumphini & East Sathon Map p112
8 Th Sukumvit Map pp118–19

Skytrain extension due to open early 2009

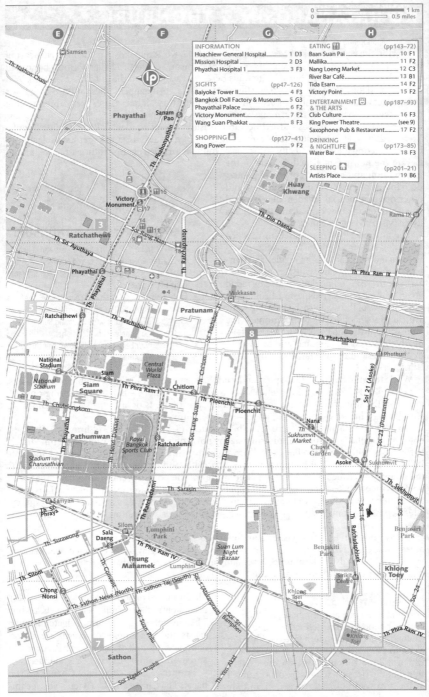

0   1 km
0   0.5 miles

INFORMATION	
Huachiew General Hospital	1 D3
Mission Hospital	2 D3
Phyathai Hospital 1	3 F3

SIGHTS	(pp47–126)
Baiyoke Tower II	4 F3
Bangkok Doll Factory & Museum	5 G3
Phayathai Palace	6 F2
Victory Monument	7 F2
Wang Suan Phakkat	8 F3

SHOPPING	(pp127–41)
King Power	9 F2

EATING	(pp143–72)
Baan Suan Pai	10 F1
Mallika	11 F2
Nang Loeng Market	12 C3
River Bar Café	13 B1
Tida Esarn	14 F2
Victory Point	15 F2

| ENTERTAINMENT | (pp187–93) |
& THE ARTS	
Club Culture	16 F3
King Power Theatre	(see 9)
Saxophone Pub & Restaurant	17 F2

| DRINKING | (pp173–85) |
& NIGHTLIFE	
Water Bar	18 F3

SLEEPING	(pp201–21)
Artists Place	19 B6

Eating p154; Shopping p128; Sleeping p202

Bordering the eastern bank of Mae Nam Chao Phraya, Ko Ratanakosin is the historic heart of Bangkok and is a veritable Vatican City of Thai Buddhism. Several of Thailand's most honoured and holy sites stand inside burly white walls here, Wat Phra Kaew and the Grand Palace (opposite), Wat Pho (p57) and the Lak Meuang (p58) being the most notable. As it happens, these are also Bangkok's most spectacular tourist attractions – and most obligatory sights – so expect camera-toting crowds rather than exotic eastern mysticism.

This collection of religious and architectural treasures wasn't accidental. Rama I (King Buddha Yodfa; r 1782–1809) intended to re-create the glory of the sacked Siamese capital of Ayuthaya by constructing a new island city – one that would be fortified against future attacks – and to elevate the newly established dynasty in the imagination and adoration of the populace. Both intentions succeeded. The Burmese and other noncommercial invaders never staged an assault on the new capital and the Chakri dynasty survives to the present day.

The ancient city has matured in modern times and is now a lively district of contradictions that only Thailand can juggle. The temples, with their heavenly status, are tethered to earth by nearby food markets shaded by faded green umbrellas clustered like mushrooms. In the shadows of the whitewashed temple walls are Buddhism's ancient companions – the animistic spirits who govern fortune and fate, neatly packaged into amulets and being sold by the thousand in the markets along Thanon Maharat (p59).

top picks

KO RATANAKOSIN & THONBURI

- Amulet market (p129) Traders, monks and collectors bartering for countless sacred amulets
- Wat Arun (p65) Mosaic-decorated stupa on the far bank of the river
- Wat Phra Kaew & Grand Palace (opposite) The Holly-wood blockbusters of Thai architecture
- Wat Pho (p57) A rather large Reclining Buddha and rambling complex of hidden sights
- Deck (p154) Unbeatable sunset views over the river and Wat Arun

While the glimmering golden spires and Buddha images of the big-ticket sights are must-sees, the charm of Ko Ratanakosin is felt just as much – if not more – by just wandering on foot, taking in the street life, stopping for lunch at local restaurants or at the Deck (p154) and mixing with young Thais in Thammasat (p62) and Silkaporn (p61) universities.

Opposite Ko Ratanakosin, across the busy waters of Mae Nam Chao Phraya, Thonburi (p64) enjoyed a brief 15-year promotion from sleepy port town to royal seat of power immediately before the capital moved to Bangkok. If it weren't for timing, it might otherwise be a footnote in Thai history. Instead it is still revered as a patriotic and divinely inspired step in reuniting the country after the fall of Ayuthaya. The stories of the postwar reunification are filled with poetic symbolism: General Taksin, who expelled the Burmese and subdued rival factions, came across this spot in the river at dawn and pronounced it Ayuthaya's successor. But Taksin was later deposed by a more strategic leader, who decided on a more strategic position across the river for his capital.

Today Thonburi is a rarely visited gem for anyone looking to experience the less commercial, quieter side of Bangkok life. Where Bangkok's *khlong* have largely been concreted over to create traffic-packed roads in Thonburi they remain an integral part of daily life. To really experience this unique neighbourhood, stay at the Thai House (p221).

KO RATANAKOSIN

Forming almost a tear-drop shape, Ko Ratanakosin's boundaries are defined by Mae Nam Chao Phraya on the western side, Th Phra Pin Klao on the northern side and Th Atsadang, which follows Khlong Lawt, on the eastern side. The district's attractions are concentrated in the area south of Sanam Luang (p60) and are ideally visited on foot (see the Walking Tour, p63), preferably in the morning before it gets too hot. The pavements that circumnavigate the main sights and the temple courtyards are almost completely devoid of shade, so a hat, sunscreen and even an umbrella can be a good idea.

Four river piers – Tha Phra Chan, Tha Maharat, Tha Chang and Tha Tien – service this district, making transport a scenic, convenient and relaxed experience. It's also a popular area from which to hire longtail boats for tours into Thonburi's canals.

South of Th Na Phra Lan is primarily a tourist zone with a few warehouses abutting the river as reminders that a measure of traditional life still exists. North of the Grand Palace is Sanam Luang, an expansive park where joggers shuffle along in the early morning hours. Alongside Sanam Luang the National Museum and the National Theatre stand with stoic resolve and people gather to celebrate and protest the kingdom's milestones. On the far eastern side of Wat Phra Kaew are government ministry buildings reflecting a pronounced Western architectural influence – an interesting contrast to the flamboyant Thai architecture across the street.

Rip-off artists prowl the tourist strip, using the country's legendary hospitality to earn a dishonest day's wages. Disregard any strangers who approach you inquiring about where you are from (usually followed by 'oh, my son/daughter is at university there'), where you are going or (the classic opening gambit) telling you the attractions are closed. Save the one-on-one cultural exchange for genuine people outside the tourist zone.

WAT PHRA KAEW & GRAND PALACE
Map p56

วัดพระแก้ว/พระบรมมหาราชวัง

☎ 0 2222 6889; Th Na Phra Lan; admission to wat, palace & Dusit Park 250B; ☷ 8.30am-3.30pm; ☗ Tha Chang (N9), ☖ air-con 503, 508 & 512, ordinary 2 & 25

The Temple of the Emerald Buddha (Wat Phra Kaew) gleams and glitters with so much colour and glory that its earthly foundations seem barely able to resist the celestial pull. Architecturally fantastic, the temple complex is also the spiritual core of Thai Buddhism and the monarchy, symbolically united in what is the country's most holy image, the Emerald Buddha. Attached to the temple complex is the former royal residence, once a sealed city of intricate ritual and social stratification.

If you're suitably dressed (see the boxed text, p59), enter Wat Phra Kaew and the Grand Palace complex through the third gate from the river pier. Tickets are purchased inside the complex; anyone telling you it's closed is a gem tout or con artist.

Past the ticket counters you'll meet the *yaksha*, brawny guardian giants from the

Ramakian (the Thai version of the Indian Ramayana epic). Beyond the gate is a courtyard where the central *bòt* (chapel) houses the Emerald Buddha (p58). The spectacular ornamentation inside and out does an excellent job of distracting first-time visitors from paying their respects to the image. Here's why: the Emerald Buddha is only 66cm tall and sits so high above worshippers in the main temple building that the gilded shrine is more striking than the small figure it cradles. There are always postcards if you miss it.

Outside the main *bòt* is a stone statue of the Chinese goddess of mercy, Kuan Im, and nearby are two cow figures, representing the year of Rama I's birth.

In the 2km-long cloister that defines the perimeter of the complex are 178 murals depicting the Ramakian in its entirety, beginning at the north gate and moving clockwise around the compound. If the temple grounds seem overrun by tourists, the mural area is usually mercifully quiet and shady.

Adjoining Wat Phra Kaew is the Grand Palace (Phra Borom Maharatchawang), a former royal residence that today is used by the king only for certain ceremonial occasions; the current monarch lives in Chitralada Palace, which is closed to the public. Visitors are allowed to survey the Grand Palace grounds and exteriors of the four remaining palace buildings, which are interesting for their royal bombast.

At the eastern end, Borombhiman Hall is a French-inspired structure that served as a residence for Rama VI (King Vajiravudh; r 1910–25). In April 1981 General San Chitpatima used it as headquarters for an attempted coup. Amarindra Hall, to the west, was originally a hall of justice but is used today for coronation ceremonies.

TRANSPORT: KO RATANAKOSIN

There's no Skytrain or Metro to Ko Ratanakosin, so the easiest and most enjoyable ways to get here are by river ferry or on foot. From Banglamphu just walk through Thammasat University or Sanam Luang; from almost anywhere else take either a ferry direct or the Skytrain to Saphan Taksin and a ferry from there.

Bus Air-con 503, 508, 511 and 512, ordinary 3, 25, 39, 47, 53 and 70

Ferry Tha Rajinee (N7), Tha Tien (N8) and Tha Chang (N9)

KO RATANAKOSIN & THONBURI

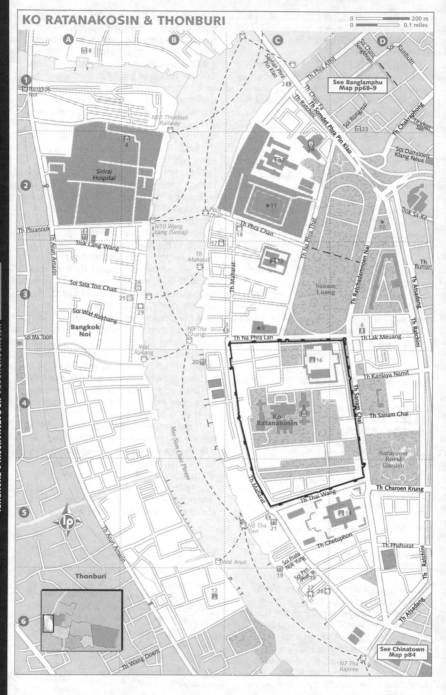

See Banglamphu Map pp68–9

See Chinatown Map p84

Bangkok Noi

Siriraj Hospital

Sanam Luang

Ko Ratanakosin

Thonburi

Saranrom Royal Garden

Mae Nam Chao Phraya

Bangkok Noi

KO RATANAKOSIN & THONBURI

INFORMATION

Bangkok Bank.................................1 C5
Bangkok Tourist Division (BTD)...2 C1
Siam City Bank...........................3 C3

SIGHTS & ACTIVITIES   (pp54–66)

Amulet Market.......................(see 17)
Emerald Buddha....................(see 16)
Forensic Medicine Museum........4 B2
Grand Palace.............................5 C4
Lak Meuang..............................6 D3
National Museum......................7 C2
Reclining Buddha..................(see 14)
Royal Barges National Museum...8 A1
Silpakorn University...................9 C3
Statue of Mae Thorani.............10 D2
Thammasat University.............11 C2

Wat Arun.................................12 B6
Wat Mahathat.........................13 C3
Wat Mahathat's International
    Buddhist Meditation Centre..(see 13)
Wat Pho..................................14 D5
Wat Pho Thai Traditional
    Massage School..................15 C6
Wat Phra Kaew.......................16 C4

SHOPPING 🛍   (pp127–41)

Amulet Market........................17 B3
Traditional Medicine Shops.......18 C2

EATING 🍴   (pp143–72)

Deck.......................................19 C6
Rachanawi Samosawn (Navy
    Club Restaurant)..................20 B4

Rub Aroon................................21 C5
Wang Lang Market.................22 A2

ENTERTAINMENT 🎭
& THE ARTS   (pp188–93)

National Gallery.......................23 D1
National Theatre......................24 C2
Patravadi Theatre....................25 B3
Silpakorn University.................(see 9)
Studio 9...............................(see 25)
Supatra River House................26 B3

SLEEPING 🛏   (pp201–21)

Arun Residence....................(see 19)
Aurum: The River Place...........27 C6
Chakrabongse Villas...............28 C6
Ibrik Resort.............................29 B3

The largest of the palace buildings is the triple-winged Chakri Mahaprasat (Grand Palace Hall). Completed in 1882 following a plan by British architects, the exterior shows a peculiar blend of Italian Renaissance and traditional Thai architecture, a style often referred to as *faràng sài chá-daa* (Westerner wearing a Thai classical dancer's head-dress), because each wing is topped by a *mondòp* (a layered, heavily ornamented spire). It is believed the original plan called for the palace to be topped with a dome, but Rama V was persuaded to go for a Thai-style roof instead. The tallest of the *mondòp*, in the centre, contains the ashes of Chakri kings; the flanking *mondòp* enshrine the ashes of Chakri princes who failed to inherit the throne.

The last building to the west is the Ratanakosin-style Dusit Hall, which initially served as a venue for royal audiences and later as a royal funerary hall.

Until Rama VI decided one wife was enough for any man, even a king, Thai kings housed their huge harems in the inner palace area (not open to the public), which was guarded by combat-trained female sentries. The intrigue and rituals that occurred within the walls of this cloistered community live on in the fictionalised epic *Four Reigns,* by Kukrit Pramoj, which follows a young girl named Ploi growing up within the Royal City.

The admission fee to Wat Phra Kaew also includes entry to Dusit Park (p80).

WAT PHO Map p56

วัดโพธิ์(วัดพระเชตุพน)

☎ 0 2622 3533; www.watpho.com; Th Sanam Chai; admission 50B; ☽ 8am-5pm; 🚢 Tha Tien (N8), 🚌 air-con 503, 508 & 512, ordinary 12 & 53

Of all Bangkok's temples, Wat Pho is arguably the one most worth visiting for both its remarkable Reclining Buddha image and its sprawling grounds. The temple boasts a long list of credits: the oldest and largest wat in Bangkok, the longest Reclining Buddha and the largest collection of Buddha images in Thailand, and the earliest centre for public education. For all that, it's less of an attraction than neighbouring Wat Phra Kaew and retains a more laid-back, less commercial feel.

A temple has stood on this site since the 16th century, but in 1781 Rama I ordered the original Wat Photharam to be completely rebuilt as part of his new capital. Under Rama III (King Nang Klao; r 1824–51), the massive Reclining Buddha was built and Wat Pho became Thailand's first university. Today it maintains that tradition as the national headquarters for the teaching and preservation of traditional Thai medicine, including Thai massage.

Narrow Th Chetuphon divides the grounds in two, and it's well worth entering from this quiet street to avoid the touts and tour groups of the main entrance on Th Thai Wang. You'll come into the eastern courtyard of the northern compound (the southern part is closed to the public), where the main *bòt* is constructed in Ayuthaya style and is strikingly more subdued than Wat Phra Kaew. Rama I's remains are interred in the base of the presiding Buddha figure in the *bòt*.

The images on display in the four *wíhăan* (sanctuaries) surrounding the main *bòt* are worth investigation. Particularly beautiful are the Phra Jinnarat and Phra Jinachi Buddhas in the western and southern chapels, both rescued from Sukhothai by relatives

THE EMERALD BUDDHA

The Emerald Buddha's lofty perch in Wat Phra Kaew signifies its high status as the 'talisman' of the Thai kingdom. No-one knows exactly where the Buddha comes from or who sculpted it, but it first appeared on record in 15th-century Chiang Rai in northern Thailand. Legend says it was sculpted in India and brought to Siam by way of Ceylon (Sri Lanka), but stylistically it seems to belong to Thai artistic periods of the 13th to 14th centuries. Despite the name, the sacred sculpture is actually carved from a single piece of nephrite, a type of jade.

Some time in the 15th century, this Buddha is said to have been covered with plaster and gold leaf and placed in Chiang Rai's own Wat Phra Kaew. Many valuable Buddha images were masked in this way to deter potential thieves and marauders during unstable times. Often the true identity of the image was forgotten over the years until a 'divine accident' exposed its precious core. The Emerald Buddha experienced such a divine revelation when it was being transported to a new location. In a fall, the plaster covering broke off, revealing the brilliant green inside. But this coming out was not the beginning of this Buddha's peaceful reign.

During territorial clashes with Laos, the Emerald Buddha was seized and taken to Vientiane in the mid-16th century. Some 200 years later, after the fall of Ayuthaya and the ascension of the Bangkok-based kingdom, the Thai army marched up to Vientiane, razed the city and hauled off the Emerald Buddha. The return of this revered figure was a great omen for future fortunes of this new leadership. The Buddha was enshrined in the then capital, Thonburi, before the general who led the sacking of Vientiane assumed the throne and had it moved to this location.

A tradition that dates back to this time is the changing of the Buddha's seasonal robes. There are now three royal robes: for the hot, rainy and cool seasons. The three robes are still solemnly changed at the beginning of each season. This duty has traditionally been performed by the king, though in recent years the crown prince has presided over the ceremony.

---

of Rama I. The galleries extending between the four chapels feature no fewer than 394 gilded Buddha images.

Encircling the main *bòt* is a low marble wall with 152 bas-reliefs depicting scenes from the Ramakian. You'll recognise some of these figures when you exit the temple past the hawkers with the mass-produced rubbings for sale; these are made from cement casts based on Wat Pho's reliefs.

A collection of towering tiled stupas commemorates the first four Chakri kings and there are 91 smaller stupas. Rama IV ordered that the four stupas be surrounded by a wall to prevent future kings joining the memorial. Note the square bell shape with distinct corners, a signature of Ratanakosin style. Other smaller *chedi* (stupa) clusters contain the ashes of royal descendants.

Small rock gardens and hill islands interrupt the tiled courtyards providing shade, greenery and quirky decorations. Inherited from China, these rockeries are cluttered with topiary, miniature waterfalls and small statues depicting daily life. Khao Mor is the most distinctive of the rock gardens, festooned with figures of the hermit credited with inventing yoga in various healing positions. According to the tradition, a few good arm stretches should cure idleness.

In the northwest corner of the site you'll find Wat Pho's main attraction, the enormous, tremendous Reclining Buddha.

The 46m-long and 15m-high supine figure illustrates the passing of the Buddha into nirvana. It is made of plaster around a brick core and finished in the gold leaf that gives it a serene luminescence that keeps you looking, and looking again, from different angles. The 3m-high feet are a highlight, with mother-of-pearl inlay depicting 108 different auspicious *láksànà* (characteristics of a Buddha).

On the temple grounds, there are nonair-conditioned massage pavilions; air-con rooms are available in the massage school (p197), across the street from the temple. The two pavilions located nearby contain visual depictions of the body meridians and pressure points that were used to record the oral knowledge of the practice and are used as a teaching tool.

LAK MEUANG Map p56
ศาลหลักเมือง

☎ 0 2222 9876; Cnr Th Sanamchai & Th Lak Meuang; admission free; ☯ 6am-6pm; ⚓ Tha Chang (N9), ⛴ air-con 508, 511 & 512, ordinary 15, 47, 53 & 59

What would otherwise be an uninteresting mileage marker has both religious and historical significance in Thailand. Lak Meuang is the city shrine, a wooden pillar erected by Rama I in 1782 to represent the founding of the new Bangkok capital. From this point, distances are measured to

TEMPLE ETIQUETTE

Wats are sacred places and should be treated with respect. At all wats you must remove your shoes as you enter – if you see empty shoes scattered around a doorway or threshold, this is your cue. At some temples, and especially at Wat Phra Kaew and the Grand Palace grounds, dress rules are strictly enforced. If you're wearing shorts or a sleeveless shirt you will not be allowed into the temple grounds – this applies to men and women. Long skirts and three-quarter length pants are not appropriate, either. If you're flashing a bit too much calf or ankle, expect to be shown into a dressing room and issued with a sarong. Once suitably attired, you'll be allowed in. For walking in the courtyard areas you are supposed to wear shoes with closed heels and toes. Sandals and thongs (flip-flops) are not permitted, though the guards are less zealous in their enforcement of this rule.

all other city shrines in the country. But its importance doesn't stop there. The pillar is endowed with a spirit, Phra Sayam Thewathirat (Venerable Siam Deity of the State), and is considered the city's guardian. To the east of the main shrine are five other idols added during the reign of Rama V (King Chulalongkorn; r 1868–1910).

Like the sacred banyan trees and the holy temples, Lak Meuang receives daily supplications from Thai worshippers, some of whom commission classical Thai dancers to perform *lákhon kâe bon* (shrine dancing) as thanks for granted wishes. Offerings also include those morbidly cute pigs' heads with sticks of incense sprouting from their foreheads.

Lak Meuang is across the street from the eastern wall of Wat Phra Kaew, at the southern end of Sanam Luang.

THANON MAHARAT Map p56
ถนนมหาราช

Btwn Th Phra Chan, Th Na Phra Lan & Mae Nam Chao Phraya; 🚢 Tha Chang (N9), 🚌 air-con 503, 508 & 512, ordinary 47 & 53

The northern stretch of this street is one of Bangkok's most interesting. On the opposite side of Wat Mahathat's whitewashed walls, the street is monopolised by ancient Thai industries: herbal apothecaries and amulet dealers. In the cool season, medicinal bowls of ginger-infused broth are sold from steaming cauldrons to stave off winter colds. Outdoor displays of pill bottles are lined up and dusted daily like prized antiques. Each remedy bears a picture of a stoic healer, a marketing pitch that puts a human face on medicine. Further along, the amulet market (*talàat phrá khrêuang*; p129) spills out of its medieval warren into the street, forcing pedestrians to run zigzag patterns through the spread blankets on which the tiny images are displayed.

This is a great place to just wander and watch men (because it's rarely women) looking through magnifying glasses at the tiny amulets, seeking hidden meaning (and value). The market stretches all the way to the riverside, where a narrow alley leads north to wooden kitchens overhanging the water. Each humble kitchen garners a view of the river; students from nearby Thammasat University congregate here for cheap eats before heading off to class. The food reflects Bangkok's peculiar student menu: a motley mix of Thai comforts and Western adaptations.

The municipal government has grand plans for this area to be demolished and redeveloped as a cultural theme park with more river vistas and shops catering to tourists. The proposal has met with fierce

STONE COLD STARE: WAT PHO'S ROCK GIANTS

Aside from monks and sightseers, Wat Pho is filled with an altogether stiffer crowd; dozens of giants and figurines carved from granite. The rock giants first arrived in Thailand as ballast aboard Chinese junks and were put to work in Wat Pho (and other wats, including Wat Suthat), guarding the entrances of temple gates and courtyards.

Look closely and you'll see an array of Chinese characters. The giants with bulging eyes and Chinese opera costumes were inspired by warrior noblemen and are called *Lan Than*; notice their swords tucked behind their ornate robes. The political nobleman wears his hair and moustache below his shoulders and carries a scroll in one hand; his long cloak indicates that he is a member of the aristocracy. The figure in a straw hat is a farmer, forever interrupted during his day's work cultivating the fields. And can you recognise the guy in the fedora-like hat with a trimmed beard and moustache? Marco Polo, of course, who introduced such European styles to the Chinese court.

resistance from residents, and many hope that this is one of the many Bangkok pipe dreams that ultimately gets smoked. But with Bangkok's love of reinvention, it is better to savour its few remaining medieval corners while they last.

NATIONAL GALLERY Map p56
หอศิลปแห่งชาติ

☎ 0 2282 2639; Th Chao Fa; admission 30B;
🕑 9am-4pm Wed-Sun; 🚲 Tha Phra Athit (N13),
🚌 air-con 508, 511 & 512, ordinary 47 & 53

Housed in a weather-worn early Ratanakosin-era building just north of Sanam Luang, the National Gallery displays traditional and contemporary art, mostly by artists receiving government support. Secular art is a fairly new concept in Thailand and some of the country's best examples of fine art reside in temples rather than galleries. Most of the permanent collection documents Thailand's homage to modern styles. One noteworthy exception is the *Musical Rhythm* sculpture, by Khien Yimsiri, which is considered one of the most remarkable fusions of Western and Thai styles of the mid-20th century. More uniquely Thai expressions can be seen in the rotating exhibitions by young artists. The general opinion is that this gallery is not Thailand's best, but with air-conditioning and its historic setting it is a quiet place to escape the crowds and the sun. A weekend art market, set up in the museum courtyard, is accessible without having to pay admission.

NATIONAL MUSEUM Map p56
พิพิธภัณฑสถานแห่งชาติ

☎ 0 2224 1402; www.thailandmuseum.com; Th Na Phra That; admission 50B; 🕑 9am-4pm Wed-Sun;
🚌 air-con 508, 511 & 512, ordinary 12, 47 & 53;
🚲 Tha Chang (N9)

Thailand's National Museum is the largest museum in Southeast Asia and covers a broad range of subjects, from historical surveys to religious sculpture displays. The buildings were originally constructed in 1782 as the palace of Rama I's viceroy, Prince Wang Na. Rama V turned it into a museum in 1884.

The history wing presents a succinct chronology of events and figures from the prehistoric, Sukhothai, Ayuthaya and Bangkok eras. Despite the corny dioramas, there are some real treasures here: look for King Ramakamhaeng's inscribed stone pillar (the oldest record of Thai writing), King Taksin's throne and the Rama V section.

The other parts of the museum aren't as well presented, but this might be part of the charm. Dimly lit rooms, ranging in temperature from lukewarm to boiling, offer an attic-like collection of Thai art and handicrafts.

In the central exhibits hall, there are collections of traditional musical instruments from Thailand, Laos, Cambodia and Indonesia, as well as ceramics, clothing and textiles, woodcarving, royal regalia, and Chinese art and weaponry. The art and artefact buildings cover every Southeast Asian art period and style, from Dvaravati to Ratanakosin. The collection is impressive but hard to digest due to poor signage and sheer volume.

The museum grounds also contain the restored Phutthaisawan (Buddhaisawan) Chapel. Inside the chapel (built in 1795) are some well-preserved original murals and one of the country's most revered Buddha images, Phra Phuttha Sihing. Legend claims the image came from Ceylon, but art historians attribute it to the 13th-century Sukhothai period.

The museum runs (highly recommended) free tours in English and French on Wednesday and Thursday, Japanese on Wednesday and German on Thursday. All tours start from the ticket pavilion at 9.30am.

SANAM LUANG Map p56
สนามหลวง

Bounded by Th Na Phra That, Ratchadamnoen Nai & Na Phra Lan; 🚌 air-con 503, 508, 511 & 512, ordinary 15, 47, 53 & 59, 🚲 Tha Chang (N9)

On a hot day, Sanam Luang (Royal Field) is far from charming – a shadeless expanse of dying grass ringed by flocks of pigeons and homeless people. Despite its shabby appearance, however, it has been at the centre of both royal ceremony and political upheaval since Bangkok was founded. Indeed, the yellow-shirted masses who protested for months before Thaksin Shinawatra was ousted in a coup d'état often used this field to air their grievances.

Less dramatic events staged here include the annual Royal Ploughing Ceremony, in which the king (or more recently the crown prince) officially initiates the rice-growing season (p13). After the rains, the kite-flying season (mid-February to April) sees the open space filled with butterfly-shaped Thai kites. Matches are held between teams flying either a 'male' or 'female' kite in a particular territory; points are won if they can force a competitor into their zone.

Large funeral pyres are constructed here during elaborate, but infrequent, royal cremations.

In a way the park is suffering a career crisis, having lost most of its full-time employment to other locales or the whims of fashion. Until 1982 Bangkok's famous Weekend Market was regularly held here (it's now at Chatuchak Park; see p140). Previously the wealthy came here for imported leisure sports; these days they head for the country club. Today the cool mornings and evenings still attract a health-conscious crowd of joggers, walkers and groups playing *tàkrâw*. If you fancy a big-crowd experience, Sanam Luang draws the masses in December for the King's Birthday (5 December), Constitution Day (10 December) and New Year.

Across Th Ratchadamnoen to the east is the statue of Mae Thorani, the earth goddess (borrowed from Hindu mythology's Dharani), which stands in a white pavilion. Erected in the late 19th century by Rama V, the statue was originally attached to a well that provided drinking water to the public.

SARANROM ROYAL GARDEN
Map p56

สวนสราญรมย์

Btwn Th Ratchini & Charoen Krung; 5am-9pm; Tha Tien (N8), air-con 503, 508 & 512, ordinary 12, 25 & 53
Easily mistaken for a European public garden, this Victorian-era green space was originally designed as a royal residence in the time of Rama IV (King Mongkut; r 1851–68). After Rama VII abdicated in 1935, the place served as the headquarters of the People's Party, the political organisation that orchestrated the handover of the government. The open space remained and in 1960 was opened to the public.

Today a wander through the garden reveals a Victorian gazebo, paths lined with frangipani and a moat around a marble monument built in honour of Rama V's wife, Queen Sunantha, who died in a boating accident. The queen was on her way to Bang Pa-In Summer Palace in Ayuthaya when her boat began to sink. The custom at the time was that commoners were for-

top picks

FOR CHILDREN

Aside from the play centres found on the top floors of several major shopping centres, Bangkok has plenty to keep kids amused (at least until they're exhausted by the heat).

- Tha Thewet (Map p79; Th Krung Kasem; 7am-7pm) Join the novice monks and Thai children as they throw food (bought on the pier) to thousands of flapping fish.
- Wat Prayoon (Map p84; 24 Th Prachathipok, cnr Thetsaban Soi 1; 8am-6pm; from Tha Pak Talat/Atsadang) This artificial hill beside the Memorial Bridge is cluttered with miniature shrines and a winding path that encircles a pond full of turtles.
- Children's Discovery Museum (p123) Fun, and they might learn something too.
- Queen Saovabha Memorial Institute (Snake Farm; p107) Cool snake shows and a chance to touch some cool snake skin.
- Lingam Shrine (p101) Face it, your kids are probably going to love this stand of giant stone and wooden phalluses.
- Theme parks (p248) There are plenty to choose from.

bidden to touch royalty, which prevented her attendants saving her from drowning.

The satellite corners of the park are filled with weightlifting equipment where a túk-túk driver might do some leg crunches in between telling tourists that the sights they are looking for have closed. As the day cools various aerobics and dance classes practise their synchronisation.

SILPAKORN UNIVERSITY Map p56

มหาวิทยาลัยศิลปากร

0 2623 6115; www.su.ac.th; 31 Th Na Phra Lan; Tha Chang (N9), air-con 508 & 512, ordinary 47 & 53
Thailand's universities aren't usually repositories for interesting architecture, but the country's premier art school breaks the mould. Partly housed in a former palace, the classical buildings form the charming nucleus of what was an early Thai aristocratic enclave and the traditional artistic temperament still survives. The building immediately facing the Th Na Phra Lan gate

BANGKOK STREET SMARTS

Keep the following in mind and you won't join the list of tourists sucked in by Bangkok's numerous scam artists, and will survive the traffic.

- Good jewellery, gems and tailor shops aren't found through a túk-túk driver.
- Skip the 10B túk-túk ride unless you have the time and will-power to resist a heavy sales pitch in a tailor or gem store.
- Ignore 'helpful' locals who tell you that tourist attractions and public transport are closed for a holiday or cleaning; it's the beginning of a con, most likely a gem scam.
- Don't expect any pedestrian rights; put a Bangkokian between you and any oncoming traffic, and yield to anything with more metal than you.
- Walk outside the tourist strip to hail a taxi that will use the meter – tell the driver 'meter'. If the driver refuses to put the meter on, get out.

was once part of a palace and now houses the Silpakorn University Art Centre (Map p56; ☎ 0 2218 2965; www.art-centre.su.ac.th; ☺ 9am-7pm Mon-Fri, 9am-4pm Sat), which showcases faculty and student exhibitions. To the right of the building is a shady sculpture garden displaying the work of Corrado Feroci (also known as Silpa Bhirasri), the Italian art professor and sculptor who came to Thailand at royal request in the 1920s and later established the university (which is named after him) and sculpted parts of the Democracy Monument (p73), among other works.

Not surprisingly, the campus has an arty, contemporary vibe and is a good place to sit and watch sketchers doing their thing. Stop by the Art Shop beside the gallery for unique postcards and books.

THAMMASAT UNIVERSITY Map p56
มหาวิทยาลัยธรรมศาสตร์

☎ 0 2221 6111; www.tu.ac.th; 2 Th Phra Chan; ⚓ Tha Chang (N9), 🚌 air-con 508, 511 & 512, ordinary 47 & 53

Much of the drama that followed Thailand's transition from monarchy to democracy has unfolded on this quiet riverside campus. Thammasat University was established in 1934, two years after the bloodless coup that deposed the monarchy. Its remit was to instruct students in law and political economy, considered to be the intellectual necessities for an educated democracy.

The university was founded by Dr Pridi Phanomyong, whose statue stands in Pridi Ct at the centre of the campus. Pridi was the leader of the civilian People's Party that successfully advocated a constitutional monarchy during the 1920s and '30s. He went on to serve in various ministries, organised

the Seri Thai movement (a Thai resistance campaign against the Japanese during WWII) and was ultimately forced into exile when the postwar government was seized by a military dictatorship in 1947.

Pridi was unable to counter the dismantling of democratic reforms, but the university he established continued his crusade. Thammasat was the hotbed of prodemocracy activism during the student uprising era of the 1970s. On 14 October 1973 (sìp-sìi tù-laa) 10,000 protesters convened on the parade grounds beside the university's Memorial Building demanding the government reinstate the constitution. The military and police opened fire on the crowd, killing 77 and wounding 857. The massacre prompted the king to revoke his support of the military rulers and for a brief period a civilian government was reinstated. Thammasat was the site of more bloody protests on 6 October 1976 (hòk tù-laa), when at least 46 students were shot dead while rallying against the return from exile of former dictator Field Marshal Thanom Kittikachorn. A plaque on the parade grounds commemorates these events.

Walk south from Th Phra Athit in Banglamphu and you'll go straight through Thammasat, emerging at the south end near Tha Chang pier.

WAT MAHATHAT Map p56
วัดมหาธาตุ

☎ 0 2222 6011; Th Mahathat; admission by donation; ☺ 7am-6pm; ⚓ Tha Chang (N9), 🚌 air-con 503, 508 & 512, ordinary 47 & 53

While other temples in the area claim all the fame, Wat Mahathat goes about the everyday business of a temple. Saffron-robed monks file in and out of the whitewashed gates, grandmas in their best silks come to make merit, and world-weary *soi* dogs haul themselves out of the shade in search of food, if not nirvana.

Founded in the 1700s, Wat Mahathat is a national centre for the Mahanikai monastic sect and is home to the first of Bangkok's two Buddhist universities, Mahathat Rajavidyalaya. The university is the most important place of Buddhist learning in mainland Southeast Asia – the Lao, Vietnamese and Cambodian governments send selected monks to further their studies here.

Entered through the Thawornwathu Building, Mahathat and the surrounding area have developed into an informal Thai cultural centre. The monastery offers meditation instruction in English (see p257).

Ko Ratanakosin Stroll
WALKING TOUR

Bangkok's most famous sites are cradled in Ko Ratanakosin (Ratanakosin Island), which owes its island status to the hand-dug Khlong Banglamphu and Khlong Ong Ang canals. When Rama I moved the capital from Thonburi to here he had the canals enlarged in an effort to re-create the island city of Ayuthaya (Thailand's former capital, which was sacked by the Burmese).

This circular walk starts at Tha Chang, accessible by Chao Phraya river ferries or, if you're staying in Banglamphu, by an easy walk from Th Phra Athit through Thammasat University. It's best to start this walk soon after lunch, so you can be sure of seeing the palace before it closes at 3.30pm. Alternatively, start early and you can do this walk and the Chinatown walk (p86) in a single day.

1 Silpakorn University From the pier, file east past the market towards Th Na Phra Lan. On your left-hand side turn into Silpakorn University (p61), Thailand's first fine-arts university. The campus includes part of an old Rama I palace and an art gallery showing works by students and professors.

2 Wat Mahathat Continue north through the campus and left to get back to Th Maharat. Turn right on Th Maharat and wander past the blankets and tables displaying herbal apothecaries and amulets. On your right is Wat Mahathat (opposite), Thailand's most respected Buddhist university.

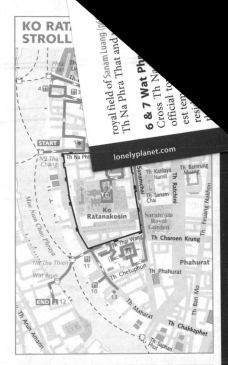

lonelyplanet.com

WALK FACTS

Start **Tha Chang (river ferry, N9)**
End **Tha Tien (river ferry, N8)**
Distance **4.6km to 5.7km**
Duration **3½ to six hours, depending on how much time you spend looking, eating, drinking and getting massaged**
Fuel Stops **Rub Aroon (p154), the Deck (p154) and the Trok Nakhon food vendors**

3 Amulet Market (p129) Turn into the narrow alley immediately after Trok Mahathat to the amulet market (p129), a warren of vendors selling *phrá khrêuang* (religious amulets) representing various Hindu and Buddhist deities.

4 Food Vendors If you're hungry, snake your way back to Th Maharat (or weave your way north along the riverside part of the market) and continue to the next alley, Trok Nakhon. This leads past more amulet stalls and stores selling graduation gowns, eventually coming to food vendors, serving delicious Thai dishes.

5 Sanam Luang Take Th Phra Chan east past Thammasat University to the vast open

63

). Turn right along
walk to the end.

a Kaew & Grand Palace
Phra Lan and turn left to the
rist entrance to Thailand's holi-
ple, Wat Phra Kaew, and the formal royal
dence, the Grand Palace (p55). All visitors to
e palace and temple grounds must be appropriately attired; see p59 for details.

8 Lak Meuang Exiting via the same gate,
take a right and cross Th Ratchadamnoen Nai
to reach Lak Meuang (City Pillar; p58), a shrine to
Bangkok's city spirit and the foundation stone
embodying the city's guardian deity. This
shrine is one of Bangkok's most important
sites of animistic worship; watch as believers
offer flowers, incense, fruit and even the odd
bottle of fiery local whisky.

9 Wat Pho From Lak Meuang, follow Th
Sanam Chai beside the white palace wall until
you come to Th Chetuphon (the second street
on your right after the palace walls end, approximately 600m from the pillar). Turn right
onto Th Chetuphon and enter Wat Pho (p57)
through the second portico. Meander through
the grounds on your way to the massive Reclining Buddha.

Options, options Okay, so now you have
to decide. Depending on the time, levels of
interest, energy, hunger and thirst – and how
many litres of sweat you've already lost today
– you can finish your walk in various ways. Get
your timing right and you can do some or all
of these and still watch the sun set behind Wat
Arun with a cold drink and a freshly de-knot-
ted body. Remember that the last ferry leaves
Tha Tien soon after 7pm, and taxis around
here are notorious for refusing to put the meter
on – if you need one, insist on the meter.

10 Deck Exit beside the Reclining Buddha,
turn left on Th Maharat and then right at Th
Soi Pratu Nok Yung. Walk past the old Chinese godowns to the end of the *soi* and the Deck
(p154), a restaurant with spectacular views of
the river and Wat Arun. The upstairs bar here
is easily the best place to finish this tour, but
unfortunately it doesn't open until 6pm.

11 Rub Aroon Exit beside the Reclining
Buddha, turn left on Th Maharat and settle
into Rub Aroon (p154), a friendly café serving Thai
standards and fresh fruit drinks.

12 Wat Arun Exit beside the Reclining Buddha, walk to Tha Tien (N8) and take the regular cross-river ferry to Wat Arun (p65) to see its
striking Hindu-Khmer stupa.

13 Get a massage Wat Pho (see stop 9) is
the national repository for traditional massage
and offers massages on the wat grounds (no
air-con) and at the nearby training school (p197).
A thoroughly sensible choice, and it's very
conveniently open until 6pm.

THONBURI
Thonburi has lived in the shadow of Bangkok
for more than 200 years and is today a not
entirely fashionable suburb of the capital. Fashion, of course, is a subjective thing. There aren't
that many raised freeways, expensive cars or
modern transportation systems on this side of
Mae Nam Chao Phraya. Instead Thonburi retains enough of the traditional transport corridors – the *khlong* that once caused Bangkok to
be known as the 'Venice of the East' and Thais
to call themselves *jâo náam* (water lords) –
to give it a decidedly different feel. A day exploring them is likely to be one of the most
memorable of your stay in the Thai capital.

The network of canals and river tributaries
still carries a motley fleet of watercraft, from
paddled canoes to rice barges. Homes, trading
houses and temples are built on stilts with front
doors opening out to the river. According to
residents, these waterways protect them from
the seasonal flooding that plagues the capital.

Khlong Bangkok Noi is lined with greenery
and historic temples, reaching deep into the
Bang Yai district, a brief five-minute ride from
the concrete entanglements of central Bangkok.
Khlong Bangkok Yai was in fact the original
course of the river until a canal was built to
expedite transits. Today the tributary sees a
steady stream of tourists on longtail boat tours
en route to floating markets, the Royal Barges
Museum (opposite) or Wat Intharam, where a
chedi contains the ashes of Thonburi's King
Taksin, assassinated in 1782. Fine gold-and-
black lacquerwork adorning the main *bòt* doors
depicts the mythical *naariiphŏn* tree, which
bears fruit shaped like beautiful maidens.

Most tourists meet only the river-facing
part of Thonburi between Khlong Bangkok
Noi and Khlong Bangkok Yai, directly across
from Ko Ratanakosin, leaving the interior
of the community predominantly Thai with
hardly an English sign or pestering *túk-túk*
driver in sight. As the river ferries ricochet

Bus Air-con 507 and 509, ordinary 21, 42 and 82

Ferry A tour of Thonburi by longtail boat is fun and easy, but for a more local experience that's also much cheaper consider taking the public ferries. Bang Yai-bound boats from Tha Chang leave every 30 minutes between 6am and 8am, every hour from 9am to 3pm, and depart when the boat is full between 3pm and 9pm. The main Chao Praya Express ferries stop at a few key Thonburi piers, most notably Wang Lang (Siriraj, N10), Thonburi Railway (N11) and Saphan Phra Pin Klao (N12). Several cross-river ferries also connect to Bangkok piers.

from stop to stop, a steady stream of commuters is shuttled to and from jobs in downtown Bangkok, impatient for the Skytrain to be extended to their dormitory community.

Two major bridges fuse the two banks together – Saphan Phra Pin Klao and Saphan Phra Phuttha Yot Fa (Memorial Bridge) – and husky cross-river ferries plod from one side to another in stress-relieving slow motion. The few major roads include those delivering passengers to the southern bus station. Thonburi has two minor rail services: one departs from Bangkok Noi (near Siriraj Hospital and about 900m from the Thonburi Railway ferry pier) and trundles west to Kanchanaburi; the other is a commuter line that goes from Wong Wian Yai to the gulf coast suburbs (see p236).

WAT ARUN Map p56
วัดอรุณฯ

☎ 0 2891 1149; www.watarun.org; Th Arun Amarin; admission 20B; ⏰ 8am-6pm; 🚤 from Tha Tien (N8) to Tha Thai Wang

The missile-shaped temple that rises from the banks of the Mae Nam Chao Phraya is known as Temple of Dawn and named after the Indian god of dawn, Aruna. It was here that, in the wake of the destruction of Ayuthaya, King Taksin stumbled upon a small shrine used by the local population and interpreted the discovery as an auspicious sign for building a new Thai capital. King Taksin built a palace beside the shrine, which is now part of Navy Headquarters, and a royal temple that housed the Emerald Buddha for 15 years before Taksin was assassinated and the capital moved across the royal river to Bangkok.

The central feature is the 82m-high Khmer-style *praang* (spire), constructed during the first half of the 19th century by Rama II (King Buddha Loetla; r 1809–24) and Rama III. From the river it is not apparent that this corn-cob shaped steeple is adorned with colourful floral murals made of glazed porcelain, a common temple ornamentation in the early Ratanakosin period, when Chinese ships calling at Bangkok used broken porcelain as ballast.

Also worth a look is the interior of the *bòt*. The main Buddha image is said to have been designed by Rama II; you can judge his artistic ability. The murals date to the reign of Rama V; impressive is one that depicts Prince Siddhartha (the Buddha) encountering examples of birth, old age, sickness and death outside his palace walls, an experience that led him to abandon the worldly life. The ashes of Rama II are interred in the base of the *bòt*'s presiding Buddha image.

On the periphery of the temple grounds are simple wooden cut-outs of Thai dancers, luring visitors to photograph each other with their mugs above the figures – for an extra 40B.

Wat Arun is located directly across from Wat Pho on the Thonburi side of the river. A lot of people visit the wat on expensive river tours, but it's dead easy and more rewarding to just jump on the 3.50B cross-river ferry from Tha Tien. For our money, visiting Wat Arun in the late afternoon is best, with the sun shining from the west lighting up the *praang* and the river behind it. Photographers – or indeed anyone with a romantic bone in their body – can then take the ferry back to Tha Tien, walk south for five minutes and perch on a stool in the Amarosa Bar, upstairs at the Deck (p154) restaurant. Wat Arun is directly across the river and there are few sights in Bangkok as serene as watching the sun sink below the horizon as the lights on the *praang* come spectacularly up while barges and ferries motor past in the twilight.

If you come earlier, consider taking a stroll away from the river on Th Wang Doem, a quiet tiled street of wooden shophouses.

ROYAL BARGES NATIONAL MUSEUM
Map p56
เรือพระที่นั่ง

☎ 0 2424 0004; Khlong Bangkok Noi; admission 30B, still/video camera fee 100/200B; ⏰ 9am-5pm; 🚤 tourist shuttle boat from Tha Phra Athit (N13) or Tha Saphan Phra Pin Klao (N12)

ountry has its famous reli-
ents and museums, but how
neir own fleet of royal boats on
a former riverine culture, Thai-
naintains the royal barges, once
y by the royal family for outings
and events and now used only for grand
ceremonies.

The royal barges are slender like their
mainstream cousins, the longtail boats, and
are fantastically ornamented with religious
symbolism. The largest is more than 45m
long and requires a rowing crew of 50 men,
plus seven umbrella bearers, two helms-
men and two navigators, as well as a flag
bearer, rhythm keeper and chanter.

Suphannahong, or 'Golden Swan', is
the king's personal barge and is the most
important of the boats. Built on the orders
of Rama I after an earlier version had been
destroyed in the sacking of Ayuthaya,
this barge is made from a single piece of
timber, making it the largest dugout in
the world. Appropriately, a huge swan's
head is carved into the bow. More recent
barges feature bows carved into other
Hindu-Buddhist mythological shapes such
as the seven-headed naga (sea dragon) and
Garuda (Vishnu's bird mount).

To mark auspicious Buddhist calendar
years, the royal barges in all their finery set
sail during the royal *kàthǐn*, the ceremony
that marks the end of the Buddhist retreat
(or *phansǎa*) in October or November.
During this ceremony, a barge procession
travels to the temples to offer new robes
to the monastic contingent and countless
Bangkokians descend on the river to watch.

The museum consists of sheds near the
mouth of Khlong Bangkok Noi. Getting
here is easiest by regular tourist boat from
N13 Tha Phra Athit, but is also possible on
foot from Saphan Phra Pin Klao (N12) river
ferry pier.

YOU, YOU, WHERE YOU GO?

A direct translation of a standard Thai inquiry *'Pai nai?'*,
the English phrase 'Where you go?' will be hurled at
you by money-struck *túk-túk* and taxi drivers as if it
were a military interrogation. Despite that nagging
feeling of rudeness, you don't have to respond and the
best answer is to master the public transport system,
which is cheap and reliable, and won't steer you to
its cousin's tailor shop. If that doesn't work, you can
always retaliate with a playground comeback like 'I've
come to see you'.

FORENSIC MEDICINE MUSEUM
Map p56

พิพิธภัณฑ์นิติเวชศาสตร์ส งกรานต์นิยมเสน
☎ 0 2419 7000; 2nd fl, Forensic Medicine Bldg,
Siriraj Hospital; admission 40B; ◷ 9am-4pm Mon-
Sat; 🚢 Tha Rot Fai (Thonburi Railway Pier, N11) or
Tha Wang Lang (Tha Siriraj, N10)

Pickled body parts, ingenious murder weapons and other crime-scene evidence are on
display at this medical museum, intended
to educate rather than nauseate. Among
the grisly displays is the preserved cadaver
of Si Ouey, one of Thailand's most prolific
and notorious serial killers who murdered
– and then ate – more than 30 children
in the 1950s. Despite being well and truly
dead (he was executed), today his name is
still used to scare misbehaving children into
submission: 'Behave yourself or Si Ouey will
come for you'. There are another five dusty
museums on the hospital premises, all with
variations on the medical theme.

Given the huge construction project at
the northern edge of the hospital grounds,
the best way to get here is by express ferry
or cross-river ferry to Tha Wang Lang (Tha
Siriraj) in Thonburi, then walk north through
the hospital grounds almost to the end, turn
left and follow the signs; or just say 'Si Ouey'
and you'll be pointed in the right direction.

Eating p155; Shopping p130; Sleeping p203

Banglamphu is old Bangkok. Once an aristocratic and artistic enclave of teak houses and tended gardens, here trees still outnumber high-rises, fashion comes from the market not the malls and you're more likely to see monks than chauffeurs.

Most of the district is a mazelike circuit board of streets and two-storey shophouses, each decorated with terracotta water gardens or potted plants and low-hanging shades that block out the sun. During the Chinese New Year, merchants do a little 'spring cleaning'. Workers scour pavements, mop floors and polish neon signs. Once all the soap is rinsed away, the scene looks inexplicably just like it did before. These shops sell ordinary items that fill wardrobes, utility closets and kitchen pantries in a typical Thai home.

But the most famous draw is Th Khao San, the backpacker enclave of guesthouses and amenities that has become the benchmark by which backpacker ghettos are measured the world over. These days 'ghetto' is a little bit harsh, as the lodgings increasingly cater to 'flashpackers', and the lodgings themselves have spread in a 1km radius from its namesake street. (For the Khao San story see p72.)

Long before Banglamphu landed on travellers' itineraries, this was the original residential district for farmers and produce merchants from Ayuthaya who followed the transfer of the royal court to Bangkok in the late 18th century. The name means 'Place of Lamphu', a reference to the *lamphuu* tree *(Duabanga grandiflora)* that was once prevalent in the area. By the time of King Rama IV, Banglamphu had developed into a thriving commercial district by day and an entertainment spot by night, a role it continues to fulfil today.

top picks

BANGLAMPHU

- Th Khao San (p72) Soak up the atmosphere in this backpacker mecca that's unlike any other place on earth (or beyond).
- Wat Saket & Golden Mount (left) Take in the panoramic views and divine your future on this artificial mount.
- Chote Chitr (p155) Taste genuine Bangkok-style food – especially the *mìi kràwp* (sweet-and-spicy crispy fried noodles).
- Taksura (p177) Join the Thai artsy crowd in this old mansion-cum-bar.
- Wat Suthat (p71) Sit and gaze at the huge Buddha and sky-high murals in this peaceful temple.

Banglamphu spreads from the river north of Th Phra Pin Klao and eventually melts into Dusit and Thewet beyond Khlong Padum Kaseng. The royal boulevard of Th Ratchadamnoen Klang (royal passage), suitably adorned with billboard-sized pictures of the king, queen and other royal family members, links the Grand Palace in Ko Ratanakosin with the new palace in Dusit. This central section of the royal road is lined by identical Art Deco–influenced low-rise buildings that were built in the early 1940s to house the administration of the new democratic Thailand. Plans to upgrade them and make Th Ratchadamnoen Klang a cultural promenade documenting Thailand's transition to democracy have stalled, with only King Prajadhipok Museum (p73) and the long-established Queen's Gallery (p192) currently welcoming visitors. Running south from Th Ratchadamnoen Klang is Th Tanao, one of Bangkok's most famous food streets.

Running parallel to the river to the west of Th Khao San, Th Phra Athit is known as the avenue of mansions built to house Thai nobility during the late 19th and early 20th centuries. Among the most splendidly restored Ratanakosin-era buildings is Ban Phra Athit (201/1 Th Phra Athit), which once belonged to Chao Phraya Vorapongpipat, finance minister during the reigns of Rama V, VI and VII. It now belongs to a private company, but a coffee shop within the grounds is open to the public.

WAT SAKET & GOLDEN MOUNT
Map pp68–9

วัดสระเกศ

☎ 0 2223 4561; soi off Th Boriphat; admission to summit of Golden Mount 10B; ☷ 7.30am-5.30pm; 🚍 air-con 511 & 512, ordinary 2, 🚢 khlong boat to Tha Saphan Phan Fah

Before glass and steel towers began growing out of the flat monotony of Bangkok's riverine plain, the massive Golden Mount (Phu Khao Thong) was the only structure to make any significant impression on the horizon. At the eastern entrance to Banglamphu, the mount was commissioned

BANGLAMPHU

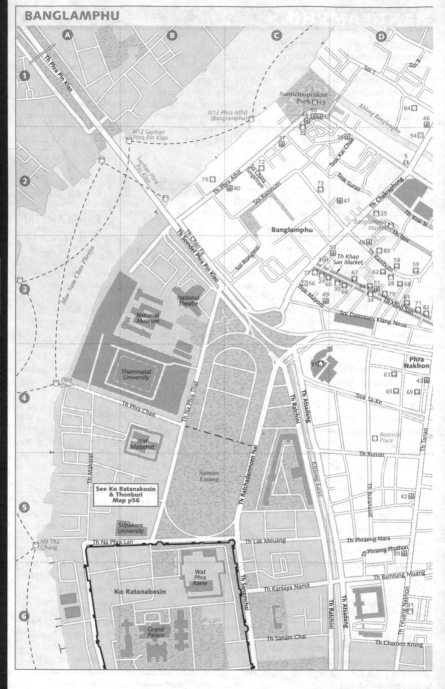

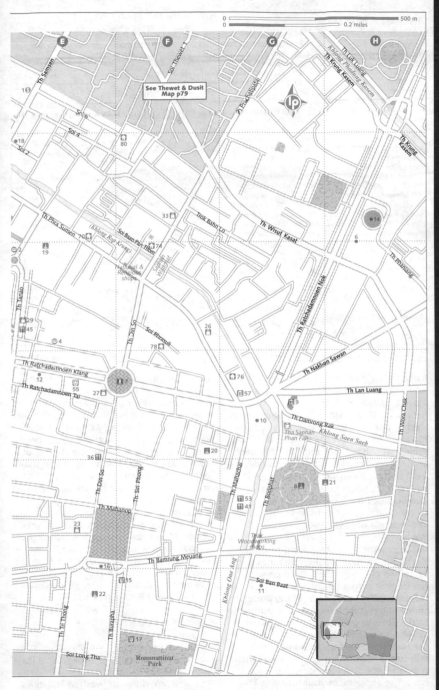

BANGLAMPHU

INFORMATION
Bangkok Bank.............................. 1 E1
Banglamphu Post Office............. 2 E3
Chana Songkhram
    Police Station........................3 C3
Post Office.................................. 4 E3
Siam Commercial Bank.............. 5 D2
TAT Information Compound...... 6 H3

SIGHTS   (pp67–77)
Democracy Monument.............. 7 F4
Golden Mount............................ 8 G5
King Prajadhipok Museum......... 9 G4
Mahakan Fort........................... 10 G4
Monk's Bowl Village................. 11 G6
October 14 Memorial................ 12 E4
Phra Sumen Fort...................... 13 C1
Ratchadamnoen Stadium...........14 H2
Saan Jao Phitsanu.................... 15 F6
Sao Ching-Cha......................... 16 E5
Thewa Sathaan........................ 17 F6
Velo Thailand........................... 18 E2
Wat Bowonniwet...................... 19 E3
Wat Ratchanatda...................... 20 F4
Wat Saket................................ 21 G5
Wat Suthat.............................. 22 E6

SHOPPING   (pp127–41)
Charoen Chaikarnchang
    Shop.................................... 23 E5
It's Happened To Be A Closet... 24 C3
Nittaya Curry Shop................... 25 D2
Passport.................................. 26 F3
Rim Khob Fah Bookstore.......... 27 E4
Saraban................................... 28 D3

Shaman Bookstore................... 29 E3
Shaman Bookstore................... 30 D3
Suksit Siam.............................. 31 D6
Taekee Taekon..........................32 C1
Thai Nakorn............................. 33 F2
Thalon Khao San Market.......... 34 D3

EATING   (pp143–72)
Ann's Sweet.............................35 C1
Arroi....................................... 36 E4
Baan Phra Arthit....................... 37 C2
Café Primavera........................ 38 D2
Chote Chitr.............................. 39 D5
Hemlock.................................. 40 C2
It's Happened To Be A Closet..(see 24)
Jay Fai.................................... 41 G5
Kaiyang Boran.......................... 42 D5
Kim Leng................................. 43 D4
Krua Noppharat........................ 44 C1
May Kaidee..............................45 E3
May Kaidee.............................. 46 D1
May Kaidee's Vegetarian Thai
    Cooking School.................(see 46)
Oh My Cod!............................. 47 D2
Pan... 48 D3
Ranee's Guesthouse................. 49 C3
Roti-Mataba.............................50 C1
Scoozi..................................... 51 D3
Shoshana................................. 52 D3
Thip Samai.............................. 53 G5

ENTERTAINMENT   (pp188–93)
& THE ARTS
Ad Here the 13th...................... 54 D2
Brick Bar..............................(see 71)

Café Democ..............................55 E4
Gazebo....................................56 C3
Queen's Gallery........................ 57 G4

DRINKING
& NIGHTLIFE   (pp173–85)
Bua Sa-ad................................ 58 D3
Buddy Bar..........................(see 71)
deep.. 59 D3
Hippie de Bar........................... 60 C3
Lava Club................................. 61 D3
Molly Bar................................. 62 D3
Phranakorn Bar........................ 63 D4
Roof Bar.................................. 64 D3
Sa-Ke Coffee Pub..................... 65 D4
Shamrock Irish Pub................... 66 D3
Silk Bar................................... 67 D3
Susie Pub................................. 68 D3
Taksura.................................... 69 D4

SLEEPING   (pp201–21)
Boworn BB................................70 E2
Buddy Lodge............................ 71 D3
Erawan House........................... 72 C2
Lamphu House.......................... 73 C2
Lamphu Treehouse.....................74 F3
New Siam Riverside....................75 B2
Old Bangkok Inn....................... 76 G4
Prakorp's House........................ 77 C3
Prasuri Guest House.................. 78 F3
Rikka Inn................................. 79 D3
Roof View Place........................80 F2
Royal Hotel.............................. 81 C4
Shambara................................. 82 D3
Viengtai Hotel.......................... 83 D3
Villa Guest House..................... 84 D1

by Rama III. He ordered that the earth that was dug out to create Bangkok's expanding *khlong* network be piled up to build an enormous, 100m-high, 500m-wide *chedi*. As the hill grew, however, the weight became too much for the soft soil beneath and the project was abandoned until Rama IV built a small gilded *chedi* on its crest and added trees to stave off erosion. Rama V later added to the structure and interred a Buddha relic from India (given to him by the British government) in the *chedi*. The concrete walls were added during WWII.

Today serpentine steps wind through gnarled trees, past small tombstones and up to two platforms that afford panoramic views across the city. At the topmost level Thais pray to a central Buddha shrine and test their fortune at a shrine to the Chinese goddess of mercy, Kuan Im. Make a small donation then shake the numbered *siem see* sticks until one falls to the floor. The piece of paper with the corresponding number gives a no-nonsense appraisal of your future in Thai, English and Chinese. It's a fun diversion,

but hopefully you receive a more positive prognosis than ours, which included, 'Lost items could never be recovered. Illness condition unfavourable. No lucks. Should be careful.' Well, great! At least we now know that: 'Forthcoming child shall be baby girl.' When Thais are the subject of such a dire forecast (ahm, try not to shake out stick number 10) they burn it on the spot (the fortune, not the stick), or at least leave it at the temple.

If your fortune is so disturbing you feel the need to seek assistance from a higher power, it's comforting to know that peaceful Wat Saket is just next door. In November the grounds host a festival that includes an enchanting candlelight procession up the Golden Mount, and a similar procession is held at Makha Bucha in February.

MAHAKAN FORT Map pp68–9
ป้อมมหากาฬ

Th Ratchadamnoen Klang; 🕑 **8.30am-6pm;** 🚌 **air-con 511 & 512, ordinary 2,** ⛴ **khlong boat to Tha Saphan Phan Fah**

The area around white-washed Mahakan Fort, one of two surviving citadels that defended the old walled city, has recently been converted into a small park overlooking Khlong Ong Ang. The octagonal fort is a picturesque stop en route to Golden Mount, but the story of its conversion is probably more interesting. For more than 13 years the community of 55 simple wooden houses that surrounded the fort fought for its survival against the Bangkok municipal government, which wanted to demolished it in order to create a 'tourist' park, the modern term for urban renewal. The community blocked progress and even proposed the development of another tourist attraction: a lí-keh museum honouring the dance tradition that traces its creation to a school located here in 1897. Some of the homes were demolished, resulting in the park you see today. But behind the fort others remain, and just before we went to print residents, city authorities and tourism authorities were still arguing about the creation (or not) of a 'living museum'.

MONK'S BOWL VILLAGE Map pp68–9
บ้านบาตร

Soi Ban Baat, Th Boriphat; 🚍 ordinary 12 & 42, 🚤 khlong boat to Tha Saphan Phan Fah
This is the only remaining village of three established in Bangkok by Rama I for the purpose of handcrafting bàat (monk's bowls), the ceremonial bowls used to collect alms from the faithful every morning. As cheaper factory-made bowls are now the norm, the artisanal tradition has shrunk to about half a dozen families. You can usually observe the process of hammering the bowls together from eight separate pieces of steel said to represent Buddhism's

Eightfold Path. The joints are then fused with melted copper wire, and the bowl is beaten, polished and (usually) coated with several layers of black lacquer. A typical bàat-smith's output is one large bowl per day; more for smaller bowls.

The alms bowls are sold for between 600B and 2000B and make great souvenirs. But the village itself is just as interesting. When we visited, an elderly woman intercepted us just nanoseconds after we'd walked into the soi and quickly ushered us through her living room, and out the back door down a series of tiny lanes populated by kids, sleeping cats and cockroaches, and delivered us to one of the bowl makers, who showed us his bowls and others making them. Competition is certainly keen for your tourist baht, but you wouldn't call it touristy. More a raw, poor Bangkok community, and a chance for you to experience that side of life and maybe buy a bowl. To find the village, walk south on Th Boriphat, south of Th Bamrung Meuang, then follow the signs into narrow Soi Ban Baat.

WAT SUTHAT Map pp68–9
วัดสุทัศน์

☎ 0 2224 9845; Th Botphram; admission 20B; ⏰ 8.30am-9pm; 🚍 ordinary 12 & 42, 🚤 khlong boat to Tha Saphan Phan Fah
Wat Suthat's truly remarkable Buddha image, acres of colourful murals and – during most of the year – relative tranquillity make it arguably the most attractive of all of Bangkok's Buddhist temples. The main attraction is Thailand's largest wíhǎan (main chapel). Set inside a large cloister that is itself lined with gilded Buddha images, it houses the 8m-high Phra Si Sakayamuni, Thailand's largest surviving Sukhothai-period bronze, a serene-looking gilded masterpiece that was cast in the former capital in the 14th century. In 1808 it was retrieved from Sukhothai and floated on a barge down Mae Nam Chao Phraya to be installed in this temple and serve as both the centre of Bangkok and a representation of Mt Meru, the mythical centre of the universe. Today the ashes of Rama VIII (King Ananda Mahidol, the current king's older brother; r 1935–46) are contained in the base of the image.

The colourful, if now somewhat faded, Jataka (murals depicting scenes from the Buddha's life) cover every wall and pillar;

TRANSPORT: BANGLAMPHU

Bus Air-con 511 and 512, ordinary 3, 15, 32 and 53

Ferry Tha Phra Athit (aka Tha Banglamphu)

Khlong boat Pier at Th Lan Luang and Th Ratchadamnoen Klang

From Banglamphu to anywhere by road can be a traffic nightmare, so using the river ferry (for Chinatown, riverside and the Skytrain at Central Pier) is both fast and much more fun. For the shopping megaplexes around Siam Sq, walk to Tha Saphan Phan Fah and take a khlong boat. For the royal sights of Ko Ratanakosin, it's easiest to just walk.

NEIGHBOURHOODS BANGLAMPHU

WHAT'S SO LONELY ABOUT THE KHAO SAN ROAD?

Thanon Khao San, better known as the Khao San Road, is genuinely unlike anywhere else on earth. It's an international clearing house of people either entering the liberated state of travelling in Southeast Asia or returning to the coddling bonds of first-world life, all together in a neon-lit melting pot in Banglamphu. Its uniqueness is probably best illustrated with a question: apart from airports, where else could you share space with the citizens of dozens of countries at the same time, people ranging from first-time backpackers scoffing banana pancakes to 75-year-old grandparents ordering G&Ts, via hippies, trendies, squares, style queens, package tourists, global nomads, people on a week's holiday and those taking a gap year, people of every colour and creed looking at you looking at them looking at everyone else?

Th Khao San – pronounced 'cow sarn' and meaning 'uncooked rice' – is perhaps the most high-profile bastard child of the age of independent travel. Of course, it hasn't always been this way. For its first two centuries or so it was just another unremarkable road in old Bangkok. The first guesthouses appeared in 1982 and as more backpackers arrived through the '80s, so one by one the old wooden homes were converted into low-rent dosshouses. By the time Alex Garland's novel *The Beach* was published in 1997, with its opening scenes set in the seedier side of Khao San, staying here had become a rite of passage for backpackers coming to Southeast Asia.

The publicity from Garland's book and the movie that followed pushed Khao San into the mainstream, romanticising the seedy and stereotyping as unwashed and counter-culture the backpackers it attracted. It also brought the long-simmering debate about the relative merits of Th Khao San to the top of backpacker conversations across the region. Was it cool to stay on KSR? Was it uncool? Was this 'real travel' or just an international anywhere surviving on the few baht Western backpackers spent before they headed home to start their high-earning careers? Was it really Thailand at all?

Perhaps one of Garland's characters summed it up most memorably when he says: 'You know, Richard, one of these days I'm going to find one of those Lonely Planet writers and I'm going to ask him, what's so fucking lonely about the Khoa San Road?'

Today more than ever the answer would have to be: not that much. With the help of all that publicity Khao San continued to evolve, with bed-bug–infested guesthouses replaced by boutique hotels, and downmarket TV bars showing pirated movies transformed into hip design bars peopled by flashpackers in designer threads. But the most interesting change has been in the way Thais see Khao San.

Once written off as home to cheap, dirty *faràng kîi ngók* ('stingy foreigners'), Banglamphu has become just about the trendiest district in Bangkok. Attracted in part by the long-derided independent travellers and their modern ideas, the city's own counter-culture kids have moved in and given the whole area a decidedly more hip feel. Indeed, Bangkok's indie crowd has proved to be the Thai spice this melting pot always lacked.

Not that Khao San has moved completely away from its backpacker roots. The strip still anticipates every traveller need: meals to soothe homesickness, cafés and bars for swapping travel tales about getting to the Cambodian border, tailors, travel agents, teeth whitening, secondhand books, hair braiding and a new generation of Akha women trying to harass everyone they see into buying wooden frogs.

see how many crabs (or crab claws) you can find, and not just in the murals. The deep-relief wooden doors are also impressive and were carved by artisans including Rama II himself.

Behind the *wíhǎan*, and accessed via a separate entrance on Th Burapha, the ordination hall is the largest in the country. Wat Suthat holds the rank of Rachavoramahavihan, the highest royal temple grade, and maintains a special place in the national religion because of its association with the Brahman priests who perform important ceremonies, such as the Royal Ploughing Ceremony (p13) in May. These priests also perform religious rites at two Hindu shrines near the wat – the Thewa Sathaan (Devi Mandir) on Th Siri Phong, and the smaller Saan Jao Phitsanu (Vishnu Shrine) on Th Din

So. The former shrine contains images of Shiva and Ganesha while the latter shrine is dedicated to Vishnu.

SAO CHING-CHA Map pp68–9
เสาชิงช้า

☎ 0 2222 6951; Th Botphram, btwn Th Tri Thong & Th Burapha; 🚌 ordinary 12, 42, ⚓ khlong boat to Tha Saphan Phan Fah

It is easy to forget the powers of the Brahmans in Thai Buddhism, unless you happen upon the giant red poles of Sao Ching-Cha (the Giant Swing). During the second lunar month (usually in January), Brahman beliefs dictate that Shiva comes down to earth for a 10-day residence and should be welcomed by great ceremonies (and apparently great degrees of daring) including the acrobatics of the Great Swing. The ceremony saw the brave or foolish swing in ever-higher arcs in an effort to reach a bag of gold suspended from a 15m bamboo pole.

The Brahmans enjoyed a mystical position within the royal court, primarily in the coronation rituals. But after the 1932 revolution the Brahmans' waning power was effectively terminated and the festival, including the swinging, was discontinued during the reign of Rama VII.

Sao Ching-Cha is two long blocks south of the Democracy Monument and outside Wat Suthat. Despite no longer being used, the Giant Swing was recently replaced with a newer model, made from six giant teak logs. The original is kept at the National Museum.

DEMOCRACY MONUMENT Map pp68–9
อนุสาวรีย์ประชาธิปไตย
Traffic circle of Th Ratchadamnoen Klang & Th Din So; 🚍 air-con 511 & 512, ordinary 2 & 82
The Democracy Monument is the focal point of the grand, European-style boulevard that is Th Ratchadamnoen Klang. It was designed by Thai architect Mew Aphaiwong and the relief sculptures were created by Italian Corrado Feroci who, as Silpa Bhirasri, gives his name to Silpakorn University. As the name suggests, it was erected to commemorate Thailand's momentous transformation from absolute to constitutional monarchy. Feroci combined the square-jawed 'heroes of socialism' style popular at the time with an Art Deco influence and a keen sense of relevant revolutionary dates.

There were 75 cannonballs around the base, to signify the year BE (Buddhist Era) 2475 (AD 1932). The four wings of the monument stand 24m tall, representing 24 June, the day the constitution was signed, and the central plinth stands 3m high (June was then the third month in the Thai calendar) and supports a chiselled constitution. Each wing has bas-reliefs depicting soldiers, police and civilians who helped usher in the modern Thai state.

During the era of military dictatorships demonstrators often assembled here to call for a return to democracy, protests that ended in violence and death on 17 May 1972 and 14 October 1973.

While you're in this area, if you head north from the Democracy Monument

on Th Din So you'll see many shophouses that date to the reigns of Rama V (King Chulalongkorn; r 1868–1910) and Rama VII (King Prajadhipok; r 1925–35). As the entire block to the northwest of the Democracy Monument belongs to Wat Bowonniwet (p74), the shop owners pay rent directly to the temple.

OCTOBER 14 MEMORIAL Map pp68–9
อนุสาวรีย์14ตุลาคม
Th Ratchadamnoen Klang; 🚍 air-con 511 & 512, ordinary 2 & 82
A peaceful amphitheatre commemorates the civilian demonstrators who were killed on 14 October 1973 by the military during a prodemocracy rally. Over 200,000 people assembled at the Democracy Monument and along the length of Th Ratchadamnoen to protest against the arrest of political campaigners and continuing military dictatorship. More than 70 demonstrators were killed when the tanks met the crowd. The complex is an interesting adaptation of Thai temple architecture for a secular and political purpose. A central *chedi* is dedicated to the fallen and a gallery of historic photographs lines the interior wall. The stalled redevelopment of Th Ratchadamnoen Klang called for a museum to be created in the underground portion of the amphitheatre.

KING PRAJADHIPOK MUSEUM
Map pp68–9
พิพิธภัณฑ์พระบาทสมเด็จพระปกเกล้า
เจ้าอยู่หัว
☎ 0 2527 7830; www.kpi.ac.th/museum; 2 Th Lan Luang; ⏰ 9am-4pm Tue-Sun; admission 40B; 🚤 khlong boat to Tha Saphan Phan Fah, 🚍 air-con 511 & 512, ordinary 2
A visit to a royal museum might sound like a royal bore, but this collection uses modern techniques to relate the rather dramatic life of King Prajadhipok (Rama VII; r 1925–35) and neatly documents Thailand's transition from absolute to constitutional monarchy. As you wander among the exhibits in the neocolonial-style former administrative building, you'll learn that Prajadhipok did not expect to become king. However, once on the throne he showed considerable diplomacy in dealing with what was, in effect, a revolution fomented by a new intellectual class of Thais who had returned home from European educations

WHAT'S A WAT?

Bòt A consecrated chapel where monastic ordinations are held.

Chedi (stupa) A large bell-shaped tower usually containing five structural elements symbolising (from bottom to top) earth, water, fire, wind and void; relics of the Buddha or a Thai king are housed inside.

Praang A towering phallic spire of Khmer origin serving the same religious purpose as a *chedi*.

Wat Temple monastery.

Wíhaan The main sanctuary for the temple's Buddha sculpture and where laypeople come to make their offerings. Classic architecture typically has a three-tiered roof representing the triple gems, Buddha (the teacher), Dharma (the teaching) and Brotherhood (the followers).

Buddha Images

Elongated earlobes, no evidence of bone or muscle, arms that reach to the knees, a third eye: these are some of the 32 rules, originating from 3rd-century India, that govern the depiction of Buddha in sculpture and denote his divine nature. Other symbols to be aware of are the 'postures', which depict periods in the life of Buddha.

Sitting Teaching or meditating. If the right hand is pointed towards the earth, Buddha is shown subduing the demons of desire. If the hands are folded in the lap, Buddha is meditating.

Reclining The exact moment of Buddha's passing into *parinibbana* (postdeath nirvana).

Standing Bestowing blessings or taming evil forces.

Walking Buddha after his return to earth from heaven.

with dreams of democracy. Prajadhipok's reign eventually ended when he abdicated while in England in 1935, just two months after the sesquicentenary of the Chakri dynasty.

PHRA SUMEN FORT & SANTICHAIPRAKAN PARK Map pp68–9
ป้อมพระสุเมร/สวนสาธารณะสันติชัยปราการ
Cnr Th Phra Athit & Th Phra Sumen; 🕙 **5am-10pm;** 🚢 **Tha Phra Athit,** 🚌 **ordinary 15, 30 & 53**
Beside Mae Nam Chao Phraya in Banglamphu stands one of Bangkok's original 18th-century forts. Built in 1783 to defend against potential naval invasions and named for the mythical Mt Meru (Phra Sumen in Thai) of Hindu-Buddhist cosmology, the octagonal brick-and-stucco bunker was one of 14 city watchtowers that punctuated the old city wall alongside Khlong Rop Krung (now Khlong Banglamphu but still called Khlong Rop Krung on most signs). Apart from Mahakan Fort, this is the only one still standing.

Alongside the fort and fronting the river is a small, grassy park with an open-air pavilion, river views, cool breezes and a bohemian mix of alternative young Thais and backpackers, the latter often wearing fisherman pants and trying to learn the current backpacking fad of twirling fire sticks.

It's an interesting place to sit, people-watch and see what are said to be the last two *lamphu* trees in Banglamphu.

From the park a walkway zigzags south along the river – and in some cases is suspended right over it – from the fort all the way to Saphan Phra Pin Klao. Follow this walk and along the way you can catch glimpses of some of Th Phra Athit's classic old Ratanakosin-style mansions that are not visible from the street, including those housing parts of the Buddhist Society of Thailand and the UN's Food & Agriculture Organization.

WAT BOWONNIWET Map pp68–9
วัดบวรนิเวศ
☎ **0 2281 2831; www.watbowon.org; Th Phra Sumen; admission free;** 🕙 **8.30am-5pm;** 🚢 **Tha Phra Athit,** 🚌 **air-con 511**
Founded in 1826, Wat Bowonniwet (commonly known as Wat Bowon) is the national headquarters for the Thammayut monastic sect, a reformed version of Thai Buddhism. The Thammayuts focused on reinstating purer rituals (based on Mon traditions) and orthodox theology expunged of folk beliefs. Rama IV, who set out to be a scholar, not a king, founded the Thammayuts and began the royal tradition of ordination at this temple. In fact, Mongkut

was the abbot of Wat Bowon for several years. Rama IX (King Bhumibol; r 1946–) and Crown Prince Vajiralongkorn, as well as several other males in the royal family, have been temporarily ordained as monks here.

Bangkok's second Buddhist university, Mahamakut University, is housed at Wat Bowon. Selected monks are sent from India, Nepal and Sri Lanka to study here. Because of its royal status, visitors should be particularly careful to dress properly for admittance to this wat – shorts and sleeveless clothing are not allowed.

WAT RATCHANATDA Map pp68–9
วัดราชนัดดา

☎ 0 2224 8807; Th Mahachai; admission free; ⏰ 8am-5pm; 🚌 air-con 511 & 512, ordinary 2, 🚤 khlong boat to Tha Saphan Phan Fah

Across Th Mahachai from the Golden Mount, this temple is most stunning at night when the 37 spires of the all-metal Loha Prasat (Metal Palace) are lit up like a medieval birthday cake. Displaying Burmese influences, it dates from the mid-19th century and was built under Rama III in honour of his granddaughter. The design is said to derive from metal temples built in India and Sri Lanka more than 2000 years ago.

Behind the formal gardens is a well-known market selling Buddhist *phrá khrêuang* in all sizes, shapes and styles. The amulets feature images not only of the Buddha, but also famous Thai monks and Indian deities. Full Buddha images are also for sale.

PHRA NAKHON MEANDER
Walking Tour

If the tourist buses and touting *túk-túks* around the Ko Ratanakosin sights threaten to do your head in, the more local feel of this part of Banglamphu should be more appealing. The area south of Wat Saket combines old wooden and terrace houses, parks, shops selling religious paraphernalia aimed purely at locals and a wat that will leave you wondering why no-one else is there. Begin at the Tha Saphan Phan Fah *khlong* boat pier, or walk from the Khao San area accommodation. If you don't have much time and don't mind sweating, you could follow this walk with the Chinatown tour (p86) or Ko Ratanakosin walk (p63).

1 King Prajadhipok Museum Oppos. the *khlong* boat pier is the handsome, modern King Prajadhipok Museum (p73), whichdetails Thailand's turbulent pre-democracy years.

2 Golden Mount From the museum, cross over Saphan Phan Fah to Golden Mount (p67) for a panoramic view of the city and a chance to have your fortune foreseen: your trip to Bangkok might have you 'discovering a mate who could become a satisfactory match', but then again, you might also 'like being dumb' and have to 'be careful'. *Chok dee!* (Good luck!)

3 Monk's Bowl Village Leave the Golden Mount and turn left (south) along Th Boriphat, where you'll walk past shops selling carved teak lintels and other decorations for turning your apartment into a Thai restaurant. Cross Th Bamrung Meuang and turn left at Soi Ban Baat to see (actually, it's more of an experience) Monk's Bowl Village (p71), the artisan village of beaten steel bowls and life amid atmospheric, eye-opening alleys.

4 Religious Shops Backtrack to Th Bamrung Meuang, turn left across the bridge and go straight ahead. The religious shops on this stretch, and others in the crescent-shaped area of shophouses on the corner of Th Din So and Bamrung Meuang, are where Bangkokians come to buy the sort of goods needed in temples. These are primarily Buddha images of all shapes and sizes, though usually only one colour – gold. Wealthy families make merit by donating these items to their local temples. Of course, you can't actually 'own' a Buddha image so technically these Buddhas are rented, not sold. If you're lucky you'll see a new Buddha 'shipment' arrive, the huge figures delivered aboard pick-ups, all wrapped up like abductees in monks' robes. Then begins the touch-up process on their golden paint jobs, and the wait for an 'adoption'.

5 Sao Ching-Cha Continue to the spindly red Sao Ching-Cha (Giant Swing; p72), a gatelike structure that once hosted a death-defying (or sometimes not) Brahmain spectacle.

6 Marble Sign To the right of the Giant Swing is the Bangkok City Hall (BMA building), which is thoroughly unremarkable except for the marble sign in front of the square spelling out Bangkok's official Thai name; a quirky photo-op recommended for travellers

planet.com

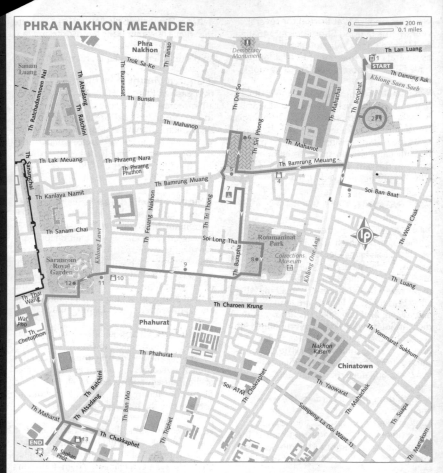

PHRA NAKHON MEANDER

WALK FACTS

Start Tha Saphan Phan Fah (*khlong* boat)
End Tha Saphan Phut (river ferry)
Distance 4km
Duration Two to three hours
Fuel Stops *Khlong*-side noodle shops and Thai restaurants on Th Din So

with very wide-angle lenses. If you're hungry, wander north on Th Din So to choose from several long-established restaurants in old shophouses.

7 Wat Suthat Passing the Giant Swing, turn left into Wat Suthat (p71), one of the biggest, holiest, most beautiful and most undertouristed temples in Thailand.

8 Rommaninat Park Leave Wat Suthat via the east entrance onto Th Burapha and turn right (south). You can re-enter Wat Suthat to see the Ordination Hall, or continue for a few minutes and turn left into **Rommaninat Park**, a pretty green space of fountains, walking paths, piped music, sleeping people and *soi* dogs. On the far side of the park is the **Corrections Museum** (admission by donation; ⊙ 9am-4pm Mon-Fri), a rehabilitated colonial building covering the park's former career as a prison in the early 1900s. Most displays are in Thai but the maintenance staff and other hangers-on turn the tour into a social event, giggling at the gruesome displays of torture used in the good old days.

9 Khlong Exit the park at the southwest corner, cross the street and follow the small *khlong* through the neighbourhood on Soi Long Tha, past fruit vendors, drying laundry, the neighbourhood shrine, a newly renovated Chinese temple and noodle and soup vendors. This is what Bangkok looked like when the city's footpaths were riverbanks and, provided the *khlong* isn't having one of its especially stinky days, this is a good place to stop for a real local meal.

10 Shopfronts At Fuang Nakhon turn left and then right on Soi Phra Si past the heavily ornamented shopfronts decorated in a style often referred to as Sino-Portuguese. In the early 20th century these buildings were the height of fashion and sold new luxury goods, like motor cars, to the modernising country. Today the fashions have shifted to downtown malls and the old buildings are either warehouses or offer more mundane items – like car parts.

11 Saphan Hok Cross Th Atsadang to Saphan Hok, a simple lever bridge across Khlong Lawt, the inner-city moat that cut off royal Ko Ratanakosin from the plebeian Bangkok. Small trading ships from Mon settlements would dock near here on trading missions.

12 Saranrom Royal Garden Enter the Saranrom Royal Garden (p61), a park favouring English Victorian gardens with tropical perfumes and earnest exercisers.

13 Pak Khlong Market Exit near the fountain to the old ministry buildings and turn left on Th Sanam Chai all the way to Th Triphet and Pak Khlong Market (p132), Bangkok's wholesale flower and vegetable market.

Eating p157; Sleeping p207

Formerly a fruit orchard north of the royal island of Ratanakosin, Dusit was transformed into a mini-European city by Rama V (King Chulalongkorn), complete with wide avenues and shady walkways. The area begins east of Th Samsen and follows Th Phitsanulok and Th Sri Ayuthaya to the district's most famous sites: Dusit Park (p80), Dusit Zoo (p81) and Wat Benchamabophit (p81). Further east is the present monarch's residence of Chitralada Palace, which is open to the public only by appointment and with a good reason.

But for all the elegance of Dusit Park and the European-style grandeur of its buildings and boulevards, the district is hollow in spirit precisely because this is Bangkok, not London or Paris. You can walk for blocks without spotting any of the things that make Bangkok wonderful: street vendors, motorcycle taxis, random stores selling random stuff. Or, as Somerset Maugham put it when driving through Dusit's streets in 1923, 'They seem to await ceremonies and procession. They are like the deserted avenues in the park of a fallen monarch.'

top picks

THEWET & DUSIT

- Dusit Park (p80) Witness the Victorian sense and Thai sensibilities merging in this royal enclave.
- Ratchadamnoen Stadium (p199) Makes Steven Seagal look soft as a pillow.
- Kaloang Home Kitchen (p157) Soak up the view of the Saphan Rama VIII while chowing down on cheap seafood.
- Wat Benchamabophit (p81) Does this Italian-marble temple remind you of an ice palace?
- Dusit Zoo (p81) Where kids can stretch their legs and imaginations.

Devotion to the venerated monarch is the primary purpose of an average Bangkokian's visit to Dusit. Many people come to make merit at the bronze equestrian statue of Rama V, which stands in military garb at the Royal Plaza. Although originally intended as mere historical commemoration, the statue has quite literally become a religious shrine, where every Tuesday evening Bangkok residents come to offer candles, flowers (predominantly pink roses), incense and bottles of whisky.

Rama V is also honoured with an annual festival on 23 October that celebrates his accomplishments in modernising the country, abolishing slavery and maintaining the country's independence when all other Southeast Asian countries were being colonised – avoiding such a fate is a matter of enormous pride to Thais. During this festival thousands of visitors converge on the plaza, accompanied by cacophonous loudspeakers and attendant food vendors, briefly disrupting Dusit's aloofness with Bangkok's engaging chaos. For visitors accustomed to more subdued places, Dusit and its well-maintained green spaces will provide a necessary break from Bangkok's incessant noise. Dusit is also home to the prime minister's residence at Government House (Map p79; Th Phitsanulok), several ministries and the UNESCAP complex, the United Nations' vast Southeast Asian headquarters.

Cradled between Th Samsen and the river, the riverside section of the district is referred to as Thewet, after the nearby temple, Wat Ratchathewet. Thewet shelters Thewet Flower Market (Map p79; Th Krung Kasem; ☉ 8am-6pm), a popular flower market beside the *khlong*, and a refreshingly quiet backpacker scene existing cheek-by-jowl with a lively wet market selling vegetables, meat, fish and other sundries that makes a great local breakfast or lunch experience. In spite of the scores – or sometimes hundreds – of backpackers staying here at any one time, the neighbourhood has resisted the temptation to transform its businesses into the internet cafés, tattoo parlours, bars or souvenir shops that usually pop up where travellers go. Instead vendors prefer the traditional course of business with the Thais, allowing the foreigners to adjust to local customs. Largely a residential neighbourhood, at rush hour Thewet is packed with uniform-clad residents climbing aboard rickety buses for a sweaty commute to the office districts of Silom or Sukhumvit, while Th Samsen is a near-continuous stream of rattletrap buses and screaming túk-túk.

Street stalls and food markets are most prolific near Thewet, but be sure to be well watered and fed before venturing into food-free Dusit on foot.

THEWET & DUSIT

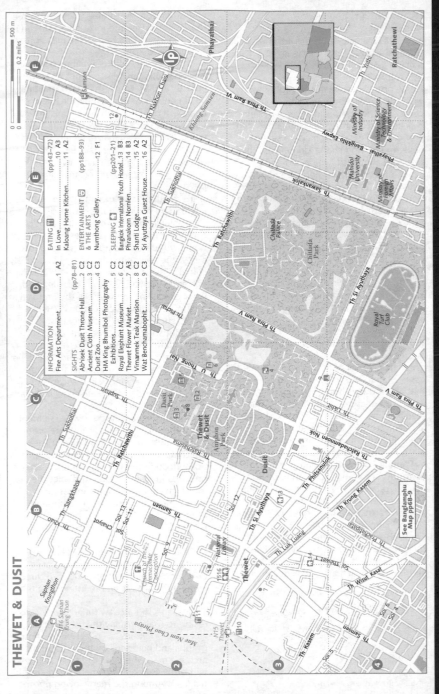

INFORMATION	(pp143–72)
Fine Arts Department............1	A2

SIGHTS	(pp78–81)
Abhisek Dusit Throne Hall.........2	C2
Ancient Cloth Museum............3	C2
Dusit Zoo...........4	C3
HM King Bhumibol Photography	
Exhibitions...........5	C2
Royal Elephant Museum...........6	C2
Thewet Flower Market...........7	A3
Vimanmek Teak Mansion...........8	C2
Wat Benchamabophit...........9	C3

EATING	(pp143–72)
In Love...........10	A3
Kaloang Home Kitchen...........11	A2

ENTERTAINMENT & THE ARTS	(pp188–93)
Numthong Gallery...........12	F1

SLEEPING	(pp201–21)
Bangkok International Youth Hostel..13	B3
Phranakorn Nornlen...........14	B3
Shanti Lodge...........15	A2
Sri Ayuttaya Guest House...........16	A2

See Banglamphu
Map pp68–9

DUSIT PARK Map p79
สวนดุสิต

☎ 0 2628 6300; bounded by Th Ratchawithi, Th U Thong Nai & Th Ratchasima; admission adult 100B, with Grand Palace ticket free; ☯ 9.30am-4pm; 🚌 510 & 70, 72

Please note: because this is royal property, visitors should wear long pants (no capri pants) or long skirts and shirts with sleeves.

A modern country, King Chulalongkorn pronounced, needed a modern seat of government. And so the king moved the royal court to Dusit, where he had built Beaux Arts institutions and Victorian manor houses. The royal residence was removed from the cloistered city of Ko Ratanakosin to the open and manicured lawns of Dusit Park. Confectioneery buildings of European and Thai fusions housed members of the royal family in a style that must have seemed as futuristic as today's skyscrapers. The maturing art of architecture has been kind to the romantic Victorian period and Dusit Park is a worthwhile escape from Bangkok's chaos and egg-carton Bauhaus and blue-glass buildings.

The highlight of the park is Vimanmek Teak Mansion, said to be the world's largest golden teak mansion, built with nary a single nail. For all of its finery, grand staircases, octagonal rooms and lattice walls that are nothing short of magnificent, it is surprisingly serene and intimate. The mansion was originally constructed on Ko Si Chang in 1868 as a retreat for Rama V; the king had it moved to its present site in 1901. For the following few years it served as Rama V's primary residence, with the 81 rooms accommodating his enormous extended family. The interior of the mansion contains various personal effects of the king and a treasure-trove of early Ratanakosin and European art objects and antiques. Compulsory English-language tours of the building start every 30 minutes and last an hour, though it's a lucky dip as to whether your guide will actually speak decent

English or not. Try to time your visit to see the Thai classical and folk dances staged in an open-sided *sala* beside the mansion at 10.30am and 2pm.

Immediately behind Vimanmek mansion is Abhisek Dusit Throne Hall. Visions of Moorish palaces and Victorian mansions must have still been spinning around in the king's head when he commissioned this intricate building of porticoes and fretwork fused with a distinctive Thai character. Built as the throne hall for the palace in 1904, it opens onto a big stretch of lawn and flowerbeds, just like any important European building.

Inside, the heavy ornamentation of the white main room is quite extraordinary, especially if you've been visiting a lot of overwhelmingly gold temples or traditional wooden buildings. Look up to just below the ceiling to see the line of brightly coloured stained-glass panels in Moorish patterns. The hall displays regional handiwork crafted by members of the Promotion of Supplementary Occupations & Related Techniques (SUPPORT) charity foundation sponsored by Queen Sirikit. Among the exhibits are *mát-mìi*–style (a form of tie-dying) cotton and silk textiles, *málaeng tháp* collages (made from metallic, multi-coloured beetle wings), damascene and nielloware, and *yaan líphao* basketry (made with a type of vine).

Built in the early 1900s by Italian architects, the great neoclassical dome of the Ananta Samakh anchors Royal Plaza. The building is still used for its intended purpose: hosting foreign dignitaries. Frescoes on the gilded dome ceiling depict the monarchs and the important works of the early Chakri dynasty. The first meeting of the Thai parliament was held in this building before being moved to a facility nearby.

Beside the Th U Thong Nai gate, the Royal Elephant Museum (opposite) showcases two large stables that once housed three white elephants; it's more interesting than it sounds.

Near the Th Ratchawithi entrance, two residence halls display the HM King Bhumibol Photography Exhibitions, a collection of photographs and paintings by the present monarch – a man who even today is rarely seen without a Canon SLR camera slung around his neck. Among the many loving photos of his wife and children are pictures of the

---

TRANSPORT: THEWET & DUSIT

Bus Air-con 505 and 510, ordinary 3, 16, 18, 32, 53, 70 and 72

Ferry Tha Thewet

With no Skytrain or Metro connections, peak hour traffic gets very busy around here.

THE ORIGINAL WHITE ELEPHANTS

Think 'white elephant' and things like Howard Hughes' *Spruce Goose* wooden plane and the Millennium Dome/O2 Arena in London come to mind. But why is it that these and other supposedly valuable, but hugely expensive and basically useless items are known as white elephants? The answer lies in the sacred status given to albino elephants by the kings of Thailand, Laos and Burma.

The tradition derives from the story in which the Buddha's mother is said to have dreamt of a white elephant presenting her with a lotus flower – a symbol of purity and wisdom – just before she gave birth. Extrapolating this, a monarch possessing a white elephant was regarded as a just and benign ruler. Across the region any genuinely albino elephant automatically became crown property; the physical characteristics used to rank white elephants are outlined in the Royal Elephant Museum (Dusit Park; 9.30am-4pm). Laws prevented sacred white elephants from working, so despite being highly regarded they were of no practical use and still cost a fortune to keep.

In modern Thailand the white elephant retains its sacred status, and one is kept at Chitralada Palace, home to the current Thai king. The museum houses sculptural representation of that elephant. Draped in royal vestments, the statue is more or less treated as a shrine by the visiting Thai public.

king playing clarinet with Benny Goodman and Louis Armstrong in 1960. The Ancient Cloth Museum presents a beautiful collection of traditional silks and cottons that make up the royal cloth collection.

DUSIT ZOO Map p79
สวนสัตว์ดุสิต(เขาดิน)

0 2281 9027; www.zoothailand.org; Th Ratchawithi; adult/child 100/50B; 8am-6pm; aircon 510, ordinary 18 & 28

The collection of animals at Bangkok's 19-hectare zoo comprises more than 300 mammals, 200 reptiles and 800 birds, including relatively rare indigenous species. Originally a private botanic garden for Rama V, Dusit Zoo (Suan Sat Dusit or *khǎo din*) was opened in 1938 and is now one of the premier zoological facilities in Southeast Asia – though that doesn't mean all the animal enclosures are first-rate. The shady grounds feature trees labelled in English plus a lake in the centre with paddle boats for rent. There's also a small children's playground.

If nothing else, the zoo is a nice place to get away from the noise of the city and observe how the Thais amuse themselves –

mainly by eating. There are a few lakeside restaurants that serve good, inexpensive Thai food. Be warned, Sundays can be awfully crowded.

WAT BENCHAMABOPHIT Map p79
วัดเบญจมบพิตร(วัดเบญฯ)

0 2282 7413; cnr Th Si Ayuthaya & Th Phra Ram V; admission 20B; 8.30am-5pm; ordinary 72

The closest Thailand will come to an ice palace, this temple of white Carrara marble (hence its alternative name, 'Marble Temple') was built at the turn of the century under Rama V. The large cruciform *bòt* is a prime example of modern Thai temple architecture. The base of the central Buddha image, a copy of Phra Phuttha Chinnarat in Phitsanulok, holds the ashes of Rama V. The courtyard behind the *bòt* has 53 Buddha images (33 originals and 20 copies) representing every *mudra* (gesture) and style from Thai history, making this the ideal place to compare Buddhist iconography. If religious details aren't for you, this temple offers a pleasant stroll beside landscaped canals filled with blooming lotus and Chinese-style footbridges.

CHINATOWN

Eating p158; Shopping p131; Sleeping p207

Although many generations removed from the mainland (see boxed text, opposite), Bangkok's China-town could be a bosom brother of any Chinese city. The streets are crammed with shark-fin restaurants, gaudy yellow-gold and jade shops and flashing neon signs in Chinese characters. But these characteristics are just window dressing for the relentlessly entrepreneurial soul of the neighbourhood.

Chinatown fans out along Mae Nam Chao Phraya between Saphan Phra Phuttha Yot Fa to the west and Hualamphong Railway Station (opposite) to the southeast, near where are the relatively quite lanes of Talat Noi (opposite). Th Yaowarat and Th Charoen Krung are the main arteries and provide the greatest diversity of services, from shopping and eating to promenading (as much as you can when the pavements are heaving with vendors) in the latest mainland Chinese styles. The whole district is buzzing from dawn until after dusk, with only the overfed *soi* dogs splayed out on footpaths seeming in any way relaxed. And where the narrow market *soi* can be a world of elbows during the day, things are marginally more mellow by night, when banquet dining and dazzling neon contribute to a carnival atmosphere.

top picks

CHINATOWN

- Talat Noi (opposite) Stroll through this cramped neighbourhood of oil-stained machine shops.
- Phahurat (opposite) Bollywood-style markets of flashy colours and sequins galore.
- Sampeng Lane (p131) Regimented chaos and commerce are staged deep in the bowels of this outdoor market.
- Wat Traimit (p85) Meet the temple's Buddha made of 5.5 tonnes of gold.

Until the 1970s Chinatown was, in effect, the country's most important market, supplying and wholesaling pretty much anything that could be bought in the kingdom from stores self-segregated by profession – whole streets or blocks are dedicated to sign making, gold and jewellery stores, and machine and tyre shops. However Bangkok's ongoing affair with consumerism, and its resulting brood of lust children in the form of multistorey megamalls, have seen a steady decline in the area's commercial importance. Much of the middle class has moved out of the cramped district to the villas and condos of Bangkok's new suburbs *(mùu bâan)*.

It's a slow process, though, and after shouldering your way through the claustrophobic commercial chaos of Trok Itsaranuphap (p86) you'll find it difficult to imagine it could ever have been busier. Chinese remains the district's primary language, and goods, people and services are on a continuous conveyor belt into and out of the area. All of which makes this one of Bangkok's most rewarding areas to simply set out and explore.

To do this you could follow the walking tour (p86), or perhaps starve yourself for two days before embarking on a voyage of street food discovery, or just make it up as you go along. Whichever option you choose, expect it to be memorable.

At the western edge of Chinatown, near the intersection of Th Phahurat and Th Chakraphet, is a small but thriving Indian and Islamic district, generally called Phahurat or Little India. The dim alleys and affinity for commerce tie these two heritages together, although their particular expressions provide a fascinating diversity. Th Chakraphet is home to several cheap Indian restaurants (p159) that serve delicious food.

CHURCH OF SANTA CRUZ Map p84

☎ 0 2466 0347; Soi Kuti Jiin, Thonburi; ⊗ Sat & Sun; 🛳 from Tha Pak Talat/ Atsadang

Centuries before Sukhumvit became the international district, the Portuguese claimed *faràng* (Western) supremacy and built the Church of Santa Cruz in the 1700s. The land was a gift from King Taksin in appreciation for the loyalty the Portuguese community had displayed after the fall of Ayuthaya. The surviving church dates to 1913. Very little activity occurs on the grounds itself, but small village streets break off from the main courtyard into the area known as Kuti Jiin. On Soi Kuti Jiin 3, several houses sell the Portuguese-inspired cakes.

HUALAMPHONG RAILWAY STATION
Map p84

สถานีรถไฟหัวลำโพง

Th Phra Ram IV; ⊕ air-con 501, ordinary 25 & 75; Ⓜ Hualamphong

At the southeastern edge of Chinatown, Bangkok's main train station was built by Dutch architects and engineers just before WWI. It is one of the city's earliest and most outstanding examples of the movement towards Thai Art Deco. If you can zone out of the chaos for a moment, look for the vaulted iron roof and neoclassical portico that were a state-of-the-art engineering feat, and the patterned, two-toned skylights that exemplify pure de Stijl Dutch modernism.

PHAHURAT Map p84

พาหุรัด

West of Th Chakrawat; 🚢 Tha Saphan Phut (Memorial Bridge, N6), 🚌 ordinary 53 & 73

Fabric and gem traders set up shop in this small but bustling Little India, where everything from Bollywood movies to bindis is sold by enthusiastic small-time traders. Behind the more obvious storefronts are winding alleys that criss-cross Khlong Ong Ang, where merchants grab a bite to eat or make travel arrangements for trips home – it's a great area to just wander, stopping for masala chai or lassi as you go.

Just off Th Chakraphet is Sri Gurusingh Sabha (Th Phahurat; 🕙 6am-5pm), a gold-domed Sikh temple best viewed from Soi ATM. Basically it's a large hall, somewhat reminiscent of a mosque interior, devoted to the worship of the Guru Granth Sahib, the 17th-century Sikh holy book, which is itself considered the last of the religion's 10 great gurus. *Prasada* (blessed food offered to Hindu or Sikh temple attendees) is distributed among devotees every morning around 9am, and if you arrive on a Sikh festival day you can partake in the *langar* (communal Sikh meal) served in the temple. If you do visit this shrine, be sure to climb to the top for panoramic views of Chinatown. Stores surrounding the temple sell assorted religious paraphernalia.

TALAT NOI Map p84

ตลาดน้อย

Bounded by the river, Th Songwat, Th Charoen Krung & Th Yotha; 🚢 Tha Si Phraya

This microcosm of *soi* life is named after a *noi* (little) market that sets up between Soi 22 and Soi 20, off Th Charoen Krung, selling goods from China. Wandering here you'll find streamlike *soi* turning in on themselves, weaving through people's living rooms, noodle shops and grease-stained machine shops. Opposite the River View Guesthouse, San Jao Sien Khong (unnamed soi; admission by donation; 🕙 6am-6pm) is one of the city's oldest Chinese shrines, which is guarded by a playful rooftop terracotta dragon. A former owner of the shrine made his fortune collecting taxes on bird-nest delicacies.

WAT MANGKON KAMALAWAT (LENG NOI YEE) Map p84

วัดมังกรกมลาวาส

Th Charoen Krung; 🕙 6am-5.30pm; 🚌 air-con 508, ordinary 16, 73, 75 & 93, 🚢 Tha Ratchawong

Explore the cryptlike sermon halls of this busy Chinese temple (also known as Leng

BANGKOK: A CHINESE STORY

The longer you spend in Thailand the more you realise that, unlike most of the rest of the country, the face of Bangkok has a noticeable Chinese look. Indeed, the influence of the Chinese and their integration within the Bangkok community means that as many as half of all Bangkokians claim some Chinese ancestry.

For many that ancestry dates to a mass migration from China's Teochew region in the late 1700s, when peasants came to labour first on the new capital of Thonburi and, later, on Bangkok. The Chinese, who had lived in the Ko Ratanakosin area while working in Thonburi, were moved outside the walls of the new capital to a neighbourhood that went on to become Chinatown. In the best Chinese traditions, impoverished peasants started menial jobs and worked their way up eventually to establish business empires. A pepper grinder who had a stall on Th Charoen Krung tugged at his bootstraps hard enough to corner the country's herbal export trade. Chinatown was a breeding ground for such rags-to-riches stories, and many immigrant families' names are now affixed to some of the country's largest businesses and economic engines.

Thais have been ambivalent about their long-running relationship with Chinese immigrants. The peasant newcomers were despised until their fortunes turned; today attitudes are complimentary, now that affluence, rather than poverty, is the norm. The umbilical cord to the cultural motherland is still strong and can be seen in such events as the Vegetarian Festival (p13). But many descendants of immigrants consider themselves 100% Thai.

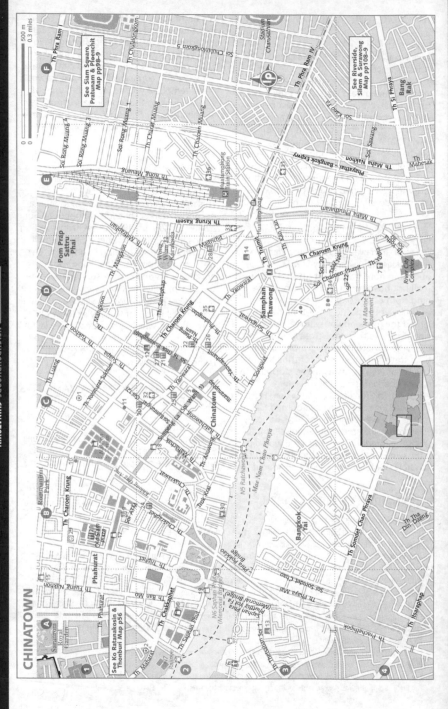

CHINATOWN

See Siam Square, Pratunam & Ploenchit Map pp98–9

See Riverside, Silom & Suravong Map pp108–9

See Ko Ratanakosin & Thonburi Map p56

CHINATOWN

INFORMATION		SHOPPING 🛍	(pp127–41)	ENTERTAINMENT 🎭	(pp188–93)
Police............................1 C1		Johnny's Gems.........................15 A1		& THE ARTS	
Police Station............................2 A2		Pak Khlong Market...................16 A2		About Café/About	
			17 B1	Studio.................................28 D2	
SIGHTS	(pp82–8)	Sampeng Lane..........................18 C2		Sala Chalermkrung..................29 B1	
Bangkok Bank...........................3 C2		Saphan Phut Night			
Chao Sua Son House.................4 D3		Bazaar................................19 A2		DRINKING	
Chinatown Gate........................5 D3				& NIGHTLIFE 🍺 🎵	(pp173–85)
Church of Santa Cruz................6 A2		EATING 🍴	(pp143–72)	Nang Nual Riverside Pub.........30 B2	
Holy Rosary Church...................7 D4		Chiang Kii................................20 C2			
San Jao Sien Khong...................8 D3		Hong Kong Noodles................21 C2		SLEEPING 🛏	(pp201–21)
Sri Gurusingh Sabha...................9 B1		Hua Seng Hong.......................22 D2		Baan Hualampong...................31 E3	
Talat Khlong Ong Ang.............10 B1		Old Siam Plaza........................23 B1		Grand China Princess..............32 C2	
Talat Khlong Thom..................11 C1		Royal India..............................24 B2		Krung Kasem Srikung	
Wat Mangkon Kamalawat.......12 C2		Shangarila Restaurant.............25 C2		Hotel...................................33 E2	
Wat Prayoon...........................13 A3		Tang Jai Yuu...........................26 C2		River View Guest House..........34 D3	
Wat Traimit (Golden Buddha)...14 D3		Thai Charoen...........................27 C2		Shanghai Inn...........................35 D2	
				Train Inn.................................36 E2	

Noi Yee) to find Buddhist, Taoist and Confucian shrines. During the annual Vegetarian Festival (p13), religious and culinary activities are centred here. But almost any time of day or night this temple is busy with worshippers lighting incense, filling the ever-burning altar lamps with oil and making offerings to their ancestors. Offering oil is believed to provide a smooth journey into the afterlife and to fuel the fire of life. Mangkon Kamalawatt means 'Dragon Lotus Temple'. Surrounding the temple are vendors selling food for the gods – steamed lotus-shaped dumplings and oranges – that are used for merit making.

WAT TRAIMIT Map p84
วัดไตรมิตร

☎ 0 2225 9775; cnr Th Yaowarat & Th Charoen Krung; admission Golden Buddha/temple 20B/free; ⏰ 8am-5pm; 🚤 Tha Ratchawong, 🚌 ordinary 25 & 53, Ⓜ Hualamphong
Wat Traimit (Temple of the Golden Buddha) is home to the world's largest gold Buddha image, a gleaming, 3m-tall, 5.5-tonne behemoth whose story is probably the most interesting aspect of a visit here. Sculpted in the graceful Sukhothai style (notice the hair curls and elongated earlobes), the image was only 'rediscovered' some 50 years ago when it was dropped from a crane while being moved. This divine act cracked a plaster exterior that was, it is thought, applied to disguise it from marauding hordes in either the late Sukhothai or the Ayuthaya period, when the Burmese repeatedly threatened and eventually pillaged Siam.

Wat Traimit is on every tour guide's itinerary, and the seemingly endless procession of tour groups seems to have scared off most of the genuine worshippers. The spectacle can be underwhelming. After viewing the image, head to the main bòt and the mechanical horoscope machines outside, which look like an import from a boardwalk amusement strip. Put a coin in the machine that corresponds to the day of the week you were born, lights flash mystically and then a number appears that corresponds to a printed fortune.

TRANSPORT: CHINATOWN

Bus Air-con 507 and 508, ordinary 53, 73 and 75

Ferry Tha Ratchawong (N5), Tha Saphan Phut (Memorial Bridge, N6)

Metro Hualamphong

While we list bus numbers here, traffic in Chinatown is so dire that you're strongly advised to avoid all forms of road transport. Instead, plan your route and arrive by river ferry to Tha Ratchawong or Tha Saphan Phut, or take the Metro to Hualamphong and walk. Following the walking tour (p86), or just making up your own as you wander, is undoubtedly the most interesting (and, ahm, hot, crowded, slow and sweaty) way to get around. If it all gets too much, at weekends a hop-on hop-off tourist bus loops from opposite Hualamphong station up Th Yaowarat and back down Th Charoen Krung.

CHINATOWN'S SHOPPING STREETS

Chinatown is the neighbourhood version of a big-box store divided up into categories of consumables.

Th Charoen Krung (Map p84) Chinatown's primary thoroughfare is a prestigious address. Starting on the western end of the street, near the intersection of Th Mahachai, is a collection of old record stores. Talat Khlong Ong Ang consumes the next block, selling all sorts of used and new electronic gadgets. Nakhon Kasem is the reformed thieves' market where vendors now stock up on nifty gadgets for portable food prep. Further east, near Th Mahachak is Talat Khlong Thom, a hardware centre. West of Th Ratchawong, everything is geared towards the afterlife and the passing of life.

Th Yaowarat (Map p84) A hundred years ago this was a poultry farm; now it is gold street, the biggest trading centre of the precious metal in the country. Shops are always painted like the interior of a Chinese shrine: blood red and decorated with well-groomed toy dogs that look down on the neighbourhood's fat *soi* dogs in every way except literally. Near the intersection of Th Ratchawong, stores shift to Chinese and Singaporean tourists' tastes: dried fruit and nuts, chintzy talismans and accoutrements for Chinese festivals. The multistorey buildings around here were some of Bangkok's first skyscrapers and a source of wonder for the local people. Bangkok's skyline has grown and grown, but this area retains a few Chinese apothecaries, smelling of wood bark and ancient secrets.

Th Mittraphan (Map p84) Sign makers branch off Wong Wian 22 Karakada, near Wat Traimit and the Golden Buddha; Thai and Roman letters are typically cut out by a hand-guided lathe placed prominently beside the pavement.

Th Santiphap (Map p84) Car parts and other automotive gear make this the place for kicking tyres.

Sampeng Lane (Soi Wanit 1; Map p84) Plastic cuteness in bulk, from pencil cases to pens, stuffed animals, hair flotsam and enough bling to kit out a rappers convention, all hang out near the eastern end of the alley. Closer to Phahurat, the main merchandise changes to bolts of fabric from India.

Soi 16, Th Charoen Krung (Trok Itsaranuphap; Map p84) This ancient fresh market splays along the cramped alley between Th Yaowarat and Th Charoen Krung. It's fascinating, but anyone who suffers even the mildest form of claustrophobia should not contemplate it. North of Th Charoen Krung funerary items for ritual burnings dominate the open-air stalls.

HOLY ROSARY CHURCH Map p84

☎ 0 2266 4849; 1318 Th Yotha, near River City;
✪ Mass Mon-Sat 6am, Sun 6.15am, 8am & 10am;
🛥 Tha Si Phraya

Portuguese seafarers were among the first Europeans to establish diplomatic ties with Siam and their influence in the kingdom was rewarded with prime riverside real estate. When a Portuguese contingent moved across the river to the present-day Talat Noi district of Chinatown in 1787 they were given this piece of land and built the Holy Rosary Church, known in Thai as Wat Kalawan, from the Portuguese 'Calvario'. Over the years the Portuguese community dispersed and the church fell into disrepair. However, Vietnamese and Cambodian Catholics displaced by the Indochina wars adopted it and now constitute most of the parish. This old church has a splendid set of Romanesque stained-glass windows, gilded ceilings and a Christ statue that is carried through the streets during Easter celebrations.

CHINATOWN WANDER
Walking Tour

Chinatown is packed – every inch of it is used to make a living. From the fresh-food market festooned with carcasses to alleys full of endless bling, the commerce never rests. This walking tour plunges into the claustrophobic alleys of chaotic dealing for which the district is famous, some quiet hidden lanes and the touristy but impressive Golden Buddha before finishing in the relatively peaceful *soi* of Talat Noi. Be prepared for crowds and smells, and bring your camera. Depending on where you want to go afterwards and what time it is (the ferries stop soon after 7pm), finish either at the Tha Marine Department river ferry or Hualamphong MTR, a 10-minute walk back from Talat Noi.

1 Phahurat (Little India) Starting from the river ferry at Tha Saphan Phut (Memorial Bridge Pier), walk north along jam-packed Th Chakraphet, past the Constitutional Court and into Phahurat, aka Little India. If it's already lunchtime you could stop for a curry, or plunge into the retail madness of Trok Huae Med.

2 Trok Huae Med There's no sign, but the old stores, street stalls and mass of people reveal you're at the beginning of Trok Huae Med, a largely Indian extension of Sampeng Lane.

CHINATOWN

After 50m cross a *khlong* (or wander right for more informal curry houses) and continue.

3 Sampeng Lane You'll soon be in Sampeng Lane, signposted (if you can see it) as Soi Wanit 1. This is Chinatown's oldest shopping strip, where the Chinese first set up shop after being moved from Ko Ratanakosin in 1782. Today it's a shopping fun house, where the sky is completely obscured and bargains lie in ambush – that is, if you really want 500 Hello Kitty pens or a tonne of stuffed animals. This initial stretch is now dominated by Indian fabric merchants.

4 Chinese shophouses After a few minutes you'll come to Th Mahachak, where to the right dozens of battered old Vespas wait for their next delivery job (there's no space for trucks around here). Turn left (northeast), walk about 30m and turn left again through a covered passage. On the far side are rows of photogenic, stuccoed yellow Chinese shophouses. It's pretty peaceful here, so it makes a nice intermission in the market tour.

5 Bangkok Bank Return to Sampeng Lane and continue east. This stretch is dominated

WALK FACTS

Start Tha Saphan Phut (Memorial Bridge, river ferry N6)
End Tha Marine Department (river ferry, N4) or Hualamphong Metro
Distance 4km
Duration three hours
Fuel Stop Hong Kong Noodles (p159) or the streetside kitchens on Th Plaeng Naam

by a mind-boggling array of cheap plastic stuff from China; a thousand different varieties of hair-pin, anyone? When you come to Th Mangkon, find somewhere you won't be run over by a trolley full of overstuffed boxes and admire two of Bangkok's oldest commercial buildings, a Bangkok Bank and the venerable Tang To Kang gold shop, both more than 100 years old. The exteriors of the buildings are classic early Ratanakosin, showing lots of European influence; the interiors are heavy with hardwood panelling.

6 Trok Itsaranuphap Turn left (north) on Th Mangkun and walk up to manic Th Yaowarat, Chinatown's main drag. Turn right

87

GOING WITH THE FLOW

For a day of sightseeing, you'll need a good map, comfortable shoes, patience, and coins and small notes to buy water. Don't bring your Western concept of pavement etiquette. You're in Asia now, and the rules of personal space – not to mention the laws of physics – are completely different. Human traffic in Bangkok acts like flowing water: if there is an empty space, it will quickly be filled with a body, regardless of who was where in some unspoken queue. With an increase of mass (a motorcycle or pushcart), a solid state is achieved and the sea of pedestrians can be pushed out of the way in a textbook example of might-makes-right – or size matters. Once you master these simple concepts, you can enjoy shuffling along with the flow.

past the street's famous gold shops (gold is sold by the *bàat*, a unit of weight equal to 15g, and prices are good). After 100m or so, gird your loins and cross Th Yaowarat, then head straight into a tiny lane known variously as Soi Charoen Krung 16 and Trok Itsaranuphap. There's no sign, but you'll know by the queue of people shuffling into the alley one at a time. If you thought Soi Sampeng was busy, this crush of humanity, also known as Talaat Mai (New Market), will have your head spinning like Linda Blair in *The Exorcist*.

7 Talat Leng-Buai-la A short way along on the left is Talat Leng-Buai-la. A spry 80 years old, it was once the city's central vegetable market but today sells mainly Chinese ingredients such as fresh cashews, lotus seeds and shiitake mushrooms. The first section is lined with vendors purveying cleaned chickens, plucked ducks, scaled fish, unnaturally coloured vats of pickled food and prepackaged snacks – hungry yet? Hong Kong Noodles (p159), on the left side of the alley, does a rollicking business catering to appetites aroused by such sights.

8 Wat Mangkon Kamalawat You will, eventually, pop out the far end onto Th Charoen Krung. Cross over and go a short way down Soi Charoen Krung 21 to Wat Mangkon Kamalawat (p83), one of Chinatown's largest and liveliest temples. Along this stretch of the street neighbouring shops sell fruit, cakes, incense and ritual burning paper, all for offering at the temple.

9 Thanon Plaeng Naam Head back to Th Charoen Krung, turn left (east) and walk one

block and turn right on Th Plaeng Naam. This atmospheric street of shophouses and street food is a more leisurely place for a feed, particularly at the two streetside kitchens at the north end.

10 Thanon Yaowarat Continue south, then turn left onto hectic Th Yaowarat. This is the neon-side of Chinatown; great for photos in the late afternoon and early evening. After passing a couple of old Art Deco buildings that have seen better days, turn left at the Odeon Circle, with its distinctive Chinese gate, onto Th Mitthaphap (aka Th Traimit).

11 Wat Traimit & the Golden Buddha A couple of minutes along this street of brushes and wicker furniture is Wat Traimit and its 5.5 tonnes of Golden Buddha (p85). If you've timed your run to get here in late afternoon (but before it closes at 5pm), it should be free of the usual tour buses and make a welcome respite from all those markets.

12 Talat Noi If you're knackered, it's a short walk eastwards to Hualamphong and the Metro. But if it's anywhere near sunset, we strongly recommend heading back to Odeon Sq, braving the traffic and heading down Soi Yaowarat 1. Follow this road of machine shops, then continue onto Soi Charoen Phanit into the local Talat Noi neighbourhood. Follow the signs to the River View Guest House (p208), where the 8th-floor restaurant-bar has cheap beer and amazing sunset views. It's not far from here to the Tha Maritime Department ferry pier, but remember the last boats pass a little after 7pm.

LOCAL VOICES

Like all great cities, Bangkok acts like a tractor beam for people from all over Thailand and around the world. The city has been the capital of Thailand for almost 230 years so people have certainly been born here, but whether it's for work, family, education, escape or just to experience life in the big smoke, the City of Angels has drawn millions more from all walks of life.

As you'll see from the Bangkokians we interviewed while researching this book, each contributes something different to Bangkok's stated aim of becoming a 'world city' to rival Hong Kong and Singapore. They reflect the dynamic nature of a place where opportunities are chased and lives changed faster than condos rise out of the flat earth. Equally, they speak to the mix of modern and traditional attitudes that coexist, often jarringly, and are central to Bangkok's character. There is the woman whose ancestor was a royal palace chef and who continues the tradition in the 80-year-old family restaurant, or the man who started as a dishwasher in an opium den and is now a taxi driver with a sideline in refereeing *muay thai* (Thai boxing). There's the young woman who has found her first job in Bangkok, and the expat who brings needed skills to the city.

These, and millions of others, are the Bangkok locals. Go out and meet some.

Street-food vendor serving the masses in Sanam Luang (p60)

Name Surachit Eurfua
Age 66
Occupation Thai boxing referee/taxi driver
Residence Greater Bangkok (Ladphrao)

Experience the thrill of a muay thai (kickboxing) match (above; p199). Get carried away with the hustle and bustle of China-town's main drag, Trok Itsaranuphap (middle; p87). Bangkok's taxis (bottom; p254) are among the best value on earth.

Describe your working life. I grew up in a poor family and left school to start working when I was 12. I worked as a dishwasher at an opium den. I earned 40B a month!

How did you get interested in Thai boxing? I started out with Thai boxing as a way to defend myself, and it became a good way to earn money to send back to my mother.

How long have you been working as a boxing referee? For 43 years now.

And how long have you been a taxi driver? Four years.

What's it like being a taxi driver in Bangkok? I'm happy driving a taxi and I like being independent.

And being a boxing referee? I'm the only referee who doesn't have an education, but I'm honest. I'm proud of the fact that I've never taken a bribe or made an unfair call. Everybody wants money, but a good reputation is much harder to find.

Is it hard to balance two jobs? I drive my taxi to work at the boxing stadium. Everybody is surprised!

Name Nathamon Jaidet
Age 53
Occupation Cook at Poj Spa Kar
Residence Banglamphu

If you can't get fresh fruit and veg from Or Tor Kor market (above; p171), you're not trying. Below: When in doubt, one of Bangkok's delicious curries (bottom; p149) always hits the right spot.

How long have you worked at Poj Spa Kar? Just over 10 years. My husband's grandmother, a former royal palace chef, started the restaurant 80 years ago.

Have you always been interested in cooking? Yes, since I was young. I've been cooking all my life, but when I got the job here, my husband's family had to teach me how to make this kind of food.

What kind of food do you serve at your restaurant? Old-fashioned Thai food. We still use the same recipes from 80 years ago and the flavours are strong, just like in the past.

Can your foreign customers eat 'real' Thai food? Sure, they order *tôm yam kûng*, green curry, fried rice. One regular customer always orders a very spicy *yam wún sên*!

Where do you like to eat? I like *phàt thai*, but I don't have much time to eat outside because I'm in the kitchen all day.

What do you think about the popularity of Western-style fast food nowadays? It's good because it's convenient, but people should still eat Thai food!

What dish would you recommend to visitors? 'Look rock soup', a broth with pork and egg. It takes a lot of work to make but is very good.

Name Niphon Maunthas
Age 60
Occupation Owner of traditional silk business
Residence Baan Krua

Shop for genuine Thai silk, hand-woven in Baan Krua (above left; p100). Thai silk for sale in Pratunam (above right; p101). Explore the intriguing teak mansion of Jim Thompson's House (bottom; p97).

How long have you lived in Baan Krua? I was born in this village and still live here.

How has the village changed over the years? Life here is mostly the same as it was when I was a boy. Most of the houses are the same, though my parents did give one building to Jim Thompson when he built his house. Some people have moved out and people from Isaan have moved in, but about 60% are still original Muslim families.

What about the weaving? The women are older, but this room and the looms are like they were when I was a boy and Mr Jim [Thompson] came to visit us every morning. But not many people weave in Baan Krua now; we are the only original weaving family still weaving.

But the area around Baan Krua must have changed? Oh God! So many high buildings! I went away for a year when I was 26, and when I came back there were many new condos. That has continued, and then there are the shopping centres...

Do you think your children will work with silk? Both my children have studied overseas. My daughter is back now and she is making a website for us. My son wants to live in London for a while. Maybe he'll be back after two or three years... maybe.

Name Patti Chuaysri
Age I never tell anyone my age, and I'm not going to start with you
Occupation Artist/bar owner
Residence Pratunam

Grab a drink and browse the artwork at Café Trio (above; p175). Dinner and then dancing at Bed Supperclub (middle; p183). Soi Dogs jamming at Living Room (bottom; p181).

How long have you lived in Bangkok and where did you grow up? My family is from Chumphon in the south. I've lived here for nearly 15 years, and five years ago I started my Café Trio.

What's good about running a Bangkok bar? I meet lots of different people from all over the world and they get to see my art. The art is very important because while we're a jazz bar first and gallery second, I make more from the art than the drinks.

What's bad? Some men think they can get sex in any Bangkok bar, but when they try that here I kick them out. Sometimes people try to tell me how to run my bar – if they're rude, I kick them out, too.

What's the best thing about this neighbourhood? This street (Soi Lang Suan) is the best street in Bangkok. It used to be a royal area and a lot of the land is still owned by the royal family. It's convenient to everything and there are no girlie bars.

Where do you go out? If I want dancing I go to Tapas (p184) or Bed Supperclub (p183), and for jazz I go to Living Room (p181).

Name Gunn Aramwit
Age 27
Occupation Marketing officer
Residence Lad Phrao

Waiting for the Skytrain (above; p254). Live music at the Saxophone Pub (middle; p181). Bangkok's notorious traffic congestion (bottom; p41).

Where are you originally from and why are you here? I grew up in Songkhla Province, near the Malaysian border, and moved here four years ago to study at university.

What do you like about Bangkok? Actually, at first I didn't like Bangkok at all – it's complex and very expensive. But professionally this is the place to be and many young people come to Bangkok. There are a lot of job opportunities that just don't exist elsewhere and the music scene, for example, is just different from the rest of Thailand…in a good way.

What don't you like? The traffic. I usually take the *khlong* boat to work so that's pretty easy, and the Skytrain and Metro are great, if they go where you want. But I do everything I can to avoid buses – they are so slow. Fortunately I have a motorbike, which is good for cutting through traffic but is dangerous because trucks and buses just act like you're invisible.

What's it like being a lesbian here? This is absolutely the best place in Thailand if your lesbian, gay, *kathoey* – anything. I never get hassled here, ever. No-one cares.

Where do you like to go out? I like the bars in Banglamphu, particularly Hippie de Bar (p176) and the Fabriq.

Name Rasafe Samphan
Age 28
Occupation Whistle-blower on the Chao Phraya Express Boat
Residence Greater Bangkok (Nonthaburi)

The gleaming and glistening Wat Phra Kaew (above left; p55). All aboard the Chao Phraya Express (above right; p253). Keeping a watchful eye on the Chao Phraya Express (bottom).

Where are you from originally? Satun, in southern Thailand.

How long have you been in Bangkok? 15 years.

Why did you come to Bangkok? There's more work here, and more opportunity for education.

How long have you worked on the Chao Phraya Express boats? Only six months, but I've been working on boats for 10 years.

What is your favourite section of the Chao Phraya River? I like the area from Sirirat Hospital to Saphan Taksin. There are lots of things to see, like famous temples and big hotels.

What's the best thing about your job? I get to use English and meet people.

What's the worst thing about working with tourists? Many people don't understand the rules on the boats. For instance, people are not allowed to stand in the yellow area at the back of the boat. If anything happens to a passenger it's my responsibility.

Has anybody ever fallen into the river? Yes, twice foreign kids have fallen in the water at Banglamphu Pier. I threw the lifebuoy then dove in after them. I was able to save both of them!

Name Steven Pettifor
Age 40
Occupation Critic/curator/artist
Residence Th Sukhumvit

Check out the student exhibitions at Silpakorn University Art Gallery (above; p192). An aerial perspective of the Mae Nam Chao Phraya (middle; p18). Pull up a stool with the other faràngs at Cheap Charlie's (bottom; p175).

How long have you been in Bangkok? 15 years.

How has Bangkok changed over the years? In the past 'anything went', but in recent years the city has become a lot more comfortable in terms of traffic, infrastructure and the variety of things to see and do.

What is the best thing about your neighbourhood? It's still a very Thai area, but there's an international mix, which means there are great restaurants, bars and galleries.

What is the worst thing about Bangkok? The lack of green space.

Any Bangkok guilty pleasures? None that I can think of.

How would you describe Bangkok's current art scene? With the current international interest in Asian art, the art scene in Bangkok is finally receiving the attention it deserves. The greater number of galleries offering a diversity of art is also helping to encourage the growth of Thai art domestically and abroad.

Your favourite galleries in Bangkok? I like the Bangkok University Gallery and the Chulalongkorn Art Centre. They aren't commercial and tend to be more experimental in the type of work they show.

SIAM SQUARE, PRATUNAM, PLOENCHIT & RATCHATHEWI

Eating p160; Shopping p132; Sleeping p209

It's not often that you'll see 'Bangkok' and 'organisation' used in the same sentence. But this central shopping district is surprisingly well connected, and it can be dangerously convenient for unleashing cash. At first glance this neighbourhood is all about shopping, a shrine to modern consumerism where mega-malls cater to every whim and exclusive brands outbid each other for the prime, ground-floor storefronts in the most exclusive malls (currently that's Siam Paragon, p132).

This is modern Bangkok, where flimsy fashion is no longer a saffron monks' robe but a flouncy skirt and clicky heels. Packs of teenagers shuffle across the concrete pathways, breaking all the social mores their ancestors ever created. Female students wear miniskirts that could easily be mistaken for wide belts, cutesy couples stroll hand in hand, hipsters (dèk naew) assume gangster styles from ghettos they've only heard rapped about. Give Bangkok another 10 years of disposable income and the city – which is rightly proud of its creative side – will rival Tokyo and New York for pop power.

The centre of the action is Siam Skytrain station, the interchange for both Skytrain lines, which acts as the heart of the district. Through its network of concrete walkway veins it pumps thousands of passengers into nearby Siam Sq (p135), an ageing ground-level mall peopled by baht-flexing students – in black and white uniforms – who trawl through the closet-sized boutiques that dictate what's hot and what's not. Exit to the north and you'll arrive in the air-conditioned atmosphere of Siam Paragon (p135), with its super-expensive boutiques, European sports cars and world-class oceanarium (p101) or the more affordable (and more funky) Siam Discovery Center (p135). Further along Bangkok's miracle mile of shopping centres on Th Phra Ram I (aka Rama I) are Mahboonkrong (MBK, p134) to the west and the vast Central World Plaza (p133), plus others, to the east. Beware of consumer euphoria.

All the action here, coupled with the massive Skytrain station that looms above everything, means the area is constantly buffeted by a cacophonous din and suffocating exhaust fumes, which also make this area alone a significant contributor to Bangkok's image as an unpleasant and difficult place to visit.

Mercifully, respite is near at hand. If you spend enough time you'll find cinemas (p190) abound. For something more cerebral head to Bangkok Art & Culture Centre (p191), which should be open by the time you read this. And there's a chance to step out of the air-conditioned, international city entirely and enter old Bangkok at the famous Jim Thompson's House (below) or, across Khlong Saen Saeb in Pratunam district, the much less touristed and thoroughly original Muslim village of Baan Krua (p100). Pratunam is also home to Thailand's tallest skyscraper, the Baiyoke Tower II (Map pp52–3).

South of Th Phra Ram I and west of Th Phayathai the Pathumwan district is filled with the National Stadium (Map pp98–9) and surrounding sports facilities, and the huge campus of Chulalongkorn University, one of Thailand's most prestigious universities.

Heading east at the intersection of Th Phra Ram I and Th Ratchadamri the area known as Ratchaprasong supports a clutch of luxury hotels, more malls and the Erawan Shrine (p102). The area extending east along Th Ploenchit includes the tree-lined Soi Lang Suan, with its expensive condos and serviced apartments, and Th Withayu (Wireless Rd), which is home to embassies and expatriates.

JIM THOMPSON'S HOUSE Map pp98–9
บ้านจิมทอมป์สัน

☎ 0 2216 7368; www.jimthompsonhouse.org; 6 Soi Kasem San 2, Th Phra Ram I; adult/concession 100/50B; ⊙ 9am-5pm; ⊛ khlong boat Hua Chang Pier; ⊠ National Stadium

In 1959, 12 years after he discovered the fine silks being woven across the khlong in Baan Krua and single-handedly turned Thai silk into a hugely successful export business, American Jim Thompson bought this piece of land on Khlong Saen Saeb and built himself a house. It wasn't, however, any old house. Thompson's love of all things Thai saw him buy six traditional wooden homes and reconstruct them in the jungle-like garden here. Some of the homes were brought from the old royal capital of Ayuthaya; others were pulled down and floated across the khlong from

SIAM SQUARE, PRATUNAM & PLOENCHIT

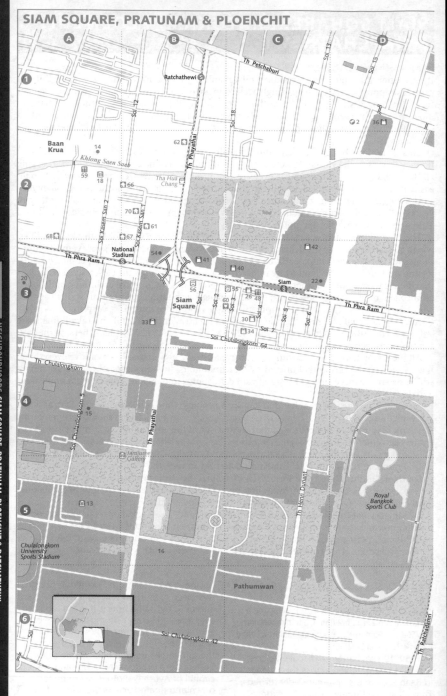

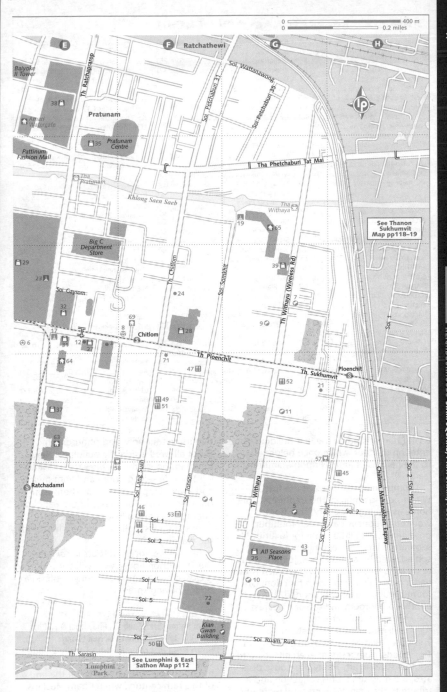

400 m
0.2 miles

E

Baiyoke
II Tower

38

Amari
Watergate

Pratunam

35
Pratunam
Centre

Pattinum
Fashion Mall

F Ratchathewi

Th Ratchaprarop

Soi Petchaburi 31

Soi Wattanawong

Soi Petchaburi 35

G

H

lp

Tha Phetchaburi Tat Mai

Tha
Pratunam

Khlong Saen Saeb

29

23

Big C
Department
Store

Soi Gaysorn

32

Th Chitlom

Tha
Withaya

19

65

Soi Somkhit

39

Th Withayu (Wireless Rd)

7

See Thanon
Sukhumvit
Map pp118–19

NEIGHBOURHOODS SIAM SQUARE, PRATUNAM, PLOENCHIT & RATCHATHEWI

24

69

8

17
34 12
27

6

64

Chitlom

9

28

3

Th Ploenchit

71

47

52

Th Sukhumvit

21

Ploenchit

11

37

63

58

Ratchadamri

Soi Lang Suan

49
51

Soi Tonson

57

45

46

44

53
Soi 1

Th Withayu

Soi Ruam Rudi

Soi 2

Chalerm Mahanakhon Expwy

Soi 2 (Soi Phasak)

4

5

Soi 2

Soi 2

Soi 3

All Seasons
Place

43

25

Soi 4

10

Soi 5

72

Soi 6

Kian
Gwan
Building

Soi 7

50

Th Sarasin

Soi Ruam Rudi

See Lumphini & East
Sathon Map p112

Lumphini
Park

SIAM SQUARE, PRATUNAM & PLOENCHIT

INFORMATION
AAA Thai Language Center....(see 24)
EU Embassy.................................1 FG
Indonesian Embassy....................2 D1
Maneeya Centre..........................3 E3
Netherlands Embassy...................4 F5
New Zealand Embassy.................5 G5
Police Station...............................6 E3
Siam Family Dental Clinic........(see 48)
South African Embassy..........(see 24)
Swiss Embassy.............................7 G3
Thai Knowledge Park.............(see 29)
TOT Office...................................8 F3
UK & Northern Ireland Embassy..9 G3
US Embassy................................10 G6
Vietnamese Embassy.................11 G4

SIGHTS   (pp89–115)
Absolute Yoga..........................12 E3
Art Centre..................................13 A5
Baan Krua..................................14 A2
Chulalongkorn Thai Pavilion....15 A4
Chulalongkorn University..........16 B5
Erawan Shrine............................17 E3
Jim Thompson Art Center.......(see 18)
Jim Thompson's House..............18 A2
Lingam Shrine............................19 G2
National Stadium........................20 A3
Pilates Studio.............................21 G4
Rachaprasong Intersection
   Shrines...............................(see 17)
Siam Ocean World.....................22 C3
Trimurthi Shrine.........................23 E3
Yoga Elements Studio................24 F3

SHOPPING   (pp127–41)
Asia Books...............................(see 41)
Asia Books...............................(see 42)
Asia Books...............................(see 29)
Asia Books...............................(see 37)
B2S...(see 28)

B2S...(see 29)
B2S...25 G5
Bookazine................................(see 25)
Bookazine................................(see 32)
Bookazine..................................26 C3
Bookazine (Bargain
   Outlet)...................................27 E3
Central Chidlom.........................28 F3
Central World Plaza...................29 E3
DJ Siam.....................................30 C3
Erawan Bangkok.......................31 E3
Gaysorn Plaza...........................32 E3
Kinokuniya..............................(see 42)
Mahboonkrong (MBK)..............33 B3
Marco Tailors.............................34 C3
Narayana Phand.........................35 E2
Pantip Plaza..............................36 D1
Peninsula Plaza..........................37 E4
Pratunam Market........................38 E1
Promenade Arcade....................39 G3
Siam Center...............................40 C3
Siam Discovery Center...............41 B3
Siam Paragon............................42 C3
Uthai's Gems.............................43 G5

EATING   (pp143–72)
Air Plane....................................44 F5
Bali..45 H5
Calderazzo.................................46 F5
Crystal Jade La Mian Xiao Long
   Bao.....................................(see 31)
Fifth..(see 33)
Food Loft................................(see 28)
Four Seasons.............................(see 63)
Gianni Ristorante.......................47 F4
Kuaytiaw Reua Tha Siam...........48 C3
MBK Food Court.......................(see 33)
No 43..49 F4
Paesano.....................................50 F6
Pan Pan.....................................51 F4
Sanguan Sri...............................52 G4

ENTERTAINMENT   (pp188–93)
& THE ARTS
100 Tonson Gallery....................53 F5
Bangkok Art & Culture Centre...54 B3
Calypso Cabaret.....................(see 62)
EGV...(see 41)
Foreign Correspondents' Club of
   Thailand (FCCT)..................(see 3)
Jim Thompson Art Center.......(see 18)
Lido Multiplex............................55 C3
Major Cineplex........................(see 29)
Scala Multiplex..........................56 B3
SF Cinema City........................(see 33)
Whitespace..............................(see 55)

DRINKING
& NIGHTLIFE   (pp173–85)
Bacchus Wine Bar......................57 G4
Café Trio....................................58 E5
Garimmin & Sobereen...............59 A2
To Sit...60 C3

SLEEPING   (pp201–21)
A-One Inn..................................61 B2
Asia Hotel..................................62 B2
Four Seasons Hotel....................63 E4
Grand Hyatt Erawan..................64 E3
Nai Lert Park Hotel....................65 G2
Pathumwan House......................66 B2
Reno Hotel.................................67 B2
Siam@Siam................................68 A2
VIP Guest House/Golden
   House....................................69 F3
Wendy House.............................70 B2

TRANSPORT   (pp250–5)
Avis..(see 64)
Cathay Pacific Airways...............71 F4
China Airlines..........................(see 37)
Hertz.......................................(see 24)
Malaysia Airlines.....................(see 71)
United Airlines...........................72 F6

Baan Krua – including the first building you enter on the tour, which once belonged to the parents of Khun Niphon Manuthas (see p92).

Thompson became one of the first Westerners to embrace the traditional Thai home as a thing of beauty. Thai homes would traditionally have been multipurpose affairs, with little room for luxuries like separate living and sleeping rooms. Thompson adapted his six buildings, joining some, to create a larger home in which each room had a more familiar Western function. One room became an air-conditioned study, another a bedroom and the one nearest the *khlong* his dining room.

As well as having good taste in silk, Thompson was an eagle-eyed collector of Thai goods, from residential architecture to Southeast Asian art. Today the house operates as a museum for his collection and a tribute to the man. Viewing is by regularly departing tour only, and photography is not allowed inside the buildings. New buildings house the Jim Thompson Art Center (p192), a café selling drinks and light meals and a vast shop flogging Jim Thompson-branded goods. For a taste of the Bangkok Thompson grew to love (and cheaper drinks and silks), follow your visit here with the walking tour, p105.

Beware well-dressed touts in *soi* near the Thompson house who will tell you it is closed and then try to haul you off on a dodgy buying spree.

BAAN KRUA Map pp98–9
Btwn Khlong Saen Saeb, Th Phayathai & Th Phra Ram VI; 🚤 khlong boat Tha Hua Chang
Baan Krua (literally 'Muslim Family Village') is one of Bangkok's oldest communities. It dates to the turbulent years at the end of the 18th century, when Cham Muslims from Cambodia and Vietnam fought on

top picks

SIAM SQUARE, PRATUNAM & PLOENCHIT

- Erawan Shrine (p102) A splash of religion in the midst of all the money
- Jim Thompson's House (p97) A teak mansion with a jungle-like garden and informative tours
- Baan Krua (opposite) The Muslim village where Jim Thompson first encountered silk
- Khlong Saen Saeb Canal Boats p253 Commute with the locals the old-fashioned way, along this atmospheric (in more ways than one) *khlong*
- Mahboonkrong (MBK; p134) Indulge in air-con, junk food, a million mobile phones, clothes and plastic stuff
- Wang Suan Phakkat (p104) Pretend you're a minor Thai royal in the quiet museum grounds
- Sanguan Sri (p160) Ignore the surrounds and dive in for the red curry with duck breast
- Siam Sq (p132) Immerse yourself in the epicentre of Thai teen culture in the cafés and boutiques of Siam Sq

the side of the new Thai king and were rewarded with this plot of land east of the new capital. The immigrants brought their silk-weaving traditions with them, and the community grew with the arrival of other Muslims and when the residents built the *khlong* to better connect them to the river.

The 1950s and '60s were boom years for Baan Krua, after Jim Thompson (see p102) hired the weavers and exported their silks across the globe. Production was moved elsewhere following Thompson's disappearance, and many Muslims have moved out of the area; today about 30% of the population is Muslim, the rest primarily immigrants from northeast Thailand. However, it retains its Muslim character, and one of the original families is still weaving silk on old teak looms; see p92 for an interview with Niphon Manuthas. The village consists of old, tightly packed homes threaded by tiny paths barely wide enough for two people to pass. It has been described as a slum, but the house-proud residents are keen to point out that they might not live in high-rise condos, but that doesn't make their old community a slum.

The best way to visit Baan Krua is to wander; see the DIY Walking Tour, p105, to get started.

SIAM OCEAN WORLD Map pp98–9

☎ 2687 2000; www.siamoceanworld.com; basement, Siam Paragon, Th Rama 1; adult/child 750/600B; ⏰ 9am-10pm (last entry 9pm); 🚇 Siam Southeast Asia's largest oceanarium is also one of its most impressive. Hundreds species of fish, crustaceans and even penguins populate this vast underground facility. The oceanarium is divided into several zones accommodating specific species. The main tank is the highlight, with an acrylic tunnel allowing you to walk beneath sharks, rays and all manner of fish. Diving with sharks is also an option if you have your licence (for a fee), though you'll have almost as much fun timing your trip to coincide with the shark and penguin feedings; the former are usually at 1pm and 4pm, the latter at 12.30pm and 4.30pm – check the website for details.

LINGAM SHRINE (SAAN JAO MAE THAP THIM) Map pp98–9
ศาลเจ้าแม่ทับทิม
Nai Lert Park Hotel, Th Withayu; 🚤 khlong boat to Tha Withayu; 🚇 Ploenchit
Every village-neighbourhood has a local shrine, either a sacred banyan tree tied up with coloured scarves or a spirit house. But it isn't everyday you see a phallus garden like this lingam shrine, tucked back behind the staff quarters of the Nai Lert Park Hotel. Clusters of carved stone and wooden shafts surround a spirit house and shrine built by millionaire businessman Nai Loet to honour Jao Mae Thap Thim, a female deity thought

TRANSPORT: SIAM SQUARE, PRATUNAM & PLOENCHIT

Bus Air-con 141, 183, 204, 501, 508 and 547, ordinary 15, 16, 25, 47 and 73, among other grid-locked rattlers

Khlong boat Tha Hua Chang for Siam Sq shopping centres, Jim Thompson's House and Baan Krua, Tha Pratunam for Central World and Pantip Plaza, Tha Withayu for Lingham Shrine and Central World

Skytrain Siam, National Stadium, Chitlom and Ploenchit

Even by Bangkok standards, traffic around here is nightmarish. If you're coming from the Silom, Sathon or Sukhumvit areas, or from north towards Chatuchak Market, take the Skytrain. Coming from Banglamphu and the Th Khao San area, take the *khlong* boat.

to reside in the old banyan tree on the site. Someone who made an offering shortly after the shrine was built had a baby, and the shrine has received a steady stream of worshippers – mostly young women seeking fertility – ever since.

If facing the entrance of the hotel, follow the small concrete pathway to the right, which winds down into the building beside the car park. The shrine is at the end of the building next to the *khlong*.

RATCHAPRASONG INTERSECTION SHRINES Map pp98–9

Cnr Th Ratchadamri & Th Ploenchit; 🚇 Chitlom

A crowd in this part of town usually means a bargain market is nearby. But in this case the continuous activity revolves around the Hindu shrines credited with making this commercial corridor a success. It's a fascinating place to come and just watch the way modern Thais have pragmatically adapted their beliefs – and their hopes – to the perceived reality that success breeds success, especially with the deities on your side.

The primary focus is the Erawan Shrine (Map pp98–9; San Phra Phrom; 🕑 6am-10.30pm), on the corner beside the Grand Hyatt Erawan Hotel. Brahma, the four-headed Hindu god of creation, holds court here. Brahma would normally command great respect in Thai Buddhism but not nearly enough to warrant this sort of idolatry. The human traffic jam can be directly attributed to the perceived powers of the shrine since it was established in 1954. Originally, a simple Thai spirit house occupied this spot during the construction of the first Erawan Hotel (named after Indra's three-headed elephant mount). After several serious mishaps delayed the hotel's construction, the developers erected this Brahman shrine to ward off future injuries. The Erawan Hotel was finished, business boomed and eventually the shrine took on a cult of its own, being seen as a harbinger of material success.

There is a constant cycle of worshippers seeking divine assistance for good luck, health, wealth and love. Most people offer marigold garlands or raise a cluster of joss sticks to foreheads in prayer. The flowers are left on the shrine for a few minutes, before attendants gather them up to be resold. Not everyone goes for that, however, and one ex-student told us how, in her university days, a Big Mac would be offered, left for a few minutes and then retrieved; why waste it?

When wishes are granted, the worshippers show their gratitude by commissioning shrine musicians and dancers for a performance. The tinkling tempo, throaty bass and colourful dancers are in marked contrast to the ordinary street corner on which the shrine stands, surrounded by idling cars and self-absorbed shoppers – though most of them will still offer a passing *wai* (bringing the hands together in a prayer-like manner at chest level).

JIM THOMPSON: INTERNATIONAL MAN OF MYSTERY...AND SILK

Born in Delaware in 1906, Jim Thompson was a New York architect who served in the Office of Strategic Services (a forerunner of the CIA) in Thailand during WWII. After the war he found New York too tame compared to his beloved Bangkok. When in 1947 he spotted some silk in a market and was told it was woven in Baan Krua (see walking tour, p105), he found the only place in Bangkok where silk was still woven by hand.

Thompson thought he could sell the fine silk from Baan Krua to a postwar world with a ravenous appetite for luxury goods. He attracted the interest of fashion houses in New York, Milan, London and Paris, and gradually built a worldwide clientele for a craft that had, just a few years before, been in danger of dying out. They were heady days for the poor Muslim weavers of Baan Krua. Thompson was noted for both his idealism and generosity, and when he set up the Thai Silk Company in 1948 he insisted that his contract weavers became shareholders.

By 1967 Thai Silk had annual sales of almost US$1.5 million. In March that year, when Thompson went missing while out for an afternoon walk in the Cameron Highlands of western Malaysia, his success as a businessman and background as a spy made it an international mystery. Thompson has never been heard from since, but the conspiracy theories – fuelled even further by the murder of his sister in the USA during the same year – have never stopped. Was it communist spies? Business rivals? A man-eating tiger? The most recent theory is that the silk magnate was accidentally run over by a Malaysian truck driver who hid his remains.

The Legendary American: The Remarkable Career & Strange Disappearance of Jim Thompson, written by his long-time friend William Warren, is an excellent account of Thompson's life.

The businesses posted on the other corners of the intersection have erected their own Hindu shrines in order to counter and/or copy the power of the Erawan Shrine. This godly one-upmanship sees Lakshmi, the wife of Vishnu, standing atop Gaysorn Plaza while Vishnu himself is mounted upon Garuda at the Intercontinental Hotel. Another Garuda can be found in the Police Hospital, while Indra is appropriately placed outside the Amarin Plaza, beside the Erawan.

If your head is spinning, you could settle for crossing diagonally from the Erawan Shrine to the square outside Central World for a look at elephant-headed Ganesha – whose presence is no great surprise given his parents are Lakshmi and Vishnu. On the same corner, most likely as a cosmic mediator between all these rival deities, is the Trimurthi Shrine (San Trimurthi). This shrine depicts the three supreme Hindu gods (Shiva, Vishnu and Brahma) and symbolises creation, destruction and preservation. Note that 'love' is not mentioned here, but peace and love aren't that far removed and that's enough to have Thai teenagers descending on the shrine on Thursdays to seek romantic success.

CHULALONGKORN UNIVERSITY
Map pp98–9

จุฬาลงกรณ์มหาวิทยาลัย

☎ 0 2215 0871; www.chula.ac.th; 254 Th Phayathai; 🚌 air-con 502, ordinary 21; 🚇 Siam; Ⓜ Samyan

Thailand's oldest and most prestigious university is nestled in a leafy enclave south of busy Th Phra Ram I. The centrepiece of the campus is the promenade ground on the east side of Th Phayathai where a seated statue of Rama V (King Chulalongkorn) is surrounded by purple bougainvillea and offerings of pink carnations. The showcase buildings display the architectural fusion the monarch favoured, a mix of Italian revival and Thai traditional. The campus has a parklike quality, with noble tropical trees considerately labelled for plant geeks. Of the many species that shade the campus, the rain trees with their delicate leaves are considered symbolic of the university, even commemorated in a school song, and the deciduous cycle matches the beginning and ending of each school year.

The university has two art galleries, Jamjuree and the Art Centre (Map pp98–9; ☎

top picks

IT'S FREE

The value of the Thai baht in international currencies might turn misers into spendthrifts, but there are still plenty of cheap and even free thrills in Bangkok.

- Hotel river boats (p113) Take a free hotel ferry from Central Pier or River City to the plush hotel of your choice; whether you have a drink when you get there is up to you
- Erawan Shrine (opposite) See traditional Thai dancing, paid for by a Bangkokian making merit
- Lumphini Park (p106) Sweat in synchrony at the free evening aerobics classes
- Victory Monument Skytrain station (Map pp52–3) See break dancers practising their moves, young couples flirting, fashion trendies exhibiting themselves, and illegal markets on the elevated walkway leading to this station

0 2218 2911; www.car.chula.ac.th/art; Centre of Academic Resources Bldg, 7th fl, Chulalongkorn University, Th Phayathai; ⏰ 9am-7pm Mon-Fri, 9am-4pm Sat; 🚇 Siam, Ⓜ Samyan). The latter shows Chula professors as well as major names in the Thai and international modern art scene; permanent exhibits include Thai art retrospectives.

On the west side of Th Phayathai is the teak Thai Pavilion, in which the Center of Arts and Culture performs cultural displays on the first Friday of each month.

RATCHATHEWI

Spreading north of Pratunam is Ratchathewi, an area that attracts few tourists but does have some sights. The area around Victory Monument is also an interesting area to find bars and restaurants that are very much the staples of the Thai middle class.

VICTORY MONUMENT Map pp52–3
อนุสาวรีย์ชัยสมรภูมิ

Th Ratchawithi & Phayathai; 🚇 Victory Monument; 🚌 ordinary 12, 62

A busy traffic circle revolves around this obelisk monument that was built in 1941 to commemorate a 1939 Thai victory against the French in Laos. But the monument is only a landmark for observing the social universe of the local university students. An elevated walkway circumnavigates the roundabout, funnelling the pedestrian traffic in and out of the Skytrain station as well as providing a gathering spot for break dancers, flirters and lots of fashion experiments. The neighbourhood around Victory Monument is less cosmopolitan and more reminiscent of provincial towns elsewhere in Thailand, but that doesn't mean it's hicksville. Nearby bars and cafés cater to the university crowd – try the rooftop Skytrain Bar on the corner of Th Rang Nam. If you wander down Th Rang Nam you'll find local *lûuk thûng* and *phleng phêua chii-wit* (songs for life) places with live music most evenings.

BAIYOKE II TOWER Map pp52–3

☎ 2656 3000; 22 Th Ratchaprarop; admission 200B; ⏰ 10am-10pm; 🚤 khlong boat Tha Pratunam

Thailand's tallest tower, if not its most architecturally attractive, the Baiyoke II tower soars to 88 storeys, the upper of which are often clad with some truly huge advertising. The main, and indeed the only, attraction here is the 77th floor observation deck. The views are as impressive as you'd expect (unless its too smoggy) but only just compensate for the tacky décor and uninspiring restaurant. If you have a choice, the rooftop bars are better.

WANG SUAN PHAKKAT Map pp52–3

วังสวนผักกาด

☎ 0 2245 4934; Th Si Ayuthaya, btwn Th Phayathai & Th Ratchaprarop; admission 100B; ⏰ 9am-4pm; 🚌 ordinary 72; 🚉 Phayathai

Everyone loves Jim Thompson's house, but few have even heard of Wang Suan Phakkat (Lettuce Farm Palace), another noteworthy traditional Thai house museum. Once the residence of Princess Chumbon of Nakhon Sawan, the museum is a collection of five traditional wooden Thai houses linked by elevated walkways containing varied displays of art, antiques and furnishings. The landscaped grounds are a peaceful oasis complete with ducks, swans and a semi-enclosed, Japanese-style garden.

The diminutive Lacquer Pavilion at the back of the complex dates from the Ayuthaya period (the building originally sat in a monastery compound on the banks of Mae Nam Chao Phraya, just south of Ayuthaya) and features gold-leaf *Jataka* and Ramayana murals as well as scenes from daily Ayuthaya life. Larger residential structures at the front of the complex contain

displays of Khmer, Hindu and Buddhist art, Ban Chiang ceramics and a collection of historic Buddhas, including a beautiful late-U Thong–style image. In the noise and confusion of Bangkok, the gardens offer a tranquil retreat.

PHAYATHAI PALACE Map pp52–3

King Mongkut Hospital, ☎ 0 2354 7732; 315 Th Ratchawithi; admission free; ⏰ 9am-4pm Sat; 🚉 Victory Monument

West of the Victory Monument roundabout, Phayathai Palace was built by King Chulalongkorn (Rama V) in 1909 as a cottage for retreats into what was then the country. The surviving throne hall, encased in French glass doors and a fanciful tiered roof, is now part of a hospital complex and is open to the public. Note the limited hours; tours are conducted at 9.30am and 1.30pm on Saturdays. The grounds are open at other times. There isn't much in the way of tourist displays, but it's worth a visit to survey the architecture of the buildings and escape the sightseeing masses.

BANGKOK DOLL FACTORY & MUSEUM Map pp52–3

พิพิธภัณฑ์ตุ๊กตาบางกอกดอล

☎ 0 2245 3008; www.bangkokdolls.com; 85 Soi Ratchataphan (Soi Mo Leng), Th Ratchaprarop; admission free; ⏰ 8.30am-5pm Mon-Sat; 🚌 ordinary 62 & 77

Khunying Tongkorn Chandevimol became interested in dolls while living in Japan. Upon her return to Thailand, she began researching and making dolls, drawing from Thai mythology and historical periods. Today her personal collection of dolls from all over the world and important dolls from her own workshop are on display. You can also view the small factory where family members continue to craft the figures that are now replicated and sold throughout Thailand's tourist markets. A large selection of her dolls are also for sale.

It is difficult to find this well-hidden spot, but perseverance will reward any doll lover, especially the pint-sized connoisseurs. The museum is in Ratchathewi and is best approached via Th Si Ayuthaya heading east. Cross under the expressway past the intersection with Th Ratchaprarop and take the *soi* to the right of the post office. Follow this windy street until you start seeing signs.

DIY BAAN KRUA
Walking Tour

We could tell you to take lefts and rights down little alleys, but exploring this historic Muslim village is more fun if you just venture forth and find your own way. But we will get you into the village... Start this DIY tour when you finish your tour of Jim Thompson's House (p97); head left to the *khlong* and left again. You'll soon come to Garimmin & Sobereen, a make-shift, *khlong*-side place selling food and cold drinks, which is a great spot to sit and watch the *khlong* boats motor by while observing village life on the other side: men dressed in white dishdashas, exotic caged birds yapping and women selling food and everyday items from tiny stores that are a world away from the nearby mega-malls.

Refreshed, cross the footbridge and dive in. Wander around and try to keep a smile on your face. The local people are welcoming and enjoy a bit of banter, but don't enter anyone's house unless you're invited. You can spend as little or long as you like wandering

WALK FACTS

Start Jim Thompson's House
End Wherever you like
Distance not very far
Duration 15 minutes to one hour
Fuel Stops Corner stores in Baan Krua, or Garimmin & Sobereen across the footbridge.

through Baan Krua, but do try to see the silk weavers in action. You'll probably hear the clickety clack of the looms before you see them; if you can't find them ask for directions (hint: they are in an alley leading off the *khlong*-side path).

Of the two, Phamai Baan Krua (☎ 0 2215 7458) is the easiest in which to watch the weaving and (if he's around) owner Niphon Manuthas speaks English and German; see p92 for an interview with him. The high-quality handwoven silk that originally attracted Jim Thompson is still sold here, and prices are very reasonable compared with the chic store across the *khlong*.

RIVERSIDE, SILOM & LUMPHINI

Eating p160; Shopping p136; Sleeping p211

During Bangkok's shipping heyday, the city faced outward toward the river to welcome foreign trading ships and European envoys. All along the Mae Nam Chao Phraya are the remnants of this mercantile era: the ornate French and Portuguese embassies, crumbling Customs House and the elegant Oriental Hotel (p212). Little lanes wind through abandoned warehouses, gated headquarters of historic shipping companies, and the Muslim and Indian communities that replaced the European presence.

Th Charoen Krung, which runs parallel to the river and links Th Silom with Chinatown, was Bangkok's first paved road – built at the behest of European residents who wanted a place for their horses and buggies. How times have changed. The water-based society was so taken by this innovation that, one by one, nearly all the canal routes were concreted over to become roads. Today the southern end of Th Charoen Krung is lined with silk and jewellery businesses that sell to wealthy tourists staying at the luxury riverside hotels. But not far away, back behind the commercial façade, are the residential areas where curry shops are more likely to serve Indian-style roti than rice, and silken headdresses distinguish Muslim Thais from their Buddhist sisters.

As industries changed the financial district migrated inland along Th Silom, which runs from Th Charoen Krung northeast to Lumphini Park and Th Phra Ram IV and was once the outskirts of the riverside city. Windmills (silom) once dotted the landscape, conveying water to the area's rice fields.

Today Silom experiences a daily tide of people. Workers flood into the office towers in the morning, are released into the streets for lunch and return home aboard public transport in the evening. Foreigners sweat in their imported suits, maintaining the corporate appearance of New York and London in styles that are ill suited for the tropics. Thai secretaries prefer polyester suits that are sold off the rack at small markets, alongside bulk toiletries and thick-heeled sandals. Workers returning to the office after lunch are usually loaded down with plastic bags of food for midafternoon snacks: in Thailand the snack table is the equivalent of the Western water cooler.

Parallel to Th Silom are Th Surawong to the north and Th Sathon to the south, which is divided into northbound Th Sathon Neua and southbound Th Sathon Tai, running either side of the remains of the khlong it has now replaced. None of these streets is especially well blessed with traditional 'sights', but wedged between Silom and Surawong, uncannily convenient to the heart of the business zone, is Bangkok's most infamous attraction, the Patpong strip of bars and clubs (p111).

Th Sathon is home to several embassies (p258), three of Bangkok's best hotels and endless speeding traffic. One of those hotels hosts the dreamy, decadent Moon Bar at Vertigo (p177), while State Tower on the corner of Th Silom and Th Charoen Krung is crowned with Sirocco (p177). Both host some of the most breathtaking, cocktail-enhanced sunset views on earth.

At the eastern end of this neighbourhood is delightfully, mercifully green Lumphini Park, the city's central green space where kids learn to ride bikes, grandmas stretch out stiff joints, office workers work out and (relatively) fresh air never tasted so good. Lumphini Park is bounded by Th Sarasin, Th Phra Ram IV, Th Withayu (Wireless Road) and Th Ratchadamri. East of the park is Suan Lum Night Bazaar (p137), a shopping mecca with an uncertain future, and Lumphini Stadium (p199). Just off the southeastern corner of the park is the area known as Soi Ngam Duphli, the backpacker predecessor of Th Khao San's guesthouse scene.

LUMPHINI PARK Map p112
สวนลุมพินี

☼ 5am-8pm; 🚌 air-con 505, ordinary 13; Ⓜ Lumphini & Silom; 🚈 Sala Daeng & Ratchadamri

Named after Buddha's birthplace in Nepal, this is Bangkok's largest and most popular park. An artificial lake in the centre is surrounded by broad, well-tended lawns, wooded areas, walking paths and, around sunset, the odd ambling turtle – it's the best outdoor escape from Bangkok without leaving town.

One of the best times to visit the park is in the early morning before 7am, when the air is fresh (well, relatively so for Bangkok) and legions of Chinese are practis-

top picks

RIVERSIDE, SILOM & LUMPHINI

- **Oriental Hotel (p212)** Relive the steamship era of globetrotting aristocrats with tea and crumpets at this legendary establishment
- **Lumphini Park (opposite)** Relax Bangkok-style among the exercisers and exercise-observers in this peaceful park
- **Patpong (p185)** Ping pong? Well, not exactly…
- **Queen Saovabha Memorial Institute (right)** Confront your fear of snakes at this humanitarian snake farm
- **Cy'an (p161)** Eat where Bangkok's best chefs choose to eat
- **Cocktail hour** Soak up the sunset views and knock back a cocktail or two at Bangkok's tower-top bar-restaurants, **Moon Bar at Vertigo (p177)** and **Sirocco (p177)**

ing t'ai chi, doing their best to mimic the aerobics instructor or doing the half-run half-walk version of jogging that, you have to agree, makes a lot of sense in this oppressive humidity. Meanwhile, vendors set up tables to dispense fresh snake's blood and bile, considered health tonics by many Thais and Chinese. A weight-lifting area in one section becomes a miniature 'muscle beach' on weekends. Facilities include a snack bar, an asphalt jogging track, a picnic area, toilets and a couple of tables where women serve Chinese tea. There are no shops inside the park, but cold drinks are available at the entrance.

During the kite-flying season (from mid-February to April), Lumphini becomes a favoured flight zone, with kites *(wâo)* for sale in the park.

OLD CUSTOMS HOUSE Map pp108–9
กรมศุลกากร

Soi 36, Th Charoen Krung; ⛴ **Tha Oriental**
The Old Customs House was once the gateway to Thailand, levying taxes on traders moving in and out of the kingdom. Designed by an Italian architect and built in the 1880s, the front door opened onto its source of income (the river) and the grand façade was ceremoniously decorated in columns and transom windows. Today it's a crumbling yet hauntingly beautiful home

to the fire brigade, with sagging shutters, peeling colonial yellow paint and laundry flapping on the unpainted balconies. Plans to resurrect this building as a luxurious Aman Resort seem to have stalled, so anyone with a large wad of spare cash and ambitions as a hotelier should contact the government. It's not open to the public, but it is OK to wander around…as long as you don't get in the way of the volleyball game.

BANGKOKIAN MUSEUM Map pp108–9

☎ 0 2233 7027; 273 Soi 43, Th Charoen Krung, Bangrak; admission free; ☀ 10am-4pm Wed-Sun; ⛴ Tha Si Phraya
This collection of three wooden houses illustrates an often-overlooked period of Bangkok's history, the 1950s and '60s. The main building was built in 1937 as a home for the Surawadee family and, as the signs inform us, was finished by Chinese carpenters on time and for less than the budgeted 2400B (which would barely buy a door handle today). This building and the large wooden one to the right, which was added as a boarding house to help cover costs, are filled with the detritus of family life and offer a fascinating window into the period. The third building, at the back of the block, was built in 1929 as a surgery for a British doctor, though he died soon after arriving in Thailand.

QUEEN SAOVABHA MEMORIAL INSTITUTE (SNAKE FARM) Map pp108–9
สถานเสาวภา

☎ 0 2252 0161; 1871 Th Phra Ram IV, Lumphini; adult/child 200/50B; ☀ 9.30am-3.30pm Mon-Fri, 9.30am-1pm Sat & Sun; 🚌 air-con 507, ordinary 4, 47 & 50; 🚉 Sala Daeng; Ⓜ Silom

TRANSPORT: RIVERSIDE, SILOM & LUMPHINI

Bus Air-con 502 and 505, ordinary 15, 22 and 62

Ferry Tha Si Phraya (N3), Tha Oriental (N1) and Tha Sathon (Central Pier)

Skytrain Sala Daeng, Chong Nonsi and Surasak

Metro Silom and Lumphini

Th Silom is busy at almost every hour, and the Skytrain is a better alternative for reaching destinations on this street. Traffic moves more regularly on Th Sathon, though U-turn possibilities are rare.

RIVERSIDE, SILOM & SURAWONG

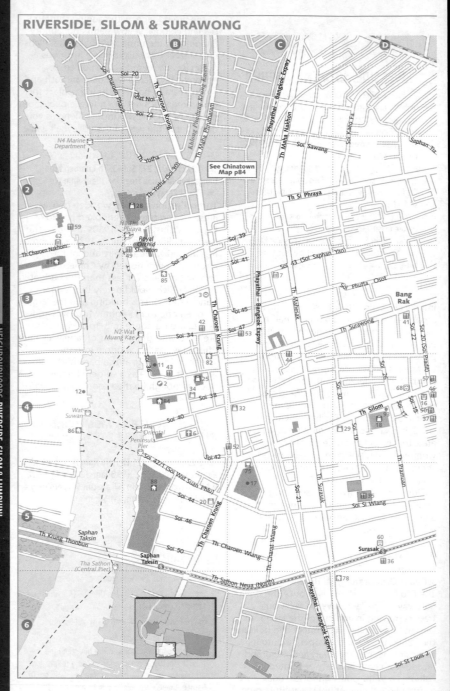

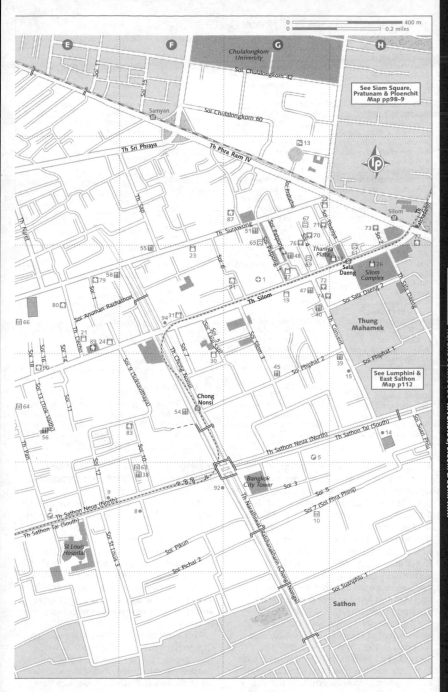

See Siam Square,
Pratunam & Ploenchit
Map pp98–9

See Lumphini &
East Sathon
Map p112

RIVERSIDE, SILOM & SURAWONG

INFORMATION			EATING 🍴	(pp143–72)	H Gallery	63	F5
Bangkok Christian Hospital	1	G3	Ban Chiang	35 D5	Kathmandu Photo Gallery	64	E4
French Embassy	2	B4	Blue Elephant	36 D5	Lucifer	65	G2
Main Post Office	3	B3	Blue Elephant Cooking School..(see 36)		Neilson Hays Library Rotunda		
Myanmar Embassy	4	E5	Chennai Kitchen	37 D4	Gallery	66	E3
Singapore Embassy	5	G4	Chocolate Bar	(see 86)	Noriega's	67	G2
			Circle of Friends	38 F5	Sala Rim Nam	(see 84)	
SIGHTS		(pp106–15)	D'Sens	(see 77)	Silom Village	68	D4
Assumption Cathedral	6	B4	Eat Me Restaurant	39 H4	Tang Gallery	(see 29)	
Bangkokian Museum	7	C3	Epicurean Kitchen Thai		Tapas Room	69	G3
Bank of Asia (Robot Building)	8	F5	Cooking School	40 G3	Thavibu Gallery	(see 29)	
Healthland Spa & Massage	9	E5	Foo Mui Kee	41 D3	Three Sixty	(see 81)	
Kukrit Pramoj House	10	G5	Harmonique	42 B3			
Old Customs House	11	B4	Home Cuisine Islamic		DRINKING		
Oriental Spa	12	A4	Restaurant	43 B4	& NIGHTLIFE 🍸	(pp173–85)	
Queen Saovabha Memorial			Indian Hut	44 C4	Balcony	70	G2
Institute (Snake Farm)	13	G2	Jay So	45 G4	Barbican Bar	71	G2
Red Bull X Park	14	H4	Khrua Aroy Aroy	46 D4	Coyote On Convent	72	G3
Ruen-Nuad Massage & Yoga	15	H4	La Boulange	47 G3	DJ Station	73	H2
Sri Mariamman Temple	16	D4	Le Bouchon	48 G3	Molly Malone's	74	G3
State Tower	17	C5	Le Normandie	(see 84)	Sirocco & Sky Bar	75	C5
			Loy Nava	49 B3	Telephone	76	G2
SHOPPING 🛍		(pp127–41)	Mashoor	50 D4			
Asia Books	(see 33)		Mizu's Kitchen	51 G2	SLEEPING 🛏	(pp201–21)	
B2S	(see 18)		Muslim Restaurant	52 C4	Dusit Thani	77	H2
Baan Silom	18	D4	Naaz	53 C3	Ibrik Resort	78	D6
Bookazine	19	G3	Oriental Hotel Thai Cooking		La Résidence Hotel	79	E3
Bookazine	(see 26)		School	(see 84)	Lub*D	80	E3
Chiang Heng	20	B5	Ran Nam Tao Hu Yong Her	54 F4	Millennium Hilton	81	A3
House of Chao	21	E3	Scoozi	55 F3	New Road Guesthouse	82	B4
Jim Thompson	22	G2	Shanghai 38	(see 89)	Niagara Hotel	83	F4
Jim Thompson Factory			Silom Thai Cooking School	56 E4	Oriental Hotel	84	B4
Outlet	23	F3	Soi Pradit Market	57 D4	P&R Residence	85	B3
Niks/Nava Import Export	24	E3	Somboon Seafood	58 E3	Peninsula Hotel	86	A4
OP (Oriental Plaza) Place	25	B4	Wan Fah	(see 49)	Rose Hotel	87	G2
Orchid Press	26	H3	Yok Yor Restaurant	59 A2	Shangri-La Hotel	88	B5
Patpong Night Market	27	G3			Sofitel Silom Bangkok	89	E3
River City	28	B2	ENTERTAINMENT 🎭	(pp188–93)	Triple Two Silom	90	E4
Silom Galleria	29	D4	& THE ARTS		Urban Age	91	G3
Soi Lalai Sap	30	F4	Ad Makers	60 D5			
Sunny Camera	31	F3	Bamboo Bar	(see 84)	TRANSPORT	(pp250–5)	
Sunny Camera	32	C4	Eat Me Restaurant	(see 39)	Air Canada	92	F5
Tamnan Mingmuang	33	H3	G O D (Guys On Display)	61 H3	Air France	93	D4
Thai Home Industries	34	B4	Gallery Ver	62 A2	Air New Zealand	94	F3
					KLM-Royal Dutch Airlines	(see 93)	

Venomous snakes such as the formidable cobra, banded krait and pit viper live a peaceful and – though they probably don't know it – altruistic existence at this institute affiliated with the Thai Red Cross. And watching the snakes being milked of their venom (daily at 11am) or, in the case of the python, draped around tourist necks (2.30pm Monday to Friday) – which feels surprisingly pleasant, smooth and cool – has become such a tourist draw that a new and very interesting serpentarium was opened in early 2008.

Of course, all the fun isn't just for the amusement of tourists. The institute was founded in 1923, when it was only the second of its kind in the world (the first was in Brazil), and has gone on to become one of the world's leading centres in the study of snakes. The venom collected during the milkings is used to make snake-bite anti-venins, which are distributed throughout the country.

It's best to arrive 30 minutes before the advertised show time to see a video presentation about the institute and its work (usually in Thai with English subtitles). Outside show times you can stroll the small garden complex where the snakes are kept in escapeproof cages. The snakes tend to be camera shy during nonperformance times, though you could get lucky and spot a camouflaged king cobra poised to strike.

This institution is named in honour of Queen Saovabha, wife of Rama V, who championed a wide variety of medical causes and education, including a school for midwives and other modern birthing practices.

PUSSY GALORE

Super Pussy! Pussy Collection! The neon signs leave little doubt about the dominant industry in Patpong, the world's most infamous strip of go-go bars and clubs running 'exotic' shows. There is enough skin on show in Patpong to make Hugh Hefner blush, and a trip to the upstairs clubs could mean you'll never look at a ping-pong ball or a dart the same way again.

For years opinion on Patpong has polarised between those who see it as an exploitative, immoral place that is the very definition of sleaze, and others for whom a trip to Bangkok is about little more than immersing themselves in planet Patpong (or Nana, or Soi Cowboy – p185). But Patpong has become such a caricature of itself that in recent times a third group has emerged: the curious tourist. Whatever your opinion, what you see in Patpong or any of Bangkok's other high-profile 'adult entertainment' areas depends as much on your outlook on life as on the quality of your vision.

Prostitution is actually illegal in Thailand but there are as many as 2 million sex workers, the vast majority of whom – women and men – cater to Thai men. Many come from poorer regional areas, such as Isaan in the northeast, while others might be students helping themselves through university. Sociologists suggest Thais often view sex through a less moralistic or romantic filter than Westerners. That doesn't mean Thai wives like their husbands using prostitutes, but it's only recently that the gradual empowerment of women through education and employment has led to a more vigorous questioning of this very widespread practice.

Patpong actually occupies two *soi* that run between Th Silom and Th Surawong in Bangkok's financial district. The two streets are privately owned by – and named for – the Thai-Chinese Patpongpanich family, who bought the land in the 1940s and initially built Patpong Soi 1 and its shophouses; Soi 2 was laid later. During the Vietnam War the first bars and clubs opened to cater to American soldiers on 'R&R'. The scene and its international reputation grew through the '70s and peaked in the '80s, when official Thai tourism campaigns made the sort of 'sights' available on Patpong a pillar of their marketing.

These days Patpong has mellowed considerably, if not matured. Thanks in part to the popular tourist night market that fills the *soi* after 5pm, it draws so many tourists that it has become a sort of sex theme park. There are still plenty of the stereotypical middle-aged men ogling pole dancers, sitting in dark corners of the so-called 'blow-job bars' and paying 'bar fines' to take girls to hotels that charge by the hour. But you'll also be among other tourists and families who come to see what all the fuss is about.

Most tourists go no further than stolen glances into the ground-floor go-go bars, where women in bikinis drape themselves around stainless-steel poles, between bouts of haggling in the night market. Others will be lured by men promising 'fucky show' to the dimly lit upstairs clubs. But it should be said that the so-called 'erotic' shows usually feature bored-looking women performing shows that feel not so much erotic as demeaning to everyone involved. Several of these clubs are also infamous for their scams, usually involving the nonperforming (ie clothed, if just barely) staff descending on wide-eyed tourists like vultures on fresh meat. Before you know it you've bought a dozen drinks and racked up a bill for thousands of baht, followed by a loud, aggressive argument flanked by menacing-looking bouncers and threats of 'no money, no pussy'.

Were we saying that Patpong had mellowed? Oh yes, there is a slightly softer side. Several bars have a little more, erm, class, and in restaurants such as the French bistro Le Bouchon (p162) in Patpong 2 and Mizu's Kitchen (p162), a divey place that has been running more than 50 years, you could forget where you are – almost.

SRI MARIAMMAN TEMPLE Map pp108–9
วัดพระศรีมหาอุมาเทวี(วัดแขก)

☎ 0 2238 4007; cnr Th Silom & Th Pan; admission free; ⏰ 6am-8pm; 🚢 Tha Oriental; 🚇 Chong Nonsi or Surasak

Arrestingly flamboyant, this Hindu temple is a wild collision of colours, shapes and deities. Built in the 1860s by Tamil immigrants, the principal temple features a 6m façade of intertwined, full-colour Hindu deities. The temple's main shrine contains three supremes: Jao Mae Maha Umathewi (Uma Devi; also known as Shakti, Shiva's consort) at the centre; her son Phra Khanthakuman (Khanthakumara or Subramaniam) on the right; and her elephant-headed son Phra Phikkhanesawora (Ganesha) on the left. Along the left interior wall sit rows of Shivas, Vishnus and other Hindu deities, as well as a few Bud-

LUMPHINI & EAST SATHON

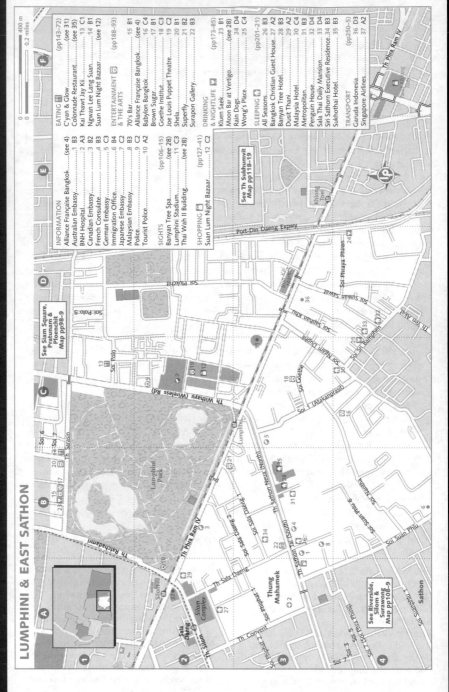

INFORMATION	
Alliance Française Bangkok............(see 4)	
Australian Embassy...........................1 B3	
BNH Hospital......................................2 A3	
Canadian Embassy.............................3 B2	
French Consulate................................4 B3	
German Embassy.................................5 C3	
Immigration Office.............................6 B4	
Japanese Embassy...............................7 C2	
Malaysian Embassy.............................8 B3	
Police..9 C2	
Tourist Police...................................10 A2	

SIGHTS	(pp106–15)
Banyan Tree Spa...........................(see 28)	
Lumphini Stadium...........................11 C3	
Thai Wah II Building......................(see 28)	

SHOPPING	(pp127–41)
Suan Lum Night Bazaar..................12 C2	

EATING	(pp143–72)
C'yan & Glow.................................(see 31)	
Colonnade Restaurant...................(see 35)	
Kai Thawt Jay Kii............................13 C1	
Ngwan Lee Lang Suan....................14 B1	
Suan Lum Night Bazaar...............(see 12)	

| **ENTERTAINMENT** | (pp188–93) |
& THE ARTS	
70's Bar...15 B1	
Alliance Française Bangkok...........(see 4)	
Babylon Bangkok............................16 C4	
Brown Sugar....................................17 B1	
Goethe Institut................................18 C3	
Joe Louis Puppet Theatre...............19 C2	
Shela...20 B1	
Superfly...21 B2	
Surapon Gallery..............................22 B3	

| **DRINKING** | (pp173–85) |
& NIGHTLIFE	
Kluen Saek.......................................23 B1	
Moon Bar at Vertigo....................(see 28)	
Rain Dogs...24 D4	
Wong's Place....................................25 C4	

SLEEPING	(pp201–21)
All Seasons.......................................26 B3	
Bangkok Christian Guest House.....27 A2	
Banyan Tree Hotel..........................28 B3	
Dusit Thani.......................................29 A2	
Malaysia Hotel.................................30 C4	
Metropolitan....................................31 B3	
Penguin House.................................32 D4	
Sala Thai Daily Mansion..................33 D4	
Siri Sathorn Executive Residence...34 B3	
Sukhothai Hotel...............................35 B3	

TRANSPORT	(pp250–5)
Garuda Indonesia............................36 D3	
Singapore Airlines...........................37 A2	

See Siam Square, Pratunam & Ploenchit Map pp98–9

See Th Sukhumvit Map pp118–19

See Riverside, Silom & Surawong Map pp108–9

Lumphini Park

Thung Mahamek

Khlong Toei

Port–Din Daeng Expwy

0   400 m
0   0.2 miles

ON THE RIVER

Getting out on the Mae Nam Chao Phraya is a great way to escape the Bangkok traffic and experience the city's maritime past. So it's fortunate that the city's riverside hotels also have some of the most attractive boats shuttling along the river. In most cases these free services run from Tha Sathon (Central Pier) and River City to their mother hotel, departing every 10 or 15 minutes. There's no squeeze and no charge, and the uniformed crew help you on and off. The Millennium Hilton boat has arguably the most polite crew and runs the most useful route. The boat services usually finish at about 10pm.

dhas. While most of the people working in the temple are of Subcontinental origin, you'll likely see plenty of Thai and Chinese devotees praying here because the Hindu gods figure just as prominently in their individualistic approach to religion.

The official Thai name of the temple is Wat Phra Si Maha Umathewi, but sometimes it is shortened to its colloquial name Wat Khaek – *khàek* is a common expression for people of Indian descent. The literal translation is 'guest', an obvious euphemism for any group of people not particularly wanted as permanent residents; hence most Indian Thais don't appreciate the term.

BANK OF ASIA Map pp108–9
ธนาคารเอเชีย
Cnr Th Sathon Tai & Soi Pikun
During the crazy 1980s, when no building project was too outlandish or expensive, architect Sumet Jumsai created his now-famous 'Robot Building' for the Bank of Asia. Few were keen on it at the time, but now it seems quaint and retro. The building is not open to the public; its whimsical façade is best viewed on the Skytrain between Surasak and Chong Nonsi stations.

KUKRIT PRAMOJ HOUSE Map pp108–9
บ้านหม่อมราชวงศ์คึกฤทธิ์ปราโมช
☎ 0 2286 8185; Soi 7 (Phra Phinij), Th Narathiwat Ratchankharin; admission adult/uniformed student 50/20B; ☼ 9.30am-5pm Sat & Sun; ▣ Chong Nonsi
Author and statesman Mom Ratchawong Kukrit Pramoj once resided in this charming complex now open to the public for tours. Surrounded by a manicured garden,

five teak buildings introduce visitors to traditional Thai architecture and to the former resident, who wrote more than 150 books (including the highly respected *Four Reigns*) and served as prime minister of Thailand.

ASSUMPTION CATHEDRAL Map pp108–9
☎ 0 2234 8556; Soi Oriental, Th Charoen Krung, Bangrak; ☼ 7am-7pm; ▲ Tha Oriental; ▣ Saphan Taksin
Marking the ascendancy of the French missionary influence in Bangkok during the reign of Rama II, this Romanesque church with its rich golden interior dates from 1910 and hosted a mass by Pope John Paul II in 1984. The schools associated with the cathedral are considered some of the best in Thailand, and you'll probably need to walk through one to reach the red-brick building.

RIVERSIDE RAMBLE
Walking Tour
There's more to the riverside district of Bangrak than large luxury hotels. Once Thailand's gateway to the world, its quiet tree-lined *soi* retain enough of their past character – in the form of old shophouses, embassies and godowns converted into antique stores – for an interesting couple of hours of walking and looking. The starting point is one of the most accessible in Bangkok, at the end of the Skytrain and the main river ferry terminal. If you plan to start after lunch it should be easier to justify regular drink stops in the hotel bars.

1 Bangrak Market Walk away from the river and turn left onto Th Charoen Krung. The street is lined with street food sellers and eventually opens into Bangrak Market, either of which makes a cheap, tasty pit stop.

2 Assumption Cathedral Continue along Th Charoen Krung, past the monumentally ugly neoclassical State Tower at the corner of Th Silom. Turn left through a schoolyard-cum-parking lot and walk through to red-brick Assumption Cathedral (above), in the midst of Bangkok's former centre of international commerce.

3 East Asiatic Company building Exit the cathedral through the front door, walk

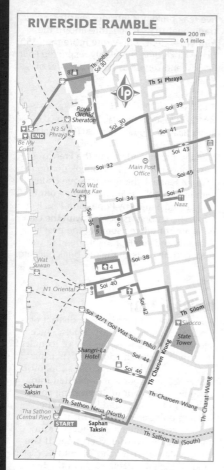

RIVERSIDE RAMBLE

0 ————— 200 m
0 ————— 0.1 miles

Th Jonha Soi 30

Th Si Phraya

Royal Orchid Sheraton

Soi 39

Soi 41

Soi 43

Soi 45

Soi 47

Naaz

N3 Si Phraya

Be My Guest

END

Soi 30

Soi 32

Main Post Office

N2 Wat Muang Kae

Soi 34

Soi 36

Soi 38

Wat Suwan

Soi 40

N1 Oriental

Soi 42/1 (Soi Wat Suan Phlu)

Soi 42

Th Silom

Sirocco

State Tower

Th Charoen Krung

Shangri-La Hotel

Soi 44

Soi 46

Saphan Taksin

Soi 50

Th Sathon Neua (North)

Tha Sathon (Central Pier)

START

Saphan Taksin

Th Sathon Tai (South)

Th Charoen Wiang

Th Charat Wiang

WALK FACTS

Start Tha Sathon (Central Pier) or Skytrain Saphan Taksin
End River City
Distance 4km walking, plus travel for drinking spot
Duration 1½ to two hours
Fuel Stops Naaz (p164)

through the small park and then right, beneath an overhead walkway linking two buildings. Here, in front of Tha Oriental, is the fading classical Venetian-style façade of the East Asiatic Company, built in 1901. Much of Thailand's foreign trade was conducted through this building, with goods coming and going from the surrounding godowns.

4 Oriental Hotel Walk east down Soi 40 and turn left into the Oriental Hotel (p212), Bangkok's oldest and most storied hotel. Have a wander around, stop for a drink in Lord Jim's, and be sure to check out the Authors' Wing (note that the 'smart, casual' dress code bans open shoes).

5 Old Customs House Exit the hotel, head away from the river and turn left past the Oriental Plaza (OP), built as a department store in 1905 and now housing expensive antique shops. Pass the walls of the French embassy and turn left; local Muslim restaurants offer sustenance here. Head towards the river and the big, decrepit Old Customs House (p107). Rehabilitation plans seem to have stalled and it remains a fire station, but it's OK to take a look around.

6 Haroon Village Leave the way you entered and turn left down a narrow lane behind Old Customs House. You're now in Haroon village, a Muslim enclave full of sleeping cats, playing kids, wooden houses and family-run stores selling essentials (including drinks and ice creams). Make your own way through Haroon and you'll eventually come to a larger street running away from the river. Follow this road, cross Th Charoen Krung and turn right and immediately left into a dead-end *soi*.

7 Naaz If you haven't already found food in Haroon Village, duck down the end of this soi to Naaz (p164) for one of the richest biryanis in town.

8 Bangkokian Museum Returning to Th Charoen Krung, turn right and walk past the imposing, Art Deco General Post Office and turn right on Soi 43. Walk beneath the expressway and past the street food vendors to the Bangkokian Museum (p106) for a taste of postwar Bangkok. Once you're done, head back the way you came and turn left down a lane just before Th Charoen Krung. At its end is Naaz (p164), which serves one of the richest biryanis in town.

9 River City Head back to Th Charoen Krung to take your life in your hands again crossing the street, and turn right. Continue to the next corner and turn left on Soi 30, aka Soi Captain Bush. Follow this road past the tacky 'antique' shops and the walls of the Portuguese embassy, Bangkok's oldest. You could finish your tour here, and take the river express boat from Tha Si Phraya, which is down a lane before the Sheraton Hotel. Alternatively, continue to River City (p137). This is a great place to view artefacts from across Southeast Asia, but be aware that anything of Cambodian origin might not be strictly kosher, as Cambodian law prohibits the export of most cultural artefacts in an attempt to maintain the cultural heritage of the country. Other countries might have different laws, but the effect of buying is the same. For more information see www .heritagewatch.org.'

10 Drinkies From River City you have several options. This is a departure point for Chao Praya dinner cruises, leaving at 7pm. More appealing are the free shuttle boats to the riverside hotels. Our recommendations: if it's after 5pm, you could take the ferry to the Oriental and walk up to State Tower for a rooftop cocktail at Sirocco (p177), or take the Hilton boat just across the river and head to the penthouse jazz bar Three Sixty (p180), which is definitely better if it's raining. For a lesser, but still great, view and much cheaper drinks, take the Hilton boat and walk left from the

THANON SUKHUMVIT

Eating p165; Shopping p138; Sleeping p216

The Sukhumvit neighbourhood starts at the fleshpots of Nana in what could be loosely called central Bangkok and tracks its namesake street for 20km all the way to the Gulf of Thailand. Like Bangkok as a whole, it has no real centre and numerous distinct personalities. Apart from the Skytrain, which looms above much of the street, the thing that brings it all together is money. This is Bangkok's most exclusive residential area, one packed with the city's most expensive apartments, villas, restaurants, shops, spas, cars, hospitals and, not surprisingly, its wealthiest residents.

Sukhumvit's two main personality blocks are either side of Soi 21 (Asoke). West of Soi Asoke, the *soi* branching off the main road are dominated by the sleazy sex tourist scene around Nana Entertainment Plaza (p185) and Soi Cowboy (p185), which tends to attract the expat (sexpat) and repeat visitor market. On Th Sukhumvit itself the scantily clad bargirls share space with men using battered laminated cards to tout eye-opening shows and a night market flogging fake DVDs, T-shirts and other junk to tourists. But it's not all sex and souvenirs. Several chic boutique hotels embellish these *soi*, and the city's most fashionable nightclubs, including Bed Supperclub (p183) and Q Bar (p184), can be found on Soi 11. Meanwhile down at Soi 3/1 you can feast on cheap Middle Eastern food in what is known as Little Arabia, where we recommend Nasser el Massry (p168).

West of Soi Asoke is where the bulk of the international residents and wealthy Thais live. During the postwar period, the green swathes of rice paddy were initially developed into large, contemporary villas occupying even larger blocks; for a prime example dine at Spring (p167). Over the years these huge blocks have proved prime targets for developers looking to cash in on the Thai infatuation with the high-rise apartment building. It's a continuing trend – there is almost nowhere in the neighbourhood where you can't hear the sweet sounds of construction.

This area is the primary address for the city's most recent expat arrivals, from Japanese engineers to Lebanese importers. Whole neighbourhoods are populated by company families temporarily transplanted to the tropics. Middle-class lives in the West are transformed into upper-class status in Thailand, and families are expected to contribute to the local economy by hiring maids, gardeners and other household staff. However, the majority of residents are still Thai, from both the established old families who run Thailand and the ranks of wannabe young professionals. Mixed Thai–*faràng* households are also very common in this area.

Most *faràng* live between Soi 21 (Asoke) and Soi 63 (Ekamai), near the Eastern bus station. Beyond here is primarily Thai, though that could change as the Skytrain extension comes online from 2009 (hopefully). And while the long noses, expensive restaurants and air-conditioned shops can sometimes have you wondering what country you're in, you only need to walk to the mouth of almost any *soi* to be reminded you're in a Thai city: street food vendors, motorcycle taxis waiting to cart you home for 10B and the ubiquitous 7-Eleven store, known hereabouts as a 'severrn'. For street food, *soi* 20, 23, 33 and 38 are particularly good.

Sukhumvit doesn't boast much in the way of bona fide sights, with temples to mammon and bacchanalian pleasure more prevalent than those to the Buddha; the restaurants are probably the main draw.

BENJAKITI PARK Map pp118–19
สวนเบญจกิติ

Th Ratchadaphisek; 5am-8pm; M Sirikit Centre
The latest addition to Bangkok's emaciated green scene, this 130-rai (20.8-hectare) park encircles a large lake on the former grounds of the Tobacco Monopoly, just behind the Queen Sirikit Convention Centre, and marks the queen's sixth cycle (72nd birthday). Another 300 rai (48 hectares) of former factory buildings is earmarked for transformation into a manmade rainforest, though it hass yet to open. The park makes a pleasant walk between the Sukhumvit strip and the Lumphini area.

SIAM SOCIETY & BAN KAMTHIENG
Map pp118–19
สยามสมาคม/บ้านคำเที่ยง

02661 6470; www.siam-society.com; 131 Soi Asoke (Soi 21), Th Sukhumvit; admission 100B; 9am-5pm; Asoke; M Sukhumvit
Stepping off cacophonous Soi Asoke and into the Siam Society's Ban Kamthieng

TRANSPORT: THANON SUKHUMVIT

Bus Air-con 501, 508, 511 and 513, ordinary 2, 25, 30 and 48

Skytrain Fom Nana east to On Nut stations are all along Th Sukhumvit. Stations beyond On Nut are due to open by 2009

Metro Sirikit Centre, Sukhumvit & Phetchaburi (Phetburi)

All odd-numbered *soi* branching off Th Sukhumvit head north, while even numbers run south. Unfortunately, they don't line up sequentially (eg Soi 11 lies directly opposite Soi 8, Soi 39 is opposite Soi 26). Some larger *soi* are known by alternative names, such as Soi Nana (Soi 3), Soi Asoke (Soi 21), Soi Phrom Phong (Soi 39) and Soi Thong Lor (Soi 55). Traffic on Th Sukhumvit is notorious; use the Skytrain if you can.

house museum is as close to a northern Thai village as you'll come in Bangkok. Ban Kamthieng is a traditional 19th-century home that was located on the banks of Mae Ping in Chiang Mai. Now relocated to Bangkok, the house presents the daily customs and spiritual beliefs of the Lanna tradition. Communicating all the hard facts as well as any sterile museum (with detailed English signage and engaging video installations), Ban Kamthieng instils in the visitor a sense of place, from the attached rice granary and handmade tools to the wooden loom and woven silks. You can't escape the noise of Bangkok completely, but the houses are refreshingly free of concrete and reflecting glass and make a pleasant, interesting break.

Next door are the headquarters of the prestigious Siam Society, publisher of the renowned *Journal of the Siam Society* and a valiant preserver of traditional Thai culture. Those with a serious interest can use the reference library, which has the answers to almost any question you could have about Thailand (outside the political sphere, since the society is sponsored by the royal family).

THAILAND CREATIVE & DESIGN CENTER Map pp118–19
ศูนย์สร้างสรรค์งานออกแบบ
☎ 0 2664 8448; www.tcdc.or.th; 6th fl, Emporium, Th Sukhumvit; ⏲ 10.30am-9pm Tue-Sun; Ⓡ Phrom Phong

Move over Scandinavian minimalism, this is the dawning of Thai style. This centre is a government-backed initiative intended to incubate design innovation, which is seen as Thailand's next step in the global marketplace now that labour is no longer competitive. The centre acts as both showroom and shop for Thai design, and is a good place to buy quality (if more expensive) Thai products and souvenirs. Rotating exhibitions feature profiles of international products and retrospectives of regional handicrafts and creativity. Material ConneXion is a permanent library of design-related materials, the first of its kind in Asia. In 2008 it was suggested the centre could be moving; call before you go.

MARKET, PARK & SPA
Walking Tour

This walk takes in the teeming commerce of Bangkok's largest market, the contrasting quiet of one of the city's newer parks, a bit of northern Thai culture and a massage to help you recover from it all. Khlong Toey market is busiest between about 5am and 10am, so if you want to be in the thick of the action start early. It's

top picks

THANON SUKHUMVIT

- Ban Kamthieng (opposite) An informative, well-presented taste of northern Thailand in this pretty teak building
- Tuba (p178) If you fancy a drink in a used furniture store, look no further
- Soi 11 Clubs Dance your way down Bangkok's premier clubbing *soi*, where new compete with favourites Bed Supperclub (p183) and Q Bar (p184)
- International restaurants (p165) Pasta, sushi, tapas, hommus – Sample Sukhumvit's huge selection of foreign cuisine
- Skytrain (p254) Peek into the neighbourhood's many fortressed mansions from this moving vantage point

THANON SUKHUMVIT

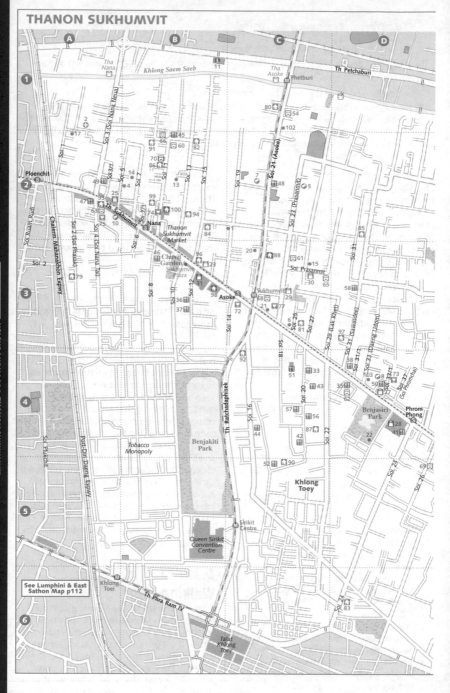

0   500 m
0   0.3 miles

E   F   G   H

Tha Wat
Maichonglam
16

Khlong Saem Saeb

Kamphaeng Phet 7

Th Petchaburi

59

Tha Thong
Lor

24

Ekamai Soi 21

18   78

55   67
76   34
Soi Promsri
3
9
19
Soi Prommit
Prommit
Hospital

71   Soi 10   6A

Khlong
Tan

Th Sukhumvit
26

Soi Thong Lor
32
53

12

Thong
Lo

Soi 34   54

Yaek 2   95
89
39
40
101   Ekamai

Th Sukhumvit

THANON SUKHUMVIT

INFORMATION
Bangkok Dental Spa.................... 1 C2
Bumrungrad International
    Hospital.....................................2 A1
Dental Hospital...........................3 F3
Foodland Pharmacy.....................4 B2
Indian Embassy.......................... 5 C2
Indian Visa Outsourcing
    Office......................................6 C3
Israeli Embassy.......................... 7 C2
Norwegian Embassy................... 8 D4
Rutnin Eye Hospital.................(see 0)
Samitivej Sukhumvit Hospital...... 9 E3
Swedish Embassy...................... 10 A2
TAT Main Office....................... 11 B1

SIGHTS   (pp116–22)
Absolute Yoga.......................... 12 F5
Ambassador Hotel Fitness
    Centre................................... 13 B2
Buathip Thai Massage............... 14 B2
Mulberries............................... 15 C3
Ozono Complex........................ 16 E1
Pirom Spa: The Garden Home
    Spa....................................... 17 A2
Play Gallery.............................. 18 G3
Rasayana Retreat...................... 19 E4
Siam Society & Ban
    Kamthieng............................20 C3
Thailand Creative & Design
    Center...............................(see 28)
Thailish Language School.......... 21 C3
World Fellowship of
    Buddhists..............................22 D4

SHOPPING 🛍   (pp127–41)
Asia Books..............................(see 28)
Asia Books............................... 23 B3
Asia Books..............................(see 31)
Basheer.................................... 24 G2
Bookazine................................ 25 A2
Dasa Book Café........................26 E4
Elite Used Books....................... 27 D4
Emporium Shopping Centre...... 28 D4
Kinokuniya.............................(see 28)
L' Arcadia................................. 29 C3
Nandakwang............................ 30 C3
Times Square............................ 31 B3

EATING 🍴   (pp143–72)
Ana's Garden...........................32 F5
Bed Supperclub.....................(see 60)
Bei Otto....................................33 C4
Boon Tong Kiat Singapore
    Hainanese Chicken Rice........ 34 G3
Bourbon St Bar & Restaurant.... 35 D4
Cabbages & Condoms.............. 36 B3
Crêpes & Co............................. 37 B3
Duc de Praslin.......................... 38 D4
Emporium Food Hall...............(see 28)
Face...39 F6
Great American Rib Company...40 E6
Greyhound Café....................(see 28)
Imoya...................................... 41 D4
Je Ngor.................................... 42 C4
Kalapapreuk on First..............(see 28)
Komala's..................................43 C4
Kuppa......................................44 C4
La Piola....................................45 B2
Le Banyan................................46 B3
Marriott Café........................... 47 A2
Memay Café............................. 48 C2
Nasser Elmassry Restaurant.......49 A2
Park Food Hall.......................(see 28)
Ramentei.................................. 50 D4
Rang Mahal.............................. 51 C4
Ruen Mallika............................ 52 C5
Scoozi...................................... 53 F5
Soi 38 Night Market..................54 F5
Spring...................................... 55 E3
Tamarind Café.......................... 56 C4
Tapas Café.............................(see 99)
Thonglee.................................. 57 C4
Yuy Lee.................................... 58 D3

ENTERTAINMENT 🎭   (pp188–93)
& THE ARTS
Bangkok Playhouse...................59 G2
Bed Supperclub.........................60 B2
Gallery F-Stop........................(see 56)
Glow.. 61 C3
Living Room...........................(see 98)
Mambo Cabaret........................ 62 D4
Nana Entertainment Plaza.........63 A2
Nang Len................................. 64 G4
Narcissus..................................65 C3
Q Bar.......................................66 B2

SFV..(see 28)
Santika.................................... 67 G3
Soi Cowboy.............................. 68 C3
Teo+Namfah Gallery..............(see 16)
Tokyo Joe's.............................. 69 D5
Twisted Republic.......................70 B2
Witch's Tavern......................... 71 G4

DRINKING
& NIGHTLIFE 🍸   (pp173–85)
Black Swan............................... 72 C3
Bull's Head & Angus
    Steakhouse........................... 73 D4
Cheap Charlie's.........................74 B2
Jool's Bar & Restaurant............. 75 A2
Nest......................................(see 91)
Opera Riserva Winetheque.......76 E3
Ship Inn................................... 77 C3
Tuba.. 78 H3

SLEEPING 🛏   (pp201–21)
Atlanta.................................... 79 A3
Bangkok Boutique Hotel...........80 C1
Bangkok Centre Sukhumvit 25..81 C3
Citichic....................................82 B2
Davis....................................... 83 D6
Dream.....................................84 B2
Eugenia................................... 85 D2
Federal Hotel............................86 B2
Grand Mercure Park Avenue.... 87 C4
Grand Millennium Sukhumvit... 88 C3
HI Sukhumvit...........................89 F6
House By The Pond.................. 90 C5
Le Fenix.................................. 91 B2
Ma Du Zi................................. 92 C4
Majestic Suites......................... 93 A2
Miami Hotel..............................94 B2
Napa Place Bed & Breakfast.......95 E6
S15.. 96 B3
Seven...................................... 97 D3
Sheraton Grande Sukhumvit.. 98 B3
Suk 11..................................... 99 B2
Swiss Park Hotel......................100 B2

TRANSPORT   (pp250–5)
Air India................................(see 10)
Eastern Bus Terminal.............. 101 G6
Lufthansa Airlines....................102 C1
PB Air..................................... 103 D4

WORKING FROM HOME: ARTISAN VILLAGES

Long before multinational factories, Bangkok was a town of craftspeople who lived and worked in artisan villages, inheriting their skills and profession from their parents. Many villages made stylised arts and crafts for the palace and minor royalty living along the fashionable avenues of the time. Today most of the villages still remain, but the descendants of the craftspeople have become office workers commuting to jobs no longer based in their homes.

Soi Ma Toom (Map p56; off Th Arun Amarin) is a surviving example of the old home-and-factory paradigm. This quiet lane, just off a traffic-clogged artery in Thonburi, across from the Naval Department, is where the *ma toom* (bael fruit) is peeled, cut into horizontal slices and soaked in palm sugar to make a popular candy.

Surviving primarily on tourist patronage, the Monk's Bowl Village (p71) dates back to the first Bangkok king and continues to create ceremonial pieces used by monks to collect morning alms.

The silk weavers of Baan Krua (p100) no longer weave for Jim Thompson, but a couple of families are still producing high-quality silks from looms in their living rooms.

Near the old timber yards and saw mills, Woodworking Street (Map pp124–5; Soi Pracha Narumit, Th Pracharat, Bang Sue) is still going strong with small Thai-Chinese–owned factories fashioning wooden eaves, furniture and shrines. Shops are open daily, and an annual street fair is celebrated in January.

ENGLISH: BEYOND EXPECTATION

Peppering documents, ad campaigns, magazine covers and pop songs with English is a sure-fire status symbol in Thailand. This isn't unconscious fluency but premeditated posturing. The thinking goes like this: the language associated with the richest nations of the world will surely divert just a little of that wealth to the business venture that masters a few key phrases.

The most creative and excessive uses of English as a good omen are found on billboard ads for new condominiums. 'Beyond expectation' is a common sales pitch. 'The ultimate in luxury living in prestige village' is another superlative-laden line that might make Muhammad Ali blush. The residents in the ads are always beautiful *lûuk khrêung* (half-Thai, half-*faràng*) impeccably dressed and enjoying a sweat-free existence in the tropics. They stare out at a misty future enjoying 'the best of tomorrow today, in the most extravagant, exciting, trendy place in the universe'.

most easily reached via the Khlong Toey Metro station and a walk.

1 Khlong Toey Market Despite being Bangkok's biggest market, and the distribution point for countless goods going to countless other stores, Khlong Toey market sees very few tourists. It's authentic and a photographer's dream.

2 Benjakiti Park Once you've had enough of the market, head out and cross busy Th Phra Ram IV, then west across Th Ratchadaphisek and north past the Stock Exchange of Thailand and finally into Benjakiti Park (p116).

Head across to the far side of the lake and walk north.

3 Ban Kamthieng At the far north end of the park, step back out onto Th Ratchadaphisek and continue north to Th Sukhumvit. Cross over (the new overpass should be finished by now), and continue north on busy Soi Asoke to Ban Kamthieng (p116), the traditional Lanna wooden home relocated to Bangkok. Adjoining is the welcome air-con of Black Canyon Coffee, which also serves cheap, tasty light lunches.

4 Massage time Refreshed enough that you're no longer dripping with sweat, brave the traffic and cross Soi Asoke, then walk through the Grand Millennium Hotel driveway to Soi 23. Turning right, there are a few local restaurants, and you have a choice of massage places. Those on Soi 23 itself are cheap (less than 300B an hour) but the women wear suspiciously short skirts so asking for an 'oil massage' might get you more than you bargained for (foot massages are a safer bet). If you walk along to the T-junction and turn left, just beyond the next corner Mulberries offers a more spa-like experience, with more professional English-speaking masseuses.

5 Soi Cowboy Rejuvenated, return to Soi 23, turn left (north) and walk along until you come to neon-filled Soi Cowboy (p185). Depending on the time, you'll find the bars sleepy or just warming up – fun photos if

MARKET, PARK & SPA

WALK FACTS

Start Khlong Toei Metro station
End Asoke Skytrain station
Distance 4km
Duration Two to four hours
Fuel Stops Naaz (p164)

NEIGHBOURHOODS THANON SUKHUMVIT

the neon is on. At the far end turn left and after a few metres left again into the Metro station, which connects under Soi 21 (Asoke) to Asoke Skytrain.

We apologise for not ending this tour with a drinking spot with a view (though some will want to stop for the views in Soi Cowboy), but it is supposed to start early. If you've managed to stretch it out to the end of the day, consider walking down to Cheap Charlies (p175) in Soi 11, and be sure to check out the Sukhumvit restaurants (p165).

GREATER BANGKOK

Once rice fields, voracious Bangkok has expanded in every possible direction with few concessions to charm. Surrounding the previously defined neighbourhoods are seemingly endless flat residential suburbs with a small number of scattered attractions. Some of these sights are conveniently located along the Skytrain route, making them easily accessible from downtown. Chatuchak and Victory Monument are both on the northern branch of the Skytrain, while Rama IX Royal Park is in the far-eastern part of town, currently beyond the last Skytrain stop but not for long.

The other attractions listed here will require several forms of public transport (and lots of time and patience) or personal transport. The prisons are located west of Chatuchak and north of central Bangkok.

BANG KWANG & KHLONG PREM PRISONS Map pp124–5
เรือนจำบางขวางและคลองเปรม

Bang Kwang ☎ 0 2967 3311; fax 0 2967 3313; Th Nonthaburi, Nonthaburi; 🚢 Nonthaburi **Khlong Prem** ☎ 0 2580 0975; 33/3 Th Ngam Wang Wan, Chatuchak; 🚢 Nonthaburi; 🚇 Mo Chit

Thailand's permissive reputation is juxtaposed by strict antidrug laws that often land foreign nationals in a prison system with feudal conditions. A sobering and charitable expedition is to visit an inmate, bringing them news of the outside, basic supplies and reading materials. The regulations for visits are quite involved and require pre-arrival research (see p261). You must dress respectfully (long sleeves and long pants), bring your passport for registration purposes, and have the name and building number of the inmate you plan to visit. Inmate information can be obtained from most embassies. Visiting hours and days vary depending on the building the inmate is housed in.

Male inmates who have received sentences of 40 years to life (often for drug offences) are detained in Bang Kwang Prison, north of central Bangkok. To reach the prison, take the Mae Nam Chao Phraya ferry north to Nonthaburi (the last stop); the prison is 500m from the pier.

Women sentenced to seven to 40 years are detained in the Bang Khen section of Khlong Prem Prison. From Nonthaburi, take a minibus (15B) to the prison, or take the Skytrain to Mo Chit and then a taxi to the prison gates.

For more information, see www.phaseloop .com/foreignprisoners/prisoners-thailand .html or www.bangkwang.net.

CHILDREN'S DISCOVERY MUSEUM Map pp124–5
พิพิธภัณฑ์เด็กกรุงเทพมหานคร

☎ 0 2618 6509; www.bkkchildrenmuseum.com; Queen Sirikit Park, Th Kamphaeng Phet 4; adult/ child 70/50B; 🕘 9am-5pm Tue-Fri, 10am-6pm Sat & Sun; 🚇 Mo Chit

Through hands-on activities, learning is well disguised as fun at this museum opposite Chatuchak Weekend Market (p140). Kids can stand inside a bubble, see how an engine works, or role-play as a firefighter. Most activities are geared to primary-school–aged children. There is also a toddlers' playground at the back of the main building.

RAMA IX ROYAL PARK Map pp124–5
สวนหลวง ร.๙

Soi 103 (Soi Udom Suk), Th Sukhumvit; admission 10B; 🕘 5am-6pm; 🚌 ordinary 2, 23 & 25, transfer to green minibus at Soi 103

Opened in 1987 to commemorate King Bhumibol's 60th birthday, this green area, about 15km southeast of central Bangkok, covers 81 hectares and has a water park and botanic garden. Since its opening, the garden has become a significant horticultural research centre. A museum with an exhibition about the king's life sits at the park's centre. There are resident lizards, tortoises and birds. A flower and plant sale is held here in December. From Th Sukhumvit it's about 7km along Soi 103, after it bends left.

SAFARI WORLD Map pp124–5
ซาฟารีเวิลด์

☎ 0 2518 1000; www.safariworld.com; 99 Th Ramindra 1, Minuburi; adult/child 750/450B; 🕘 9am-5pm

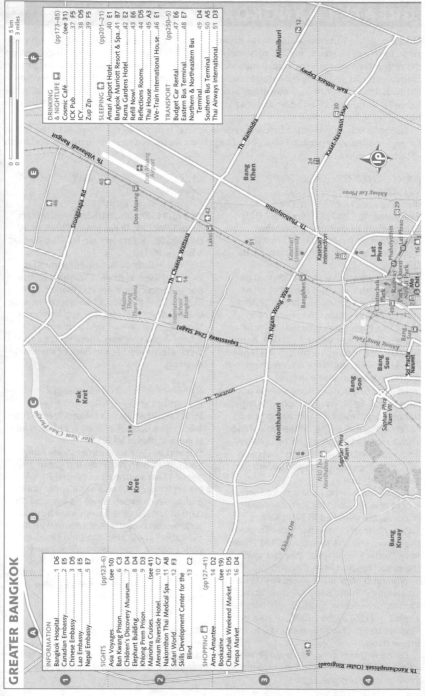

INFORMATION
Bangkok Hospital................................1 D6
Canadian Embassy...............................2 E5
Chinese Embassy.................................3 D5
Lao Embassy.......................................4 E5
Nepal Embassy....................................5 E7

SIGHTS   (pp123–6)
Asia Voyages...............................(see 10)
Ban Kwang Prison................................6 C3
Children's Discovery Museum.................7 D4
Elephant Building................................8 D4
Khlong Prem Prison..............................9 D3
Manohra Cruises...........................(see 41)
Menam Riverside Hotel......................10 C7
Nakornthon Thai Medical Spa.......11 A8
Safari World..12 F3
Skills Development Center for the
  Blind...13 C2

SHOPPING   (pp127–41)
Ama-Amantee.....................................14 D2
Bookazine....................................(see 19)
Chatuchak Weekend Market...........15 D5
Vespa Market.....................................16 D4

DRINKING
& NIGHTLIFE   (pp173–85)
Cosmic Café...............................(see 31)
ICK Pub..37 F5
ICY..38 D5
Zup Zip..39 F5

SLEEPING   (pp201–21)
Amari Airport Hotel...........................40 E1
Bangkok Marriott Resort & Spa...41 B7
Rama Gardens Hotel..........................42 E2
Refill Now!...43 E6
Reflections Rooms..............................44 D5
Thai House...45 A3
We-Train International House.......46 E1

TRANSPORT   (pp250–6)
Budget Car Rental..............................47 E6
Eastern Bus Terminal..........................48 E7
Northern & Northeastern Bus
  Terminal...49 D4
Southern Bus Terminal........................50 A5
Thai Airways International..................51 D3

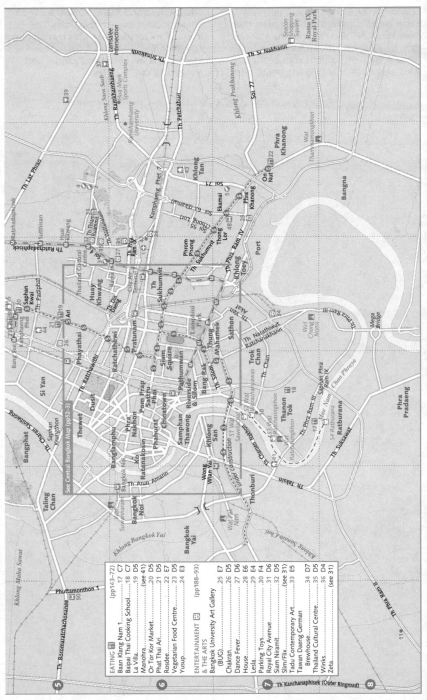

EATING		(pp143–72)
Baan Klang Nam 1	17	C7
Baipai Thai Cooking School	18	C7
La Villa	19	D5
Manohra	(see 41)	
Or Tor Kor Market	20	D5
Phat Thai Ari	21	D5
Rosdee	22	E7
Vegetarian Food Centre	23	D5
Yusup	24	E3

ENTERTAINMENT		(pp188–93)
& THE ARTS		
Bangkok University Art Gallery		
(BUG)	25	E7
Chakran	26	D5
Dance Fever	27	D6
House	28	E6
Lesla	29	E4
Parking Toys	30	F4
Royal City Avenue	31	D6
Siam Niramit	32	D5
Slim/Flix	(see 31)	
Tadu Contemporary Art	33	E5
Tawan Daeng German		
Brewhouse	34	D7
Thailand Cultural Centre	35	D5
Winks	36	D4
Zeta	(see 31)	

Claiming to be world's largest 'open zoo', Safari World is divided into two parts the drive-through Safari Park and the Marine Park. In the Safari Park, visitors drive through different habitats with giraffes, lions, zebras, elephants, orang-utans, and other African and Asian animals. A panda house displays rare white pandas. The Marine Park focuses on stunts by dolphins and other trained animals. Safari World is 45km northeast of Bangkok, and is best reached by car.

top picks

- Chatuchak Weekend Market (p140)
- MBK (Mahboonkrong; p134)
- Pak Khlong Market (p132)
- Pantip Plaza (p132)
- River City Complex (p137)
- Siam Square (p135)

SHOPPING

Commerce and shopping are so ubiquitous in Bangkok that they appear to be genetic traits of the city's inhabitants. Hardly a street corner in the city is free from a vendor, hawker or impromptu stall, and Bangkok is also home to one of the word's largest outdoor markets, not to mention Southeast Asia's largest mall. There's something here for just about everybody, and often genuine and knock-off items live happily side by side. Although the tourist brochures tend to tout the upmarket malls, Bangkok still lags slightly behind Singapore and Hong Kong in this area, and the open-air markets are where the best deals and most-original items are found.

Bargaining is part of the culture at markets and small family-run shops where prices aren't posted. When engaging in this ancient sport, remember that it requires finesse rather than force, and the best approach is one of camaraderie. If you're interested in buying, ask the vendor the price and then ask if they could lower it. You can then counter with a lower sum that will tug the return offer closer to a comfortable range. Figures are sometimes volleyed back and forth at this point, but stay calm and cool. It is poor form to haggle over a difference of 10B. Prices aren't negotiable when a price is posted.

Thais are generally so friendly and laid-back that some visitors are lulled into a false sense of security, forgetting that Bangkok is a big city with untrustworthy characters. While your personal safety is rarely at risk in Thailand, you may be unwittingly charmed out of an unfair amount of the contents of your wallet. See opposite for more information about scams.

SHOPPING AREAS

The area around Siam Sq has the greatest concentration of shopping malls for designer and department-store goods. Street markets for souvenirs and pirated goods are on Th Khao San, Th Sukhumvit and Th Silom. Thai-style housewares and handicraft items can be found in the older parts of Bangkok, such as Banglamphu or around Th Charoen Krung.

OPENING HOURS

Most family-run shops are open from 10am to 7pm daily. Street markets are either daytime (from 9am to 5pm) or night-time (from 8pm to midnight). Note that streetside vendors are forbidden by city ordinance to clutter the pavements on Mondays, but do so every other day. Shopping centres are usually open from 10am to 10pm.

SHOPPING GUIDE

The city's intense urban tangle sometimes makes orientation a challenge in finding intimate shops and markets. Like having your own personal guide, *Nancy Chandler's Map of Bangkok* (www.nancychandler.net) tracks all sorts of small, out-of-the-way shopping venues and markets as well as dissecting the innards of the Chatuchak Weekend Market (p140). The colourful map is sold in bookshops throughout the city.

KO RATANAKOSIN & THONBURI

The leafy lanes of Bangkok's oldest district specialise in the ancient arts of health, safety and fortune. Locals come to inspect sacred amulets and pick up pellet-sized pills of Thai traditional medicines.

TRADITIONAL MEDICINE SHOPS
Map p56   Health Supplies
Th Maharat from Thammasat University to Wat Pho, Ko Ratanakosin; ☾ 8am-7pm; ⊟ air-con 503, ordinary 32, 53 & 203, ⚓ Tha Chang
Bangkok's commercial medicine cabinet occupies the riverside thoroughfare of Th Maharat. Packaged in plastic pill bottles bearing an unsmiling photo of a trusted authority, commercial formulas combine various herbal ingredients – such as galingale, lemon grass, kaffir lime and other flavourings used in Thai dishes – to target a specific disease or to promote general wellness.

Shops carrying massage supplies cater to practitioners and to students at the nearby Wat Pho massage training school. Keep an eye out for the dumpling-shaped herbal compresses that are heated and pressed onto the body during sessions of Thai herbal massage.

BUYER BEWARE

The disparity between the Thai baht and foreign currencies often clouds the judgment of otherwise eagle-eyed shoppers. Do your homework and approach each expensive transaction with a healthy amount of scepticism.

Antiques

Real Thai antiques are rare and costly and reserved primarily for serious collectors. Everything else is designed to look old and most shopkeepers are happy to admit it. Reputable antique dealers will issue an authentication certificate. Contact the Department of Fine Arts (☎ 0 2226 1661) to obtain the required licence for exporting religious images and fragments, either antique or reproductions.

Gems & Jewellery

Thailand is one of the world's largest exporters of gems and ornaments, but scams are more prevalent than bargains. Don't buy goods from a shop that claims to have a 'one-day' sale or wants you to deliver uncut gems to your home country for resale.

Reputable dealers don't pay commissions to túk-túk drivers but are known by customer referrals. Most are members of the Jewel Fest Club, established jointly by the Tourism Authority of Thailand (TAT; ☎ 0 2250 5500; www.tourism thailand.org; ☼ 8.30am-4.30pm Mon-Fri) and the Thai Gem Jewellery Traders Association (www.thaigemjewelry .com). When you purchase from a member shop, a certificate detailing your purchase will be issued and a refund is guaranteed (less 10% to 20%). A list of members offering government guarantees is available from TAT, or visit the association's website for buying information.

The latest trend is to open a gem 'museum', charging a hefty admission price, with an attached jewellery store. Proceed with caution.

Tailor-Made Clothes

Tailors are as prolific as massage parlours in Bangkok and so are the scams. Workmanship and fabric quality ranges from shoddy to excellent.

Good tailors don't have to advertise; their reputation precedes them in the well-dressed circles of the diplomatic corps. Commission a few small pieces from a reputable shop (one that doesn't have hawkers out the front) before committing to high-dollar items, and know your fabrics before being duped by synthetics.

AMULET MARKET

Map p56   Outdoor Market

Several small soi off Th Maharat, along Th Maharat near Wat Mahathat, Ko Ratanakosin; ☼ 8am-6pm; ⊞ air-con 503, ordinary 32, 53 & 203, ⚓ Tha Chang

Catholics with their parade of saints and protective medals will recognise a great kinship with this streetside amulet market. Ranging from pendant-sized to medallion-sized, *phrá khrêuang* (amulets) come in various classes, from rare objects or relics (like antlers, tusks, or the dentures of abbots) to images of Buddha or famous monks embossed in bronze, wood or clay. Itinerant dealers spread their wares on blankets along the broken pavement across from the temple, and more-permanent shops proliferate in the sunless alleyways along the river. Taxi drivers, monks and average folk squat alongside the displays inspecting novel pieces like practised jewellers. Mixed in with certain amulets are pulverised substances: dirt from a special temple, hair from a monk, or powerful herbs.

When the serious collectors aren't perusing the market, they are flipping through amulet magazines that discuss noteworthy

TAX REFUNDS

Thailand allows for value added tax (VAT) refunds but some complicated rules apply. First you need to qualify as a VAT recipient, which excludes Thais and airline crew members. Each receipt must be for more than 2000B spent on one day and must be issued by a participating VAT shop, which must also supply other accompanying paperwork. Your total purchases need to exceed 5000B in order to qualify. You also must have been in Thailand for less than 180 days in a calendar year and be leaving the country by plane. Call the VAT Refund for Thailand Office (☎ 0 2272 9387) for more information.

CLOTHING SIZES

Women's clothing

Aus/UK	8	10	12	14	16	18
Europe	36	38	40	42	44	46
Japan	5	7	9	11	13	15
USA	6	8	10	12	14	16

Women's shoes

Aus/USA	5	6	7	8	9	10
Europe	35	36	37	38	39	40
France only	35	36	38	39	40	42
Japan	22	23	24	25	26	27
UK	3½	4½	5½	6½	7½	8½

Men's clothing

Aus	92	96	100	104	108	112
Europe	46	48	50	52	54	56
Japan	S		M	M		L
UK/USA	35	36	37	38	39	40

Men's shirts (collar sizes)

Aus/Japan	38	39	40	41	42	43
Europe	38	39	40	41	42	43
UK/USA	15	15½	16	16½	17	17½

Men's shoes

Aus/UK	7	8	9	10	11	12
Europe	41	42	43	44½	46	47
Japan	26	27	27½	28	29	30
USA	7½	8½	9½	10½	11½	12½

Measurements approximate only – try before you buy

specimens. While money changes hands between vendor and customer, both use the euphemism of 'renting' to get around the prohibition of selling Buddhas.

BANGLAMPHU

The spectrum of goods available in this district ranges from backpacker staples along Th Khao San to delicious Thai curry pastes and high-quality handicrafts in the more traditional areas nearby. In recent years the twain have met, and Th Khao San has expanded into the silver business with souvenir-grade baubles sold in bulk to importers.

IT'S HAPPENED TO BE A CLOSET

Map pp68–9   Clothing
☎ 0 2629 5271; 32 Th Khao San, Banglamphu; 🕑 1-11pm; 🚌 air-con 511 & 512, ordinary 15, 30 & 65, 🚤 Tha Phra Athit

Hidden in the same courtyard as Tom Yam Kung restaurant, the only kinship this

women's clothing shop seems to have with Th Khao San is its Bohemian roots. Bright colours and bold patterns rule among the Thai-designed and -made togs, and the elegant shop even features a restaurant and café, a hair and nail salon, and private rooms for movie viewing. You may never need to leave.

NITTAYA CURRY SHOP Map pp68–9   Food
☎ 0 2282 8212; 136-40 Th Chakhraphong, Banglamphu; 🕑 10am-7pm; 🚌 air-con 3, 32 & 49, ordinary 30, 32, 33 & 65, 🚤 Tha Phra Athit

Follow your nose; Nittaya is famous throughout Thailand for her pungent but high-quality curry pastes. Pick up a couple of take-away canisters for prospective dinner parties or peruse the snack and gift sections, where visitors to Bangkok load up on local specialities for friends back in the provinces.

TAEKEE TAEKON Map pp68–9   Handicrafts
☎ 0 2629 1473-4; 118 Th Phra Athit, Banglamphu; 🕑 10am-5pm Mon-Sat; 🚌 ordinary 3, 6, 15 & 82, 🚤 Tha Phra Athit

This atmospheric shop has a decent selection of Thai textiles from the country's main silk-producing areas, especially northern Thailand, as well as assorted local knick-knackery and interesting postcards not widely available elsewhere.

THAI NAKORN Map pp68–9   Handicrafts
☎ 0 2281 7867; 79 Th Prachathipathai, Banglamphu; 🕑 10am-6pm Mon-Sat; 🚌 ordinary 10

This family-owned enterprise has been in business for 70 years and often fills commissions from the royal family for nielloware and silver ornaments. Silver-moulded cases and clutches, ceremonial bowls and tea sets are also among the offerings. If you can navigate the language, ask to go behind the showroom to witness the aged artisans at work.

THANON KHAO SAN MARKET
Map pp68–9   Outdoor Market
Th Khao San, Banglamphu; 🕑 10-2am Tue-Sun; 🚌 air-con 511 & 512, ordinary 15, 30 & 65, 🚤 Tha Phra Athit

The main guesthouse strip in Banglamphu is a day and night shopping bazaar, selling all but the baby and the bath water. Cheap T-shirts, trendy purses, wooden frogs, fuzzy puppets, bootleg CDs, hemp clothing, fake

SHOPPING CHINATOWN

READING FRENZY

The Banglamphu area is home to nearly all of Bangkok's independent bookstores. In addition, Th Khao San is virtually the only place in town to go for used English-language books. You're not going to find any deals here, but the selection is decent.

Passport (Map pp68–9; ☎ 0 2629 0694; 523 Th Phra Sumen, Banglamphu) Although the vast majority of the titles here are in Thai, the shop is worth a visit for its artsy atmosphere and tasty drinks.

Rim Khob Fah Bookstore (Map pp68–9; ☎ 0 2622 3510; 78/1 Th Ratchadamnoen, Banglamphu) Without having to commit loads of your suitcase space, you can sample an array of slim scholarly publications from the Fine Arts Department on Thai art and architecture. The academic texts in English have also been joined by your standard-issue travel books and region-specific titles.

Saraban (Map pp68–9; ☎ 0 2629 1386; 106/1 Th Rambutri, Banglamphu) Stocking the largest selection of international newspapers and new Lonely Planet guides, this claustrophobic shop also has a good selection of used yarns.

Shaman Bookstore (Map pp68–9; ☎ 0 2629 0418; D&D Plaza, 68-70 Th Khao San; 127 Th Tanao, Banglamphu) This longstanding shop spans two locations on Th Khao San and has the area's largest selection of used books. Titles can conveniently be searched using a computer program.

Suksit Siam (Map pp68–9; ☎ 0 2225 9531; 113-5 Th Fuang Nakhon, Banglamphu) Opposite Wat Ratchabophit, this shop specialises in books on Thai progressive politics and Buddhism. It also has mainstream titles on Thailand and Asia in both English and Thai.

student ID cards, knock-off designer wear, souvenirs, corn on the cob, orange juice... You name it, they've got it.

CHAROEN CHAIKARNCHANG SHOP
Map pp68–9   Religious

☎ 0 2222 4800; 87 Soi Nava, Th Bamrung Muang, Banglamphu; ⏱ 9am-6pm; 🚌 air-con 508, ordinary 5, 35 & 56, khlong taxi Tha Phan Fah

Easily the largest and most impressive religious shop in an area of impressive religious shops. The workshop at the back produces gigantic bronze Buddha images for wáts all over Thailand. You might be unlikely to buy a life-sized Buddha, but looking is fun and who knows when you might need to do a great deal of merit making.

CHINATOWN

The Phahurat and Chinatown districts have interconnected markets selling fabrics, clothes and household wares, as well as wholesale shops for every imaginable bulk item. There are a few places selling gems and jewellery.

JOHNNY'S GEMS Map p84   Gemstones

☎ 0 2224 4065; 199 Th Fuang Nakhon, Chinatown; ⏱ 9.30am-6pm Mon-Sat; 🚌 air-con 508

A long-time favourite of Bangkok expats, Johnny's Gems is a reliable name in an unreliable business. The namesake founder

has since passed away, but his son carries on the spic-and-span reputation, primarily in rubies and emeralds from fun to serious.

PHAHURAT MARKET
Map p84   Outdoor Market

Th Phahurat & Th Triphet, across from Old Siam Plaza, Phahurat; ⏱ 9am-6pm; 🚌 air-con 73, 🚤 Tha Saphan Phut

If it sparkles, then this market has it. Phahurat proffers boisterous Bollywood-coloured textiles, traditional Thai dance costumes, tiaras, sequins, wigs and other accessories to make you look like a cross-dresser, a *măw lam* (Thai country music) performer, or both. This is cloth city, and amid the colour spectacle are also good deals on machine-made Thai textiles and children's clothes.

SAMPENG LANE
Map p84   Outdoor Market

Soi Wanit 1, Th Ratchawong, Chinatown; ⏱ 8am-6pm; 🚌 air-con 4, 49, 73 & 507, ordinary 40, 49, 73, 85 & 159, 🚤 Tha Ratchawong

Sampeng Lane is a narrow artery running parallel to Th Yaowarat and bisecting the commercial areas of Chinatown and Phahurat. The Chinatown portion of Sampeng is lined with wholesale shops of hair accessories, pens, stickers, household wares and beeping, flashing knick-knacks. Near Th Chakrawat, gem and jewellery shops

lonelyplanet.com

abound. Weekends are horribly crowded, and it takes a gymnast's flexibility to squeeze past the pushcarts, motorcycles and other roadblocks.

SAPHAN PHUT NIGHT BAZAAR
Map p84   Outdoor Market
Th Saphan Phut, Chinatown; 8pm-midnight Tue-Sun; air-con 60, 73 & 512, ordinary 5 & 8, Tha Saphan Phut
On either side of the Memorial Bridge (Saphan Phut), this night market has bucket loads of cheap clothes, late-night snacking and a lot of people-watching. As Chatuchak Weekend Market (p140) becomes more design oriented, Saphan Phut has filled the closets of the fashion-forward, baht-challenged teenagers.

PAK KHLONG MARKET
Map p84   Plants & Flowers
Th Chakkaphet & Th Atsadang, Chinatown; 24hr; air-con 60, 73 & 512, ordinary 5 & 8, Tha Saphan Phut
This sprawling wholesale flower market has become a tourist attraction in its own right. The endless piles of delicate orchids, rows of roses and stacks of button carnations are a sight to be seen, and the shirtless porters wheeling blazing piles of colour set the place in motion. The best time to come is late at night, when the goods arrive from upcountry.

During the morning Pak Khlong Market is also one of the city's largest wholesale vegetable markets.

SIAM SQUARE, PRATUNAM & PLOENCHIT

If you like your retail upscale and air-conditioned, head directly for the centre of town. Bangkok's ever-expanding repertoire of luxury malls is a major draw for tourists from Asia and the Middle East, and can be found near the intersection of Th Phra Ram I and Th Phayathai, and further east at Th Ratchadamri.

If you're looking for something a bit more homegrown, designs by Thailand's emerging fashion designers are available at shops in and around Siam Sq.

For penny-pinchers and/or wholesalers the ultimate destination is Pratunam district, where a daily open-air bazaar fuels both locally made and cheap import goods.

Keep an eye out for end of season and payday sales, as well as the citywide sales spree in June.

PANTIP PLAZA
Map pp98–9   Computer Equipment
0 2656 5030; 604 Th Phetburi, Pratunam; 10am-10pm; Phayathai
If you can tolerate the crowds and annoying pornography vendors ('DVD sex? DVD sex?') Pantip, a multistorey computer and electronics warehouse, might just be your kinda paradise. Shiny new hardware isn't really Pantip's speciality, but grey market goods are. Technorati will find pirated software and music, gear for hobbyists to enhance their machines, flea market–style peripherals and other odds and ends. Up on the 6th floor is IT City (0 2656 5030), a reliable computer megastore that gives VAT refund forms for tourists.

UTHAI'S GEMS
Map pp98–9   Gems & Jewellery
0 2253 8582; 28/7 Soi Ruam Rudi, Th Ploenchit, Ploenchit; 10am-6pm Mon-Sat; Ploenchit
With 40 years in the business, Uthai's fixed prices and good service, including a money-back guarantee, make him a popular choice among expats. The showroom boasts a huge stock, and gems can be custom-cut to order.

FROM NYMPH TO JUMBO
In your home town, you may be considered average or even petite, but based on the Thai measuring stick you're an extra large, clearly marked in the tag as 'LL' or, worse still, 'XL'. If that batters the body image, then skip the street markets, where you'll bust the seams from the waist up – if you can squirm that far into the openings. Only street vendors on Th Khao San accommodate foreign women's natural endowments in the shoulders, bust and hips. If you're larger than a US size 10 or an Australian size 12, you strike out altogether. Men will find that they exceed Thai clothes in length and shoulder width, as well as shoe sizes. For formal wear, many expats turn to custom orders through tailors. For ready-to-wear, many of the vendors at Pratunam Market (opposite), and several stalls on the 7th floor of MBK (p134) stock the larger sizes.

HOT ON THE TRAIL

Walk into a store, any store, in Bangkok and you'll be followed by a sales assistant from rack to rack. They smile, you smile. 'Would you like to look, madame?' They open up the display case, remark 'how lovely', then follow you to the next shiny object. This is the definition of service in a Thai store, not an anti-shop-lifting measure. A sales assistant who doesn't stay glued to a customer's elbow isn't doing a good job. Even the Western-style department stores are over-staffed with such attention. You can politely decline help, which will gain you a few feet of breathing room.

PRATUNAM MARKET

Map pp98–9   Outdoor Market

Cnr Th Phetburi & Th Ratchaprarop, Pratunam; 9am-midnight; khlong taxi Tha Pratunam, Chitlom

The emphasis here is on clothes, in particular T-shirts, and the Baiyoke Garment Center, the immense open-air market that comprises much of the area, is the best place in town to buy that black Iron Maiden T-shirt you've had your eye on.

The greater market area occupies the neighbourhood behind the shopfronts on the corner of Th Phetburi and Th Ratch-aprarop, and also includes several like-minded malls, such as: Indra Square, which carries mostly women's clothing; Pratunam Centre, featuring a decent selection of Thai handicrafts and silver; City Complex and Krung Thong Plaza, two nearly identical wholesale clothing malls; and across the street, the five-storey Platinum Fashion Mall sports the latest in no-brand couture, including a base-ment-level Jeans Zone, featuring 100 shops.

CENTRAL CHIDLOM

Map pp98–9   Shopping Centre

☎ 0 2793 7777; www.central.co.th; 1027 Th Ploen-chit, Ploenchit; 10am-10pm; Chidlom

Central is a modern Western-style depart-ment store with locations throughout the city. This flagship store, Thailand's largest, is the snazziest of all the branches.

The ground floor carries all the big names in cosmetics, with eager perfume spritzers and the token ladyboy sales agent who pulls off blush better than those born with the double-X chromosomes.

Foreigner-sized clothing is one of the shop's strengths. The helpful sales staff will bluntly steer you to slimming colours and relatively huge sizes to fit your sturdy frame.

A decent selection of English-language books and magazines, not to mention stationery and music, is available at B2S on the 7th floor.

CENTRAL WORLD PLAZA

Map pp98–9   Shopping Centre

☎ 0 2635 1111; www.centralworld.co.th; cnr Th Ploenchit & Th Ratchadamri, Ploenchit; 10am-10pm; Chidlom

Once one of the city's dying shopping cen-tres, this is now the latest in a line of Queer Eye for the Straight Guy–type makeovers, boasting seven floors of unadulterated commercial bliss. We fancy the concrete-floored F section that features cool do-mestic brands with barely pronounceable names such as Playground! Manga, Qcon-ceptstore and Flynow III.

Up on the 8th floor, the Thai Knowledge Park (TK Park; ☎ 0 2250 7620; www.tkpark.or.th) is part of a government initiative to cultivate reading and learning habits in children. The centre features various libraries, including a fun music library and a children's reading area, and heaps of computers for internet access.

ERAWAN BANGKOK

Map pp98–9   Shopping Centre

☎ 0 2250 7777; www.erawanbangkok.com; 494 Th Ploenchit, Ploenchit; 10.30am-8.30pm; Chidlom

Bangkok's chi-chi crowd has a new stomp-ing ground: the shopping wing of the Erawan Hotel. Luxury matrons occupy the 1st floor, while street-smarts chill on the 2nd floor, fusing the generation gap with a shared closet. The top floor is a dedicated wellness centre, should conspicuous con-sumption prove hazardous to your health. The ladies who lunch can often be found in the basement-level Urban Kitchen or the 2nd-floor Erawan Tea Room.

GAYSORN PLAZA

Map pp98–9   Shopping Centre

☎ 0 2656 1149; www.gaysorn.com; cnr Th Ploen-chit & Th Ratchadamri, Ploenchit; 10am-10pm; Chidlom

A haute couture catwalk, Gaysorn has spiral-ling staircases, all-white halls and mouth-fuls of top-name designers. The 2nd floor 'Urban Street Chic' zone is a crash course

top picks

LOCAL BUYS

Right, you've got gems, silks and elephants on your Bangkok shopping list, but there are loads of local buys that won't make your home look like a beachfront souvenir shop. Add some class to your space with these local products.

- **Zebra Stainless Steel Kitchenware** This 40-year-old company based in Rayong scooped out a market niche with its high-quality Chinese soup spoons. It has since expanded into nesting bowls, Thai-style lunchboxes and soup pots that would cost a fortune for comparable quality back home. Available at department stores and housewares markets.

- **Harnn & Thann** Smell good enough to eat with these botanical-based spa products: lavender massage lotion, rice bran soap, and jasmine compresses. Products are all natural, rooted in Thai traditional medicine, and stylish enough to share space with brand-name beauty. Available at Gaysorn (p133).

- **Niwat Cutlery** Born out of the ancient sword-making traditions of Ayuthaya province, the NV Aranyik company, a family-owned business, produces distinctively Thai cutlery. Available at Gaysorn (p133).

- **Mr P Lamp** Thai designer Chaiyut Plypetch dreamed up Propaganda's signature character, devilish Mr P who appears in anatomically correct cartoon lamps and other products. Available at Siam Discovery Center (opposite) and Emporium (p138).

- **Beyond Living** Colourful and textured woven rugs, cushions and handbags draw inspiration from natural Thai materials and handicraft traditions with a distinctly modern flair. Available at Gaysorn (p133).

in the local fashion industry. Start chronologically with Fly Now and Senada Theory, and then visit the young fabric wizards, like the boudoir-inspired flounces of Stretis and a little bit of everything at Fashion Society, an umbrella store for smaller domestic labels.

Stores on the 3rd floor offer the same level of sophistication for your home. The open-air D&O Shop is the first retail venture of an organisation created to encourage awareness of Thai design abroad. Triphum has mock Sukhothai-era ceramics, lacquerware scripture chests and other high-quality Asian reproductions.

MAHBOONKRONG (MBK)

Map pp98–9   Shopping Centre

☎ 0 2620 9111; www.mbk-center.com; cnr Th Phra Ram I & Th Phayathai, Siam Sq; ⏱ 10am-10pm; ⓡ National Stadium

This unbelievably immense shopping mall is quickly becoming one of Bangkok's top attractions. Half of the city filters through the glass doors on weekends, stutter-stepping on the escalators, stuffing themselves with junk food or making stabs at individualism by accessorising their mundane school uniforms with high slits or torturous heels. You can buy everything you need here: cellphones, accessories, shoes, name brands, wallets, handbags, T-shirts. The middle-class Tokyu department store also sells good-quality kitchenware.

The 4th floor resembles something of a digital produce market. A confusing maze of stalls sell all the components to send you into the land of cellular – a new phone, a new number and a SIM card. Even if you'd rather keep yourself out of reach, do a walk through to observe the chaos and the mania over phone numbers. Computer print-outs displaying all the available numbers for sale turn the phone numbers game into a commodities market. The luckier the phone number, the higher the price; upwards of thousands of dollars have been paid for numbers composed entirely of nines, considered lucky in honour of the current king, Rama IX, and because the Thai word for 'nine' is similar to the word for 'progress'.

MBK is also one of the more convenient one-stop shopping destinations for photo equipment. Foto File, on the ground floor, has a good selection of used gear, although be sure to inspect the quality closely. The shop's sister venture, Photo Thailand, stocks all manner of new photo-related gear on the 3rd floor. Sunny Camera on the 3rd floor contains shelves of gleaming new Nikon and Mamiya equipment.

PROMENADE ARCADE

Map pp98–9   Shopping Centre

Nai Lert Park, Th Withayu, Ploenchit; ⏱ 10am-6pm; khlong taxi Tha Withayu, ⓡ Ploenchit

A low-key but noteworthy stop, Promenade Arcade shelters several of Bangkok's influential décor designers. On the 2nd floor, Gub features the creations of ML Chiratorn Chirapravati and Kongpat Sakdapitak; the pair, along with other like-minded designers, have created a bright, irreverent world of lamps, chandeliers and paintings, and their showroom is like a thrift store on acid. Sakul Intakul, the acclaimed floral designer, displays his flower vessels (that's a 'vase', kiddo) that bring couture to home arrangements. His floral sculptures can also be seen in the Sukhothai Hotel (p215).

SIAM CENTER & SIAM DISCOVERY CENTER Map pp98–9 Shopping Centre
Cnr Th Phra Ram I & Th Phayathai, Siam Sq; 10am-10pm; National Stadium & Siam

These linked shopping malls are surprisingly subdued, almost comatose compared with frenetic MBK. Thailand's first shopping centre, Siam Center was built in 1976 but, since a recent nip and tuck, hardly shows its age. Its 3rd floor is one of the best locations to check out local labels such as Fly Now, Senada Theory and Tango.

In the attached Siam Discovery Center, the 4th floor continues to be a primary outpost for the Thai design scene. Panta creates modern furnishings and *objets d'art* out of uniquely Asian materials, such as water hyacinth and bamboo. Bangkok-based French designer Gilles Caffier and his store, 2 Gilles Caffier, sells hand-beaded vases, palm-wood chopsticks and other Asian-esque decorative objects that have landed his designs in Alain Ducasse's restaurant. Nearby is a huge branch of Asia Books, which carries a wide selection of design magazines, Thailand fiction titles, and new guidebooks.

Upstairs, Doi Tung-Mae Fah Luang is a royally funded crafts shop selling handmade cotton and linen from villages formerly involved with poppy production. Check out the beautiful handmade rugs. The only Southeast Asian branch of Habitat, the European décor outlet, is also located on this floor.

DO THE WALK

Bangkokians generally avoid walking as a matter of course, shopping being the main exception to this. In an effort to link the various megamalls in the Siam/Chitlom area, the Sky Walk, an elevated walkway linking Siam and Chitlom BTS stations, was completed in 2006. Now it's possible to walk from Siam Paragon to Central World, Erawan Bangkok and Gaysorn Plaza without having to descend to the commonalities of street level. We're wondering when the moving walkway will be installed.

Siam Discovery Center is also, somewhat incongruously, one of the best places in town to stock up on camping gear. Within tent-pitching distance of each other on the 3rd floor are Pro Cam-Fis, Equinox Shop, Rockcamp Climbing Shop and the North Face.

SIAM PARAGON Map pp98–9 Shopping Centre
0 2690 1000; www.siamparagon.co.th; 991/1 Th Phra Ram I, Siam Sq; 10am-10pm; Siam

Paragon epitomises the city's fanaticism for the new, the excessive, and absurd slogans. The 'peerless' venue is the largest mall in Southeast Asia, sprawling over 500,000 sq metres, and is a showcase for luxury retailers, like Van Cleef & Arpels and Mikimoto, who had not previously had a pedestal in the country. There's a Lamborghini dealer on the 2nd floor should you need a ride home, and one floor up a True Urban Park 'lifestyle centre' featuring a café, internet access and a shop selling books, music and camera equipment. Bookworms will fancy Kinokuniya (3rd fl), the largest bookstore in Thailand, as well as an expansive branch of Asia Books (2nd fl).

Even more audacious than the retail sections are Siam Ocean World (p101), a spectacular aquarium and an IMAX theatre. Whew.

SIAM SQUARE Map pp98–9 Shopping Centre
Th Phra Ram I, near Th Phayathai, Siam Sq; 11am-9pm; Siam

It doesn't look like much, just an ageing open-air shopping area divided into 12 *soi* (lanes), but Siam Sq is ground zero for teenage culture. Pop music blares out of tinny speakers, and gangs of hipsters in various costumes ricochet between fast-food restaurants and closet-sized boutiques. DJ Siam (Soi 4) carries all the Thai indie (like Modern Dog) and T-pop albums you'll need to speak 'teen'. Small shops peddle pop-hip styles along Soi 2 and Soi 3, but most outfits require a barely-there waist. Centerpoint (Soi 7) plugs in on weekends with concerts from the latest bands, b-boys (breakdancers) and perky models. And intertwined are fast-food joints, sweets, snacks and drinks.

NARAYANA PHAND Map pp98–9 Souvenirs
0 2309 5800; 1st fl, Pratunam Center, Cnr Th Phetburi & Th Ratchaprarop, Pratunam; 10am-8pm; Chitlom

Souvenir-quality handicrafts are given fixed prices and comfortable air-conditioning at this government-run facility. You won't find anything here that you haven't already seen at all of the tourist street markets, but it is a good stop if you're pressed for time or spooked by haggling.

MARCO TAILORS Map pp98–9   Tailor
☎ 0 2251 7633; 430/33 Soi 7, Siam Sq; ☽ 10am-5pm Mon-Fri; ▣ Siam
Dealing solely in men's suits, this long-standing and reliable tailor has a wide selection of banker-sensibility wools and cottons. Marco requires at least two weeks and two fittings.

RIVERSIDE, SILOM & LUMPHINI

Those looking for a painting by a contemporary Burmese artist, or an Ayuthaya era Buddhist manuscript cabinet will undoubtedly find something interesting in this part of town. Considering the prices, much of what's on sale in this area is better for browsing than buying. However, if petty issues such as budget or luggage weight restrictions aren't obstacles, you're sure to find a shiny new toy at one of the numerous antique shops and art galleries.

HOUSE OF CHAO Map pp108–9   Antiques
☎ 0 2635 7188; 9/1 Th Decho, Silom; ☽ 9am-7pm; ▣ Chong Nonsi, 🚍 air-con 504, 514, 544 & 547, ordinary 15, 76, 115, 162, 163 & 164
This three-storey antique shop, housed, appropriately, in an antique house, has everything necessary to deck out your fantasy colonial-era mansion. Particularly interesting are the various weatherworn doors, doorways, gateways and trellises that can be found in the covered area behind the showroom.

ORCHID PRESS Map pp108–9   Books
☎ 0 2231 3300; www.orchidbooks.com; 4th fl, Silom Complex, 191 Th Silom; ☽ 10am-8pm; ▣ Sala Daeng, Ⓜ Silom
The venerable Asiana publisher Orchid Press now has a Bangkok showroom. Titles span the region from academic to glossy art books, as well as a few out of print or rare titles.

NIKS/NAVA IMPORT EXPORT
Map pp108–9   Cameras
☎ 0 2235 2929; www.niksthailand.com; 166 Th Silom; ☽ 11am-4pm Mon-Fri; ▣ Chong Nonsi,

🚍 air-con 504, 514, 544 & 547, ordinary 15, 76, 115, 162, 163 & 164
On the northwest corner of Soi 12, Thailand's biggest camera importer sells all types of professional equipment, including Nikon, Mamiya and Rollei. It's also the best place to bring your sick Nikon for a check-up.

SUNNY CAMERA Map pp108–9   Cameras
☎ 0 2236 8365; 144/23 Th Silom; ☽ 10am-6pm Mon-Sat; ▣ Chong Nonsi
Dedicated Nikon-heads should head directly to Sunny Camera to satisfy their gear addiction. There are other branches on the 3rd floor of MBK (☎ 0 2620 9293) and on Th Charoen Krung (☎ 0 2235 2123; 1267-1267/1 Th Charoen Krung).

TAMNAN MINGMUANG
Map pp108–9   Handicrafts
☎ 0 2231 2120; 3rd fl, Thaniya Plaza, Th Silom; ☽ 11am-8pm; ▣ Sala Daeng, Ⓜ Silom
As soon as you step through the doors of this museumlike shop, the earthy smell of dried grass and stained wood rush to meet you. Rattan, *yan lipao* (a fern-like vine), water hyacinth woven into silk-like patterns, and coconut shells carved into delicate bowls are among the exquisite pieces that will outlast flashier souvenirs available on the streets.

THAI HOME INDUSTRIES
Map pp108–9   Handicrafts
☎ 0 2234 1736; 35 Soi Oriental, Th Charoen Krung, Riverside; ☽ 9am-6.30pm Mon-Sat; 🚍 ordinary 35, 36, 75 & 93, ⚓ Tha Oriental
A visit to this templelike building, a former monks' quarters, is like discovering an abandoned attic of Asian booty. On a recent visit, the display cases absentmindedly held cotton farmer shirts, handsome stainless-steel flatware, and delicate mother-of-pearl spoons. Despite the odd assortment of items and lack of order (not to mention the dust), it's heaps more fun than the typically faceless Bangkok handicraft shop.

CHIANG HENG Map pp108–9   Kitchen Supplies
☎ 0 2234 7237; 1466 Th Charoen Krung, Riverside; ☽ 10.30am-7pm; ▣ Saphan Taksin
In need of a handmade stainless-steel wok, old-school enamel-coated crockery, or a manually operated coconut milk strainer? Then we suggest you stop by this third-generation family-run kitchen supply store.

EXTREME WINDOW SHOPPING

Having trouble working the 20B entrance fee for the National Museum into your daily budget? Not a problem: a visit to the Silom area's numerous antique shops and galleries is a poor person's alternative to a trip to the museum.

Beginning at River City (below), accessible via a free boat from Tha Sathon pier, head directly to the antique shops on the 3rd and 4th floors, bearing in mind that in this 'museum' if you break it, you buy it. Exiting along Soi 30, stop by the various antique shops, keeping your eye open for things you'll buy when you win the lottery. Upon reaching Th Charoen Krung, continue until Soi 38 and stop by OP (Oriental Plaza) Place (Map pp108–9; ☎ 0 2266 0186; 30/1 Soi Oriental; 🕙 10.30am-7pm), an upmarket antique mall, and Thai Home Industries (opposite), an atmospheric handicraft shop where, if you're willing to forfeit lunch, you might actually be able to afford something.

Continuing until Th Silom, cross the road and enter Silom Galleria (p138) and check out the posters in the lobby to see what free exhibitions of contemporary Asian art are on. Crossing Th Silom, enter Th Decho and stop by House of Chao (opposite), where you can convince yourself that it really is the size, rather than the price, that's keeping you from buying that beautiful antique teak doorway.

Even if your cabinets are already stocked, a visit here is a glance into the type of specialised, cramped but atmospheric shops that have all but disappeared from Bangkok.

PATPONG NIGHT MARKET
Map pp108–9　　　　Outdoor Market
Soi Patpong 1 & Soi Patpong 2, Th Silom; 🕙 6pm-midnight; 🚉 Sala Daeng, Ⓜ Silom
You'll be faced with the competing distractions of strip-clubbing or shopping on this infamous street. And true to the area's illicit leanings, pirated goods (in particular watches) make a prominent appearance even amid a wholesome crowd of families and straight-laced couples. Bargain with determination, as first-quoted prices tend to be astronomically high.

SOI LALAI SAP Map pp108–9　Outdoor Market
Soi 5, Th Silom; 🕙 9am-8pm; 🚉 Sala Daeng, Ⓜ Silom
The ideal place to buy an authentic Thai secretary's uniform, this 'money-dissolving soi' has mobs of vendors selling insanely cheap but frumpy clothing, as well as heaps of snacks and housewares.

SUAN LUM NIGHT BAZAAR
Map p112　　　　Outdoor Market
Cnr Th Withayu & Th Rama IV, Silom; 🕙 6pm-midnight; Ⓜ Lumphini
Like Chatuchak without the hot weather and crowds, the Night Bazaar specialises in modern Thai souvenirs, clothes and handicrafts. Highlights among the 3700 stalls include handmade jewellery, one-of-a kind designer T-shirts and a unique furniture and home décor section. If you can find it,

Nancy Chandler's map (p128) outlines interesting shopping at the bazaar. If shopping's not your idea of fun, the central outdoor beer garden is the perfect place to nurse an imported beer while the family is hunting for gifts.

At the time of writing, the bazaar is scheduled to be replaced by, surprise, surprise, a megamall in late 2008, but don't hold your breath – we certainly aren't.

BAAN SILOM Map pp108–9　Shopping Centre
Cnr Soi 19, Th Silom; 🕙 10.30am-7pm; 🚌 air-con 504, 514, 544 & 547, ordinary 15, 76, 115, 162, 163 & 164, 🚉 Surasak
This open-air colonial-style shopping centre is the art-school kid brother of Bangkok malls. Changing exhibitions of contemporary art can be taken in at La Lanta Fine Art, and ultra-funky Thai-designed necklaces, rings and bracelets are available at Kit-Ti's Jewellery. Art and design books are available at a branch of B2S.

RIVER CITY Map pp108–9　Shopping Centre
☎ 0 2237 0077; www.rivercity.co.th; 23 Th Yotha, off Th Charoen Krung, Riverside; 🕙 10am-9pm; 🚌 ordinary 35, 36, 75 & 93, ⚓ Tha Si Phraya
Near the Royal Orchid Sheraton, this multistorey centre is an all-in-one stop for old-world Asiana, much of it too large to fit in the bag of most travellers. Several high-quality art and antique shops occupy the 3rd and 4th floors, including the Verandah, which deals in 'tribal' art from Borneo and abroad, and Hong Antiques, with 50 years of experience in decorative pieces. Acala is a gallery of unusual Tibetan and Chinese artefacts. And Old Maps & Prints proffers one of the best selections of one-of-a-kind,

rare maps and illustrations. As with many antique stores in Bangkok, the vast majority of pieces at River City appear to come from Myanmar (Burma). Many shops are closed on Sunday.

SILOM GALLERIA
Map pp108–9   Shopping Centre
☎ 0 2630 0944; Soi 19, Th Silom; ☺ 10am-8pm; ☒ air-con 504, 514, 544 & 547, ordinary 15, 76, 115, 162, 163 & 164, ☒ Surasak
The only reason to visit this spooky half-deserted mall is for the contemporary Asian art exhibitions hosted by the various galleries inside. To avoid disappointment proceed directly to the back, or alternatively, check the posters in the lobby to see what's on display at the better galleries such as Thavibu (p193) or Tang (p193).

JIM THOMPSON Map pp108–9   Thai Silk
☎ 0 2632 8100; www.jimthompson.com; 9 Th Surawong, Silom; ☺ 9am-6pm; ☒ Sala Daeng, Ⓜ Silom
The surviving business of the international promoter of Thai silk, the largest Jim Thompson shop sells colourful silk handkerchiefs, placemats, wraps and cushions. The styles and motifs appeal to older, somewhat more conservative tastes. There are also branches at Jim Thompson's House museum (p97), the Emporium (right), and at a Factory Outlet (☎ 0 2235 8931; 149/4-6 Th Surawong), just up the road, which sells discontinued patterns at a significant discount.

THANON SUKHUMVIT
Supplies for the recently arrived expat can be found in the shops that line never-ending Th Sukhumvit. Furniture, clothes and household knick-knacks hang out on upper Sukhumvit, while tourist souvenirs are centred around Soi 11. Reputable tailors have low-key presences in this neighbourhood, and Th Thong Lor is home to several of the city's 'lifestyle' malls.

L'ARCADIA Map pp118–19   Antiques
☎ 0 2259 9595; 12/2 Soi 23, Th Sukhumvit; ☺ 9am-10pm; ☒ Asoke
The buyer at L'Arcadia has a sharp eye for collectables from Myanmar, Cambodia and Thailand, including cute red-lacquer containers, Khmer-style sandstone figures and carved wooden temple decorations. If you

simply can't resist that colonial-era lounge chair, the shop can also arrange to have it shipped home for you.

NANDAKWANG Map pp118–19   Handicrafts
☎ 0 2258 1962; www.nandakwang.com; 108/2-3 Soi 23 (Soi Prasanmit), Th Sukhumvit; ☺ 9am-6pm Mon-Sat & 10am-5pm Sun; ☒ Asoke, Ⓜ Sukhumvit
A Bangkok satellite of a Chiang Mai–based store, Nandakwang sells a fun and handsome mix of cloth, wood and glass products. The cheery hand-embroidered pillows and bags are particularly attractive. There is also a branch on the 3rd floor of Siam Discovery Center (p135).

THANON SUKHUMVIT MARKET
Map pp118–19   Outdoor Market
Th Sukhumvit, Soi 3 & Soi 15; ☺ 11am-11pm; ☒ Nana
Leaving on the first flight out tomorrow morning? Never fear about gifts for those back home; the street vendors will find you with faux Fendi handbags, soccer kits, 'art', sunglasses and jewellery, to name a few. You'll also find stacks of nudie DVDs, Chinese throwing stars, penis-shaped lighters and other questionable gifts for your high-school-aged brother.

EMPORIUM SHOPPING CENTRE
Map pp118–19   Shopping Centre
☎ 0 2269 1000; www.emporiumthailand.com; 622 Th Sukhumvit, cnr Soi 24; ☺ 10am-10pm; ☒ Phrom Phong
Once Bangkok's most chi-chi shopping centre, Emporium is finally starting to show its age in comparison to its hipper and younger siblings, Siam Paragon and the recently remodelled Central World.

The ground floor is filled with Euro fashion labels, like Prada, Miu Miu and Chanel. The 2nd floor is more casual, with homegrown contenders, such as Soda, which has snipped punk into haute wear, and imagemaker Greyhound. Staid Jim Thompson even gets a face-lift with its branch here. On the 3rd floor, indigenous kitschy-cool gifts and home décor can be found at Propaganda.

Even more impressive than the resident fashionistas is the Thailand Creative & Design Centre (☎ 0 2664 8448; www.tcdc.or.th; 6th fl) a design museum with an attached gift shop selling cool souvenirs related to the various exhibits, and a design library.

SHOPPING THANON SUKHUMVIT

BONDING WITH BOOKS

For new books and magazines, Asia Books, B2S and Bookazine have extensive selections and several branches throughout the city.

Asia Books

Central World Plaza (Map pp98–9; ☎ 0 2255 6209; 6th fl, Th Ratchadamri, Siam Sq)

Emporium Shopping Centre (Map pp118–19; ☎ 0 2664 8545; 3rd fl, cnr Soi 24, Th Sukhumvit)

Peninsula Plaza (Map pp98–9; ☎ 0 2253 9786; 2nd fl, Th Ratchadamri, Ploenchit)

Siam Discovery Center (Map pp98–9; ☎ 0 2658 0418; 4th fl, Th Phra Ram I, Siam Sq)

Siam Paragon (Map pp98–9; ☎ 0 2610 9609; 2nd fl, Th Phra Ram I, Siam Sq)

Thaniya Plaza (Map pp108–9; ☎ 0 2231 2106; 3rd fl, Soi Thaniya, 52 Th Silom)

Thanon Sukhumvit (Map pp118–19; ☎ 0 2651 0428; 221 Th Sukhumvit btwn Soi 15 & Soi 17)

Times Sq (Map pp118–19; ☎ 0 2250 0162; 2nd fl, Times Sq, 221 Th Sukhumvit btwn Soi 12 & Soi 14)

B2S

Baan Silom (Map pp108–9; ☎ 0 2684 1527; cnr Soi 19, Th Silom, Silom)

Central Chidlom (Map pp98–9; ☎ 0 2947 5566; 7th fl, 1027 Th Ploenchit, Ploenchit)

Central World Plaza (Map pp98–9; ☎ 0 2646 1270; levels 1-3, Th Ratchadamri, Siam Sq)

Bookazine

Chitlom (Bargain Outlet) (Map pp98–9; ☎ 0 2256 9304; 3rd fl, Amarin Plaza, 496-502 Th Ploenchit)

Gaysorn Plaza (Map pp98–9; ☎ 0 2656 1039; cnr Th Ploenchit & Th Ratchadamri)

La Villa (Map pp124–5; ☎ 0 2613 0558; 2nd fl, La Villa, 356 Th Phaholyotin, Greater Bangkok)

Patpong (Map pp108–9; ☎ 0 2231 0016; 1st fl, CP Tower, 313 Th Silom)

Siam Sq (Map pp98–9; ☎ 0 2255 3778; 286 Th Phra Ram I, btwn Soi 3 & Soi 4) Opposite Siam Center.

Silom Complex (Map pp108–9; ☎ 0 2231 3135; 2nd fl, cnr Th Silom & Th Phra Ram IV)

Thanon Sukhumvit (Map pp118–19; ☎ 0 2655 2383; Nailert Bldg, north side btwn Soi 3 & Soi 5, Ploenchit)

Wireless (Map pp98–9; ☎ 0 2685 3863; 2nd fl, All Seasons Pl, 87 Th Withayu, Ploenchit)

New titles are also available at Kinokuniya at Emporium (opposite) and Siam Paragon (p135).

Art books can be found at Basheer (Map pp118–19; ☎ 0 2391 9815; www.basheergraphic.com; H1, 998 Soi 55, Th Sukhumvit; 🚇 Thong Lo) and Rim Khob Fah (p131). Politicos should trot over to Suksit Siam (see p131).

Used titles are easy to find in Banglamphu (see p131), but are rare elsewhere. If you're tied to New Bangkok, try Elite Used Books (Map pp118–19; ☎ 0 2258 0221; 593/5 Soi 33/1, Th Sukhumvit; 🚇 Phrom Phong) or Dasa Book Café (Map pp118–19; ☎ 0 2661 2993; btwn Soi 26 & 28, Th Sukhumvit).

GREATER BANGKOK

Markets really capture the hubbub of Bangkok and the real reason to visit the 'burbs is the world famous Chatuchak Weekend Market (p140).

ÁMANTEE Map pp124–5   Antiques/Art
☎ 0 2982 8694; www.amantee.com; 131/3 Soi 13, Th Chaeng Wattana, Greater Bangkok; ⏰ 9am-8pm; taxi from 🚇 Mor Chit

Although well outside of the city centre, this 'repository of Oriental and Tibetan art and antiques' is well worth the trip. Consisting of several interconnecting wooden Thai houses holding a variety of classy items, the peaceful compound also boasts a café (⏰ 9am-5pm), accommodation and occasional cultural events.

A Thai-language map for taxi drivers can be downloaded from the website.

lonelyplanet.com

KING POWER Map pp52–3 Duty Free

☎ 0 2677 8899; www.kingpower.com; 8 Th Rang Nam, Ratchathewi; ⏰ 10am-9pm; 🚇 Victory Monument

Towering over leafy Soi Rang Nam, this 'sensory extravaganza' has taken duty-free shopping from the airport to the streets of suburban Bangkok. The selection and prices are the same as that of the airport, but occasional discounts and promotions can make it worth the trek. Featuring the largest watch centre in Southeast Asia, the ultramodern complex also includes a hotel, buffet restaurant and, at the King Power Theater, a branch of the Traditional Thai Puppet Theatre (see p189).

To make duty-free purchases here, bring your passport and flight information and register at the lobby. Purchases of domestic goods can be taken away the same day, while imported goods are picked up at the airport on your day of departure.

King Power even offers a pick-up service (☎ 0 2205 8888; ⏰ 10am-7pm) to and from hotels in the centre of the city.

CHATUCHAK WEEKEND MARKET

Map pp124–5 Market

Th Phahonyothin, Greater Bangkok; ⏰ 9am-6pm Sat & Sun; 🚇 Mo Chit, Ⓜ Kamphaeng Phet

Imagine if all the city's markets, with their green shade umbrellas and narrow walkways, were fused together in one great big market-style concentration camp. Now add in a little artistic flair, a climate like a sauna, the energy of bargaining crowds and you've got a rough sketch of Chatuchak (also spelled 'Jatujak' or nicknamed 'JJ'). More than 15,000 stalls cater to hundreds of thousands of visitors during the two days of the week when the market is in full operation (on other days, only certain portions are open).

Everything is sold here, from live chickens and snakes to vintage fans and *măw lam* CDs. Once you're deep in the bowels, it will seem like there is no order and no escape, but Chatuchak is arranged into sections: crafts, clothing, plants, pets, etc. Nancy Chandler's map (p128) has a handy breakdown and there are posted maps within the complex. An information centre and several ATMs with foreign-exchange booths are located near the Chatuchak Park offices, towards the northern end of the market's Soi 1, Soi 2 and Soi 3. Come

early to beat the heat and the crowds and watch your valuables carefully as sticky fingers love JJ too.

Clothing dominates most of the market, starting in Section 8 and continuing through the even-numbered sections to 24. Stalls sell the usual ethnic garb, army surplus, and other modest and immodest duds. In section 5, funky secondhand clothes get a minor role, selling grease-monkey work shirts with sewn-on name labels, so that Matthews can become Leroys. Tourist-sized clothes and textiles are in Sections 10 and 8.

In years past, Chatuchak was more of a working-class market, selling housewares and gravel. But as Bangkok becomes more self-assured, the weekend market has moved more towards boutique. Young designers and artists cut their teeth in these little stalls hoping to graduate to a more permanent space. Section 7 is becoming an arty bastion with little galleries and knick-knack stalls. More-traditional arts and crafts, like musical instruments, hill-tribe crafts, religious amulets and antiques, hang out in Sections 25 and 26. Sections 2 and 3, currently Chatuchak's most valuable real estate, have a variety of shops selling original décor items and trendy clothing.

Across from the southern side of the market on Th Kampaengphet 2 is a strip of stores selling traditional wood furniture, vintage fans and phonographs and other treasures of yore. Keep an eye out for water-hyacinth rugs, every apartment-dweller's dream accent.

Lots of Thai-style eating and snacking will stave off Chatuchak rage (cranky behaviour brought on by dehydration or hunger). Numerous food stalls set up between Sections 6 and 8, and particularly enticing are Foon Talop (Section 26, Soi 1), an incredibly popular Isan restaurant, and Café Ice (Section 7, Soi 3), a Western-Thai fusion joint with tasty fruit shakes. As evening draws near, down a beer at Viva's (Section 26, Soi 1), a café-bar that features live music and stays open late, or cross Th Kamphaengphet 2 to the cosy whisky bars that keep nocturnal hours.

Or Tor Kor Market (p171) sets up opposite the south side of Chatuchak Weekend Market, selling an amazing array of fruits and prepared foods.

Considering the current obsession with malls in Bangkok, it was really only a matter of time before JJ Mall, an air-conditioned

SHOPPING GREATER BANGKOK

Chatuchak wannabe, opened directly north of the market in 2007. A sanitised version of the real thing; its generous air-conditioning is the only justification we can find for making the trudge over.

VESPA MARKET Map pp124–5   Outdoor Market
Cnr Th Rachadaphisek & Th Lat Phrao, Greater Bangkok; ✆ **6-11pm Sat;** Ⓜ **Lad Phrao**

Uniting urban cowboys, hip-hoppers, wannabe mods and pissed-off punks, this expansive outdoor market is a virtual melting pot of Bangkok youth subculture. The original emphasis was on vehicles, and you can still find heaps of vintage Vespas and Lambrettas, Volkswagens and Austin Minis for sale or show betwixt quirky T-shirts, used sneakers and modern antiques.

top picks

- **Chote Chitr** (p155) Thai
- **Cy'an** (p161) International
- **Face** (p166) Thai and Indian
- **Gianni Ristorante** (boxed text, p160) Italian

EATING

HISTORY & CULTURE

In Thailand, food is culture, and vice versa. Appreciation of the national cuisine is so central to their cultural identity that Thais often assume that foreigners are unable to partake in it unless they have been trained in the difficult art of feeling exhilarated over a bowl of well-prepared *kǔaytǐaw* (noodle soup). You will not be asked simply whether you like to eat Thai food, but *'Kin aahǎan thai pen mái?'* ('Do you know how to eat Thai food?').

Nowhere else is this reverence for food more evident than in Bangkok. The city's characteristic odour is a unique blend of noodle stalls and car exhaust, and in certain parts of town, restaurants appear to form the majority of businesses, often flanked by streetside hawker stalls and mobile snack vendors. To the outsider, the life of an average Bangkokian can appear to be little more than a string of meals and snacks punctuated by the odd stab at work, not the other way around. If you can adjust your gutteral clock to fit this schedule, we're confident your stay in Bangkok will be a delicious one indeed.

Just about every regional Thai cooking style is available in Bangkok, although much like the region's language and culture, central Thai cooking has come to be regarded as the mainstream of Thai cuisine. Thus, central Thai-style dishes such as *tôm yam* or *kaeng khǐaw wǎan* (green curry) can be found across the country – and nowadays even across the globe. This school of cooking is characterised by a fondness for sweet flavours, ample use of coconut cream, a palpable Chinese influence, and an emphasis on presentation, possibly the result of the 'royal' cuisine of the capital's palaces.

Other regional Thai cuisines have also helped to shape Bangkok's culinary landscape. Due to the massive influx of migrant labourers, taxi drivers and prostitutes from the poorer northeast, there are quite possibly more Isan (northeastern Thai) eateries in Bangkok than in the entire northeast. As a result, *sôm-tam* (papaya salad) – essentially a Lao dish – is arguably the most popular and ubiquitous snack in Bangkok. The city's southern Thai community largely resides along the ultra-urban stretch of road known as Th Ramkhamhaeng, where one can find bright-yellow curries and authentic Thai-Muslim eateries.

Particularly associated with the Bangkok style of cooking are the various Thai-Chinese amalgams, especially those employing noodles such as *phàt thai, kǔaytǐaw yen taa fo* and *phàt sii-íw*. With well over 25% of the population claiming Chinese ancestry, it comes as no surprise that Chinese is the probably the biggest influence on the Bangkok kitchen. Although Chinese traders had lived along Chao Phraya's riverbanks for hundreds of years, during the royal capital's late-18th-century

MUITO OBRIGADO

Try to imagine a Thai curry without the chillies, *phàt thai* without the peanuts, or papaya salad without the papaya. Many of the ingredients used on a daily basis by Thais are in fact relatively recent introductions, courtesy of European traders and missionaries. During the early 16th century, while Spanish and Portuguese explorers were first reaching the shores of Southeast Asia, expansion and discovery was taking place in the Americas. The Portuguese in particular were quick to seize the exciting new products coming from the New World and market them in the East, thus introducing modern-day Asian staples such as tomatoes, potatoes, corn, lettuce, cabbage, chillies, papaya, guava, pineapples, pumpkins, sweet potatoes, peanuts and tobacco.

Chillies in particular seem to have struck a chord with Thais, and are thought to have first arrived in Ayuthaya via the Portuguese around 1550. Before their arrival, the natives got their heat from bitter-hot herbs and roots such as ginger and pepper.

And not only did the Portuguese introduce some crucial ingredients, but also some enduring cooking techniques, particularly in the area of sweets. The bright-yellow duck egg and syrup-based treats you see at many Thai markets are direct descents of Portuguese desserts known as *fios de ovos* ('egg threads') and *ovos moles*. And in the area surrounding Bangkok's Church of Santa Cruz (p82), a former Portuguese enclave, you can still find *khànǒm faràng*, a bun-like snack baked over coals.

shift from Ayuthaya to Bangkok the Chinese were moved to a single area of town known as Sampeng or Yaowarat—the city's Chinatown. Today this is still the best area to find authentic Chinese food, as well as delicious Thai-Chinese dishes. Since most Chinese immigrants trace their ancestry back to southern China, you'll mainly find southern Chinese cooking styles including Cantonese, Teo Chew and Hokkien.

The Phahurat district is home to much of Bangkok's Indian community. A stroll down Th Chakraphet will bring you nose to nose with a rich variety of Indian tea shops, Punjabi sweets vendors, samosa carts and tiny restaurants serving cuisines from nearly every region of northern India.

In recent decades, other cuisines have also taken a foothold in the city. Th Sukhumvit's Soi 3, known as Nana, began attracting a heavy concentration of residents and visitors from Middle Eastern and North African countries in the 1970s. The number of restaurants and food vendors along Soi 3 and adjacent smaller *soi* (lanes) continues to multiply and today there are dozens of different Middle Eastern food venues in the neighbourhood.

Elsewhere, a slight French accent can be detected along the leafy boulevard of Th Convent, off Th Silom, where you'll find open-air cafés, a French bakery and butcher, as well as a wine shop and a French restaurant. An even more established Japanese enclave can be found at Th Sukhumvit, across from the Emporium shopping centre, and at the corner of Th Sukhumvit Soi 12 there is a multistorey shopping mall colloquially known as 'Korea Town'. Although the contributions of these latter cuisines to the indigenous central Thai kitchen are negligible, they are the latest culinary additions to a city that has been readily accepting foreign food cultures since its birth.

ETIQUETTE

While Thai table manners would hardly ever be described as 'formal' in the Western sense, there are plenty of subtleties to be mastered, and using the correct utensils and eating gestures will garner much respect from Thais.

Originally Thai food was eaten with the fingers, and it still is in certain regions. In the early 1900s Thais began setting their tables with fork and spoon to affect a 'royal' setting, and it wasn't long before fork-and-spoon dining became the norm in Bangkok and later

lonelyplanet.com

THE RIGHT TOOL FOR THE JOB

If you're not offered chopsticks, don't ask for them. Thai food is eaten with fork and spoon, not chopsticks. When *faràng* (Westerners) ask for chopsticks to eat Thai food, it only puzzles the restaurant proprietors.

Chopsticks are reserved for eating Chinese-style food from bowls, or for eating in all-Chinese restaurants. In either case you will be supplied with chopsticks without having to ask. Unlike their counterparts in many Western countries, restaurateurs in Thailand won't assume you don't know how to use them.

spread throughout the kingdom. Some foods, such as *khâo nǐaw* (sticky rice), are eaten by hand everywhere.

The *sâwm* (fork) and *cháwn* (spoon) are placed to the left of the plate, and usually wrapped in a paper or cloth napkin. In simpler restaurants, these utensils are laid bare on the table or may not arrive until the food is served. Some restaurants place a supply of clean forks and spoons in a steel or glass container on each table.

To use these tools the Thai way, use a spoon to take a single mouthful of food from a central dish, and ladle it over a portion of your rice. Then use the fork to push the portion back onto the spoon, with which you place the food in your mouth.

Tàkìap (chopsticks) are reserved for dining in Chinese restaurants or for eating Chinese noodle dishes (see above). Noodle soups are eaten with a spoon in the left hand (for spooning up the broth) and chopsticks in the right.

Whether at home or in a restaurant, Thai meals are always served 'family style', that is, from common serving platters. Traditionally, the party orders one of each kind of dish, perhaps a curry, a fish, a stir-fry, a *yam* (hot and tangy salad), a vegetable dish and a soup, taking care to balance cool and hot, sour and sweet, salty and plain. One dish is generally large enough for two people. One or two extras may be ordered for a large party.

Dishes are usually served more or less all at once rather than in courses. If the host or restaurant staff can't bring them all to the table at the same time, then the diners typically wait until everything has arrived before digging in. One exception to this rule is if a *yam* or other *kàp klâem* is ordered: these are sometimes served as an appetiser with drinks before the main meal. When these dishes come out with everything else they will be eaten first.

THE CULT OF SÔM-TAM

Pounded green papaya salad, known in Thai as *sôm-tam*, probably has its origins in Laos, but is today one of the most popular dishes in Bangkok. It is made by taking strips of green unripe papaya and bruising them in a clay or wood mortar along with garlic, palm sugar, green beans, tomatoes, lime juice, fish sauce and a typically shock-inducing amount of fresh chillies. *Sôm-tam laao*, the 'original' version of the dish, employs heartier chunks of papaya, sliced eggplants, salted field crabs, and a thick unpasteurised fish sauce known as *plaa rôa*. Far more common in Bangkok is *sôm-tam thai*, which includes dried shrimp and peanuts, and is seasoned with bottled fish sauce. Almost always made by women, *sôm-tam* is also primarily also enjoyed by women, often as a snack rather than an entire meal – the intense spiciness provides a satisfying mental 'full'.

Thais aren't fussy about dishes being served piping hot, so no-one minds if the dishes sit untouched for a while. The one exception to the cooling rule is noodle dishes, which are typically consumed immediately.

Empty plates are placed in front of every person at the beginning of the meal, and the diners take a little from each serving platter onto these plates. When serving yourself from a common platter, put no more than one spoonful onto your plate at a time. It's customary at the start of a shared meal to eat a spoonful of plain rice first – a gesture that recognises rice as the most important part of the meal.

For the most part, *tôm yam* (chilli and lemon-grass soup) and other soups aren't served in individual bowls except in more elegant restaurants or those aimed at tourists. You serve yourself from the common bowl, spooning broth and ingredients over your rice or into your own spoon. Sometimes serving spoons are provided. If not, you simply dig in with your own spoon.

Don't pick up a platter to serve yourself. Etiquette requires that the platter stays on the tabletop: reach over to it with your spoon, even if it means stretching your arm across the table. If you can't reach, hand your plate to someone near the platter who will place some food on your plate. Most Thais will do this automatically if they notice you're out of platter range.

Thais are constantly looking out for each other at meal times – making sure no-one's plate is empty – and will usually give you more food than you can eat. Don't be surprised if another diner in your party spoons food directly onto your plate, just like your mother did when you were a child. This is a completely normal gesture in Thai dining custom and carries no particular import other than showing hospitality towards a foreign guest.

Thais want you to enjoy the food, and at some point in the meal your host or one of your dining companions will pause for a second, smile and ask, '*Àràwy maí?*' ('Is it delicious?'). The expected answer, of course, is *àràwy* (delicious) or *àràwy mâak* (very delicious).

Cigarettes often appear both before and after a meal, but it is considered impolite to smoke during a meal. Thais will often step away from the table to smoke, mainly because ashtrays aren't usually placed on dining tables. It's not customary in Thailand to ask permission to smoke before lighting up, though this is beginning to change in Bangkok society. To be on the safe side, always ask, '*Sùup bùrìi dâi mái?*' ('Is it OK to smoke?'). Note that a recent law bans smoking in any public area, bars and restaurants included.

HOW THAIS EAT

Aside from the occasional indulgence in deep-fried savouries, most Thais sustain themselves on a varied and healthy diet of many fruits, rice and vegetables mixed with smaller amounts of animal protein and fat. Satisfaction seems to come not from eating large amounts of food at any one meal, but rather from nibbling at a variety of dishes with as many different flavours as possible throughout the day.

Thais extend a hand towards a bowl of noodles, a plate of rice or a banana-leaf-wrapped snack with amazing frequency. There are no 'typical' times for meals, though in Bangkok diners tend to cluster in local restaurants at the customary noon to 1pm lunch break.

Nor are certain kinds of food restricted to certain times of day. Practically anything can be eaten first thing in the morning, whether it's sweet, salty or chilli-ridden. *Khâo kaeng* (curry over rice) is a very popular morning meal, as are *khâo nĭaw mŭu thâwt* (deep-fried pork with sticky rice) and *khâo man kài* (sliced chicken cooked in chicken broth and served over rice).

Lighter morning choices, especially for Thais of Chinese descent, include *paa thâwng kô* (deep-fried bits of dough) dipped in warm *náam tâo hûu* (soya milk). Thais also eat noodles, whether fried or in soup, with great gusto in the morning, or as a substantial snack at any time of day or night.

As the staple with which almost all Thai dishes are eaten (noodles are still seen as a Chinese import), rice *(khâo)* is considered an absolutely indispensable part of the daily diet. Most Bangkok families will put on a pot of rice, or start the rice cooker, just after rising in the morning to prepare a base for the day's menu. All other dishes, aside from noodles, are considered *kàp khâo* (side dishes) that supplement this *aahǎan làk* (staple).

Plaa (fish) finds its way into almost every meal, even if it's only in the form of *náam plaa* (a thin amber sauce made from fermented anchovies), which is used to salt Thai dishes, much as soy sauce is used in eastern Asia. Pork is undoubtedly the preferred protein, with chicken in second place. Beef is seldom eaten in Bangkok, particularly by Thais of Chinese descent who subscribe to a Buddhist teaching that forbids eating 'large' animals.

Thais are prodigious consumers of fruit. Vendors push glass-and-wood carts filled with a rainbow of fresh sliced papaya, pineapple, watermelon and mango, and a more muted palette of salt-pickled or candied seasonal fruits. These are usually served in a small plastic bag with a thin bamboo stick to use as an eating utensil.

Because many restaurants in Thailand are able to serve dishes at an only slightly higher price than they would cost to make at home, Thais dine out far more often than their Western counterparts. Any evening of the week you'll see small groups of Thais – usually males – clustered around roadside tables or in outdoor restaurants, drinking beer or rice liquor while picking from an array of common dishes, one morsel at a time. These are *kàp klâem*, dishes specifically meant to be eaten while drinking alcoholic beverages, often before an evening meal or while waiting for the larger courses to arrive. *Kàp klâem* can be as simple as a plate of *mét mámûang thâwt* (fried cashews) or as elaborate as one of the many types of *yam*, containing a blast of lime, chilli, fresh herbs and a choice of seafood, roast vegetables, noodles or meats.

Thais tend to avoid eating alone. Dining with others is always preferred because it means everyone has a chance to sample several dishes. When forced to fly solo by circumstances – such as during lunch breaks at work – a single diner usually sticks to one-plate dishes such as fried rice or curry over rice.

STAPLES & SPECIALITIES

Bangkok's central position, and more importantly its wealth relative to the rest of the country, means that spices, seasonings and produce hailing from any corner of the kingdom are easily available. Coconuts from the south, bamboo shoots from the north, *maengdaa* (water beetle) from the northeast – all find their way into Bangkok markets.

Rice

Bangkok sits right in the middle of the Mae Nam Chao Phraya delta, the country's 'rice bowl'. Although Thailand's role as the largest producer of rice was recently taken over by Vietnam, its product is still considered the best in the world. Thailand's *khâo hǎwm málí* (jasmine rice) is so coveted that there is a steady underground business in smuggling bags of the fragrant grain to neighbouring countries.

Rice is so central to Thai food culture that the most common term for 'eat' is *kin khâo* (literally 'consume rice'), and one of the most common greetings is, '*Kin khâo réu yang?*' ('Have you eaten rice yet?'). All the dishes eaten with rice – whether curries, stir-fries, soups or other food preparations – are simply classified as *kàp khâo* ('with rice' – side dishes). Only two dishes incorporating rice as a principal ingredient are common in Thailand, *khâo phàt* (fried rice) and *khâo mòk kài* (chicken biryani), neither of which is native to Thailand.

top picks

INTERNATIONAL FASHION PLATES

- Bed Supperclub (p165) Futuristic chic with top-notch international fare
- Cy'an (p161) Nouveau Mediterranean amid polished minimalism
- Eat Me (p161) Bangkok's favourite cosmo maven
- Hazara (p166) Indian 'Frontier cuisine' tamed and brought to the city
- Tapas Café (p168) Slurp your gazpacho under the gaze of the latest art exhibition.

PERK UP YOUR NOODLE

Much as chicken soup is viewed as something of a home remedy for colds in the West, rice-noodle soups in Thailand are often eaten to ward off colds, hangovers or general malaise. When you face a bowl of noodles and the array of condiments available to season them, you must be prepared to become your own pharmacist, mixing up the ingredients to create the right flavour balance.

If you see a steel rack containing four lidded glass bowls or jars on your table, it's proof that the restaurant you're in serves *kŭaytĭaw* (rice noodles). Typically these containers offer four choices: *náam sôm phrík* (sliced green chillies in white vinegar), *náam plaa* (fish sauce), *phrík pon* (dried red chilli, flaked or ground to a near powder) and *náamtaan* (plain white sugar).

In typically Thai fashion, these condiments offer three ways to make the soup hotter – hot and sour, hot and salty, and just plain hot – and one to make it sweet.

The typical noodle-eater will add a teaspoonful of each one of these condiments to the noodle soup, except for the sugar, which in sweet-tooth Bangkok usually rates a full tablespoon. Until you're used to these strong seasonings, we recommend adding them a little at a time, tasting the soup along the way to make sure you don't go overboard. Adding sugar to soup may appear strange to some foreign palates, but it does considerably enhance the flavour of *kŭaytĭaw náam*.

Cooked rice is usually referred to as *khâo sŭay* – literally 'beautiful rice', yet another clue as to how thoroughly Thais esteem this staple. When you order plain rice in a restaurant you may use this term or simply *khâo plào*, 'plain rice'. Restaurants may serve rice by the plate (*jaan*) or you can order a *thŏ* or large bowl of rice, lidded to keep it warm and moist, and notched along the rim to accommodate the handle of a rice scoop. *Thŏ* may be practical thick-sided plastic affairs or more elaborate engraved, footed aluminium bowls with fancy serving spoons to match.

In Chinese-style eateries, *khâo tôm* ('boiled rice'), a watery porridge sometimes involving brown or purple rice, is a common carb.

Noodles

Exactly when the noodle reached Thailand is difficult to say, but it probably arrived along trade routes from China, since the preparation styles in contemporary Thailand are similar to those of contemporary southern China.

You'll find four basic kinds of noodle in Bangkok. Hardly surprising, given the Thai fixation on rice, is the overwhelming popularity of *sên kŭaytĭaw*, noodles made from pure rice flour mixed with water to form a paste, which is then steamed to form wide, flat sheets. The sheets are then folded and sliced into *sên yài* (flat 'wide line' noodles 2cm to 3cm wide), *sên lék* ('small line' noodles about 5mm wide) and *sên mìi* ('noodle line' noodles only 1mm to 2mm wide). *Sên mìi* dry out so quickly that they are sold only in their dried form.

At most restaurants or vendor stands specialising in *kŭaytĭaw*, you are expected to specify which noodles you want when ordering.

The king of Thai noodles, *kŭaytĭaw* comes as part of many dishes. The simplest and most ubiquitous, simply called *kŭaytĭaw mŭu*, takes the form of noodles served in a bowl of pork stock accompanied with balls of ground pork, and perhaps a handful of mung bean sprouts. Season your noodle soup by choosing from a rack of small glass or metal containers on the table (see boxed text above).

In recent years, one of the most popular types of *kŭaytĭaw* in Bangkok has been *yen taa fo*, an intimidating-looking mixture of assorted fish balls, cubes of blood, water spinach and rice noodles in a bright-red broth. The dish is probably the biggest culinary contribution by the Teo Chew, an ethnic group originally from southern China that comprises the largest group of Chinese in Bangkok. The *yen taa fo* sold next door to the Sri Mariamman Temple (p111), the Hindu temple off Th Silom (known locally as Wát Khàek), is said to be the most authentic.

Chilli-heads must give *kŭaytĭaw phàt khîi mao* ('drunkard's fried noodles') a try. A favourite lunch or late-night snack, this spicy stir-fry consists of wide rice noodles, holy basil leaves, meat (typically seafood, but also chicken or pork), seasonings and an eye-opening dose of fresh sliced chillies and garlic. Jay Fai (p155) makes the most lauded – and most expensive *phàt khîi mao* in town.

Probably the most well-known *kŭaytĭaw* dish among foreigners is *kŭaytĭaw phàt thai*, usually called *phàt thai* for short. Taking the form of thin rice noodles stir-fried with dried or fresh shrimp, bean sprouts, tofu, egg and seasonings, the dish is traditionally served with lime halves and a few stalks of Chinese chives and a sliced banana flower. Thip Samai (p156), a nondescript shophouse restaurant in Banglamphu, is generally regarded as the best place in Bangkok to try this dish.

Two other ways to order Thai rice noodles include *kŭaytĭaw hâeng* (dry *kŭaytĭaw*) and *kŭaytĭaw râat nâa* (*kŭaytĭaw* with gravy). For *kŭaytĭaw hâeng*, rice noodles are momentarily doused in very hot water to heat them up and soften them, then tossed in a soup bowl with the usual ingredients that make up *kŭaytĭaw náam*, save the broth. *Kŭaytĭaw râat nâa* involves braising the noodles in a slightly slimy gravy made with cornstarch-thickened stock, adding meats and seasonings to taste and serving the finished product on an oval plate. A seafood version of the latter, *kŭaytĭaw râat nâa tháleh*, is one of the most popular versions in Bangkok. *Râat nâa* (or *lâat nâa*, as it's more typically pronounced in Bangkok), the shortened name for any *kŭaytĭaw râat nâa* dish, is frequently used when ordering.

Another kind of noodle, *khànŏm jiin*, is produced by pushing a fermented rice-flour paste through a sieve into boiling water, in much the same way as pasta is made. *Khànŏm jiin* is eaten topped with various curries. The most standard curry topping, *náam yaa* (herbal sauce), contains a strong dose of *kràchaay* (Chinese key), a root of the ginger family used as a traditional remedy for a number of gastrointestinal ailments, along with ground fish.

The third kind of noodle, *bà-mìi*, is made from wheat flour and sometimes egg (depending on the noodle-maker or the brand). It's yellowish in colour and is sold only in fresh bundles. After being briefly parboiled, the noodles are mixed with broth and meat, typically barbecued pork or crab, to create *bà-mìi náam*. Served in a bowl with a small amount of garlic oil and no broth, it's *bà-mìi hâeng*.

Restaurants or vendors who sell *bà-mìi* typically also sell *kíaw*, a square of *bà-mìi* dough wrapped around ground pork or ground fish. These dumplings may be boiled and added to soup, or deep-fried to make *kíaw thâwt*. One of the most popular *bà-mìi* dishes in Bangkok is *kíaw puu náam*, a soup containing *kíaw* and *puu* (crab).

Finally there's *wún-sên*, an almost clear noodle made from mung-bean starch and water. Sold only in dried bunches, *wún-sên* (literally 'jelly thread') is easily prepared by soaking in hot water for 10 to 15 minutes. It's used for only three dishes in Bangkok. The most native, *yam wún-sên*, is a hot and tangy salad made with lime juice, fresh sliced *phrík khîi nŭu* ('mouse-dropping chilli'), shrimp, ground pork and various seasonings. *Puu òp wún-sên* is bean-thread noodles baked in a lidded clay pot with crab and seasonings. Lastly, *wún-sên* is a common ingredient in *kaeng jèut*, a bland, Chinese-influenced soup containing ground pork, soft tofu and a few vegetables.

Curries

In Thai, *kaeng* (pronounced similarly to 'gang') is often translated as 'curry', but it actually describes any dish with a lot of liquid and can thus refer to soups (such as *kaeng jèut*) as well as the classic chilli paste–based curries such as *kaeng phèt* (red curry) for which Thai cuisine is famous. The preparation of all chilli-based *kaeng* begins with a *khrêuang kaeng*, created by mashing, pounding and grinding an array of fresh ingredients with a stone mortar and pestle to form an aromatic, extremely pungent-tasting and rather thick paste. Typical ingredients in a *khrêuang kaeng* include dried chilli, galingale (also known as Thai ginger), lemon grass, kaffir lime zest, shallots, garlic, shrimp paste and salt. Dried spices such as coriander seeds and cumin are added for certain kinds of curries.

Most *kaeng* are blended in a heated pan with coconut cream, to which the chef adds the rest of the ingredients (meat, poultry, seafood and/or vegetables), along with diluted coconut milk to further thin and flavour the *kaeng*. Some recipes omit coconut milk entirely, such as *kaeng pàa* (jungle curry), a fiery soup that combines a mixture of vegetables and meat. Another *kaeng* that does not use coconut milk is *kaeng sôm* (sour curry), made with dried chillies, shallots, garlic and Chinese key ground with salt and shrimp paste (*kà-pì*). Cooked with tamarind juice and green papaya to create an overall tanginess, the result is a soupy, salty, sweet-and-sour ragout that most Westerners would never identify with the word 'curry'.

Thai curry cuisine revolves around three primary *kaeng*. *Kaeng phèt* (hot curry), also known as *kaeng daeng* (red curry) and *kaeng phèt daeng* (red hot curry), is the most traditional and is often used as a base to create other curries. This curry paste should be quite spicy, with its deep red colour coming from a copious number of dried chillies. *Kaeng phánaeng*, by contrast, is a relatively mild curry where the heat is brought down by the presence of crushed peanuts. *Kaeng khĭaw wăan*, literally 'sweet green curry', substitutes fresh green chillies for red, and somewhat unusually, dried spices such as cumin and coriander.

Although Thais are familiar with international curry powder (*phŏng kàrìi*), it's employed only in a few Hokkien Chinese-influenced dishes such as *puu phàt phŏng kàrìi* (cracked crab stir-fried with bottled curry powder and eggs). The use of the Anglo-Indian term 'curry' (*kàrìi*) Thai, is applied only to *kaeng kàrìi kài*, the one dish in Thailand's culinary repertoire that most approximates a true Indian curry. The word *kàrìi* also happens to be Thai slang for 'prostitute', and is thus the source of an endless series of puns that intentionally confuse cooking with sex.

A few extra seasonings such as *bai makrùut* (kaffir lime leaves), *bai hohráphaa* (sweet basil leaves) and *náam plaa* (fish sauce) may be added to taste just before serving. Bangkok Thais like their curries a bit sweeter than other regions of Thailand.

Most Bangkokians eat curries only for breakfast or lunch, hence the average *ráan khâo kaeng* (rice-curry shop) is only open from 7am to 2pm. It is considered a bit odd to eat curries in the evening, and hence most restaurants (tourist restaurants excepted) don't offer them on the evening menu.

To witness a truly amazing selection of curries, check out the vendors at the Or Tor Kor Market (p171). In general, the best place to find authentic curries is at a *ráan khâo kaeng* such as Khrua Aroy Aroy (p163), rather than a regular restaurant.

Hot & Tangy Salads

Standing right alongside *kaeng* in terms of Thainess is the ubiquitous *yam*, a hot and tangy salad containing a blast of lime, chilli, fresh herbs and a choice of seafood, roast vegetables, noodles or meats. Bangkokians prize *yam* dishes so much that they are often eaten on their own, without rice, before the meal has begun.

Lime juice provides the tang, while the abundant use of fresh chilli produces the heat. Other ingredients vary considerably, but plenty of leafy vegetables and herbs are usually present, including lettuce (often lining the dish) and *khêun châi* (Chinese celery). Lemon grass, shallots and mint may also come into play. Most *yam* are served at room

temperature or just slightly warmed by any cooked ingredients.

On Thai menus, the *yam* section will often be the longest. Yet when these same menus are translated into English, most or all of the *yam* are omitted because Thai restaurateurs harbour the idea that the delicate *faràng* (Western) palate cannot handle the heat or pungency. The usual English menu translation is either 'Thai-style salad' or 'hot and sour salad'.

Without a doubt, *yam* are the spiciest of all Thai dishes, and a good *yam* to begin with if you're not so chilli-tolerant is *yam wún-sên*, bean-thread noodles tossed with shrimp, ground pork, Chinese celery, lime juice and fresh sliced chilli. Another tame *yam* that tends to be a favourite among Thais and foreigners alike is *yam plaa dùk fuu*, made from fried shredded catfish, chilli and peanuts with a shredded-mango dressing on the side. Because of the city's proximity to the Gulf of Thailand, Bangkok eateries serve a wide variety of seafood yam, and at seafood restaurants such as Kaloang Home Kitchen (p157) these are a very good choice. *Yam* may also be made primarily with vegetables, such as the decadent *yam hŭa plii*, banana blossom salad, at Chote Chitr (see p155).

Stir-Fries & Deep-Fries

The simplest dishes in the Thai culinary repertoire are the stir-fries (*phàt*), brought to Thailand by the Chinese, who are of course world famous for being able to stir-fry a whole banquet in a single wok.

The list of *phàt* dishes seems endless. Most are better classified as Chinese, such as *néua phàt náam man hăwy* (beef in oyster sauce). Some are clearly Thai–Chinese hybrids, such as *kài phàt phrík khĭng*, in which chicken is stir-fried with ginger, garlic and chilli – ingredients shared by both traditions – but seasoned with fish sauce. Also leaning towards Thai – because cashews are native to Thailand but not to China – is *kài phàt mét mámûang hĭmáphaan* (sliced chicken stir-fried in dried chilli and cashews), a favourite with *faràng* tourists.

Perhaps the most Thai-like *phàt* dish is the famed lunch meal *phàt kàphrao*, a chicken or pork stir-fry with garlic, fresh sliced chilli, soy and fish sauce, and lots of holy basil. Another classic is *phàt phèt* (literally 'hot stir-fry'), in which the main ingredients are quickly stir-fried with red curry paste and tossed with sweet basil leaves before serving. This recipe usually includes seafood or freshwater fish, such as shrimp, squid, catfish or eel.

Stir-fry chicken, pork, beef or shrimp with black pepper and garlic and you have *phàt phrík thai kràthiam*, a relatively mild recipe often ordered as a 'fill-in' dish during a larger meal. For lovers of fresh vegetables, *phàt phàk khanáa* (Chinese kale stir-fried with a fermented soy-bean sauce) is worth looking out for, as is *phàt phàk bûng fai daeng*, flash-fried morning glory. For above-average fried dishes, the best destination is the street stalls of Chinatown (see p161).

Thâwt (deep-frying in oil) is mainly reserved for snacks such as *klûay thâwt* (fried bananas) or *paw-pía* (egg rolls). An exception is *plaa thâwt* (deep-fried fish), which is the most common way any fish is prepared. Many Thai recipes featuring whole fish require that it be fried first, usually in a wok filled with cooking oil (until the outside flesh is crispy to a depth of at least 1cm). Although to Western tastes this may appear to dry the fish out, in Thailand most fish fried in this way will then be topped with some sort of sauce – lime or a cooked chilli-onion mixture – which will remoisten the dish. Some fish, such as mackerel, will be steamed first, then lightly pan-fried in a smaller amount of oil to seal in the moisture.

A very few dishes require ingredients to be dipped in batter and then deep-fried, such as *kài thâwt* (fried chicken) and *kûng chúp pâeng thâwt* (batter-fried shrimp).

Soups

Thai soups fall into two broad categories, *tôm yam* and *kaeng jèut,* that are worlds apart in terms of seasonings. *Tôm yam* is almost always made with seafood, though chicken may also be used. *Tôm yam kûng* (*tôm yam* with shrimp) can be found in nearly all Thai restaurants as well as in many serving non-Thai cuisine. It is often translated on English menus as 'hot and sour Thai soup', although this often misleads non-Thais to think of Chinese hot and sour soup, which is milder and thinner in texture, and includes vinegar.

Lemon grass, kaffir lime leaf and lime juice give *tôm yam* its characteristic tang. Galingale is also added to *tôm yam* and, like its friends, is not meant to be eaten, but rather simply to add flavour. Fuelling the fire beneath *tôm yam*'s often velvety surface are fresh *phrík khîi nǔu* (tiny spicy chillies) and sometimes half a teaspoonful of *náam phrík phǎo* (a paste of dried chilli roasted with *kà-pì*). In addition to the tart-inducing ingredients, coriander leaf is an important garnish for both appearance and fragrance.

Keep in mind that *tôm yam* is meant to be eaten with rice, not sipped alone. The first swallow of this soup often leaves the uninitiated gasping for breath. It's not that the soup is so hot, but the chilli oils that provide the spice tend to float on top.

Of the several variations on *tôm yam* that exist, probably the most popular with Westerners is the milder *tôm khàa kài* (literally 'boiled galingale chicken', but often translated as 'chicken coconut soup'). The chilli is considerably muted in this soup by the addition of coconut milk.

Kaeng jèut covers the other end of the spectrum with a soothing broth seasoned with little more than soy or fish sauce. Although the variations on *kaeng jèut* are many, common ingredients include *wún-sên* (mung-bean starch noodles), *tâo hûu* (tofu), *hǔa chái tháo* (Chinese radish) and *mǔu sàp* (ground pork). Krua Nopparat (p156) in Banglamphu does a few very tasty *kaeng jèut,* and Thai-Chinese eateries such as Ngwan Lee Lang Suan (p164) excel in hot and spicy soups such as *tôm yam.*

Fruit

The omnipresent *phǒn-lá-mái* (literally 'fruit of the tree', a general term for all fruit) testifies to the Thais' great fondness for fruit, which they appear to consume at every opportunity. An evening meal is normally followed by a plate of sliced fresh fruit, not pastries or Western-style desserts – no doubt one reason Thais stay so slim, as a rule.

Other common year-rounders include *máphráo* (coconut), *faràng* (guava; also colloquial name for Westerner), *khànǔn* (jackfruit), *màkhǎam* (tamarind), *sôm khǐaw wǎan* (mandarin orange), *málákaw* (papaya), *sôm oh* (pomelo), *taeng moh* (watermelon) and *sàppàrót* (pineapple). All are most commonly eaten fresh, and sometimes dipped in a mixture of salt, sugar and ground chilli. Fruit juices of every kind are popular as beverages. Probably the best, if not most expensive, place to shop for fruit is Or Tor Kor Market (p171).

No discussion of Thai fruit is complete without a mention of durian (*thúrian*), dubbed the king of fruits by most Southeast Asians yet despised by many foreigners. A member of the aptly named Bombacaceae

SEASONAL FRUITS

The watchful visitor could almost fix the calendar month in Thailand by observing the parade of fruits appearing – sweet mangoes in March, mangosteens in April, rambeh in May, custard apples in July, golden-peel oranges in November and so on.

Chom-phûu (Rose apple) Small, apple-like texture, very fragrant; April to July.

Lamyai (Longan) 'Dragon's eyes'; small, brown, spherical, similar to rambutan; July to October.

Lámút (Sapodilla) Small, brown, oval, sweet but pungent smelling; July to September.

Máfai (Rambeh) Small, reddish-brown, sweet, apricot-like; April to May.

Mámûang (Mango) Several varieties and seasons.

Mangkhút (Mangosteen) Round, purple fruit with juicy white flesh; April to September.

Náwy nàa (Custard apple) July to October.

Ngáw (Rambutan) Red, hairy-skinned fruit with grapelike flesh; July to September.

family, this heavy, spiked orb resembles an ancient piece of medieval weaponry. Inside the thick shell lie five sections of plump, buttery and pungent flesh. Legions of connoisseurs as well as detractors have laboured to describe the durian's complex flavour. The durian's ammonia-like aroma is so strong that many hotels in Thailand, as well as Thai Airways International, ban the fruit from their premises.

Sweets

English-language Thai menus often have a section called 'Desserts', even though the concept doesn't exist in Thai cuisine, nor is there a direct translation for the word. The closest equivalent, khǎwng wǎan, simply means 'sweet stuff' and refers to all foods whose primary flavour characteristic is sweetness, although many also have a salty element as well. Sweets mostly work their way into the daily Thai diet in the form of between-meal snacks, so you won't find khǎwng wǎan in a traditional Thai restaurant at all. Instead, they're prepared and sold by market vendors or, more rarely, by shops specialising in khǎwng wǎan.

Khǎwng wǎan recipes and preparation techniques tend to require more skill than other dishes. The cook spends the morning making up khǎwng wǎan, which are bundled into banana leaves or cut into colourful squares. These are then arranged on large trays and taken to local markets or wheeled on carts through the streets to be sold by the chín (piece).

Prime ingredients for many Thai sweets include grated coconut, coconut milk, rice flour (from white rice or sticky rice), cooked sticky rice (whole grains), tapioca, mung-bean starch, boiled taro and various fruits. For added texture and crunch, some sweets may also contain fresh corn kernels, sugar-palm kernels, lotus seeds, cooked black beans and chopped water chestnuts. Egg yolks are a popular ingredient for khǎwng wǎan – including the ubiquitous fǎwy thawng (literally 'golden threads') – probably influenced by Portuguese desserts and pastries introduced during the early Ayuthaya era (see p144).

Thai sweets similar to the European concept of 'sweet pastry' are called khànǒm. Here again the kitchen-astute Portuguese were influential. Probably the most popular type of khànǒm in Thailand are the bite-sized items wrapped in banana leaves, especially khâo tôm kà-thí and khâo tôm mát. Both consist of sticky rice grains steamed with kà-thí (coconut milk) inside a banana-leaf wrapper to form a solid, almost toffeelike, mass. Khâo tôm kà-thí also contains fresh grated coconut, while khâo tôm mát usually contains a few black beans or banana. Tàkôh, a very simple but popular steamed sweet made from tapioca flour and coconut milk over a layer of sweetened seaweed gelatine, comes in small cups made from pandanus leaves. A similar blend, minus the gelatine and steamed in tiny porcelain cups, is called khànǒm thûay (cup pastry). The best place to try many of these sweets is Bangkok's open-air markets, such as Or Tor Kor (p171) or the Nang Loeng Market (p170), the latter particularly celebrated for its high-quality central Thai–style sweets.

Coconut milk also features prominently in several soupier sweets with colourful names. In the enormously popular klûay bùat chii ('bananas ordaining as nuns'), banana chunks float in a white syrup of sweetened and slightly salted coconut milk. Bua láwy ('floating lotus') consists of boiled sticky rice dumplings in a similar coconut sauce. Substitute red-dyed chunks of fresh water chestnut and you have *tháp thim kràwp* ('crispy rubies'). As at a modern ice-cream parlour, you can often order extra ingredients, such as black beans, sugar-palm kernels or corn kernels, to be added to the mix. Crushed ice is often added to cool the mixture.

Although foreigners don't seem to immediately take to most Thai sweets, one dish few visitors have trouble with is *ai tim kà-thí*, Thai-style coconut ice cream. At more traditional shops, the ice cream is garnished with toppings such as kidney beans or sticky rice, and is a great snack on a sweltering Bangkok afternoon.

WHERE TO EAT

Wherever you go in Bangkok, there is food. *Rót khěn* (vendor carts) are deployed across the city outfitted with portable woks, charcoal stoves or deep fryers ready to whip up a quick snack or a sit-down meal. There is so much variety on the streets themselves that you can go weeks without stepping inside a restaurant.

When you make the leap inside, your best options for great Thai food are Spartan closets run by mum, dad, and the kids. Some of the most famous food shops that get written up in the Thai-language press are a few tables shy of being a home kitchen and look more like a carport than a palace. For folks more interested in food than finery, Bangkok is the great liberator from tablecloth suffocation and penguin-suit waiters. Even when karma has delivered fame and fortune, the elite don't abandon street eats. Your fellow diners at a famous outdoor stall might have just returned from a semester abroad and are shuttled around town in a chauffeured car. When it comes to good eats, Asia's famous obsession with status takes a back seat. Best of all, in these proven grub shops, unlike in New York City or London, you can eat well for much less than the cost of a car payment.

That doesn't mean you can't dine in decadence. As a cosmopolitan centre, Bangkok loves to spend money and has many stylish spots that cater to a mood, from sky-high perches to riverside pavilions and contemporary minimalism. Italian is king in the fine-dining sphere, with Japanese and Mediterranean–Californian styles not far behind. Those refreshing flavours of citrus and sea-food translate better into this tropical climate than the heavy sauces of traditional French cuisine, the usual haute contender.

Bangkok also offers a host of homesick cures for its many immigrant communities. Chinatown is naturally a good area for Chinese food, particularly from the southern regions of that country. In a corner of Chinatown known as Phahurat and around Th Silom, Indian residents keep themselves and the culinary traveller well fed. In the crowded bazaar-like area of Little Arabia, just off Th Sukhumvit, there is such fabulous Arabic cuisine that no one would fault you for doing one too many hummus nights. And elsewhere, meat pies, nachos, cornbread, runny eggs – whatever mama used to make – is likely to have been re-created by an expat entrepreneur for those far-from-home cravings.

PRACTICALITIES
Opening Hours

Restaurants serving Thai food are generally open from 10am to 8pm or 9pm, although some places are open later. Foreign-cuisine restaurants tend to keep only dinner hours, although this varies. Thais are consummate eaters and are always within reach of a snack or a light meal, so meal times are quite flexible, although restaurants can get crowded around 8pm.

Muslim-run restaurants sometimes close in observance of religious or cultural holidays, some close on Fridays, while others close on Mondays. Most Thai and Chinese restaurants view holidays as a chance to feed more customers and therefore rarely lock up the metal gates for the day.

Bangkok has recently passed a citywide ordinance banning street vendors from setting up shop on Mondays. The footpaths are so uncluttered on these days that a roadside eater might feel both hungry and abandoned.

How Much?

A bowl of noodles or a stir-fry dish bought from a street vendor should cost 25B to 30B, depending on the portion size and ingredients. Climbing up the scale are the canteen shops that have a selection of pre-made dishes, sturdier chairs and a roof. For these luxuries, you'll probably pay 30B to 40B.

Thai restaurants with an army of servers and laminated menus usually offer main dishes for around 60B to 120B. Add ambience, air-con and fancy uniforms, and a main jumps to about 120B to 200B. Anything above 300B will deliver you into the arms of some of the city's fanciest restaurants. An exception is the restaurants in top-end hotels, which feature prices close to what you'd expect to pay at any flash hotel in the world.

In most parts of the city, Western food occupies the high end of the scale, costing from 200B to 350B. One obvious exception is Banglamphu, where *faràng* food comes in under 200B a plate.

Note also that nearly all hotel restaurants include '++', which implies an additional 7% for VAT (value added tax) and a 10% 'service charge' on top of your total bill.

Booking Tables

If you have a lot of friends in tow or will be attending a formal restaurant (including hotel restaurants), reservations are recommended. Bookings are also recommended for Sunday brunch and dinner cruises.

Otherwise, you shouldn't have a problem scoring a table at the vast majority restaurants in the city, especially if you arrive during off-peak hours. Following the European tradition (or because of the wretched evening commute), peak dinner time starts around 8pm. The lunchtime crush typically starts around noon and lasts for close to an hour.

Tipping

You shouldn't be surprised to learn that tipping in Thailand isn't as exact as it is in Europe (tip no-one) or the USA (tip everyone). Thailand falls somewhere in between, and some areas are left open to interpretation. Everyone agrees that you don't tip streetside vendors, although some add a little surcharge when tallying up a bill for a foreigner. To avoid getting annoyed about this double-pricing scheme, consider it an implicit tip.

When eating at a restaurant, tipping becomes more a game of finesse. Some people leave behind roughly 10% at any sit-down

EATING KO RATANAKOSIN & THONBURI

PRICE GUIDE

$$$	more than 500B
$$	200-500B a meal
$	less than 200B a meal

Price is for a meal for one person, including an appetiser or dessert, a main course and a drink.

restaurant where someone fills their glass every time they take a sip. Others don't. Most upmarket restaurants will apply a 10% service charge to the bill. Some patrons leave extra on top of the service charge; others don't. The choice is yours.

KO RATANAKOSIN & THONBURI

Despite the riverfront setting, there are surprisingly few restaurants along this stretch of the Chao Phraya River.

DECK Map p56 International/Thai $$
☎ 0 2221 9158; www.arunresidence.com; Arun Residence, 36-38 Soi Pratu Nok Yung, Ko Ratanakosin; mains 170-690B; ☑ 11am-10pm; ▣ air-con 508 & 512, ordinary 32 & 53, ⚓ Tha Tien
The Deck's claim to fame is its commanding views over Wat Arun, but the restaurant's short but diverse menu, ranging from duck confit to Thai-style pomelo salad, sweetens the pot. After dinner, take a drink at the hotel's open-air rooftop bar.

RACHANAWI SAMOSAWN (NAVY CLUB RESTAURANT) Map p56 Thai $
☎ 0 2222 0081; 77 Th Maharat, Ko Ratanakosin; mains 70-150B; ☑ 8am-6pm; ▣ air-con 508 & 512, ordinary 32 & 53, ⚓ Tha Chang
Commanding one of the few coveted riverfront locations along this stretch of the Chao Phraya, this restaurant has a reputation among locals in the know for cheap and delicious seafood-based Thai nosh.

To find the restaurant, use the entrance near the ATM machines at Tha Chang.

RUB AROON Map p56 Thai $
☎ 0 2622 2312; rub_ar_roon_cafe@yahoo.co.th; 310-312 Th Maharat, Ko Ratanakosin; mains 60-95B; ☑ 8am-6pm; ▣ air-con 508 & 512, ordinary 32 & 53, ⚓ Tha Tien
Perfectly situated for a post-temple refresher, this café across the street from Wat Pho also throws in great old-word atmosphere and a few simple dishes.

WANG LANG MARKET Map p56 Thai $
Th Phra Chan & Trok Wang Lang, Thonburi; mains 20-60B; ⚓ Tha Wang Lang
Beside Siriraj Hospital is a busy market that sprawls west from Tha Wang Lang. Many of the vendors prepare fiery southern-style

curries and dishes such as *phàt phèt sataw* (spicy red curry stir-fry with stink beans). The theory is that southern Thai food took root here because of the nearby train station that served southern destinations.

BANGLAMPHU

Bangkok's most traditional district is not surprisingly one of the best places to try authentic central Thai-Bangkok–style nosh. Every alley wide enough to hold a wok is claimed as a makeshift dining room and, because of the backpacker presence, Western and vegetarian food is also plentiful and cheap.

CAFÉ PRIMAVERA Map pp68–9   Pizza $$

☎ 0 2281 4718; 56 Th Phra Sumen, Banglamphu; mains 95-325B; ⏰ 9am-11pm; 🚌 ordinary 3, 6, 15 & 82, ⚓ Tha Phra Athit

If the coffee was just a tad better, this dark-wood and marble-topped table trattoria is just the kind of place we'd like to make our local café. The pizzas and homemade gelati offer more hope, and the friendly and efficient staff seal the deal.

JAY FAI Map pp68–9   Thai $$

☎ 0 2223 9384; 327 Th Mahachai, Banglamphu; mains 200-250B; ⏰ 5pm-midnight Sun-Fri; 🚌 ordinary 5, 35 & 159, khlong taxi Tha Phan Fah

You wouldn't think so by looking at her bare-bones dining room, but Jay Fai is known far and wide for serving Bangkok's most expensive *phat khii mao* (drunkard's noodles). The price is justified by the copious fresh seafood, as well as Jay Fai's distinct frying style that results in a virtually oil-free finished product.

HEMLOCK Map pp68–9   Thai $$

☎ 0 2282 7507; hemlockeyes@hotmail.com; 56 Th Phra Athit, Banglamphu; mains 80-200B; ⏰ 4pm-midnight; 🚌 ordinary 3, 6, 15 & 82, ⚓ Tha Phra Athit

Taking full advantage of its cosy shop-house location, this perennial favourite has enough style to feel like a special night out, but doesn't skimp on flavour or preparation. The eclectic menu reads like an ancient literary work, reviving old dishes from the aristocratic kitchens across the country. Try the flavourful *mîang kham* (wild tea leaves wrapped around ginger, shallots, peanuts, lime and coconut flakes) or *yam khàmoi* (thieves' salad).

top picks

DINING WITH A VIEW

- Emporium Food Hall (p166) The cheapest view in town
- Face (p166) Thai teak, jungle and carp ponds complete the vista
- Rang Mahal (p169) A sea of concrete towers meets the horizon from this rooftop perch
- River Bar (p170) Sassy and classy glass box overlooking the Chao Phraya River
- Deck (opposite) The prime seat for sunset over Wat Arun

OH MY COD! Map pp68–9   English/Thai $$

☎ 0 2282 6553; www.fishandchipsbangkok.com; 95d, Soi Rambuttri Village Inn, Soi Rambuttri I, Banglamphu; mains 70-200B; ⏰ 7.30am-11pm; 🚌 air-con 3, 32 & 49, ordinary 30, 32, 33 & 65, ⚓ Tha Phra Athit

English cuisine bears the burden of a negative reputation, but is there anything more satisfying than fish and chips? An order here takes the form of a puffy filet accompanied by thick-cut chips (French fries) and peas, prepared 'garden' or 'mushy' style. Breakfast is served all day, and parched Anglophiles can enjoy a proper cuppa in the sunny courtyard dining area.

SHOSHANA Map pp68–9   Israeli $

☎ 0 2282 9948; 88 Th Chakraphong, Banglamphu; mains 90-150B; ⏰ 11am-11pm; 🚌 air-con 3, 32 & 49, ordinary 30, 32, 33 & 65, ⚓ Tha Phra Athit

One of Khao San's longest-running Israeli restaurants, Shoshana resembles your grandparents' living room down to the tacky paintings and perpetual re-runs of 'Seinfeld'. The 'I heart Shoshana' T-shirts worn by the wait staff may be a hopelessly optimistic description of employee morale, but the gut-filling chips-falafel-and-hummus plates leave nothing to be desired.

CHOTE CHITR Map pp68–9   Thai $

☎ 0 2221 4082; 146 Th Phraeng Phuton, Banglamphu; mains 60-150B; ⏰ 11am-10pm; 🚌 air-con 508, ordinary 5, 35 & 56, khlong taxi Tha Phan Fah

If you can ignore the occasional dog napping on the tables, a meal at this local legend will undoubtedly change your opinions about cuisine. Chote Chitr (which is pronounced *chôht jìt*) puts out delicious, dictionary-definition central Thai fare, and is particularly renown for its *mìi kràwp*, sweet-and-spicy crispy fried noodles, still made the old-school way. But just about anything from the exceedingly extensive menu will impress.

RANEE'S GUESTHOUSE

Map pp68–9   Thai Vegetarian $

☎ 0 2282 4072; 77 Trok Mayom off Th Tanao, Banglamphu; mains 70-120B; ☷ 7am-midnight; ▣ air-con 511 & 512, ordinary 15, 30 & 65, ⚓ Tha Phra Athit

In addition to meat-free Thai, this 'flash-packer' oasis now fancies itself as a bakery, and puts out some better-than-decent pizza, pasta and bread. Dining with new friends in the cool leafy courtyard, we double-dare you to miss the bad old days of cheap guesthouse eats.

KRUA NOPPHARAT Map pp68–9   Thai $

☎ 0 2281 7578; 130-132 Th Phra Athit, Banglam-phu; mains 60-100B; ☷ 10.30am-2.30pm & 5-9pm Mon-Sat; ▣ ordinary 3, 6, 15 & 82, ⚓ Tha Phra Athit

A few dusty paintings are the only effort at interior design at this family-run standby. Where flavour is concerned, however, Krua Noppharat is willing to expend consider-ably more energy. Krua Noppharat is as popular among foreigners as it is among Thais, but thankfully does not tone down its excellent central and southern-style Thai fare for the former.

KAIYANG BORAN Map pp68–9   Thai $

☎ 0 2622 2349; 474-476 Th Tanao, Banglamphu; mains 40-100B; ☷ 10am-10pm; ▣ air-con 508, ordinary 5, 35 & 56, khlong taxi Tha Phan Fah

In a neighbourhood filled with old-school Bangkok-style grub, Kaiyang Boran's una-bashedly Isan menu stands out. It is even more incongruous considering that the owner is Thai-Chinese and had never eaten the fiery dishes of the northeast until he met his wife from Chaiyapoom. The com-fortable setting and air-conditioning make this an ideal spot for overheated neat freaks made nervous by streetside dining.

BAAN PHRA ARTHIT Map pp68–9   Café $

☎ 0 2280 7878; baanphraarthit@hotmail.com; 102/1 Th Phra Athit, Banglamphu; mains 50-90B;

☷ 7am-8pm; ▣ ordinary 3, 6, 15 & 82, ⚓ Tha Phra Athit

When only air-conditioning will do, why not do it in style? This classy café features a few basic Western–Thai fusion dishes, decent coffee, and even better cakes and sweets. And all of this for less than the price of a latté back at home.

PAN Map pp68–9   Thai $

☎ 0 83817 4227; Th Rambutri, Banglamphu; mains 50-90B; ☷ 11.30am-10pm; ▣ air-con 3, 32 & 49, ordinary 30, 32, 33 & 65, ⚓ Tha Phra Athit

If you're looking for authentic Thai, but don't want to stray far from the comforts of Th Khao San, this streetside eatery (next to Viengtai Hotel) is your best bet. Simply look for the overflowing tray of raw ingredients, point to what you want and Pan will mix it up for you. The clientele is decidedly inter-national, but the flavours wholly domestic.

ROTI-MATABA Map pp68–9   Thai-Muslim $

☎ 0 2282 2119; 136 Th Phra Athit, Banglamphu; mains 50-90B; ☷ 7am-10pm Tue-Sun; ▣ ordinary 3, 6, 15 & 82, ⚓ Tha Phra Athit

This classic eatery appears to have become a bit too big for its britches in recent years, but still serves tasty Thai-Muslim dishes such as roti, *kaeng mátsàmàn* (Muslim curry), a brilliantly sour fish curry, and *mátàbà* (a sort of stuffed Indian pancake). An upstairs air-con dining area and outdoor tables provide barely enough seating for its loyal fans.

THIP SAMAI Map pp68–9   Thai $

☎ 0 2221 6280; www.thipsamai.com; 313 Th Ma-hachai, Banglamphu; mains 25-120B; ☷ 5.30pm-1.30am; ▣ ordinary 5, 35 & 159, khlong taxi Tha Phan Fah

Brace yourself, but you should be aware that the fried noodles sold from carts along Th Khao San have nothing to do with the dish known as *phàt thai*. Luckily, less than a five-minute túk-túk drive away lies Thip Samai, also known by locals as *phàt thai pratuu phǐi*, and home to the most legen-dary *phàt thai* in town. For something a bit different, try the delicate egg-wrapped ver-sion, or the *phàt thai* fried with *man kûng*, decadent shrimp fat.

KIM LENG Map pp68–9   Thai $

☎ 0 2622 2062; 158-160 Th Tanao, Banglamphu; mains 40-80B; ☷ 10am-10pm Mon-Sat; ▣ air-con 508, ordinary 5, 35 & 56, khlong taxi Tha Phan Fah

A WILD CAKE HUNT

Few Westerners, even those who've lived here for decades, seem to take to the hyp
khǎwng wǎan and *khànǒm* (traditional Thai sweets and desserts). Luckily, in recent ye
dance of high-quality, domestically made Western-style cakes, ice creams and chocola

The best place to begin your search for the sweet is undoubtedly the basement of
this expansive temple to indulgence, cake lovers will be delighted to find branches of t
Nôtre and Vanilla Brasserie. Stop by Le Gourmet for chocolate orbs of pleasure, and Gela
supermarket, makes excellent Italian-style ice cream served in freshly made waffle cone

If the thought of dining in a mall gives you hives, take a seat at the marble-topped
pp108–9; ☎ 0 2631 0354; www.la-boulange.com; 2-2/1 Th Convent, Silom). This longst̶a̶n̶d̶i̶n̶g̶ French-owned bakery
makes a huge variety of admirable cakes and Viennoiserie.

Duc de Praslin (Map pp118–19; ☎ 0 2258 3200; www.gallothai.com; ground fl, Fenix Tower, Soi 31, Th Sukhumvit), a Belgian-owned chocolatier, has opened several of its classy European cafés at various locations around town. As
well as the spot-on bon-bons, try a hot cocoa, made in front of your eyes by steaming milk with shards of rich chocolate.
About 2km up the road at Visage, part of Face (p166), Eric Perez prepares many of the same near-perfect pastries and
chocolates he made at the French Embassy and the Ritz in Washington DC.

Nowadays even the Thais need their tiramisu and tartes, and respectable Western-style desserts can be found
along Th Phra Athit in Banglamphu. Anshada of Ann's Sweet (Map pp68–9; ☎ 0 86889 1383; 138 Th Phra Athit,
Banglamphu) makes some pretty fly cakes for a Thai girl, and the decadent desserts at Baan Phra Arthit (opposite)
and It's Happened to be a Closet (p130) leave little to be desired.

Want a home-cooked meal, but having trouble convincing random strangers on the street to make one for you? A visit to this eatery excelling in the foods of central Thailand is a decent substitute. As with much of the food of the capital, sweet intermingles with spicy here, and you can't go wrong with Kim Leng's *hàw mòk* (steamed curry) or *náam phrík kà-pì* (shrimp paste dip served as a set with veggies and deep-fried fish).

MAY KAIDEE
Map pp68–9   Thai Vegetarian $
☎ 0 2281 7699; www.maykadee.com; sub-soi off Th Tanao, Banglamphu; mains 50B; 11am-9.30pm; air-con 511 & 512, ordinary 15, 30 & 65, Tha Phra Athit

May Kaidee started doing non-meat around the same time that fisherman pants became the backpacker uniform. She knows her audience: easy on chillies, heavy on coconut milk. And she doesn't even wince when new arrivals ask for chopsticks for their curries.

To find this restaurant from Th Khao San, cross Th Tanao and follow the little *soi* near Sirinthip Guesthouse; take the first left for 50m. There is a second branch just over the bridge on Th Samsen that also offers cooking lessons (see p158).

ARROI
Map pp68–9   Thai Vegetarian $
152 Th Din So, Banglamphu; mains 20-30B; 7am-8pm; air-con 508, ordinary 5, 35, 56 & 159, khlong taxi Tha Phan Fah

Employing a variety of tasty meat substitutes and sticking to a repertoire of classic Thai dishes, this tiny restaurant will even make flesh eaters happy.

THEWET & DUSIT

The primary draw to this sleepy neighbourhood is the riverside restaurants that drink in the cool river breezes and grill whole fish for communal picking.

IN LOVE
Map p79   Thai $$
☎ 0 2281 2900; Th Krung Kasem, Thewet; mains 150-200B; 11am-10pm; air-con 506 & 53, Tha Thewet

This recently remodelled perch straddling the Chao Phraya River has undergone a transformation from homey to chic, reflecting much of the change in today's newfangled Bangkok. Slate grey and minimalist décor now define your settings, but the seafood-heavy menu, thankfully, still has its head in the past.

KALOANG HOME KITCHEN
Map p79   Thai $$
☎ 0 2281 9228; 2 Th Si Ayuthaya, Thewet; mains 80-200B; 11am-11pm; 9am-6pm; air-con 3, 16, 32, 49, 505, ordinary 30, 32, 33, 64 & 65, Tha Thewet

Don't be alarmed by the peeling paint and the dilapidated deck; Kaloang Home

EATING THEWET & DUSIT

...COOKING

...ed everything Bangkok has to offer is one thing, but imagine the points you'll rack up if you can make ...nes for your friends back at home. A visit to a Thai cooking school has become a must-do for many Bangkok ...es, and for some visitors it is a highlight of their trip.

...ourses range in price and value: a typical half-day course should include at least a basic introduction to Thai ingredients and flavours, and a hands-on chance to both prepare and cook several dishes. Most schools offer a revolving cast of dishes that changes on a daily basis, making it possible to study for a week without repeating a dish, if desired. Many courses include a visit to a market, and nearly all lessons include a set of printed recipes and end with a communal lunch consisting of your handiwork. At the more expensive schools, students are also usually given an apron and a gift box of Thai cooking ingredients.

Baipai Thai Cooking School (Map pp124–5; ☎ 0 2294 9029; www.baipai.com; 150/12 Soi Naksuwan, Th Nonsee, Greater Bangkok; lessons 1800B) Housed in an attractive suburban villa, and taught by a small army of staff, Baipai offers two daily lessons (9.30am to 1.30pm and 1.30pm to 5.30pm Tuesday to Sunday) of four dishes each. Transport is available.

Blue Elephant Cooking School (Map pp108–9; ☎ 0 2673 9353; www.blueelephant.com; 233 Th Sathon Tai, Silom; lessons 2800B) Bangkok's most chi-chi Thai cooking school offers two lessons a day (8.45am to 12.30pm and 1.15pm to 5pm) Monday to Saturday. The morning class squeezes in a visit to a local market, while the afternoon session includes a detailed introduction to Thai ingredients.

Epicurean Kitchen Thai Cooking School (Map pp108–9; ☎ 0 2631 1119; www.thaikitchen.com; 10/2 Th Convent, Th Silom; lessons 2000B) This cramped but classy school offers daily lessons (9.30am to 1pm Monday to Friday) that encompass a whopping eight dishes, as well as a one-hour 'short course' of four dishes.

May Kaidee's Vegetarian Thai Cooking School (Map pp68–9; ☎ 0 2281 7699; www.maykaidee.com; 33 Th Samsen, Banglamphu; lessons 1200B) One of the few places around offering a truly meat-free cooking experience, May's classes (9am to 1pm) offer a brief visit to a local market and instruction in 10 veggie versions of traditional Thai dishes.

Oriental Hotel Thai Cooking School (Map pp108–9; ☎ 0 2659 9000; www.mandarinoriental.com; 48 Soi 38, Th Charoen Krung, Riverside; lessons 4500B) Located across the river in an antique wooden home, the Oriental's cooking class features a daily revolving menu of four dishes. The lessons (9am to 12.30pm Monday to Saturday) are less 'hands on' than elsewhere, and cooking is done in teams, rather than individually.

Silom Thai Cooking School (Map pp108–9; ☎ 0 84726 5669; www.bangkokthaicooking.com; 68 Soi 13, Th Silom; lessons 1000B) Although the facilities are basic, Silom crams a visit to a local market and instruction of six dishes into 3½ hours (9.30am to 1pm), making it the best bang for your baht. Transport available.

Kitchen certainly isn't. The laid-back atmosphere and seafood-heavy menu will quickly dispel any concerns about sinking into the Chao Phraya, and a beer and the breeze will temporarily erase any scarring memories of Bangkok traffic.

Finding this restaurant is part of the fun: follow Th Si Ayuthaya toward the river and turn right at the temple past the kids playing badminton till the end of the street.

CHINATOWN

Although Chinatown seems to be dominated by restaurants serving shark-fin and bird's nest soup, noodles usually prepared by the street vendors that line Th Yaowarat after dark are the true Chinatown meal. During the annual Vegetarian Festival (opposite), the neighbourhood embraces meatless meals with yellow-flagged street stalls.

Phahurat, Bangkok's Little India, has several inconspicuous Indian restaurants and an afternoon samosa vendor near Soi ATM.

SHANGARILA RESTAURANT
Map p84   Chinese $$$
☎ 0 2224 5933; 306 Th Yaowarat, Chinatown; mains 220-500B; ⏱ 11am-10pm; 🚌 air-con 4, 49, 73 & 507, ordinary 40, 49, 73, 85 & 159, 🚢 Tha Ratchawong

This massive, banquet-style restaurant prepares a variety of banquet-sized Cantonese dishes for ravenous families. The dim sum lunches are worth the effort of muscling your way past the outdoor steam tables.

TANG JAI YUU Map p84   Chinese $$$
☎ 0 2224 2167; 85-89 Th Yaowaphanit, Chinatown; mains 220-500B; ⏱ 11am-10pm; 🚌 air-con 4, 49, 73 & 507, ordinary 40, 49, 73, 85 & 159, 🚢 Tha Ratchawong

EATING CHINATOWN

In Thailand, policemen and big-haired women are usually a tip-off for good eats, not suspicious activity, and Tang Jai Yuu is no exception. This place specialises in Teo Chew and Chinese-Thai specialities with an emphasis on seafood, and you can't go wrong choosing a fresh fish from the tank out the front and letting the boys grill it for you.

CHIANG KII Map p84   Thai-Chinese $$

54 Soi Bamrungrat, Chinatown; mains 250B; ☺ 5pm-10pm; ⊟ air-con 4, 49, 73 & 507, ordinary 40, 49, 73, 85 & 159, ⚓ Tha Ratchawong

At 250B, Chiang Kii's *khâo tôm plaa* (rice soup with fish) is among the most expensive in town. Before balking at the price, witness the care that the elderly Thai-Chinese owners put into every bowl, not to mention the generous amount of exceedingly fresh fish, and it begins to make sense.

HUA SENG HONG
Map p84   Thai-Chinese $$

☎ 0 2222 0635; 371-373 Th Yaowarat, Chinatown; mains 100-300B; ☺ 10am-midnight; ⊟ air-con 4, 49, 73 & 507, ordinary 40, 49, 73, 85 & 159, ⚓ Tha Ratchawong

Shark-fin soup may draw heaps of Asian tourists into this place, but Hua Seng Hong's varied menu, including dim sum, braised goose feet and noodles, make it a delicious destination for anybody craving Chinese.

ROYAL INDIA Map p84   Indian $$

☎ 0 2221 6565; 392/1 Th Chakraphet, Phahurat; mains 100-250B; ☺ 10am-10pm; ⊟ air-con 73, ordinary 8, ⚓ Tha Saphan Phut

A windowless dining room of 10 tables in a creepy alley may not be everybody's ideal lunch destination, but this legendary north Indian place continues to draw foodies despite the lack of aesthetics. Try any of the delicious breads or saucy curries, and finish with a homemade Punjabi sweet.

OLD SIAM PLAZA Map p84   Thai $

cnr Th Phahurat & Th Triphet, Phahurat; mains 30-90B; ☺ 10am-5pm; ⊟ air-con 73, ordinary 8, ⚓ Tha Saphan Phut

Wedged between the western edge of Chinatown and the northern edge of Phahurat, this shopping plaza has a decent 3rd-floor food centre serving Thai and Chinese food. Even better yet, the 1st floor is a virtual crash course in Thai desserts, with vendors selling all the streetside sweets in a quieter and more sanitary setting.

HONG KONG NOODLES
Map p84   Chinese $

136 Trok Itsaranuphap, Th Charoen Krung, Chinatown; mains 30B; ☺ 9am-6pm; ⊟ air-con 4, 49, 73 & 507, ordinary 40, 49, 73, 85 & 159, ⚓ Tha Ratchawong

Deep in the heart of the vendor-lined *soi* known as Talaat Mai (New Market), this claustrophobic shop does a busy trade in steaming bowls of wheat-and-egg noodles. If you can find a seat, there's a nice vista of the surrounding commerce.

THAI CHAROEN Map p84   Thai-Chinese $

☎ 0 2221 2633; 454 Th Charoen Krung, Chinatown; mains 20-30B; ☺ 9am-7pm; ⊟ air-con 4, 49, 73 & 507, ordinary 40, 49, 73, 85 & 159, ⚓ Tha Ratchawong

Simply look for the table of delicious-looking eats out front. This unassuming restaurant specialises in cheap and delicious Thai-Chinese specialities such as stuffed-squid, stir-fried eggplant, and *jàp chǎi* (a Chinese vegetable 'stew').

EATING CHINATOWN

WAVING THE YELLOW FLAG

During the annual Vegetarian Festival (in September/October), Bangkok's Chinatown becomes a virtual orgy of non-meat cuisine. The festivities centre on Wat Mangkon Kamalawat, on Th Charoen Krung, and in the Talaat Noi area, but food shops and stalls all over the city post yellow flags to announce their meat-free status.

Celebrating alongside the ethnic Chinese are Thais who look forward to the special dishes that appear during the festival period. Most restaurants will put their normal menus on hold and instead prepare soy-based substitutes for standard Thai dishes like *tôm yam*, *kaeng mátsàmàn*, and *kaeng khǐaw wǎan*. Even Thai regional cuisines are sold – without the meat, of course. Of the special festival dishes, yellow Hokkien-style noodles appear in stir-fried dishes along with meaty mushrooms and big hunks of vegetables.

Along with abstinence from meat, the 10-day festival is celebrated with special visits to the temple, often requiring worshippers to dress in white.

BANGKOK'S LITTLE ITALY

Italian is the most prevalent foreign cuisine in Bangkok, and the city's greatest concentration of Italian restaurants can be found between the leafy streets of Th Lang Suan and Soi Tonson. Although the majority of the kitchens reach for the upper echelon of the dining market, there is a decent mix of the quirky and the exclusive to slake your pasta craving.

Air Plane (Map pp98–9; ☎ 0 2252 4630; airplanerest@hotmail.com; 63 Soi Lang Suan, Ploenchit; mains 90-250B; ⏰ 11am-2.30pm & 6-11pm) Located in a refurbished home, the starched tablecloths and varied menu make this a step up from the average corner spaghetti shack.

Calderazzo (Map pp98–9; ☎ 0 2252 8108; 59 Soi Lang Suan, Ploenchit; mains 200-800B; ⏰ 11am-2.30pm & 6-11pm) Specialising in southern Italian cuisine, the chic dining room and imported furniture leave no doubt that this is the poshest of the area's Italian immigrants. Located just across the street is the slightly more casual Calderazzo Bistro.

Gianni Ristorante (Map pp98–9; ☎ 0 2252 1619; www.giannibkk.com; 34/1 Soi Tonson, Ploenchit; mains 260-600B; ⏰ 11am-2pm & 6-11pm) Generally considered the best of the lot, this restaurant nearly singlehandedly upped the bracket for Italian dining in Bangkok. Homemade sausages, lobster-stuffed raviolis and braised lamb shank transport tastebuds to the Adriatic. Wine lovers rave about the huge and unique selection.

No. 43 (Map pp98–9; ☎ 0 2658 7444; Cape House, 43 Soi Lang Suan, Th Ploenchit; ⏰ 11am-11pm) If you prefer quantity over quality, this chain-like restaurant offers an acceptable Italian lunch buffet for 300B.

Paesano (Map pp98–9; ☎ 0 2252 2834; 96/7 Soi Tonson, Ploenchit; mains 150-550B; ⏰ 11am-2pm & 5.30-10.30pm) This Bangkok institution combines old-school atmosphere with an even older-school menu.

Pan Pan (Map pp98–9; ☎ 0 2252 7104; 45 Soi Lang Suan, Ploenchit; mains 80-220B; ⏰ 11am-11pm) Open since 1976, this is undoubtedly where many Bangkok Thais got their first taste of Italy. Local office workers still comprise the majority of the clientele at what is probably the cheapest of the area's Italian joints.

SIAM SQUARE, PRATU-NAM & PLOENCHIT

Welcome to Mall Land. Although the plastic façades of famous franchises seem to prevail, there are some noteworthy independent eats, both with and without amenities such as air-conditioning and shopping families. Soi Lang Suan is a virtual Little Italy of Italian restaurants, and the area around Th Withayu is home to a few longstanding Thai restaurants.

CRYSTAL JADE LA MIAN XIAO LONG BAO Map pp98–9   Chinese $$

☎ 0 2250 7990; Urban Kitchen, Basement Erawan Bangkok, 494 Th Ploenchit; mains 120-300B; ⏰ 10am-10pm; ☒ Chitlom

The tongue-twistingly long name of this excellent Singaporean chain refers to the restaurant's signature wheat noodles (la mian) and the famous Shanghainese steamed dumplings (xiao long pao). If you order the hand-pulled noodles (which you should do) allow the staff to cut them with kitchen shears, otherwise you'll end up with ample evidence of your meal on your shirt.

KUAYTIAW REUA THA SIAM
Map pp98–9   Thai $

☎ 0 2252 8353; Soi 3, Siam Sq, Th Phra Ram 1; mains 40-100B; ⏰ 9am-9pm; ☒ Siam

Back in the days when canals were the city's thoroughfares, the noodle boat floated from house to house. Now that life has moved to solid ground, this restaurant and others like it pay tribute to those days by serving bowls from decidedly land-locked vessels. The restaurant's namesake, *kŭaytĭaw reua* (boat noodles) are, like the chain's surprisingly decent Isan food, intensely spicy and satisfying.

SANGUAN SRI Map pp98–9   Thai $

☎ 0 2252 7637; 59/1 Th Withayu, Ploenchit; mains 60-150B; ⏰ 10am-3pm Mon-Sat; ☒ Ploenchit

This restaurant, resembling a concrete bunker filled with furniture circa 1973, can afford to remain decidedly *choei* (old-fashioned) simply because of its reputation. Mimic the area's hungry office staff and try the excellent *kaeng phèt pèt yâang*, red curry with grilled duck breast served over snowy white *khànŏm jeen* noodles.

RIVERSIDE, SILOM & LUMPHINI

Riverside Bangkok is often associated with hotel fine dining, but this is actually one of the city's most diverse eating districts. Those willing to try something different can poke into one of the numerous Thai-Muslim or In-

BIG DEAL

Although the prices at Bangkok's best restaurants may seem like chump change when compared to those of their brethren in New York City or London, a few nights of eating out at this level is going to make a dent in just about anyone's wallet. To ease the pain but still savour the flavour, we suggest dining at lunch, when many of Bangkok's most revered upmarket eateries offer some fantastic set-lunch specials.

The three-course set lunch at Gianni Ristorante (opposite) for a mere 350B++ is a downright steal, and three set courses at Cy'an (below) for 680B++ also had us wondering if there was some sort of catch. Other standouts include a fun three-tapas lunch set at Tapas Café (p168) for 280B++, the three-course lunch for 1000B++ at the Dusit Thani's elegant French restaurant D'Sens (below), and for 1050B++, a three-course lunch at what is the city's poshest eatery, the Oriental Hotel's Le Normandie (below).

dian restaurants near the intersection with Th Charoen Krung. Authentic foreign food can be found at the eastern end of Th Silom, near BTS Sala Daeng, and several old-school eating houses can be found at the river end. And if you're set on decadent dining, but can't justify the price tag, consider lunch, when many of Bangkok's most famous hotel restaurants offer cut-rate specials to entice diners.

CY'AN & GLOW
Map p112   International $$$
☎ 0 2625 3333; www.metropolitan.como.bz; Metropolitan Hotel, 27 Th Sathon Tai, Silom; 7-course meal 2800B; ☉ 6am-10.30am, noon-2pm & 6.30-10.30pm; Ⓜ Lumphini
Resembling the school cafeteria that Philippe Starck never designed, Cy'an is the perfect forum for the mix-and-match creations of Australian chef Daniel Moran, a protégé of Neil Perry. Combining vibrant Mediterranean and Moroccan flavours, a healthy obsession with the finest seafood, and a chic yet intimate atmosphere, the result is quite possibly the most faultless fine-dining experience in town.

The hotel's 'fresh food' restaurant, Glow has a sanatorium effect with health-conscious spa food to offset the ill effects of guzzling Bangkok's toxic sludge.

LE NORMANDIE
Map pp108–9   French $$$
☎ 0 2236 0400; Oriental Hotel, Soi 38, Th Charoen Krung, Riverside; 3/7 course meals 1000/4000B; ☉ noon-2.30pm & 7pm-10.30pm, closed lunch Sun; 🚌 ordinary 35, 36, 75 & 93, 🚢 Tha Oriental
For decades Le Normandie was synonymous with fine dining in the city. And although today's Bangkok boasts a plethora of upmarket choices, Le Normandie has maintained its niche, and is still the only place to go for a genuinely old-world 'continental' dining experience. A revolving cast

of Michelin-starred guest chefs and some of the word's most decadent ingredients keep up the standard, and appropriately formal attire (including jackets) is required.

BLUE ELEPHANT
Map pp108–9   Thai $$$
☎ 0 2673 9353; www.blueelephant.com; 233 Th Sathon Tai, Silom; mains 200-500B; ☉ 11.30am-2.30pm & 6.30-10.30pm; 🚇 Surasak
The Blue Elephant got its start in Brussels more than two decades ago as an exotic outpost of royal Thai cuisine. After spreading to other cities, the owners boldly chose Bangkok, the cuisine's birth mother, as its ninth location. Set in a stunning Sino-Portuguese colonial building with service fit for royalty, the restaurant also features an impressive cooking school (see p158).

D'SENS
Map pp108–9   French $$$
☎ 0 2200 9000; www.dusit.com; 22nd fl, Dusit Thani Hotel, 946 Th Rama IV, Silom; mains 130-500B; ☉ 11.30am-2pm Mon-Fri & 6-10pm Mon-Sat; 🚇 Sala Daeng, Ⓜ Lumphini
Located in what looks like a control tower at the top of the Dusit Thani Hotel. Bangkok's swankiest diners come to D'Sens for vibrant contemporary French cuisine as designated by the Michelin star–lauded brothers, Jacques and Laurent Pourcel. Gracious service and one of the best views of Bangkok round out the package.

EAT ME RESTAURANT
Map pp108–9   International $$$
☎ 0 2238 0931; Soi Phiphat 2, off Th Convent, Silom; mains 200-400B; ☉ 3pm-1am; 🚇 Sala Daeng, Ⓜ Silom
A little bit of Sydney has blossomed here off Th Silom, helping to give Bangkok more cosmo cred. Chic, minimalist décor is accessorised by rotating art exhibits supplied by H Gallery, the city's leading contemporary

gallery. And lest we forget, the food is creative and modern, spanning the globe from pumpkin risotto to tuna tartare.

LE BOUCHON Map pp108–9 French $$$

☎ 0 2234 9109; Soi Patpong 2, Silom; mains 150-350B; ☷ noon-3pm & 6pm-midnight; ☷ Sala Daeng, ☷ Lumphini

Cast aside any preconceived notions of pretentious waiters and intimidating menus; this homely bistro smack-dab in the middle of one of Bangkok's more 'colourful' districts is a capable and fun introduction to French cooking. Choose your dishes from the blackboard menu toted around by the cheery waiting staff, but it'd be a shame to miss the garlicky frogs' legs or the savoury foie gras pâté.

INDIAN HUT Map pp108–9 Indian $$

☎ 0 2635 7876; www.indian-hut.com; 311/2-5 Th Surawong, Silom; mains 130-250B; ☷ 11am-10.30pm; ☷ ordinary 35, 36, 75 & 93, ☷ Tha Oriental

This Indian restaurant, across from the Manorha Hotel, specialises in Nawabi (Lucknow) cuisine. Try the vegetarian samosas, fresh prawns cooked with ginger or the homemade paneer in tomato and onion curry.

BAN CHIANG Map pp108–9 Thai $$

☎ 0 2236 7045, 14 Soi Si Wiang, Th Surasak, Silom; mains 90-150B; ☷ 11.30am-2pm & 5.30-10.30pm; ☷ Surasak

Named after the archaeological site in northeastern Thailand, Ban Chiang is a

tourist spot that deserves referrals. Traditional Thai and Isan cuisine fills the menu in a cosy wooden house with eclectic décor.

MIZU'S KITCHEN
Map pp108–9 Japanese/Steak $$

☎ 0 2233 6447; 32 Soi Patpong 1, Th Silom; mains 90-400B; ☷ noon-1am; ☷ Sala Daeng, Metro Silom

This certifiable hole-in-the-wall oozes character, not to mention the beefy essence of thousands of steaks served over the decades. Do order the house Sarika steak, and do take a hint from the regulars and use your chequered tablecloth to protect your clothes from the spray of the hot plate when it arrives.

SCOOZI Map pp108–9 Italian $$

☎ 0 2234 6999; www.scoozipizza.com; 174 Th Surawong, Silom; mains 150-350B; ☷ 10.30am-11pm; ☷ Chong Nonsi

At this chic pizzeria you can witness your pie being skilfully tossed and topped before it's blistered in a wood-burning oven from Italy. Go minimalist for once and order the tasty napoletana, a pizza topped with little more than mozzarella, anchovies and olives. The ever-expanding Scoozi empire now boasts branches at Thanon Khao San (Map pp68–9; ☎ 0 2280 5280; 201 Soi Sunset) and Thonglor (Map pp118–19; ☎ 0 2391 5113; Fenix Thonglor, Soi 1, Soi 55 (Thonglor), Th Sukhumvit).

SOMBOON SEAFOOD Map pp108–9 Thai $$

☎ 0 2233 3104; www.somboonseafood.com; cnr Th Surawong & Th Narathiwat Ratchanakharin, Silom; mains 150-250B; ☷ 4pm-midnight; ☷ Chong Nonsi

Somboon, a classy seafood hall with a reputation far and wide, is known for doing the best curry-powder crab in town. Soy-steamed sea bass (*plaa kràphong nêung sii-íw*) is also a speciality and, like all good Thai seafood, should be enjoyed with an immense platter of *khào phàt puu* (fried rice with crab) and as many friends as you can gather together.

CHENNAI KITCHEN
Map pp108–9 Indian Vegetarian $

☎ 0 2234 1266; 10 Thanon Pan, Th Silom; mains 50-120B; ☷ 10am-3pm; ☷ air-con 504, 514, 544 & 547, ordinary 15, 76, 115, 162, 163 & 164, ☷ Surasak

This thimble-sized restaurant near the Hindu temple puts out some of the most

top picks

OLD-SKOOL BANGKOK DINING

- **Chote Chitr** (p155) The flavours of Olde Bangkok served up in an antique shophouse
- **Foo Mui Kee** (opposite) Where else can you have your ox tongue stew and eat it in an 80-year-old restaurant too?
- **Mizu's Kitchen** (right) Travel back in time to the R&R days of the 'American' War
- **Muslim Restaurant** (p164) Pull up a booth and enjoy dishes that haven't changed in nearly a century
- **Sanguan Sri** (p160) Party like it's 1969; fortunately the food is that of the timeless variety

solid southern Indian vegetarian around. Yard-long *dosai* (a crispy southern Indian bread) is always a good choice, but if you're feeling indecisive (and/or exceptionally famished) go for the banana-leaf thali that seems to incorporate just about everything in the kitchen.

CIRCLE OF FRIENDS Map pp108–9 Thai $
☎ 0 2237 0080; Soi 10, Th Sathorn, Silom; mains 60-100B; � 10am-8pm Mon-Fri, 4pm-8pm Sat & Sun; 🚇 Surasak
Somehow remaining cool and shady on even the hottest days, this leafy café shares space with the adjacent Saeng-Arom Ashram. With each day of the week comes two attractive set-menu options, and refreshing herbal and fruit drinks abound.

FOO MUI KEE Map pp108–9 Thai/Chinese $
☎ 0 2234 6648; 10-12 Soi 22 (Prachoom), Silom; mains 20-50B; � 10am-9pm; 🚌 air-con 504, 514, 544 & 547, ordinary 15, 76, 115, 162, 163 & 164, 🚇 Chong Nonsi
Foo Mui Kee has been serving a unique mixture of Thai, Chinese and European dishes for nearly 80 years. In some cases, such as the stewed ox tongue served with rice, the boundaries between cuisines are not so distinct, although the bottle of Worcestershire sauce on each table is a giveaway of the restaurant's Western leanings.

HARMONIQUE Map pp108–9 Thai $
☎ 0 2237 8175; Soi 34, Th Charoen Krung, Silom; mains 60-150B; � 11am-10pm Mon-Sat; 🚌 ordinary 35, 36, 75 & 93, ⚓ Tha Oriental
A tiny oasis squeezed into a former Chinese residence, Harmonique is an expat staple for thrifty romantic dinners. The dishes are unabashedly designed for folks fearful of chillies and fish sauce, but the ambience of fairy lights, a central banyan tree and marble-topped tables have spared Harmonique from our chopping block.

HOME CUISINE ISLAMIC RESTAURANT Map pp108–9 Thai-Muslim $
☎ 0 2234 7911; 196-198 Soi 36, Th Charoen Krung, Riverside; mains 45-130B; � 11am-10pm Mon-Sat, 6-10pm Sun; ⚓ Tha Oriental
Hidden in a leafy corner mercifully distant from hectic Th Charoen Krung, this bungalow-like restaurant does tasty Thai-Muslim with an endearing Indian accent. Sit out on the breezy patio and try the simultaneously

rich and sour fish curry, accompanied ideally by a flaky roti or three.

JAY SO Map pp108–9 Thai $
☎ 0 85999 4225; 146/1 Soi Phiphat 2, Th Silom; mains 20-50B; � 10am-5.30pm; 🚇 Sala Daeng, Ⓜ Lumphini
This bright blue crumbling shack is living proof that, where authentic Thai food is concerned, ambiance is often considered more a liability than an asset. Fittingly, Jay So has no menu as such, but a mortar and pestle and a huge grill are the telltale signs of ballistically spicy *sôm-tam*, sublime herb-stuffed grilled catfish and other Isan specialties.

KAI THAWT JAY KII (SOI POLO FRIED CHICKEN) Map p112 Thai $
☎ 0 1252 2252; 137/1-3 Soi Polo, Th Withayu, Lumphini; mains 30-150B; � 7am-10pm; 🚇 Ploenchit, Ⓜ Lumphini
This Cinderella of a former street stall has become virtually synonymous with fried chicken. Although the *sôm-tam*, sticky rice and *lâap* (spicy 'salad' of minced meat) give the impression of an Isan eatery, the restaurant's namesake deep-fried bird is more southern in origin. Regardless, smothered in a thick layer of crispy deep-fried garlic, it is none other than a truly Bangkok experience.

KHRUA AROY AROY Map pp108–9 Thai $
☎ 0 2635 2365; Th Pan, Th Silom; mains 30-70B; � 6am-6pm; 🚌 air-con 504, 514, 544 & 547, ordinary 15, 76, 115, 162, 163 & 164, 🚇 Surasak
Despite being the kind of family-run Thai restaurant where nobody seems to mind a cat slumbering on the cash register, Khrua Aroy Aroy ('Delicious Delicious Kitchen') lives up to its lofty name. Stop by for some of the richest curries around, as well as the interesting daily specials including, on Thursdays, *khâo khlúk kà-pì*: rice cooked in shrimp paste and served with sweet pork, shredded green mango and other toppings.

MASHOOR Map pp108–9 Indian Vegetarian $
☎ 0 2234 9305; 38 Th Pan, Th Silom; mains 50-120B; � 9am-9pm; 🚌 air-con 504, 514, 544 & 547, ordinary 15, 76, 115, 162, 163 & 164, 🚇 Surasak
Indian–Nepali vegetarian cuisine via Myanmar may sound like an entirely new cuisine altogether, but somehow it tastes

DINNER CRUISES

The Chao Phraya River is lovely in the evenings, with the skyscrapers' lights twinkling in the distance and a cool breeze chasing the heat away. A dozen or more companies run regular dinner cruises along the river. Some are mammoth boats so brightly lit inside that you'd never know you were on the water; others are more sedate and intimate, allowing patrons to see the surroundings. Several of the dinner boats cruise under the well-lit Saphan Phra Ram IX, the longest single-span cable-suspension bridge in the world.

Loy Nava (Map pp108–9; ☎ 0 2437 4932; www.loynava.com; set menu 1618B) Two cruises (from 6pm to 8pm and 8pm to 10pm) travel from Tha Si Phraya aboard a converted rice barge.

Manohra (Map pp124–5; ☎ 0 2477 0770; www.manohracruises.com; Bangkok Marriott Resort & Spa, 257/1-3 Th Charoen Nakorn; 1550B) Another restored rice barge, Manohra is the grandest them all. Cruises at 7.30pm to 10pm.

Wan Fah (Map pp108–9; ☎ 0 2222 8679; www.wanfah.com; 1200B) Also departing from Tha Si Phraya, Wan Fah's barge cruise (7pm to 9pm) is the cheaper of the lot.

Yok Yor Restaurant (Map pp108–9; ☎ 0 2439 3477; www.yokyor.co.th; dinner 300-320B) This long-running floating restaurant on the Thonburi side of the river also runs a dinner cruise (8pm to 10pm) for the average folks, mainly Thais celebrating birthdays. Add 120B surcharge to the prices quoted here.

just right. This informal kitchen, operated by a Burmese cook of Nepali descent, assembles a mean meat-free thali. Cap off your meal with a visit to Kathmandu (p192), the photography gallery across the street, and you'll soon forget which part of Asia you're actually in.

MUSLIM RESTAURANT
Map pp108–9   Thai-Muslim $

☎ 0 2234 1876; 1354-56 Th Charoen Krung, Riverside; mains 30-90B; ☾ 10am-8pm; ☒ ordinary 35, 36, 75 & 93; ☒ Tha Oriental
Plant yourself in any random wooden booth of this ancient eatery for a glimpse into what restaurants in Bangkok used to be like back in the day. The menu, much like the interior design, doesn't appear to have changed much in the restaurant's 70-year history, and the biryanis, curries and samosas are still more Indian-influenced than Thai.

NAAZ Map pp108–9   Thai-Muslim $

☎ 0 2234 4537; 24/9 Soi 45, Th Charoen Krung, Riverside; mains 40-90B; ☾ 8.30am-10pm Mon-Sat; ☒ ordinary 35, 36, 75 & 93, ☒ Tha Oriental
Hidden in a nondescript alleyway is Naaz (pronounced Nát), a tiny living-room kitchen serving some of the city's richest khâo mòk kài (chicken biryani). Various daily specials include chicken masala and mutton korma, but we're most curious to visit on Thursdays when the restaurant serves something called Karai Ghost.

NGWAN LEE LANG SUAN
Map p112   Thai-Chinese $

☎ 0 2250 0936; cnr Soi Lang Suan & Th Sarasin, Lumphini; mains 150-300B; ☾ 6pm-3am; ☒ Ratchadamri
This cavern-like staple of copious consumption is still going strong after all these decades. If you can locate the entrance, squeeze in with the post-clubbing crowd and try some of those dishes you never dare to order elsewhere, such as jàp châi (Chinese-style stewed veggies) or hŏy laay phàt náam phrík phǎo (clams stir-fried with chilli sauce and Thai basil).

RAN NAM TAO HU YONG HER
Map pp108–9   Chinese $

☎ 0 2635 0003; 68 Th Narathiwat, Silom; mains 40-205B; ☾ 11am-10pm; ☒ Chong Nonsi
Although the name of this blink-and-you'll-miss-it shophouse eatery translates as 'soy milk restaurant', the emphasis here is on northern Chinese cuisine – a rarity in Bangkok. Try the Shanghainese speciality xiao long bao (described on the menu as 'Small steamed bun'), steamed dumplings encasing a pork filling and rich hot broth that pours out when you bite into them.

SOI PRADIT MARKET Map pp108–9   Thai $
Soi 20, Th Silom; ☾ 10am-10pm; mains 25-75B; ☒ air-con 504, 514, 544 & 547, ordinary 15, 76, 115, 162, 163 & 164, ☒ Surasak
This blue-collar street market is a virtual microcosm of Thai cuisine. Muslims deep-fry marinated chicken in front of the mosque,

lonelyplanet.com

while across the way Chinese vendors chop up stewed pork leg and Isan women pound away at mortars of *sôm-tam*. Live on the edge a little and proceed past the stalls with English signs peddling the predictables.

SUAN LUM NIGHT BAZAAR
Map p112   Thai $

Th Phra Ram IV, Lumphini; mains 50-150B;
☾ 6pm-midnight; Ⓜ Lumphini

Find a seat (as far from the stage as possible if you value your eardrums), order a draught *hefeweizen* and a dish of deep-fried soft-shell crabs, and settle down for an evening of typically tasty Thai entertainment. Although the live music performances might not be to everybody's taste, the combo of decent eats and copious beer tends to tip the scales. There is talk that Suan Lum is slotted for the wrecking ball in 2008, but until the bulldozers arrive, we're remaining sceptical.

THANON SUKHUMVIT

Th Sukhumvit is Bangkok's international avenue. Running through the immigrant community of Little Arabia at Soi 3/1, past the girlie bars around Nana, and skirting the well-heeled Thai and executive expat neighbourhoods further east, there's hardly a cuisine not represented here. You wouldn't come to Sukhumvit to eat Thai, but you do come for everything else, from hummus to burgers.

LE BANYAN Map pp118–19   French $$$
☎ 0 2253 5556; www.le-banyan.com; 59 Soi 8, Th Sukhumvit; mains 350-2000B; ☾ 6.30-9.30pm Mon-Sat; Ⓡ Nana

Sukhumvit's trendy diners demand change every six months: new menu, new décor, new chef, anything to chase away restaurant boredom. But for the monogamous eaters who value a stiff-lipped experience, this classy French restaurant proves its dinosaur wisdom with formal efficient service and traditional fare. A lush garden surrounds the charming house illuminated with candles and gleaming wine glasses. The house speciality is pressed duck, but the seared foie gras steals the show.

BED SUPPERCLUB
Map pp118–19   International $$$
☎ 0 2651 3537; www.bedsupperclub.com; 26 Soi 11, Th Sukhuvmit; set menu 1000B; Ⓡ Nana

It's the modern equivalent of breakfast in bed, except that it's not breakfast, and your 'bed' is a gigantic white tube that you share with other diners. Regardless, leave your nightclothes at home and come by on Fridays when Kiwi head chef Paul Hutt takes the best of what he can get his mitts on and transforms it into a surprise four-course menu. There are three seatings per evening Sunday to Thursday and one seating at 8.30pm on Friday and Saturday.

LA PIOLA Map pp118–19   Italian $$$
☎ 0 2250 7270; lapiolabkk@hotmail.com; 31/4 Soi 11, Th Sukhumvit; full/small set menu 1200/900B; ☾ 6-10pm Tue-Sat; Ⓡ Nana

What a charming Italian eatery this is. The highlight here is the fixed menu; the only choice you make is what to drink. Three courses, including antipasto, three pasta mains and dessert, will effortlessly appear while the crowd is serenaded with Italian karaoke. You'll leave unimaginably full and drunk with flavours.

BEI OTTO Map pp118–19   German $$$
☎ 0 2262 0892; www.beiotto.com; 1 Soi 20, Th Sukhumvit; mains 170-850B; ☾ 6-11.30pm Mon-Sat, 11.30am-2.30pm Sun; Ⓡ Asoke, Ⓜ Sukhumvit

Claiming a Bangkok residence for nearly 20 years, Bei Otto's major culinary bragging point is its pork knuckles, reputedly the best in town. A good selection of German beers and an attached delicatessen with brilliant breads and super sausages make it even more attractive to go Deutsch.

KUPPA Map pp118–19   International $$$
☎ 0 2663 0450; 39 Soi 16, Th Sukhumvit; mains 180-420B; ☾ 10.30am-11.30pm Tue-Sun; Ⓡ Asoke, Ⓜ Sukhumvit

For Bangkok's ladies who lunch, Kuppa is something of a second home. Resembling an expansive living room, this place fancies itself as a 'tea and coffee trader' and the coffee is truly among the best in town. Thankfully the eats are just as good, in particular the spot-on Western-style pastries and sweets.

Kuppa is located a long walk down Soi 16; to find it, simply look for the Mercedes-laden car park peopled with loitering chauffeurs.

FOOD COURT FRENZY

For most residents of Bangkok, eating is as important a part of shopping, as er… shopping is. Thus every mall worth its escalators has some sort of food court. In the recent past these were the abode of middle-class Thais; the food was cheap, the settings bland, and you were even expected – horror of horrors – to carry your own tray. In recent years, however, food courts have moved upmarket, and the setting, cuisine and service have elevated accordingly.

Central Chitlom's Food Loft (Map pp98–9; 7th fl, Central Chitlom, Sukhumvit) pioneered the concept of the upmarket food court, and mock-ups of the various Indian, Italian, Singaporean and other international dishes aid in the decision-making process. The Loft also features monthly promotions that highlight such cuisines as Spanish, or dishes using organic produce from the north of Thailand. Upon entering, you'll be given a temporary credit card and will be led to a table. You have to get up again to order at the counters, but the dishes will be brought to you. Paying is done on your way out.

The MBK Food Court (Map pp98–9; 6th fl, Mahboonkrong Centre, Siam Sq), the granddaddy of the genre, offers tens of vendors selling food from virtually every corner of Thailand and beyond. Standouts include an excellent vegetarian food stall (stall C8), whose mock-meat mushrooms almost taste better than the real thing, and a very decent Isan food vendor (C22). The Fifth, on the 5th floor of the same mall, emphasises international eats in a slightly more upmarket setting.

Emporium's Park Food Hall (Map pp118–19; 5th fl, Emporium, Sukhumvit) brings together some of the city's most well-known international food vendors, including Indian food by Face at aloo, Vietnamese by Madam Nga, Italian by Fallabella and even acceptable Tex-Mex at Sunrise Tacos. Emporium Food Hall, on the same floor, features cheaper, mostly Thai-Chinese food, and what must be the cheapest meal with a view in town. Try the mercilessly spicy curries at Sakul, or the Phitsanulok-style noodles, served topped with the Thai equivalent of tempura. As with most food courts of this manner, paying is done by buying coupons at the windows in the entrance. Be sure to leave these in your pocket until the next day when it's too late to get a refund; it's an integral part of the food court experience.

GREAT AMERICAN RIB COMPANY
Map pp118–19   American $$$

☎ 0 2661 3801; www.greatrib.com; 32 Soi 36, Th Sukhumvit; mains 165-400B; 11.30-11.30pm; Thong Lor

The term 'barbecue' often inspires images of grilled meat, but slow-cooking as it's done in the American south is entirely another beast altogether. Avoid the burgers at this blandly named but popular joint, and stick to the fall-apart-at-the-touch Memphis-style ribs and rich pulled pork.

RUEN MALLIKA Map pp118–19   Thai $$$

☎ 0 2663 3211; www.ruenmallika.com; sub-soi off Soi 22, Th Sukhumvit; 11am-11pm; mains 200-350B; Asoke

Thai restaurateurs have tourists figured out: convert an old teak house into a restaurant and the crowds will come, regardless of the food. Ruen Mallika ups the ante by offering exquisite dishes, like dizzyingly spicy náam phrík (a thick dipping sauce with vegetables and herbs) and soulful chicken wrapped in banana leaves. The surrounding garden supplies the ingredients for the deep-fried flower dish, a house speciality. The restaurant is a little tricky to find; approach from Soi 22 off Th Ratchadapisek.

FACE Map pp118–19   Indian/Thai $$$

☎ 0 2713 6048; www.facebars.com; 29 Soi 38, Th Sukhumvit; mains 150-400B; 6.30-10pm Mon-Fri, 6.30-11pm Sat & Sun; Thong Lor

Housed in several interconnected Thai-style wooden structures, this handsome dining complex is essentially two very good restaurants in one. Lan Na Thai does flawless domestic with an emphasis on regional Thai dishes, while Hazara dabbles in exotic-sounding 'North Indian frontier cuisine.' To make matters even better, Visage, the café-bakery next door, prepares some of the best cakes and chocolates in Bangkok.

CRÊPES & CO Map pp118–19   French $$

☎ 0 2653 3990; 18/1 Soi 12, Th Sukhumvit; mains 140-350B; 9am-midnight; Asoke, Sukhumvit

Want to pretend you're part of Bangkok's expat community? This cute cottage crêperie, another 50m down the same soi as Cabbages & Condoms, is a good place to start. The homely setting and excellent service, not to mention a menu that offers much more than the restaurant's name suggests, keep the desperate housewives of Bangkok's diplomatic corps coming back again and again.

TAMARIND CAFÉ
Map pp118–19   International Vegetarian $$

☎ 0 2663 7421; www.tamarind-cafe.com; 27 Soi
20, Th Sukhumvit; mains 120-320B; ⏲ 3pm-
midnight Mon-Fri, 10am-midnight Sat & Sun;
🚇 Asoke, Ⓜ Sukhumvit

Sporting a recent face-lift, this chic but
casual vegetarian restaurant-photography
gallery is looking better than ever. Enjoy
innovative and fresh dishes under the gaze
of the latest exhibition, or sneak up to the
top-floor patio to sip wine and nibble on
desserts with the night breezes.

BOURBON ST BAR & RESTAURANT
Map pp118–19   American $$

☎ 0 2259 0328; www.bourbonstbkk.com; 29/4-6
Soi 22, Th Sukhumvit; mains 150-300B; ⏲ 10am-
2am; 🚇 Phrom Phong

Although the 'spicy' reputation of New
Orleans cuisine will probably make most
Thais chuckle at most, any restaurant run
by a man who owns a crayfish farm, stuffs
his own andouille, and has written a cook-
book on spicy food is obviously serious
about eats. Stop by on Monday, when the
traditional New Orleans dinner of red beans
and rice is served buffet-style. It's behind
the Washington Theatre.

SPRING Map pp118–19   International $$

☎ 0 2392 2747; 199 Soi Promsri 2, Soi 39, Th
Sukhumvit; mains 140-350B; ⏲ 11.30am-2.30pm
& 5-10.30pm; 🚇 Phrom Phong

The expansive lawn of this smartly recon-
verted '70s-era house is probably the only
chance you'll ever have to witness Bangkok's fair and beautiful willingly exposing
themselves to the elements. The pan-Asian
cuisine can be hit and miss, but the desserts, with names like Better Than Sex, are
as almost good as they sound.

KALAPAPREUK ON FIRST
Map pp118–19   Thai/International $$

☎ 0 2664 8410; 1st fl, Emporium, cnr Soi 24, Th
Sukhumvit; mains 150-300B; ⏲ 11am-10pm;
🚇 Phrom Phong

When Thai society types give their cooks a
day off, they wander over to this airy café
in the Emporium mall for ahǎan faràng
(Western food) or regional Thai specialities.
The dining room is not as in-your-face hip
as much of the Sukhumvit scene, but in this
part of town it's pleasant to find a place
where flavour takes a front seat.

ANA'S GARDEN Map pp118–19   Thai $$

☎ 0 2391 1762; 67 Soi 55, Th Sukhumvit; mains
150-250B; ⏲ 5pm-midnight; 🚇 Thong Lor

Ana's lush garden of broad-leafed palms
and purring fountains will almost make
you forget about the urban jungle on the
other side. The spicy yam thùa phluu (wing
bean salad) and the house speciality grilled
chicken, on the other hand, will leave no
doubts about which city you're in.

GREYHOUND CAFÉ
Map pp118–19   International $$

☎ 0 2664 8663; 2nd fl, Emporium, btwn Soi 22
& 24, Th Sukhumvit; mains 110-270B; ⏲ 11am-
10pm; 🚇 Phrom Phong

Conspicuous consumption is part of many
Bangkok menus, but Greyhound still sets
the pace. You could crawl into the techno
soundtrack of the sleek dining room, but
everyone knows that the best seats are
along the main pedestrian hallway – the
better to be seen. Despite the emphasis on
style, the menu is diverse, the food decent,
and it's good value to boot.

CABBAGES & CONDOMS
Map pp118–19   Thai $$

☎ 0 2229 4611; Soi 12, Th Sukhumvit; mains 150-
200B; ⏲ 11am-10pm; 🚇 Asoke, Ⓜ Sukhumvit

'Be fed and be sheathed' is the motto of
the restaurant outreach program of the
Population & Community Development
Association (PDA), a sex education/AIDS
prevention organisation. And likewise,

top picks

AUTHENTIC IMPORTS

- Gianni Ristorante (p160) Italian not necessarily
  the way mama made it, but even better
- Great American Rib Company (opposite) A manly
  meal of big slabs of slow-roasted southern
  barbecue
- Le Bouchon (p162) You'll be the only one speaking
  English at this Francophile outpost
- Ramentei (p168) Feel like an authentic Japanese
  sarariman as you slurp your noodles
- Ran Nam Tao Hu Yong Her (p164) One of the few
  places in town to get your northern Chinese on

for many visitors to Bangkok, this quirky garden restaurant has served as an equally 'safe' introduction to Thai food. Thankfully it's done relatively well. This is a good place to gauge the Thai staples, such as the rich green curry, or the briny *phàt phàk bûng fai daeng* (flash-fried water spinach). Instead of after-meal mints, diners receive packaged condoms, and all proceeds go towards PDA educational programmes in Thailand.

NASSER ELMASSRY RESTAURANT
Map pp118–19   Egyptian $$
☎ 0 2253 5582; 4/6 Soi 3/1, Th Sukhumvit; mains 80-350B; ☼ 8am-5am; 🚇 Nana
Part restaurant, part shrine to the glories of stainless steel furnishings, this popular Egyptian joint simply can't be missed. This is Muslim food, and the emphasis is on meat, meat and more meat, but the kitchen also knocks off some brilliant veggie mezze as well. Enhance your postprandial digestion and catch up on the Arabic-language TV news with a puff on the shishah in the super-casual smoking room upstairs.

BALI Map pp98–9   Indonesian $$
☎ 0 2250 0711; 15/3 Soi Ruam Rudi, Th Sukhumvit; mains 100-200B; ☼ 11am-2pm & 6-10pm; 🚇 Phloen Chit
With the proprietors living directly above the dining room, homely atmosphere takes a literal interpretation at Bangkok's only Indonesian restaurant. Despite the name, the food here is not Balinese, but rather pan-Indonesian, and the restaurant serves all the expected standards (satay, gado-gado, *rijstaffel*), as well as a few, slightly more unusual dishes (young jackfruit salad, a variety of *sambels* (spicy Indonesian/ Malaysian dips).

JE NGOR Map pp118–19   Thai-Chinese $$
☎ 0 2258 8008; 68/2 Soi 20, Th Sukhumvit; mains 90-600B; ☼ 11am-2pm & 5-11pm; 🚇 Asoke, Ⓜ Sukhumvit
Je Ngor proffers banquet-sized servings of tasty Thai-Chinese dishes in a banquet-like setting. The Sukhumvit branch of this lauded Thai franchise is probably not an ideal choice for a first date, but it would be a great locale for grandma's birthday dinner. The relatively short, seafood-heavy menu features rarities such as *sôm-tam puu dawng* (papaya salad with preserved crab) and baked rice with preserved olive.

TAPAS CAFÉ Map pp118–19   International $$
☎ 0 2651 2947; www.tapasiarestaurants .com; 1/25 Soi 11, Th Sukhumvit; mains 90-550B; ☼ 11.30am-11.30pm; 🚇 Nana
Although it's the least expensive of Bangkok's three Spanish joints, a visit to this newcomer is in no way a compromise. Vibrant tapas, refreshing sangria and an open, airy atmosphere make Tapas Café well worth the visit. Come before 7pm, when tapas are buy-two, get-one-free. Tapas Café is located nearly next door to Suk 11 Hostel.

RAMENTEI Map pp118–19   Japanese $$
☎ 0 2662 0050; 593/23-24 Soi 33/1, Th Sukhumvit; mains 120-300B; ☼ 11am-midnight; 🚇 Phrom Phong
The sight of French maid–clad Thai waitresses speaking Japanese may have you wondering what you've been smoking, but the spot-on Japanese comfort food will bring you back to your senses. Located smack dab in the middle of Bangkok's Little Tokyo, this workaday ramen joint serves up a variety of authentic noodle dishes to the city's sizable Japanese expat community. Choose a seat at the open kitchen to witness your bowl being prepared, or hide yourself behind a Japanese magazine in one of several booths.

KOMALA'S Map pp118–19   Indian Vegetarian $
☎ 0 2663 5971; 15 Soi 20, Th Sukhumvit; mains 80-200B; ☼ 11am-10pm Mon-Fri, 10am-11pm Sat & Sun; 🚇 Asoke
Welcome to the McDonald's of Indian food – in atmosphere, at least. If you can forgive the form-fitting plastic furniture and reckless use of teal, this Singaporean chain puts out some wonderful south Indian vegetarian staples. Go with the crispy pancake-like *dosai*, or impress your date and order the beach ball–sized *bhattura*, a deep-fried bread that unceremoniously deflates when pierced.

BOON TONG KIAT SINGAPORE HAINANESE CHICKEN RICE
Map pp118–19   Singaporean $
☎ 0 2390 2508; 440/5 & 396 Soi 55, Th Sukhumvit; mains 50-100B; ☼ 10am-10pm; 🚇 Thong Lor
The unofficial national dish of Singapore is treated with holy reverence at this humble eatery. After taking in the exceedingly detailed and ambitious chicken rice mani-

HOTEL BUFFET BONANZA

Perhaps we're food curmudgeons, but we've been under-whelmed by many of the highly touted hotel restaurants, which have more in common with graduation dinners at the country club than culinary orgasms. Where the hotels really excel is the mind-blowingly decadent buffets, with their fountains of chocolate, oysters on the half shell, pretty pink salmon, and dishes from every major cuisine. Move over Roman vomitoriums, we've got to do another buffet round.

At the high-end hotels, lunch buffets are typically 1000B, and dinner and brunch buffets 1500B to 2000B. Smaller hotels are significantly cheaper. Reservations are required.

Chocolate Bar (Map pp108–9; ☎ 0 2861 2888; Jester's, 1st fl, Peninsula Bangkok, 333 Th Charoen Nakhorn, Riverside; ⏲ 7-11.30pm Fri & Sat) Every Friday and Saturday evening the Peninsula Bangkok offers an entirely chocolate-based buffet featuring unorthodox sweet bites such as chocolate sushi and wontons filled with ganache and essence of Earl Grey.

Colonnade Restaurant (Map p112; ☎ 0 2344 8888; 1st fl, Sukhothai Hotel, 13/3 Th Sathon, Silom; ⏲ 11am-2.30pm Sun) Dah-ling you've got to brag to the neighbours about this cherry-on-top Sunday brunch. Free-flowing champagne, made-to-order lobster bisque, caviar, imported cheeses and foie gras, and a jazz trio for background music. Reservations essential, months in advance.

Four Seasons (Map pp98–9; ☎ 0 2250 1000; Four Season Hotel, 155 Th Ratchadamri, Ploenchit; ⏲ 11.30am-3pm Sun) The Four Seasons' highly regarded restaurants, Shintaro, Biscotti and Madison, set up steam tables for their decadent Sunday brunch buffet.

Marriott Café (Map pp118–19; ☎ 0 2656 7700; JW Marriott, 4 Soi 2, Th Sukhumvit; ⏲ 11.30am-2.30pm & 6.30-10.30pm) American-style abundance fills the buffet tables with fresh oysters, seafood, pasta and international nibbles at its daily buffet. There are also activities for children.

Oriental Hotel (Map pp108–9; ☎ 0 2655 9900; Oriental Hotel, Soi Oriental, Th Charoen Krung, Riverside) The Oriental has two options: Lord Jim's is a chic glass-enclosed restaurant that overlooks the river and serves a weekend brunch buffet of seafood. The Riverside Terrace serves evening barbecue buffets within fishing distance of the river.

Rang Mahal (Map pp118–19; ☎ 0 2261 7100; 26th fl, Rembrandt Hotel, 19 Soi 18, Th Sukhumvit; ⏲ 11am-2.30pm Sun) Couple views from this restaurant's 26th floor with an all-Indian buffet, and you have one of the most popular Sunday destinations for Bangkok's South Asian expat community.

Shanghai 38 (Map pp108–9; ☎ 0 2238 1991; Sofitel Silom, 188 Th Silom; ⏲ 11.30am-2.30pm) Perched on the 38th floor, this Chinese restaurant dishes up a daily dim-sum buffet and a panoramic view. On weekends the buffet includes roast suckling pig and Peking duck.

festo written on the walls, order a plate of the restaurant's namesake and witness how a dish can be so simple, yet so delicious. And while you're there you'd be daft not to order *rojak*, the spicy/sour fruit 'salad', which is referred to here tongue-in-cheek as 'Singapore Som Tam'.

IMOYA Map pp118–19 *Japanese $*
☎ 0 2663 5185; 3rd fl, Terminal Shop Cabin, 2/17-19 Soi 24, Th Sukhumvit; mains 40-120B; ⏲ 6pm-midnight; ⓡ Phrom Phong
Temporarily set aside thoughts of Bangkok and whisk yourself back to 1950s Tokyo. A visit to this well-hidden Japanese restaurant, with its antique ads, wood panelling and wall of sake bottles, is like taking a trip in a time machine. Even the prices of the better-than-decent eastern-style pub grub haven't caught up with modern times.

THONGLEE Map pp118–19 *Thai $*
☎ 0 2258 1983; Soi 20, Th Sukhumvit; mains 40-70B; ⏲ 9am-8pm, closed 3rd Sun of month; ⓡ Asoke, Ⓜ Sukhumvit
With the owners' possessions overflowing into the dining room, a heavily laden spirit shrine and tacky synthetic tablecloths, Thonglee is the epitome of a typical Thai restaurant. However, in the sea of foreign food that is Th Sukhumvit, this is exactly what makes it stand out. Thonglee offers a few dishes you won't find elsewhere, like *mǔu phàt kà-pì* (pork fried with shrimp paste) and *mìi kràwp* (sweet-and-spicy crispy fried noodles).

SOI 38 NIGHT MARKET
Map pp118–19 *Thai-Chinese $*
Soi 38, Th Sukhumvit; mains 30-60B; ⏲ 8pm-3am; ⓡ Thong Lor

It's not the best street food in town by a long shot, but after a hard night of clubbing on Sukhumvit, you can be forgiven for believing so. If you're going sober, stick to the knot of 'famous' vendors tucked into an alley on the right-hand side as you enter the street; the flame-fried *phàt thai* and herbal fish ball noodles are musts.

YUY LEE Map pp118–19   Thai $
☎ 0 2258 4600; 25 Soi 31, Th Sukhumvit; mains 25-60B; ☺ 10am-8pm Mon-Sat; ☒ Asoke, Ⓜ Sukhumvit
This aged but spotless eatery serves a variety of dishes, but most folks come for the northern Thai noodle duo of *khâo sawy* (wheat noodles in a curry broth) and *khànŏm jiin náam ngíaw* (fresh rice noodles in a tomato and pork broth). The former, although not bad for Bangkok, can't compete with the real deal from Chiang Mai, but the latter is an excellent take on a hard-to-find dish.

GREATER BANGKOK

Although it will involve something of a schlep for most visitors, an excursion to Bangkok's suburbs can be a profoundly tasty experience. The northern reaches of the city in particular are home to heaps of restaurants that wouldn't even consider toning down their food to suit foreigners. The city's outskirts are also a particularly great place to sample regional Thai cuisine.

BAAN KLANG NAM 1 Map pp124–5   Thai $$$
☎ 0 2292 0175; www.baanklangnam.net; 3792/106 Soi 14, Th Phra Ram III, Greater Bangkok; mains 200-400B; ☺ 11am-midnight; taxi from Saphan Taksin BTS station
Near Khlong Toey Port, this rustic wooden house is a favourite of the Thai matriarchs and guests at nearby Montien Riverside. The seafood is a little more expensive here than other riverside restaurants, but so is the quality. Crab, prawns, and whole white fish are among the hits that make people swoon.

LA VILLA Map pp124–5   International $$
Cnr Soi 6, Th Phaholyothin, Greater Bangkok; mains 180-300B; ☺ 10am-10pm; ☒ Ari
This new mini-mall features a handsome selection of eateries, including a branch of Greyhound Café, several Japanese restau-

rants, and delicious domestic ice cream at the local chain, iberry. Homesick foreigners will also appreciate the large branch of Villa, which carries an impressive variety of imported foodstuffs.

RIVER BAR CAFÉ Map pp52–3   Thai $$
☎ 0 2879 1747; www.riverbar.com; 405/1 Soi Chao Phraya, Th Rachawithi, Thonburi; mains 180-300B; ☺ 5pm-midnight; ☒ to Krung Thon Bridge pier
Sporting a picture-perfect riverside location, good food and live music, River Bar Café is the epitome of a Bangkok night out. Take a seat on the deck to soak up the breezes and to avoid the enthusiastic but loud live bands inside.

NANG LOENG MARKET
Map pp52–3   Market $
Btw Soi 8-10, Th Nakhon Sawan, Central Bangkok; ☺ 10am-2pm Mon-Sat; ☒ air-con 72
Dating back to 1899, this atmospheric fresh market is a wonderful glimpse of old Bangkok, not to mention a great place to grab a bite. Although it seems not to have entirely recovered from a fire a few years ago, Nang Loeng is still known for its Thai sweets, and at lunchtime is also an excellent place to fill up on savouries. Try a bowl of handmade egg noodles at Rung Rueng (☎ 0 2281 9755; 62/147 Soi 8, Th Nakhon Sawan), or the wonderful curries across the way at Ratana (☎ 0 2281 0237).

ROSDEE Map pp124–5   Thai-Chinese $
☎ 0 2331 1375; 2357 Th Sukhumvit, cnr Soi 95/1, Greater Bangkok; mains 40-120B; ☺ 8am-9pm; ☒ On Nut

top picks

REGIONAL VICTUALS

- Jay So (p163) Supreme northeastern Thai – if you can handle the heat
- Khrua Aroy Aroy (p163) The closest you'll get to an authentic southern Thai curry shack without hopping on a train
- Nang Loeng Market (above) A variety of vendors hawking true Central Thai flava
- Wang Lang Market (p154) A market of finger-lickin' good southern Thai
- Yuy Lee (left) Northern-style noodles – in the heart of Bangkok

EATING GREATER BANGKOK

FORAGING OFF THE BEATEN TRACK

Hop on the Skytrain heading north of central Bangkok for an impromptu food-tourist outing. Come lunchtime, Soi Ari, off Th Phahonyothin, is a street food paradise and virtually the entire spectrum of Isan and Thai-Chinese dishes is available. Excellent *phàt thai* can be got at the lauded Phat Thai Ari (Map pp124–5; ☎ 0 2270 1654; 2/1 Soi Ari, Greater Bangkok; ☻ 10am-10pm). Soi Rang Nam near the Victory Monument is another grazing option with lots of regional Thai restaurants such as Mallika (Map pp52–3; ☎ 0 2248 0287; 21/36 Th Rang Nam, Greater Bangkok; ☻ 10am-10pm Mon-Sat), specialising in the foods of Thailand's southern provinces, and tasty Isan at Tida Esarn (Map pp52–3; ☎ 0 2247 2234; 1/2-5 Th Rang Nam, Greater Bangkok; ☻ 11am-10pm).

This stodgy family eating hall is never going to make it on to any international magazine's 'Hot Lists' of places to dine, but the elderly bow-tied staff does give the place a certain element of charm. Instead, Rosdee is known for its consistently tasty, well-executed Thai-Chinese favourites such as the garlicky *aw sùan* (oysters fried with egg and a sticky batter), or the house speciality, braised goose.

YUSUP Map pp124–5 Thai-Muslim $
☎ 0 85136 2864; Kaset-Navamin Hwy, Greater Bangkok; mains 30-90B; ☻ 11am-2pm; taxi from ® Mor Chit
The Thai-language sign in front of this restaurant boldly says *Raachaa Khâo Mòk* (King of Biryani) and Yusup backs it up with flawless biryani (try the unusual but delicious *khâo mòk plaa*, fish biryani), not to mention mouth-puckeringly sour oxtail soup and decadent *kaeng mátsàmàn*. For dessert try *roti wǎan*, a paratha-like crispy pancake topped with sweetened condensed milk and sugar – a dish that will send most carb-paranoid Westerners running away screaming.

To find Yusup, get in a taxi heading north from Mor Chit BTS station and tell the driver to take you to Th Kaset-Navamin (also locally known as the *sên tàt mài*). Turn right at the Kaset intersection and continue about 1km past the first stop light; Yusup is on the left-hand side (look for the giant wind socks advertising the restaurant).

OR TOR KOR MARKET Map pp124–5 Thai $
Th Kampangphet, Greater Bangkok; mains 30-60B; ☻ 10am-5pm; Ⓜ Kampheng Phet
Or Tor Kor is Bangkok's highest-quality fruit and agricultural market, and sights such as the toddler-sized mangoes and dozens of pots full of curries are reason enough to visit. The vast majority of vendors' goods are takeaway only, but a few informal restaurants exist, including Rot Det, which does excellent stir-fries and curries, and sublime Isan at Sut Jai Kai Yaang, just south of the market.

To get here, take the MRT to Kampheng Phet station and exit on the side opposite Chatuchak (the exit says 'Marketing Organization for Farmers').

VICTORY POINT Map pp52–3 Thai $
Th Phayathai & Th Ratwithi, Ratchathewi; mains 30-60B; ☻ 6pm-midnight; ® Victory Monument
In Bangkok, the best meals are always in unlikely places. Far from the foreign forces of inner Bangkok, Victory Point can be as provincial as it wants, with a squat village of concrete stalls lit in neon and a mix of super casual and delicious food vendors.

BAAN SUAN PAI Map pp52–3 Thai Vegetarian $
☎ 0 2615 2454; Th Phahonyothin, Greater Bangkok; mains 25B; ☻ 11am-9pm; ® Ari
This vegetarian food centre offers a huge selection of meat-free meals served up by several vendors. Everything is strictly vegetarian, even lacking the ubiquitous fish sauce. Most plates offer the choice of three stir-fries, but there's also sushi and noodles. Don't miss the handmade ice cream of such exotic flavours as passionfruit, lemon grass and lotus root.

Purchase coupons from the woman at the desk near the entry. The coupons are printed with Thai numbers only, but the denominations are colour-coded: green – 5B; purple – 10B; blue – 20B; red – 25B.

The restaurant is just past the petrol station before Soi 4.

VEGETARIAN FOOD CENTRE
Map pp124–5 Thai Vegetarian $
Th Kamphaeng Phet, Greater Bangkok; mains 10-30B; ☻ 8am-noon Tue-Mon; Ⓜ Kamphaeng Phet, ® Mor Chit

lonelyplanet.com

Operated by the Asoke Foundation, this wholly vegetarian food centre near the Weekend Market is one of Bangkok's oldest. To find it, cross the footbridge above Th Kampaengphet, heading away from the market, and towards the southern end of Th Phahonyothin. Take the first right onto a through street heading into the car park, and walk past the nightclubs and bars. Turn right, and you'll see a new block of buildings selling bulk food stuff. The restaurant is at the end of this strip. Prices are ridiculously low (around 10B per dish) and you buy tickets at the front desk.

DRINKING & NIGHTLIFE

top picks

- Cheap Charlie's (p175)
- Club Culture (p183)
- The Living Room (p181)
- Parking Toys (p181)
- Thanon Khao San & Thanon Rambutri (p176)

Disregard the tired cliché of Bangkok's nightlife as a one-trick pony. The infamous girlie-bar scene may still be going just as strong as it has been for the last 30 years but, despite what your uncle told you, having a good time in Bangkok doesn't have to involve ping-pong balls or bar fines. Just like any other big international city, Bangkok's drinking and partying scene ranges from points classy to trashy, and touches on just about everything in between.

The powers that be, however, take a slightly different view on fun, and would seemingly rather have us watching traditional dance performances and tucked into bed by 9pm. Since 2004 the vast majority of Bangkok's bars and clubs have been ordered to close by 1am. A complicated zoning system sees venues in designated 'entertainment areas', including RCA (Royal City Avenue), Th Silom, and parts of Th Sukhumvit, open until 2am, but even these are subject to police whimsy. Despite the resulting financial losses and negative impact on tourism (not to mention Bangkok's reputation), the policy has been popular among Thais, and there's little chance of seeing any changes in the near future.

The good news is that everything old is new again. Th Khao San, that former outpost of foreigner frugality, has undergone something of an upscale renaissance and is now more popular with the locals than ever. And RCA, a suburban nightclub zone previously associated with gum-snapping Thai teenagers, has finally graduated from high school and is drawing in dancers and drinkers of all ages and races.

DRINKS

FRUIT DRINKS

With the abundance of fruit growing in Thailand, the variety of juices and shakes available in markets, street stalls and restaurants is extensive. The all-purpose term for fruit juice is *náam phŏn-lá-mái*. When a blender or extractor is used, you've got *náam khán* (squeezed juice), hence *náam sàppàrót khán* is freshly squeezed pineapple juice. *Náam âwy* (sugarcane juice) is a Thai favourite and a very refreshing accompaniment to *kaeng* dishes. A similar juice from the sugar palm, *náam taan sòt*, is also very good, and both are full of vitamins and minerals. Mixed fruit blended with ice is *náam pan* (literally 'mixed juice'), as in *náam málákaw pan*, a papaya shake.

BEER

Advertised with such slogans as '*pràthêht rao, bia rao*' ('our land, our beer'), the Singha label is considered the quintessential Thai beer by *faràng* (Westerners) and locals alike. Pronounced *sǐng*, this pilsner claims about half the domestic market. Singha's original recipe was formulated in 1934 by Thai nobleman Phya Bhirom Bhakdi, the first Thai to earn a brewmaster's diploma in Germany. The barley for Singha is grown in Thailand, the hops are imported from Germany and the alcohol content is a heady 6%. It is sold in brown glass bottles (330ml and 660ml) with a shiny gold lion on the label, as well as in cans (330ml). It is available on tap as *bia sòt* (draught beer) – much tastier than either bottled or canned brew – in many Bangkok pubs and restaurants.

Singha's biggest rival, Beer Chang, pumps the alcohol content up to 7%. Beer Chang has managed to gain an impressive following mainly because it retails at a significantly lower price than Singha and thus offers more bang per baht.

Boon Rawd (the makers of Singha) responded with its own cheaper brand, Leo. Sporting a black-and-red leopard label, Leo costs only slightly more than Beer Chang but is similarly high in alcohol.

Dutch-licensed but Thailand-brewed Heineken comes third after Singha and Chang in sales rankings. Similar 'domestic imports' include Asahi and San Miguel. Other Thai-brewed beers, all at the lower end of the price spectrum, include Cheers and Beer Thai. More variation in Thai beer brands is likely in the coming years as manufacturers scramble to command market share by offering a variety of flavours and prices.

RICE WHISKY

Rice whisky is a favourite of the working class in Bangkok, since it's more affordable than beer. It has a sharp, sweet taste not unlike rum, with an alcohol content of 35%. The most famous brand for many years was Mekong (pronounced 'mee kong'), but currently the most popular brand is the slightly more expensive Sang Som. Both come in 750ml bottles called *klom* or in 375ml flask-shaped bottles called *baen*. Thais normally drink whisky with ice and plenty of soda water.

More-expensive Thai whiskies produced from barley and appealing to the can't-afford-Johnnie-Walker-yet set include Blue Eagle, 100 Pipers and Spey Royal, each with a 40% alcohol content. These come dressed up in shiny boxes, much like the expensive imported whiskies they're imitating.

DRINKING

Bangkok's watering holes cover the spectrum from English-style pubs where you can comfortably sit with a pint and the paper, to chic dens where the fair and beautiful go to be seen, not to imbibe. A laundry list of beverages is available, though alcohol prices are relatively more than, say, cab rides or street food.

Because food is so integral to any Thai outing, most bars have tasty dishes that are absent-mindedly nibbled between toasts. Bars don't have cover charges, but they do strictly enforce closing time at 1am, sometimes earlier if they suspect trouble from the cops.

BACCHUS WINE BAR Map pp98–9   Wine Bar
☎ 0 2650 8986; www.bacchus.tv, info@bacchus.tv; 20/6-7 Soi Ruam Rudi, Ploenchit; 5pm-1am; Ploenchit
Wine bars are still a new and relatively uncommon concept in Bangkok. Bacchus was among the first, and still sets the aesthetic standard with exposed brick walls, floating stairs and sculpture seating. Despite the slightly upscale setting, it's a friendly enough place to down a glass or two of one of the 400 varieties of wine, or cop a nibble from the lengthy menu of tapas and appetisers.

BARBICAN BAR Map pp108–9   Bar
☎ 0 2234 3590; www.greatbritishpub.com; 9/4-5 Soi Thaniya, Th Silom; 6pm-1am; Sala Daeng, M Silom
Decked out in slate-grey and blonde wood, this upscale-ish pub is an oasis of subdued cool in a strip consisting mostly of Japanese-frequented massage parlours. Where else could you suck down a few cocktails with friends from Thailand, Singapore and

Norway, and then stumble out to find a line of Thai women dressed like cheap prom dates reciting 'Hello, massage' in faulty Japanese?

BLACK SWAN Map pp118–19   Bar/Restaurant
☎ 0 2626 0257; www.blackswanbkk.com; 326/8-9 Th Sukhumvit; 9-1am; Asoke, M Sukhumvit
Liable to bring a tear to the eye of a homesick Brit, the combination of supping mates, dining families and bad décor make the Black Swan the most authentic of Bangkok's numerous English pubs. Come on Friday when you can enjoy your draught bitter with fresh fish flown directly from Scotland.

BULL'S HEAD & ANGUS STEAKHOUSE
Map pp118–19   Bar/Restaurant
☎ 0 2259 4444; www.greatbritishpub.com; 595/10-11 Soi 33/1, Th Sukhumvit; 6pm-midnight; Phrom Phong
Worn wood panelling, imported draught beer and admirable pub grub take the Bull's Head just beyond the realm of the 'theme' pub. With friendly management and staff, and more events and activities than a summer camp, this is a good place to meet people, particularly those of the British persuasion.

CAFÉ TRIO Map pp98–9   Bar
☎ 0 2252 6572; 36/11-12 Soi Lang Suan, Th Ploenchit; 6pm-1am, closed 2nd & 4th Sun of month; Chitlom
This jazz bar/art gallery also offers live music on an irregular basis – it's best to check ahead. The real highlights are the laid-back local atmosphere and the proprietor, Patti, whose artwork graces the walls and whose laughter and boisterous conversation have the ability to render music redundant.

CHEAP CHARLIE'S Map pp118–19   Bar
Soi 11, Th Sukhumvit; 6pm-1am Mon-Sat; Nana
You're bound to have a mighty difficult time convincing your Thai friends to go to Th Sukhumvit only to sit at an outdoor wooden shack decorated with buffalo skulls and wagon wheels. Fittingly, Charlie's draws a staunchly foreign crowd who don't mind a bit of kitsch and sweat with their Singha.

THANON KHAO SAN & THANON RAMBUTRI

Not just for foreigners any more, in recent years Th Khao San has become an acceptable destination among Thai fun-seekers, and correspondingly, the scene has diversified. You can still sit directly on the street and watch the freak show while nursing the cheapest beer in town, but if you fancy a martini and a soundtrack, such things can be arranged.

A visible sigh can be heard as people cross to quieter Th Rambutri. Slightly more upscale in places, and thus more popular with Thais, there's still a bar to suit every taste.

Here is a brief cross-section of what's available.

- Buddy Bar (Map pp68–9; ☎ 2629 4477; Th Khao San, Banglamphu) Clean and cool colonial-themed bar for folks who find Bangkok too dirty.
- Bua Sa-ad (Map pp68–9; Th Rambutri, Banglamphu) Named after the elegant house that contains it, this street-side bar is one of the few in the area serving imported beers.
- deep (Map pp68–9; ☎ 0 2629 3360; 329/1-2 Th Rambutri, Banglamphu) If you're willing to wait out the perpetual queue, inside you'll find a dark den packed to the gills with young Thai hipsters.
- Hippie de Bar (Map pp68–9; Th Khao San, Banglamphu) Retro décor, pool tables and chill DJs.
- Lava Club (Map pp68–9; ☎ 0 2281 6565; 249 Th Khao San, Banglamphu) Moody basement lounge spinning all genres of electronica.
- Molly Bar (Map pp68–9; ☎ 0 2629 4074; 108 Th Rambutri, Banglamphu) Mellow sidewalk beer garden for audible conversations.
- Roof Bar (Map pp68–9; ☎ 0 2629 2300; 3rd fl, Th Khao San, Banglamphu) Although the live acoustic soundtrack is hit-and-miss, the views are solid from this rooftop pub. Next to Khao San Palace Hotel.
- Shamrock Irish Pub (Map pp68–9; 2nd fl, Khao San Centre, Th Khao San, Banglamphu) Loud live bands and cheap Guinness.
- Silk Bar (Map pp68–9; ☎ 0 2281 9981; 129-131 Th Khao San, Banglamphu) An open-air cocktail bar for the visiting Sukhumvit entourage crowd.
- Susie Pub (Map pp68–9; ☎ 0 2282 4459; 108/5-9 Th Rambutri, Banglamphu) Before Khao San was a hip place for Thais to hang out, Susie was a local outpost for university students to play pool and drink in candy pop music.

Th Khao San and Th Rambutri run parallel to each other between Th Chakraphong and Th Tanao, north of Th Ratchadamnoen Klang. Take the river ferry to Tha Phra Athit, air-con bus 511 or 512, or ordinary bus 15, 30 or 65.

COSMIC CAFÉ Map pp124–5 Bar
☎ 0 2641 5619; Zone C Royal City Ave, off Th Phra Ram IX, Greater Bangkok; admission free; ⏰ 7pm-2am; Ⓜ Rama IX

Cosmic calls itself a café and looks like a club but in reality is more of a bar… Despite the slight identity crisis, this is a fun place to drink and meet Thai-style. Come on Wednesday night when the DJ spins Thai music from the '80s.

COYOTE ON CONVENT
Map pp108–9 Bar/Restaurant
☎ 0 2631 2325; www.coyoteonconvent.com; 1/2 Convent Rd, Th Silom; ⏰ 11-1am; Ⓡ Sala Daeng, Ⓜ Lumphini

Coyote serves decent but pricey Mexican nosh with a relatively light dose of kitsch. But what really keeps people coming, in particular Bangkok's female half, are the 75+ varieties of margaritas. Come Wednesday evening the icy drinks are distributed free to all women who pass through the door. On other days the frosty drinks are buy-one-get-one-free from 3pm to 7pm.

JOOL'S BAR & RESTAURANT
Map pp118–19 Bar/Restaurant
☎ 0 2252 6413; Soi 4 (Soi Nana Tai), Th Sukhumvit; ⏰ 11am-midnight; Ⓡ Nana

With the walls virtually covered with pictures of the bar's regulars, you'll feel like part of the crowd even if you're drinking alone. When things are buzzing, lots of Nana Plaza girly-bar vets take a breather here for a good-natured romp with beer buddies.

MOLLY MALONE'S
Map pp108–9 Pub
☎ 0 2266 7160; www.mollymalonesbangkok.com; 1/5-6 Convent Rd, Th Silom; ⏰ 11-1am; Ⓡ Sala Daeng, Ⓜ Silom

The third and, we hope, final reincarnation of this Bangkok Irish staple has retained much of the faux-shamrock charm of its predecessor. Like most of its countryfolk, Molly's is equal parts game for a quiet pint alone or a rowdy night out with your friends.

MOON BAR AT VERTIGO Map p112 Bar

☎ 0 2679 1200; www.banyantree.com; Banyan Tree Hotel, 21/100 Th Sathon Tai, Silom; ⊗ 6.30-11pm, weather permitting; Ⓜ Lumphini
Bangkok is one of the few big cities in the world where nobody seems to mind if you set up the odd restaurant or bar on the top of a skyscraper. Now nearly forgotten, the restaurant Vertigo and the attached Moon Bar started the trend. Come dressed up and grab a coveted seat to the right of the bar for impressive views at sunset.

NANG NUAL RIVERSIDE PUB
Map p84 Pub

☎ 0 2223 7686; Trok Krai, Th Mahachak, Chinatown; ⊗ 4pm-midnight; ⬛ air-con 60, 73 & 512, ordinary 5 & 8, 🚢 Tha Saphan Phut
In the best Thai tradition, this riverside deck blurs the lines between a restaurant and a bar. Groups of friends gather around the whisky set and plates of *kàp klâem* (drinking food) to watch the river and the night flow by. At certain times, the bar's blaring pop music competes for valuable air space with the Muslim call to prayer from the temple across the river.

NEST Map pp118–19 Bar/Restaurant

☎ 0 2255 0638; www.nestbangkok.com; Rooftop, Le Fenix Hotel, 33/33 Soi 11, Th Sukhumvit; admission free; ⊗ 5pm-2am; 🚇 Nana
Perched on the roof of the Le Fenix Hotel, Nest is a chic maze of cleverly concealed sofas and inviting daybeds. A DJ soundtrack and one of the most interesting pub grub menus in town bring things back down to ground level.

OPERA RISERVA WINETHEQUE
Map pp118–19 Wine Bar

☎ 0 2258 5601; www.operariserva.com; 53 Soi 39, Th Sukhumvit; ⊗ 5.30pm-1am; 🚇 Phrom Phong
Decked out in leather and wood and sporting a speakeasy feel, Opera's wine bar is more for the discreet conversationalist than the sensationalist. You're more than likely to find something you'll fancy from the week's wine pics, and an attractive and extensive menu of wine-friendly Italian-style meals and snacks is also available.

PHRANAKORN BAR Map pp68–9 Bar

☎ 0 2282 7507; 58/2 Soi Damnoen Klang Tai, Banglamphu; ⊗ 6pm-midnight; ⬛ air-con 511 & 512, ordinary 15, 30 & 65, 🚢 Tha Phra Athit

It must have taken a true visionary to transform this characterless multilevel building into a warm, fun destination for a night out. Students and arty types make Phranakorn Bar a home away from hovel with eclectic décor, gallery exhibits and, the real draw, a rooftop terrace for beholding the old district's majesty.

RAIN DOGS BAR & GALLERY
Map p112 Bar

☎ 0817 206 989; 16 Soi Phraya Phiren, off Soi Sawan Sawat, off Phra Ram IV; Lumphini; ⊗ 7pm-1am; Ⓜ Klongtoei
Tucked away down a dead-end street, you'd never find Rain Dogs unless you knew about it. Run by and for local and expat artists, photographers and journalists, it feels refreshingly grungy in increasingly slick Bangkok. Rain Dogs has regular events, but can also be empty, so call ahead to see what's on. To get there, walk from Klongtoei Metro (cross under the freeway, turn left down the small lane to the dead end) or get a taxi driver to call for the address.

SHIP INN Map pp118–19 Bar

9/1 Soi 23, Th Sukhumvit; ⊗ 11am-midnight; 🚇 Asoke
Only steps away from Soi Cowboy but a world away in ambience, Ship Inn provides a mature embrace for a quiet drinking crowd. The mock-Tudor bar is as well stocked as a ship captain's quarters, and the music is gracefully at conversational volume.

SIROCCO Map pp108–9 Bar

☎ 0 2624 9555; The Dome at State Tower, 1055 Th Silom; ⊗ 5pm-1am; Ⓜ Saphan Taksin
Yet another of Bangkok's rooftop bars, the Sky Bar at Sirocco provides heart-stopping views over the Chao Phraya River, not to mention much of Bangkok. Come here for a drink and the view, not the overpriced cuisine.

TAKSURA Map pp68–9 Bar

☎ 0 2622 0708; 156/1 Th Tanao, Banglamphu; ⊗ 5pm-1am; ⬛ air-con 511 & 512, ordinary 15, 30 & 65, 🚢 Tha Phra Athit
There are no signs to lead you to this seemingly abandoned 93-year-old mansion in the heart of old Bangkok, which is all the better according to the cool uni-artsy

NIGHTLIFE ANTHROPOLOGIST

Honestly, Bangkok's nightlife is never going to measure up to that of the world-class cities, but Bangkok's nightcrawling characters are a lot easier to gain access to than those in New York City's exclusive clubs.

The nightspots and night owls that a foreigner might encounter can be divided into three genres: hi-so, *dèk naew* (trendy child) and lo-so. The high society types split their time between Bangkok and Europe and have pioneered Bangkok's fascination with wine, London lounge, mid-century minimalism and international cuisine – the usual tastes of the rich and famous. You'll find them snacking at Bacchus (p175) or nodding to live jazz at the Living Room (p181).

Younger and more fashion-fearless are *dèk naew*. This scene can range from arty and creative to pop and parodying. Bakery Music (p32) and other alternative labels were funded by the buying power of *dèk naew*, and the '80s fashion revival sprouted amid Siam Sq's hipsters before it hit the equivalent neighbourhoods in San Francisco. *Dèk naew* who choose not to stray far from their Siam stomping grounds go to To Sit (below), while others trudge over to Banglamphu for Taksura (p177) or to Ekamai for Nang Len (p183).

At the bottom of the feeding chain are the lo-sos ('low society'), the ordinary middle class who prefer Thai rock to international electronica and drink whisky sets instead of gin and tonics. Lat Phrao, Pattanakan and other suburban neighbourhoods are where the 'real' Thais live and party. Places like Tawan Daeng German Brewhouse (p182) and Water Bar (below) attract average Thais doing average Thai things.

Foreigners are somehow exempt from this spectrum and can be found anywhere, from trendy dens such as Barbican Bar (p175) or Opera Riserva Winetheque (p177), to fun dives such as Wong's (below) or Cheap Charlie's (p175).

crowd who frequent the place. Take a seat outside to soak up the breeze, and go Thai by ordering some spicy nibbles with your drinks.

TO-SIT Map pp98–9 Bar

☎ 0 2658 4001; www.tosit.com; Siam Sq, Soi 3, Th Phra Ram 1; ⏰ 6pm-1am; ⧠ Siam
Live, loud and sappy music, cheap and spicy food, good friends and cold beer: To-Sit epitomises everything a Thai university student could wish for on a night out. There are branches all over town (check the website), but the Siam Sq location has the advantage of being virtually the only option in an area that's buzzing during the day, but dead at night.

TUBA Map pp118–19 Bar/Restaurant

☎ 0 2622 0708; 30 Soi 21, Soi 63 (Ekamai), Th Sukhumvit; ⏰ 6pm-2am; ⧠ Ekamai
Used-furniture shop by day, Italian restaurant-bar by night. Oddly enough, this business formula is not entirely unheard of in Bangkok. Pull up a leatherette lounge and take the plunge and buy a whole bottle for once. And don't miss the delicious chicken wings.

WATER BAR Map pp52–3 Bar

☎ 0 2642 7699; 107/3-4 Soi Rang Nam, Th Phayathai, Ratchathewi; ⏰ 5pm-1am; ⧠ Victory Monument
Every new arrival should learn the whisky-set routine, a drinking tradition more at home than at Thai family gatherings than in flash hotels. At this misnomered bar, a short walk from Victory Monument, the Sang Som set (see p182) still reigns as the tipple of choice. The attentive waiters will keep your glass filled to the right proportions (three fingers whisky, a splash of Coke, the rest soda), after which you should offer up a toast and drain the night away.

WONG'S PLACE Map p112 Bar

27/3 Soi Sri Bumphen, off Soi Ngam Duphli, Th Phra Ram IV, Lumphini; ⏰ 8pm-late; Ⓜ Lumphini
An odd choice for an institution if there ever was one, this dusty den is a time warp into the backpacker world of the early 1980s. The namesake owner died several years ago, but a relative removed the padlock and picked up where Wong left off. Wong's works equally well as a destination or a last resort, but don't bother knocking until midnight, keeping in mind that it stays open until the last person crawls out.

GAY & LESBIAN BANGKOK

Is there a more gay-friendly city on the planet? While stepping off the Western shelf is a gamble for many, Bangkok's male-gay nightlife is out and open with bars, discos and *kàthoey* cabarets. Night spots for Thai lesbians (*tom-dee*) aren't as prominent or as segregated.

The city's most stylish gays mix with the beautiful people at whatever watering hole is elite enough for their attention (Eat Me (p161) is a gracious dinner date). Most gay foreign men find themselves at one of the bars or dance clubs that line Soi 2 and Soi 4 (Map pp108–9), off Th Silom. A more local crowd of students hangs out on the *sois* (lanes) around Ramkhamhaeng University on Th Ramkhamhaeng (Map pp124–5) near the Lamsalee intersection, or on Th Kamphaeng Phet (Map pp124–5), across from Chatuchak Weekend Market. The strip of bars along Th Sarasin (Map p112) has also become a popular destination among young gay Thais. Bed Supperclub (p165) hosts a hugely popular 'pink' night on Sunday, and other posh locales play host to weekend-long 'circuit parties' (visit www .gcircuit.com to find out when and where the next one is).

The city's lesbian entertainment scene is still rather new, and limited to a handful of dedicated venues: Lesla, Shela and Zeta. For comprehensive lesbian-specific information online, visit Bangkok Lesbian (www.bangkoklesbian .com), maintained by a New Yorker and her Thai girlfriend.

The *Utopia Guide to Thailand* covers gay-friendly businesses in 18 Thai cities, including Bangkok. Its website, www.utopia-asia .com, is also a good, if slightly outdated, source of information. More up-to-date listings and events can be found at www.fridae. com. Both gays and lesbians are well advised to visit Bangkok in mid-November, when the city's small but fun Pride Festival (www.bangkokpride .org) is in full swing. Dinners, cruises, clubbing and contests are the order of the week.

BALCONY Map pp108–9 Bar/Restaurant
☎ 0 2235 5891; www.balconypub.com; 86-88 Soi 4, Th Silom; ⏰ 5.30pm-2am; 🚇 Sala Daeng, Ⓜ Silom
Instantly recognisable by its perky T-shirt-and-shorts clad staff, Balcony is a lively bar with dancing and karaoke inside and chill-out tables on the terrace.

DJ STATION Map pp108–9 Bar
☎ 0 2266 4029; www.dj-station.com; 8/6-8 Soi 2, Th Silom; ⏰ 10pm-2am; 🚇 Sala Daeng, Ⓜ Silom
Massively popular with the younger crowd and among the most well-known gay destinations in town, this place has pounding dance music, flamboyant costume parties and *kàthoey* cabaret at 11pm.

ICK PUB Map pp124–5 Pub
☎ 0 81442 9472; Soi 89/2, Th Ramkhamhaeng, Greater Bangkok; ⏰ 8pm-1am; Ⓜ Rama IX
Near the end of the *soi*, ICK is a poster-child for Ramkhamhaeng's gay student hangouts, and is full of bubble-gum pop music and late-night schedules.

ICY Map pp124–5 Bar
Th Kamphaengphet, Greater Bangkok; ⏰ 8pm-1am; 🚇 Kamphaeng Phet
Located in the jumble of straight and gay bars near Chatuchak Weekend Market, this long-running pub is consistently loud, crowded and very local.

KLUEN SAEK Map p112 Bar
☎ 0 2254 2962; 297 Th Sarasin, Lumphini; ⏰ 6pm-1am; 🚇 Ratchadamri
One of a strip of bars along Th Sarasin that are becoming gayer by the day, Kluen Saek is barely able to contain a mixed crowd of ravers in its cool grey grip.

SA-KE COFFEE PUB Map pp68–9 Bar
☎ 0 2225 6000; Trok Sa-Ke, cnr Trok Sa-Ke & Th Rachadamnoen Tai, Banglamphu; ⏰ 8pm-1am; 🚌 air-con 511 & 512, ordinary 15, 30 & 65, ⛴ Tha Phra Athit
Near the Khok Wua intersection, 'Sa-gay' is in the middle of a mini gay scene happening just steps from Khao San.

TELEPHONE Map pp108–9 Bar/Restaurant
☎ 0 2234 3279; www.telephonepub.com; 114/11-13 Soi 4, Th Silom; ⏰ 6pm-1am; 🚇 Sala Daeng, Ⓜ Silom
At 20 years of age, Bangkok's oldest gay bar/restaurant still features telephones so that patrons can 'ring' each other. The café-like seating in front is probably the best place from which to watch the virtual gay-pride parade that is Soi 4.

ZUP ZIP Map pp124–5 Bar/Restaurant
☎ 0 81734 2759; 674 Soi 101, Th Lat Phrao; ⏰ 6pm-2am; 🚌 air-con 172, ordinary 44
This lesbian-owned locale in the northern suburbs features a friendly atmosphere, homey Thai-Chinese fare and supping tom-dees.

G.O.D. (GUYS ON DISPLAY)
Map pp108–9 Club
☎ 0 2632 8032; Soi 2/1, Th Silom; admission 280B; ⏰ 7pm-late; 🚇 Sala Daeng, Ⓜ Silom

The former Freeman has been reincarnated as this popular after-hours destination. Open late and, as the name suggests, not averse to a bit of shirtless dancing. Located on the tiny alley between Soi 2 and Soi Thaniya.

LESLA Map pp124–5   Club
☎ 0 2618 7191; www.lesla.com; Chit Chat Club, Soi 85, Soi Choke Chai 4, Th Lad Phrao; admission 200B; ⊙ 8pm-1am Sat; taxi from Ⓜ Lad Phrao
Bangkok's biggest lesbian group date is held every Saturday at Chit Chat Pub in Bangkok's northern outskirts.

SHELA Map p112   Club
☎ 0 2254 6463; www.shelacorner.com; 106/12-13 Soi Lang Suan (cnr Soi Lang Suan & Th Sarasin), Lumphini; admission free; ⊙ 7pm-2am; Ⓡ Ratchadamri
Owned by the same women who run Zeta, Shela draws a slightly more mature crowd with live music, a pool table and food. Women only.

ZETA Map pp124–5   Club
☎ 0 2203 0994; www.zetabangkok.com; 29 Royal City Ave, off Phra Ram IX, Greater Bangkok; admission free; ⊙ 10pm-2am; Ⓜ Rama IX
This exceedingly popular lesbian club on the quiet end of RCA is packed to the gills with young tom-dees on weekends. It's for women only.

BABYLON BANGKOK
Map p112   Sauna
☎ 0 2679 7984; www.babylonbangkok.com; 34 Soi Nantha, off Soi 1, Th Sathon, Sathon; ⊙ 3-11pm; Ⓜ Lumphini
This four-storey gay sauna has been described as one of the top 10 of its kind in the world. Facilities include a bar, roof garden, gym, massage room, steam and dry saunas, and spa baths. The spacious, well-hidden complex also has accommodation.

CHAKRAN Map pp124–5   Sauna
☎ 0 2279 1359; www.utopia-asia.com/chakran; 32 Soi 4, Soi Ari, Th Phaholyothin, Greater Bangkok; ⊙ noon-11.30pm; Ⓡ Ari
This upmarket multistorey complex comes fully loaded with an indoor pool, large spa, steam, sauna, gym, video room and karaoke areas, as well as a restaurant and poolside bar. The crowd is generally Thai/Asian, but it's starting to see more faràng as well.

LIVE MUSIC
As Thailand's media capital, Bangkok is also the centre of the Thai music industry, packaging and selling pop, crooners, lûuk thûng, and the recent phenomenon of indie bands.

Music is a part of almost every Thai social gathering. The matriarchs and patriarchs like dinner with an easy-listening soundtrack: typically a Filipino band and a synthesizer. Patrons pass their request (on a napkin) up to the stage. An indigenous rock style, phleng phêua chii-wít (songs for life), makes appearances at a dying breed of country-and-western bars decorated with buffalo horns and pictures of Native Americans. Several dedicated bars throughout the city feature blues and rock bands, but are quite scant on live indie-scene performances. Up-and-coming garage bands occasionally pop up at free concerts where the kids hang out: Santichaiprakan Park (Th Phra Athit), Th Khao San and Siam Sq. Music festivals like Noise Pop and Fat Festival also feature the new breed.

Some of the steam that fuelled Th Phra Athit's (Map pp68–9) arty resurrection has dissipated, but the street still retains several closet-sized bars where bohemian Thais and university students mix and mingle with whisky sets and acoustic singalongs. The strip clusters around the block starting directly in front of the river ferry pier. The shopfront bars on Th Phra Athit typically feature a squeaky guitar and a solo singer, performing to an audience of young Thai folk who always know all the words.

For a schedule of live shows, check out Eastbound Downers (www.eastbound-downers.com), a promo site for indie bands, and Bangkok Gig Guide (www.bangkokgigguide.com), a comprehensive schedule of shows across the city. For more on the ins and outs of the Thai music scene, see p31.

AD HERE THE 13TH Map pp68–9   Bar
13 Th Samsen, Banglamphu; ⊙ 6pm-midnight; 🚌 air-con 3, 32 & 49, ordinary 30, 32, 33 & 65, 🚤 Tha Phra Athit
Please don't blame the drummer if you're accidentally smacked by a stray drumstick; things can get a bit tight in here. Featuring a soulful house band that plays at 10pm nightly, Ad Here is one of those places that somehow manages to be both raucous and intimate.

AD MAKERS Map pp108–9   Bar
☎ 0 2634 5227; 142 Th Sathon Tai; ☯ 11am-10.30pm; ⓡ Surasak
Now at new digs on Th Sathon, this live-music staple is going strong after all these years. The house band still puts out heart-felt Thai folk and other classic-rock stand-ards, and an expanded menu means more flavour with your tunes.

BAMBOO BAR Map pp108–9   Bar
☎ 0 2659 9000; Oriental Hotel, Soi 38 (Oriental), Th Charoen Krung, Riverside; ☯ 11-1am; ⌷ ordinary 35, 36, 75 & 93, ⚓ Tha Oriental
Rubber-plantation barons and colonial mansions are not exactly part of Bangkok's history, but Bamboo Bar, in the historic Oriental Hotel, exudes oodles of bygone charm. Internationally recognized jazz bands hold court within a brush stroke of the audience to set a mellow lounge mood.

BRICK BAR Map pp68–9   Bar
☎ 0 2629 4477; basement, Buddy Lodge, 265 Th Khao San, Banglamphu; ☯ 8pm-1am; ⌷ air-con 511 & 512, ordinary 15, 30 & 65, ⚓ Tha Phra Athit
Resembling Liverpool's Cavern Club circa 1960, Brick Bar is an underground den that hosts a nightly revolving cast of live music for an almost exclusively Thai crowd. Come before midnight, wedge yourself into a table a few inches from the horn section, and lose it to Teddy Ska, one of the most energetic live acts in town.

BROWN SUGAR Map p112   Pub
☎ 0 2250 1825; www.brownsugarbangkok.com; 231/20 Th Sarasin, Lumphini; ☯ 6pm-1.30am; ⓡ Ratchadamri
Be careful upon entering Brown Sugar lest you trip over the bass player. With Crescent City informality, Friday and Saturday nights see this perpetually packed pub's house band giving inspired performances that blend soul, jazz, rock and just about everything else.

GAZEBO Map pp68–9   Pub
☎ 0 2629 0705; www.gazebobkk.com; 3rd fl, 44 Th Chakrapong, Banglamphu; ☯ 7pm-late; ⌷ air-con 511 & 512, ordinary 15, 30 & 65, ⚓ Tha Phra Athit
Like an oasis above Th Khao San, this vaguely Middle-Eastern themed pub draws backpackers and locals alike with fun cover bands, mist-blowing fans and fez-topped sheesha attendants. Its elevated location

also appears to lend it some leniency with the city's strict closing times.

LIVING ROOM Map pp118–19   Lounge Bar
☎ 0 2649 8888; www.sheratongrandesukhumvit.com; Level I, Sheraton Grande Sukhumvit, 250 Th Sukhumvit; ☯ 9pm-1am; ⓡ Asoke, Ⓜ Sukhumvit
Although it's not exactly a smoky den filled with finger-snapping hep cats, every night the Sheraton Grande Sukhumvit's deceptively bland hotel lounge transforms into one of the city's best venues for live jazz. Check ahead of time to see which sax master or hide hitter is currently in town.

NORIEGA'S Map pp108–9   Bar/Pub
☎ 0 2233 2813; Soi 4, Th Silom; ☯ 6pm-1am; ⓡ Sala Daeng, Ⓜ Silom
All the way at the end of the *soi*, where the rainbow flag ceases to fly, Noriega's doesn't play the techno game. It prefers the raw noise of rotating bands of every genre, from salsa to Irish. The scene is also the unofficial headquarters of Bangkok's Hash House Harriers ('The drinking club with a running problem').

PARKING TOYS Map pp124–5   Bar
☎ 0 2907 2228; 17/22 Soi Mayalap, Kaset-Navamin Hwy, Greater Bangkok; ☯ 5pm-1am; taxi from ⓡ Mor Chit
If you're willing to make the long schlep north of town, this bizarrely named bar is quite possibly Bangkok's best-kept live-music secret. A rambling hall decked out with vintage furniture, Parking Toys hosts an eclectic revolving cast of fun bands ranging in genre from acoustic/classical ensembles to electro-funk jam acts. Get a taxi from Mor Chit BTS station and tell the driver to take you to Th Kaset-Navamin (also locally known as the *sên tàt mài*). Turn right at the Kaset intersection and continue until you pass the second stop light. Keep an eye out for the Heineken sign immediately on your left.

SAXOPHONE PUB & RESTAURANT
Map pp52–3   Pub/Restaurant
☎ 0 2246 5472; www.saxophonepub.com; 3/8 Th Phayathai, Ratchathewi; ☯ 6pm-midnight; ⓡ Victory Monument
Don't leave town without a visit to this venerable music club. Whether you're toasting distance from the band or perched in the

THE WHISKY SET

Thai beer is generally more miss than hit, so the next time you're out on the town, why not drink like the Thais do and order a bottle of whisky?

Your first step is to choose a brand. For a particularly decadent night out, the industry standard is a bottle of *bláek* (Johnnie Walker Black Label). Those on a budget can go for the cheaper imported labels such as Red Label or Benmore, and a rock-bottom, but fun, night can be had on domestic spirits such as 100 Pipers or Sang Som. And it's not unusual to bring your own bottle to many Thai bars, although some might charge a modest corkage fee.

As any Thai can tell you, your next immediate concern is mixers. These will take the form of several bottles of soda water and a bottle or two of Coke, along with a pail of ice. Most waiters will bring these to you as a matter of course.

Mixing is the easiest step and requires little or no action on your part; your skilled waiter will fill your glass with ice, followed by a shot of whisky, a splash of soda, a top -ff of Coke and, finally, a swirl with the ice tongs to bring it all together.

If you can't finish your bottle, shame on you, but don't fret, as it's perfectly normal to keep it at the bar. Simply tell your trusted waiter, who will write your name and the date on the bottle and keep it for your next visit.

2nd-floor alcove, Saxophone's intimate space draws the crowd into the laps of great jazz and blues musicians. The music changes each night – jazz during the week; rock, blues and beyond on weekends. Reggae-fusion worships define Sunday nights.

TAWAN DAENG GERMAN
BREWHOUSE Map pp124–5   Beer Hall/Pub
☎ 0 2678 1114; www.tawandaeng1999.com; 462/61 Th Narathiwat Ratchanakharin (cnr Th Phra Ram III), Greater Bangkok; ⏰ 5pm-midnight; access by taxi

Despite its hangar-like girth, this Thai version of a Bavarian beer hall manages to pack 'em in just about every night. The Thai-German food is tasty, the house-made brews more than potable, and the nightly stage shows make singing along a necessity. Most people come for the Wednesday performance of Fong Nam (see p32). Music starts at 8.30pm.

THREE SIXTY Map pp108–9   Bar
☎ 0 2442 2000; 32nd fl, Millennium Hilton, 123 Th Charoen Nakorn, Thonburi; ⏰ 5pm-1am; ⚓ Tha Sathon

Feeling frustrated with Bangkok? A set or two of live jazz in this elegant glass-encased perch 32 floors above the city will help you forget some of your troubles, or at the very least, give you a whole new perspective on the city.

TOKYO JOE'S Map pp118–19   Bar
☎ 0 2259 6268; www.tokyojoesbkk.com; 25/9 Soi 26, Th Sukhumvit; ⏰ 5pm-1am; 🚇 Phrom Phong

Recently relocated to something of a residential district – what do the neighbours

think of the noise? Despite the move, the bar's die-hard regulars still file in to witness a revolving cast of jazz, blues and rock. To see what the place is really about, come on Sunday evening, when the infamous Joe's World Famous Blues Jam kicks off at 9.30.

WINKS Map pp124–5   Pub
☎ 0 2939 5684; cnr Soi 37, Th Phahonyothin, Greater Bangkok; ⏰ 7pm-1am; 🚌 air-con 512 & 524, ordinary 24, 26, 28

Starting to wonder where the Thai people actually hang out? Join wannabe musicians, Kasetsart University students, the odd *dara* (star) and any others who can't be bothered with the Sukhumvit scene at this fun local boozer. The live bands aren't quite as good as they are loud, but after a couple ofdrinks and some new friends, you'll wish you could take the bar home with you.

WITCH'S TAVERN Map pp118–19   Pub
☎ 0 2391 9791; 306/1 Soi 55 (Thong Lor), Th Sukhumvit; ⏰ 6pm-1am; 🚇 Thong Lor

This spacious joint claims to be an English pub, but it's closer to a hotel lobby geared toward down-to-earth Thai professionals. Jazz and folk bands start up around 8.30pm, and at 10.30pm the house cover band takes to the stage, accepting requests from the audience. Ballads get the biggest round of applause.

CLUBBING

Fickleness is the reigning characteristic of the Bangkok club scene, and venues that were pulling in thousands a night just last year are often only vague memories today. What used to be a rotating cast of hotspots has slowed to a few standards on the *sois* off Sukhumvit, Silom, Ratchadapisek and RCA (Royal City Ave), the city's 'entertainment zones', which qualify for the 2am closing time. Most places don't begin filling up until midnight and cover charges run as high as 600B and usually include a drink. You'll need an ID to prove you're legal (20 years old); they'll card even the grey hairs.

To keep the crowds from growing bored, clubs host weekly theme parties and visiting DJs that ebb and flow in popularity. To get an idea of current happenings around town, check Bangkok Spin (www.bangkokspin.com), *BK*, the *Bangkok Post*'s Friday supplement, Guru, and the Bangkok Recorder's online mag (www.bangkokrecorder.com).

70'S BAR Map p112 Club
☎ 0 2253 4433; 231/16 Th Sarasin, Lumphini; 🕑 6pm-1am; admission free; 🚇 Ratchadamri
A tad too small to be a club proper, this retro-themed bar spins all the hits from the Me generation in the ultimate Me city. Like much of the strip, the clientele is mixed, but often verges on the pink side of the fence.

808 CLUB Map pp124–5 Club
www.808bangkok.com; Block C, Royal City Ave, off Th Phra Ram IX, Greater Bangkok; admission 200-400B; 🚇 Rama IX
Named after the infamous beat machine, this club fills the space previously occupied by Astra and looks to follow the tradition of big-name DJs and insanely crowded events.

BED SUPPERCLUB Map pp118–19 Club
☎ 0 2651 3537; www.bedsupperclub.com; 26 Soi 11, Th Sukhumvit; admission 500-600B; 🕑 8pm-1am; 🚇 Nana
Bed has basked in the limelight for a few years now, but has yet to lose any of its futuristic charm. Arrive at a decent hour to squeeze in dinner (see p165), or if you've only got dancing on your mind, come on Tuesday for the hugely popular hip-hop night.

CAFÉ DEMOC Map pp68–9 Club
☎ 0 2622 2571; www.cafe-democ.com; 78 Th Ratchadamnoen, Banglamphu; admission free; 🕑 8pm-1am Tue-Sun; 🚌 air-con 511 & 512, ordinary 15, 30 & 65
Up-and-coming DJs present their turntable dexterity at this narrow unpretentious

club in Olde Bangkok. Hip-hop, break beat, drum 'n' bass and tribal fill the night roster, but only special events actually fill the floor.

CLUB CULTURE Map pp52–3 Club
☎ 0 89497 8422; www.club-culture-bkk.com; Th Sri Ayuthaya (opposite Siam City Hotel), Ratchathewi; admission 250B; 🕑 7pm-late Wed, Fri & Sat; 🚇 Phayathai
Housed in a unique 40-year-old Thai-style building and run by the same folks who ran RCA's popular Astra, Culture is the biggest and quirkiest recent arrival on Bangkok's club scene. Come to enjoy internationally recognised DJs and the best sound system in town.

DANCE FEVER Map pp124–5 Club
☎ 0 2247 4295; 71 Th Ratchadaphisek, Greater Bangkok; 🕑 8pm-2am; 🚇 Rama IX
Like taking a time machine back to the previous decade, Dance Fever is a holdover from the days when a night out in Bangkok meant corny live stage shows, wiggling around the whisky set table, and neon, neon, neon.

GLOW Map pp118–19 Club
☎ 0 2261 3007; www.glowbkk.com; 96/4-5 Soi 23, Th Sukhumvit; admission 200B; 🕑 6pm-1am; 🚇 Asoke, 🚇 Sukhumvit
Another club reincarnation, the former Faith is a small venue with a big reputation. Boasting a huge variety of vodkas and a recently upgraded sound system, the tunes range from hip-hop (Friday) to electronica (Saturday), and everything in between.

LUCIFER Map pp108–9 Club
☎ 0 2234 6902; www.luciferdisko.com; 76/1-3 Soi Patpong 1, Silom; admission 150B; 🕑 9pm-1am; 🚇 Sala Daeng, 🚇 Silom
Meet the Miltonian side of Lucifer: a fun-loving hedonist. Nestled in the heart of Patpong, Lucifer kicks off the night with a few brave travellers who wander in from the night market. By 11pm the crowd shifts to a younger, prettier persuasion with serious dance-floor know-how. Another wave of recruits arrives at hook-up time.

NANG LEN Map pp118–19 Club
☎ 0 2711 6564; 217 Soi 63 (Ekamai), Th Sukhumvit; admission free; 🕑 6pm-1am; 🚇 Ekamai
Young, loud and Thai; Nang Len (literally 'sit and chill') is a ridiculously popular

PARTY LIKE A BUTTERFLY

If you're having commitment issues, try these streets for a club buffet.

You might already be there, but Th Khao San (p176) has become so diverse lately that you don't really have to leave to get a good dose of Bangkok nightlife.

A young crowd flocks to RCA (Map pp124–5; an extension of Phra Ram IX known as Royal City Ave), a district of loud, flashy bars that was once a Thai teen playground but now has something for all danceable ages. Th Ratchadapisek Soi 4 (Map pp124–5) has sprouted a recent growth of very Thai teenybopper clubs to capitalise on its designation as an entertainment zone.

The party spills out onto the sidewalks of *sois* near Patpong off Th Silom. Soi 4 (Map pp108–9) is a boisterous carnival of blaring techno, parading drag queens, muscle boys, and a lot of exhibitionism. Tapas Room (below) is one of the saner options along the row.

A string of café-bars south of Chatuchak Park on Th Kampaengphet (Map pp124–5) wind up at nights as the weekend market winds down.

Ekamai and Thong Lor (Map pp118–19) epitomise Bangkok cool, but the bars change so frequently it's hard for a clunky guidebook to keep up. Check the nightlife rags for leads.

sardine tin of live music and uni students on popular Th Ekamai. Get in before 10pm or you won't get in at all.

NARCISSUS Map pp118–19   Club

☎ 0 2261 3991; www.narcissusclubbangkok.com; 112 Soi 23 (Prasanmit), Th Sukhumvit; admission 500B; 9pm-1am; Asoke

Faux-Roman decadence (think gratuitous marble and pillars) makes Narcissus one of Bangkok's most ostentatious clubs. It doesn't see as much action as it did in years past, but the whole city turns up when Paul Oakenfold graces this palace with his presence.

Q BAR Map pp118–19   Club

☎ 0 2252 3274; www.qbarbangkok.com; 34 Soi 11, Th Sukhumvit; admission 400-500B; 9am-1am; Nana

In club years, Q Bar is fast approaching retirement age, but still rules the techno-rati with slick industrial style. The dance floor is monopolized by working girls and pot-bellied admirers, but Sunday theme parties and celebrity DJs bring in everybody else in town. Q also boasts perhaps Thailand's largest range of drinks – 27 types of vodka and 41 brands of whisky/bourbon.

SANTIKA Map pp118–19   Club

☎ 0 2711 5887; 235/11 Soi 63 (Ekamai), Th Sukhumvit; admission 200-400B; 8pm-1am; Ekamai

One of several same-same-but-different mega-clubs that line Ekamai, whose crowd comprises a predictable cross-section of Thai jet-setters, children of politicians, and

lûuk khrûeng models. But even the mon-eyed Thais like their drinks affordable and their disco music deafening.

SLIM/FLIX Map pp124–5   Club

☎ 0 2203 0504; 29/22-32 Royal City Avenue, off Th Phra Ram IX, Greater Bangkok; admission free; 8pm-2am; Rama IX

Ideal for the indecisive raver, this immense three-in-one complex dominating one end of RCA features chilled house on one side (Flix), while the other (Slim) does the hip hop/R&B soundtrack found across much of the city. Oh, and there's a restaurant thrown in there somewhere as well. Despite its size, this place is packed on weekends.

SUPERFLY Map p112   Club

☎ 0 2633 9990; cnr Phra Ram IV & Soi 1, Th Sala Daeng, Lumphini; admission 200B; 9pm-late; Sala Daeng, Lumphini

This gargantuan dance hall is a decent middle ground in the jungle of Bangkok clubs; not too trendy, with music that the majority of us can shake to. As with many places in town, the cover charge gets you one drink.

TAPAS ROOM Map pp108–9   Club

☎ 0 2234 4737; www.tapasroom.net; 114/17-18 Soi 4, Th Silom; admission 100B; 9pm-1am; Sala Daeng, Silom

Although it sits staunchly at the front of Bangkok's pinkest street, this longstanding box manages to bring in just about everybody. Come Thursday to Saturday, when the combination of DJs and live percussion brings the body count to critical level.

TWISTED REPUBLIC Map pp118–19   Club

☎ 0 2651 0800; www.twistedrepublic.com; 37 Soi 11, Th Sukhumvit; admission 300B; ⏱ 8pm-1am; 🚇 Nana

Neighbour to Bed and Q Bar, Twisted truly is the new kid on the block. Promising an 'ultimate interactive clubbing experience', the fresh-faced club boasts an impressive roster of DJs, both domestic and imported.

GO-GO BARS

Whole neighbourhoods of Bangkok are dedicated to the sex trade, from massage parlours to go-go bars, and tales about these places comprise the majority of English-language literature about the city. Like the sex industry in other parts of the world, issues of exploitation, human trafficking and HIV/AIDS are ever-present.

Looming large in the visitor's imagination is the notorious Patpong district of pingpong and 'fucky' shows. Along two narrow *soi* (Soi Patpong 1 and Soi Patpong 2, off Th Silom), blaring neon bars with subtle names such as Pussy Collection, Supergirls and Pussy Galore cater mainly to a gawking public (both male and female) with circus-like sexual exploits.

The gay men's equivalent of Patpong can be found on nearby Soi Pratuchai and Soi Anuman Ratchathon, where bars feature go-go dancers and live sex shows.

A more direct legacy of the Vietnam R&R days is Soi Cowboy (Map pp118–19), a strip of hostess and go-go bars targeted at the consumer, not the curious.

Nana Entertainment Plaza (Map pp118–19) is a three-storey complex featuring topless dancing and strip shows. The 'female' staff at Casanova consists entirely of Thai transvestites and transsexuals; this is a favourite stop for foreigners visiting Bangkok for sex reassignment surgery.

Asian tourists – primarily Japanese, Taiwanese and Hong Kong males – flock to the Ratchada entertainment strip, part of the Huay Khwang district (Map pp124–5), along wide Th Ratchadaphisek between Th Phra Ram IX and Th Lat Phrao. Lit up like Las Vegas, this stretch of neon boasts huge, male-oriented, massage-snooker-and-karaoke and go-go complexes with names like Caesar's Sauna and Emmanuelle, which are far grander in scale.

ENTERTAINMENT & THE ARTS

top picks

Bangkok has some outstanding art galleries.
- 100 Tonson Gallery (p191)
- Bangkok University Art Gallery (p191)
- H Gallery (p192)
- Jim Thompson Art Center (p97)
- National Gallery (p192)

ENTERTAINMENT & THE ARTS

Although Bangkok's hyper-urban environment seems to cater to the inner philistine in all of us, the city has a significant but low-key art scene. Largely encouraged and nurtured by the city's expat community, art in today's Bangkok ranges from beautifully benign *objets d'art* to increasingly sophisticated displays of social commentary. The city's galleries are also a diverse lot, and include a refurbished wooden house and several chic restaurant-cum-galleries. In recent years, new ones seemed to have been opening on a weekly basis. Bangkok also acts as something of a regional art hub, showing many works by emerging artists from places like Burma and Cambodia.

The performing arts have a long history in Bangkok. Dancing in particular, whether it be classically trained performers at a shrine or ladyboys camping about on stage, seems to form a large part of the entertainment options for many visitors to the city.

For profiles of Thai modern artists and movements, pick up a copy of *Flavours: Thai Contemporary Art*, by Steven Pettifor, a leading Bangkok art critic. Rama IX Museum (www.rama9art .org) is an online resource for artists' portfolios and gallery profiles.

THEATRE & DANCE

High art–wise, Bangkok's heyday passed with the dismantling of the royal court. Today Thai preservationists cling to the classical dance-dramas, which attract little government funding or appreciation, as the city races to be more modern than it was the day before.

There is a handful of companies performing Western arts and interesting fusions of Thai–Western traditions, but the number of arts venues are abysmally small compared with more-profitable and less-cultural businesses. The city's daily newspapers and monthly magazines maintain a calendar of cultural events.

Performances are typically advertised in the *Bangkok Post* or online at www.bangkokcon certs.org. Reservations are recommended for events. Tickets can be purchased through Thai Ticket Major (www.thaiticketmajor.com).

BANGKOK PLAYHOUSE Map pp118–19
☎ 0 2319 7641; 2884/2 Th Phetchaburi, Sukhumvit; tickets 300-600B; ☽ shows Fri-Sun; ▣ Phetchaburi
Open since 1993, this modern private theatre hosts modern drama and other performing arts, as well as the occasional visual-art exhibition. Show times and prices vary; call ahead for details.

NATIONAL THEATRE Map p56
☎ 0 2221 0171; Th Ratchini, Ko Ratanakosin; tickets 40-80B; ▣ air-con 503, ordinary 32, 53 & 203, ⚓ Tha Chang
Thailand's National Theatre is the country's centre stage for Thai drama and *khŏn* (see

p36). Exhibitions of Thai classical dancing and music are held on the last Friday and Saturday of each month and, on occasion, the theatre also offers international performances.

The National Theatre temporarily closed for renovations in 2005 and is still under construction in some parts, although performances are continuing as usual.

PATRAVADI THEATRE Map p56
☎ 0 2412 7287; www.patravaditheatre.com; 69/1 Soi Wat Rakhang, Thonburi; tickets 300-800B; ☽ shows 7pm Fri-Sun; ⚓ from Tha Chang to Tha Wat Rakhang
Patravadi is Bangkok's leading modern-dance venue. A stylish open-air theatre that also includes a gallery and restaurant, the concept is the brainchild of Patravadi Mejudhon, a famous Thai actor and playwright. The dance troupe performance is a blend of traditional Thai dance and modern choreography, music and costume. The theatre is also the primary venue for the Bangkok International Fringe Festival, held in January and February.

SALA CHALERMKRUNG Map p84
☎ 0 2222 0434; www.salachalermkrung.com; 66 Th Charoen Krung, Chinatown; tickets 1000-2000B; ☽ shows 8.30pm Fri & Sat; ▣ air-con 73, ordinary 8, ⚓ Tha Saphan Phut
This Art Deco Bangkok landmark, a former cinema dating to 1933, is one of the few remaining places *khŏn* can be witnessed. The traditional Thai dance-drama is enhanced here by laser graphics and hi-tech audio.

GET THEE SOME CULTURE

Bangkok's various cultural centres extend an open invitation to the entire city for monthly art exhibits, film screenings, stage performances and annual festivals.

- Alliance Française Bangkok (Map p112; ☎ 0 2670 4200; www.alliance-francaise.or.th; 29 Th Sathon Tai, Sathon)
- Goethe Institut (Map p112; ☎ 0 2287 0942; 18/1 Soi Goethe, off Soi 1 (Atakanprasit, Th Sathon Tai, Silom; ☺ 8am-4.30pm Mon-Fri) Also hosts Bangkok Poetry slams and Christmas Art Fair.
- Japan Foundation (Map pp118–19; ☎ 0 2260 8560; www.jfbkk.or.th; 10th fl, Serm-Mit Tower, Soi 21, Th Sukhumvit; ☺ 9am-7pm Mon-Fri, 9am-5pm Sat)
- Neilson Hays Library Rotunda Gallery (Map pp108–9; ☎ 0 2233 1731; 195 Th Surawong, Silom; ☺ varies)

Concerts and other events are also held – check website for details.

SIAM NIRAMIT Map pp124–5

☎ 0 2649 9222; www.siamniramit.com; 19 Th Thiam Ruammit, Greater Bangkok; tickets 1500B; ☺ shows 8pm; Ⓜ Thailand Cultural Centre

A cultural theme park, this enchanted kingdom transports visitors to a Disneyfied version of ancient Siam with a technicoloured stage show depicting the Lanna Kingdom, the Buddhist heaven and Thai festivals. Elaborate costumes and sets are guaranteed to be spectacular both in their grandness and their indigenous interpretation. It is popular with tour groups.

THAILAND CULTURAL CENTRE
Map pp124–5

☎ 0 2247 0028; www.thaiculturalcenter.com; Th Ratchadaphisek btwn Th Thiam Ruammit & Th Din Daeng, Greater Bangkok; Ⓜ Thailand Cultural Centre

Bangkok's primary performing-arts facility, the Thailand Cultural Centre is the home of the Bangkok Symphony Orchestra and hosts the International Festival of Dance and Music in September. Classical dance performances, and regional Thai concerts like lûuk thûng (Thai country music) and Khorat Song, also cycle through the yearly calendar.

On performance days, a free shuttle picks up passengers from the subway's exit 1.

TRADITIONAL THAI PUPPET
THEATRE Map p112

☎ 0 2252 9683; www.thaipuppet.com; Suan Lum Night Bazaar, 1875 Th Rama IV, Lumphini; tickets 600B; ☺ shows 7.30pm & 9.30pm; Ⓜ Lumphini

The ancient art of Thai puppetry (lákhawn lék) was rescued by the late Sakorn Yang-khiawsod, more popularly known as Joe Louis, in 1985. Joe's children now carry on the tradition. His creations are controlled by three puppeteers and can strike many humanlike poses. Modelled after the characters in the epics Ramayana and Phra Aphaimani, the puppets perform nightly at this air-conditioned theatre, conveniently located in the Suan Lum Night Bazaar, as well as at the King Power Theater (p140).

DINNER THEATRE

Another option for viewing Thai classical dance is through dinner theatre. Most dinner theatres in Bangkok are heavily promoted through hotels to an ever-changing clientele, so standards are poor to fair. They can be tolerably worthwhile if you accept them as cultural tourist traps.

SALA RIM NAM Map pp108–9

☎ 0 2437 3080; www.mandarinoriental.com/bangkok/; Oriental Hotel, Soi 38, Th Charoen Krung, Riverside; tickets 1800B; ☺ dinner & show 7pm-10pm; 🚌 ordinary 35, 36, 75 & 93, ⛴ Tha Oriental

The historic Oriental Hotel hosts dinner theatre in a sumptuous Thai pavilion located across the river in Thonburi. Free shuttle boats transfer guests across the river from the hotel's dock. The price is well above average, reflecting the means of the hotel's client base.

SILOM VILLAGE Map pp108–9

☎ 0 2234 4448; www.silomvillage.co.th; 286 Th Silom; mains 150-350B; ☺ 6-10pm; 🚇 Surasak

More relaxed than most dinner shows, Silom Village delivers comfort, accessibility and decent dinners. Picky eaters swear by the crispy pork and cashew chicken, and the demonstrations of Thai dance and martial arts strike one 'to do' off the itinerary.

ENTERTAINMENT & THE ARTS KÀTHOEY CABARET

SHRINE DANCING

Although scheduled performances are grand, lasting memories are often unscripted and the serendipity of catching a shrine dance is unforgettable, like spotting a rainbow. If you hear the din of drums and percussion from a temple or shrine, follow the sound to see traditional *lákhawn kâe bon* (shrine dancing). At Lak Meuang (p58); cnr Th Ratchadamnoen Nai & Th Lak Meuang) and the Erawan Shrine (p102); cnr Th Ratchadamri & Th Ploenchit), worshippers commission costumed troupes to perform dance movements that are similar to classical *lákhawn*, but not as refined, as they are specially choreographed for ritual purposes.

STUDIO 9 Map p56

☎ 0 2412 7287; www.patravaditheatre.com; Patravadi Theatre, 69/1 Soi Wat Rakhang, Thonburi; ☺ shows 7.30pm-midnight Fri & Sat; ⚓ from Tha Chang to Tha Wat Rakhang

The country's top modern-dance theatre recently began combining highbrow entertainment and dining. Performances are plucked from a diverse menu of music, dance, puppetry and theatre; check ahead of time to see what's in store.

SUPATRA RIVER HOUSE Map p56

☎ 0 2411 0305; www.supatrariverhouse.net; 266 Soi Wat Rakhang, Thonburi; set menu 800-1150B; ☺ dinner shows 8.30-9pm Fri & Sat; restaurant shuttle from Tha Mahathat

This stylishly restored teak house garners the famous dual-temple view of Wat Arun as well as the Grand Palace. An outdoor stage hosts dance performances by graduates of the affiliated Patravadi Theatre. The food and service, however, are hit and miss.

KÀTHOEY CABARET

Along with sacred temples and longboat tours of the Chao Phraya River, *kàthoey* (ladyboys) are the latest addition to the itineraries of many visitors to Bangkok. This largely takes the form of *kàthoey* cabaret, where convincing ladyboys take to the stage with elaborate costumes, MTV-style dance routines and rehearsed lip-synching to pop hits. Calypso Cabaret (Map pp98–9; ☎ 0 2653 3960-2; www.calypsocabaret.com; 1st fl, Asia Hotel, 296 Th Phayathai, Siam Sq; tickets 1000B; ☺ shows 8.15pm & 9.45pm) and Mambo Cabaret (Map pp118–19; ☎ 0 2259 5715; Washington Sq, Th Sukhumvit

btwn Soi 22 & Benjasiri Park; tickets 600-800B; ☺ shows 8.30pm & 10pm) do family- and tourist-friendly shows of pop and Broadway camp.

CINEMAS

To offset the uncomfortable humidity, Bangkok's cinemas offer even more than just a movie screening: they pamper. These hi-tech, well-air-conditioned palaces offer VIP decadence (reclining seats and table service) in addition to the familiar fold-down seats and sticky floors. All movies are preceded by the king's anthem, during which everyone is expected to stand respectfully.

Hollywood movies are released in Bangkok's theatres in a timely fashion. But as homegrown cinema grows bigger, more and more Thai films, often subtitled in English, fill the roster. Bangkok also hosts several annual film festivals, including the Bangkok International Film Festival in January.

At the cinemas listed here, English movies are subtitled in Thai rather than dubbed. Ticket prices range from 100B to 180B for regular seats, and up to 500B for VIP seats. For movie listings and reviews, check the *Nation*, *Bangkok Post*, *Metro*, Movie Seer (www.movieseer.com) and Thai Cinema (www.thaicinema.org).

Alliance Française Bangkok (Map p112; ☎ 0 2670 4200; www.alliance-francaise.or.th; 29 Th Sathon Tai, Sathon; Ⓜ Lumphini) French films at the French cultural centre.

EGV (Map pp98–9; ☎ 0 2812 9999; www.egv.com; Siam Discovery Centre, 6th fl, Th Phra Ram I, Siam Sq) Ⓡ Siam) Bangkok's poshest venue to view all the mainstream movies.

Goethe Institut (Map p112; ☎ 0 2287 0942; 18/1 Soi Goethe, off Soi 1 (Atakanprasit), Th Sathon Tai, Silom; Ⓜ Lumphini) German films at the German cultural centre.

House (Map pp124–5; ☎ 0 2641 5177; www.houserama.com; 3rd fl, UMG Cinema, RCA, Th Phra Ram IX, Greater Bangkok; Ⓜ Rama IX) Bangkok's first art-house cinema showing lots of foreign flicks of the non-Hollywood type.

Lido Multiplex (Map pp98–9; ☎ 0 2251 1265; Th Phra Ram I, btwn Soi 2 & Soi 3, Siam Sq; Ⓡ Siam) Arty and independent movies.

Major Cineplex (Map pp98–9; ☎ 0 2515 5810; www.majorcineplex.com; Central World Plaza, 7th fl, Th Ratchadamri, Ploenchit; Ⓡ Chitlom) All the amenities and mainstream hits.

Paragon Cineplex (Map pp98–9; ☎ 0 2525 5555; www.paragoncineplex.com; Siam Paragon, Th Phra Ram I, Siam Sq; Ⓜ Siam) Bangkok's newest, biggest and baddest

CINEMA STRATEGY

Cinemas are a very big deal in Bangkok. It's unlikely that any other city in the world has anything like EGV's Gold Class, a ticket that grants you entry into a cinema with fewer than 50 seats, and where you're plied with blankets, pillows, foot-warming stockings and, of course, a valet food-and-drink service. There's also Major Cineplex's Emperor Class seat which, for the price of a sticky stool back home, entitles you to a sofa-like love seat designed for couples. And if you find Paragon Cineplex's 16 screens and 5000 seats a bit plebeian, you can always apply for Enigma, a members-only theatre.

Despite the heat and humidity on the streets, keep in mind that Bangkok's movie theatres pump the air-conditioning with such vigour that a jumper is an absolute necessity – unless you're going Gold Class, that is.

cinema offers both quantity (more than a dozen screens) and quality (several classes of viewing).

Scala Multiplex (Map pp98–9; ☎ 0 2251 2861; Soi 1, Th Phra Ram I, Siam Sq; ⊠ National Stadium) Last of the old-style theatres, in the heart of Siam Sq.

SF Cinema City (Map pp98–9; ☎ 0 2268 8888; www.sfcinemacity.com; 7th fl, MBK Centre, Th Phra Ram I, Siam Sq; ⊠ National Stadium) Multiplex showing Hollywood blockbusters.

SFV (Map pp118–19; ☎ 0 2260 9333; 6th fl, Emporium Shopping Centre, Th Sukhumvit, cnr Soi 24; M Phrom Phong) Creature comforts trimmings and varied screenings.

GALLERIES

In typical Bangkok style, the art scene lacks a centre – artists and galleries are peppered throughout the city. The more-conservative, generally government-sponsored art can be found in the older parts of town, particularly around the Banglamphu area, while the commercial galleries prefer the business districts of Th Silom and Th Sukhumvit.

For maps of the city's art scene, pick up BAM! (Bangkok Art Map), the *Thailand Art & Design Guide*, or check the lifestyle magazines for exhibition opening nights.

100 TONSON GALLERY Map pp98–9

☎ 0 2684 1527; www.100tonsongallery.com; 100 Soi Tonson, Th Ploenchit; ⊠ 11am-7pm Thu-Sun; ⊠ Chitlom

Housed in a spacious residential villa, and largely regarded as the city's top commercial gallery, 100 Tonson hosts a variety of contemporary exhibitions of all genres by local and international artists.

ABOUT CAFÉ/ABOUT STUDIO
Map p84

☎ 0 2639 8057; 418 Th Maitrichit, Chinatown; ⊠ varies; M Hualamphong

Formerly the cool cat in town for cutting-edge local artists, in recent years About has

only been open on a sporadic basis. Be sure to call ahead.

BANGKOK ART & CULTURE CENTRE
Map pp98–9

Cnr Th Phayathai & Th Phra Ram I, Siam Sq; ⊠ National Stadium

This large, modern building in the centre of Bangkok is the most recent addition to the city's arts scene. In addition to a permanent exhibition and several floors of galleries, the 11-storey building also boasts a theatre, library, shops and restaurants in an effort to appeal to today's 'culture-consuming lifestyle'.

BANGKOK UNIVERSITY ART GALLERY (BUG) Map pp124–5

☎ 0 2350 3500; http://fab.bu.ac.th/buggallery; 3rd fl, Bldg 9, City Campus, Th Phra Ram IV, Greater Bangkok; ⊠ 9.30am-7pm Tue-Sat; ⊠ Phra Khanong

This spacious new compound is located at what is currently the country's most cutting-edge art school. Recent exhibitions have encompassed a variety of media by some of the country's top names, as well as the work of internationally recognised artists.

EAT ME RESTAURANT Map pp108–9

☎ 0 2238 0931; Soi Phiphat 2, off Th Convent, Silom; ⊠ 3pm-1am; ⊠ Sala Daeng, M Silom

This chic restaurant also houses bi-monthly rotating exhibitions of photography and painting, often but not exclusively with a gay emphasis, organised by H Gallery.

FOREIGN CORRESPONDENTS' CLUB OF THAILAND (FCCT) Map pp98–9

☎ 0 2652 0580; www.fcctthai.com; Penthouse, Maneeya Center, 518/5 Th Ploenchit; ⊠ noon-2.30pm & 6pm-midnight; ⊠ Chitlom

A bar-restaurant, not to mention gathering place for the city's hacks and photogs, the FCCT also hosts art exhibitions ranging in genre from photojournalism to contemporary painting.

GALLERY F-STOP Map pp118–19

☎ 0 2663 7421; www.talisman-media.com/fstop; Tamarind Café, 27 Soi 20, Th Sukhumvit; ☻ 3pm-midnight Mon-Fri, 10am-midnight Sat & Sun; ⓡ Asoke, Ⓜ Sukhumvit

Gallery F-Stop holds a variety of photographic exhibitions on the walls of Tamarind Café (p167). The bright open space can accommodate photographs that are too large for the more cramped locales.

GALLERY VER Map pp108–9

☎ 0 2861 0933; www.verver.info; 2nd fl, 71/31-35 Klongsarn Plaza, Th Charoen Nakhorn, Thonburi; ☻ noon-7pm Wed-Sun; ⓦ Millenium Hilton ferry from Tha Sathon

Owned by Rirkrit Tiravanija, Thailand's most internationally recognised artist, this gallery on the Thonburi side of the river hosts a rotating display of typically edgy, installation-type conceptual art. The easiest way to reach Ver is to take the cross-river ferry from Tha Si Phraya. The gallery is directly behind the pier on the Thonburi side.

H GALLERY Map pp108–9

☎ 0 2234 7556; www.hgallerybkk.com; 201 Soi 12, Th Sathon, Silom; ☻ noon-6pm Thu-Sat; ⓡ Chong Nonsi

Housed in a refurbished colonial-era wooden building, H is generally considered among the city's leading private galleries. It is regarded as a jumping-off point for Thai artists with international ambitions, such as Jakkai Siributr and Somboon Hormthienthong.

JIM THOMPSON ART CENTER
Map pp98–9

☎ 0 2216 7368, 0 2215 0122; www.jimthompsonhouse.org; Jim Thompson House, 6 Soi Kasem San 2, Th Phra Ram I, Siam Sq; ☻ 9am-5pm; khlong taxi to Tha Ratchathewi, ⓡ National Stadium

This popular tourist destination has added an entire new gallery wing with rotating displays ranging from the contemporary to the traditional. Recent exhibitions have included a display of traditional Lao textiles, as well as an interactive work by Pinaree Sanpitak, one of the country's top female artists.

KATHMANDU PHOTO GALLERY
Map pp108–9

☎ 0 2234 6700; www.kathmandu-bkk.com; 87 Th Pan, Th Silom; ☻ 11am-7pm Sun-Fri; ⓡ Surasak

Bangkok's only gallery truly dedicated to photography is housed in an attractively restored Sino-Portuguese shophouse. The owner, photographer Manit Sriwanichpoom, wanted Kathmandu to resemble photographers' shops of old, where customers could flip through photographs for sale. Manit's own work is on display on the ground floor, and the small but airy upstairs gallery plays host to changing exhibitions by local and international artists and photographers.

NATIONAL GALLERY Map p56

☎ 0 2282 2639; Th Chao Fa, Ko Ratanakosin; admission 30B; ☻ 9am-4pm Wed-Sun; ferry Tha Phra Athit, ⓦ air-con 508, 511 & 512, ordinary 47, 53

Housed in a weatherworn colonial building, the National Gallery displays traditional and contemporary art, mostly by artists receiving government support. In general, the gallery's permanent exhibition is a rather dusty and dated affair. One noteworthy exception is the *Musical Rhythm* sculpture, by Khien Yimsiri, which is considered one of the most remarkable fusions of Western and Thai styles. More interesting are the rotating exhibits held in the spacious rear galleries.

NUMTHONG GALLERY Map p79

☎ 0 2243 4326; www.numthonggallery.com; Room 109, Bangkok Co-op Housing Bldg, 1129/29 Th Toeddamri, Dusit; ☻ 11am-6pm Mon-Sat; ⓡ Ari

A proving ground for Thai contemporary artists, Numthong has featured work by the cream of the crop of Thailand's avant-garde, including Vasan Sitthiket, Michael Shaowanasai and Kamin Lertchaiprasert.

QUEEN'S GALLERY Map pp68–9

☎ 0 2281 5360; www.queengallery.org; 101 Th Ratchadamnoen Klang, Banglamphu; ☻ Thu-Tue 10am-7pm; admission 20B; ⓦ ordinary 5, 35 & 159, khlong taxi Tha Phan Fah

This royal-funded museum presents five floors of rotating exhibitions of modern and traditionally influenced art. The building is sleek and contemporary and the artists hail from the upper echelons of the conservative Thai art world. The attached shop is filled with fine arts books and gifts.

SILPAKORN UNIVERSITY Map p56

☎ 0 2623 6115; www.su.ac.th; 31 Th Na Phra Lan, Ko Ratanakosin; ⓦ air-con 503, ordinary 32, 53 & 203, ⓦ Tha Chang

GALLERY GROWTH

In the not-so-distant past, Bangkok's art galleries were either dusty state-run museums or sleek commercial entities, without any real middle ground. However, in recent years the city has seen an explosion in the number of small- and medium-size galleries, including two spaces maintained by some of the country's leading artists.

Photographer Manit Sriwanichpoom, best known for his 'Pink Man' series of photographs that criticise consumerism in modern Thai society, opened Kathmandu (opposite), the city's first true photography gallery, in 2006. To date Kathmandu has showcased the work of outspoken senator Kraisak Choonhavan, elegant black-and-white photos by the elder statesperson of Thai photography, Surat Osathanugrah, and a haunting personal look at methamphetamine addiction by Olivier Pin-Fat. Manit's work is on permanent display and, in typical eclectic style, the gallery also holds lessons in meditation and yoga.

Rirkrit Tiravanija is Thailand's best-known artist abroad, and his Gallery Ver (from the Thai pronunciation of over, meaning extreme or overboard; opposite), has featured challenging installations by Patiroop Chychookiat and Udomsak Krisanamis and conceptual paintings by Thakon Khao sa-ad. The gallery has a unique text-free magazine of the same name and, fittingly, a MySpace page (www.myspace.com/vergallery).

Thailand's universities aren't usually repositories for interesting architecture, but the country's premier art school breaks the mould. Housed in a former palace, the classical buildings form the charming nucleus of an early Thai aristocratic enclave. The building immediately facing the Th Na Phra Lan gate houses the university's art gallery, which showcases faculty and student exhibitions. To the right of the building is a shady sculpture garden displaying the work of Corado Ferroci (aka Silapa Bhirasri), the Italian art professor who helped establish Silpakorn's fine arts department.

SURAPON GALLERY Map p112

☎ 0 2638 0033-4; www.rama9art.org/gallery/surapon/index.html; 11am-6pm Mon-Sat; 1st fl, Tisco Tower, 48/3 Th Sathon Tai, Silom; Sala Daeng, M Lumphini

Perhaps the most 'Thai' of the city's contemporary galleries, Surapon has featured work by some of the country's most renowned artists such as painters Chatchai Puipia and Muangthai Busamaro.

TADU CONTEMPORARY ART
Map pp124–5

☎ 0 2645 2473; www.tadu.net; 7th fl, Barcelona Motors Bldg, 99/2 Th Thiam Ruammit, Greater Bangkok; Mon-Sat 9.30am-6pm; M Thailand Cultural Centre

Emphasising the work of domestic artists, Tadu is a leading exhibition space for those working largely in the realms of performance and installation art.

TANG GALLERY Map pp108–9

☎ 0 2630 1114; basement, Silom Galleria, 919/1 Th Silom; 11am-7pm Mon-Sat; air-con 504, 514, 544 & 547, ordinary 15, 76, 115, 162, 163 & 164, Surasak

Bangkok's primary venue for modern artists from China has edged its way to become among the city's top contemporary galleries. Check the posters in the lobby of the Galleria to see what's on.

TEO+NAMFAH GALLERY Map pp118–19

☎ 0 2259 6117; www.teonamfahgallery.com; 2nd fl, Ozono Complex, Soi 39, Th Sukhumvit; 11.30am-8.30pm; Phrom Phong

Named after the children of the American-Thai couple that owns it, this new gallery is quickly earning a reputation for exhibiting a broad diversity of international artists. Teo+Namfah also houses an impressive permanent collection, as well as a space devoted to selling high-quality art supplies.

THAVIBU GALLERY Map pp108–9

☎ 0 2266 5454; www.thavibu.com; 3rd fl, Silom Galleria, 919/1 Th Silom; 11am-7pm Tue-Sat, noon-6pm Sun; air-con 504, 514, 544 & 547, ordinary 15, 76, 115, 162, 163 & 164, Surasak

Thavibu is an amalgam of Thailand, Vietnam and Burma. The gallery specialises in contemporary paintings by younger and emerging artists from the three countries.

WHITESPACE Map pp98–9

☎ 0 2252 2900; www.whitespaceasia.com; 2nd fl, Lido Bldg, Soi 3, Siam Sq, Th Rama I; 11.30am-8pm Tue-Sun; Siam

An active design studio, Whitespace also includes a small non-commercial gallery that features a diverse array of exhibitions by emerging artists.

SPORTS & ACTIVITIES

top picks

- Wat Pho Thai Traditional Massage School (p197)
- Lumphini Stadium (p199)
- Ruen-Nuad Massage & Yoga (p197)

Although the climate is not conducive to exercise, Bangkokians like to work up a sweat doing more than just climbing the stairs to the Skytrain station. All the popular Thai sports are represented in the capital city: from the top-tier *muay thai* (Thai boxing) to a pick-up game of *tàkrâw* (Siamese football).

Thais also consider traditional massage an integral component of health, so you can always pay someone else to do all the work. In tandem with the massage tradition, Bangkok is emerging as one of the world's spa capitals, with facilities to satisfy almost any whim or budget.

HEALTH & FITNESS

Whether you're looking to sweat out the toxins or have them pampered away, Bangkok should be able to satisfy.

SPAS & MASSAGE

According to traditional Thai healing, the use of herbs and massage should be part of a regular health and beauty regimen, not just an excuse for pampering. The variations on this theme range from storefront traditional Thai massage to an indulgent spa 'experience' with service and style. Bangkok's spas have begun to focus more on the medical than the sensory, and the growing number of plush resort-style spas offer a huge variety of treatments.

Although it sounds relaxing, traditional Thai massage *(nûat phaen boraan),* will seem more closely related to *muay thai* than to shiatsu. It is based on yogic techniques for general health involving pulling, stretching, bending and manipulating pressure points. If done well, a traditional massage will leave you sore but revitalised.

Full-body massages will usually include camphor-scented balms or herbal compresses, or oil in cheaper establishments. Note that 'oil massage' is sometimes taken as code for 'sexy massage'; see the boxed text, opposite, for the lowdown. Sightseeing aches and pains can usually be treated effectively with a quick foot massage. Depending on the neighbourhood, prices for massages in small parlours are about 200B to 350B for a foot massage and 300B to 500B for a full-body massage. Spa experiences start at about 800B and climb like a Bangkok skyscraper. For a fuller idea of what's available see www.spasinbangkok.com.

BANYAN TREE SPA Map p112
☎ 0 2679 1052; banyantreespa.com/bangkok; Banyan Tree Hotel & Spa, 21/100 Th Sathon Tai; packages from 5800B; Ⓜ Lumphini

This hotel spa delivers modern elegance and world-class pampering. The womblike spa rooms look out over a silent and peaceful vision of Bangkok from on high. Thai, Swedish and Balinese massages, body scrubs using aromatic oils and herbs with medicinal properties, and beauty treatments comprise the spa's offerings. 'Spa vacation' packages include accommodation.

BUATHIP THAI MASSAGE Map pp118–19
☎ 0 2251 2627; 4/13 Soi 5, Th Sukhumvit; 1hr massage 270B; ☺ 10am-midnight; ⓡ Nana

On a small sub-*soi* (lane) behind the Amari Boulevard Hotel, this tidy shopfront is in a decidedly sleazy part of town, but inside is a professional masseur whose focused concentration could melt metal.

NAKORNTHON THAI MEDICAL SPA
Map pp124–5
☎ 0 2416 5454; www.nakornthonhospital.com; 12th fl, Nakornthon Hospital, Th Phra Ram II; packages from 1000B; access by taxi

The wellness centre of this Bangkok hospital has a traditional Thai medicine wing, combining spa therapy with ancient Thai techniques. The primary practice is the use of *tamrub thong*, which uses the application of gold leaf and herbs to rejuvenate skin and restore collagen. Other treatments focus on nutritional evaluations and aromatherapy to ensure the balance of the body's essential elements: earth, wind, water and fire.

ORIENTAL SPA Map pp108–9
☎ 0 2659 0444; www.mandarinoriental.com; Oriental Hotel, 48 Soi 38, Th Charoen Krung; half-day packages from 8400B; ⓡ Saphan Taksin, ⛴ from Oriental Hotel

This award-winning spa, set in a delightful riverside location opposite the Oriental

BANGKOK MASSAGE 101

Bangkok has hundreds of massage options, from tiny shops with a couple of masseuses to resort-style spas that have honed pampering down to a fine art, via venerable training institutions such as Wat Pho, where centuries of tradition are maintained and passed on. Parlours offering Thai traditional massage are the most prevalent, typically with massage beds in the front window, colourful reflexology charts on the walls and foot or full-body massages selling for very reasonable rates.

But the world of Bangkok massage parlours can sometimes throw up unexpected scenarios. If you're a woman you can rest easy in the knowledge that you'll get, with varying degrees of quality, the massage you asked for. For men, however, your full-body 'oil massage' might involve techniques you didn't have in mind and which are definitely not on the curriculum at Wat Pho.

The tough part about this is that you never really know when you walk into a studio whether the massage is going to extend further up your inner thigh than is normally considered proper. It's not as if the parlours actually advertise 'Happy Endings 200B extra'. Indeed, many parlours actively discourage the practice, but masseuses are poorly paid and the opportunity to earn a bigger tip is often too hard to ignore.

So what should you do? First, if you're not actually looking for a 'happy ending' then start by avoiding massage parlours in Bangkok's sleazier neighbourhoods – Nana, Sukhumvit near Soi Cowboy or around Patpong. You can also avoid trouble by walking past the shops with young, attractive women in miniskirts sitting outside and chorusing 'Hello sir, massage?' Look instead for the older, stronger-looking women, who normally give better massage. Parlours off the main path are often a good bet.

Once you've chosen your parlour, choosing not to undress completely – or wearing the unisex disposable knickers provided – will go some way toward deterring wandering hands. But it's no guarantee. If your masseuse's 'innocent' rubbing goes too far it will deliberately be left open to your interpretation; you'll need to either ignore it both physically and verbally, or deal with it verbally.

Hotel, offers a full range of massage and health treatments. Privacy is the spa's main strength, with individual and couples' suites (shower, massage tables and steam room) keeping camera-shy celebs happy. Bookings are essential.

RASAYANA RETREAT Map pp118–19
☎ 0 2662 4803; www.rasayanaretreat.com; 41/1 Soi Prommit off Soi 39, Th Sukhumvit; massage/packages from 500B/2800B; ⑨ Phrom Phong
Rasayana combines basic beauty and massage treatments with holistic healing techniques, such as detoxification, colonic irrigation and hypnotherapy, for reasonable prices.

RUEN-NUAD MASSAGE & YOGA
Map pp108–9
☎ 0 2632 2663; 42 Th Convent, Th Silom; ⑨ 10am-10pm; 1hr traditional massage 350B; ⑨ Sala Daeng, Ⓜ Silom
Just the right mix of old and new, Ruen-Nuad is set in a charming converted wooden house opposite BNH Hospital. It has partitioned massage stations, creating a mood of pampering and privacy typical of spa facilities, but at very reasonable parlour prices.

SKILLS DEVELOPMENT CENTER FOR THE BLIND Map pp124–5
☎ 0 2583 7327; 78/2 Soi 1, Th Tiwanon, Pak Kret; 1½-hr massage in fan/air-con room 120/160B; ⑨ 7am-6pm; ⚓ Tha Pak Kret
This outreach centre north of central Bangkok trains the blind in the ancient techniques of Thai traditional massage, developing what many people consider to be expert masseurs. Getting out here can be half the fun. Take the Chao Phraya Express (p253) north to Tha Nonthaburi, where you will connect to a Laem Thong boat (5.45am to 5.45pm) to Tha Pak Kret. From the pier, hire a motorcycle taxi to take you to the Skills Development Center (one way 10B). You'll need to speak a little Thai to pull this off (ask for *suun pháthánaa sàmàtthàphâap khon taa bàwt*), but Pak Kret villagers are pretty easy-going and willing to listen to foreigners massacre their language. The easier option is to just get in a taxi and get the driver to call the centre for directions.

WAT PHO THAI TRADITIONAL MASSAGE SCHOOL Map p56
☎ 0 2221 3686; www.watpomassage.com; Soi Penphat, Th Sanamchai; 1hr Thai massage 300B, foot massage 250B; ⑨ 8am-5pm; ⚓ Tha Tien
The school affiliated with Wat Pho is the

country's primary training centre for Thai traditional massage. You can choose from the fan-conditioned *sǎlaa* (pavilions) in the southeast corner of the temple grounds and air-conditioned rooms in the massage training centre in Soi Penphat, the unsigned *soi* closer to the river.

YOGA & PILATES

You might think Thais don't need any extra relaxation, but the international yoga revolution has found many a believer in Bangkok. Yoga studios – and enormous accompanying billboards of smiling gurus – have popped up faster than mushrooms at a full-moon party.

ABSOLUTE YOGA Map pp98–9

☎ 0 2252 4400; www.absoluteyogabangkok.com; 4th fl, Amarin Plaza, Th Ploenchit, Pathumwan
The largest and most commercial yoga studio group, teaching Bikram hot yoga plus a host of other styles. Another popular branch is Thong Lor (Map pp118–19; ☎ 0 2381 0697; 2nd fl, 55th Plaza, Soi Thong Lor 2, Th Sukhumvit).

YOGA ELEMENTS STUDIO Map pp98–9

☎ 0 2655 5671; www.yogaelements.com; 29 Vanissa Bldg, 23rd fl, Th Chitlom
Run by American Adrian Cox, who trained at Om in New York and teaches vinyasa and ashtanga, this is probably the most respected studio in the city. The high-rise location helps you rise above it all, too.

PILATES STUDIO Map pp98–9

☎ 0 2650 7797; www.pilatesbangkok.com; 888/58-9 Mahatun Plaza, Th Ploenchit
One of three in this group, the name pretty much covers it.

GYMS

Bangkok is well stocked with gyms, ranging in style from the long-running open-air affairs in spaces such as Lumphini Park (p106), to ultramodern mega-gyms complete with hi-tech equipment, bars selling exotic vegetable drinks and a roster of stunningly good-looking members and instructors. Most large hotels have gyms and swimming pools, as do a growing number of small hotels. If your hotel doesn't, or you prefer the fashion-gym experience, both California Wow (www.californiawowx.com) and True Fitness (www.truefitness.co.th) have several branches in the Sukhumvit, Silom and Siam Sq areas, and offer

pricey day memberships (about 700B). For something more old-school, the Ambassador Hotel Fitness Centre (Map pp118–19; ☎ 0 2254 0444; www.amtel .co.th; Soi 11, Th Sukhumvit; per day 300B; ☿ 6am-10pm; ☒ Nana) isn't bad and has instructors who can give you a game of squash.

ACTIVITIES

If your hotel pool is more like a bathtub than a venue for lapping, the National Stadium (Map pp98–9; ☎ 0 2214 0120; Th Phra Ram I; ☒ National Stadium) has a public pool plus basketball and volleyball courts and other sports facilities. You might also pick up a game of basketball at the Red Bull X Park (Map pp108–9; ☎ 0 2670 8080; Th Sathon Tai, opposite Evergreen Laurel Hotel; ☿ 10am-9pm; ☒ Chong Nonsi, Ⓜ Lumphini, Silom).

GOLF

Bangkok's outer suburbs are well stocked with golf courses with green fees ranging from 250B to 5000B, plus the customary 200B tip for caddies. The website Thai Golfer (www.thaigolfer .com) rates every course in Thailand. Rental equipment is available and some courses are closed on Monday, while others are open at night for cooler tee-off times.

JOGGING & CYCLING

Lumphini Park, Sanam Luang and Benjakiti Park all host early-morning and late-evening runners. Benjakiti has less shade and fewer people than the others, and also has bikes for rent. Several Hash groups meet for weekly runs, including the Bangkok Hash House Harriers (men only), Bangkok Monday Hash (mixed) and the Harriettes (mixed). The Bangkok Hash House Mountain Bikers meet monthly on Sunday afternoon for a 20km to 30km mountain-bike ride. See www.bangkokhhh .com for details.

SPECTATOR SPORTS

Thais have embraced an increasingly diverse range of sports in recent years – tennis, golf, diving and motor racing, among others – but it's football and home-grown *muay thai* that inspire the most devoted support.

FOOTBALL

Thais, and particularly Bangkokians, have been caught up in the rapid internationalisation of football in recent years. Thailand has a national league, but apart from a few stars of the underperforming national team (90th in the FIFA world rankings in April 2008), most Thais will be happier watching Ronaldo, Rooney, Torres and ex-PM Thaksin Shinawatra's club, Manchester City, on TV than their own league. Still, if you want to see a match, nine of the 16 Thai Premier League teams are based in Bangkok; two play at the conveniently central Chulalongkorn University Sports Stadium (Map pp98–9).

MUAY THAI (THAI BOXING)

Quintessentially Thai, almost anything goes in *muay thai*, the martial art more commonly known elsewhere as Thai boxing or kick boxing (below). If you don't mind the violence, a Thai boxing match is well worth attending for the pure spectacle – the wild musical accompaniment, the ceremonial beginning of each match and the frenzied betting.

The best of the best fight at Bangkok's two boxing stadiums. Built on royal land at the end of WWII, the Art Deco–style Ratchadamnoen Stadium (Sanam Muay Ratchadamnoen; Map pp68–9;

☎ 0 2281 4205; 1 Th Ratchadamnoen Nok; ☺ bouts 5-8pm & 8.30-midnight Sun, 6.30-11.30pm Mon, Wed & Thu; ☒ aircon bus 503, ordinary 70) is the original and has a relatively formal atmosphere. Lumphini Stadium (Sanam Muay Lumphini; Map p112; ☎ 0 2252 8765; www .muaythailumpini.com; Th Rama IV; ☺ bouts 6.30-11pm Tue & Fri, 5-8pm & 8.30-11.30pm Sat; Ⓜ Lumphini) was constructed by the Thai army in 1956 and has a looser and more populist atmosphere than at Ratchadamnoen. Lumphini is also more encouraging of non-Thai boxers. Plans to move Lumphini Stadium have apparently been shelved.

Admission fees are the same at both stadiums and vary according to seating. Ringside seats (2000B) are the most expensive and will be filled with VIPs; tourists usually opt for the 2nd-class seats (1500B); and die-hard *muay thai* fans bet and cheer from the fenced-off bleachers in 3rd class (1000B). If you're thinking these prices sound a bit steep for your average fight fan (taxi drivers are big fans and they make about 600B a day), then you're right. *Faràng* (Western) prices are more than double what Thais pay.

There is much debate about which seats are better. Ringside gives you the central action,

KICKING & SCREAMING

More formally known as Phahuyut (from the Pali-Sanskrit *bhahu* or 'arm' and *yodha* or 'combat'), Thailand's ancient martial art is arguably one of the kingdom's most striking national icons. Overflowing with colour and ceremony as well as exhilarating moments of clenched-teeth action, the best matches serve up a blend of such skill and tenacity that one is tempted to view the spectacle as emblematic of Thailand's centuries-old devotion to independence in a region where most other countries fell under the European colonial yoke.

Many martial arts aficionados agree that *muay thai* is the most efficient, effective and generally unbeatable form of ring-centred hand-to-hand combat practised today. And according to legend, it has been for a while.

After the Siamese were defeated at Ayuthaya in 1767, several expert *muay boran* (from which *muay thai* is derived) fighters were among prisoners hauled off to Burma. A few years later a festival was held and one of the Thai fighters, Nai Khanom Tom, was ordered to take on prominent Burmese boxers for the entertainment of the king, and to determine which martial art was most effective. He promptly dispatched nine in a row and, as legend has it, was offered money or beautiful women as a reward; he promptly took two new wives. Today a *muay thai* festival (p12) in Ayuthaya is named after Nai Khanom Tom.

Unlike some martial disciplines, such as kung fu or qi gong, *muay thai* doesn't entertain the idea that esoteric martial-arts techniques can be passed only from master to disciple in secret. Thus the *muay thai* knowledge base hasn't fossilised and in fact remains ever open to innovation, refinement and revision. Thai champion Dieselnoi, for example, created a new approach to knee strikes that was so difficult to defend that he retired at 23 because no-one dared to fight him anymore.

Another famous *muay thai* champion is Parinya Kiatbusaba, aka Nong Thoom, a transvestite from Chiang Mai who arrived for weigh-ins wearing lipstick and rouge. After a 1998 triumph at Lumphini, Parinya used the purse to pay for sex-change surgery and in 2003 the movie *Beautiful Boxer* was made about her life. While Bangkok has long attracted foreign fighters, it wasn't until 1999 that French fighter Mourad Sari became the first non-Thai fighter to take home a weight-class championship belt from a Bangkok stadium.

Several Thai *nák muay* (fighters) have gone on to triumph in world championships in international-style boxing. Khaosai Galaxy, the greatest Asian boxer of all time, successfully defended his World Boxing Association super flyweight world title 19 times before retiring in 1991.

but gambling is prohibited and the crowd is comprised of subdued VIPs. The 2nd-class seats are filled with numbers-runners who take bets from the die-hard fans in 3rd class. Akin to being in a stock-exchange pit, hand signals communicating bets and odds fly between the 2nd- and 3rd-class areas. The 3rd-class area is the rowdiest section. Fenced off from the rest of the stadium, most of the die-hard fans follow the match (or their bets) too closely to sit down. If you need more entertainment than two men punching each other, then the crowd in the 3rd-class seats will keep you amused.

Most programs have eight to 10 fights of five rounds each. English-speaking 'staff' outside the stadium, who will practically tackle you upon arrival, hand you a fight roster and steer you to the foreigners' ticket windows; they can also be helpful in telling you which fights are the best match-ups (some say that welterweights, between 61.2kg and 66.7kg, are the best.). To keep everyone honest, however, remember to purchase tickets from the ticket window, not from a person outside the stadium (you don't need help to buy a ticket, no matter what you're told). For more on the fighters and upcoming programs, see www.muaythai2000.com.

The Isan restaurants on the north side of Ratchadamnoen stadium are well known for their *kài yâang* (grilled chicken) and other northeastern dishes, something of a fight-night tradition.

TÀKRÂW

Sometimes called 'Siamese football' in old English texts, *tàkrâw* refers to a game in which a woven rattan (or sometimes plastic) ball about 12cm in diameter is kicked around. *Tàkrâw* is also popular in several neighbouring countries and is a hotly contested sport in the Southeast Asian Games.

Traditionally *tàkrâw* is played by men standing in a circle (the size of which depends on the number of players) and simply trying to keep the ball airborne by kicking it soccer style. Points are scored for style, difficulty and variety of kicking manoeuvres. Like watching someone juggling a football, there is something quite mesmeric about watching the best players stand about 8m apart and volley the *lûuk tàkrâw* back and forth, sometimes hitting it with their heel while completely unsighted after it has sailed over their heads. Modern competitive *tàkrâw* is played with a volleyball net, using feet and head instead of hands.

Pick-up games are played throughout the city, most commonly in Lumphini Park (Map p112; Th Phra Ram IV; Ratchadamri, Saladaeng, Lumphini) and National Stadium (Map pp52–3; 0 2214 0120; Th Phra Ram I; National Stadium).

lonely planet Hotels & Hostels

Want more Sleeping recommendations than we could ever pack into this little ol' book? Craving more detail — including extended reviews and photographs? Want to read reviews by other travellers and be able to post your own? Just make your way over to **lonelyplanet.com/hotels** and check out our thorough list of independent reviews, then reserve your room simply and securely.

SLEEPING

top picks

See also our top views (p203) and top romantic lodgings (p203).

- **Sukhothai Hotel** (p215)
- **Peninsula Hotel** (p212)
- **Oriental Hotel** (p212)
- **Old Bangkok Inn** (p204)
- **Phranakorn Nornlen** (p207)
- **Reflections Rooms** (p221)
- **Eugenia** (p217)
- **Ma Du Zi** (p217)
- **Refill Now!** (p221)
- **Rose Hotel** (p214)

SLEEPING

After a decade of little excitement, Bangkok has been going through a veritable hotel-building boom during the last couple of years. Particularly in the midrange and top-end, where even the Millennium Hilton (p212) was finally completed, new properties have been competing to outdo each other and the established dames. And Thai designers have given the long-suffering midrange fans several new options that sit firmly in the chic, urbane 21st century. Put simply, Bangkok is home to some of the finest hotels in the world.

Like the city itself, Bangkok's accommodation is spread far and wide. Your choices are modern Sukhumvit, the business centre around Silom, the scenic riverside, the backpacker enclave of Banglamphu, the shopping district around Siam Sq, or boisterous Chinatown. To get a feel for which neighbourhood you might fancy before you book, see our cheat sheet on p204. And remember, Bangkok traffic can be almost apocalyptic...so if you can be near the Skytrain, Metro or river ferry you'll save time.

If money is your main consideration, then there's a good chance you'll end up on or near the famous Th Khao San backpacking mecca (p72). Th Silom and Th Sukhumvit cater mainly to midrange and top-end budgets. Interesting options in the low end of the midrange can be found in Siam Sq, Ko Ratanakosin and Chinatown.

The best way to get a discount is to book online (p208). Indeed, you're likely to pay significantly more if you just walk into a top-end hotel. The best time for discounts is outside Bangkok's peak season, November to March and July and August. Discounts can also be had through Thai travel agencies or at Bangkok's airport hotel desks. With few exceptions, Bangkok accommodation wants you to check in at 2pm and check out at noon.

LONGER-TERM RENTALS

Bangkok is loaded with serviced apartment buildings aimed at the executive market. While not cheap, they work out very well when compared with hotels offering similar (or more often inferior) rooms and suites; internet specials are common and some apartments were renting for US$62 a day when we looked. Rates usually include daily cleaning, kitchenette, internet and direct-dial telephones, plus on-site business and fitness centres and a pool.

Several options are concentrated on centrally located Soi Lang Suan, between Chid Lom and Lumphini, while others gather on the other side of Lumphini Park in the Silom business district. The Centrepoint group (www.centrepoint.com) is the biggest manager of serviced apartments, with seven buildings across Bangkok. Others that we like include:

Siri Sathorn (Map p112; ☎ 0 2266 2345; www.sirisathorn.com; 27 Soi Sala Daeng 1, Th Silom; daily from 5000B, per month 1-bedroom 80,000-98,000B, 2-bedroom 120,000-240,000B; 🅿 🖵 🛋) Chic modern apartments starting at 60 sq metres; shuttle bus, satisfying service.

House By The Pond (Map pp118–19; ☎ 0 2259 3543; www.housebythepond.com; 230/3 Soi Sainumthip 2, Soi 22, Th Sukhumvit; daily 1600-2800B, per month 22,000-43,000B; 🅿 🖵 🛋) Older and more affordable.

Pathumwan House (p211) has more modest rooms at more modest prices, or if you're on a microscopic budget the guesthouses around Soi Ngam Duphli welcome long stayers. Check the 'Property Guide' in the *Bangkok Post* on Thursdays for rental listings, or:

www.sabaai.com Most professional site for apartments

www.mrroomfinder.com Wide range, detailed search options

www.bangkokapartments.info Cheap places

bangkok.craigslist.co.th Mainly long leases

KO RATANAKOSIN & THONBURI

Bangkok's oldest districts, the royal island of Ko Ratanakosin and Thonburi across the river, make an excellent base for exploring the city's major historic sights and experiencing life by the Mae Nam Chao Phraya. Until relatively recently, however, the Banglamphu budget area (opposite) at the northern end of Ko Ratanakosin was the only place you could stay.

That has changed with the opening of four small, intimate riverside abodes that are among the most atmospheric lodgings in the city. Given their small number of rooms, advance bookings are recommended.

CHAKRABONGSE VILLAS

Map p56   Hotel $$$

☎ 0 2622 3356; www.thaivillas.com; 396 Th Maharat, Ko Ratanakosin; villas 10,000-25,000B; ⚲ Tha Tien; ✲ ⚇

Prince Chakrabongse Bhuvanath's 19th-century mansion has been converted and adapted to become a luxurious slice of history with a private, personal touch. Set around a garden adorned with a modest pool are four villas fittingly kitted out with traditional furnishings and silks, plus modern luxuries, in both Thai and Chinese styles. An open-sided dining pavilion is literally right on the river, with splendid views across to Wat Arun; meals are cooked to order using the freshest ingredients – delightful.

AURUM: THE RIVER PLACE

Map p56   Hotel $$

☎ 0 2622 2248; www.aurum-bangkok.com; 396 Th Maharat, Ko Ratanakosin; tw/d 3600/4100B; ⚲ Tha Tien; ✲

At the river end of a row of old Chinese godowns, the Aurum manages to feel at home here despite its faux-Parisian style. The 12 tastefully furnished rooms are by no means big, but the windows are and make the most of the not-wholly-uninterrupted river views. Breakfast is included.

ARUN RESIDENCE Map p56   Hotel $$

☎ 0 2221 9158; www.arunresidence.com; 396 Th Maharat, Ko Ratanakosin; d 3100-5000B; ⚲ Tha Tien; ✲ ▣

A couple of minutes' walk from Wat Pho along another *soi* (lane) of godowns, the Arun Residence is a romantic retreat because of its Deck restaurant (p154), bar and unrivalled views across to Wat Arun. All rooms are fitted out in charismatic midcentury décor and modern luxuries (including wi-fi and cable broadband), but some are dark and only the larger suite has clear views (from its private terrace). Wherever you stay, you'll find it hard to drag yourself away from the sunset views from the bar.

top picks

ROMANTIC STAYS

Money is No Object
- Ma Du Zi (p217) Contemporary luxury, relaxed chic
- Oriental (p212) Conrad, Maugham, Coward...and you
- Eugenia (p217) Explorer-style escapism
- Chakrabongse Villas (left) Riverfront royal residence

Affordable Romance
- Ibrik Resort (below) Simple west-bank seclusion
- Arun Residence (left) Sunsets over Wat Arun
- Old Bangkok Inn (p204) Luxury shop house living, family feel
- River View Guest House (p208) Million-baht views from front, upper rooms

IBRIK RESORT Map p56   Boutique $$

☎ 0 2848 9220; www.ibrikresort.com; 256 Soi Wat Rakhang, Th Arun Amarin, Thonburi; d 3200-3500B; ⚲ Tha Wang Lang; ✲

Fancy being near the river? If you roll out of bed in this three-room resort you could quite literally roll right into the river (which, given this is the Chao Phraya, is not recommended). The resort is in a white wooden house and with silks and four-post beds the rooms are perfect for a romantic getaway that won't feel forced. Note the Moonlight room has no view, but occupants can use the communal riverside terrace. Price includes breakfast. There is also a sister property in town on Th Sathon (Map pp108–9; ☎ 0 2211 3470; 235/16 Th Sathon Tai).

BANGLAMPHU

At the northern end of Ko Ratanakosin is Banglamphu (p67), a truly unique backpacker phenomenon and the world's greatest clearing house of international travellers. Centred around Th Khao San – better known simply as 'the Khao San Road' or 'KSR' – Banglamphu has graduated from the days of Spartan cells for 50B to include a fast-growing range of midrange options. Of course, dirt-cheap rooms are still available and whatever budget you're travelling with, fierce competition means you'll get the best value for your baht in Banglamphu.

WHERE SHOULD I STAY?

If you don't have time to read through the Neighbourhoods chapter (p48) before booking your hotel – or can't be arsed – these words and phrases should help give you an idea of what Bangkok's various neighbourhoods (and their *soi* dogs) have to offer. If your stay inspires other adjectives, by all means share them with us at www.lonelyplanet.com/talk2us.

Ko Ratanakosin & Thonburi (p54) Historic centre, royal palace, temples, golden spires, reclining Buddha, tourists, river ferry, sunsets, amulets, students, godowns, lazy *soi* dogs.

Banglamphu (p67) Old Bangkok, shop houses, village feel, hidden bars, the Khao San Rd, ultra budget beds, crossroads of people, fashion parade, sandals and flip-flops, braids, touts, neon, traffic, mangy *soi* dogs.

Thewet & Dusit (p78) Parkland, European palaces, soulless space, village wet market, street food, few hotels, no trains, royal *soi* dogs.

Chinatown (p78) Noise, energy, flavours, tiny lanes, street food, shop houses, stalls, wholesalers, temples, Golden Buddha, túk-túks, battered Vespas, fat *soi* dogs.

Siam Sq, Pratunam & Ploenchit (p78) Shopping, malls, business, air-conditioning, fashion, miniskirts, shopping, students, Jim Thompson's, quiet Muslim village, noisy roads, shopping, traffic, *soi* dogs underfoot, shopping.

Riverside, Silom & Lumphini (p78) Diplomatic, professional, establishment, views, river boats, classic hotels, rooftop bars, park, kickboxing, night bazaar, aerobics, release.

Th Sukhumvit (p116) Modern, frivolous, international and frenetic, lots of hotels, fine restaurants, boutique, wannabe-boutique, classy, sleazy *sois*, loud, Skytrain, healthy-looking *soi* dogs (some with collars).

Booking ahead is recommended in peak season, particularly in the more expensive places and, let's face it, anywhere listed in this book. Some cheapies don't take bookings, but most now do. Still, if you're a bit flexible you should be able to wander around and find something at any time of year.

Banglamphu's popularity has seen lodgings spread out within about a 1km radius of its KSR epicentre. The district can be sliced into three main personalities centred around the following streets: Th Khao San, Soi Rambutri/Th Phra Athit and Th Samsen.

Th Khao San itself has upgraded its image (sort of) and certainly its prices. Most of the grim little rooms with paper-thin walls and resident communities of bedbugs (we still remember you bedbug class of '98, good riddance to you and the filthy mattresses you rode in on!) have been moved on and replaced by comfortable if not-exactly-inspiring mid-rises with air-con and lifts. Prices are more suited to the barely 20s travelling with robust credit cards than the every-baht-is-sacred crowd of yore. Savvy budgeters should shop around for the latest makeover or newcomer luring new business with cut-rate promotions. Or better yet, step off KSR to find better value. For budget travellers who want to stay near KSR and are happy to forfeit cleanliness, privacy and quiet for the sheer thrill of paying close to nothing, monastic 150B to 250B rooms can still be found along Soi Damnoen Klang and Trok Mayom, alleys running parallel to Khao San where small wooden houses are divided into even smaller rooms.

Along leafy Soi Rambutri and the river-facing Th Phra Athit is a more mature and slightly less crowded scene. Hotels have more creature comforts, there's less techno music to keep you awake and outdoor parties wind up earlier. It's all a short walk from Th Khao San – cut through the little Tel Aviv of the Secret Garden guesthouse – and conveniently near Tha Phra Athit and the express boats to major historical sites along the river.

Heading north across Khlong Rop Krung (aka Khlong Banglamphu), Th Samsen runs parallel to the river heading north to Thewet. Small *soi* branching off the road shelter a couple of tired no-tell hotels on the east side, and nearer to the river a mix of newer cheap hotels and family-run guesthouses amid a typical village world of thick-hipped mothers, freshly bathed babies and neighbours shuffling off to the nearest shopkeeper to buy sundries. It's a great area to wander.

Finally, we're listing the Banglamphu guesthouses we like most, but there are loads of others that are clean and – quite possibly – cheaper.

OLD BANGKOK INN   Map pp68–9   Hotel $$
☎ 0 2629 1787; www.oldbangkokinn.com; 609 Th Phra Sumen; d 3190-3990B, r 6590B; 🚍 air-con 511, 512 & 516, ordinary 2, 12, 68 & 82, khlong taxi Tha Phan Fah; ✖ 🖳
Occupying several adjoining shophouses that were once a neighbourhood noodle house, this boutique hotel is now pleasingly decorated in colours that will evoke

visions of desserts: crème caramel walls, dark cocoa furnishings, persimmon silk bedspreads and flowing white mosquito nets. The 10 rooms occupy unconventional and sometimes cramped spaces, including mezzanine floors, attics and, in the family-size Lemongrass room, a walk-though bathroom to a garden bathtub. They all evoke the historic feel of the district, which is what you're here for, while catering to modern needs with internet-ready computer terminals. Service is excellent, and rates include breakfast.

BUDDY LODGE Map pp68–9 Hotel $$
☎ 0 2629 4477; www.buddylodge.com; 265 Th Khao San; d 2400-2900B; 🚇 Tha Phra Athit, 🚌 air-con 511 & 512, ordinary 2 & 82; 🗙 💻 🖵
It was when we arrived on Khao San in 2001 and saw a Rolls Royce parked outside the grand new Buddy Lodge that we knew the road had changed forever. With its middle-of-the-action location, rooftop pool and 76 attractive, tropical-manor style rooms, Buddy has been booming ever since – so get up early (or don't go to bed) if you want a sun lounge. The McDonald's in the lobby is cheesier than a cheeseburger and service is patchy, but if you're not budgeting it's a good choice.

VIENGTAI HOTEL Map pp68–9 Hotel $$
☎ 0 2280 5434; www.viengtai.co.th; 42 Th Rambutri; s/tw 2000/2000B; 🚇 Tha Phra Athit, 🚌 air-con 511 & 512, ordinary 2 & 82; 🗙 💻 🖵
The Viengtai has been a Banglamphu fixture since 1953 – long, long before the first reefer-toting backpackers strung up hammocks on the Khao San Road. But as the area has taken off, so the basic Chinese-style hotel has renovated and extended itself firmly into the midrange. The 200 rooms are completely devoid of personality, but peace and comfort are givens. Plus those Lucy-and-Desi twin beds are charmingly old fashioned.

LAMPHU TREEHOUSE Map pp68–9 Hotel $$
☎ 0 2282 0991-92; www.lamphutreehotel.com; Soi Baan Pan Thom, 155 Wanchat Bridge, Th Prachatipatai; s/d 1250/1450B; 🚌 ordinary 9, 12 & 56; 🗙 💻 🖵
Accessed via a khlong-side footpath running west from Wanchat Bridge, the newly built Lamphu is no treehouse, but it is a very good-value new hotel. The terracotta-coloured lobby opens onto a modest pool where backpackers loiter and, together with the engaging staff, give the place a pleasantly social ambience. The 40 rooms on four levels (with lift) are colourful, comfortable and don't have TVs.

NEW SIAM RIVERSIDE Map pp68–9 Hotel $$
☎ 0 2629 3535; www.newsiam.net; 21 Th Phra Athit; d 1190-2190B; 🚇 Tha Phra Athit, 🚌 air-con 511 & 512, ordinary 2 & 82;
The fortunes of the New Siam guesthouse empire are a metaphor for the rise and rise of Banglamphu itself. With this, the fourth and newest New Siam that opened in 2007, they've boldly stepped onto the Chao Phraya riverfront with a 104-room orange behemoth. With a riverside pool, café, well-equipped and vaguely stylish rooms and attractive Phra Athit location, it's one of the best options in the district – if you pay for a room with a view (from 1590B). The price includes breakfast. The New Siams II and III are also very popular.

ERAWAN HOUSE Map pp68–9 Hotel $$
☎ 0 2629 2121; www.erawanhouse.net; 17 Soi Chana Songkhram, Th Phra Athit; r 1000B; 🚇 Tha Phra Athit, 🚌 ordinary 15, 30 & 53; 🗙 💻
Bringing a dash of 'boutique' to this soi of veteran guesthouses beyond the wát, the Erawan has made the most of globe-like lampshades and a lobby atrium. Rooms are comfortable but modestly fitted out, which helps keep the rates at these very reasonable levels.

RIKKA INN Map pp68–9 Hotel $
☎ 0 2282 7511; www.rikkainn.com; 259 Th Khao San; s/d 600/950B; 🚇 Tha Phra Athit, 🚌 air-con 511 & 512, ordinary 2 & 82; 🗙 💻 🖵
If you want a pool but don't want to spend money on rooms with fancy decorations (or, in many cases, a window), then the fairly stylish minimalism of the Rikka will appeal. The lobby promises more contemporary style than the small rooms deliver, but credit where it's due – for this price they're more than fine. The rooftop pool is super.

SHAMBARA Map pp68–9 Guesthouse $
☎ 0 2282 7968; www.shambarabangkok.com; 138 Th Khao San; r 700-950B; 🚇 Tha Phra Athit, 🚌 air-con 511 & 512, ordinary 2 & 82; 🗙 💻

Just 50m from the noise and neon of Khao San, Shambara feels a world away. The century-old traditional wooden home has nine tiny rooms that share two clean showers and toilets. For the rooms alone it's not great value, but you're buying into the chilled, convivial atmosphere. Price includes coffee and toast; wi-fi is 1B per minute.

ROOF VIEW PLACE Map pp68–9   Hotel $

☎ 081-805 8846; Soi 6, Th Samsen; s 450B, d 550-800B; ⚓ Tha Phra Athit or Tha Thewet; ⊠ 🖥
Opened in 2007, the Roof View embraces a sparse but – at this price – relatively stylish minimalism that makes it the pick among an otherwise uninspiring bunch in this quiet village area. The rooms we saw were squeaky clean and very white. The sixth-floor roof does indeed have fine district views, but so far nowhere to sit. There's a winch for backpacks but no lift. Wi-fi costs 50B per day, and guests can use the kitchen in the lobby.

BOWORN BB Map pp68–9   Guesthouse $

☎ 0 2629 1073; www.bowornbb.com; 335 Th Phra Sumen; r 600-700B; ⚓ Tha Phra Athit, 🚌 air-con 511 & 512, ordinary 2 & 82; ⊠ 🖥
Cultural chameleons will love this antique neighbourhood of green-and-yellow sho-phouses and flip-flop-clad families with hardly a sign of tourist incursions. Boworn has bland but clean rooms with wet-all-over bathrooms and a fresh coat of paint. But it's the familial atmosphere centred around the café-lobby and the garden rooftop that are most attractive – and the *aroi* (delicious) green curries. Wi-fi is available for 100B per day.

LAMPHU HOUSE Map pp68–9   Guesthouse $

☎ 0 2629 5861; www.lamphuhouse.com; 75-77 Soi Rambutri, Th Chakraphong; d from 590B; ⚓ Tha Phra Athit, 🚌 ordinary 15, 30 & 53; ⊠ 🖥
A refreshing oasis, Lamphu House creates a mellow mood with its hidden, relatively quiet location and breezy, smartly deco-rated rooms. The building was a hospital in another era and the spirit of cleanliness lives on. Some have balconies overlook-ing the green courtyard, and cheaper fan rooms with shared bathrooms are also available. All up, great value – book as far ahead as you can.

VILLA GUEST HOUSE

Map pp68–9   Guesthouse $

☎ 0 2281 7009; 230 Soi 1, Th Samsen; s 300B, d 400-600B; ⚓ Tha Phra Athit, 🚌 air-con 506, ordinary 53
Hidden behind a wooden door at the end of a nondescript lane, the long-running Villa is a quiet garden oasis amid the village life of Soi 1. The dark interiors of this 19th century nobleman's teak house ooze his-tory, written in 70 years worth of detritus accumulated by the family of the current owners. It is also home to 10 simple rooms (all with fan and shared bathroom); reserva-tions are strongly recommended.

PRASURI GUEST HOUSE

Map pp68–9   Guesthouse $

☎ 0 2280 1428; prasuri_gh_bkk@hotmail.com; Soi Phrasuli; s 220-380B, d 280-420B; ⚓ Tha Phra Athit; 🚌 air-con 511 & 512, ordinary 2 & 82; ⊠ 🖥
It doesn't get much more everyday Thai than this simple old guesthouse in a leafy *soi* northeast of Th Khao San. Appropriately in a neighbourhood of family-run shop-houses, the Prasuri doubles as a 30B restau-rant, shop for random grocery items and internet café that sees crowds of uniformed Thai schoolchildren battling it out on video games during lunch and after school. The rooms are tired but quiet and clean, and all have bathrooms.

PRAKORP'S HOUSE

Map pp68–9   Guesthouse $

☎ 0 2281 1345; fax 0 2629 0714; 52 Th Khao San; s/d 160/250B; ⚓ Tha Phra Athit, 🚌 air-con 511 & 512, ordinary 2 & 82
One of the last old-style guesthouses on Th Khao San, Prakorp's offers both the good and bad of the street's past: a charismatic old wooden house set back from the road and dire concrete cells in the older street-front building. Staff are friendly (significant because this is not always the case on KSR) and the food is delicious. The five simple rooms in the old house are obviously the ones to go for.

If you're arriving late in the day in peak sea-son, rooms can be hard to find if you don't have a reservation. An alternative is:
Royal Hotel (Map pp68–9; ☎ 0 2222 9111-26; fax 0 2224 2083; cnr Th Ratchadamnoen Klang & Th Atsadang; d 1200-1700B; ⊠ 🖥) Bangkok's third-oldest hotel

GREEN HOTELS

Hotels might seem to be gobbling up the landscape, but many are watching what they eat when it comes to world resources. Green Leaf Foundation, a collaborative environmental organisation, has recognised a number of Bangkok hotels for cutting energy and water use and garbage output, and raising awareness of environmental issues among their staff. Among them, green hotels we recommend include Bangkok Marriott Resort & Spa Hotel (p220), Banyan Tree Hotel (p215), Dusit Thani (p213), Grand China Princess (p208), Grand Hyatt Erawan (p210) and the Malaysia Hotel (p215). See www.greenleafthai.org for specifics of what they have done.

Several smaller hotels have also adopted social and environmentally responsible practices, notably Phranakorn Nornlen (below) and Reflections Rooms (p220).

(aka Hotel Ratanakosin), so yes, rather old. Rooms vary markedly.

THEWET & DUSIT

The district north of Banglamphu near the National Library is known as 'Thewet'. Guesthouses line the *soi* side of Th Sri Ayuthaya, popular with Asia-savvy budgeters who are generally a little older than the Khao San crowd. This is a lovely, leafy area with a morning market, a busy neighbourhood temple and easy access to the river ferry. The only drawbacks are that downtown Bangkok is many traffic jams away and the street is prone to flooding during the rainy season.

The surrounding neighbourhood of Dusit has a few large package-tour hotels.

PHRANAKORN NORNLEN
Map p79   Boutique Hotel $$
☎ 0 2628 8188-90; www.phranakorn-nornlen
.com; 46 Thewet Soi 1, Th Krung Kasem, Thewet;
s/d 1800/2200B; ☷ Tha Thewet; ⌘ ▯
Everyone seems to love this small, arty boutique hotel where smiles come readily to faces. Maybe it's the garden setting in which the converted wooden building stands, or perhaps the individual rooms with tall showers and rustic charm. Or perhaps it's the social and environmental responsibility of the owners, who provide a very healthy organic breakfast but also encourage guests to head out and patronise the local businesses; the owners also run an NGO to help children. For us it was the community ambience, fostered by the wonderfully engaging staff. It's highly recommended.

SHANTI LODGE Map p79   Hostel $
☎ 0 2281 2497; Th Si Ayuthaya, Thewet; dm 200B,
s 400B, d 750-850B; ☷ Tha Thewet, ⌘ ordinary
53 & 30; ⌘ ▯

Nobody does backpacker chic like Shanti Lodge, where a rambling wooden house with a maze of artfully decorated air-con rooms crouches above a blissed-out garden café downstairs; think lolling, guitar-strumming, story-swapping and good coffee. The staff are, and have been for years, prone to a certain ice-queen indifference that annoys some travellers but is ignored by most. That aside, it's a real gem.

SRI AYUTTAYA GUEST HOUSE
Map p79   Hostel $
☎ 0 2282 5942; Th Si Ayuthaya, Thewet; s 350B,
d 600-850B; ☷ Tha Thewet, ⌘ ordinary 53 & 30;
⌘ ▯
Offering a decent alternative to Shanti Lodge, the Sri Ayuttaya has romantic air-con rooms with pretty hardwood floors, exposed brick and other stylish touches. It's not as social as Shanti, and service isn't much more forthcoming, either. But it's still superior to many Khao San–area flophouses charging the same dough.

BANGKOK INTERNATIONAL
YOUTH HOSTEL Map p79   Hostel $
☎ 0 2282 0950; www.hihostels.com; 25/2 Th Phit-
sanulok, Dusit; dm 120-170B, r 250-500B; ☷ Tha
Thewet, ⌘ ordinary 16 & 509; ⌘ ▯
In a dull location east of Th Samsen and the Thewet budget abodes, this HI was being expanded when we passed. The old rooms and dorms, however, remained cramped and tired. The main reason to stay is the generally enthusiastic nature of the guests and the Thai volunteers who lead free tours for a chance to practise their English. Take 50B off if you're a member.

CHINATOWN

Many visitors venture into this neighbourhood in search of a little more cultural immersion than can be found in the multicultural

Disneyland of Khao San. By and large China-town's hotels suffer from the same sort of total charisma bypass familiar in, well, Chinese cities. But the rates and rooms communi-cate in the international language for 'value', and recent additions have added some class. The edges of the district and the area around Hualamphong train station have some appeal-ing cheap options among the dross, while the Indian district of Phahurat is less expensive and caters to low-end business travellers from the subcontinent. But do watch your pockets and bags around the Hualamphong area.

SHANGHAI INN Map p84 Boutique $$

☎ 0 2221 2121; www.shanghai-inn.com; 479 Th Yaowarat; r 2800-4000B; Ⓜ Hualamphong, 🛥 Tha Ratchawong, 🚍 air-con 507, ordinary 73; ▨
The Shanghai is a real boutique place that brings a technicolour interpretation of '30s Shanghai to manic Th Yaowarat. The 55 excellent-value rooms are kitted out in Chi-nese-style four-post beds, bright-painted walls and as many as 10 hanging silk lights. Wi-fi is available throughout, and breakfast is included. The best place in Chinatown.

GRAND CHINA PRINCESS
Map p84 Hotel $$
☎ 0 2224 9977; www.grandchina.com; 215 Th Yaowarat; r 2200-4200B; Ⓜ Hualamphong,

🛥 Tha Ratchawong, 🚍 air-con 507, ordinary 73; ▨ 🖳 🛥
A certifiable monstrosity from the outside, this hotel in the heart of Chinatown is popular with groups and has nondescript, but comfortable rooms buoyed by great views. The top floor has a panoramic ro-tating restaurant to make your dreams of gaudy Asia complete. There's pretty good service and big discounts online.

KRUNG KASEM SRIKUNG HOTEL
Map p84 Hotel $
☎ 0 2225 8900; srikrung_htl@yahoo.com; 1860 Th Krung Kasem; d 650B; 🚍 ordinary 25, 35 & 53, Ⓜ Hualamphong; ▨
Across the khlong from Hualamphong sta-tion, this institutional-style high-rise won't win any design awards but the clean, siz-able rooms are fair value. Rear rooms (with even numbers) are better because while the front rooms have train station views, they are buffeted by street noise.

RIVER VIEW GUEST HOUSE
Map p84 Guesthouse $
☎ 0 2234 5429; www.riverviewbkk.com; 768 Soi Phanurangsi, Th Songwat; r 450-900B; Ⓜ Hualam-phong, 🛥 Tha Si Phraya, 🚍 ordinary 36 & 93; ▨
Overlooking a bend in the river, the aptly named River View has an awesome and af-

BOOKING ONLINE: JUST DO IT

'You know,' said the woman as she glanced conspiratorially around the reception of one of Bangkok's top hotels, 'if you book online the rates are much cheaper…about 30% usually.' We were offered similar surprisingly honest advice several times while researching this guide, with the general message being that for midrange and top-end hotels booking ahead gets you discounts you can't even contemplate when you walk in.

As another front office manager explained: 'Sorry, but you probably won't get anywhere bargaining with the front desk girls because they take a commission on any rooms they sell, so they want to keep the price as high as possible.' Ah, so that's it. Then she handed over a hotel business card and said: 'Here, call this number and you'll get a discount automatically.' So, in theory, we could have called from the guest phone in the lobby, reserved a room at the discount rate, had a drink in the bar and checked in 15 minutes later having saved 30%.

Even during the January peak season hefty discounts can be found by looking around online, particularly in the midrange. And even Th Khao San budget places offer modest advance booking discounts, though the cheapest places might still engage in a bit of old-style, person-to-person haggling.

Of course, online booking also has its dangers…read LP author Karla Zimmerman's account of her unwitting transformation into voyeur in the boxed text, p216.

Recommended Sites

For independent reviews rather than endless superlatives, Lonely Planet's Hotels & Hostels (www.lonelyplanet.com) features thorough reviews from authors and traveller feedback, and a booking facility. For an idea of the sort of discounts you're looking at, independent website Travelfish (www.travelfish.org) has a very handy list of nothing more than the hotel name and current online price at the bottom of its Bangkok pages.

ROOM RATES – WHAT YOU GET FOR YOUR MONEY

Accommodation in this book is broken down into three categories. We've listed the mid-season rates and they include the ++, which means 10% service and 7% government tax. These are the walk-in rates quoted to us, and it should be noted that big discounts are available most of the time if you book online (see the boxed text, opposite).

$$$ more than 4500B a night

$$ 1000B to 4500B a night

$ less than 1000B a night

So what do you get for your money? Bangkok's growing array of top-end hotels start at about 4500B and climb many times higher. In the top tier rooms start at more than 10,000B, but in most of the luxurious design and boutique hotels, and the vast majority of the international brands, you're looking at about 6000B to 9000B, before online discounting.

You can pay up to 4500B for a midrange room, too, though with discounting most are available for between 3000B and 4000B. Of course, more-modest properties have more-modest rates – modesty seemingly defined by the style of the décor. Thus the older places are often quite cheap, while trendier new places are more pricey.

The days of 50B beds in Banglamphu are over, but those on wafer-thin budgets can still get a dorm bed for between 150B and 400B, with a shared bathroom. More comfortable and stylish rooms are available for upwards of 800B, price rising with size and location.

fordable location between Silom and Chinatown, steps from the river. The front rooms with small balconies have views you'd pay several times as much for in the nearby top-end hotels, and the rooftop bar-restaurant is one of the best sunset views in town. Most are fan-conditioned; air-con costs more.

River View is hidden among small lanes and can be tough to find. Heading north on Th Charoen Krung from Th Si Phraya, take a left on to Th Songwat (before the Chinatown Arch), then the second left onto Soi Phanurangsi. You'll start to see signs at this point.

TRAIN INN Map p84 — Hostel $
☎ 0818-195 544; www.thetraininn.com; 428 Th Hualamphong; r 450-900B; Ⓜ Hualamphong exit 3, Ⓑ ordinary 36 & 9; ✲ ▯
In a strip of tired old budget places directly opposite the train station, the clean, secure and relatively funky Train Inn is a breath of fresh air. Owner Jana maintains a young, friendly and helpful atmosphere and her 41 rooms are hostel-style compact; the '1st class' rooms are best; others can be noisy, so ask to see a few. Cable broadband is included in the 1st-class price and 200B per day in other rooms.

BAAN HUALAMPONG
Map p84 — Guesthouse $
☎ 0 2639 8054; www.baanhualampong.com; 336/20 Soi 21, Th Charoen Krung; dm 220B, s 290B, d 520-700B; Ⓜ Hualamphong; ✲ ▯

Off a relatively quiet soi a few minutes' walk from the station, this old-style wood-and-concrete guesthouse has developed a loyal following among those seeking a mix of family atmosphere and backpacker self-sufficiency, centred around the communal areas and kitchen. The owner speaks English and German and is a font of knowledge – see the website for the cheapest possible ways of getting here.

SIAM SQUARE & PRATUNAM

As central as Bangkok gets, this area is conveniently located on the Skytrain near shopping centres and loads of high-rise chain hotels. In the midrange, a devoted cast of túk-túk and taxi drivers throng the entrances of hotels zealously pouncing on every map-toting victim. If you're a pedestrian wanderer, you'll be happier at a smaller hotel that is less of a target. Soi Kasem San 1, off Th Phra Ram I, has a cluster of nice guesthouses for the early-to-bed, early-to-rise travellers. For more on the Siam Sq and Pratunam district, see p97.

FOUR SEASONS HOTEL
Map pp98–9 — Luxury Hotel $$$
☎ 0 2250 1000; www.fourseasons.com/bangkok; 155 Th Ratchadamri; d from 9000B; Ⓡ Ratchadamri; ✲ ▯ ⌨
A spectacular mural descending a grand staircase, ceilings adorned with neck-craning

209

THE INTERNET: MINIMUM SERVICE OR EXPENSIVE LUXURY?

If you're paying big bucks for a room should you then have to pay extortionate rates to use the internet? For most travellers, no matter how wealthy they are, the answer is a resounding 'no'. Most Bangkok hotels and a growing number of guesthouses provide either wi-fi or cable broadband (or sometimes both) in their rooms and public spaces. But as we researched Bangkok's hotels for this edition, too often we found ourselves in conversations something like this:

LP: 'So, does this room come with internet?'
Hotel: 'Yes, all our rooms have high-speed/wi-fi internet.'
LP: 'That's great. Is it free, or do I have to pay?'
Hotel, somewhat sheepishly: 'It costs 17B a minute but you only pay to a maximum of 717B per day.'
LP: '17B a minute!!! That's more than 50c a minute! I'd reach 717B in... (calculating)...42 minutes!' Uncomfortable silence.
Hotel: 'Umm...now if you look out here you can see these rooms have wonderful views....'

Right. To put this into perspective, the owner of one small boutique hotel (which like many smaller Bangkok properties charges lower room rates and *doesn't* charge extra for internet use) explained that her total monthly broadband internet bill was less than 800B. Total. So internet costs in Bangkok are low.

Sure, if you can afford to spend hundreds of dollars on a room (or you're on the corporate tab) the extra US$25 might not matter. But even (especially?) billionaires know value, or as one executive told us, know 'highway robbery' when they see it.

So what can you do? Put simply, stay with someone else. A growing number of Bangkok hotels are including internet use in the price, so finding one to match your budget shouldn't be too hard. Indeed, cheaper hotels seem to be leading the way on this front, and many midrange places have joined in. Ask or check their website to find out.

artwork and a library-quiet lobby punctuated with muscular columns give the Four Seasons a tone of relaxed opulence that continues into the lauded restaurants – especially Biscotti and Madison. These, and an open-air jungle courtyard, are probably more attractive than the 353 rooms.

GRAND HYATT ERAWAN
Map pp98–9   Luxury Hotel $$$
☎ 0 2254 1234; www.bangkok.hyatt.com; 494 Th Ratchadamri; d from 8800B; 🚇 Chitlom; ✕ 🖥 🛅

The Erawan's neoclassical lobby, embellished with mature tropical trees, sets the tone in what is one of Bangkok's most-respected hotels. The 320 rooms are relatively big and well designed, with smart use of mirrors and well-positioned desks complementing an attractive modern Asian décor of hardwoods, silks and white marble. Rooms on the west side have the best views, overlooking the prestigious Bangkok Royal Sports Club racetrack. Annoyingly, the wi-fi internet costs a staggering 17B per minute, or a maximum of 717B for 24 hours.

NAI LERT PARK HOTEL
Map pp98–9   Luxury Hotel $$$
☎ 0 2253 0123; www.swissotel.com/bangkok-nai lertpark; 2 Th Withayu (Wireless Rd); d from US$185; 🚇 Ploenchit 🚤 Tha Withayu; ✕ 🖥 🛅

Aiming for the *Wallpaper* crowd, new owner Raffles has taken the old Hilton, rebranded it as Swissotel and done as much as possible to convert it to Zen, but there's only so much you can do with a classic 1980s atrium (hang a lot of shiny stuff from the ceiling, apparently). Still, the rooms are impressive and, best of all, boast soothing views onto the jungle garden and shaded pool.

SIAM@SIAM Map pp98–9   Boutique $$$
☎ 0 2217 3000; www.siamatsiam.com; 865 Th Phra Ram I; d from 5700B; 🚇 National Stadium; ✕ 🖥 🛅

From the moment you walk into this new hotel you get the feeling this 'design hotel and spa' has taken the concept of industrial design pretty much as far as it can go. Wire sculptures stand on polished concrete while railway sleepers seem to cover every exposed pylon. The 203 rooms occupy the 14th to 25th floors and have city views – those looking at National Stadium are best. Inside they are a world of concrete, rust, copper and wood, with dashes of orange; note that twin rooms have adjoining beds. Rates include breakfast and wi-fi internet.

ASIA HOTEL Map pp98–9   Hotel $$
☎ 0 2215 0808; www.asiahotel.co.th; 296 Th Phayathai; r from 2600B; 🚇 Ratchathewi; ✕ 🛅

The appropriately named Asia is the classic Asian midranger, sporting a wannabe luxurious lobby of polished granite floors, faux chandeliers and the constant din of noisy tourists. Rooms are reliable – nothing more – with the superior and deluxe options worth the extra baht. A covered walkway connects to the Skytrain.

VIP GUEST HOUSE/GOLDEN HOUSE
Map pp98–9   Hotel $$

☎ 0 2252 9535; www.goldenhouses.net; 1025/5-9 Th Ploenchit; r from 1400B; 🚇 Chitlom; ✂
The 27 clean, quiet and mainly bright rooms make this a good lower midrange choice in this otherwise pricey part of town. The price includes breakfast.

These next five places are in a mainly quiet *soi* just a few minutes walk west of the Siam shopping extravaganza. If you prefer spending your baht on shopping rather than sleeping, it's for you.

PATHUMWAN HOUSE
Map pp98–9   Hotel $$

☎ 0 2612 3580; www.pathumwanhouse.com; 22 Soi Kasem San 1, Th Phra Ram I; d daily 1200-2300B, monthly 15,000-34,000B; 🚇 National Stadium; ✂
Tucked back in the crook of the *soi*, this friendly high-rise is mainly a long-term hotel but lots of dailies cycle through after striking out elsewhere. Rooms are a decent size but the cheapest are almost devoid of natural light, and the bathrooms we saw had showerheads mounted at about navel height. Your comings and goings will be announced by a collection of chirping caged birds.

RENO HOTEL
Map pp98–9   Hotel $$

☎ 0 2215 0026; www.renohotel.co.th; 40 Soi Kasem San 1, Th Phra Ram I; d 1180-1550B; 🚇 National Stadium; ✂ ▢ ▤
This Vietnam War veteran has embraced the new millennium with colour and flair, making the best of its retro features (check out the monogrammed pool) and funking up the foyer and café, in particular. The 70 rooms remain fairly simple, the best being those with a balcony overlooking the pool, and service can be reluctant. But for the money (price includes breakfast), the Reno is a great, central deal.

WENDY HOUSE
Map pp98–9   Hostel $$

☎ 0 2214 1149-50; www.wendyguesthouse.com; Soi Kasem San 1, Th Phra Ram I; s/tw 900/1100B; 🚇 National Stadium; ✂ ▢
Wendy is a cheery backpacker joint with small but well-scrubbed rooms and tiled bathrooms. The 20 rooms are all nonsmoking, which is refreshing in this price bracket. Desk staff are sweet and the well-lit lobby is the sort of place you're likely to end up swapping stories with fellow travellers. Breakfast is included.

A-ONE INN
Map pp98–9   Guesthouse $

☎ 0 2215 3029; www.aoneinn.com; 25/13-15 Soi Kasem San 1, Th Phra Ram I; d 600-850B; 🚇 National Stadium; ✂
A small family operation, busy A-One has 25 cosy and clean rooms with hardwood floors that live up to its advertising, offering value 'in the heart of town'. A-One is a wi-fi hotspot.

RIVERSIDE & SILOM

Bangkok's most established and famous luxury hotels form a necklace along this stretch of the Mae Nam Chao Phraya. This is romantic Bangkok, where old colonial buildings wilt under the elements and twinkling fairy lights reflect in the water. If the top end is out of reach, there are a couple of cheapies that pass the mould-free test. For more on this part of Bangkok, see p106.

The Silom, Lumphini and Sathon areas are rather different to the riverside and bring a different range of accommodation. From stylish to spinster, Silom's hotels sit in Bangkok's primary business district and are mainly popular with business travellers, airline staff and first-time tourists wanting to be near the neon and flesh of Patpong Market, Suan Lum Night Bazaar and easy access to the river.

Along east Th Sathon near Lumphini Park the trendy Sukhothai and Metropolitan hotels and the spa-like Banyan Tree make a splash among the sober embassies and office buildings. Just around the corner, but galaxies apart in price and comfort, are the survivors of Bangkok's original backpacker ghetto.

RIVERSIDE

A combination of the Skytrain to Saphan Taksin and either a walk or ferry ride on the complimentary hotel ferries is the way to reach the

FROM LITERATI TO GLITTERATI

Now a famous grand dame, the Oriental Hotel started its career as the seafarers' version of a Th Khao San guesthouse. The original owners, two Danish sea captains, traded the nest to Hans Niels Andersen, the founder of the formidable East Asiatic Company. Andersen transformed the hotel into a civilised palace of grand architecture and luxury standards. He hired an Italian architect, S Cardu, to design what is now the Author's Wing, which was the city's most fantastic building not constructed by the king.

The rest of the hotel's history relies on its famous guests. A Polish-born sailor named Joseph Conrad stayed here in 1888. The hotel brought him good luck: he got his first command on the ship *Otago*, from Bangkok to Port Adelaide, which in turn gave him ideas for several early stories. W Somerset Maugham stumbled into the hotel with an advanced case of malaria. In his feverish state, he heard the German manager arguing with the doctor about how a death in the hotel would hurt business. Maugham's overland Southeast Asian journey is recorded in *Gentleman in the Parlour: A Record of a Journey from Rangoon to Haiphong*, which gave literary appeal to the hotel. Other notable guests have included Noel Coward, Graham Greene, John le Carré, James Michener, Gore Vidal and Barbara Cartland. Some modern-day writers claim that an Oriental stay will overcome writer's block – though we suspect any writer staying these days would need a very generous advance indeed.

riverside's top-end hotels. We've got to say, the hotel ferries are a very civilised – and enjoyable – way to get around in Bangkok. Most hotels also run boats to River City (p137).

ORIENTAL HOTEL Map pp108–9   Hotel $$$
☎ 0 2659 9000; www.mandarinoriental.com/bangkok; 48 Soi 38, Th Charoen Krung; r from US$360; 🛥 Tha Oriental, 🚇 Saphan Taksin; ✄ ▢ ▣
Dating to 1876, the Oriental Hotel is one of southeast Asia's grand colonial-era hotels and one of the most luxurious and most respected in the region. The hotel's storied history of steamer travel and famous guests (see the boxed text, above) lives on in the original Author's Wing, a Victorian-era, gingerbread-style residence with rooms and suites dedicated to the famous writers who bedded and penned here.

The management prides itself on highly personalised service – once you've stayed here the staff will remember your name and what you like to eat for breakfast – though it's more formal and less relaxed than some younger competitors. Most of the 400 rooms are in the ageing River and Tower wings, which have contemporary Thai decorations, spacious bathrooms and river terraces. The establishment feel extends to the famed Normandie French restaurant and the bars, though you should find the sublime spa, on the Thonburi side of the river, more relaxing.

PENINSULA HOTEL Map pp108–9   Hotel $$$
☎ 0 2861 2888; www.bangkok.peninsula.com; 333 Th Charoen Nakhon; d from US$330; 🛥 private ferry dock near the Oriental Hotel; ✄ ▢ ▣

The Peninsula is world class, with all the international accolades to prove it. The lobby is poised and polished, an Asian-esque temple of squared black marble hallways and confident power players. Being on the Thonburi side of the river, the Peninsula enjoys views of both the river and the skyline beyond. The 370 tech-filled rooms boast oversized desks and private fax numbers to go with the understated style. All of this is complemented by classic, unpretentious service, fine restaurants and one of the city's finest spas. It's hard to beat.

SHANGRI-LA HOTEL Map pp108–9   Hotel $$$
☎ 0 2236 7777; www.shangri-la.com; 89 Soi Wat Suan Phlu, Th Charoen Krung; d from US$200, ste from US$300; 🛥 Tha Oriental, 🚇 Saphan Taksin; ✄ ▢ ▣
The Shangri-La might be 20 years old but it has aged gracefully enough that it could be said to have matured…which is a description equally at home with most of its guests. The 799 rooms are done in an understated, New Asia aesthetic that works well. Particularly so in the well-designed main wing, where the curved sides ensure everyone gets a river view (still, it's worth asking for a room close to the river). It's within the luxury sphere, yet families won't feel like bulls in a china shop. The Krung Thep wing has lower-rise terraces overlooking the river.

MILLENNIUM HILTON
Map pp108–9   Hotel $$$
☎ 0 2442 2000; bangkok.hilton.com; 123 Th Charoennakorn, Klongsan; d from 6000B; 🛥 private ferry from River City & Central Pier; ✄ ▢ ▣

After a decade as a 32-storey concrete skeleton on the far bank of the Chao Phraya, the Millennium Hilton finally opened in 2006 and now stands proudly, like a sailor in his cap, among the riverside top-end matrons. The modern Asian design creates a more stylish and less formal atmosphere than its neighbours. Flow buffet café sets the tone with fresh food and river views, The Beach makes the most of a modest-sized pool by putting the sunbeds in the water, and ThreeSixty bar fills out that sailor's cap with jazz and unrivalled views – nice. The 543 rooms aren't huge but every one has cinemascopic views; the executive plus suites are the pick. A private ferry connects to River City and Saphan Thaksin Skytrain.

P&R RESIDENCE Map pp108–9   Hotel $$
☎ 0 2639 6091-93; pandrresidence@gmail.com; 34 Soi 30, Th Charoen Krung, Bangrak; r 1000-1200B; 🚲 Tha Si Phraya, 🚉 Saphan Thaksin; 🏊
There's nothing fancy about the P&R, but its rooms are comfortable and clean and it's very fairly priced for this atmospheric old part of town. Ask for a front room, which will have views into the historic Portuguese embassy. Breakfast is 80B extra, and payment is by cash only.

ARTISTS PLACE Map pp52–3   Guesthouse $
☎ 0 2862 0056, www.geocities.com/theartistsplace; 63 Soi Thiam Bunyang, off Soi Krung Thonburi 1, Th Krung Thonburi; d 350-400B; 🚉 Saphan Taksin to bus 106
You wouldn't complain about the beds if you were staying with a friend, and this is what it's like staying with resident artist Charlee at the Artists Place in Thonburi. It's the space and the ambience you're here for, and if this is your bag then don't be surprised if you stay longer than anticipated. See the website or call for detailed directions.

NEW ROAD GUESTHOUSE
Map pp108–9   Guesthouse $
☎ 0 2630 6994-98; www.jysk-rejsebureau.dk; 1216/1 Th Charoen Krung, Bangrak; dm 90B, d 600-1300B, r 2500B; 🚲 Tha Si Phraya, 🚉 Saphan Thaksin; 🏊 💻
In this galaxy full of hotel stars light years from Banglamphu, the New Road is a welcome surprise. Run by young Danish guys

whose names all seem to end in –sen, it has recently expanded to become the go-to budget lodging in this part of town. Rooms range from some uber simple dorms to very comfortable doubles and a four-room apartment that's ideal for families. It's a good place to meet other travellers and the JYSK office sells a load of budget-priced tours.

SILOM

Parts of Silom are well served by the Skytrain, with Sala Daeng and Chong Nonsi stations most useful, which is a relief because traffic crawls day and night. Cars move faster along Sathon's multilane corridor. The east end of Silom is also served by the Metro at Silom station.

DUSIT THANI Map pp108–9   Hotel $$$
☎ 0 2200 9000; www.dusit.com; 946 Th Phra Ram IV, cnr Th Silom; r from 6100B; 🚲 Sala Daeng, Ⓜ Silom; 🏊 💻 🔊
The Dusit Thani defined Bangkok glamour in the 1970s when it reigned as the city's tallest skyscraper. From the outside its distinctively '60s look remains, with balconies off every room and triangular layout. But rather than embracing this with a thoughtful retrovation, the Dusit's renovation in the global Zen style has left it with an identity crisis. Despite this, the Dusit remains a favourite among Thais and *faràng* alike, and there is a palpable buzz of excitement as Thais in their finest arrive and depart for wedding banquets or conferences. It also boasts one of Bangkok's best restaurants (and killer views) in D'Sens (p161).

top picks

PANORAMAS

If you like to spend time in your room looking out of it, these beanpoles have guaranteed angel's-eye views in the City of Angels. Just remember to ask for a room on an upper floor.

- Millennium Hilton (opposite)
- Banyan Tree Hotel (p215)
- Peninsula Hotel (opposite)
- Dusit Thani (above)

SOFITEL SILOM BANGKOK
Map pp108–9   Hotel $$$

☎ 0 2238 1991; www.sofitel.com; 188 Th Silom; r from 6000B; 🚇 Chong Nonsi; 🍽 🖳
Coffee and liqueur colours add a spike of cool to this otherwise suburban-minded hotel. Rooms are more cosy than expansive, and the design is more safe than cutting edge. But they're clean, comfortable and everything works. Ride up to the 37th floor for a wine with a view at V9.

TRIPLE TWO SILOM Map pp108–9   Hotel $$

☎ 0 2627 2222; www.tripletwosilom.com; 222 Th Silom; r/ste 4500/5900B; 🚇 Chong Nonsi; 🍽 🖳
How do you take a bland Bangkok shopping mall and turn it into a classy boutique? The answer lies in this four-storey, 75-room hotel in the middle of stylish Th Silom. The 2004 makeover delivered a lot of white marble, dark wood and old-timey photographs, which come together in a pleasing pan-Asian mode. Rooms are large and kitted out with both wi-fi and ADSL internet at the desk. Guests can use the roof garden, but will have to go next door to the sister Narai Hotel for the swimming pool and fitness centre.

LA RÉSIDENCE HOTEL Map pp108–9 Hotel $$

☎ 0 2233 3301; www.laresidencebangkok.com; 173/8-9 Th Surawong; d/ste 2000/3700B; 🚇 Chong Nonsi; 🚌 air-con 16, ordinary 93; 🍽
La Résidence is a charming boutique inn with 26 playfully and individually decorated rooms that, according to the manager, have been 'changing all the time, one at a time for the last 15 years'. They're fantastic value! Micro-mini-sized rooms start at 1200B but for 2000B, you get a more voluptuous abode with blood-red walls, modern Thai motifs and crystal-clean bathroom. The overall effect is a casual sophistication that will delight anyone who gets twitchy in chain hotels.

LUB*D Map pp108–9   Hostel $$

☎ 0 2634 7999; www.lubd.com; 4 Th Decho, Th Surawong; dm/d 550/1800B; 🚇 Chong Nonsi; 🍽 🖳
From the owners of Triple Two Silom comes Lub*D (meaning 'sleep well'), a flashpacker haunt that will no doubt be described as a 'boutique hostel' before long. Opened in 2008, the four storeys of dorms (including a ladies-only wing) and

rooms with and without bathrooms are an industrial mix of raw concrete, exposed iron beams, woodchip doors and stencilled signs. The atmosphere is young and hip, with free internet in the streetside bar-cum-lobby, and security is tight (even the dorm rooms have key cards). If you want backpacker atmosphere but fancy (and can afford) a bit of comfort, Lub*D won't disappoint.

ROSE HOTEL Map pp108–9   Hotel $$

☎ 0 2266 8268-72; www.rosehotelbkk.com; 118 Th Surawong, Silom; r from 1700B; 🚇 Sala Daeng, Ⓜ Silom; 🅿 🍽 🖳 🖳
Hidden down a lane beside the much larger Montien, the Rose is another Bangkok veteran that has had some much-needed cosmetic surgery. The result is more Halle Berry than Jocelyne Wildenstein, with the 70 spacious rooms sporting a stylish mix of coloured walls, dark tiles and sleek bathrooms. This Rose is a very cheap date, too, considering she comes with a small gym (three machines), sauna and Thai restaurant in an old teak house set around an oasis-like pool. With breakfast included and wi-fi for 100B an hour, it's one of the best deals in town.

URBAN AGE Map pp108–9   Hostel $

☎ 0 2634 2680; theurbanage@hotmail.com; 130/6 Soi 8, Th Silom; dm/d 250/800B; 🚇 Chong Nonsi; 🍽 🖳
The Urban Age is a sort of new age version of the classic Bangkok budget haunt, in a quiet soi within crawling distance of the Silom nightspots. Small rooms, all without bathrooms and some without windows, have just enough draped fabric and minor touches to make it more appealing than the prison-cell style competition. The friendly girls who run the place (English spoken only from 8am to 5pm) are a highlight. The only downside is that the dorms are six storeys up, all stairs.

NIAGARA HOTEL Map pp108–9   Hotel $$

☎ 0 2635 0676-85; 26 Soi 9, Th Silom; d from 1000B; 🚇 Chong Nonsi; 🍽
From the outside, Niagara looks like another shady no-tell motel, with a well-hidden car park for midday breaks and a weather-beaten facade. The '60s-vintage lobby doesn't look much better, but the squeaky clean rooms, gleaming white bath-

rooms and friendly owner make this a good deal for the area. It seems this place takes guest entertainment seriously, too, with three channels of 24-hour pornography.

LUMPHINI & EAST SATHON

Access to Lumphini Park and the business and diplomatic areas of Th Sathon are the main reasons to stay in this part of Bangkok. Concentrated on Soi Ngam Duphli and Soi Sri Bamphen, the ultra-budget, pre-Khao San flophouses are popular with long-term expats – often teachers – who like the price, location near to Lumphini Metro station and the fact it's not Banglamphu.

The leafy area between the east ends of Th Sathon and Th Silom is home to several executive apartment buildings.

BANYAN TREE HOTEL
Map p112   Hotel $$$
☎ 0 2679 1200; www.banyantree.com; Thai Wah II Bldg, 21/100 Th Sathon Tai, Sathon; d from 10,500B; Ⓜ Lumphini; ⌗ ▯ ☲
The Banyan Tree is housed in one of Bangkok's most recognisable buildings, a sleek wafer of a skyscraper with a huge circular hole through it and a rooftop fitted out with the dreamy Moon Bar and Vertigo grill (p177). The mood is more spa than hotel, with the fragrance of gardenias and the sound of splashing water in the foyer and no less than six levels of spa facilities. Rooms are smart and views expansive. All up an excellent top-end choice, but with a few too many stairs for families with young kids.

METROPOLITAN Map p112   Hotel $$$
☎ 0 2625 3322; www.metropolitan.como.bz; 27 Th Sathon Tai, Sathon; d from US$290; Ⓜ Lumphini; ⌗ ▯ ☲
The very essence of urban cool – with the members-only Met Bar to prove it – the Metropolitan has been Bangkok's 'it' place since it was reborn from the ashes of, of all things, a YMCA. The techno-cool lobby leads to sleek modern rooms with white-on-black contrasts. But the ghost of hostels past is still apparent in the cramped and overpriced City rooms, where minimalist becomes torturous, though the bathrooms remain big enough for rock-star primping.

The suites are more humane and the two-storey suites are the ultimate in expansive expensive luxury. The two in-house restaurants, and particularly C'yan (p161), are excellent.

SUKHOTHAI HOTEL Map p112   Hotel $$$
☎ 0 2344 8888; www.sukhothai.com; 13/3 Th Sathon Tai; r 14,000-100,000B; Ⓜ Lumphini; ⌗ ▯ ☲
If you're sick of the cookie-cutter international hotels where you need to remind yourself what city you're in, stay at the Sukhothai. Architect Ed Tuttle's uniquely Thai modernism embraces both classic Thai features – think winged roofs, hardwood floors and six acres of garden full of brick stupas reminiscent of the ancient capital of Sukhothai – and a modern minimalism that is deeply satisfying. The 210 rooms carry the theme and most have views of the extensive gardens and ponds; though expect the view to suffer somewhat as a the owners build a tower in 2008 and 2009. All up, very classy, with restaurants Celadon and La Scala rounding it out.

ALL SEASONS Map p112   Hotel $$
☎ 0 2343 6333; www.allseasons-asia.com; 31 Th Sathon Tai; r 1800-2500B; Ⓜ Lumphini; ⌗ ▯
After a 2008 makeover hauling it into the 21st century, the All Seasons, nee King, offers 78 spacious, high-ceilinged rooms for an attractive price amid the embassies. The ambience is modern Asia, with yellow, red and green on white, and comforts include rain shower, desk with free wi-fi and cable broadband, and flat-screen TV on the wall. Superior and deluxe rooms are best; the rooftop 'exclusive' rooms are small.

MALAYSIA HOTEL Map p112   Hotel $
☎ 0 2679 7127; www.malaysiahotelbkk.com; 54 Soi Ngam Duphli; s 738-838B, d 848-928B; Ⓜ Lumphini; ⌗ ▯ ☲
The Malaysia was celebrating its 36th anniversary in a sea of pink shirts (complete with singing poodles) when we dropped in, and while its glory days as Bangkok's most famous budget travellers' hotel are long gone, it remains very busy. It has a reputation as a gay pick-up scene, though the manager assured us that 'anyone is welcome, not only gays'. The 119 rooms are a good size and good value.

THE PERILS OF ONLINE BOOKING Karla Zimmerman

Neon bikinis: that's odd, we thought, as our taxi drove out of the snarled traffic on Th Sukhumvit and up to our hotel. The building across the street was bursting with women clad in glowing skimp-wear. German oom-pah songs wafted through the air, and advertisements for 'bratwursts' covered menu boards at the surrounding restaurants.

Yes, we were jet-lagged, having just spent 21 hours to reach Bangkok, and it was the middle of the night, when strange things tend to happen. But bratwursts and fluorescent bikinis?

We entered the hotel lobby, where Western men and young Thai women nuzzled on all the available couches. That's when the light bulb popped over our heads, and we realised our situation: the room we'd booked on the internet – a room of 'luxurious comfort' with 'teakwood decorations and cable TV' – was located in a de facto brothel. We'd arrived at the Nana Entertainment Plaza.

A quick amble around the hotel grounds brought us to bars like Hollywood Strip (Pool! Shows! Girls! Darts!), Carnival (GoGo Girls, Girls, Girls!) and G-Spot (250 Girls Upstairs!). The latter's dancers made the neon-bikini group look practically Amish by comparison.

Despite the distraction of drinking one's beer and eating one's *phàt thai* in venues where most of the patrons were getting hand jobs, we appreciated our unplanned bite of this classic slice of Bangkok. Next time, though, we'll be more careful when booking online. While a hotel that touts 'easy access, 24 hours' can't be faulted for false advertising, it's wise to remember that words have multiple meanings.

PENGUIN HOUSE Map p112   Guesthouse $
☎ 0 2679 9991; 27/23 Soi Sri Bamphen; r 800-900B; M Lumphini; ✷

With some rooms big enough for a ping-pong game and real furniture with a hint of décor, the Penguin is rightly popular in this area of tired old-timers. Rear rooms will be quieter, and there are a couple of interior rooms that sleep two couples. Weekly and monthly rates are also available. There's a two-night minimum stay.

SALA THAI DAILY MANSION
Map p112   Guesthouse $
☎ 0 2287 1436; sub-soi off Soi Sri Bamphen; s 200-500B; d 400-600B; M Lumphini

The Sala Thai looks little different than it did in its pre–Khao San salad days, but the occupants of the 15 clean, cheap, but basic, rooms (shared bathrooms) are mainly long-termers. Owner Anong (aka artist A-Za Tan) is a delight and, aside from the breezy rooftop terrace, is the main reason to stay. After-hours guests aren't welcome. Sala Thai is at the end of a lane off a sub-*soi* with other ultra-cheap places; look for the red-and-white signs.

BANGKOK CHRISTIAN GUEST HOUSE
Map p112   Guesthouse $$
☎ 0 2233 6303; www.bcgh.org; 123 Soi Sala Daeng 2, Th Convent; s/d/tr 1100/1500/1800B; 🚉 Sala Daeng, M Silom; ✷

This Christian guesthouse is steps away from Patpong's strip clubs, proving that vice and morality are constant companions.

The rooms are institutional but adequate and family-style meals provide fellowship as well as sustenance. A small outdoor playground is available. The price includes breakfast.

THANON SUKHUMVIT

Much of Bangkok's recent rush to build condos, offices and hotels has been played out in a sea of cranes and jackhammers along Th Sukhumvit. More than 10 new hotels have opened between 2006 and 2008, mostly falling into the style, boutique or wannabe boutique categories. So there's plenty of choice.

Sukhumvit is the newest, most cosmopolitan part of Bangkok, home to thousands of expats and hi-so Thais whose spending power supports hundreds of restaurants – Italian and Japanese being the most common. Th Sukhumvit itself is dominated by the Skytrain, which runs above it for several kilometres (and soon a few stops further) and at points creates a canyon-like sound trap that can be very noisy.

Down on the ground the street is divided into two distinct districts. West of Soi Asoke (Soi 21) is the main tourist sector where the 1960s R&R days live on in *soi* full of girlie bars. It's easy enough to avoid these, though escaping the streetside stalls flogging cheap souvenirs and fake DVDs is impossible (though the touting is more Marley than manic). Soi 11 hosts plenty of lower midrange hotels with rate sheets that often include 'joiner fees'; the Swiss Park Hotel (Map pp118–19; ☎ 0 2254 0228; 155/23 Soi

11/1, Th Sukhumvit; s/d 1800/2100B; ☒) is among the best, while one block east the '60s-era Miami (Map pp118–19; ☎ 0 2253 1266; 2 Soi 13, Th Sukhumvit; ☒ ☒) has replaced the GIs with friendly *kàthoey* (ladyboy) staff and guests collecting material for 'novels'. East of Soi Asoke, the girlie bars are replaced with residential areas, package-tour hotels and some more quirky places too.

Sukhumvit traffic is diabolical, but by using the Skytrain you can rise above most of it when heading west to the shopping areas and the riverside. The Metro connects at Asoke and is by far the easiest way to get to the northern bus station and Hualamphong train station.

MA DU ZI Map pp118–19 Boutique $$$
☎ 0 2615 6400; www.maduzihotel.com; cnr Th Ratchadapisek & Sukhumvit Soi 16; r 15,000-33,000B; ☒ Asoke, ☒ Sukhumvit; ☒ ☒
Ma Du Zi means 'come and see' and it seems this recently opened luxury hotel won't have any shortage of people wanting to come and stay. Ma Du Zi is a master-piece of design, with every detail thought of and the appointments of the highest order – each of the 41 rooms has a work desk with fax/copier/printer, an espresso machine, original artwork, and a restrained but very stylish luxury in white marble, blond wood and black furniture – some even have remote-controlled bath tubs. Rooms are huge, starting at 49 sq m, and in fairness, so too are the prices and there is no pool. But they do include everything, from airport pickup through wi-fi to the minibar. The French restaurant is also excellent. Reservations only, no walk-in.

GRAND MILLENNIUM SUKHUMVIT
Map pp118–19 Hotel $$$
☎ 0 2204 4111; www.grandmillenniumskv.com; 30 Soi Asoke, Th Sukhumvit; r from 7500B, ste 13,500B; ☒ Asoke, ☒ Sukhumvit; ☒ ☒ ☒
Looking like a giant glass zipper opening from the top down, the ambitious new Grand Millennium is set to shake up Bangkok's business hotel scene. Its 325 bright, spacious (minimum of 38 sq m) and tastefully furnished rooms are set around a triangular atrium fronted by acres of glass. If you don't suffer from vertigo, they're great for business, with decent-sized desks, free wi-fi and ADSL internet – there's even a putting green in the carpark. Just days before it opened in late 2007 we watched from our apartment as the newly completed 'Millennium' sign atop the hotel was hurriedly replaced with 'Grand Millennium'. In most respects this hotel is worth the grander classification, but in the tacked-together suites you can see its more humble original ambition.

DAVIS Map pp118–19 Boutique $$$
☎ 0 2260 8000; www.davisbangkok.net; Soi 24, Th Sukhumvit; d from 5000B; ☒ Phrom Phong, ☒ Sirikit Centre; ☒ ☒ ☒
One of Bangkok's original 'boutique' offerings, the Davis mixes 'design rooms' in regal themes, such as a Raj's palace, a Kyoto hermitage or a Burmese plantation, with a dizzying range of large, stylish, but sometimes quite dark, spaces. Some suites boast their own sauna and orgy-sized Jacuzzi for when size (of the tub) really matters. Born for the pages of *Architectural Digest*, the detached Thai wood villas are polished to a burnished gold, with deep sleigh beds and big sunny windows arranged around a private lap pool and garden.

SHERATON GRANDE SUKHUMVIT
Map pp118–19 Hotel $$$
☎ 0 2649 8888; www.sheratongrandesukhumvit .com; 250 Th Sukhumvit; r from 10,000B; ☒ Asoke, ☒ Sukhumvit; ☒ ☒ ☒
The Sheraton is a hit with corporate travellers for its 420 large (from 45 sq m) and meticulously appointed rooms, with handy details like irons, extra-large deposit boxes and big tubs as standard. The sky-high, jungle-fringed pool is an oasis and, if you have a spare 38,000B, the Thai-styled Rama suite challenges the Davis with party-sized indoor and outdoor Jacuzzis. Ask for a lake-view room.

EUGENIA Map pp118–19 Boutique $$$
☎ 0 2259 9017; www.theeugenia.com; 267 Soi 31, Th Sukhumvit; r 5800-7200B; ☒ Prom Pong; ☒ ☒ ☒
The Eugenia is a truly unique boutique. Dreamt up by 'Taiwanese Indiana Jones' Eugene Yu-Cheng Yeh, the 12-room residence is modelled on the colonial mansions of Africa and the Subcontinent. Think Livingston/Hemingway/Indian Raj, with the rooms and public spaces packed full of art, books, antique furniture, beaten copper bathtubs and dead animals (we counted

zebra, warthog, crocodile, various antelope, peacock and duck). It's not, however, devoid of modern luxuries, with wi-fi internet, VoIP telephony and minibar all included in the rate. Our only criticism is that the rooms aren't huge, especially the tiny Siam suites. Ask about the airport trips in the vintage Mercedes and Jags.

DREAM Map pp118–19 Boutique $$$

☎ 0 2254 8500; www.dreambkk.com; 10 Soi 15, Th Sukhumvit; r from US$200; ⓡ Asoke, Ⓜ Sukhumvit; ✕ 🖳 🖾

We must have looked doubtful about the blue neon glow in the bedroom, and the woman showing us around sounded like she'd seen the reaction often enough. 'The blue lights are the Dream signature,' she explained, 'we have some scientific studies that prove it makes you sleep deeper.' The blue-lit rooms are just one of the features that set Dream apart from your average boutique or design hotel. It's totally different. The 195 rooms in two buildings are a rock-star world of cream leather, mirrors, silver and blue motifs and, in the uber-chic Flava lounge bar-cum-restaurant, a white tiger (yes, blue stripes) and pink leopard. Rooms come with free wi-fi (Dream 1 only) or ADSL, coffee machines and big flat-screen TVs. At almost US$1000, the suites are ludicrously priced for a bit more room and 'a free plate of fresh fruit'.

S15 Map pp118–19 Boutique $$

☎ 0 2651 2000; www.s15hotel.com; 217 Th Sukhumvit, cnr Soi 15; d 4500-6000B; ste 7700B; ⓡ Asoke, Ⓜ Sukhumvit; ✕ 🖳

Among the better 'boutique' openings along Sukhumvit in 2007, sleek S15 has at least half an eye on the business market, with free wi-fi and a business centre and meeting room to go with the central location. The reasonably sized rooms are a mix of the browns and whites so preferred by boutique hotels, augmented with modern Asian ornaments. It works pretty well, though better value is available. If you find yourself yearning for something more grungy, the classic little restaurant on the opposite corner of Soi 15 should satisfy.

SEVEN Map pp52–3 Hotel $$

☎ 081-616 2636; www.sleepatseven.com; 3/15 Soi 31, Th Sukhumvit, r 3100-6000B; Ⓜ Prom Pong; ✕ 🖳

Six rooms, seven colours. This brand-new design hotel from the designers of London's Ministry of Sound comes with a boutique concept that reminds you're in Thailand. Thais believe each day has its own colour (eg Monday is yellow, and everyone wears a yellow shirt for the king), and each room (plus the lobby) is decorated in its own colour. The rooms are not big, but they're well appointed with free mobile phones, wi-fi and iPods. Seven will appeal to hip young singles and couples looking for design and relaxed, homey service.

LE FENIX Map pp52–3 Hotel $$

☎ 0 2305 4000; www.lefenix-sukhumvit.com; 33 Soi 11, Th Sukhumvit; r 2590B; Ⓜ Phetburi; ✕ 🖳

It was inevitable the big hotel companies would co-opt the 'boutique' idea, as Accor did in 2007 with this 147-room, eight-floor place at the end of busy Soi 11. It's aimed at young, party-oriented tourists and is reasonable value. It looks contemporary enough with a lobby daubed in orange and white opening onto a 'look at me' bar. Down lounge-music-filled corridors the small rooms are, well, small. All have two single mattresses on a single base, which can be pushed apart only a few inches. To explain this design we were told 'this is a boutique hotel'…but perhaps they should add 'mainly for couples and very close acquaintances'. Service was disorganised when we visited, but should improve. Rooms have both wi-fi and broadband cable internet.

CITICHIC Map pp118–19 Hotel $$

☎ 0 2342 3888; www.citichichotel.com; 34 Soi 13, Th Sukhumvit; r from 2300B; ⓡ Nana or Asoke, Ⓜ Sukhumvit; ✕ 🖳 🖾

'Small hotel, small pool…see, everything's small.' The guy showing me around was right – pretty much everything about this new midranger is noy, from the foyer to the 37 rooms on five floors, the gym with four machines and the 3m by 9m rooftop pool. And while the self-applied 'boutique' classification is stretching it, they have managed to squeeze a lot into the rooms; desk, broadband internet and 'chic' bathroom, some with tubs. Add in the personable service and it's a good deal.

BANGKOK BOUTIQUE HOTEL
Map pp118–19   Boutique Hotel $$

☎ 0 2261 2850; www.bangkokboutiquehotel
.com; 241 Soi Asoke, Th Sukhumvit; r from 2900B;
Ⓜ Phetburi; ❇ ▣

At the north end of Soi Asoke, one of Bangkok's busiest and noisiest office-building strips, the low-rise Bangkok Boutique combines a minimalist, polished-concrete mode with hi-tech gadgetry (free wi-fi and cable broadband internet, and wireless keyboards plugged into the big flatscreen TVs so you can surf from bed) in targeting the mid-range business market. Superior rooms are the best value; ask for one away from the street. The price includes breakfast.

NAPA PLACE BED & BREAKFAST
Map pp118–19   Hotel $$

☎ 0 2661 5525; www.napaplace.com; 11/3 Yaek 2, Soi 36, Th Sukhumvit; d 2750-4800B; Ⓡ Thong Lo; ❇ ▣

The Napa maintains a genuinely homey B&B atmosphere despite having 12 rooms. Tucked away in a quiet *soi* off Soi 36 and seven minutes' walk to Thong Lo Skytrain, it appeals to families because it has huge rooms (36 to 67 sq m), plenty of communal space, solid security and free buffet breakfasts. Cable broadband is also free. In short, it's superb value.

MAJESTIC SUITES   Map pp118–19   Hotel $$

☎ 0 2656 8220; www.majesticsuites.com; 110-110/1 Th Sukhumvit btwn Soi 4 & Soi 6; s/d from 1400/1900B; Ⓡ Nana; ❇ ▣

Love-for-money is prevalent in this part of Th Sukhumvit, but Majestic's hermetically sealed rooms deliver privacy and quiet. The hotel is small and friendly and rooms facing Sukhumvit have a bird's-eye view of the street's traffic-snarled grandeur. Gym and pool facilities are available at the sister Majestic Grande, making this a central, value midranger.

GRAND MERCURE PARK AVENUE
Map pp118–19   Hotel $$

☎ 0 2262 0000; www.grandmercure-asia.com; 30 Soi 22, Th Sukhumvit; r from 2400B; Ⓡ Phrom Phong; ❇ ▣

A palette of cocoa and black brings a splash of global Zen to Soi 22. Not quite the Park Avenue of international repute, this large hotel does a convincing job of acting like

THE NOSE KNOWS

Top-end and some midrange hotels have smoking and nonsmoking floors. If you've got a nose for stale cigarette smoke, which has amazing endurance in the tropics, state your preference at the time of booking.

an intimate boutique. Bathrooms are Mini-Me sized and the price includes breakfast.

FEDERAL HOTEL   Map pp118–19   Hotel $$

☎ 0 2253 0175; www.federalbangkok.com; 27 Soi 11, Th Sukhumvit; d 1000-1500B; Ⓡ Nana; ❇ ▣
Club Fed, as the Pattaya crowd calls it, was once an R&R stop for American GIs and remains a Soi 11 fixture more for its frangipani-lined swimming pool and time-warped coffee shop than its rooms. It's laid out like a '60s motel but you'll need to have a wide sentimental streak to really appreciate the dated furnishings and old-hotel smell. Avoid the ground-floor rooms as they occasionally flood in the rainy season. Old-timers might be comfortable in the Fed, but youngsters should look elsewhere.

ATLANTA   Map pp118–19   Hotel $

☎ 0 2252 6069, 0 2252 1650; fax 0 2656 8123; 78 Soi 2 (Soi Phasak), Th Sukhumvit; d from 800B; Ⓡ Nana, Ploenchit; ❇ ▣
The oldest hotel in the Th Sukhumvit area (and proud of it), the Atlanta enjoys cultlike status with return budget travellers who shun the Banglamphu 'tourist' scene. And rightly so. The hotel was started as the Atlanta Club in 1952 by Dr Max Henn, a former secretary to the Maharajah of Bikaner and owner of Bangkok's first international pharmacy. And while it looks thoroughly grim from outside, the perfectly preserved midcentury lobby, complete with old-fashioned writing desks and a grand-entrance staircase sweeping up five floors (there's no lift), make you want to hang around waiting for Bogart to slip in. The rooms are functional; those on the top floor aren't good at all. But the just-kempt jungle-landscaped pool is very welcome in this price bracket. Note: 'The Atlanta does not welcome sex tourists and does not try to be polite about it.'

SUK 11   Map pp118–19   Guesthouse $

☎ 0 2253 5927-28; www.suk11.com; sub-soi off Soi 11, Th Sukhumvit; dm 250B, d 480-800B; Ⓡ Nana; ❇ ▣

Stepping between the potted plants and into the wooden-fronted oasis of Suk 11 is to step into Sukhumvit's primary outpost of backpacker culture, and a definite atmosphere of post-beach chill. Hidden down a small and relatively silent sub-*soi* off Soi 11, expect a lobby crowded with travellers from all over sitting around, drinking and swapping tales. Upstairs the 80 (yes, 80!) rooms stretch above the stores almost the length of the *soi*, with plank walkways and terracotta accents embellishing otherwise plain rooms with and without bathrooms. Outside is a spa, restaurant and Cheap Charlie's (p175) for the cheapest beers outside 7-Eleven.

BANGKOK CENTRE SUKHUMVIT 25
Map pp118–19   Hotel $$
☎ 0 2259 6869; www.thailandhotel.com; Soi 25, Th Sukhumvit; dm/s/d 390/1200/1500B; 🚇 Asoke; 🅿 🖳
Opened in 2006, this HI-affiliated place looks a bit institutional but feels friendly and communal. The large, clean rooms come with cable TV, fridge and clean bathrooms – including the dorms (though they need three people for the air-con to be turned on). Prices here are for non-members, but sign up for 200B per person

and save 100/300/500B on a dorm/single/double; breakfast is included.

HI SUKHUMVIT Map pp118–19   Hostel $
☎ 0 2391 9338; www.hisukhumvit.com; 23 Soi 38, Th Sukhumvit; dm 300B, d 800-900B, r 1200; 🚇 Thong Lo; 🅿 🖳
Seemingly lost in a galaxy where budget lodgings usually fear to go, the clean, simple dorms and rooms and welcoming family owners make this budget place a real find. The breezy rooftop is a good place to chill out, wash clothes and watch another Bangkok condo emerge from the ground, and the nearby night market is a great place to eat.

GREATER BANGKOK
If you're staying outside central Bangkok, choose a place near the Skytrain for zippy commutes. Options in Thonburi are less accessible but more local.

BANGKOK MARRIOTT RESORT & SPA
Map pp124–5   Hotel $$$
☎ 0 2476 0022; www.marriot.com; 257 Th Charoen Nakhon, Samrae, Thonburi; r from 6000B; 🚢 hotel shuttle boat from Tha Sathon & Tha Oriental; 🅿 🖳 🚲

AIRPORT ACCOMMODATION

Most people will use the new Suvarnabhumi International Airport, which takes all international flights, but old Don Muang airport still hosts some domestic services. See p251 for transport details.

Suvarnabhumi International Airport

Novotel Suvarnabhumi Airport Hotel (☎ 0 2131 1111; www.novotel.com; r from 5000B; 🅿 🖳) Boasts 600-plus luxurious rooms in the airport.

Grand Inn Come Hotel (☎ 0 2738 8189; www.grandinncome-hotel.com; 99 Moo 6, Th Kingkaew, Bangplee; s/tw from 1800/2000B; 🅿 🖳) Solid midranger 10km from the airport; airport shuttle; 'lively' karaoke bar.

Refill Now! (see opposite) Nearest good budget option.

Don Muang Airport

Amari Airport Hotel (Map pp124–5; ☎ 0 2566 1020; www.amari.com; 333 Th Choet Wutthakat; r from US$90; 🅿 🚲) Opposite Don Muang, most popular airport hotel and has well-equipped day-use rooms from US$85.

Rama Gardens Hotel (Map pp124–5; ☎ 0 2561 0022; www.ramagardenshotel.com; 9/9 Th Vibhavadi Rangsit; r from 4700B; 🅿 🚲) Tranquil garden setting and very comfortable deluxe wings with deep-soak tubs. Shuttle buses to airport.

We-Train International House (Map pp124–5; ☎ 0 2967 8550-54; www.we-train.co.th; 501/1 Muu 3, Th Dechatungkha, Sikan, Don Muang; dm 200B, r 800-1100B; 🅿 🚲) Quiet place with good-value rooms 3km from airport. Run by the Association for the Promotion of the Status of Women. Take a taxi (about 80B) from outside Amari Hotel.

Set amid the lushest landscaped gardens by the river, this is the nearest thing to a resort you'll find in Bangkok. Going downriver from busy Bangkok is a mental and physical relaxant – ably abetted by the pool area and rooms. If you want to get away from it all in an international-style resort – without leaving Bangkok – this might be for you.

REFILL NOW! Map pp124–5   Hostel $$
☎ 0 2713 2044; www.refillnow.co.th; 191 Soi Pridi Banhom Yong 42, Soi 71, Th Sukhumvit; dm/s/d 560/1085/1470B; ⊠ Phra Kanong; ✄ ▢ ▣
From the fertile imaginations of two young Thai architects based in California, Refill promises 'high-style low-cost'. It delivers with spotless white private rooms and dorms that have flirtatious pull screens between each double-bunk; women-only dorms are also available. Some people might balk at paying this much for shared bathrooms. But the hip-but-unpretentious vibe that emanates from the funky bar and communal areas make it well worth the money. A pool is planned for 2008. Refill Now! is near trendy Thong Lo and only 20 minutes from the airport. To get there, take a taxi or moto taxi from the Skytrain down Soi 71, turn right on Soi 42 and left; or come by *khlong* taxi and walk.

REFLECTIONS ROOMS Map pp124–5 Hotel $$
☎ 0 2270 3344; www.reflections-thai.com; 224/2-18 Th Pradipat btwn Sois 18 & 20; r 1850-3450B; ⊠ Saphan Kwai; ✄ ▢

A room bedecked entirely in black-and-white spiral psychedelia; another sporting portraits of playful puffed-up ladies; and another decorated completely in recycled goods. These are just three of the 39 rooms at Reflections Rooms, each styled by a different artist, designer or celebrity, and probably the most arty, trippy, kitschy and totally cool hotel in Thailand. Recently moved north to Th Pradipat, a 10-minute walk from Saphan Kwai Skytrain, Reflections have been thoroughly revitalised. The rooms are still Starbucks-sized: small is really big and large is mega, each also fitted with DVD player and free wi-fi. Check out the rooms online to book the one you want; front rooms are noisy.

THAI HOUSE   Guesthouse $$
☎ 0 2903 9611; www.thaihouse.co.th; 32/4 Mu 8, Tambon Bang Meuang, Bang Yai, Nonthaburi; s/d 1400B/1600B
For an experience of traditional Thai life, surrounded by fruit trees and river music and feeling far from Bangkok's urban snarl, it's hard to beat the Thai House. The teak home built with wing-shaped roofs is pure, old-fashioned Siam, with a welcome as warm as you could hope for. Rates include breakfast, and many guests choose to do the cooking courses taught on the premises. By river, take a public boat from Tha Chang to Bang Yai in Nonthaburi, via Khlong Bangkok Noi. Once you reach the public pier in Bang Yai, charter a boat to Thai House's own pier – all the boat pilots know it. By taxi, get the driver to call for directions.

EXCURSIONS

EXCURSIONS

Believe it or not, there is life after Bangkok. The city's central location, not to mention its role as the country's transportation hub, makes it a convenient base to explore much of what central Thailand has to offer. Destinations range from renowned beaches to critter-laden jungles, and can be done either as a day trip or a more relaxed overnighter. Much of the tourism surrounding Bangkok is geared towards the natives, and as such there's an emphasis on religious pilgrimages and food – the latter ranging from 'famous' restaurants to buzzing night markets for socialising and dining. Both of these also allow for fascinating insights into Thai culture. Bangkok's outlying areas also have many theme parks and animal attractions that will entertain children who are sick of humouring their parents.

BACK TO NATURE

Going from concrete jungle to real jungle is not as hard as you'd think, and a couple hours on a bus will take you to places so wild you can count elephants and tigers among your neighbours.

To the northeast, the Dangrek Mountains geographically fuse Thailand and Cambodia and break the fertile central plains around Bangkok. Occupying this wooded landscape is Khao Yai National Park (p246), one of Thailand's biggest and best preserves. Its mountainous monsoon forests dress and undress with the comings and goings of the seasons and claim hundreds of resident species. Visitors can take quick dips into nature while staying at a nearby resort, playing golf and touring start-up wineries. And hard-core nature types can immerse themselves completely in rustic park shelters in the forest. Waterfalls tend to dominate Khao Yai itineraries, but in between you might be lucky enough to spot the big game, though don't get your hopes up too high – the wildlife is, erm, wild, and unlikely to just wander up for a quick chat and a beer.

West of Bangkok, limestone hills rise out of the sun-parched land like a great ruined city. Kanchanaburi (p242) is the best base for exploring this area of waterfalls, caves and tropical jungle. Bike rides will take you past shaggy fields of sugar cane being harvested by hand and lovingly tended spirit houses guarding uninhabited woods. Organised tours take visitors on whirlwind outings by land, water and rail.

Moving south along Thailand's rugged border with Myanmar (Burma), Kaeng Krachan National Park (p241), the country's largest, is a paradise for birders and others looking to do some camera hunting.

TIME TRAVEL

Thailand's heroic ancient capital, Ayuthaya (p226), is a Unesco World Heritage Site and a major pilgrimage site for anyone interested in Thai history. The remaining red-brick temples, which resisted the Burmese siege in the 18th century, are now resisting the pull of gravity. It is hard to imagine today, but this modern city of temple ruins was once a golden city that bewitched European traders in the heyday of the Asian trade route. Nearby Bang Pa-In, a royal summer palace, is a surviving homage to the world's architectural styles that convened near this port city.

More recent masterpieces of Thai art can be seen in the vivid wall paintings and graceful stucco façades of Phetburi's (p238) numerous temples. A day of wandering can provide views into several of the recognised masterpieces of central Thai art.

The Ancient City (p248), an architectural museum in Samut Prakan, has reproduced Thailand's great monuments into a tastefully arranged park. Like Ayuthaya, the Ancient City is best explored by bicycle, when the peaceful grounds and impressive structures will inspire further-flung excursions throughout the country.

Modern history is only a train ride away in Kanchanaburi (p242) where vivid museums, themed excursions and touching monuments bring home the area's tragic setting as a WWII labour camp.

THAI LIFE

The Mahachai Rail Line (p236) will transport you directly to the rhythms of daily life outside the capital. The destinations, a string of gulfside market towns, are just as interesting as the villages and markets that comprise the journey.

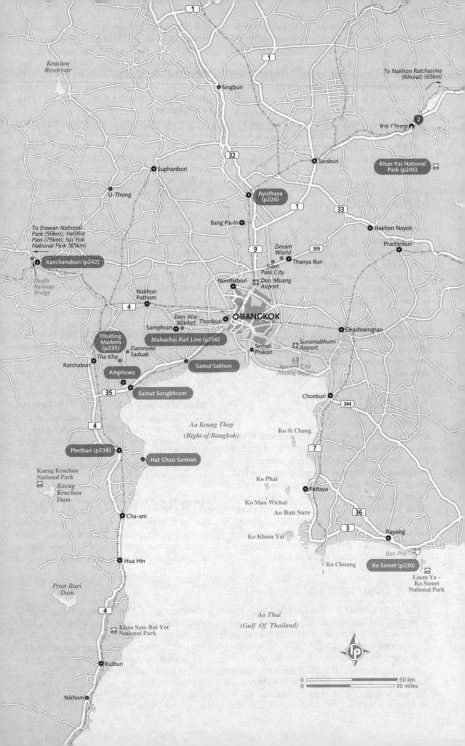

Phetburi's (p238) twisting back lanes, peak-roofed Thai-style wooden houses and rambling morning market combine to form the epitome of central Thai life.

Outside the capital, village life is still tied to the *khlong* (canals) and rivers that knit the land to the sea. Amphawa's (p236) canalside setting and ancient wooden houses are straight out of a movie set, and homestays provide a first-hand view of this uniquely Thai community. Elsewhere, largely touristy floating markets (p235) are the last remnants of a traditional Thai lifestyle that has all but disappeared.

SAND & SUN

With its emerald seas, languid breezes and blonde strips of sand, Ko Samet (p230) is an easy weekend getaway for urban warriors. Small bungalows dot the various bays, which are connected by footpaths traversing rocky outcrops. You can claim a piece of sand and watch the day expire, dine at beachside barbecues and listen to the music of the hidden insects.

Hat Chao Samran (p241), a short jaunt from Phetburi, provides all the necessary elements of sand, cosy accommodation and cheap seafood necessary for a proper Thai-style beach getaway.

AYUTHAYA

พระนครศรีอยุธยา

Drawn by the prospect of ancient ruins, the majority of visitors to this former Thai capital do so from a big bus on a tight schedule. If you're willing to explore rather than be led, you'll find that not only does Ayuthaya offer a glimpse into the past, but it is also a great break from city life. Throw in excellent riverfront dining, cheap but comfortable accommodation and the chance to see the temples in the cool, quiet dawn, and you might even be persuaded to stay a night or two.

Built at the confluence of three rivers (Chao Phraya, Pa Sak and Lopburi), this island city was the seat of a powerful Siamese kingdom that dominated the region for 400 years. Both courted and aided by foreign interests, the empire eventually extended its control deep into present-day Laos, Cambodia and Myanmar (Burma).

Ayuthaya remained one of the world's most splendid and cosmopolitan cities until 1767, when the Burmese, after several attempts, eventually conquered and destroyed it. The surviving Thai army fled south to re-establish control in Thonburi and, 15 years later, to the founding of the new capital, Bangkok.

The famed capital suffered greatly at the hands of the invading Burmese army. Many of the city's temples were levelled, and the sacred Buddha figures were decapitated as if they were enemy combatants. Although Thailand's Fine Arts Department has done extensive restoration work on the ancient capital, it is still rare to find an unscarred Buddha amid Ayuthaya's ruins.

Getting a handle on the religious and historical importance of the temples is difficult without some preliminary research. Ayuthaya Historical Study Centre (☎ 0 3524 5124; Th Rotchana; adult/student 100/50B; ☀ 9am-4.30pm Mon-Fri, 9am-5pm Sat & Sun) has informative, professional displays that paint a clear picture of the ancient city. Other museums in town include Chao Sam Phraya National Museum (☎ 0 3524 1587; cnr Th Rotchana & Th Si Sanphet; admission 30B; ☀ 9am-4pm Wed-Sun), which features a basic roundup of Thai Buddhist sculpture with an emphasis on Ayuthaya pieces, and Chantharakasem National Museum (☎ 0 3525 1587; Th U Thong; admission 30B; ☀ 9am-4pm Wed-Sun), a museum piece in itself, in the northeast corner of town.

AYUTHAYA HISTORICAL PARK

The Ayuthaya Historical Park is separated into two geographical districts. Ruins 'on the island', in the central part of town west of Th Chee Kun, are best visited on bicycle or

---

JUST ANOTHER TOWN?

Since 1991 Ayuthaya has been included on Unesco's prestigious World Heritage List. Referred to as the Historic City of Ayutthaya and Associated Historic Towns, the designation is a point of pride among many Thais, and a selling point for many of the tourists who visit the ruins. However, along with the prestige comes a strict set of rules detailing land use near the historic sites. In late 2007 increasing land encroachment and rapid development were rumoured to have threatened the city's Unesco status. The news unleashed a series of emotional newspaper editorials in which the greed of local entrepreneurs was likened to the invading Burmese originally responsible for the city's destruction. Thailand's Culture Minister admitted that being removed from the list would be 'unfortunate and embarrassing', and has pledged to work with local authorities and Thailand's Fine Arts Department to remedy the situation.

TRANSPORT: AYUTHAYA

Distance from Bangkok 85km

Direction North

Travel Time One hour by bus; 1½ hours by train

Bus 1st-class air-con (72B) and 2nd-class air-con (61B) buses depart Bangkok's Northern and Northeastern Bus Terminal (also called Mo Chit; Map pp124–5) to Th Naresuan in Ayuthaya every 20 minutes between 5am and 7pm. On Th Naresuan in Ayuthaya, a minivan service shuttles passengers to and from Bangkok's Victory Monument (Map pp52–3) from 5am to 5pm (60B).

Train Northbound trains leave from Bangkok's Hualamphong station (Map p84) roughly every 30 minutes between 6.20am and 9.30am, and 6pm and 10pm. The 3rd-class fare is 20B. You can also take the train from Bangkok's Don Muang airport to Ayuthaya (20B) roughly every hour from 6am to 9am and 3pm to 10pm. From Ayuthaya's train station, the quickest way to reach the city is to walk straight west to the river, where you can take a short ferry ride (3B) across. Alternatively, a túk-túk to any point in old Ayuthaya should be around 30B to 50B.

Boat Many boat companies in Bangkok offer scenic boat tours to Ayuthaya; see p264.

Getting Around Guesthouses rent bicycles for 50B per day or motorcycles for 250B; túk-túk tours cost 200B per hour. A longtail boat trip (one-hour evening trip 600B) involves a semicircular tour of the island, as well as views of river life. Arrange at the pier behind Hua Ro Market.

motorbike; those 'off the island', opposite the river from the centre, are best visited on an evening boat tour. You can also take a bicycle across the river by boat from the pier near Pom Phet fortress, inside the southeast corner of the city centre. At many of the ruins a 30B admission fee is collected from 8am to 6.30pm.

On the Island

Wat Phra Si Sanphet was once the largest temple in Ayuthaya and was used as the royal temple–palace by several kings. Built in the 14th century, the compound contained a 16m standing Buddha coated with 250kg of gold, which was melted down by the Burmese conquerors. Its three Ayuthaya-style *chedi* (stupas) have come to be identified with Thai art more than any other style. The adjacent Wat Phra Mongkhon Bophit, built in the 1950s, houses one of the largest bronze seated Buddhas in Thailand.

Wat Phra Mahathat, on the corner of Th Chee Kun and Th Naresuan, has one of the first *prang* (Khmer-style tower) built in the capital and a Buddha head engulfed by fingerlike tree roots – one of the most photographed sites in Ayuthaya. Across the road, Wat Ratburana contains *chedi* and faded murals that are among the oldest in the country. Neighbouring Wat Thammikarat features overgrown *chedi* ruins and lion sculptures.

Wat Lokayasutharam features an impressive 28m-long reclining Buddha, ostensibly dating back to the early Ayuthaya period.

Wat Suwandaram's two main structures boast attractive murals, including a modern-era depiction of a famous Ayuthaya-era battle in the *wíhăan* and classic *Jataka* (stories from the Buddha's lives) in the adjacent *bòt* (ordination hall). Nearby Pom Phet served as the island's initial line of defence for centuries. Only crumbling walls remain today, but the spot features breezy views and is also home to a river crossing ferry to the mainland.

Off the Island

Southeast of town on Mae Nam Chao Phraya, Wat Phanan Choeng was built before Ayuthaya became a Siamese capital. The temple's builders are unknown, but it appears to have been constructed in the early 14th century, so it's possibly Khmer. The main *wíhăan* (central sanctuary) contains a highly revered 19m sitting Buddha image from which the wat derives its name. The area surrounding the temple was once home to a large Chinese community, and at weekends it is crowded with Buddhist pilgrims from Bangkok who pay for lengths of saffron-coloured cloth to be ritually draped over the image.

The ruined Ayuthaya-style tower and *chedi* of Wat Chai Wattanaram, on the western bank of Mae Nam Chao Phraya, boast the most attractive setting of any of the city's temples. The manicured Thai-style compound across the river belongs to the Thai royal family.

Wat Yai Chai Mongkhon is southeast of the town proper; it can be reached by white-and-green

AYUTHAYA

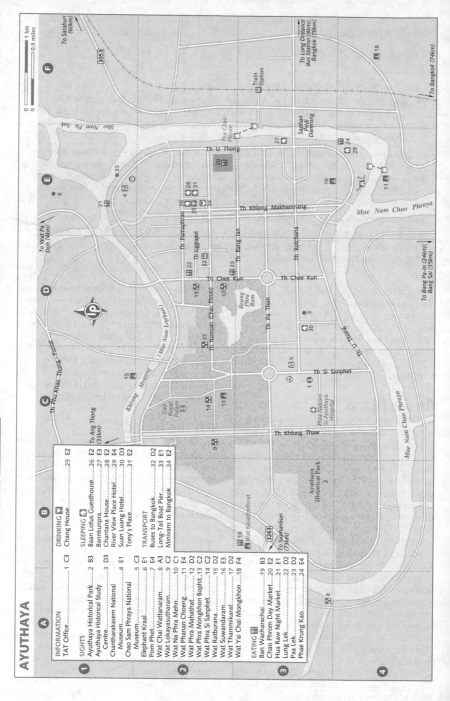

INFORMATION
TAT Office..........................1 C3

SIGHTS
Ayuthaya Historical Park.........2 B3
Ayuthaya Historical Study
  Centre.............................3 D3
Chantharakasem National
  Museum..........................4 E1
Chao Sam Phraya National
  Museum..........................5 C3
Elephant Kraal.....................6 E1
Pom Phet............................7 F4
Wat Chai Wattanaram............8 A3
Wat Lokayasutharam.............9 C2
Wat Na Phra Mehn................10 C1
Wat Phanan Choeng.............11 F4
Wat Phra Mahathat..............12 D2
Wat Phra Mongkhon Bophit..13 C2
Wat Phra Si Sanphet..............14 C2
Wat Ratburana.....................15 D2
Wat Suwandaram................16 E3
Wat Thammikarat................17 D2
Wat Yai Chai Mongkhon.......18 F4

EATING
Ban Wacharachai................19 B3
Chao Phrom Day Market.......20 E2
Hua Raw Night Market..........21 E1
Lung Lek............................22 D2
Paa Lek.............................23 D2
Phae Krung Kao..................24 E4

DRINKING
Chang House......................25 C3

SLEEPING
Baan Lotus Guesthouse........26 E2
Bannkunpra.......................27 E3
Chantana House.................28 E2
River View Place Hotel..........29 E4
Suan Luang Hotel................30 D3
Tony's Place........................31 E2

TRANSPORT
Buses to Bangkok................32 D2
Long-Tail Boat Pier..............33 E1
Minivans to Bangkok...........34 E2

EXCURSIONS AYUTHAYA

BANG PA-IN
บางปะอิน

This postcard-perfect palace lies just 24km south of Ayuthaya. A hodgepodge of international architectural styles reflects the eclectic tastes of Rama IV (King Mongkut; r 1851–68) and his son and heir Rama V (King Chulalongkorn; r 1868–1910), both of whom used the residence as a retreat from the summer rains. The winged-eaved Thai-style pavilion, the ornate Chinese-style Wehat Chamrun Palace and a Swiss chalet mansion (the preferred residence of Rama V) are all on display. A flamboyant lookout tower (Withun Thatsana) gave the king fine views over the gardens and lakes.

At the nearby Royal Folk Arts & Crafts Centre (☎ 0 3536 6252; admission 100B; ☼ 9am-5pm Mon-Fri, 9am-7pm Sat & Sun) at Bang Sai you can see traditional Thai handicrafts and artwork being made. The centre is also home to Thailand's largest freshwater aquarium.

Bang Pa-In can be reached by blue *săwngthăew* (pick-up truck; 13B; 45 minutes) or minibus (30B) from Ayuthaya's Chao Phrom Market (Map p228) on Th Naresuan. From Bangkok there are buses (50B) every half-hour from the Northern & Northeastern Bus Terminal (Mo Chit; Map pp124–5). You can also reach Bang Pa-In by two morning trains from Bangkok (3rd class, 12B).

minibus 6. It's a quiet place built in 1357 by King U Thong and was once famous as a meditation centre. The compound contains a very large *chedi,* and a community of *mâe chii* (Buddhist nuns) lives here.

North of the city, the Elephant Kraal is a restoration of the wooden stockade once used for the annual roundup of wild elephants. A huge fence of teak logs planted at a 45-degree angle enclosed the elephants. The king had a raised observation pavilion for the thrilling event.

North of the old royal palace *(wang lŭang)* grounds is a bridge to Wat Na Phra Mehn. This temple is notable because it escaped destruction in the 1767 Burmese capture, though it has undergone restoration over the years. The main *bòt* (central chapel) was built in 1546 and features fortress-like walls and pillars. The *bòt* interior contains an impressive carved wooden ceiling and a splendid 6m-high sitting Buddha in royal attire. Inside a smaller *wíhăan* behind the *bòt* is a green-stone, European-pose (sitting in a chair) Buddha from Ceylon, said to be 1300 years old. The walls of the *wíhăan* show traces of 18th- or 19th-century murals.

INFORMATION

Tourist Authority of Thailand (TAT; ☎ 0 3524 6076; 108/22 Th Si Sanphet; ☼ 9am-5pm) Occupying an imposing building dating back to 1941, TAT provides maps, bus schedules and information about Loi Krathong festivities. Ask for a free copy of *Ayutthaya*, the excellent illustrated booklet published by TAT.

EATING

Ban Wacharachai (☎ 0 3532 1333; Wat Kasattrathirat; dishes 60-150B; ☼ 10-2am) A must for visiting foodies, this hidden gem is legendary among locals and regular visitors alike for its perfectly executed central Thai–style dishes, not to mention a pleasant riverfront location. The smoked snakehead fish is sublime. To get there, cycle or take a *túk-túk* to Wat Kasattrathirat (known as Wat Kasat); the rambling restaurant is hidden in a thick garden directly north of the temple.

Hua Raw Night Market & Chao Phrom Day Market (Th U Thong) These markets are the highlight of Ayuthaya noshing. The former features several vendors preparing Thai-Muslim dishes.

Phae Krung Kao (Th U Thong; dishes 60-100B; ☼ 10-2am) On the southern side of the bridge, this floating restaurant is so popular that Thai locals even rouse their geriatric grandmas for a night out.

In the past, Ayuthayans got their noodle fix from boat-based vendors who hocked their bowls along the city's canals and rivers. Today the vessels are all landlocked, but the famous *kŭaytĭaw ruea* (boat noodles) remain as popular as ever. Lung Lek (Th Chee Kun; dishes 15B; ☼ 9am-4pm) serves incredibly intense *kŭaytĭaw ruea* with pork or beef. Look for the open-air tent-like structure. Slightly more popular, but not as spicy, is Paa Lek (Th Chee Kun; dishes 10B; ☼ 9am-4pm), a sprawling roadside stall next door to the city's telephone authority.

Sweet snacks associated with Ayuthaya include *roti saay mai* (thin pancake-like sheets wrapped around candy floss), available from numerous vendors near Phra Nakorn Si Ayuthaya Hospital. *Khànŏm bà bin* (tiny pancakes made from sticky rice flour and shredded coconut meat) can be found at the market behind Wat Phra Mongkhon Bophit.

EXCURSIONS AYUTHAYA

KO KRET
เกาะเกร็ด

Bangkok's closest green getaway is this artificial 'island', the result of a canal being dredged to shorten an oxbow bend in the Chao Phraya River nearly 300 years ago. Today Ko Kret's claim to fame is the hand-thrown terracotta pots that are sold at markets throughout Bangkok. This island and the pottery tradition date back to one of Thailand's oldest settlements of Mon people, who were a dominant tribe of central Thailand between the 6th and 10th centuries AD. There are two pottery centres on the island where you can buy the earthenware and watch the potters work; one is on the east coast and the other is on the north coast. From Wat Paramai Yikawat (Wat Mon), which has an interesting Mon-style marble Buddha, go in either direction to find the pottery shops.

Even more prevalent than pottery is food. At weekends droves of Thais flock to Ko Kret to munch on old-school deep-fried savouries, *khâo châe* (a Mon dish combining savoury/sweet titbits and chilled rice) and iced coffee served in the island's distinctive pottery.

If you're thinking of staying overnight, or longer, Baan Dvara Prateep (☎ 0 2373 6457; www.baandvaraprateep .com; 53/3 Moo 5, Ko Kret) offers accommodation, not to mention multiday yoga and meditation retreats, in a traditional wooden house on the west coast of the island. At the time of writing they were taking only group bookings; call ahead for details.

The easiest way to reach Ko Kret is to take the special Chao Phraya Express boat (☎ 0 2623 6001; www.chao phrayaboat.co.th; adult/child 299/250B; ⏱ departs 10am, returns 4.30pm) directly to the island departing every Sunday from Tha Sathon (Map pp108–9). Otherwise, the easiest way is to take a bus (ordinary 52, 150, 356, air-con 150, 166) or taxi to Pak Kret and catch a cross-river ferry at Wat Sanam Nuea (1B) for the brief ride to the island.

DRINKING

Chang House (☎ 0 3532 8228; 14/10 Th Naresuan) Left your friends back in Bangkok? You won't have any problems making some new ones at this friendly open-air boozer smack dab in the middle of the lively guesthouse strip.

SLEEPING

Ayuthaya has several hotels but beyond the budget end (mainly found on the Th Naresuan strip, opposite Chao Phrom Market), there isn't a huge amount of character.

Baan Lotus Guest House (☎ 0 325 1988; 20 Th Pamaphrao; r 300-600B; ❄) Two tall wooden houses contain spotless and airy rooms, and the service here is genial and warm.

Chantana House (☎ 0 3532 3200; 12/22 Th Naresuan; r 300-450B; ❄) Calling itself the 'Local Touch Guest House', this expansive suburban villa is the most authentically domestic of the city's guesthouse accommodation. The tidy rooms are an excellent bargain.

Bannkunpra (☎ 0 3524 1978; www.bannkunpra.com; 48 Th U Thong; dm/s 250/300B, d 400-800B; ❄) This genteel old teak house is the most atmospheric place in town and has a prime riverfront location and breezy, though mostly shared-bathroom, rooms. There is also a four-bed dorm.

Tony's Place (☎ 0 3525 2578; Soi Thaw Kaw Saw, off Th Naresuan; d 200-1000B; ❄ 🖵) Tony's is a sprawling establishment with an energetic party atmosphere and busy patio restaurant and bar. Rooms are dependable, and some have balconies.

Suan Luang Hotel (☎/fax 0 3524 5537; Th Rotchana; d 500-600B; ❄) This five-storey hotel looks like a government building because it is; Suan Luang functions as a training facility for students at the neighbouring Rajabhat University. The hotel has passable air-con rooms with fridge, TV and private bathroom.

River View Place Hotel (☎ 0 3524 1444; 35/5 Th U Thong; d from 1700B; ❄ 🖭 🖵) Great river views, as the name suggests, and spacious rooms. The hotel also features an acclaimed restaurant featuring a variety of local dishes.

KO SAMET
เกาะเสม็ด

The search for sun and sand doesn't have to involve a big trip down south. Only half a day's journey from Bangkok, Ko Samet has famously squeaky sand beaches and an endless expanse of ocean. Plus it is a relatively dry island, making it an excellent place to visit during the rainy season when other island paradises are under water. Of course, all of this makes it very popular with everyone – Thais, foreigners and especially stray dogs (not really *soi* dogs; perhaps they're 'hat dogs') – especially on weekends or holidays. September is a particularly good time.

Ko Samet earned a permanent place in Thai literature when classical Thai poet Sunthorn

Phu set part of his epic *Phra Aphaimani* on its shores. The story follows the travails of a prince exiled to an undersea kingdom governed by a lovesick female giant. A mermaid assists the prince in his escape to Ko Samet, where he defeats a giant by playing a magic flute. Today the poem is immortalised on the island by a mermaid statue built on the rocky point separating Ao Hin Khok and Hat Sai Kaew.

In the early 1980s, Ko Samet began receiving its first visitors: young Thais in search of a retreat from city life. At that time there were only about 40 houses on the island. Rayong and Bangkok speculators saw the sudden interest in Ko Samet as a chance to cash in on an up-and-coming Phuket and began buying up land along the beaches. No-one bothered about the fact that Ko Samet had been a national marine park since 1981. When *faràng* (Westerners) soon followed, spurred on by rumours that Ko Samet was similar to Ko Samui '10 years ago' (one always seems to miss it by a decade), the National Parks Division stepped in and built a visitors' office on the island, ordered that all bungalows be moved back behind the tree line and started charging admission to the park.

However, the regulating hand of the National Parks Division is almost invisible beyond the admission gate. Many attempts to halt encroachment have been successfully defeated by resort operators or developers. One successful measure is a ban on new accommodation (except where it replaces old sites), ensuring that bungalows remain thinly spread over most of the island.

Most development is concentrated at the northern end of the island, though compared with Bangkok even this busiest part of Ko Samet seems as sparsely populated as the Australian outback. The further south you go, the less likely you are to be kept awake by a guesthouse party.

Boat trips (per person 600-800B) to nearby reefs and uninhabited islands, such as Ko Thalu and Ko Kuti, can easily be arranged.

Around the Island

Ko Samet is shaped like a golf tee, with the wide part in the north tapering away along a narrow strip to the south. Most boats from the mainland arrive at Na Dan Pier in the north, which is little more than a transit point. On the northeastern coast is Hat Sai Kaew (Diamond Beach), the most developed stretch of beach on the island and the best place for nightlife. Wealthy Bangkokians file straight into Hat Sai's air-con bungalows with their designer sunglasses and (small) designer dogs.

Heading south along the eastern shore is a scruffier set of beaches: Ao Hin Khok, Ao Phai and Ao Phutsa, which are fittingly claimed by backpackers. A rocky headland crossed by a footpath separates palm-shaded Ao Phutsa from beaches further south. Quiet Ao Nuan and Ao Cho (Chaw) have beaches that aren't quite

EXCURSIONS KO SAMET

TRANSPORT: KO SAMET

Distance from Bangkok **200km**

Direction **Southeast**

Travel Time **Four hours**

Bus The fastest way to reach Ko Samet by public transport is actually the most roundabout: bus to Rayong, *sǎwngthǎew* to Ban Phe and boat to the island. Buses directly to Ban Phe (140B), the pier for ferries to Ko Samet, leave from Bangkok as well, but the travel time is slower. Air-con buses to Rayong (137B, 3½ hours, every 30 minutes from 5am to 9.30pm) leave Bangkok's Eastern Bus Terminal (Ekamai; Map pp124–5). From Rayong bus station (or wherever you're dropped), take a *sǎwngthǎew* (20B, 30 minutes, every 15 minutes) to Ban Phe. Guesthouses around Th Khao San often arrange transport that costs more but is more convenient, although not necessarily faster.

Taxi Of course, you could just ditch the whole bus plan and take a taxi; almost any Bangkok taxi will be up for the job, assuming they have enough time left on their shift (mornings are good). From Bangkok it will cost about 2500B to 3000B one way, and it will take about two hours. From Suvarnabhumi Airport it's about 2300B.

Boat Boats to Ko Samet leave from Ban Phe's many piers; be sure to buy tickets directly from a boat office at the pier instead of a scammer waiting at the bus station. Most boats go to Na Dan Pier (return 100B, about an hour each way), but there are also boats to Ao Wong Deuan (return 120B) and other beaches in high season. Boat schedules vary depending on the season, so prepare to wait an hour or more unless it's very busy. You can also charter a speedboat (1200B to 2000B).

KO SAMET

0 ——— 1 km
0 ——— 0.5 miles

To Ban Phe (5km)
Laem Noi Na
To Ban Phe (5km)
To Ban Phe (5km)

Laem Phra
Ao Wiang Wan

Ao Kham

Na Dan Pier

Na Dan

Ao Phrao
Laem Ya/Ko Samet National Park
Hat Laem Yai
Laem Yai

Hat Sai Kaew
Ao Hin Khok

Ao Phai
Ao Phutsa (Ao Thap Thim)

Laem Rua Taek
Ao Nuan

Ao Cho
Ao Wong Deuan

Hat Saeng Thian
Ao Thian

Ao Kiu Na Nai

Ao Wai

Ao Thai (Gulf of Thailand)

Ao Kiu Na Nok

Laem Khut

Ao Karang

EXCURSIONS KO SAMET

INFORMATION
ATM...1 B4
Ko Samet Health Centre...................2 C2
National Park Branch Office.............3 B3
National Park Main Office................4 C2
Post Office.....................................5 C2

SIGHTS
Mermaid Statue..............................6 C2

EATING
Bamboo Restaurant.........................7 B3
Baywatch Bar............................(see 1)
Jep's.....................................(see 13)
Naga Bungalows.............................8 C2
Panorama Restaurant......................9 B1

DRINKING
Naga Bar..................................(see 8)
Silver Sand Bar.........................(see 24)
Tok Bar..................................(see 25)

SLEEPING
Ao Nuan Bungalows.......................10 B3
Ao Prao Resort.............................11 B2
Baan Thai Sang Thian Samed.........12 B4
Jep's Bungalows...........................13 C2
Le Vimarn Cottages.......................14 B2
Lima Coco..................................15 B2
Lung Dam...................................16 B4
Malibu Garden Resort....................17 B4
Paradee Resort & Spa....................18 A6
Sai Kaew Beach Resort..................19 C2
Saikaew Villa..............................20 C2
Samed Sand Sea..........................21 C2
Samed Villa................................22 B3
Samet Ville Resort........................23 B5
Silver Sand................................24 B3
Tok...25 C2
Tubtim Resort.............................26 B3
Vongdeuan Resort........................27 B4

voluptuous enough to attract crowds, and tend to attract romantics instead.

Immediately to the south is the prom queen of the bunch: Ao Wong Deuan, whose graceful stretch of sand is home to an entourage of sardine-packed sun-worshippers, screaming jet skis and honky-tonk bars akin to those in Pattaya.

Thai college kids claim Ao Thian (Candlelight Beach) for all-night guitar jam sessions, and further south is a castaway's dream of empty beaches and gentle surf, and the starting point for languid walks to the western side of the island to see fiery sunsets.

The only developed beach on the western side of the island is Ao Phrao (Coconut Beach), which hosts the island's most luxurious resort and moonlights as 'Paradise Beach' to those escaping winter climates.

INFORMATION

There is an ATM near Malibu Garden Resort.

Ko Samet Health Centre (☎ 0 3861 2999; btwn Hat Sai Kaew & Na Dan; ☼ 8.30am-8pm Mon-Fri, to 4.30pm Sat & Sun) Small public clinic with English-speaking doctors for minor health problems.

National Park entrance gates (Hat Sai Kaew; admission 200B; ☼ sunrise-sunset) There's another office on Ao Wong Deuan; wherever you arrive a ranger will find you to charge the fee.

Post office (Ao Hin Khok, next to Naga Bungalows; ☼ 8.30am-4.30pm Mon-Fri, 8.30am-noon Sat) Poste restante and internet access.

DRINKING

Naga Bar (dishes 50-160B; ☼ 8-2am) On Ao Hin Khok at Naga Bungalows, this is a good destination for post-dinner shenanigans. Ao Wong Deuan is so packed with wall-to-wall bars it's difficult to know where one ends and the next begins – but does it really matter? Tok Bar (dishes 40-150B; ☼ 7-2am), nearby, offers the same thing.

Silver Sand Bar (☎ 0 6530 2417; Ao Phai; ☼ 1pm-2am) As the clock ticks towards the witching hour, the island's night owls congregate under trippy spherical lights to watch the fire twirlers show off, grind to cheesy dance music, and knock back more than 35 types of cocktail (all served in buckets, of course).

EATING

Most guesthouses have restaurants, and many offer beachside dining in the evenings. There

BEFORE SAMET MEANT ESCAPE

If marketing minds had been involved, Ko Samet would still be known by its old name: Ko Kaew Phitsadan (Vast Jewel Isle), a reference to the abundant white sand. But the island's first cash cow, the cajeput (or *sàmèt*) tree, lent its name to the island as this valuable firewood source grew in abundance here. Locally, the *sàmèt* tree has also been used in boat building.

are several food stalls along the main drag between Na Dan pier and Sai Kaew Beach, and it's worth looking out for the nightly beach barbecues, particularly along Ao Hin Khok and Ao Phai.

Bamboo Restaurant (Ao Cho; dishes 80-150B; ☼ 8am-10pm) This restaurant offers inexpensive, but tasty, food and good service.

Baywatch Bar (☎ 08 1826 7834; Ao Wong Deuan; dishes 190-290B; ☼ 8-2am) Sorry fellas, Pam Anderson is nowhere to be found, although the delicious cocktails and international dishes are a decent consolation prize.

Jep's (Ao Hin Khok; dishes 60-400B; ☼ 8am-10pm) If you're going to leave your bungalow in search of other restaurants, try Jep's. It's on the pricier side, but the almanac-sized menu offers everything from Thai staples to Indian and French faves.

Naga Bungalows (☎ 0 3865 2448; Ao Hin Khok; dishes 150-200B; ☼ 8am-10pm) This guesthouse restaurant has a bakery with warm rolls, croissants and donuts in the morning and great sandwiches and pizza throughout the day. There are plenty of tofu dishes on the menu and weekly buffet meals.

Panorama Restaurant (Moo Ban Talay Resort, Ao Noi Na; dishes 120-300B; ☼ 11am-11pm) City sensibilities serve Asian and Western cuisine instead of guesthouse grub. It's northwest of Na Dan.

SLEEPING

Because of demand, Ko Samet's prices aren't always reflective of amenities. A ramshackle hut starts at 300B, and with air-con this can climb to 800B. Reservations aren't always honoured, so at peak times it is advisable to arrive early, poised for the hunt.

Hat Sai Kaew

Sai Kaew Beach Resort (☎ 0 2438 9771/2; www.samed resorts.com; r 3600-4800B, bungalows 4800-14,500B; ⚒) Smart, blue and white bungalows dot this fairly classy beach resort. Off-beach rooms are better than they sound, and away from the jetskis.

Saikaew Villa (☎ 0 3864 4139-48; www.saikaew.com; bungalows 700-2500B; ✖ 🖳) A huge and not especially personal complex that serves up comfortable accommodation. It's worth asking for a room away from the noisy generators.

Samed Sand Sea (☎ 0 3865 1126, 08 7508 3250; www .samedsandsea.com; r 2400-4000B; ✖) The last new place on Hai Sai Kaew (since there's now officially no more room to build), Samed Sand Sea has beautiful wooden bungalows with refreshing air-con that's borderline cryogenic.

Ao Hin Khok & Ao Phai

Jep's Bungalows (☎ 0 3864 4112; www.jepbungalow.com; r 300-1200B; ✖ 🖳) Jep's bungalows are a cheery mix of mahogany and magenta, although there are better options around if you're going to fork out more than 600B. Guests staying in the pricier pads get free breakfast. Mosquito repellent is a must.

Samed Villa (☎ 0 3864 4094; www.samedvilla.com; r incl breakfast 1800-2800B; ✖) Hugely popular place with well-maintained, tree-shaded bungalows with large verandas. The larger bungalows are large indeed and are suited to families, while the best of the lot have sea views.

Silver Sand (☎ 08 6530 2417; www.silversandresort .com; bungalows 300-1800B; ✖) This establishment has about 40 comfortable but oddly green bungalows with their own verandas and some with beach frontage. There is also a lively beach bar.

Tok (☎ 0 3864 4072; bungalows 300-800B; ✖) One of the island's first bungalow operations is still kicking along, with clean but spartan fan and air-con bungalows with and without bathroom. The hillside lodgings are popular because they are fair value.

Ao Phutsa (Ao Thap Thim) & Ao Nuan

Ao Nuan Bungalows (Ao Nuan; bungalows 600-1000B) If you blink you'll miss this beach and the secluded rustic huts scattered about the hillside. They all have shared bathrooms and intermittent electricity. It's a five-minute walk over the headland from Ao Phutsa. There's no phone and it doesn't take reservations.

Tubtim Resort (☎ 0 3864 4025; www.tubtimresort.com; r 600-2000B; ✖) Tubtim has five rows of bungalows climbing a rugged hill from the beach

up into the jungle. Spend the extra 200B and go for an upgraded fan bungalow – they have sparkling bathrooms and varnished fixtures, and are noticeably better than the rickety cheapies.

Ao Wong Deuan & Ao Thian

Baan Thai Sang Thian Samed (☎ 08 1305 9408; Ao Thian; r 1500-2500B; ✖) This newer address, featuring traditional Thai architecture with a treehouse twist, confirms quiet Ao Thian's move away from its budget backpacker origins and into the flashpacker realm.

Lung Dam (☎ 08 1659 8056; Ao Thian; bungalows 600-1200B; ✖) This is good for low-budget romance – the huts are built of scrap and junk, both organic and otherwise. It all looks as if it belonged to some settlement of castaways marooned on a deserted island.

Malibu Garden Resort (☎ 0 3864 4020; Ao Wong Deuan; bungalows 1550-7000B; ✖) This resort has well-built brick or wooden bungalows; the more expensive rooms have a fridge and TV. Breakfast is included.

Vongdeuan Resort (☎ 0 3865 1777; www.vongdeuan .com; Ao Wong Deuan; r 2000-3500B; ✖) This is the best of Ao Wong Deuan, and is quite extravagant by Ko Samet standards. Most bungalows are teak-style houses with front-row beach seating; cheaper and less attractive concrete cottages are at the back.

Other Eastern Beaches

Paradee Resort & Spa (☎ 0 2438 9771; www.samedresorts .com; villas 15,000B; ✖ 🖳 🛋) The price tag is high, but you get your own self-contained, beachfront villa on probably Ko Samet's best beach. There's gorgeous Thai furniture, a personal plunge pool, DVD player, espresso maker – even your own butler. Speedboats from Ban Phe are arranged – you'll be way too busy being pampered to have time to plan a ferry connection.

Samet Ville Resort (☎ 0 3865 1682; www.sametville resort.com; r 980-3780B; ✖) Samet Ville is a private getaway where guests can enjoy luxury and isolation in equal measure. The shaded restaurant is lovely spot for a romantic dinner. Staff can arrange speedboat transfers from Ban Phe.

Ao Phrao

Ao Prao Resort (☎ 0 2438 9771-72; www.samedresorts .com; chalets 6500-18,200B; ✖ 🖳) The oldest luxury lodging on Samet has been surpassed by younger models, but the private seclusion and all the bells and whistles still earn their keep. Ao Prao Divers, at the resort, provides diving, windsurfing, kayaking and boat trips.

Le Vimarn Cottages (☎ 0 2438 9771/2, Dhivarin Spa 0 3864 4104-7; www.samedresorts.com; r 8000-10,500B; 🕸 🖳 🖨) Possibly the island's most luxe option, Le Vimarn is manicured tranquillity with elegant and modern rooms. Facilities include the lavish Dhivarin Spa (☎ 0 3864 4104-7).

Lima Coco (☎ 0 2938 1811; www.limacoco.com; d 2500-6900B; 🕸) Formerly the Dome Bungalows, this bungalow village is built on the hillside and has a few midrange options worth investigating. The resort also offers a free ferry from Ban Phe's Chok Pitsada Pier.

FLOATING MARKETS
ตลาดน้ำ

Pictures of floating markets (tàlàat náam) jammed full of the wooden canoes pregnant with colourful exotic fruits have defined the official tourist profile of Thailand for decades. The idyllic scenes are as iconic as the Grand Palace (p54) or the Reclining Buddha (p54), but they are also almost completely contrived for, and dependent upon, tourists. Roads and motorcycles have long moved daily errands onto dry ground.

The most famous of the breed – the one you've seen photographed hundreds of times – is the Damnoen Saduak Floating Market (Khlong Damnoen Saduak; ⏱ 7am-noon). You can hire a boat from any pier that lines Th Sukhaphiban 1, which is

TRANSPORT: FLOATING MARKETS

Damnoen Saduak
Distance from Bangkok 65km
Direction Southwest
Travel Time Two hours
Bus Air-con buses (80B) go direct from Thonburi's Southern Bus Terminal (Map pp124–5) to Damnoen Saduak every 20 minutes, beginning at 6.30am. Most buses will drop you off at a pier along the khlong, where you can hire a boat directly to the floating market. The regular bus stop is in town just across the bridge. A yellow sǎwngthǎew (5B) does a frequent loop between the floating market and the bus stop in town.

Don Wai Market
Distance from Bangkok 50km
Direction Southwest
Travel Time 1½ hours
The easiest way to reach Don Wai Market is to take a minibus (45B; 35 minutes) from beside Central Pinklao (Map pp124–5) in Thonburi.

Amphawa Market
Distance from Bangkok 80km
Direction Southwest
Travel Time 1½ hours
Buses run every 40 minutes from Thonburi's Southern Bus Terminal (Map pp124–5) directly to Amphawa (72B).

Tha Kha Floating Market
Distance from Bangkok 55km
Direction Southwest
Travel Time Two hours
Tours can be organised through Baan Tai Had Resort (p236).

EXCURSIONS MAHACHAI RAIL LINE & AMPHAWA

TRANSPORT: MAHACHAI RAIL LINE

Distance from Bangkok 28km to Samut Sakhon; 74km to Samut Songkhram

Direction Southwest

Travel Time One hour to Samut Sakhon, 1½ hours to Samut Songkhram

Train Trains leave Thonburi's Wong Wian Yai station (Map pp52–3) roughly every hour starting at 5.30am to Samut Sakhon. You'll need to leave Thonburi before 8.30am in order to do the trip entirely by train. There are four departures (7.30am, 10.10am, 1.30pm and 4.40pm) from Baan Laem to Samut Songkhram. The 3rd-class train costs 10B for each leg. Returning, the last two departures are 11.30am and 3.30pm from Samut Songkhram to Baan Laem, which has hourly departures to Thonburi until 7pm.

Bus If you get a late start, you can always return to Bangkok by bus. In both Samut Sakhon and Samut Songkhram the train station is a five-minute walk from the bus terminal. Regular buses from Samut Sakhon (44B) and Samut Songkhram (65B) arrive at the Southern Bus Terminal (Map pp124–5) in Thonburi. Both cities have bus service to Damnoen Saduak (p235).

the land route to the floating market area. The going rate is 250B per person per hour. The 100-year-old market is now essentially a floating souvenir stand filled with package tourists. But beyond the market, the residential canals are quite peaceful and can be explored by hiring a boat for a longer duration. South of the floating market are several small family businesses, including a Thai candy maker, a pomelo farm and a knife crafter.

Not technically a swimmer, Don Wai Market (Talat Don Wai; 6am-6pm) claims a riverbank location in Nakhon Pathom province, having originally started out in the early 20th century as a floating market for pomelo and jackfruit growers and traders. Like many tourist attractions geared towards Thais, the main attraction here is food, including fruit, traditional sweets and *pèt phálo* (five-spice stewed duck), which can be consumed on board large boats that cruise the Nakhorn Chaisi River (one hour, 60B).

The Amphawa Floating Market (Talat Náam Amphawaa; 4pm-9pm Fri-Sun), about 7km northwest of Samut Songkhram, convenes near Wat Amphawa. If you can get your timing right, several nearby floating markets meet in the mornings on particular lunar days and tend to be mainly tourist-free zones. Tha Kha Floating Market (2nd, 7th & 12th day of waxing & waning moons, 7am-noon Sat & Sun) is one notable example, coalescing along an open, breezy *khlong* lined with greenery and old wooden houses.

INFORMATION

Baan Tai Had Resort (0 3476 7220; www.baantaihad .com; 1 Moo 2, Th Tai Had, Samut Songkhram) Rents

kayaks and organises trips for exploring the Amphawa and Tha Kha markets.

Bike & Travel (0 2990 0274; www.cyclingthailand .com) This tour company organises bike trips to Damnoen Saduak and the surrounding villages.

Damnoen Saduak Tourist Information Office (Th Sukhaphiban 1; 9am-5pm) This office, across from the floating market, can organise transport to outlying canal sites if you want a two- to three-hour tour. It also arranges for home stays and other canal trips.

MAHACHAI RAIL LINE & AMPHAWA

สายรถไฟมหาชัย

If you've got the need to get out of the city but don't know where you want to go, this might be the perfect trip. The Mahachai Line, a rail spur linking Thonburi with a string of gulfside towns scented with the fishy perfume of the sea, is a pleasant, pointless trip for sating the lust to wander. However, if you're the type that requires a destination, the quaint canalside village of Amphawa boasts enough atmosphere, accommodation and activities to warrant an overnight stay.

The adventure begins when you take a stab into Thonburi looking for the Wong Wian Yai train station (Map pp52–3; Th Taksin; bus 37). Just past the traffic circle (Wong Wian Yai) is a fairly ordinary food market that camouflages the unceremonious terminal of this commuter line.

Only 15 minutes out of the station the city density yields to squatty villages where you can peek into homes, temples and shops, many of which are arm's length from the passing trains. Further on palm trees, small rice fields and marshes filled with giant elephant ears and canna lilies form the way, tamed only briefly by little whistle-stop stations.

The wilderness and backwater farms evaporate quickly as you enter Samut Sakhon, popularly known as Mahachai because it straddles the confluence of Mae Nam Tha Chin and Khlong Mahachai. It is a bustling port town, several kilometres from the Gulf of Thailand and the end of the first rail segment.

After working your way through what must be one of the most hectic fresh markets in the country, you'll come to a vast harbour clogged with water hyacinth and wooden fishing boats. A few rusty cannon pointing towards the river testify to the town's crumbling fort, built to protect the kingdom from sea invaders. Before the 17th century, the town was known as Tha Jiin (Chinese Pier) because of the large number of Chinese junks that called here.

A few kilometres west of Samut Sakhon, further along Hwy 35, is the Ayuthaya-period Wat Yai Chom Prasat, which is renowned for the intricately carved wooden doors on its *bòt*. To reach here from Samut Sakhon, board a westbound bus (8B) heading towards Samut Songkhram. The *wát* is a short ride outside town, just across the large bridge.

OK, back to the harbour and on with the rail trip. Take the ferry across to Baan Laem (3B), jockeying for space with the motorcycles that cross back and forth, driven by school teachers and errand-running housewives. From the ferry, take a motorcycle taxi (10B) for the 2km ride to Wat Chawng Lom.

Wat Chawng Lom is home to the Jao Mae Kuan Im Shrine, a 9m-high fountain in the shape of the Mahayana Buddhist Goddess of Mercy that is popular with regional tour groups. The colourful image, which pours a perpetual stream of water from a vase in the goddess's right hand, rests on an artificial hill into which a passageway is carved, leading to another Kuan Im shrine.

Just beside the shrine is Tha Chalong, a train stop with two afternoon departures for Samut Songkhram (see opposite). Rambling out of the city, the surrounding forest is so dense that it seems the surrounding greenery might engulf the train tracks. We know it's an old cliché, but this little stretch of line genuinely feels a world away from the big smoke of Bangkok. Alas, not for long. The illusion that you've entered a parallel universe free of concrete is shattered as you enter Samut Songkhram. And to complete the seismic shift

you'll emerge directly into a hubbub of hectic market stalls, which between train arrivals and departures set up directly on the tracks hiding the station's back-door entrance.

Commonly known as Mae Klong, Samut Songkhram is a tidier version of Samut Sakhon, and offers a great deal more as a destination. Owing to flat topography and abundant water sources, the area surrounding the provincial capital is well suited to the steady irrigation needed to grow guava, lychee and grapes. A string of artificial sea-lakes used in the production of salt fill the space between Mae Klong and Thonburi.

Wat Phet Samut Worawihan, in the centre of town near the train station and river, contains a renowned Buddha image called Luang Phaw Wat Ban Laem – named after the *phrá sàksìt* (holy monk) who dedicated it, thus transferring mystical powers to the image.

However, it comes as something of a relief that the province's most famous tourist attraction is not a wat. Instead, the honour goes to a bank of fossilised shells known as Don Hoi Lot at the mouth of Mae Nam Mae Klong, not far from town. These shells come from *hǎwy làwt* (clams with a tubelike shell). The shell bank can really be seen only during the dry season when the river surface has receded to its lowest level (typically April and May). Nearby perennial seafood restaurants are popular with city folk. To get there you can hop into a *sǎwngthǎew* in front of Somdet Phra Phuttalertla Hospital at the intersection of Th Prasitwatthana and Th Thamnimit; the trip takes about 15 minutes (10B). Or you can charter a boat from the Mae Klong Market pier *(thâa tàlàat mâe klawng)*, a scenic journey of around 45 minutes (1000B).

Wat Sattatham, 500m down the road from Don Hoi Lot, is notable for its *bòt* constructed of golden teak and decorated with 60 million baht worth of mother-of-pearl inlay. The inlay completely covers the temple's interior and depicts scenes from the *Jataka* (stories from the Buddha's lives) above the windows and the Ramakian below.

If you're not ready to turn back yet, charter a boat (1000B) or hop in a *sǎwngthǎew* (9B) near the market for the 10-minute ride to Amphawa. This canalside village has become a popular destination among city folk who seek out what many consider its quintessentially 'Thai' setting. This urban influx has sparked a few signs of gentrification, but the canals, old wooden buildings, atmospheric cafés and quaint waterborne traffic still retain heaps of charm. At weekends Amphawa puts on a reasonably authentic floating market (p235); visit on a weekday if you want to have the whole town to yourself.

Steps from Amphawa's central footbridge is Wat Amphawan Chetiyaram, a graceful temple thought to be located at the place of the family home of Rama II (King Buddha Loetla; r 1809-24), and which features accomplished murals. A short walk from the temple is King Buddhalertla (Phuttha Loet La) Naphalai Memorial Park (Km 63, Route 35, Samut Songkhram; admission 20B; park 9am-6pm daily, museum 9am-6pm Wed-Sun), a museum housed in a collection of traditional central Thai houses set on four landscaped acres. Dedicated to Rama II, the museum contains rare Thai books and antiques from early-19th-century Siam.

At night longtail boats zip through Amphawa's sleeping waters to watch the star-like dance of the *hìng hâwy* (fireflies). Several operators lead tours, including Niphaa (0 81422 0726), an experienced and well-equipped outfit located at the mouth of the canal, near the footbridge. If you take a tour, be aware that people are often sleeping in the homes you'll pass, so insist the that driver doesn't make more noise than is absolutely necessary.

EATING

Khrua Chom Ao (0 85190 5677; Samut Sakhon; dishes 60-200B) This open-air seafood restaurant looks over the gulf and has a loyal local following. It is a brief walk from Wat Chawng Lom, down the road running along the side of the temple opposite the statue of Kuan Im.

Tarua Restaurant (0 3441 1084; Ferry Terminal Bldg, 859 Th Sethakit, Samut Sakhon; dishes 60-200B) Occupying three floors of the imposing ferry building, this seafood restaurant offers views over the harbour and an English-language menu.

Amphawa Floating Market (Talàat Náam Ampháwaa; dishes 20-40B; 4-9pm Fri-Sun) If you're in town on a weekend, plan your meals around this fun market (see p235) where *phàt thai* and other noodle dishes are served directly from boats.

Phu Yai Thawngyib (0 3473 5073; Amphawa; dishes 20-60B) This community development project and homestay located outside Amphawa includes a restaurant that serves authentic local dishes and sweets. Call ahead to arrange a visit.

SLEEPING

Amphawa is popular with Bangkok's weekend warriors, and it seems like virtually every other house has opened its doors to tourists

in the form of home stays. These can range from little more than a mattress on the floor and a mosquito net to upscale guesthouse-style accommodation. Baan Song Thai Plai Pong Pang (0 3475 7333; Amphawa) organises home stays and has been recognised for ecotourism excellence. Most of these places are best reached by boat, though some have road access; call ahead or get your driver to call for directions.

Reorn Pae Amphawa (0 3475 1333; 139-145 Rim Khlong Amphawa; d 800B;) A good upper-budget option is this generations-old wooden home with basic but tidy rooms.

Baan Ku Pu (0 3472 5920; Th Rim Khlong, Amphawa; d 1000B;) For something more upscale Baan Ku Pu is a self-styled 'resort' featuring wooden bungalows.

Baan Tai Had Resort (0 3476 7220; www.baantaihad .com; 1 Moo 2, Th Tai Had, Samut Songkhram; r 1750-5000B;) This new riverside resort is more worthy of the description, with bright and comfortable rooms and several activities to choose from.

Baan Amphawa Resort & Spa (22 034-752 222; 22 Bangkapom-kaewfah, Amphawa; r from 3500B;) At the top of the heap is delightful Baan Amphawa, set among the paddies and khlong and built in traditional Thai style – plus luxuries like a spa and wi-fi internet.

PHETBURI (PHETCHABURI)

เพชรบุรี

Phetburi (sometimes referred to as Phetchaburi, the 'City of Diamonds') has a bit of everything – history, nature, good eats and beaches. Given buses take only a couple of hours it can be done in a long day, though is more enjoyable as an overnight excursion. The trip down to Phetburi is stereotypical central Thailand – flat plains punctuated by shaggy sugar palms and the occasional unexpected limestone outcroppings. As you get closer to Phetburi you'll see a surprising number of wooden homes, many with the characteristically peaked roof that has all but died out elsewhere in Thailand. The town itself is a repository of traditional central Thai culture, and a walk along the town's twisting back lanes, a peek at the vivid morning market and a tour of the fabled temples provide a glimpse of a traditional lifestyle that has changed little for decades.

TRANSPORT: PHETBURI

Distance from Bangkok 166km

Direction South

Travel Time Two hours by bus; three to four hours by train

Bus There are frequent air-con bus services to/from Bangkok's Southern bus station (112B; two hours). The bus terminal for air-con buses to/from Bangkok is across from the night market.

Train Trains are less convenient than buses, unless you factor in the time taken to get to or from Bangkok's bus terminals. There are frequent services from Bangkok's Hualamphong train station, and fares vary depending on the train and class (2nd class, around 200B; 3rd class, around 100B; three hours). Getting back to Bangkok by train is a bit tougher as there are only two daytime departures, a 3rd class train at 3pm (34B; four hours) and an air-con departure at 4.40pm (358B; three hours).

Getting Around *Săamláw* and motorcycle taxis go anywhere in the town centre for 30B; you can also charter them for the whole day (from 300B). *Săwngthăew* cost 10B to 20B around town. Rabieng Rimnum Guest House (p241) rents out motorcycles (per day 250B).

Phetburi lives in the shadow of Khao Wang, a looming hill studded with wat and topped by various components of King Mongkut's 1860 palace, Phra Nakhon Khiri (☎ 0 3240 1006; admission 40B; ☽ 8.30am-4.30pm). You can make the strenuous upward climb or head to the west side of the hill and take a funicular straight up to the peak (return adult/child 70/40B). The views from here are fantastic, especially at sunset, and the entire hill teems with meandering monkeys looking for attention. The ticket office will sell you an information pamphlet (5B) that includes a map of the palace grounds.

Phetburi is known throughout Thailand for its varied collection of wat. The first temple you're likely to notice is Wat Mahathat with its imposing late Ayuthaya–early Ratanakosin adaptation of the *prang* of Lopburi and Phimai. The beautiful murals inside the *wíhăan* illustrate the *Jataka* (stories from the Buddha's lives) and also show vivid snippets of everyday Thai life during the 19th century. The roof of the adjacent *bòt* (ordination hall) holds fine examples of stucco work, a characteristic of the Phetburi school of art that can be seen on many of the city's temples. One of the earliest surviving examples of this art form, known in Thai as *poon pân*, can be seen on the crumbling Ayuthaya-era *wíhăan* of Wat Phai Lom.

Somewhat unusually for a Thai temple, contemporary stucco work portraying the violent political unrest of 1973 can be viewed at Wat Chi Prasoet.

Wat Yai Suwannaram was originally built during the 17th century and renovated during the reign of King Rama V (r 1868–1910). Legend

has it that the gash in the ornately carved wooden doors of the lengthy wooden *sălaa* dates to the Burmese attack of Ayuthaya. The faded murals inside the *bòt* (central sanctuary) date back to the 1730s. Next to the *bòt*, set on a murky pond, is a beautifully designed old *hăw trai* (Tripitaka library).

Wat Ko Kaew Sutharam (Wat Ko) dates back to the Ayuthaya era, and the *bòt* features early-18th-century murals that are among the oldest and most beautiful in Thailand. One panel depicts what appears to be a Jesuit priest wearing the robes of a Buddhist monk, while another shows other foreigners undergoing Buddhist conversions.

If you've got time to make a short trip outside town, there are two cave sanctuaries worth visiting. Khao Luang (donation encouraged; ☽ 8am-6pm) is 5km north of Phetburi, and the caverns here are filled with ageing Buddha images in various stances, many of them originally placed by King Rama IV. The best time to visit is around 5pm, when evening light pierces the ceiling, surrounding artefacts below with an ethereal glow. Khao Bandai-It (donation encouraged; ☽ 9am-4pm), 2km west of town, has English-speaking guides who can lead you through the caves and answer your questions. A *săamláw* from the city centre to either site costs about 55B; a motorcycle taxi is 40B.

INFORMATION

TAT office (☎ 0 3240 2220; Th Ratwithi; ☽ 8.30am-4.30pm) Set in a wat-like structure with random baroque chandeliers, this tourism branch doesn't have loads of brochures, but the smiley staff can point you in the direction of cheap food,

PHETBURI (PHETCHABURI)

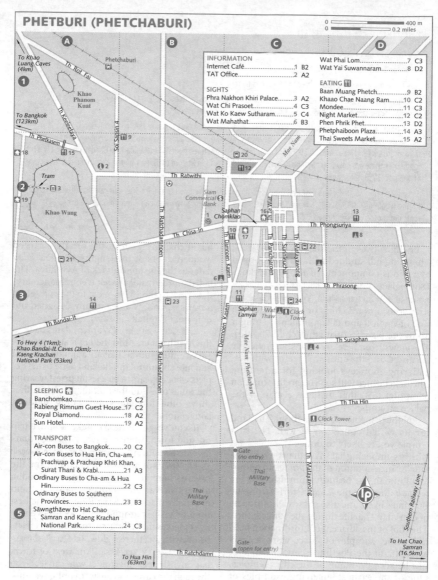

INFORMATION
Internet Café.............................1 B2
TAT Office..............................2 A2

SIGHTS
Phra Nakhon Khiri Palace.........3 A2
Wat Chi Prasoet........................4 C3
Wat Ko Kaew Sutharam............5 C4
Wat Mahathat.........................6 B3

Wat Phai Lom.........................7 C3
Wat Yai Suwannaram..............8 D2

EATING 🍴
Baan Muang Phetch.................9 B2
Khaao Chae Naang Ram..........10 C2
Mondee................................11 C3
Night Market.........................12 C2
Phen Phrik Phet.....................13 D2
Phetphaiboon Plaza................14 A3
Thai Sweets Market................15 A2

SLEEPING 🏠
Banchomkao...........................16 C2
Rabieng Rimnum Guest House..17 C2
Royal Diamond.......................18 A2
Sun Hotel..............................19 A2

TRANSPORT
Air-con Buses to Bangkok........20 C2
Air-con Buses to Hua Hin, Cha-am,
  Prachuap & Prachuap Khiri Khan,
  Surat Thani & Krabi.............21 A3
Ordinary Buses to Cha-am & Hua
  Hin..................................22 C3
Ordinary Buses to Southern
  Provinces..........................23 B3
Sǎwngthǎew to Hat Chao
  Samran and Kaeng Krachan
  National Park......................24 C3

lodging and temples. There's an internet café (Th Chisa-In; per hr 20B; ⏰ 10am-9pm) in the centre of town, not far from Rabieng Rimnum Guest House.

EATING

Phetburi is known across Thailand for its desserts, many of which claim a royal pedigree and get their sweet taste from the fruit of the sugar palms that dot the countryside. Two of the most famous sweets include *mâw kaeng* (an egg and coconut milk-based custard) and *khànǒm taan* (bright-yellow steamed buns sweetened with sugar palm kernels). The best place to sample these and others is along the Thai sweets market directly north of Khao Wang.

The town features two lively night markets, one at Phetphaiboon Plaza (Th Bandai-It; dishes 20-60B;

HAT CHAO SAMRAN
หาดเจ้าสำราญ

Lying just 18km east of Phetburi, Hat Chao Samran is one of Thailand's oldest beach resorts, dating back to Rama VI (r 1910–1925). While the Thailand of today certainly has nicer beaches, it's a pleasant enough place to laze your way through a day or two, punctuating your naps with cheap seafood binges. The area has seen a recent resurgence in popularity that has brought with it new 'boutique'-style bungalow accommodation. Typical of the lot, Blue Sky (☎ 0 3244 1399; www.blueskyresort.com; 5 Moo 2, Hat Chao Samran; bungalows 1800-5000B; ☒) offers ridiculously cute bungalows and rooms overlooking the garden or the sea. When you can relax no more, stumble next door to Jaa Piak (☎ 0 3247 8496; dishes 50-280B; ☒ 9am-9pm), which serves up all your shelled favourites, including a mean horseshoe crab egg salad (yam khài maengdaa tháleh).

To reach Hat Chao Samran, hop on a sǎwngthǎew (35 minutes; 20B) across from the clock tower near Wat Thaw.

☒ 5-11pm), and the night market (Th Rot Fai; dishes 20-60B; ☒ 5-11pm) near the Bangkok-bound bus stop.

Baan Muang Petch (☎ 0 81694 5031; 20/2-3 Soi Sapsin 4; dishes 25-60B; ☒ 10.30am-8pm) This well-situated coffee shop is an excellent place to refill on caffeine and sweets between temple visits. Simple dishes and a great sunset view of Khao Wang are also available.

Khaao Chae Naang Ram (☎ 0 84801 8395; Th Damnoen Kasem; dishes 15-20B; ☒ 8am-5pm) Khâao châe (camphor-scented chilled rice served with sweet/savoury titbits) is a dish associated with Phetburi, and a good place to sample it is at this renowned roadside stall in front of a noodle restaurant.

Mondee (☎ 0 81697 1768; Saphaan Lamyai; dishes 25-100B; ☒ 10.30am-4.30pm & 5.30-midnight) During the day, this cosy wooden shack serves khànǒm jeen (fresh rice noodles served with a variety of curries). At night Mondee takes full advantage of the breezes and river view and serves decent central Thai fare with an emphasis on seafood.

Phen Phrik Phet (☎ 0 3241 2990; 173/1 Th Phongsuriya; dishes 25B; ☒ 9am-3pm Wed-Mon) Located directly across from Wat Yai Suwannaram, this local noodle legend makes tasty kǔay tiaw mǔu

náam daeng (pork noodles in a fragrant dark broth).

SLEEPING
For a town its size with so many attractions, Phetburi is lacking in the accommodation department.

Royal Diamond (☎ 0 3241 1061; www.royaldiamond hotel.com; 555 Th Phetkasem; r 1200-2000B; ☒ ☐) Ostensibly the best in town, though the characterless hotel ambience doesn't compare with the Sun.

Sun Hotel (☎ 0 3240 0000; 43/33 Th Phetkasem 1; r 590-890B, ste 1090B; ☒) The vast, bright rooms and cheery boutique feel make this place a veritable bargain. It's a top choice.

Rabieng Rimnum Guest House (☎ 0 3242 5707; 1 Th Shesrain; s/d 120/240B) This is one of several uninspiring budget guesthouses, you can look forward to rooms that are little more than a wooden closet with a mattress. If you aren't impressed with the rooms, the owner will point across the bridge to the Banchomkao (☎ 0 3242; Th Thewet; s/d 170/250), which is same price, but here your closet is concrete. They are, however, very cheap.

KAENG KRACHAN NATIONAL PARK
อุทยานแห่งชาติแก่งกระจาน

The largest national park in Thailand and home to the gorgeous Pala-U waterfalls, Kaeng Krachan National Park (☎ 0 3245 9291; adult/child 400/200B) is easily reached from Phetburi. There are caves to explore, mountains, a huge lake and excellent bird-watching opportunities in the evergreen forest that blankets the park. Kaeng Krachan has fantastic trekking, and it is one of the few places to see Asian elephants roaming wild (if you're lucky). Intermittent sǎwngthǎew (50B) depart from near Wat Thaw and stop at the park headquarters. To get to some of the higher campgrounds you'll have to charter a vehicle from the headquarters (900B) or hitch. Rabieng Rimnum Guest House (above) arranges overnight visits (2400B per person, minimum four people).

KANCHANABURI

อ.เมือง.กาญจนบุรี

Less than two hours from Bangkok, Kanchanaburi (pronounced 'kan-cha-*na*-buri') is a convenient and refreshing retreat from city life. Framed by limestone mountains and fields of sugarcane, the city offers ample riverside accommodation options that specialise in the art of relaxing after a day of sightseeing in the scenic countryside.

But don't be fooled by Kanchanaburi's sleepy daytime demeanour. After the sun sets the river boom-booms its way through the night with disco and karaoke barges packed with Bangkokians looking to let their hair down, especially at weekends. Out-of-tune crooners and shoddy stereo systems disrupt the calm that many travellers are hoping to find in their riverside rooms. If this is you, it won't take long before you're thinking that sometimes Asia needs a mute button. An hour or so later you might be fantasising about bazookas.

The city was originally established by Rama I (King Buddha Yodfa; r 1782–1809) as a first line of defence against the Burmese who, it was commonly believed, might use the old invasion route through the Three Pagodas Pass on the Thai–Burmese border to the west. Crumbling buildings that reflect the town's age can be found on the side streets that run off and parallel to Th Song Khwae.

Despite its unspectacular appearance (it's an iron bridge), the Death Railway Bridge across Mae Nam Khwae is one of Kanchanaburi's most popular attractions. The bridge is 2km north of town and best visited by bicycle. It's possible to walk across. A railway line travels part of the original Death Railway route from Kanchanaburi west to the village of Nam Tok, across Mae Nam Khwae. Trains depart Kanchanaburi at 5.57am, 10.24am and 4.19pm for the two-hour scenic trip to Nam Tok, where you'll have a short layover before the last departure back to Kanchanaburi. Foreigners are charged 100B.

There are several other war-related sights. The WWII Museum (Th Mae Nam Khwae; admission 40B; 9am-6pm) beside the bridge has a picture-postcard view and an eclectic assortment of war and peace memorabilia, though you wouldn't call it a must-see.

Better is the Thailand-Burma Railway Centre (☎ 0 3451 0067; 73 Th Jaokannun; adult/child 80/40B; 9am-5pm), where exhibits outline Japanese aggression in Southeast Asia and detail their plans for the railway. Occasionally foreign guides, sometimes relatives of those interned, lead moving tours through the museum.

The centre stands opposite the Kanchanaburi Allied War Cemetery (Th Saengchuto; admission free; 7am-6pm), the final resting place of about 7000 prisoners who died while working on the railway. The cemetery is meticulously maintained by the Commonwealth War Graves Commission (www.cwgc.org), and the rows of headstones are identical except for the names and short epitaphs. It's just around the corner from the riverside guesthouses, or you could catch a *săwngthăew* anywhere along Th Saengchuto going north.

Less visited is the Chung Kai Allied War Cemetery (admission free; 7am-6pm), where about 1700 graves are kept a short and scenic bike ride from central Kanchanaburi. From Th Lak Meuang, take the bridge across the river

TRANSPORT: KANCHANABURI

Distance from Bangkok 130km

Direction West

Travel Time Two to three hours

Bus Regular buses leave from the Southern Bus Terminal (Map pp124–5) in Thonburi (1st class/2nd class 103/80B; every 30 minutes until 9pm) to Kanchanaburi's bus station off Th Saengchuto.

Train Kanchanaburi is a stop on the scenic but slow Bangkok Noi-Nam Tok line. The train leaves from Bangkok Noi station (Map p56) in Thonburi twice a day (7.45am and 1.35pm; 100B) and stops at Kanchanaburi's train station, just off Th Saengchuto. To return to Bangkok, there is one morning and one afternoon departure.

Getting Around Kanchanaburi is very accessible by bicycle; you can hire bikes along Th Mae Nam Khwae (per day 40B). For areas outside town, rent a motorcycle (per day 150B to 200B) from the Suzuki dealer near the bus terminal. *Săamláw* within the city cost 30B a trip. Regular *săwngthăew* (5B) cruise Th Saengchuto, but be careful you don't accidentally charter one all for yourself.

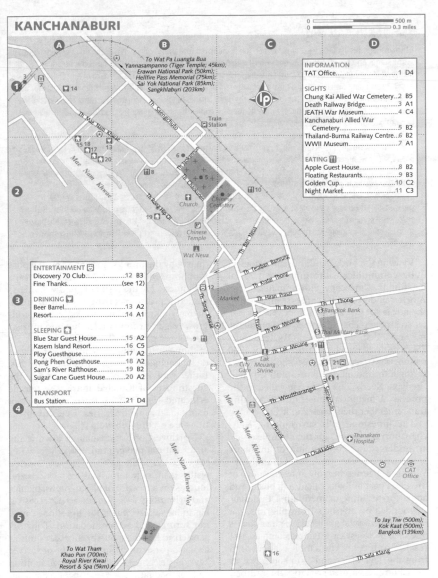

KANCHANABURI

To Wat Pa Luangta Bua
Yannasampanno (Tiger Temple; 45km);
Erawan National Park (50km);
Hellfire Pass Memorial (75km);
Sai Yok National Park (85km);
Sangkhlaburi (203km)

Train Station

Church

Chinese Cemetery

Chinese Temple

Wat Neua

Market

Bangkok Bank

Thai Military Bank

Lak Mouang Shrine

City Gate

Thanakam Hospital

CAT Office

To Wat Tham
Khao Pun (700m);
Royal River Kwai
Resort & Spa (5km)

To Jay Tiw (500m);
Kok Kaat (500m);
Bangkok (139km)

INFORMATION		
TAT Office	1	D4

SIGHTS		
Chung Kai Allied War Cemetery	2	B5
Death Railway Bridge	3	A1
JEATH War Museum	4	C4
Kanchanaburi Allied War Cemetery	5	B2
Thailand-Burma Railway Centre	6	B2
WWII Museum	7	A1

EATING		
Apple Guest House	8	B2
Floating Restaurants	9	B3
Golden Cup	10	C2
Night Market	11	C3

ENTERTAINMENT		
Discovery 70 Club	12	B3
Fine Thanks	(see 12)	

DRINKING		
Beer Barrel	13	A2
Resort	14	A1

SLEEPING		
Blue Star Guest House	15	A2
Kasem Island Resort	16	C5
Ploy Guesthouse	17	A2
Pong Phen Guesthouse	18	A2
Sam's River Rafthouse	19	B2
Sugar Cane Guest House	20	A2

TRANSPORT		
Bus Station	21	D4

through picturesque corn and sugarcane fields until you reach the cemetery on your left.

The JEATH War Museum (Th Pak Phraek; admission 40B; 8.30am-6pm) is arguably the pick of the memorials and is a moving testament to war's atrocities. The museum operates in the grounds of a local temple and has reconstructions of the bamboo huts used by the POWs as shelter. The long huts contain various photographs taken during the war, draw-

ings and paintings by POWs, maps, weapons and other war memorabilia. The acronym JEATH represents the fated meeting of Japan, England, Australia/America, Thailand and Holland at Kanchanaburi during WWII. The war museum is at the end of Th Wisuttharangsi (Visutrangsi), near the TAT office. The common Thai name for this museum is Phíphítháphan Songkhram Wát Tâi (Wat Tai War Museum).

THE DEATH RAILWAY

Kanchanaburi's history includes a brutal cameo (later promoted to starring) role in WWII. The town was home to a Japanese-run prisoner of war camp, from which Allied soldiers and others were used to build the notorious Death Railway, linking Bangkok to Burma (now Myanmar). Carving a rail bed out of the 415km stretch of rugged terrain was a brutally ambitious plan intended to meet an equally remarkable goal of providing an alternative supply route for the Japanese conquest of Burma and other countries to the west. Japanese engineers estimated that the task would take five years. But the railway was completed in a mere 16 months, entirely by forced labour that had little access to machines or nutrition. A Japanese brothel train inaugurated the line.

Close to 100,000 labourers died as a result of the hard labour, torture or starvation; 13,000 of them POWs, mainly from Britain, Australia, the Netherlands, New Zealand and America. The POWs' story was chronicled in Pierre Boulle's book *The Bridge on the River Kwai* and later popularised by the movie of the same name. Many visitors come here specifically to pay their respects to the fallen POWs at the Allied cemeteries, and you can set your watch by the arrival of the tour buses carrying Chinese or Japanese tourists who rush through the major war sites.

The original bridge was used by the Japanese for 20 months before it was bombed by Allied planes in 1945. Of what you see today, the curved spans are original and the square sections were rebuilt after the war. As for the Death Railway, only a small portion remains. Much of the original track was carted off by Karen and Mon tribespeople for use in the construction of local buildings and bridges, and other parts were used to reconstruct other Thai railways after the war.

Viewing the bridge and museums doesn't quite communicate the immense task of bending the landscape with human muscle. A better understanding comes from a visit to the Hellfire Pass Memorial (Rte 323; ☽ sunrise-sunset), an Australian-Thai Chamber of Commerce memorial dedicated to the POW labourers, 75km north of Kanchanaburi. A crew of 1000 prisoners worked for 12 weeks to cut a pass through the mountainous area dubbed Hellfire Pass. Nearly 70% of the crew died in the process. A memorial museum and walking trail remember their work and lives.

The limestone hills surrounding Kanchanaburi are famous for their temple caves, an underground communion of animistic spirit worship and traditional Buddhism. Winding arteries burrow into the guts of the caves past bulbous calcium deposits and altars for reclining or meditating Buddhas, surrounded by offerings from pilgrims. Wat Tham Khao Pun (admission by donation; ☽ 7am-4pm) is one of the closest cave temples, and is best reached by bicycle. The temple is about 4km from the TAT office and 1km southwest of the Chung Kai cemetery across the railroad tracks and midway up the hill.

One of Kanchanaburi's more bizarre tourist destinations is Wat Pa Luangta Bua Yannasampanno (www.tigertemple.org; admission 400B; ☽ 8.30am-noon & 1.30-5pm), known colloquially as the Tiger Temple. After gaining a reputation as a refuge for wounded animals, the temple received its first tiger cub in 1999 and has accumulated 17 more since. During visiting hours, the cats are led around a quarry by the monks, and for a fee, will pose for photos with tourists. Although the efforts are undeniably the result of goodwill, there's something disconcerting (not to mention surreal) about seeing monks leading full-grown tigers around on leashes and tourists posing for pictures (for extra money) with said huge cats lying in their laps. The tigers do look sedated, though the monks deny this. Either way, it's an oft-debated issue in the guesthouses of Kanchanaburi. The temple is located 45km outside town, and is part of many local tour itineraries. Detailed directions are on the website.

Northwest of Kanchanaburi town is the area's natural playground. Erawan National Park (☎ 0 3457 4222; admission 400B; ☽ 8am-4pm) sports a watery mane of waterfalls visited by locals and tourists for a day trip of photographs, picnics and swimming. Sai Yok National Park (admission 400B) has more variety: waterfalls, limestone caves, hot springs and accommodation. Tour organisers in Kanchanaburi arrange day outings to these parks on various expeditions: river kayaking, elephant trekking, waterfall spotting and bamboo rafting – Kanchanaburi has it all, plus people persuading you to do it (for some of your baht, of course).

INFORMATION

TAT office (☎ 0 3451 1200; Th Saengchuto; ☽ 8.30am-4.30pm) Provides a great provincial map with information about trips outside Kanchanaburi, as well as bus and train schedules. It's near the bus station.

DRINKING

Beer Barrel (Th Mae Nam Khwae; ⏰ 6pm-midnight) Deep in a thicket of trees, this mazelike bar of gigantic wooden tables is a soothing elixir after a day of doing nothing.

Resort (☎ 0 81847 9227; 318/2 Th Mae Nam Khwae; ⏰ 6pm-midnight) This faux colonial-era veranda boasts a nightly live band and attractive outdoor seating.

EATING

Apple Guest House (☎ 0 3451 2017; Th Rong Hip Oi; dishes 50-120B; ⏰ 8am-10pm) This guesthouse restaurant introduces newcomers to Thai food without being condescending. Both the *kaeng mát-sàmàn* (Muslim-style curry) and *phàt thai* are highly recommended.

Floating restaurants (Th Song Khwae; dishes 80-200B; ⏰ 6-11pm) Down on the river are several large floating restaurants where the quality of the food varies, but it's hard not to enjoy the atmosphere. Most cater to Thais out for a night of drinking and snacking.

Golden Cup (☎ 0 3451 3505; 284/53 Th Saengchuto; dishes 30-50B; ⏰ 8am-5pm) When only real coffee and air-conditioning will do, head to this tiny café. To bring you back to Thailand, try the shop's signature *thawng múan*, known here as 'crispy rolls', a Thai sweet associated with Kanchanaburi.

Night market (Th Saengchuto; dishes 30-60B; ⏰ 6-11pm) An expansive market featuring everything from Thai-Muslim nosh to *phàt thai* unfolds every night in front of the bus station.

One of the culinary trademarks of Kanchanaburi are the curry restaurants that sell a huge variety of local-style curries, soups and fried dishes – simply check under the lids and choose what looks good. Two that we found particularly good:

Kok Kaat (☎ 0 3451 2481; 211/1 Th Saengchuto; dishes 20-30B; ⏰ 7am-3pm) Stocks an astounding 39 dishes, displayed in rows of stainless-steels pots out front.

Jay Tiw (☎ 0 81526 4487; Th Saengchuto; dishes 20-30B; ⏰ 7am-3pm) A block away from Kok Kaat, towards the city centre, Jay Tiw boasts only 19 dishes, but emphasises quality over quantity. To reach both restaurants, hop on any *sǎwngthǎew* heading south along Th Saengchuto and ask to get off at *sǎalaa klaang jangwàt* (City Hall). The restaurants are more or less across the street – just look for the rows of stainless steel pots.

ENTERTAINMENT

If boat-bound karaoke is not your thing, head to the northern end of the floating restaurant strip where clubs with names like Discovery 70 Club and Fine Thanks have brought a whiff of urban sophistication to Kanchanaburi.

SLEEPING

The most scenic places to stay are the floating guesthouses along the river, but these are also the loudest, thanks to the nightly disco and karaoke barges. A pair of good earplugs and a night of imbibing will help to block out the bass. A *sǎamláw* (three-wheeled pedicab) or motorcycle taxi from the bus or train stations to the river area and most guesthouses should cost from 20B to 30B, although many guesthouses and hotels also offer a pick-up service.

Royal River Kwai Resort & Spa (☎ 0 3465 3297; www .royalriverkwairesort.com; Th Kanchanaburi-Sai Yok; d from 1900B; 🖳 🛏) Catching the design bug, Royal River sports the global Zen look and a riverside pool amid landscaped grounds about 3km from town.

Kasem Island Resort (☎ 0 3451 3359; in Bangkok 0 2255 3604; d 1050-1700B; 🖳 🛏) Sitting on an island in the middle of Mae Nam Mae Khlong, about 200m from Th Chukkadon, Kasem Island Resort has tastefully designed thatched cottages and house rafts. There are facilities for swimming, fishing and rafting, as well as an outdoor bar and restaurant. The resort has an office near Tha Chukkadon where you can arrange a free shuttle boat out to the island.

Ploy Guesthouse (☎ 0 3451 5804; www.ploygh.com; 79/2 Th Mae Nam Khwae; d 650-850B; 🖳) Although views of the river are slim, Ploy more than makes up for it with modern rooms and a unique garden atmosphere, and all this for half the price you'd pay back in Bangkok.

Pong Phen Guesthouse (☎ 0 3451 2981; www.phong pen.com; 5 Soi Bangladesh, off Th Mae Nam Khwae; d 330-800B;

KANCHANABURI KNOWLEDGE

Try as you might, you will find few Thais who have ever heard of the River Kwai. The river over which the Death Railway trundled is pronounced much like 'quack' without the '-ck'. If spelled phonetically, 'Kwai' should be 'Khwae'. In the mispronounced river live *plaa yìisòk*, the most common edible fish in this area and the model for the city's attractive fish-shaped street signs.

⚡ ⚡) These modern rooms set in a lush garden have more creature comforts than most budget options.

Sam's River Rafthouse (☎ 0 3462 4231; www.sams guesthouse.com; 48 Th Rong Hip Oi; d 300-400B; ⚡) Two aged but well-kept rafts sit on the river, while cheaper rooms inland escape the noise.

Blue Star Guest House (☎ 0 3451 2161; www.blue star-guesthouse.com; 241 Th Mae Nam Khwae; d 150-650B; ⚡) From the inside these rooms have a funky feel with faux stone walls and more-than-spartan furnishings. Step outside and the rows of A-frame stilted wooden houses are divided by a walkway; throw in some furry midgets, Luke and Leia and you could be in an Ewok village.

Sugar Cane Guest House (☎ 0 3462 4520; www.sugar caneguesthouse.com; 22 Soi Pakistan, off Th Mae Nam Khwae; d 150-550B; ⚡) Sugar Cane boasts some of the better raft-style accommodation, with rooms on a raft with a wide communal balcony, as well as landlocked bungalows and a social riverside restaurant.

KHAO YAI NATIONAL PARK

อุทยานแห่งชาติเขาใหญ่

Cool and lush, Khao Yai National Park is an easy escape into the primordial jungle. The 2168 sq km park, part of a Unesco World Heritage Site, spans five forest types, from rainforest to monsoon, and is the primary residence of tigers, elephants, gibbons, tropical birds and audible, yet invisible, insects. Like a diligent baker, the jungle wakes up with the dawn, making a different kind of morning noise from the city sounds: chirping insects, hooting monkeys, whooping macaques and anonymous shrieks and trills. Khao Yai is a major birding destination with large flocks of hornbills and several migrators, including the flycatcher from Europe. Caves in the park are the preferred resting place for wrinkle-lipped bats. In the grasslands, batik-printed butterflies dissect flowers with their surgical tongues.

The park has several accessible trails for self-tours, but birders or animal trackers should consider hiring a jungle guide to increase their appreciation of the environment and to spot more than the tree-swinging gibbons and blood-sucking leeches (the rainy season is the worst time for the latter). In total, there are 12 maintained trails criss-crossing

the entire park; not ideal if you want to walk end to end. Access to transport is another reason why a tour might be more convenient, although Thai visitors with cars are usually happy to pick up pedestrians.

A two-hour walk from the park headquarters leads to the Nong Pak Chee observation tower, which is a good early-morning spot for seeing insect-feeding birds, thirsty elephants and sambar deer. Reservations need to be made at the visitors' centre. Spotting the park's reclusive tigers and elephants isn't as common as adoring the frothy waterfalls that drain the peaks of the Big Mountain. The park's centrepiece is Nam Tok Haew Suwat (Haew Suwat Falls), a 25m-high cascade that is a roaring artery in the rainy season. Nam Tok Haew Narok (Haew Narok Falls) is its larger cousin with three pooling tiers and a towering 150m drop.

The cool highlands around Khao Yai are also home to a nascent wine industry. These have been dubbed the 'New Latitude' wines because grapes are not normally grown between the 14th and 18th parallels. PB Valley Khao Yai Winery (☎ 0 3622 7328; www.khaoyaiwinery.com; 102 Moo 5, Phaya Yen, Pak Chong; tastings 150B, winery day tour incl meal 700B; ⏰ 7.30am-4.30pm) and GranMonte (☎ 0 3622 7334; www.granmonte.com; 52 Th Phansuk-Kud Khala) are among the wine makers managing to coax shiraz and chenin blanc grapes from the relatively tropical climate.

The best time to visit the park is in the dry season (December to June), but during the rainy season river rafting and waterfall spotting will be more dramatic. Most guest-

---

TRANSPORT: KHAO YAI NATIONAL PARK

Distance from Bangkok 196km

Direction Northeast

Travel Time Three hours

Bus From Bangkok's Northern & Northeastern Bus Terminal (Mo Chit; ☎ 0 2936 2841-8; Map pp124–5), take a bus to Pak Chong (ordinary/air-con 95/160B, every 30 minutes from 5am to 10pm). From Pak Chong, take a *săwngthǎew* (15B, from 6am to 5pm) to the entrance gate of the park.

Getting Around From the entrance gate it's possible to charter a vehicle (400B) or flag a passing car for a ride to the visitors' centre. Chartered transportation within the park is available via the visitors centre; however, hitchhiking not an uncommon way to get around here..

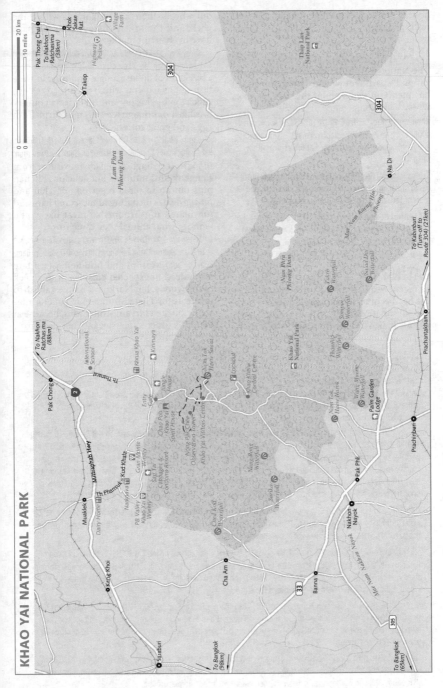

KHAO YAI NATIONAL PARK

lonelyplanet.com

EXCURSIONS KHAO YAI NATIONAL PARK

247

houses and lodges arrange jungle treks and rafting tours.

INFORMATION

The National Park, Wildlife & Plant Conservation Department website (www.dnp.go.th) has plenty of detail about the park, as does www.thaibirding.com.

Khao Yai Visitors Centre (☎ 0 81877 3127; admission 400B; ☼ 8am-6pm) Topographical maps, hiking advice, and jungle guides can be arranged at this centre within the park.

Sarika Nature Trips (☎ 0 81643 6317) This small outfit based in Nakorn Nayok offers nature and wildlife-based tours of the national park and surrounding areas.

TAT Central Region Office 8 (☎ 0 3731 2282; tatnayok@tat.or.th; 182/88 Moo 1, Th Suwannason, Nakhon Nayok) Information on guides and tours in Khao Yai.

EATING

In recent years, the area surrounding Khao Yai has become something of a minor culinary destination, with cuisines ranging from upscale Italian to Thai-Muslim. If you're without wheels, there are restaurants within the park, and the towns surrounding the park have lively night markets.

Dairy Home (☎ 0 4432 2230; www.dairyhome.co.th; Km 144, Th Mitraphap, Muak Lek; mains 50-70B; ☼ 9am-8pm) If a weekend of intense jungle exploring or wine tasting has left you with a need for Western eats, stop by this organic dairy for a country breakfast of homemade sausages, farm-fresh eggs and good coffee.

Khrua Khao Yai (☎ 0 4429 7138; Km 13.5, Th Thanarat, Pak Chong; mains 50-150B; ☼ 9am-8pm Sun-Thu, 9am-10pm Fri & Sat) Exceedingly popular with visitors from Bangkok, this informal but delicious kitchen puts out an inspired repertoire of Thai and *faràng* dishes including home-cured ham and marinated mushrooms so meat-like you'll wonder what animal they came from.

Narknava (☎ 0 81924 7091; www.narknavafarm.net; Km 8, Th Phansuk-Kud Khala, Pak Chong; mains 50-150B; ☼ 8am-7pm Tue-Sun) Muslim and Middle Eastern fare are indeed unexpected cuisines in this neck of the woods, but Narknava is an established favourite for Thai visitors seeking out its infamous chicken biryani – infamous, because at 100B it's super-expensive by Thai standards.

THEME PARKS

Just outside Bangkok are theme park playgrounds delivering everything from pachyderm dances to modern amusement parks. With or without kids some of these can be quite a lot of fun. Tour operators service all of these places, but it's just as easy and cheaper to get your hotel to write the name and flag down one of Bangkok's cheap taxis, or check their websites for other options.

Ancient City (Muang Boran; ☎ 0 2709 1644; www.ancientcity.com; 296/1 Th Sukhumvit, Samut Prakan; adult/child 300/200B; ☼ 8am-5pm) Billed as the world's largest open-air museum, the Ancient City covers more than 80 hectares of peaceful countryside scattered with 109 scaled-down facsimiles of many of the kingdom's most famous monuments. Visions of Las Vegas and its corny replicas of world treasures might spring to mind, but the Ancient City has architectural integrity and is a preservation site for classical buildings and art forms. It's a great place for long, undistracted bicycle rides (rental from the admission office is 50B), as it's usually quiet and never crowded.

Dream World (☎ 0 2533 1152; www.dreamworld-th.com; Km 7 Rangsit-Nakorn Nayok, Thanya Buri; combination ticket 1000B; ☼ 10am-5pm Mon-Fri, 10am-7pm public holidays) No-excuses fun park with roller coasters, paddle boats, stunt shows, go-carts and an artificial snow world.

Samphran Elephant Ground & Zoo (☎ 0 2295 2938; www.elephantshow.com; Km 30 Th Phetkasem, Nakhorn Pathom; adult/child 450/250B; ☼ 8.30am-6pm) Samphran is a nine-hectare zoo with elephant roundups, crocodile shows and an orchid nursery. On Labour Day (1 May), the annual Elephant Queen Parade is held for heavy-set women who can display the girth and the elegance of the elephant.

Samut Prakan Crocodile Farm & Zoo (☎ 0 2703 4891; Samut Prakan; adult/child 300/200B; ☼ 7am-6pm) More than 30,000 crocs who spend their time wallowing in mud. It also harbours elephants, monkeys and snakes. The farm has trained-animal shows, including croc wrestling and elephant performances, and the reptiles get their dinner between 4pm and 5pm.

Siam Park City (☎ 0 2919 7200; www.siamparkcity.com; 99 Th Serithai, Khannayao; water park 100-200B; combination ticket 500B; ☼ 10am-6pm Mon-Fri, 9am-7pm Sat & Sun) A water park with artificial waves, giant water slides and a flow pool. There is also an amusement park, small zoo and playground.

SLEEPING

Golf courses and upscale resorts ring the perimeter of the park. Pak Chong is the primary base-camp town, but Nakhon Nayok and Prachinburi are beginning to develop more low-key options. Most accommodation can arrange jungle tours and transport to the park.

Jungle House (☎ 0 4429 7183; www.junglehousehotel .com; 21/5 Th Thanarat, Km 19.5, Pak Chong; d 600-1200B; ⊠) An old favourite with lots of extras to keep kids entertained. Loft rooms encourage monkeylike agility.

Palm Garden Lodge (☎ 0 9989 4470; www.palmgalo .com; Prachinburi; r 400-1200B; ⊠) Woodsy gardens and rustic bungalows keep you in touch with nature. The lodge is 7km south of the park's southern entrance, near Ban Kon Khuang on Hwy 33, and arranges park tours.

Park Lodging (☎ 0 2562 0760; Khao Yai Visitors Centre) Within the park, there are three types of accommodation: villas sleeping 12 people (2400B), cabins for two (800B) and camping (150B per person with tents and bedding included).

Sap Tai Cabbages & Condoms Resort (☎ 0 3622 7065; www.pda.or.th/saptai/; 98 Moo 6, Th Phaya Yen, Pak Chong; d 1000-2200B; ⊠ ⊒) This resort, with a city hotel ambience, is the sister facility of the Bangkok restaurant (p167) with the same name that supports a great cause: HIV/AIDS education and prevention.

Village Farm (☎ 0 4422 8407-8; www.villagefarm.co.th; 103 Moo 7, Tambon Thaisamakee, Wan Nam Kheo, Nakhon Ratchasima; d 2200-9000B; ⊠ ⊒) This micro-winery is the closest thing Thailand has to a French village. Restored teak villas are cradled in 32 hectares of farmland, and the resort includes a spa and restaurant.

Kirimaya (☎ 0 4442 6099; www.kirimaya.com; 1/3 Moo 6, Th Thanarat, Pak Chong; r 9000-33,000B; ⊠ ⊒) A stunning setting and amenities including tented villas with a private indoor pool and personal golf cart have seen Kirimaya recently make a *Conde Nast Traveler* list of top 10 new hotels of the world.

TRANSPORT

Bangkok may seem chaotic and impenetrable at first but, regular traffic jams notwithstanding, its transport system works reasonably well and is not nearly as dire as legend would have it. And as urban railways continue to be built, it should keep getting better. Flights, tours and rail tickets can be booked online at www .lonelyplanet.com/travel_services.

AIR

Bangkok is a major Southeast Asian air hub, and dozens of airlines fly regularly between the Thai capital and Europe, Asia, the USA and Australia. Thailand's national carrier is Thai Airways International (THAI; www.thaiair.com), which also operates a number of domestic air routes.

Airlines
DOMESTIC

Thailand has several airlines – both full service and low cost – competing on a large network of domestic routes. All of those listed here also fly regional international routes. Nok Air, Orient Thai, PB Air and Thai Air Asia are budget airlines, Thai Airways is full service and Bangkok Airways is somewhere in between. Big discounts are often available online, and most deal only in e-tickets, so there's no reason to schlep out to their distant offices to book a fare; use a travel agent, the internet or the phone. For last-minute fares, buy at the departures level in the relevant airport.

Bangkok Airways (PG; ☎ 1771 or 0 2265 5555; www .bangkokair.com)

Nok Air (OX; ☎ 1318; www.nokair.com)

PB Air (9Q; ☎ 0 2261 0222; www.pbair.com)

THINGS CHANGE...

The information in this chapter is particularly vulnerable to change. Check directly with the airline or a travel agent to make sure you understand how a fare (and ticket you may buy) works, and be aware of the security requirements for international travel. Shop carefully. The details given in this chapter should be regarded as pointers and are not a substitute for your own careful, up-to-date research.

Thai Air Asia (AK; ☎ 0 2515 9999; www.airasia.com)

Thai Airways International (TG; ☎ 0 2232 8000; www .thaiair.com)

INTERNATIONAL
Some of the airlines flying to Thailand, with offices where they exist.

Air Asia (AK; ☎ 0 2515 9999; www.airasia.com)

Air Canada (AC; Map pp108–9; ☎ 0 2670 0400; www .aircanada.ca; Suite 1708, Empire Tower, River Wing West, Th Sathon Tai, Yannawa, Sathon)

Air France (AF; Map pp108–9; ☎ 0 2635 1191; www .airfrance.com; 20th fl, Vorawat Bldg, 849 Th Silom)

Air India (AI; Map pp118–19; ☎ 0 2653 2288; www .airindia.com; 18th fl, One Pacific Pl, 140 Th Sukhumvit)

Air New Zealand (NZ; Map pp108–9; ☎ 0 2235 8280; www.airnewzealand.com; ITF Tower, 11/4 Th Silom)

Cathay Pacific Airways (CX; Map pp98–9; ☎ 0 2263 0606; www.cathaypacific.com; 11th fl, Ploenchit Tower, 898 Th Ploenchit)

China Airlines (CI; Map pp98–9; ☎ 0 2250 9898; www .china-airlines.com; 4th fl, Peninsula Plaza, 153 Th Ratchadamri)

Garuda Indonesia (GA; Map p112; ☎ 0 2679 7371-2; www.garuda-indonesia.com; 27th fl, Lumphini Tower, 1168/77 Th Phra Ram IV)

Japan Airlines (JL; ☎ 0 2649 9500; www.jal.co.jp/en/; 12th fl, Nantawan Bldg, 161 Th Ratchadamri, Lumphini)

Jetstar (☎ 0 2267 5125; www.jetstar.com)

KLM Royal Dutch Airlines (KL; Map pp108–9; ☎ 0 2635 2400; www.klm.com; 20th fl, Vorawat Bldg, 849 Th Silom)

Lao Airlines (QV; Map pp118–19; ☎ 0 2664 0661; 10th fl, 253 Tower, 253 Soi Asoke, Th Sukhumvit)

Lufthansa Airlines (LH; Map pp118–19; ☎ 0 2264 2400; www.lufthansa.com; 18th fl, Q House Asoke Bldg, 66 Soi 21, Th Sukhumvit)

Malaysia Airlines (MH; Map pp98–9; ☎ 0 2263 0565; www.malaysiaairlines.com; 20th fl, Ploenchit Tower, 898 Th Ploenchit)

Qantas Airways (QF; ☎ 0 2627 1701; www.qantas .com.au)

Singapore Airlines (SQ; Map p112; ☎ 0 2353 6000; www.singaporeair.com; 12th fl, Silom Center Bldg, 2 Th Silom)

CLIMATE CHANGE & TRAVEL

Climate change is a serious threat to the ecosystems that humans rely upon, and air travel is the fastest-growing contributor to the problem. Lonely Planet regards travel, overall, as a global benefit, but believes we all have a responsibility to limit our personal impact on global warming.

Flying & Climate Change

Pretty much every form of motorised travel generates CO_2 (the main cause of human-induced climate change), but planes are far and away the worst offenders, not just because of the sheer distances they allow us to travel, but because they release greenhouse gases high into the atmosphere. The statistics are frightening: two people taking a return flight between Europe and the US will contribute as much to climate change as an average household's gas and electricity consumption over a whole year.

Carbon Offset Schemes

Climatecare.org and other websites use 'carbon calculators' that allow travellers to offset the level of greenhouse gases they are responsible for with financial contributions to sustainable travel schemes that reduce global warming – including projects in India, Honduras, Kazakhstan and Uganda.

Lonely Planet, together with Rough Guides and other concerned partners in the travel industry, support the carbon offset scheme run by climatecare.org. Lonely Planet offsets all of its staff and author air travel.

For more information check out our website: www.lonelyplanet.com.

Swiss (LX; ☎ 0 2204 7744; www.swiss.com; 18th fl, Q House Asoke Bldg, 66 Soi 21, Th Sukhumvit)

United Airlines (UA; Map pp98–9; ☎ 0 2253 0558; www.unitedairlines.co.th; 14th fl, Sindhorn Bldg, 130-132 Th Withayu)

Airports

Bangkok has two main airports. Opened in late 2006, Suvarnabhumi International Airport (☎ 0 2132 1888; www2.airportthai.co.th) is the vast glass-and-concrete construction 30km east of central Bangkok that acts as the main international airport. After rather a lot of teething problems, at most times Suvarnabhumi

THE HAND LUGGAGE NAZIS OF SUVARNABHUMI

Be warned! Flying from Suvarnabhumi International Airport can be an experience in loss if you carry any liquids in your hand luggage. Bottles bought inside the airport and sealed in a duty free bag will be okay, but everything else will be confiscated. That means your sun cream, moisturiser, toothpaste – look for the huge bags full of stuff being picked over by security staff near the X-ray checks. Some airlines even take 3ml vials of insulin for 'safekeeping', offering to deliver them to your seat when required during the flight. Anything liquid you don't want to lose, check it in or leave it at home.

(pronounced su-wan-a-poom) works fairly efficiently. The unofficial www.bangkokairportonline.com site has up-to-date transport information and real-time details of airport arrivals and departures. Left-luggage facilities (☉ 24 hr) are available on Level 2, beside the helpful TAT office (☎ 0 2134 4077; ☉ 24 hr). For airport hotels, see p220.

Don Muang Airport (Map pp124–5; ☎ 0 2535 1111; www2.airportthai.co.th) is 25km north of the city centre and, after being temporarily retired, it now serves some, but not all, domestic routes.

Getting to/from Don Muang you can take a taxi or bus. Taking a taxi is the fastest and most comfortable option, and fares at most times will be a very reasonable 200B to 350B depending on the traffic and how far you're going. Taxis depart from outside the arrivals hall, and there is a 50B airport charge added to the meter fare, plus expressway tolls.

Slow, crowded public bus 59 stops on the highway in front of the airport and carries on to Banglamphu, passing Th Khao San and the Democracy Monument; luggage is not allowed. Air-con buses are faster, and you might actually get a seat. Useful air-con routes include:

Bus 29 Northern Bus Terminal, Victory Monument, Siam Sq and Hualamphong train station

Bus 510 Victory Monument, Southern Bus Terminal

Bus 513 Th Sukhumvit, Eastern Bus Terminal

TRANSPORT GETTING INTO TOWN FROM SUVARNABHUMI

GETTING INTO TOWN FROM SUVARNABHUMI

Airport Bus

Airport Express runs four useful routes between Suvarnabhumi and Bangkok city. They operate from 5am to midnight for a flat 150B fare, meaning a taxi will be a comparable price if there are two people heading to central Bangkok, but more expensive if you're going to Banglamphu. The Airport Express counter is near entrance 8 on level 1. Routes stop at Skytrain stations, major hotels and other landmarks.

AE-1 to Silom (by expressway). Via Pratunam, Central World, Ratchadamri Skytrain, Lumphini Park, Th Saladaeng, Patpong, Plaza Hotel and others.

AE-2 to Banglamphu (by expressway). Via Th Phetchaburi Soi 30, Democracy Monument, Royal Hotel, Th Phra Athit, Th Phra Sumen, Th Khao San.

AE-3 to Sukhumvit Soi 52, Eastern Bus Terminal, Soi 34, 24, 20, 18, 10, 6, Central Chidlom, Central World, Soi Nana.

AE-4 to Hualamphong train station Via Victory Monument, Phayathai Skytrain, Siam Sq, MBK, Chulalongkorn University.

Local Transport

With more time and less money, you could take the Skytrain to On Nut (40B), then from near the market entrance opposite Tesco take the either bus 552 (every 20 minutes or so, 35B) or the BTS minivan (departs when full, 25B) to the airport.

Several other air-con local buses serve Suvarnabhumi for a 35B flat fare. Departures are every 20 minutes or so. Most useful are:

Bus 551 Siam Paragon Via Victory Monument

Bus 552 Klong Toei Via Sukumvit 101 and On Nut Skytrain

Buses 554 & 555 Don Muang Airport

Bus 556 Southern Bus Terminal, via Democracy Monument (for Th Khao San) and Thammasat University.

Intercity buses to places including Pattaya, Rayong and Trat stop at the Public Transportation Centre, reached via a free shuttle from the airport.

Minivan

If you are heading to the airport from Banglamphu, the hotels and guesthouses can book you on air-con minivans. These pick up from hotels and guesthouses and cost about 180B per person (you're better off using the AE bus).

Skytrain

From early 2009 (insha'Allah) a new Skytrain line will run from downstairs at the airport to a huge new City Air Terminal in central Bangkok, near Soi Asoke and Th Phetchaburi. There will be an express service (the pink line) that will take 15 minutes, and a local service (the red line) taking 27 minutes.

How useful this service will be depends on whether you're travelling alone and how far your hotel is from the City Air Terminal. Except during the worst traffic, a taxi covers the same trip in about 35 minutes for about 200B to 250B.

Taxi & Limousine

Ignore the touts and all the yellow signs pointing you to 'limousines' (actually cars costing 700B flat), walk outside on the arrivals level and join the fast-moving queue for a public taxi. Cabs booked through this desk should always use their meter, but they often try their luck so insist by saying 'meter, please'. You must also pay a 50B official airport surcharge and reimburse drivers for any toll charges (up to 60B); drivers will always ask your permission to use the tollway. Depending on traffic, a taxi to Asoke should cost 200B to 250B, Silom 300B to 350B and Banglamphu 350B to 425B. Fares are per vehicle, not per person. Break big notes before you leave the airport.

BOAT

Although many of Bangkok's *khlong* have been paved over, there is still plenty of transport along and across the Chao Phraya and up adjoining canals.

River Ferries

The Chao Phraya Express Boat Co (☎ 0 2623 6001; www.chaophrayaboat.co.th) operates the main ferry service along the Chao Phraya. The central pier is known as Sathorn, Saphan Taksin or sometimes Central Pier, and connects to the Skytrain's Saphan Taksin station. Each pier is numbered from Sathorn, and ferries run four stops south to Wat Ratchasingkhon (S4), though tourists rarely use these. Much more useful are the services running to and from Nonthaburi (N30) in northern Bangkok; the maps in this book show the piers and their numbers. Fares are cheap and differ by distance from 10B to 34B. There are four different services, differentiated by the colour of the flags on their roofs. To avoid an unwanted trip halfway to Nonthaburi be sure to keep an eye on those flags.

Local Line (no flag) The all-stops service, operating every 15 to 20 minutes mornings and evenings.

Orange Express Stops at N1, N3, N4, N5, N6, N8, N9, N10, N12, N13, N15, N18, N21, N22, N24, N30. The most common service, departing every five to 20 minutes depending on the time of day.

Yellow Express Stops at N3, N5, N10, N12, N15, N22, N24, N30. Departing every five to 20 minutes depending on the time of day.

Blue Express Nonthaburi express, stopping N10 and N30 only. Just a couple of services in the morning 7am to 7.30am and evening at 5.35pm and 6.05pm.

A special tourist boat runs between Phra Athit and Sathorn every 30 minutes between 9.30am and 3pm. A one-day pass for unlimited travel costs 120B. There is also a boat that connects Tha Phra Athit with the Royal Barges Museum in Thonburi every hour from 10am to 3.35pm for 50B.

All this is best illustrated in the small, folding maps that detail routes, prices and times and are sometimes available at ferry piers – ask for one – or on boards at the piers.

There are also dozens of cross-river ferries, which charge 3.50B and run every few minutes until late at night.

Khlong Boats

Canal taxi boats run along Khlong Saen Saep (Banglamphu to Ramkhamhaeng) and are an easy way to get from Banglamphu to Jim Thompson's House, the Siam Sq shopping centres (get off at Th Hua Chang for both), and other points further east along Sukhumvit – after a mandatory change of boat at Tha Pratunam. These boats are mostly used by daily commuters and pull into the piers for just a few seconds – jump straight on or you'll be left behind. Fares range from 7B to 20B.

BUS

Bangkok's public buses are a cheap if not always comfortable way to get around the city. They are run by the Bangkok Mass Transit Authority (☎ 0 2246 4262; www.bmta.co.th), which has a website with detailed information on bus routes. Air-con fares typically start at 10B or 12B and increase depending on distance. Fares for ordinary (fan-con) buses start at 7B or 8B. Most of the bus lines run between 5am and 10pm or 11pm, except for the 'all-night' buses, which run from 3am or 4am to midmorning.

Bangkok Bus Map by Roadway, available at Asia Books (p139) and some 7-Eleven stores, is the most up-to-date route map available.

CAR

Renting a car just to drive around Bangkok is not a good idea. Parking is impossible, traffic is frustrating, road rules can be mysterious and the alternative – taxis – are cheap and ubiquitous. But if you still want to give it a go, all the big car-hire companies have offices in Bangkok and at Suvarnabhumi airport. Rates start at around 1500B per day for a small car. An International Driving Permit and passport are required for all rentals. Most can also provide drivers (600B per day, 8am to 6pm), which gives local drivers a job and means you don't have to navigate, park or deal with overzealous police.

Reliable car-rental companies include:

Avis (☎ 0 2255 5300; www.avisthailand.com; 2/12 Th Withayu), also a branch at Grand Hyatt Erawan Hotel (Map pp98–9).

Budget (Map pp124–5; ☎ 0 2203 9200; www.budget .co.th; 19/23 Bldg A, Royal City Ave, Th Phetburi Tat Mai)

Hertz (Map pp98–9; ☎ 0 2654 1105; www.hertz.com; M Thai Tower, All Seasons Pl, 87 Th Withayu)

METRO (SUBWAY)

Bangkok's first underground railway line is operated by the Metropolitan Rapid Transit Authority (MRTA; www.mrta.co.th) and is known locally as *rót fai tâi din* or 'Metro' – no-one understands 'subway'. Recently announced plans see a series of lines running more than 300km, but for now the 20km Blue Line runs from Hualamphong Railway Station north to Bang Sue and features 18 stations. Fares cost 15B to 40B; child and concession fares can be bought at ticket windows. Trains run every seven minutes from 6am to midnight, more frequently between 6am and 9am and from 4.30pm to 7.30pm.

The Metro is more useful to residents than visitors, unless you're staying in the lower Sukhumvit area. Useful stations (from north to south) include Kamphaeng Phet and Bang Sue for Chatuchak Weekend Market; Thailand Cultural Centre; Sukhumvit, where it links to Asoke Skytrain station; Khlong Toei for the market; Lumphini Park; Silom (with access to Sala Daeng Skytrain station); and Hualamphong train station and Chinatown at its southern end.

SKYTRAIN (BTS)

The BTS Skytrain (☎ 0 2617 7340; www.bts.co.th) allows you to soar above Bangkok's legendary traffic jams in air-conditioned comfort. Known by locals as 'BTS' or *rót fai fáa* (literally 'train sky'), services are fast, efficient and relatively cheap, although rush hour can be a squeeze. Fares range from 15B to 40B, and trains run from 6am to midnight. Ticket machines accept coins and notes (when they're working), or pick up change at the staffed kiosks. One-day (120B) passes are available, but the rechargeable cards (130B, with 100B travel and 30B card deposit) are more flexible. There are two Skytrain lines, which are well represented on free tourist maps available at most stations.

Silom Line

Starting at National Stadium on Th Phra Ram I in central Bangkok, it passes the Siam interchange station and bends around via the eastern section of Th Silom and western end of Th Sathon to finish (for now) at Saphan Taksin, on the river near the intersection of Th Charoen Krung and Th Sathon. The final stop connects to the Chao Phraya river ferries (p253). A long-awaited extension west across Saphan Taksin is due to come online in 2009.

Sukhumvit Line

Running from On Nut, at distant Soi 81 of Th Sukhumvit, this line runs west right along Th Sukhumvit, connecting to the Metro at Asoke. It continues into the shopping and commercial district and the main interchange station at Siam, where it meets the Silom BTS line. From here the line turns north up to Mo Chit, near Chatuchak Weekend Market. Five more stations are due to be built at the eastern end of the line, but don't hold your breath.

TAXI

Bangkok's thousands of brightly coloured taxis are some of the best value cabs on earth. Most are new, air-conditioned and have working seatbelts in the front seat, though less often in the back. You can flag them down almost anywhere in central Bangkok. The meter charge is 35B for the first 2km, then 4.50B for each of the next 10km, 5B for each kilometre from 13km to 20km and 5.50B per kilometre for any distance greater than 20km, plus a small standing charge in slow traffic. Freeway tolls – 25B to 70B depending on where you start – must be paid by the passenger. Because of high fuel prices, there is talk of raising taxi rates.

Taxi Radio (☎ 1681; www.taxiradio.co.th) and other 24-hour 'phone-a-cab' services are available for 20B above the metered fare.

During the morning and afternoon rush hours taxis might refuse to go to certain destinations; if this happens, just try another cab. Around Th Khao San and other tourist areas, some cabbies might refuse to use the meter and try to charge a flat fee; if this happens just walk away and find another cab.

You can hire a taxi all day for 1500B to 2000B, depending on how much driving is involved. Taxis can also be hired for trips to Pattaya (1500B), Hua Hin (2300B) and Phetchaburi (1700B), among others; see www.taxiradio.co.th for fares.

Motorcycle Taxi

Motorcycle taxis serve two purposes in Bangkok. Most commonly and popularly they form an integral part of the public transport network, running from the corner of a main thoroughfare, such as Th Sukhumvit, to the far ends of *soi* (lanes) that run off that thoroughfare. Riders wear coloured, numbered vests and gather at either end of their *soi*, usually charging about 10B for the trip (without a helmet unless you ask).

Their other purpose is as a means of beating the traffic. You tell your rider where you want to go, negotiate a price (from 20B for a short trip up to about 100B going across town), strap on the helmet (they will insist for longer trips) and say a prayer to whichever god you're into. Drivers range from responsible to kamikaze, but the average trip involves some time on the wrong side of the road and several near-death experiences. It's the sort of white-knuckle ride you'd pay good money for at Disneyland, but is all in a day's work for these riders. Comfort yourself in the knowledge that there are good hospitals nearby.

TÚK-TÚK

Bangkok's iconic *túk-túk* (like motorised rickshaws) are used by Thais for short hops not worth paying the taxi flag fall for. For foreigners, however, these emphysema-inducing machines are notorious for taking little 'detours' to commission-paying gem and silk shops and massage parlours. En route to 'special' temples, you'll meet 'helpful' locals who will steer you to even more rip-off opportunities. See p265 for more on *túk-túk* scams, and ignore anyone offering too-good-to-be-true 10B trips.

The other problem is that *túk-túk* drivers always ask too much from tourists (expat *faràng* never use them). Expect to be quoted a 100B fare, if not more, for even the shortest trip. Still, it's an iconic experience so it's worth bargaining them down to about 40B for a short trip, preferably at night when the pollution (hopefully) won't be quite so bad. Once you've done it, you'll find taxis are cheaper, cleaner, cooler and quieter.

BUSINESS HOURS

Most government offices are open from 8.30am to 4.30pm Monday to Friday, but close from noon to 1pm for lunch. In recent years the government has pushed for a 'no lunch closing' policy – you might even see signs posted to this effect – but in reality government employees pay no attention and you will almost surely be disappointed if you expect to get anything done between noon and 1pm.

Regular bank hours in Bangkok are 8.30am to 3.30pm Monday to Friday, but several banks have special foreign-exchange offices that are open longer hours (generally from 8.30am to 8pm), including weekends in touristy areas. Note that all government offices and banks are closed on public holidays (see p260).

Commercial businesses usually operate between 8.30am and 5pm Monday to Friday and sometimes Saturday morning as well. Larger shops usually open from 10am to 6.30pm or 7pm, but the big malls are open later (until 9pm or 10pm) and smaller shops may open earlier and close later. Hours for restaurants and cafés vary greatly. Some local Thai places open as early as 7am, while bigger places usually open around 11am and still others are open in the evenings only. Some close as early as 9pm and others stay open all night. Bars, by law, can't open before 4pm and must close by 1am. This, however, seems to be as typically flexible as many Thai laws.

CHILDREN

Thais love children and in many instances will shower attention on your offspring, who will find ready playmates among their Thai counterparts and a temporary nanny service at practically every stop.

For the most part, parents needn't worry too much about health concerns. Aside from the usual common sense precautions (drinking lots of water, washing hands etc), it's worth warning children specifically to keep their hands off the local *soi* (lane) dog populace; while rare in Bangkok, rabies is relatively common in Thailand.

Nappies (diapers), formula and other infant requirements are available at Bangkok supermarkets, pharmacies and convenience stores.

Check out Lonely Planet's *Travel With Children* for further advice, and see p248 for a list of kid-friendly attractions.

CLIMATE

At the centre of the flat, humid Mae Nam Chao Phraya delta, Bangkok sits at the same latitude as Khartoum and Guatemala City, and can be as hot as the former and as wet as the latter.

The southwest monsoon arrives between May and July and lasts into November. This is followed by a dry period from around November to May, which begins with lower relative temperatures until mid-February (because of the influence of the northeast monsoon, which bypasses this part of Thailand but results in cool breezes), followed by much higher relative temperatures from March to May. It usually rains most during August and September, though floods in early October may find you in hip-deep water in certain parts of the city. An umbrella can be invaluable – a raincoat will just make you hot.

It's worth remembering that we're talking about the weather here, a temperamental beast if ever there was one. So all the dates above are flexible. In 2008, for example, Bangkok was flooded by a major storm in normally dry January, and the cool season stretched well into March.

For recommendations on the best times to visit Bangkok see p12; for a handy interactive weather map for Bangkok and the rest of Thailand, see www.travelfish.org/country/thailand.

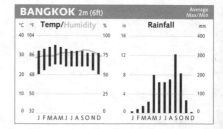

BANGKOK 2m (6ft)   Average Max/Min

COURSES

You can learn a lot in Bangkok. In half a day you could learn enough to impress your friends with a firey home-cooked Thai meal; for recommended cooking courses see the boxed text, p158. Taking a course in traditional massage will undoubtedly be well received by your special friends or, if there's someone you don't like, then a week in a Muay Thai school might help. With more time you could even learn how to talk your way out of trouble.

Language

Tuition at most Thai language schools averages around 100B to 200B per hour for group classes, more for private tutoring. We recommend the following:

AAA Thai Language Center (Map pp98–9; ☎ 0 2655 5629; www.aaathai.com; 6th fl, 29 Vanissa Bldg, Th Chitlom, Pathumwan; 🚇 Chitlom) Opened by a group of experienced Thai language teachers from other schools, good-value AAA Thai has a loyal following.

AUA Language Center (Map pp98–9; ☎ 0 2252 8170; www.auathai.com; 179 Th Ratchadamri) The most intensive language course in Bangkok, with rolling classes for listening only, from 7am to 8pm Monday to Friday; go when you like.

Thailish Language School (Map pp118–19; ☎ 0 2258 6846; www.thailanguageschool.com; 427 Th Sukhumvit, btwn Sois 21 & 23; 🚇 Asoke; Ⓜ Sukhumvit) This small, personal school looks like an antique shop and has private or small-group classes concentrating on conversation.

Meditation & Massage

Most Buddhist study centres in Bangkok specialise in *vipassana* (insight) meditation. Dharma Thai (www.dhammathai.org) has a rundown on several prominent wat and meditation centres, or speak to the World Fellowship of Buddhists (WFB; Map pp118–19; ☎ 0 2661 1284; www.wfb-hq.org; 616 Benjasiri Park, Soi 24, Th Sukhumvit; 🕙 8.30am-4.30pm Mon-Fri; 🚇 Phrom Phong), which also hosts occasional meditation classes.

International Buddhist Meditation Center (Map p56; ☎ 0 2623 6326; www.mcu.ac.th/IBMC/; Vipassana Section Room 106, Mahachula Bldg, Wat Mahathat, Th Pra Chan) Holds regular lectures on Buddhist topics in English, and meditation classes.

Wat Mahathat (Map p56; ☎ 0 2222 6011; Section 5, Wat Mahathat, Tha Maharat; Ko Ratanakosin) Separate to the IBMC, the monks here practise meditation between 4am and 2pm most days, though call ahead to make sure

the English-speaking instructors are in town. You can stay in the wat, in basic dorms, or stay outside and visit for instruction.

Wat Pho Thai Traditional Massage School (Map p56; ☎ 0 2221 3686; www.watpomassage.com; Soi Phenphat 1, Th Maharat, Ko Ratanakosin) By far the best place to learn traditional massage. Courses are held at the school headquarters across from Wat Pho on Soi Phenphat, just off Th Maharat. A 30-hour course costs 8500B.

Muay Thai

Many foreigners come to Thailand to study *muay thai* (Thai boxing). Training regimens can be *extremely* strict. See www.muaythai .com for more information.

Fairtex Muay Thai Camp (☎ 0 2755 3329; www .muaythaifairtex.com; 99/8 Soi Boonthamanusorn, Th Theparak, Samut Prakan) Training from 500B a session to 7700B-a-week residence.

Sor Vorpin (☎ 0 2282 3551; www.thaiboxings.com; 13 Trok Kasap, Th Chakkaphong) Just around the corner from Th Khao San; offers daily and weekly training schedules for foreigners. More serious training is held at a second facility outside the city. A half-day costs 500B, the weekly rate is 2500B and a month is 9000B.

CUSTOMS REGULATIONS

The white-uniformed officers of Thai customs prohibit the import or export of the usual array of goods – porn, weapons, drugs – and if you're caught with drugs, in particular, expect life never to be the same again. Otherwise, they're quite reasonable. The usual 200 cigarettes or 250g of tobacco are allowed in without duty, along with 1L of wine or spirits. Ditto for electronic goods as long as you don't look like you're planning to sell them – best to leave your third and fourth laptops at home.

For information on currency import or export, see p263. For details on exporting Buddha images and other antiquities, see p129. For hours of fun reading other customs details (useful if you're planning on moving to Thailand), check out www.customs.go.th/Customs-Eng/indexEng.jsp.

DISCOUNT CARDS

The Th Khao San trade in fake student cards is still bubbling along 20 years after it began, which means unless you're prepared to dress in the black and white uniforms of Thai schools you can forget about student discounts in Bangkok.

Most of the major shopping centres around Siam Sq and Emporium offer a standard 5% off to tourists. To get it, you need a '5% off' card, which usually comes attached to the free tourist maps from the tourist booths around town. If you don't have one, don't fret. If you don't look Thai, in most cases the staff will ask if you are a tourist and, before you can nod, will have whipped out a spare card from under the counter. Once you've paid and had your discount, they'll take you to the VAT rebate office for a bit more saving.

ELECTRICITY

Electric current is 220V, 50 cycles. Electrical wall outlets are usually of the two-pin type. Some outlets accept plugs with two flat pins, and some will accept either flat or round pins. Any electrical supply shop will carry adaptors for international plugs, as well as voltage converters.

EMBASSIES

Some Bangkok embassies are listed here. For a full and regularly updated list, go to www .mfa.go.th/web/12.php and click through to Foreign Missions in Thailand. For Thai missions click through to About the Ministry.

Australia (Map p112; ☎ 02 344 6300; www.aust embassy.or.th; 37 Th Sathon Tai; Ⓜ Lumphini)

Cambodia (Map pp124–5; ☎ 0 2957 5851; 518/4 Th Pracha Uthit, Soi Ramkamhaeng 39; Wangthonglang)

Canada (Map p112; ☎ 0 2636 0540; geo.international .gc.ca/asia/bangkok; 15th fl, Abdulrahim Bldg, 990 Th Phra Ram IV, Lumphini; Ⓡ Saladaeng; Ⓜ Silom)

China (Map pp124–5; ☎ 0 2245 0088; www.china embassy.or.th; 57 Th Ratchadaphisek, Din Daeng; Ⓜ Thailand Cultural Centre)

EU (Map pp98–9; ☎ 0 2305 2600; www.deltha.ec .europa.eu; 19th fl, Kian Gwan House II, 1410/1 Th Withayu; Ⓡ Ploenchit)

France Embassy (Map pp108–9; ☎ 0 2266 8250-6; www.ambafrance-th.org; 35 Soi 36, Th Charoen Krung); Consulate (Map p112; ☎ 0 2287 1592; 29 Th Sathon Tai; Ⓜ Lumphini)

Germany (Map p112; ☎ 0 2287 9000; www.bangkok .diplo.de; 9 Th Sathon Tai; Ⓜ Lumphini)

India Embassy (pp118-19; ☎ 0 2258 0300-6; http:// indianembassy.gov.in/bangkok; 46 Soi 23, Th Sukhumvit; Ⓡ Asoke); Consulate (pp118-19; ☎ 0 2665 2968; www .ivac-th.com; 15th fl, Glas Haus Bldg, Soi 25, Th Sukhumvit; Ⓡ Asoke; Ⓜ Sukhumvit)

Israel (Map pp118–19; ☎ 0 2204 9200; http://bangkok .mfa.gov.il; 25th fl, Ocean Tower II, 75 Soi 19, Th Sukhumvit; Ⓡ Asoke; Ⓜ Sukhumvit)

Indonesia (Map pp98–9; ☎ 0 2252 3135; 600-602 Th Phetburi, Ratchathewi; Ⓡ Ratchathewi)

Japan (p112; ☎ 0 2207 8500; www.th.emb-japan.go.jp; 177 Th Witthaya, Lumphini; Ⓜ Lumphini)

Laos (Map pp124–5; ☎ 0 2539 6667; www.bkklao embassy.com; 520/1-3 Soi Sahakarnpramoon, Th Pracha Uthit, Wangthonglong)

Malaysia (p112; ☎ 0 2679 2190-9; 33-35 Th Sathon Tai; Ⓜ Lumphini)

Myanmar (Map pp108–9; ☎ 0 2234 0278; 132 Th Sathon Neua; Ⓡ Surasak)

Nepal (Map pp124–5; ☎ 0 2390 2280; 189 Soi 71, Th Sukhumvit)

Netherlands (Map pp98–9; ☎ 0 2309 5200; www .netherlandsembassy.in.th; 15 Soi Tonson, Ploenchit; Ⓡ Chitlom)

New Zealand (Map pp98–9; ☎ 0 2254 2530-3; www .nzembassy.com; 19th fl, M Thai Tower, All Seasons Pl, 87 Th Withayu; Ⓡ Ploenchit)

Singapore (Map pp108–9; ☎ 0 2286 2111; www.mfa .gov.sg; 9th & 18th fl, Rajanakam Bldg, 129 Th Sathon Tai; Ⓡ Chong Nonsi)

South Africa (Map pp98–9; ☎ 0 2659 2900; www.sa embbangkok.com; 12th fl, M-Thai Tower, All Seasons Pl; Th Witthaya; Ⓡ Ploenchti)

Sweden (Map pp118–19; ☎ 2263 7200; www.swedenabroad .com; 20th fl, One Pacific Pl, 140 Th Sukhumvit; Ⓡ Nana)

Switzerland (Map pp98–9; ☎ 0 2253 0156-60; www .swissembassy.or.th; 5 Th Withayu Neua, Ploenchit; Ⓡ Ploenchit)

UK (Map pp98–9; ☎ 0 2305 8333; www.britishembassy .gov.uk; 1031 Th Withayu, Ploenchit; Ⓡ Ploenchit)

USA (Map pp98–9; ☎ 0 2205 4000; http://bangkok .usembassy.gov; 120-122 Th Withayu, Lumphini; Ⓡ Ploenchit, Ⓜ Lumphini)

Vietnam (Map pp98–9; ☎ 0 2251 5836-8; 83/1 Th Withayu, Ploenchit; Ⓡ Ploenchit)

EMERGENCY

The main emergency numbers are:

Ambulance (via Police ☎ 191)

Fire (☎ 199)

Police (☎ 191)

Tourist Police (☎ 1155)

You're unlikely to find any English-speaker at the fire number, so it's best to use the default

191 number. In a medical emergency it's probably best to call the hospital direct, and it will dispatch an ambulance. See p262 for recommended hospitals.

The best way to deal with most problems requiring police, most likely a rip-off or theft, is to contact the Tourist Police on the 24-hour 1155 hotline. Unlike the regular Thai police, the tourist police are used to dealing with foreigners and can be very helpful in cases of arrest. Although they typically have no jurisdiction over the kinds of cases handled by regular cops, they should be able to help with translation, contacting your embassy and/or issuing a police report you can take to your insurer.

GAY & LESBIAN TRAVELLERS

Thai culture is very tolerant of homosexuality, both male and female, and Bangkok is one of the most gay-friendly cities on Earth. Thailand does not have laws that discriminate against homosexuals, and Bangkok's gay scene, and increasingly the lesbian scene too, is way out in the open. Pride Week (p14) is in early November. These groups and organisations are a good place to start:

Dreaded Ned (www.dreadedned.com) Listings, forums, personal ads.

Gay Guide in Thailand (www.gayguideinthailand.com) What it says on the (six)-pack.

Lesbian Guide to Bangkok (www.bangkoklesbian.com) Active site run by a *faràng* (Western) lesbian, with helpful forums and news on venues. It's mainly in English.

Lesbian Adventures Thailand (www.lathailand.com) An adventure travel company owned and operated by women, exclusively for women.

Lesla (www.lesla.com) The most-established group for Thai and *faràng* lesbians, particularly younger women.

Long Yang Club (www.longyangclub.org/thailand) A 'multicultural social group for male-oriented men who want to meet outside the gay scene', with branches all over the world. The Thailand chapter hosts events in Bangkok.

Utopia (www.utopia-asia.com/thaibang.htm) Long-running and well-respected gay and lesbian website with lots of Bangkok information and member reviews.

HEALTH

While urban horror stories can make a trip to Bangkok seem frighteningly dangerous, in reality few travellers experience anything more than an upset stomach and the resulting clenched-cheek waddles to the bathroom. If you do have a problem, Bangkok has some very good hospitals in which you can recover; see p262.

Many medications can be bought over the counter without a doctor's prescription, but it can be difficult to find some newer drugs, particularly antidepressants, blood-pressure medications and contraceptive pills. Bangkok and the surrounding regions of central Thailand are entirely malaria free, so you won't need to worry about taking any antimalarial medication if you don't plan to venture beyond that area.

Food & Water

If a place looks clean and well run and the vendor also looks clean and healthy, then the food is probably safe. In general, the food in busy restaurants is cooked and eaten quite quickly with little standing around, and is probably not reheated. The same applies to street stalls. It's worth remembering that when you first arrive the change in diet is quite likely to result in a loose stool or two, but that doesn't automatically mean you've got amoebic dysentery, so hold off a bit before rushing to the doc.

All water served in restaurants or to guests in offices or homes in Bangkok comes from purified sources. It's not necessary to ask for bottled water unless you prefer it. Reputable brands of Thai bottled water or soft drinks are generally fine. Fruit juices are made with purified water and are safe to drink. Milk in Thailand is always pasteurised.

Ice is generally produced from purified water under hygienic conditions and is therefore theoretically safe. The rule of thumb is that if it's chipped ice, it probably came from an ice block (which may not have been handled well), but if it's ice cubes or 'tubes', it was delivered from the ice factory in sealed plastic.

Medical Problems & Treatment

In Bangkok medicine is generally available over the counter for much less than it costs in the West. However, fake drugs are common so try to use reputable-looking pharmacies, and check storage conditions and expiry dates before buying anything.

AIR POLLUTION

Bangkok has a bad reputation for air pollution, and on bad days the combination of heat, dust and motor fumes can be a powerful brew of potentially toxic air. The good news is that more efficient vehicles, fewer of them thanks to the Skytrain and Metro, and less industrial pollution mean Bangkok's skies are much cleaner than they used to be. To put it into perspective, the air is usually nearer to Singapore standards than diabolical Hong Kong. There's not much you can do to avoid air pollution, except to try to stay indoors – hello malls!

HEAT
By most people's standards Bangkok is somewhere between hot and seriously (expletive) hot all year round. Usually that will mean nothing more than sweat-soaked clothing, discomfort and excessive tiredness. However, heat exhaustion is not uncommon, and dehydration is the main contributor. Symptoms include feeling weak, headache, irritability, nausea or vomiting, sweaty skin, a fast, weak pulse and a normal or slightly elevated body temperature. Treatment involves getting out of the heat and/or sun and cooling the victim down by fanning and applying cool, wet cloths to the skin, laying the victim flat with their legs raised and rehydrating with electrolyte drinks or water containing a quarter teaspoon of salt per litre.

Heatstroke is more serious and requires more urgent action. Symptoms come on suddenly and include weakness, nausea, a hot, dry body with a temperature of more than 41°C, dizziness, confusion, loss of coordination, seizures and eventually collapse and loss of consciousness. Seek medical help and begin cooling by getting the victim out of the heat, removing their clothes, fanning them and applying cool, wet cloths or ice to their body, especially to the groin and armpits.

HIV & AIDS
In Thailand around 95% of HIV transmission occurs through sexual activity, and the remainder through natal transmission or through illicit intravenous drug use. HIV/AIDS can also be spread through infected blood transfusions, although this risk is virtually nil in Thailand due to rigorous blood-screening procedures. If you want to be pierced or tattooed, be sure to check that the needles are new.

HOLIDAYS
Chinese New Year (usually late February or early March) and Songkran (mid-April) are the two holiday periods that most affect Bangkok. For up to a week before and after these holidays public transport in or out of the city is extremely busy, although during the holidays themselves Bangkok tends to be quiet (except in Chinatown during Chinese New Year and Th Khao San during Songkran). Because it's peak season for foreign tourists visiting Thailand, December and January can also be very tight.

See p12 for detailed information on individual festivals and holidays.

Public Holidays
Government offices and banks close their doors on the following public holidays. For the precise dates of lunar holidays, see the TAT website www.tourismthailand.org/travel-information.

New Year's Day 1 January

Makha Bucha Day January/March (lunar)

Chakri Day 6 April (commemorates the founding of the royal Chakri dynasty)

Songkran 13 to 15 April (Thai New Year)

Labor Day 1 May

Coronation Day 5 May (commemorating the 1946 coronation of the current king and queen)

Visakha Bucha Day May/June (lunar).

Khao Phansa July/August (lunar; beginning of the Buddhist rains retreat, when monks refrain from travelling away from their monasteries)

Queen's Birthday 12 August

King Chulalongkorn Day 23 October

Ok Phansa October/November (lunar; end of Buddhist rains retreat)

King's Birthday 5 December

Constitution Day 10 December

New Year's Eve 31 December

INTERNET ACCESS
Bangkok is a very well wired town. Internet cafés are scattered throughout the city, charging from about 40B per hour up to 120B. Th Khao San (Map pp68–9) has the highest concentration of internet cafés available. Other good areas include Th Silom (Map pp108–9), Th Ploenchit and Siam Sq (Map pp98–9). Additionally, the vast majority of Bangkok guesthouses and hotels offer internet access; see the boxed text, p210, for details.

RJ11 phone jacks are the standard, though in a few older hotels and guesthouses the

DIRECTORY LEGAL MATTERS

WI-FI ACCESS

Wi-fi (wireless fidelity) is not hard to find in Bangkok. All Starbucks (www.starbucks.co.th) and Gloria Jean's (www.gloriajeanscoffees.com.au) coffee shops and growing number of cafés and bars offer free wi-fi services. Most top-end and midrange hotels have wi-fi, as do quite a few guesthouses, sometimes for free and sometimes available by prepaying for time; see p210 for details. Of the various websites listing Bangkok wi-fi spots www.bkkpages.com and www .stickman.com are the most comprehensive.

phones might still be hard wired. In the latter case you might be able to use a fax line in the office, since all fax machines in Thailand are connected via RJ11 jacks.

With so much free internet available, and so many net cafés, paying for a temporary dial-up internet account barely seems worth it. If you think it is, find a nearby 7-Eleven (which shouldn't take too long) and buy a prepaid card for a couple of hundred baht.

LEGAL MATTERS

Thailand's police don't enjoy a squeaky clean reputation but as a foreigner, and especially a tourist, you probably won't have much to do with them. While some expats will talk of being targeted for fines while driving, most anecdotal evidence suggests the men in tight (we're talking spray-on) brown shirts and dark aviators will usually go out of their way not to arrest a foreigner breaking minor laws.

The big exception is drug laws. Most Thai police view drug-takers as a social scourge and consequently see it as their duty to enforce the letter of the law; for others it's an opportunity to make untaxed income via bribes. Which direction they'll go often depends on drug quantities; small-time offenders are sometimes offered the chance to pay their way out of an arrest, while traffickers usually go to jail.

Smoking is banned in almost all indoor spaces, and the ban was extended to open-air public spaces in early 2008, which means lighting up outside a shopping centre, in particular, might earn you a polite request to butt out. If you throw your cigarette butt on the ground, however, you could then be hit with a hefty littering fine. Bangkok has a strong antilittering law, and police won't hesitate to cite foreigners and collect fines of 2000B.

If you are arrested for any offence, the police will allow you to make a phone call to your embassy or consulate in Thailand if you have one, or to a friend or relative. There's a whole set of legal codes governing the length of time and manner in which you can be detained by the police before being charged or put on trial, but the police have a lot of discretion. As a foreigner, the police are more likely to bend these codes in your favour than the reverse. However, as with police worldwide, if you don't show respect to the men in brown you will only make matters worse, so keep your hair on.

Visiting Prisoners

Visiting imprisoned foreigners in Bangkok's notorious jails (p123) has become something of a fad. Visiting details are discussed on several websites, notably www.khaosanroad.com. If you want to see a particular prisoner the best approach is to first contact the prisoner's Bangkok embassy. Consular officials can tell you whether the prisoner, or any other prisoner, wants to be seen; note that they won't give names or details unless the prisoner has authorised them to do so. If so, they can help out and advise on visiting times, which are usually only a couple of days a week. Don't try going directly to the prison without a letter from the prisoner's embassy, as you might be refused entry.

Most foreign prisoners in Thai prisons are from the UK, Australia, Africa and Europe; most American prisoners are repatriated to jails in the US.

MAPS

From the moment you enter Bangkok – literally right after you've passed immigration – you'll see your first free maps. Quality varies between useful and utter rubbish, but the *Official Airport Bangkok Map* and the *City Map of Bangkok,* both usually available at the airport, will get you around the major sights, transport routes and hotels.

Maps for sale in bookshops and some 7-Elevens are better. Lonely Planet's comprehensive *Bangkok City Map,* in a handy, laminated, fold-out form, includes a walking tour and is fully indexed. One map that is often imitated but never equalled is *Nancy Chandler's Map of Bangkok* (www.nancychandler.net), a colourful hand-drawn map with useful inset panels for Chinatown, Th Sukhumvit and Chatuchak Weekend Market.

To master the city's bus system, purchase Roadway's *Bangkok Bus Map.* For visitors who consider eating to be sightseeing, check out Ideal Map's *Good Eats* series, which has mapped mom-and-pop restaurants in three of Bangkok's noshing neighbourhoods – Chinatown, Ko Ratanakosin and Sukhumvit. Groovy Map's *Groovy Bangkok* combines up-to-date bus and transport routes and sights with a short selection of restaurant and bar reviews. Groovy Map also publishes *Roadway Bangkok*, a GPS-derived 1:40,000 driving map of the city that includes all tollways, expressways, roads and lanes labelled in Thai and English. If travelling to districts outside central Bangkok, Thinknet's *Bangkok City Atlas* is a wise way to spend 250B.

MEDICAL SERVICES

More than Thailand's main health-care hub, Bangkok has become a major destination for medical tourism, with patients flying in for treatment from all over the world. In addition to three university research hospitals, the city is home to an ever-expanding number of public and private hospitals and hundreds of private medical clinics. Bumrungrad International, widely considered the best hospital in the country, despite being a bit of a factory, has US accreditation and feels more like a hotel than a hospital; rooms have free wi-fi internet, equipment is the latest available and in the 'lobby' you'll find Starbucks and, erm, McDonalds – would you like a thick shake with that bypass?

Whether your stay is to recover from a nasty 'Thai tattoo' (burned inner right calf after a motorcycle mishap), for corrective surgery you couldn't afford or wait for at home, or for something more cosmetic – new nose, lips, breasts, Adam's apple removal – the following hospitals should be able to help. Of course, it's worth checking the websites and searching around online for feedback before booking yourself in for anything. It's worth remembering that Thai hospitals are notorious for overprescribing drugs and overcharging for them at their own dispensaries. Doctors will often speak English, but if you need another language contact your embassy for advice (p258).

Bangkok's better private hospitals include:

Bangkok Christian Hospital (Map pp108–9; ☎ 0 2235 1000-07; www.bkkchristianhosp.th.com; 124 Th Silom; Ⓜ Saladaeng)

Bangkok Hospital (Map pp124–5; ☎ 0 2310 3000; www.bangkokhospital.com; 2 Soi 47, Th Phetburi Tat Mai, Bangkapi)

BNH Hospital (Map p112; ☎ 0 2686 2700; www.bnhhospital.com; 9 Th Convent; Ⓜ Saladaeng; Ⓜ Silom)

Bumrungrad International (Map pp118–19; ☎ 0 2667 1000; www.bumrungrad.com; 33 Soi 3, Th Sukhumvit; Ⓜ Nana or Ploenchit)

Phyathai Hospital 1 (Map pp52–3; ☎ 0 2640 1111; www.phyathai.com; 364/1 Th Si Ayuthaya; Ⓜ Victory Monument)

Samitivej Sukhumvit Hospital (Map pp118–19; ☎ 0 2711 8000; www.samitivej.co.th; 133 Soi 49, Th Sukhumvit; Ⓜ Phrom Phong)

All these hospitals have substantial ophthalmological treatment facilities. The best eye specialist in the city is **Rutnin Eye Hospital** (Map pp118–19; ☎ 0 2639 3399; www.rutnin.com; 80/1 Soi Asoke; Th Sukhumvit; Ⓜ Asoke; Ⓜ Sukhumvit).

Medical spas mixing alternative therapies, massage and detoxification have taken 'the cure' a step further. See p196 for recommendations.

Chinese Medicine

In the Sampeng–Yaowarat district, along Th Ratchawong, Th Charoen Krung, Th Yaowarat and Th Songwat, you will find many Chinese clinics and herbal dispensaries, though not so much English so bring someone to translate. Larger is the **Huachiew General Hospital** (Map pp52–3; ☎ 2223 1351; hch@huachiewhospital.com; 665 Th Bamrung Meuang), a medical facility dedicated to all aspects of traditional Chinese medicine, along with modern international medicine. The team of licensed acupuncturists at Huachiew are thought to be Thailand's most skilled, though there isn't much English spoken here.

Dentists

As you wander around Bangkok it can start to seem that there is a dental clinic on every *soi*. Or maybe two or three. Business is good in the teeth game, partly because so many *faràng* are combining their holiday with a spot of cheap root canal or some 'personal outlook' care – a sneaky teeth-whitening treatment by any other name. Suggested clinics include:

Bangkok Dental Spa (Map pp118–19; ☎ 0 2651-0807; www.bangkokdentalspa.com; 27 Methawattana Bldg, 2nd fl, Soi 19, Th Sukhumvit; Ⓜ Asoke; Ⓜ Sukhumvit) This is not a typo. Combines oral hygiene with spa services (foot and body massage).

Dental Design Clinic & Lab (Map pp118–19; ☎ 0 2261 9119; www.dentaldesignclinic-lab.com; 20 Dental Design Bldg, Soi 21, Th Sukhumvit; Ⓜ Asoke; Ⓜ Sukhumvit)

Dental Hospital (Map pp118–19; ☎ 02 2260 5000-15; www.dentalhospitalbangkok.com; 88/88 Soi 49, Th Sukhumvit; ® Thong Lor) A private dental clinic with fluent English-speaking dentists.

Siam Family Dental Clinic (Map pp98–9; ☎ 0 2255 6664; www.siamfamilydental.com; 292/6 Soi 4, Siam Sq; ® Siam) Teeth-whitening is big here.

Pharmacies

Pharmacies are plentiful in the city, and in central areas most pharmacists will speak English. If you don't find what you need at the smaller pharmacies, try one of the hospitals listed above, which stock a wider range of pharmaceuticals but also charge higher prices (and you'll need to see a doctor first). The hospital pharmacies are open 24 hours; smaller pharmacies usually open around 10am and close between 8pm and 10pm. One non-hospital pharmacy that's open 24 hours is Foodland Supermarket Pharmacy (Map pp118–19; ☎ 0 2254 2247; 1413 Soi 5, Th Sukhumvit; Skytrain Nana).

MONEY

Most travellers rely on credit or debit cards to access cash in Bangkok, where ATMs are almost as common as bumholes. The basic unit of Thai currency is the baht. There are 100 *satang* in one baht – though the only place you'll be able to spend them is in the ubiquitous 7-Elevens. Coins come in denominations of 25 *satang*, 50 *satang*, 1B, 5B and 10B. Paper currency comes in denominations of 20B (green), 50B (blue), 100B (red), 500B (purple) and 1000B (beige).

By Thai law, any traveller arriving in Thailand is supposed to carry at least the following amounts of money in cash, travellers cheques, bank draft or letter of credit, according to visa category: Non-Immigrant Visa, US$500 per person or US$1000 per family; Tourist Visa, US$250 per person or US$500 per family; Transit Visa or no visa, US$125 per person or US$250 per family. Your funds might be checked by authorities if you arrive on a one-way ticket or if you look as if you're at 'the end of the road'. There is no limit to the amount of Thai or foreign currency you may bring into Thailand. Upon leaving, you are permitted to take no more than 50,000B per person without special authorisation; exportation of foreign currencies is unrestricted.

Standard banking hours are 8.30am to 3.30pm Monday to Friday, though some banks close at 4.30pm on Fridays, and almost every bank in Bangkok has at least one ATM. It's legal to open a foreign-currency account at any commercial bank in Thailand. As long as the funds originate from abroad, there are no restrictions on their maintenance or withdrawal.

ATMs & Credit Cards

You won't need a map to find an ATM in Bangkok – they're everywhere. Bank ATMs accept major international credit cards and many will also cough up cash (Thai baht only) if your account from home has a card affiliated with the Cirrus or Plus networks. You can withdraw up to 20,000B at a time from most ATMs.

Credit cards as well as debit cards can be used for purchases at many shops and pretty much any hotel or restaurant where you might need credit – you'll have to pay cash for your *phat thai*. The most commonly accepted cards are Visa and MasterCard, followed by Amex and JCB. To report a lost or stolen card, call the following numbers:

Amex (☎ 0 2273 5544)

MasterCard (☎ 001 800 11 887 0663)

Visa (☎ 001 800 441 3485)

Changing Money

Banks or legal moneychangers offer the optimum foreign-exchange rates. When buying baht, US dollars and euros are the most readily accepted currencies and travellers cheques receive better rates than cash. British pounds and Australian dollars are also widely accepted. As banks often charge commission and duty for each travellers cheque cashed, you'll save on commissions if you use larger cheque denominations.

Most banks can change foreign exchange but it can sometimes take significantly more time than the specialty exchange places. In tourist areas, such as the Siam Sq shopping district and Th Khao San, you'll often find small exchange counters outside banks; these can change cash and cheques in major currencies and are typically open from 8.30am to 8pm daily.

See the inside front cover for exchange rates. Current exchange rates are printed in the *Bangkok Post* and the *Nation* every day, or you can walk into any Thai bank and ask to see a daily rate sheet.

Tipping

Tipping is not a traditional part of Thai life and, except in big hotels and posh restaurants, tips are not expected. Having said that, Bangkok sees enough tipping tourists for those Thais who commonly deal with tourists to become increasingly familiar with tipping. Taxi drivers, for example, will automatically round the price up to the nearest 10B (Thais rarely insist on these coins). For most places, however, tips remain appreciated rather than expected.

NEWSPAPERS & MAGAZINES

Bangkok has a well-established English-language media and has possibly the largest concentration of freelance journalists and photographers of any city on Earth. The *Bangkok Post* (www.bangkokpost.net) is the major daily broadsheet, with local and international news as well as articles on culture, entertainment, dining and events. The *Nation* (www.nationmultimedia.com) is now a business paper and also publishes a free tabloid called *Daily Xpress*. The *International Herald Tribune* (IHT) is widely available, as are all major international magazines.

Targeting the young ones, *Guru* is a lifestyle insert in the Friday edition of the *Bangkok Post*. For new restaurants, current happy hours, band dates and which DJs are in town there are two good-quality independent publications: the free and irreverent weekly *BK Magazine* (www.bkmagazine.com), and the monthly *Bangkok 101*, which also has handy reviews of sights, restaurants, nightclubs and theatres, and a monthly photo essay; it costs 100B.

ORGANISED TOURS

Mastering Bangkok is the urban aficionado's version of conquering Everest. But not everyone enjoys slogging through the sprawl and heat, and for those sensible folks there are many tours available. Almost every hotel and guesthouse can book you on tours of the main historic sights, and a good number of *túk-túk* drivers will probably try their luck too (don't be tempted). Tours of the river and adjoining *khlong* are the most popular, and bicycle tours (yes, serious) are finding a growing number of happy peddlers.

River & Canal Tours

The car has long since become Bangkok's conveyance of choice, but there was a time,

and there are still places today, where roads are made of water, not asphalt. Taking to these traditional thoroughfares reveals children swimming in the muddy (or often 'filthy') waters, huge cargo barges groaning under the weight of sand being shipped to construction sites, and wake-skipping longtailed boats roaring by. At sunset the famed Wat Arun (p65) and the riverside towers of the luxury hotels are bathed in red and orange hues.

The cheapest and most local way of experiencing riverine Bangkok is by boarding the Chao Phraya Express Boat (☎ 0 2623 6001; www .chaophraya boat.co.th) at any *tha* (pier) and taking it in either direction to its final stop; see p253 for details. The company also offers a one-day river pass (100B) for unlimited trips aboard the Chao Phraya Tourist Boat, which stops at 10 major piers from 9.30am to 3pm and has a distracting loudspeaker guide. Even guidebook writers who sightsee at warp speed don't find this pass offers much better value than the average 12B fare. More appealing are the Sunday trips to Ko Kret (adult/child 299/250B; ⏱ 10am-4.30pm from Tha Sathorn or Tha Maharat) and back; see p230.

Hiring a longtail boat, sometimes known as a 'James Bond boat' after the chase scene in *The Man With the Golden Gun* that first brought them to the attention of the world, is a popular way of touring the Thonburi *khlong*. Shop around for a tour that doesn't include Wat Arun and the Royal Barge Museum, both of which can be more easily (and, let's be honest, more cheaply) visited independently. Tha Chang (Map pp52–3) is the best place to hire a boat. They can also be booked at Tha Oriental (Map pp108–9), Tha Saphan Phut (Map p84) and Tha Si Phraya (Map pp108–9); rental costs from about 400B and 800B an hour, usually nearer to 800B. You'll need two, or preferably three, hours to do it justice and, if you're on a budget, some accomplices help to split the cost.

For dinner cruises, see p164.

Asia Voyages (Map pp124–5; ☎ 0 2655 6246-8; www .asia-voyages.com; per person from 8000B) operates three stout but elegant converted rice barges called *Mekhala*, delivering passengers to Ayuthaya and Bang Pa-In as part of a two-day trip that includes an overnight stay on the boat with a candlelight dinner at the foot of a picturesque temple. Downriver trips are cheaper (from 6150B).

The restored wooden rice barges in the Manohra Cruises (☎ 0 2477 0770; www.manohracruises

.com) fleet are the grandest of all, having been converted into luxury cruisers with real character. There are several cruising options, all departing the Marriott Resort & Spa (Map pp124–5) take a hotel boat from Tha Sathon). The sunset (900B, 6pm to 7pm) and dinner cruises (2342B, 7.30pm to 10pm) are rightly popular if you have the change. If you have both time and money, then consider the two- or three-day trips between Bangkok and Ayuthaya, via Ko Kret and Bang Pa-In.

Bicycle Tours

From inside a taxi it's hard to imagine even contemplating cycling in Bangkok, which makes these trips especially cool as you discover a whole side of the city off-limits to four-wheeled transport. Half-day tours start at about 1000B, but check online for the latest prices.

Long-running ABC Amazing Bangkok Cyclist Tour (☎ 0 2665 6364; www.realasia.net) organises daily bike tours through a scenic riverside neighbourhood in Thonburi. You travel by long-tail boat to the *khlong*-crossed villages of stilt houses, green gardens and old ladies wrapped up in market sarongs. Instead of asphalt and traffic, you'll negotiate narrow concrete pathways bridging the canal below and occasionally yielding to a few motorbikes driven by 10-year-old kids. Weekend tours also take in a floating market and what is touted as a 'super special' lunch.

Grasshopper Adventures (☎ 0 2628 7067; www.grasshopperadventures.com) offers tours of Ko Ratanakosin and a cooler night tour to Thonburi, along with multiday trips throughout Southeast Asia.

Velo Thailand (☎ 089 201 7782; www.velothailand.com; 88 Soi 2, Th Samsen, Banglamphu) Ae, from Velo, works with Grasshopper but also operates his own tours, including the night tour to Thonburi. The bikes here are first class; rental, sales and repairs are also available. It's a very good choice.

Other Tours

Most Bangkok sights can be visited easily under your own steam, but every travel agent and most hotels can arrange guided tours of important sites. If you want a custom tour with an expert guide, and money is no objective, Bangkok Private Tours (www.bangkokprivatetours.com) is earning a reputation for its food tours, among others.

POST

Thailand has an efficient postal service, and both domestic and international rates are very reasonable. Bangkok's main post office (Communications Authority of Thailand, CAT; Map pp108–9; ☎ 0 2233 1050; Th Charoen Krung) is open from 8am to 8pm Monday to Friday and from 8am to 1pm Saturday and Sunday and holidays. An inexpensive packaging service can help if you've spent too much at Chatuchak Market. The parcel counter is open from 8am to 4.30pm Monday to Friday and from 8.30am to noon on Saturday; at other times an informal service is open at the centre rear of the building. If you're a Luddite, or your mum is, you might use the poste restante service here.

An international telecommunications service (including telephone, fax and internet) is located in a separate building in the northeast corner of the block; services are paid for with pre-paid cards that can also be used at Bangkok airports. The easiest way to reach the main post office is via the Chao Phraya Express to Si Phraya (N3) or Muang Khae (N2), both a short walk away.

Elsewhere, branch post offices are found throughout the city; ask your hotel for the nearest one.

RADIO

Bangkok has around 100 FM and AM stations broadcasting a huge range of music, talk and news. The place you're most likely to hear Thai radio is in a taxi. Given that most Bangkok cabbies are from the northeast Isaan region, expect them to be listening to *lûuk thûng* (Thai country music) on Luk Thung 95.0 FM. For Thai Top 40 try Hotwave 91.5 FM; for more alternative Thai tunes try Fat Radio 104.5 FM.

For a taste of what's on offer, listen to live radio online by clicking through to Thailand on www.surfmusic.de.

SAFETY

Bangkok is a safe city, and incidents of violence against tourists are rare. However, scams aimed at separating you and your hard-earned are so prevalent that the term 'gem scam' has become almost synonymous with 'Bangkok'. Con artists tend to haunt first-time tourist spots, such as the Grand Palace area, Wat Pho, the Golden Mount and Siam Sq (especially near Jim Thompson's House).

Most scams begin the same way: a friendly Thai male (or, on rarer occasions, a female) approaches and strikes up a seemingly innocuous conversation. Sometimes the con man says he's a university student or teacher; at other times he might claim to work for the World Bank or a similarly distinguished organisation. If you're on the way to Wat Pho or Jim Thompson's House, for example, he may tell you it's closed for a holiday or repairs. Eventually the conversation works its way around to the subject of the scam – the best fraudsters can actually make it seem as though you initiated the topic. The scammer might spend hours inveigling you into his trust, taking you to an alternative 'special' temple, for example, and linking with other seemingly random people, often *túk-túk* drivers, who are also in on the scam.

The scam itself almost always incorporates gems, tailor shops or card playing. With gems, the victim is invited to a gem and jewellery shop – your new-found friend is picking up some merchandise for himself and you're just along for the ride. Somewhere along the way he usually claims to have a connection in your home country (what a coincidence!) with whom he has a regular gem export-import business. One way or another, the victim is persuaded that they can turn a profit by arranging a gem purchase and reselling the merchandise at home. After all, the jewellery shop just happens to be offering a generous discount today.

There are seemingly infinite variations on the gem scam, almost all of which end up with the victim purchasing small, low-quality sapphires and posting them to their home country. Once you return home, of course, the cheap sapphires turn out to be worth much less than what you paid for them. Many have invested and lost virtually all their savings.

Even if you were able to return your purchase to the gem shop in question, chances are slim to none they'd give a full refund. The con artist who brings the mark into the shop gets a commission of 10% to 50% per sale – the shop takes the rest. The Thai police are usually of no help, believing that merchants are entitled to whatever price they can get. The main victimisers are a handful of shops who get protection from certain high-ranking government officials.

At tailor shops the objective is to get you to pay exorbitant prices for poorly made clothes. The tailor shops that do this are adept at delaying delivery until just before you leave Thailand, so that you don't have time to object to poor workmanship. The way to avoid this scam is to choose tailor shops yourself and not offer any more than a small deposit – no more than enough to cover your chosen fabrics – until you're satisfied with the workmanship.

The card-playing scam starts out very similarly to the gem scenario: a friendly stranger approaches the lone traveller on the street, strikes up a conversation and then invites him or her to the house of his relative for a drink or meal. After a bit of socialising, a friend or relative of the con arrives; it just so happens a little high-stakes card game is planned for later that day. Like the gem scam, the card-game scam has many variations, but eventually the victim is shown some cheating tactics to use with help from the 'dealer', some practice sessions take place and finally the game gets under way. The mark is allowed to win a few hands first, then somehow loses a few, gets bankrolled by one of the friendly Thais, and then loses the Thai's money. Suddenly your new-found buddies aren't so friendly any more – they want the money you lost. Sooner or later you end up sucking large amounts out of the nearest ATM. Again the police won't take any action – in this case because gambling is illegal in Thailand and you've broken the law by playing cards for money.

Other minor scams involve *túk-túk* drivers, hotel employees and bar girls who take new arrivals on city tours; these almost always end in high-pressure sales pushes at silk, jewellery or handicraft shops. In this case greed isn't the ruling motivation – it's simply a matter of weak sales resistance.

The best way to avoid all this is to follow the TAT's number-one suggestion: disregard all offers of free shopping or sightseeing help from strangers. You might also try lying whenever a stranger asks how long you've been in Thailand – if it's only been three days, say three weeks! The con artists rarely prey on anyone except new arrivals.

You should contact the Tourist Police if you have any problems with consumer fraud. Call ☎ 1155 from any phone.

TAXES & REFUNDS

Thailand has a 7% value-added tax (VAT) on many goods and services. Mid-range and top-end hotels and restaurants might also add a 10% service tax. When the two are combined this becomes the 17% king hit known as 'plus plus', or '++'.

Visitors to Bangkok who depart by air and who haven't spent more than 180 days in Thailand during the previous calendar year can apply for a VAT refund on purchases made at approved stores; look for the blue and white VAT Refund sticker. Minimum purchases must add up to 2000B per store in a single day, with a minimum total of 5000B. You must get a VAT Refund form and tax invoice from the shop. Most major malls in Bangkok will direct you to a desk dealing with VAT refunds, where they will organise the appropriate paperwork (takes about five minutes).

At the airport, large items should be declared at the customs desk, which will issue the appropriate paperwork; you can then check them in. Smaller items (such as watches and jewellery) must be hand-carried as they will need to be reinspected once you've passed immigration. Either way, you actually get your money at a VAT Refund Tourist Office (☎ 0 2272 9384-5), which at Suvarnabhumi are on Level 4 in both the east and west wings. For all the details, see www.rd.go.th/vrt.

TELEPHONE

The Bangkok telephone system is efficient enough for you to be able to direct-dial most major centres without trouble. Thailand's country code is ☎ 66.

Inside Thailand you must dial the area code no matter where you are. In effect, that means all numbers are nine digits; in Bangkok they begin with 02, then a seven-digit number. The only time you drop the initial 0 is when you're calling from outside Thailand. Calling the provinces will usually involve a three-digit code beginning with 0, then a six-digit number. Mobile phone numbers all have 10 digits, beginning with 08.

To direct-dial an international number from a private phone, first dial ☎ 001 or, if it's available, ☎ 007, which is significantly cheaper. For operator-assisted international calls, dial ☎ 100. For free local directory assistance call ☎ 1133 inside Bangkok.

You can direct-dial Home Country Direct access numbers from any private phone (most hotel phones won't work) in Thailand. Dial ☎ 001 999 followed by one of the numbers given on the Quick Reference page on the inside front cover. TOT offers a separate international service to 30 select countries (including Australia, Belgium, Canada, Denmark, France, Germany, Hong Kong, Japan, Malaysia, Singapore, UK and USA), accessed by dialling ☎ 008 first. The TOT service costs less per minute than the corresponding CAT service, so there's no reason to use the 001 route if you have a choice. For big discounts for calls to long-distance numbers or mobiles from private phones or payphones (not mobiles) within Thailand, call ☎ 1234 before the number.

A useful CAT office stands next to the main post office (Map pp108–9), and the TOT office (Map pp98–9) on Th Ploenchit is mainly an internet café but does have one phone for Home Country Direct calls – buy a phone card first.

Payphones are common throughout Bangkok, though too often they're beside the thundering traffic of a major thoroughfare. Red phones are for local calls, blue are for local and long-distance calls (within Thailand), and the green phones are for use with phonecards. Calls start at 1B for three minutes; for mobile numbers it's 3B per minute. Local calls from private phones cost 3B, with no time limit.

Internet Phone & Phonecards

The cheapest way to call internationally is via the internet, and many internet cafés in Bangkok are set up for phone calls. Some have Skype loaded and (assuming there's a working headset) you can use that for just the regular per-hour internet fee. Others might have their own VoIP service at cheap international rates.

CAT itself offers the PhoneNet card, which comes in denominations of 300B, 500B and 1000B and allows you to call overseas via Voice over Internet Protocol for a 40% to 86% saving over regular rates. The difference with PhoneNet is that you can call from any phone; landline, your mobile etc. Quality is good and rates represent excellent value; refills are available. Cards are available from any CAT office or online at www.thaitelephone.com, from which you get the necessary codes and numbers immediately. See http://thaitelephone .com/EN/RateTable/for rates.

That table also displays rates for CAT's standard ThaiCard, a prepaid international calling card selling for 300B and 500B. You can use the ThaiCard codes from either end, eg calling the UK from Thailand or calling Thailand from the UK. These are better value than Lenso cards, which are used from payphones.

Mobile Phones

If you have a GSM phone you will probably be able to use it on roaming in Thailand. If you have endless cash, or you only want to send text messages, you might be happy to do that. Otherwise, think about buying a local SIM card.

Buying a pre-paid SIM is as difficult as finding the nearest 7-Eleven store. The market is super-competitive and deals vary so check websites first, but expect to get a SIM, with 100 or 200 minutes, for between 99B and 300B. Per-minute rates start at less than 50 satang. Recharge cards are sold at the same stores. Calling internationally the network will have a promotional code (eg 009 instead of 001) that affords big discounts on the standard international rates, though you might have to go into a phone company office to get the full list of rates. The three main networks are:

AIS (www.one-2-call.com) Wide coverage across Thailand; One-2-Call is the pre-paid option.

DTAC (www.dtac.co.th) Lots of options, including Happy (www.happy.co.th) for pre-paid SIM.

True Move (www.truemove.com) Offers a Welcome SIM package for visitors, with domestic calls for 2B a minute and cheaper international rates. The network is not as good outside Bangkok.

If your phone is locked, head down to Mahboonkrong (MBK) shopping centre (p134) to get it unlocked, or to shop for a new or cheap used phone (they start at less than 2000B).

TIME

Thailand is seven hours ahead of GMT/UTC. Thus, noon in Bangkok is 9pm the previous day in Los Angeles, midnight the same day in New York, 5am in London, 6am in Paris, 1pm in Perth, and 3pm in Sydney. Times are an hour later in countries or regions that are on Daylight Savings Time (Summer Time). Thailand does not use daylight saving. See also the World Time Zones map (p295).

The official year in Thailand is reckoned from the Western calendar year 543 BC, the beginning of the Buddhist Era, so that AD 2009 is 2552 BE, AD 2010 is 2553 BE etc. All dates in this book refer to the Western calendar.

TOILETS

If you don't want to pee against a tree like the túk-túk drivers, you can stop in at any shopping centre, hotel or fast-food restaurant for facilities. Shopping centres typically charge 1B to 2B for a visit, and some of the larger shopping centres on Th Silom and Th Ploenchit have toilets for the disabled. Toilet paper is rarely provided, so carry an emergency stash or do as the locals do and use the hose (an acquired skill). In older buildings and wat you'll still find squat toilets, but in modern Bangkok expect to be greeted by a throne.

TOURIST INFORMATION

Bangkok has two organisations that handle tourism matters: the Tourism Authority of Thailand (TAT) for country-wide information, and Bangkok Tourist Division for city-specific information. Also be aware that travel agents in the train station and near tourist centres co-opt TAT as part of their name to lure in commissions.

The Bangkok Tourist Division (BTD; Map p56; ☎ 0 2225 7612-4; www.bangkoktourist.com; 17/1 Th Phra Athit; ☼ 8am-7pm Mon-Fri, 9am-5pm Sat & Sun), operated by the Bangkok Metropolitan Administration (BMA), has this main office near Saphan Phra Pinklao with well-informed staff and a wealth of brochures, maps and event schedules. Staff can assist with the chartering of boats at the adjacent pier. Kiosks and booths around town, and particularly in major shopping malls, are less useful, but do have maps; look for the symbol of a mahout on an elephant. The yellow-and-green BTD tourist information booth (Map pp68-9; ☎ 0 2281 5538; ☼ 9am-7pm Mon-Sat, 9am-5pm Sun), opposite the Chana Songkhram police station on Th Chakraphong, close to the corner of Th Khao San, has particularly useful local bus maps.

The larger TAT (☎ 1672 for assistance; www.tourism thailand.org; ☼ 8am-8pm) has two main offices in Bangkok and two at Suvarnabhumi International Airport, all well-stocked with brochures and maps covering the whole country. If you need information over the phone we strongly recommend you to call the ☎ 1672 line, not the offices themselves.

Head Office (Map pp52-3; ☎ 0 2250 5500; 1600 Phetchaburi Tat Mai; Makkasan; Ratchathewi; ☼ 8.30am-4.30pm)

Banglamphu (Map pp68-9; ☎ 0 2283 1555, ext 1556; cnr Th Ratchadamnoen Nok & Th Chakrapatdipong; ☼ 8.30am-4.30pm) Opposite the boxing stadium. It is also home to the Tourist Police (☎ 1155; ☼ 24hr).

Suvarnabhumi International Airport (☎ 0 2134 4077; International Terminal, 2nd fl, btwn Gate 2 & 5; ☼ 8am-10pm) Also in the domestic terminal.

TAT Offices Abroad

TAT has 20 offices scattered about the globe, mainly in Europe, Asia, North America and Australia. For a full list, with exhaustive contact details, see www.tourismthailand.org/tat -oversea-office.

TRAVELLERS WITH DISABILITIES

Bangkok presents one large, ongoing obstacle course for the mobility-impaired, with its high curbs, uneven pavements and nonstop traffic. Many of the city's streets must be crossed via pedestrian bridges flanked with steep stairways, while buses and boats don't stop long enough to accommodate even the mildly disabled. Aside from some Skytrain and Metro stations, ramps or other access points for wheelchairs are rare.

A few top-end hotels make consistent design efforts to provide disabled access. Other deluxe hotels with high employee-to-guest ratios are usually good about providing staff help where building design fails. For the rest, you're pretty much left to your own resources. These companies and websites might help:

Asia Pacific Development Centre on Disability (www .apcdproject.org)

Society for Accessible Travel & Hospitality (www.sath .org)

Wheelchair Tours to Thailand (www.wheelchairtours.com)

VISAS

Thailand has been much stricter in enforcing its visa laws since the coup of 2006, but the citizens of 42 countries, including most Western European countries, Australia, Canada, Hong Kong, Japan, New Zealand, Singapore and the USA, can still enter Thailand without a visa and stay for up to 30 days. Citizens of Brazil, Republic of Korea and Peru may enter without a visa for 90 days. For a list of eligible countries and other visa matters, see the Royal Thai Ministry of Foreign Affairs website www .mfa.go.th/web/12.php.

The crackdown, apparently designed to get rid of illegal workers and 'bad influences' such as sex tourists, has seen the once-ignored requirement of an onward ticket being more strictly enforced, usually by airline staff in the departing city. We've heard of several people who have had to buy an onward ticket and later have it refunded, with a penalty.

It should go without saying that the better dressed you are, the less likely you are to be hassled.

If you're planning to stay longer than 30 days it's best to get a 60-day tourist visa before you arrive. This can then be extended by 30 days at any visa office in the country; see below.

Other Visas

Thai embassies and consulates issue a variety of other visas for people on business, students or those with employment in Thailand. The Non-Immigrant Visa comes in several classifications and is good for 90 days. If you want to stay longer than 90 days in six months, this is the one to get. If you plan to apply for a Thai work permit, you'll need a Non-Immigrant Visa first. Getting a non-immigrant visa with the intention of working in Thailand can be difficult and involves a tedious amount of paperwork. If you get one, usually with the support of an employer, you'll likely end up at the One-Stop Service Centre (☎ 0 2937 1155; www.boi .go.th; 16th fl, Rasa Tower, 555 Th Phahonyothin) for several hours of paper pushing – get there early!

Citizens from a list of 14 nations, including the People's Republic of China, Taiwan and several countries in Central and South Asia, can obtain a 15-day Transit Visa (800B). You might be required to show you have 10,000B per person or 20,000B per family to obtain this visa.

For information and discussion about all things visa, see www.thaivisa.com.

Visa Extensions & Renewals

Without a long-term visa you cannot stay in Thailand for more than 90 days out of 180, and there must be a 90-day gap before you return. The 60-day Tourist Visa can be extended by up to 30 days at the discretion of Thai immigration authorities. In Bangkok, the Immigration Bureau (Map p112; ☎ 0 2287 3101; Soi Suan Phlu, Th Sathon Tai) does the deed; elsewhere any immigration office will do. A fee of 1900B will be charged, and you'll need the usual mug shots and photocopies of face and visa pages of your passport.

The 30-day, no-visa stay can be extended for a maximum of seven days for 1900B. Alternatively, you can plan your itinerary so you leave the country after 30 days and immediately return for a fresh 30 days. This can only be done up a total of 90 days within 180.

A seven-day extension of the 15-day Transit Visa is allowed only if you hold a passport from a country that has no Thai embassy.

If you overstay your visa the usual penalty is a fine of 500B for each extra day, with a 20,000B limit (after that, more trouble awaits). Fines can be paid at the airport or in advance at Room 416, in the Old Building at the Immigration Bureau. Children under 14 travelling with a parent do not have to pay the penalty.

VOLUNTEERING

Volunteering seems to be all the rage at the moment, and Thailand is one of the favourite destinations. Most volunteering positions are in rural Thailand, but there are also plenty of possibilities in Bangkok. Working in some capacity with people who need your help can make a difference and be rewarding both to you and them. But it's not all sweetness and light, and it's important to understand what you're getting yourself into. Unless you know the country, speak the language and have skills needed in a particular field (computing, health and teaching, for example), what you can offer in a short period will largely be limited to manual labour – a commodity not in short supply in Thailand. Having said that, if you can match your skills to a project that needs them, this can be a great way to spend time in Thailand.

There are two main forms of volunteering. For those interested in a long-term commitment, typically two or three years, there are a few long-established organisations that will help you learn the language, place you in a position that will, hopefully, be appropriate to your skills, and pay you (just barely). Such organisations include:

Australian Volunteers International www.australianvolunteers.com

US Peace Corps www.peacecorps.gov

Voluntary Service Overseas (VSO Canada) www.vsocanada.org

VSO UK www.vso.org.uk

Volunteer Service Abroad (VSO NZ) www.vsa.org.nz

The more popular form of volunteering, sometimes called 'voluntourism', is something you actually pay to do. This is a fast-growing market, and a quick search for 'Thailand volunteering' will turn up pages of companies offering to place you in a project in return for some of your hard-earned. In fairness, the projects can be very good, but some are not. With these companies you can be a volunteer for as little as a single week or up to six months or longer. Fees vary, but start at about €500 for four weeks. The list below is a starting point and should not be read as a recommendation. We have not worked with any of these companies so cannot speak for or against them. Do your own research and check out all the options before making a decision – and by all means call them up and ask all the hard questions you like about where your money will go. Locally focused organisations include Volunthai (www.volunthai.com), and Thai Experience (www.thai-experience.org). Other general volunteering sites worth looking at are the Global Volunteer Network (www.volunteer.org.nz), Idealist (www.idealist.org) and Volunteer Abroad (www.volunteerabroad.com), which lists available positions with a variety of companies. Multicountry organisations that sell volunteering trips include:

Cross Cultural Solutions www.crossculturalsolutions.org

Cultural Embrace www.culturalembrace.com

Global Crossroad www.globalcrossroad.com

Global Service Corps www.globalservicecorps.org

Institute for Field Research Expeditions www.ifrevolunteers.org

Open Mind Projects www.openmindprojects.org

Starfish Ventures www.starfishventures.co.uk

Transitions Abroad www.transitionsabroad.com

Travel to Teach www.travel-to-teach.org

Youth International www.youthinternational.org

WOMEN TRAVELLERS

Contrary to popular myth, Thailand doesn't receive a higher percentage of male visitors than most other countries. In fact around 40% of visitors are women, a higher ratio than the worldwide average as measured by the World Tourism Organization. The overall increase for women visitors has climbed faster than that for men in almost every year since the early 1990s.

Everyday incidents of sexual harassment are much less common in Thailand than in India, Indonesia or Malaysia, and this might lull women familiar with those countries into thinking that Thailand is safer than it is. If you're a woman travelling alone it's worth pairing up with other travellers when moving around at night or, at the least, avoiding quiet areas. Make sure hotel and guesthouse rooms are secure at night – if they're not, request another room or move to another hotel or guesthouse.

When women are attacked in Thailand it usually happens in remote beach or mountain areas, and very rarely in Bangkok. So while common sense precautions are recommended at all times, be especially vigilant if you're on a beach, and even more if you're alone and you've been drinking.

WORK

Bangkok's status as the heart of the Thai economy provides a variety of work opportunities for foreigners, and tens of thousands live and work here. Having said that, *faràng* are not allowed to work in certain professions (such as medical doctors) and it's not as easy to find a job as it is in more developed countries.

All work in Thailand requires a Thai work permit. Thai law defines work as 'exerting one's physical energy or employing one's knowledge, whether or not for wages or other benefits', so theoretically even volunteer and missionary work requires a permit. Work permits should be obtained via an employer, who may file for the permit before the employee arrives in-country. The permit itself is not issued until the employee enters Thailand on a valid Non-Immigrant Visa (see p269).

For information about work permits, contact any Thai embassy abroad or check the Ministry of Foreign Affairs website (www .mfa.go.th/web/12.php). No joy? Seek solace and advice on the message boards of www .thaivisa.com.

Busking is illegal in Thailand, where it is legally lumped together with begging.

Teaching English

As in the rest of East and Southeast Asia, there is a high demand for English speakers to provide instruction to Thai citizens. Those with academic credentials such as teaching certificates or degrees in English as a second language will get first crack at the better-paying jobs, such as those at universities and international schools. But there are perhaps hundreds of private language-teaching establishments in Bangkok that hire noncredentialled teachers by the hour. Private tutoring is also a possibility. International oil companies pay the highest salaries for English instructors, but are also quite choosy.

A website maintained by a Bangkok-based English teacher, www.ajarn.com, has tips on finding jobs and pretty much everything else you need to know about getting into the teaching game in Thailand. If you're more dedicated (or desperate) the Yellow Pages (www.yellow.co.th/Bangkok) has contact details for hundreds of schools, universities and language schools.

LANGUAGE

Learning some Thai is a wonderful way to enhance your stay in Bangkok; naturally, the more you pick up, the closer you get to Thailand's culture and people. Your first attempts to speak the language will probably meet with mixed success, but keep trying. Listen closely to the way the Thais themselves use the various tones – you'll catch on quickly. Don't let laughter

at your linguistic forays discourage you; this apparent amusement is really an expression of appreciation. Travellers are particularly urged to make the effort to meet Thai college and university students. Thai students are, by and large, eager to meet visitors from other countries. They will often know some English, so communication isn't as difficult as it may be with shop owners, civil servants etc, and they're generally willing to teach you useful Thai words and phrases.

If you'd like a more comprehensive guide to the language, get a copy of Lonely Planet's compact and comprehensive *Thai Phrasebook*.

PRONUNCIATION

Tones

In Thai the meaning of a single syllable may be altered by means of different tones. For example, depending on the tone, the syllable *mai* can mean 'new', 'burn', 'wood', 'not?' or 'not'.

The following chart represents tones to show their relative pitch values:

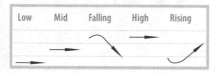

Low	Mid	Falling	High	Rising

The tones are explained as follows:

low tone – 'flat' like the mid tone, but pronounced at the relative bottom of one's vocal range. It is low, level and with no inflection, eg *bàht* (baht – the Thai currency).
mid tone – pronounced 'flat', at the relative middle of the speaker's vocal range, eg *dee* (good); no tone mark is used.
falling tone – sounds as if you are emphasising a word, or calling someone's name from afar, eg *mâi* (no/not).
high tone – pronounced near the relative top of the vocal range, as level as possible, eg *máh* (horse).
rising tone – sounds like the inflection used by English speakers to imply a question – 'Yes?', eg *sǎhm* (three).

Consonants

The majority of Thai consonants correspond closely to the English counterparts used to represent them in transliterations. The ones that will be unfamiliar to English speakers

are 'b (pronounced like a cross between 'b' and 'p', as in 'hipbag'), d (pronounced like a cross between a 'd' and a 't', as in 'hardtop') and ng (pronounced as in 'sing', but differing from English in that this consonant can come at the beginning of a word; practise by saying 'singing' and then leave off the 'si-').

Vowels

The many different vowel sounds and combinations in Thai can be tricky at first.

i	as in 'bit'
ee	as in 'feet'
ai	as in 'aisle'
ah	as the 'a' in 'father'
a	as in 'about'; half as long as 'ah'
aa	as the 'a' in 'bat' or 'tab'
e	as in 'hen'
air	as in English, but with no 'r' sound
eu	as the 'er' in 'fern', but with no 'r' sound
u	as in 'put'
oo	as in 'food'
ow	as in 'now'
or	as in 'torn', but with no 'r' sound
o	as in 'hot'
oh	as the 'o' in 'toe'
eu·a	a combination of eu and a
ee·a	as 'ee-ya'
oo·a	as the 'our' in 'tour'
oo·ay	sounds like 'oo-way'
ew	as the 'ew' in 'new'
ee·o	as the 'io' in 'Rio'
aa-ou	as the 'a' in 'cat' followed by a short 'u' as in 'put'
eh-ou	as the 'e' in bed, followed by a short 'u' as in 'put'
oy	as in 'toy'

SOCIAL
Meeting People

Hello.

สวัสดี   sà·wàt·dee

 (ครับ/ค่ะ)   (kráp/kâ) **(to m/f)**

Goodbye.

ลาก่อน   lah gòrn

Please.

กรุณา   gà·rú·nah

Thank you (very much).

ขอบคุณ(มาก)   kòrp kun (mâhk)

Yes.

ใช่   châi

No.

ไม่ใช่   mâi châi

I

ผม/ดิฉัน   pŏm/dì·chǎn **(m/f)**

you

คุณ   kun

Do you speak English?

คุณพูดภาษา   kun pôot pah·sǎh

 อังกฤษได้ไหม   ang·grìt dâi mǎi?

Do you understand?

เข้าใจไหม   kôw jai mǎi?

I understand.

เข้าใจ   kôw jai

I don't understand.

ไม่เข้าใจ   mâi kôw jai

Could you please ...?

ขอ...ได้ไหม

kŏr ... dâi mǎi?

 repeat that

 พูดอีกที   pôot èek tee

 speak more slowly

 พูดช้าลง   pôot cháh long

 write it down

 เขียนให้   kĕe·an hâi

Going Out

What's on ...?

มีอะไรทำ...

mee à·rai tam ...?

 locally

 แถวๆนี้   tăa·ou·tăa·ou née

 this weekend

 เสาร์อาทิตย์นี้   sŏw ah·tít née

today

วันนี้   wan née

tonight

คืนนี้   keun née

Where are the ...?

...อยู่ที่ไหน

... yòo têe nǎi?

 clubs

 ไนท์คลับ   nai kláp

 gay venues

 สถานบันเทิงเกย์   sà·tǎhn ban·teung gair

 places to eat

 ร้านอาหาร   ráhn ah·hǎhn

 pubs

 ผับ   pàp

Is there a local entertainment guide?

มีคู่มือสถานบันเทิงบริเวณนี้ไหม

mee kôo meu sà·tǎhn ban·teung

 bor·rí·wairn née mǎi?

PRACTICAL
Question Words

Who?	ใคร	krai?
What?	อะไร	à·rai?
When?	เมื่อไร	mêu·a rai?
Where?	ที่ไหน	têe nǎi?
How?	อย่างไร	yàhng rai?

Numbers & Amounts

0	ศูนย์	sŏon
1	หนึ่ง	nèung
2	สอง	sŏrng
3	สาม	sǎhm
4	สี่	sèe
5	ห้า	hâh
6	หก	hòk
7	เจ็ด	jèt
8	แปด	ฺbàat
9	เก้า	gôw
10	สิบ	sìp
11	สิบเอ็ด	sìp·èt
12	สิบสอง	sìp·sŏrng
13	สิบสาม	sìp·sǎhm

14	สิบสี่	sìp·sèe
15	สิบห้า	sìp·hâh
16	สิบหก	sìp·hòk
17	สิบเจ็ด	sìp·jèt
18	สิบแปด	sìp·Ъàat
19	สิบเก้า	sìp·gôw
20	ยี่สิบ	yêe·sìp
21	ยี่สิบเอ็ด	yêe·sìp·èt
22	ยี่สิบสอง	yêe·sìp·sŏrng
30	สามสิบ	săhm·sìp
40	สี่สิบ	sèe·sìp
50	ห้าสิบ	hâh·sìp
60	หกสิบ	hòk·sìp
70	เจ็ดสิบ	jèt·sìp
80	แปดสิบ	Ъàat·sìp
90	เก้าสิบ	gôw·sìp
100	หนึ่งร้อย	nèung róy
1000	หนึ่งพัน	nèung pan
2000	สองพัน	sŏrng pan
10,000	หนึ่งหมื่น	nèung mèun
100,000	หนึ่งแสน	nèung săan
1,000,000	หนึ่งล้าน	nèung láhn

Days

Monday	วันจันทร์	wan jan
Tuesday	วันอังคาร	wan ang·kahn
Wednesday	วันพุธ	wan pút
Thursday	วันพฤหัสฯ	wan pà·réu·hàt
Friday	วันศุกร์	wan sùk
Saturday	วันเสาร์	wan sŏw
Sunday	วันอาทิตย์	wan ah·tít

Banking

I'd like to ...
อยากจะ...
yàhk jà ...
   change money
   แลกเงิน   lâak ngeun
   change some travellers cheques
   แลกเช็คเดินทาง   lâak chék deun tahng

Where's the nearest ...?
...ที่ใกล้เคียงอยู่ที่ไหน
... têe glâi kee·ang yòo têe năi?

ATM
ตู้เอทีเอ็ม
đôo air·tee·em
foreign exchange office
ที่แลกเงินต่างประเทศ
têe lâak ngeun đàhng Ъrà·têt

Post

Where is the post office?
ที่ทำการไปรษณีย์อยู่ที่ไหน
têe tam gahn Ъrai·sà·nee yòo têe năi?

I want to send a ...
อยากจะส่ง...
yàhk jà sòng ...
   fax
   แฟกซ์   fàak
   parcel
   พัสดุ   pát·sà·dù
   postcard
   ไปรษณียบัตร   Ъrai·sà·nee·yá·bàt

I want to buy ...
อยากจะซื้อ...
yàhk jà séu ...
   an envelope
   ซองจดหมาย   sorng jòt·măi
   a stamp
   แสตมป์   sà·đaam

Phones & Mobiles

I want to buy a phone card.
อยากจะซื้อบัตรโทรศัพท์
yàhk jà séu bàt toh·rá·sàp
I want to make a call to ...
อยากจะโทรไป...
yàhk jà toh Ъai ...
reverse-charge/collect call
เก็บปลายทาง
gèp Ъlai tahng

I'd like a/an ...
ต้องการ...
đôrng gahn ...
   adaptor plug
   ปลั๊กต่อ
   Ъlák đòr
   charger for my phone
   เครื่องชาร์จสำหรับโทรศัพท์
   krêu·ang cháht săm·ràp toh·rá·sàp

274

mobile/cell phone for hire
เช่าโทรศัพท์มือถือ
chôw toh·rá·sàp meu tĕu
prepaid mobile/cell phone
โทรศัพท์มือถือแบบจ่ายล่วงหน้า
toh·rá·sàp meu tĕu bàap jài lôo·ang nâh
SIM card for the ... network
บัตรซิมสำหรับเครือข่ายของ...
bàt sim săm·ràp kreua kài kŏrng ...

Internet

Where's the local Internet café?
ร้านอินเตอร์เนตอยู่ที่ไหน
ráhn in·đeu·nét yòo têe năi?

I'd like to ...
อยากจะ...
yàhk jà ...

check my email
ตรวจอีเมล   đròo·at ee·mehn
get online
ต่ออินเตอร์เนต   đòr in·đeu·nét

Transport

What time does the ... leave?
...จะออกกี่โมง
... jà òrk gèe mohng?
bus
รถเมล์   rót mair
ferry
เรือข้ามฟาก   reu·a kâhm fâhk
train
รถไฟ   rót fai

What time's the ... bus?
รถเมล์...มากี่โมง
rót mair ... mah gèe mohng?
first
คันแรก   kan râak
last
คันสุดท้าย   kan sùt tái
next
คันต่อไป   kan đòr ɓai

Are you free? (taxi)
ว่างไหม   wâhng măi?
Please put the meter on.
เปิดมิเตอร์ด้วยหน่อย ɓèut mí·đeu dôo·ay
                    nòy

How much is it to ...?
ไป...เท่าไร   ɓai ... tôw·rai?
Please take me to ... .
ขอพาไป...   kŏr pah ɓai ...

FOOD

breakfast
อาหารเช้า   ah·hăhn chów
lunch
อาหารเที่ยง   ah·hăhn têe·ang
dinner
อาหารเย็น   ah·hăhn yen
snack
อาหารว่าง   ah·hăhn wâhng

Can you recommend a ...
แนะนำ...ได้ไหม
náa·nam ... đâi măi?
bar/pub
บาร์/ผับ   bah/pàp
café
ร้านกาแฟ   ráhn gah·faa
restaurant
ร้านอาหาร   ráhn ah·hăhn

For more detailed information on food and
dining out, see p144.

EMERGENCIES

It's an emergency!
เป็นเหตุฉุกเฉิน
ɓen hèt chùk chĕun!
Could you please help me/us?
ช่วยได้ไหม
chôo·ay đâi măi?
Call the police/a doctor/an ambulance!
ตามตำรวจ/หมอ/รถพยาบาลด้วย
đahm đam·ròo·at/mŏr/rót pá·yah·bahn
dôo·ay!
Where's the police station?
สถานีตำรวจที่ใกล้เคียงอยู่ที่ไหน
sà·tăh·nee đam·ròo·at têe glâi kee·ang yòo
têe năi?

HEALTH

Where's the nearest ...?
...ที่ใกล้เคียงอยู่ที่ไหน
... têe glâi kee·ang yòo têe năi?
chemist
ร้านขายยา   ráhn kăi yah

doctor/dentist

หมอ/หมอฟัน — mŏr/mŏr fan

hospital

โรงพยาบาล — rohng pá·yah·bahn

I need a doctor (who speaks English).

ต้องการหมอ(ที่พูดภาษาอังกฤษได้)
dôrng gahn mŏr (têe pôot pah·săh
ang·grìt dâi)

Could the doctor come here?

หมอมาที่นี่ได้ไหม
mŏr mah têe née dâi măi

I'm sick.

ผม/ดิฉันป่วย
pŏm/dì·chăn ฮ̀òo·ay (m/f)

I have (a) ...

ผม/ดิฉัน...
pŏm (m)/dì·chăn (f) ...

diarrhoea

เป็นโรคท้องร่วง — ฮen rôhk tórng
rôo·ang

fever

เป็นไข้ — ฮen kâi

sore throat

เจ็บคอ — jèp kor

headache

ปวดหัว — ฮòo·at hŏo·a

pain

เจ็บปวด — jèp ฮòo·at

GLOSSARY

baht – Thai currency
BMA – Bangkok Metropolitan Administration
BTS – Bangkok Mass Transit System
CAT – Communications Authority of Thailand
faràng – foreigner of European descent
Isan – isăan; general term for northeastern Thailand, from the Sanskrit name for the medieval kingdom Isana, which encompassed parts of Cambodia and northeastern Thailand.
khlong – khlawng; canal
MRTA – Metropolitan Rapid Transit Authority; agency responsible for the Metro subway.
rai – Thai unit of measurement (area); 1 rai = 1600 sq metres

Ratanakosin – style of architecture present in the late 19th to early 20th century, which combines traditional Thai and European forms; also known as 'old Bangkok'
reua hăang yao – longtail boat
rót fai fáa – BTS Skytrain
rót fai fáa máhăanákhawn – MRTA subway
soi – sawy; lane or small road
TAT – Tourist Authority of Thailand
tha – thâa; pier
THAI – Thai Airways International
thanon – thanŏn (abbreviated 'Th' in this guide); road or street
TOT – Telephone Organisation of Thailand
trok – tràwk; alleyway
wat – Buddhist temple, monastery

BEHIND THE SCENES

The first Lonely Planet guide to Bangkok was published in 1992, researched and written by Joe Cummings. This 8th edition was researched on the ground in the city by two Bangkok residents: Andrew Burke and Austin Bush. David Lukas wrote the Environment section. This guide was commissioned in Lonely Planet's Melbourne office and produced by the following:

Commissioning Editor Holly Alexander

Coordinating Editor Justin Flynn

Coordinating Cartographer Erin McManus

Coordinating Layout Designer Yvonne Bischofberger

Managing Editor Melanie Dankel

Managing Cartographer David Connolly

Managing Layout Designer Celia Wood

Assisting Editors Janice Bird, Kirsten Rawlings, Kim Hutchins, Cathryn Game

Assisting Cartographers Ross Butler, Valentina Kremenchutskaya

Assisting Layout Designer Wibowo Rusli

Cover Designer Pepi Bluck

Language Content Coordinator Quentin Frayne

Project Manager Chris Love

Thanks to Carolyn Boicos, Errol Hunt, Lisa Knights, Julie Sheridan, Tashi Wheeler, Martine Power, Bruce Evans, Chris Girdler, Daniel Corbett

Cover photographs Seller at Damnoen Saduak Floating Market, Bangkok, Bertrand Gardek/Hemis (top & back); Guardians surround the Temple of the Emerald Buddha (Wat Phra Kaew), Bangkok, Richard Nebesky/LPI (bottom).

Internal photographs p7 (#7) Austin Bush; p8 (#3) Andrew Woodley/Alamy. All other photographs by Lonely Planet Images: p92 (portrait), p92 (top left), p93 (portrait), p94 (portrait) Andrew Burke; p7 (#6), p6 (#3), p91 (portrait), p90 (portrait), p91 (top), p93 (top), p95 (bottom), p95 (portrait), p96 (portrait), p96 (bottom) Austin Bush; p7 (#4) Tom Cockrem; p4 (#3) Paolo Cordelli; p4 (#1), p5 (#4), p6 (#1), p90 (top), p93 (middle), p95 (top left), p94 (middle), p94 (top), p96 (middle) Mick Elmore; p3, p2, p90 (bottom) Greg Elms; p4 (#2), p5 (#7), p5 (#6), p5 (#5), p6 (#2), p7 (#5), p8 (#1), p89 , p91 (bottom), p90 (middle), p93 (below), p94 (bottom), p95 (top right), p96 (top) Richard I'Anson; p92 (top right) Margaret Jung; p92 (bottom) Richard Nebesky; p8 (#2), p8 (#4) Bill Wassman

All images are copyright of the photographer unless otherwise indicated. Many of the images in this guide are available for licensing from Lonely Planet Images: www.lonelyplanetimages.com.

THANKS
ANDREW BURKE

I'd like to offer a heartfelt *khàwp khun khráp* to the many people in Bangkok who helped make this book possible. First and foremost, it was great to have my wife Anne around for an entire LP job and get her feminine feedback on things Bangkok. Mason Florence and Stuart McDonald were generous with their tips, and May Nekkham, Whan Kullamas, Gun Aramwit and Tui (enjoy the monastery)

THE LONELY PLANET STORY

Fresh from an epic journey across Europe, Asia and Australia in 1972, Tony and Maureen Wheeler sat at their kitchen table stapling together notes. The first Lonely Planet guidebook, *Across Asia on the Cheap*, was born.

Travellers snapped up the guides. Inspired by their success, the Wheelers began publishing books to Southeast Asia, India and beyond. Demand was prodigious, and the Wheelers expanded the business rapidly to keep up. Over the years, Lonely Planet extended its coverage to every country and into the virtual world via lonelyplanet.com and the Thorn Tree message board.

As Lonely Planet became a globally loved brand, Tony and Maureen received several offers for the company. But it wasn't until 2007 that they found a partner whom they trusted to remain true to the company's principles of travelling widely, treading lightly and giving sustainably. In October of that year, BBC Worldwide acquired a 75% share in the company, pledging to uphold Lonely Planet's commitment to independent travel, trustworthy advice and editorial independence.

Today, Lonely Planet has offices in Melbourne, London and Oakland, with over 500 staff members and 300 authors. Tony and Maureen are still actively involved with Lonely Planet. They're travelling more often than ever, and they're devoting their spare time to charitable projects. And the company is still driven by the philosophy of *Across Asia on the Cheap*: 'All you've got to do is decide to go and the hardest part is over. So go!'

at MeMay Café helped keep me sane during months of writing. Thanks to my co-author Austin Bush and to LPHQ in Melbourne, a big thank you to my wonderfully patient and good-natured commissioning editors Holly Alexander and Errol Hunt, and to the editors and cartographers who worked hard to make this a better book.

AUSTIN BUSH

I'd like to thank the following helpful people: Andrew Burke, Yuthika Charoenrungruang, Mason Florence, Nicholas Grossman, Wesley Hsu, Steven Pettifor, Kong Rithdee, Suthon Sukphisit, Daniel Ten Kate, China Williams and the great editorial crew at LP Melbourne.

OUR READERS

Many thanks to the travellers who used the last edition and wrote to us with helpful hints, useful advice and interesting anecdotes:

Alison Anderson, Peter Antonissen, Marg Barr-Brown, Edwina Barrett, R V Beck, Lynda Beermann, Robert Bound, Leslie Burnett, Rusty Cartmill, Daniel Chernov, Agata Ciabattoni, Linda Clark, Birgitta & Andy Clift, Kay Louise Cook, Francisco Coronado, Heather Dunn, Anna Earles, Bob Eastwood, Bjoern Edenborn, Sam Evans, Kristian Faering, Paul Fichter, Jos Flachs, Yee Ling Foo, Larry Fraser, Kasper Frisch, Lydia Gilson, David Goode, Jackie Hadel, Kelly Hardwick, Danny Harvard, Claudia Hendriks, Michael Hoes, Mary Holliday, George Hooker, Prapanporn Hoono, Mariann Horn, Miki Huntington, John & Diana Hutchison, Mia Louise Knudsen, Sue Kristy, Olga Kroes, Somchai Krungthep, Efsa Kuraner, Mikelson Leong, Justin Lim, Edward M Lippe, Gianluca Lira, Paul Lithander, Sian Lucas, Kim Macdonald, Sarah Mathers, Eytan Mazori, Ian Mcgown, Rolf Michl, Jayashree Mitra, Ed Montgomery, Sjonnie En Nele, Hanne Nielsen, Dax Oliver, Margarita Passion, Sarah Paterson, Thakorn Pinsirigun, Jean-Paul Pourque, Rita Powell, Suma Prakesh, Walter Priess, Rupert Reed, Daniel Rinehart, Karin Robnik, Simon Rose, George Rothschild, Marie-Therese Le Roux, Donald Rowe, Kevin Sands, Agi & Max Schirmer, Marc Schnapp, Birgit Schrama, Heidi Schuster, Lily Seah, Eivind Seiness, Luisa Siccia, Anneke Sips, Phillipa Smyth, Hilary Spann, Tong-Khee Tan, Dider Tangelder, Nouk Tanke, Shana Taylor, Pepijn Thysse, Herbert Tyrell, Steve Walker, Arthur Wickson

SEND US YOUR FEEDBACK

We love to hear from travellers – your comments keep us on our toes and help make our books better. Our well-travelled team reads every word on what you loved or loathed about this book. Although we cannot reply individually to postal submissions, we always guarantee that your feedback goes straight to the appropriate authors, in time for the next edition. Each person who sends us information is thanked in the next edition – and the most useful submissions are rewarded with a free book.

To send us your updates – and find out about Lonely Planet events, newsletters and travel news – visit our award-winning website: www.lonelyplanet.com/contact.

Note: We may edit, reproduce and incorporate your comments in Lonely Planet products such as guidebooks, websites and digital products, so let us know if you don't want your comments reproduced or your name acknowledged. For a copy of our privacy policy visit www.lonelyplanet.com/privacy.

Notes

Notes

Notes

INDEX

See also separate
indexes for:

Drinking & Nighlife	p290
Eating	p290
Entertainment & the Arts	p291
Shopping	p292
Sights	p292
Sleeping	p293
Sports & Activites	p294
Top Picks	p294

A

accommodation 202-22, *see also* Sleeping subindex
  airport 220
  Amphawa 238
  Ayuthaya 230
  Banglamphu 203-7
  Chinatown 207-9
  costs 209
  discounts 210
  Greater Bangkok 220-2
  green hotels 207
  internet resources 202, 208
  Kanchanaburi 245-6
  Khao Yai National Park 249
  Ko Ratanakosin 202-3
  Ko Samet 233-5
  long-term rental 202
  Lumphini 215-16
  Phetburi 241
  Pratunam 209-11
  reservations 216
  Riverside 211-13
  Siam Sq 209-11
  Silom 213-15
  smoking 219
  Thanon Sukhumvit 216-20
  Thewet & Dusit 207
  Thonburi 202-3

000 map pages
000 photographs

activities 196-200, *see also individual activities*, Sports & Activities subindex
AIDS 260
air travel 250-1
  airlines 250-1
  airports 251
  to/from the airport 252
Amarindra Hall 55
Amphawa 226, 236-8
  accommodation 238
  attractions 236-8
  food 238
Amphawa Floating Market 236
amulet market 129-30, **4**
amusement parks 248
Ancient City 224, 248
Animism 44
antiques 129
Ao Cho 231-3
Ao Hin Khok 231, 234
Ao Mae Kuan Im Shrine 237
Ao Nuan 231-3, 234
Ao Phai 231, 234
Ao Phrao 233, 234-5
Ao Phutsa 231, 234
Ao Thap Thim 234
Ao Thian 233, 234
Ao Wong Deuan 233, 234
architecture 37-40
  office towers, hotels & shopping centres 39-40
  preservation 39
  temples, forts & shop-houses 37-40
artisan villages 120
arts 26-37, *see also* Entertainment & the Arts subindex
  cinema 33-6
  dance 36, 188-9
  khŏn 36
  lákhawn 36-7
  lákhawn lék 37
  lákhawn phûut 37
  líkeh 37
  literature 29-33
  modern Thai film 34-6
  sculpture 27

temple murals 28
theatre 36, 188-9
Asanha Bucha 13
Assumption Cathedral 113
At Amphawan Chetiyaram 238
ATMs 263
Ayuthaya 224, 226-30, **228**, **8**
  accommodation 230
  attractions 226-30
  drinking 230
  food 229
  information 229
  transport 227
Ayuthaya Historical Park 226-9
Ayuthaya Historical Study Centre 226

B

Baan Krua 100-1, 120
  walking tour 105
Baipai Thai Cooking School 158
Baiyoke II Tower 104
Ban Kamthieng 116-17, 121
Bang Kwang Prison 123
Bang Pa-In 229
Bangkok International Fashion Week 12
Bangkok International Film Festival 13
Bangkok Jazz Festival 14
Bangkok Pride Week 14
Bangkokian Museum 107, 114
Banglamphu 67-77, **68-9**, **6**
  accommodation 203-7
  attractions 67-77
  food 155-7
  shopping 130-1
  transport 71
  walking tour 75-7, **76**
Bank of Asia 113
bars, *see* Drinking & Nightlife subindex
bathrooms 268
beaches 231-3
beer 174

Benjakiti Park 116, 121
Bhirasri, Silpa 28
Bhumibol, King 21, 22
bicycle travel 198, 265
Blue Elephant Cooking School 158
boat travel 253
boat trips 264-5
  Amphawa 238
  dinner cruises 164
  Ko Samet 231
books 29-33, 212
Boonthawi, Kamphoon 30
Borombhiman Hall 55
Brahmanism 44
Buabusaya, Jitr 28, 29
Buddha images 74
  Amphawa 237
  Ayuthaya 227
  Khao Luang 239
  National Museum 60
  Phetburi 239
  Wat Arun 65
  Wat Benchamabophit 81
  Wat Phet Samut Worawihan 237
  Wat Pho 57, **2**, **5**
  Wat Phra Kaew 58
  Wat Suthat 71
Buddhism 43-4
bus travel 252, 253
business hours 256
  restaurants 153
  shops 128

C

cakes 157
canals 42
car travel 253
Carabao, Aed 32
cell phones 268
Chakkaphat, King 16
Chakri Mahaprasat 57
Chakri, Phaya 16-17
Chantharakasem National Museum 226
Chao Phraya Express Boat Co 253, 264, **95**
Chao Sam Phraya National Museum 226
chemists 263

children, travel with 256
  aquariums 101
  museums 123
  puppet shows 189
  theme parks 248
  zoos 81, 123-4, 248
Children's Discovery
  Museum 123
chillies 144
Chinatown 82-8, 204, **84**, **90**
  accommodation 207-9
  attractions 82-8
  food 158-9
  shopping 131-2
  transport 85
  walking tour 86-8, **87**
Chinese medicine 262
Chinese New Year 12
Chinese people 43, 83
chocolates 157
chopsticks 145
Chulalongkorn University
  103
Chulalongkorn, King 19
Chulanont, Surayud 25
Chung Kai Allied War
  Cemetery 242
Church of Santa Cruz 82
churches, *see* Sights
  subindex
cinema, *see* film
cinemas 190-1, *see*
  also Entertainment & the
  Arts subindex
climate 12, 256
climate change 251
clothing sizes 130, 132
clubs 182-5, *see also* Drinking & Nightlife subindex
Concert in the Park 14
cooking schools 158
costs 14-15
  accommodation 209
  discounts 210, 257-8
  food 153-4, 161
  taxes 266-7
courses
  cooking 158
  language 257
  massage 257
  meditation 257
  muay thai 257
credit cards 263
culture 42-4
  food 144-5
curries 149-50, **91**
customs regulations 257
cycling 198, 265

D

Damnoen Saduak Floating
  Market 235-6
dance 36
  festivals 13
  shrine dancing 190
day trips 224-49, **225**
Death Railway 244
Death Railway Bridge 242
Democracy Monument 73
dentists 262-3
dessert 152-3
Dieselnoi 199
disabilities, travellers
  with 269
discounts 210, 257-8
Don Hoi Lot 237
Don Muang Airport 251
Don Wai Market 236
Dream World 248
drinking 175-86, *see*
  also drinks, Drinking &
  Nightlife subindex
  gay & lesbian venues
  178-80
drinks 174-5, *see*
  also Drinking & Nightlife
  subindex
  beer 174
  fruit drinks 174
  rice whisky 174-5
  whisky 182
driving, *see* car travel
Duangjan, Pumpuang 31
Dusit Hall 57
Dusit Park 80, **5**
Dusit Zoo 81
duty free 257

E

East Sathon 107-15, 215-
  16, **112**
economy 43
electricity 258
Elephant Kraal 229
embassies 258
Emerald Buddha 58
emergency services 258-9
environment 40-2, 251
  green hotels 207
Epicurean Kitchen Thai
  Cooking School 158
Erawan National Park 244
etiquette 145-6
excursions 224-49, **225**
exchange rates, *see inside*
  front cover

F

fashion 12, 46
  clothing sizes 130, 132
FAT Festival 14
Feroci, Corrado 20
festivals 12-15
  beauty pageants 13
  boats 13
  Buddha ceremonies
  12, 13
  Chinese New Year 12
  dance 13
  fashion 12
  film 13, 14
  food 13, 159
  Hindu 13
  kite flying 12
  martial arts 12
  music 13, 14
  Rama V 14
  rice planting 13
  temples 14
  Thai New Year 13
film 33-6
  festivals 13, 14
fitness centres 198
floating markets 226,
  235-6
  Amphawa Floating
  Market 236
  Damnoen Saduak 235-6
  Tha Kha Floating Market
  236
  transport 235
food 144-54, **7**, *see*
  also Eating subindex
  Amphawa 238
  Ayutthaya 229
  Banglamphu 155-7
  cakes 157
  chillies 144
  Chinatown 158-9
  chocolate 157
  cooking schools 158
  costs 153-4, 161
  curries 149-50, **91**
  dessert 152-3
  dinner cruises 164
  etiquette 146-7
  festivals 13, 159
  fruit 151-2
  Greater Bangkok 170-2
  history 144-5
  hotel buffets 169
  Kanchanaburi 245
  kàp klâem 147
  Khao Yai National Park 248

Ko Ratanakosin 154-5
Ko Samet 233
Lumphini 160-5
noodles 148-9
opening hours 153
Phetburi 240-1
Ploenchit 160
Pratunam 160
reservations 154
rice 147
Riverside 160-5
salads 150
sanitation 259
Siam Sq 160
Silom 160-5
sôm-tam 146
soups 151
stir-fries 150-1
street food 171
Thanon Sukhumvit 165-70
Thewet & Dusit 157-8
Thonburi 154-5
tipping 154
vegetarian 13
football 198-9
Forensic Medicine
  Museum 66
fruit 151-2
fruit drinks 174

G

galleries 191-3
gay travellers 259
  drinking 178-80
  festivals 14
gems 129
geography 40
go-go bars 111, 185
Golden Mount 67-70, 75
golf 198
government 44-5
Grand Palace 55, 64
GranMonte 246
Greater Bangkok 123-6,
  124-5
  accommodation 220-2
  attractions 123-6
  food 170-2
  shopping 139-42
gyms 198

H

Haripitak, Fua 28
Haroon Village 114
Hat Chao Samran 226
Hat Sai Kaew 231, 233-4

lonelyplanet.com

health 259-60
heatstroke 260
Hellfire Pass Memorial 244
hiking 246
history 16-25
    2007 elections 25
    bloodless coup 25
    building Bangkok 18
    Chakri dynasty 16-17
    European influence
        19-21
    life under Thaksin 22-5
    recent past 21-5
    settlement 16
    struggle for democarcy
        21
    WWII 20
HIV 260
holidays 260, see also
    festivals
Holy Rosary Church 86
hospitals 262
hotels, see Sleeping
    subindex
Hualamphong Railway
    Station 83

I
International Festival of
    Music & Dance 13
internet access 260-1
internet resources 15
    accommodation 202, 208
itineraries 50-1

J
Janehuttakarnkit, Sriwan
    29
jazz music 14
JEATH War Museum 243
Jim Thompson's House
    97-100, 4, 92
jogging 198

K
Kaeng Krachan National
    Park 224, 241
kàhtoey caberet 190
Kanchanaburi 224, 242-6,
    243, 8
    accommodation 245-6
    attractions 242-5
    drinking 245
    food 245

000 map pages
000 photographs

information 244
    transport 242
Kanchanaburi Allied War
    Cemetery 242
kàp klâem 147
Kensaku, Turee 29
Khao Bandai-It 239
Khao Luang 239
Khao Phansa 13
Khao San Road 72, 204, 3
Khao Wang 239
Khao Yai National Park 224,
    246-9, 247
    accommodation 249
    food 248
    information 248
    transport 246
Khietkong, Chamras 28
khlong boats 253
Khlong Prem Prison 123
khôn 36
Kiatbusaba, Parinya 199
King Buddhalertla Naphalai
    Memorial Park 238
King Chulalongkorn Day 14
King Prajadhipok Museum
    73-4, 75
kites 12
Ko Kret 230
Ko Ratanakosin 17, 54-63,
    204, 56
    accommodation 202-3
    attractions 54-63
    food 154-5
    shopping 128-30
    transport 55
    walking tour 63-4, 63
Ko Samet 226, 230-5, 232
    accommodation 233-5
    attractions 230-2
    drinking 233
    food 233
    informartion 233
    transport 231
Kosayothin, Apirak 45
Kukrit Pramoj House 113

L
ladyboys 190
Lak Meuang 58-9, 64
lákhawn 36-7
lákhawn lék 37
lákhawn phûut 37
language 272-6
    courses 257
left luggage 251
legal matters 261

lesbian travellers 259
    drinking 178-80
    festivals 14
líkeh 37
Lingam Shrine 101-2
literature 29-33, 212
Loi Krathong 14, 8
Lumphini 106-15, 204, 112
    accommodation 215-16
    attractions 106-15
    food 160-5
    shopping 136-8
    transport 107
Lumphini Park 106-7, 5
lûuk khrêung 34

M
Mae Thorani statue 61
magazines 264
Mahachai 237
Mahachai Rail Line 224,
    236-8
Mahakan Fort 70-1
Makha Bucha 12
maps 261-2
markets 226, see also
    Shopping subindex
martial arts 199
    courses 257
    festivals 12
massage 196-8
    courses 257
massage parlours 197
May Kaidee's Vegetarian
    Thai Cooking School 158
medical services 262-3
meditation 257
metric conversions, see
    inside front cover
Metro 254
Miss Jumbo Queen Contest
    13
mobile phones 268
money 263-4
    costs 14-15, 153-4,
        161, 209
    refunds 267
    tipping 154, 264
Monk's Bowl Village 71,
    75, 120
Moolpramook, Piman 28
muay thai 199-200, 90
    courses 257
murals 28
music 31-3
    alternative 33
    classical Thai 31

festivals 13, 14
jazz 14
Thai pop & rock 31-3

N
Na Dan Pier 231
Nam Tok Haew Narok 246
Nam Tok Haew Suwat 246
Nandakhwang, Tawee 28
National Gallery 60
National Museum 60
national parks
    Erawan National Park
        244
    Kaeng Krachan National
        Park 224, 241
    Khao Yai National Park
        224, 246-9
    Sai Yok National Park 244
Navaratree Hindu Festival 13
newspapers 45, 264
nightclubs 182-5
Niphon 238
Nong Pak Chee observation
    tower 246
noodles 148-9

O
October 14 Memorial 73
Old Customs House 107,
    114
opening hours, see business
    hours
Ophakun, Yuengyong 32
organised tours 264-5
Oriental Hotel Thai Cooking
    School 158
Osathanugrah, Surat 193

P
parks & gardens, see Sights
    subindex
Patpong 111
PB Valley Khao Yai Winery
    246
Pestonji, Ratana 33
Phahurat 83, 86
Phamai Baan Krua 105
pharmacies 263
Phayathai Palace 104
Phetburi 224, 226, 238-41,
    240
    accommodation 241-2
    attractions 239-40
    food 240-1
    information 239-40
    transport 239

Phetchaburi, *see* Phetburi
Phetphaiboon Plaza 240
Phleungtham, Utansa 30
Phra Nakhon Khiri 239
Phra Nakhon Si Ayuthaya
  World Heritage Fair 14
Phra Sumen Fort 74
Phumisak, Jit 28
pilates 198
planning 12, 48, 50-1
  costs 14-15
  discount cards 257-8
Ploenchit 97-103, 204, **98-9**
  attractions 97-103
  food 160
  shopping 132-6
  transport 101
politics 44-5
pollution 40-1, 259-60, **94**
polygamy 18
Pom Phet 227
postal services 265
Prajadhipok, King 73-4
Pramoj, Kukrit 30
Pratunam 97-103, 204, **98-9**
  accommodation 209-11
  attractions 97-103
  food 160
  shopping 132-6
  transport 101
prostitution 111
public holidays 260, *see
  also* festivals

Q
Queen Saovabha Memorial
  Institute (Snake Farm)
  107-10

R
radio 265
Rama V 19-46
  festivals 14
Rama IX Royal Park 123
Ratanakosin Island, *see* Ko
  Ratanakosin
Ratchaprasong Intersection
  Shrines 102-3
Ratchathewi 103-5
red-light districts 185
  Patpong 111
  Soi Cowboy 121-2
refunds 267
religion
  Animism 44
  Brahmanism 44
  Buddhism 43-4

restaurants, *see* Eating
  subindex
rice 147
rice whisky 174-5
Rimsakul, Porntaweesak 29
River City 114-15
river ferries 253
Riverside 106-15, 204,
  108-9
  accommodation 211-13
  attractions 106-15
  food 160-5
  shopping 136-8
  transport 107
  walking tour 113-15,
    114
rock carvings 59
Rommaninat Park 76
Royal Barges National
  Museum 65-6
Royal Ploughing Ceremony
  13
rubbish 41

S
Saetang, Chang 28
Safari World 123-4
safety 62, 265-6
Sai Yok National Park 244
salads 150
Sampeng Lane 86, 87
Samphran Elephant Ground
  & Zoo 248
Samut Prakan Crocodile
  Farm & Zoo 248
Samut Songkhram 237
Sanam Luang 60-1, **89**
Santichaiprakan Park 74
Sao Ching-Cha 72-3
Saranrom Royal Garden
  61, 77
scams 55, 62, 265-6
sculpture 27
seum 104
sewage 41
sex trade 111, 185
shopping 128-42, *see
  also* Shopping subindex
  antiques 129
  Banglamphu 130-1
  Chinatown 131-2
  clothing sizes 130, 132
  duty free 140
  gems 129
  Greater Bangkok 139-42
  Ko Ratanakosin 128-30
  Lumphini 136-8

Ploenchit 132-6
Pratunam 132-6
Riverside 136-8
  shopping streets 86
Siam Sq 132-6
Silom 136-41
  tailors 129
  tax refunds 129
Thanon Sukhumvit 138
Thonburi 128-30
  window shopping 137
shrine dancing 190
shrines, *see* Sights
  subindex
Siam Ocean World 101
Siam Park City 248
Siam Sq 97-103, 204, **98-9**
  accommodation 209-11
  attractions 97-105
  food 160
  shopping 132-6
  transport 101
silk 100, **92**
silk trade 102
Silom 106-15, 204, **108-9**
  accommodation 213-15
  attractions 106-15
  food 160-5
  shopping 136-8
  transport 107
Silom Thai Cooking School
  158
Silpakorn University 61-2,
  63, **95**
Sitthiket, Vasan 29
Skytrain 252, 254, **94**
smoking 146, 219
soccer 198-9
Soi 16 86
Soi Cowboy 121-2
Soi Ma Toom 120
sôm-tam 146
Somtow, SP 30
Songkhram, Phibul 20
Songkran Festival 13, **8**
Songmangmee, Sweang 28
soup 151
spas 196-8
sports 196-200, *see also individual sports*, Sports &
  Activities subindex
Sri Mariamman Temple
  111-12
Srimuang, Chamlong 44-5
Sriwanichpoom, Manit
  29, 193
stir-fries 150-1

strip clubs 111, 185
Suvarnabhumi
  International Airport
  27, 251

T
table manners 145-6
tailors 129
tàkrâw 200
Taksin, Phaya 16
Talat Leng-Buai-la 88
Talat Noi 83, 88
Tantisuk, Sawasdi 28
tax refunds 129
taxes 266-7
taxis 254-5, **90**
telephone services 267-8
temples, *see* Sights
  subindex
    temple etiquette 59
    temple murals 71-2
Tha Kha Floating Market
  236
Thai boxing 199-200, **90**
  courses 257
Thailand Creative & Design
  Center 117
Thailand International
  Swan Boat Races 13
Thailand-Burma Railway
  Centre 242
Thaksin, Shinawatra 22-5
Thammasat University 62
Thanon Charoen Krung 86
Thanon Khao San 72, 204, **3**
Thanon Maharat 59-60
Thanon Mittraphan 86
Thanon Plaeng Naam 88
Thanon Santiphap 86
Thanon Sukhumvit 116-22,
  204, **118-19**
  accommodation 216-20
  attractions 116-22
  food 165-70
  shopping 138
  transport 117
  walking tour 117-22,
    121
Thanon Yaowarat 86, 88
theatre 36
theme parks 248
Thewet & Dusit 78-81,
  204, **79**
  accommodation 207
  attractions 78-81
  food 157-8
  transport 80

Thompson, Jim 97-101, 102
Thonburi 64-6, 204, **56**
  accommodation 202-3
  attractions 64-6
  food 154-5
  shopping 128-30
  transport 65
time 268
tipping 154, 264
Tiravanija, Rirkrit 193
toilets 268
tourist information 268-9
tours 264-5
train travel 254
  Death Railway 244
  Mahachai Rail Line 224,
    236-8
trekking 246
Trimurthi Shrine 103
Trok Huae Med 86-7
túk-túks 255
TV 45

U
universities
  Chulalongkorn 103
  Silpakorn 61-3, **192**
  Thammasat University 62

V
Vegetarian Festival 13-14
Victory Monument 103-4
Visakha Bucha 13
visas 269-70
volunteering 270, *see
  also* work

W
walking 246
walking tours
  Baan Krua 105
  Banglamphu 75-8, **76**
  Chinatown 86-8, **87**
  Ko Ratanakosin 63-4,
    63
  Riverside 113-15, **114**
  Thanon Sukhumvit 117-
    22, **121**
Wang Suan Phakkat 104
Wat Arun 65, **4**
Wat Benchamabophit 81
Wat Bowonniwet 74-5
Wat Chai Wattanaram 227
Wat Chi Prasoet 239

Wat Ko Kaew Sutharam
  239
Wat Lokayasutharam 227
Wat Mahathat 62-3, 239
Wat Mangkon Kamalawat
  83-4, 88
Wat Na Phra Mehn 229
Wat Pa Luangta Bua
  Yannasampanno 244
Wat Phai Lom 239
Wat Phanan Choeng 227
Wat Phet Samut
  Worawihan 237
Wat Pho 57-8, 59, 64,
  2, 5
Wat Phra Kaew 55-7,
  64, **95**
Wat Phra Mahathat 227
Wat Phra Mongkhon
  Bophit 227
Wat Phra Si Sanphet 227
Wat Ratburana 227
Wat Ratchanatda 75
Wat Saket 67-70
Wat Saket Fair 14
Wat Satthatham 237
Wat Sutha 76
Wat Suthat 71-2
Wat Suwandaram 227
Wat Thammikarat 227
Wat Traimit 85
Wat Yai Chai Mongkhon
  227-9
Wat Yai Chom Prasat 237
Wat Yai Suwannaram 239
water quality 41, 259
weather, *see* climate
whisky 182
wi-fi 261
women travellers 270-1
Wong Wian Yai 236
work 271, *see also*
  volunteering
World Film Festival 14
World Gourmet Festival 13
World Thai Martial Arts
  Festival 12
WWII 20
WWII Museum 242

Y
Yipintsoi, Misiem 28
yoga 198
Yongchaiyudh, Chavalit 22

Z
zoos 81, 123-4, 248

**DRINKING &
NIGHTLIFE**
**BAR/
RESTAURANTS**
Balcony 179
Black Swan 175
Bull's Head & Angus
  Steakhouse 175
Coyote on Convent 176
Jool's Bar & Restaurant
  176
Nest 177
Telephone 179
Tuba 178
Zup Zip 179

BARS
Ad Here the 13th 180
Ad Makers 181
Bamboo Bar 181
Barbican Bar 175
Brick Bar 181
Bua Sa-ad 176
Buddy Bar 176
Café Trio 175, **93**
Chang House 230
Cheap Charlie's 175, **96**
Cosmic Café 176
deep 176
DJ Station 179
Hippie de Bar 176
Icy 179
Kluen Saek 179
Lava Club 176
Living Room 181, **93**
Molly Bar 176
Moon Bar at Vertigo
  177, **7**
Parking Toys 181
Phranakorn Bar 177
Rain Dogs Bar & Gallery
  177
Resort 245
Roof Bar 176
Sa-ke Coffee Pub 179
Ship Inn 177
Silk Bar 176
Silver Sand Bar 233
Sirocco 177
Taksura 177
Three Sixty 182
Tok Bar 233
Tokyo Joe's 182
To-Sit 178
Water Bar 178
Wong's Place 178

CLUBS
70's Bar 183
808 Club 183
Bed Supperclub 183, **93**
Café Democ 183
Club Culture 183
Dance Fever 183
G.O.D. (Guys on Display)
  179-80
Glow 183
Lesla 180
Lucifer 183
Nang Len 183-4
Narcissus 184
Q Bar 184
Santika 184
Shela 180
Slim/Flix 184
Superfly 184
Tapas Room 184-5
Twisted Republic 185
Zeta 180

PUBS
Beer Barrel 245
Brown Sugar 181
Gazebo 181
Ick Pub 179
Molly Malone's 176
Nang Nual Riverside Pub
  177
Noriega's 181
Saxophone Pub &
  Restaurant 181, **94**
Shamrock Irish Pub 176
Susie Pub 176
Tawan Daeng German
  Brewhouse 182
Winks 182
Witch's Tavern 182

SAUNA BARS
Babylon Bangkok 180
Chakran 180

WINE BARS
Bacchus Wine Bar 175
Opera Riserva Winetheque
  177

EATING
AMERICAN
Bourbon St Bar &
  Restaurant 167
Great American Rib
  Company 166

INDEX

000 map pages
000 photographs

BRITISH
Oh My Cod! 155

CHINESE
Chiang Kii 159
Crystal Jade La Mian Xiao
Long Bao 160
Foo Mui Kee 163
Hong Kong Noodles 159
Hua Seng Hong 159
Je Ngor 168
Ngwan Lee Lang
Suan 164
Ran Nam Tao Hu Yong
Her 164
Rosdee 170-1
Shangarila Restaurant 158
Soi 38 Night Market 169
Tang Jai Yuu 158-9
Thai Charoen 159

DINNER CRUISES
Asia Voyages 264
Manohra Cruises 264-5

EGYPTIAN
Nasser Elmassy Restaurant
167

FOOD COURTS
Emporium Food Hall 166
Food Loft 166
MBK Food Court 166
Park Food Hall 166

FRENCH
Crêpes & Co 166
D'Sens 161
Le Banyan 165
Le Bouchon 162
Le Normandie 161

GERMAN
Bei Otto 165

INDIAN
Indian Hut 162
Royal India 159

INDONESIAN
Bali 168

INTERNATIONAL
Baan Muang Petch 241
Baywatch Bar 233
Bed Supperclub 165, **93**

Cy'an & Glow 161
Deck 154
Eat Me Restaurant 161-2
Golden Cup 245
Greyhound Café 167
Kuppa 165
La Villa 170
Naga Bungalows 233
Panorama Restaurant 233
Spring 167, **6**
Tapas Café 168

ISRAELI
Shoshana 155

ITALIAN
Air Plane 160
Café Primavera 155
Calderazzo 160
Gianni Ristorante 160
La Piola 165
No 43 160
Paesano 160
Pan Pan 160
Scooz 162

JAPANESE
Imoya 169
Mizu's Kitchen 162
Ramentei 168

SEAFOOD
Tarua Restaurant 238

SINGAPOREAN
Boon Tong Kiat Singapore
Hainanese Chicken
Rice 168

THAI
Amphawa Floating Market
238
Ana's Garden 167
Apple Guest House 245
Baan Klang Nam 1 170
Bamboo Restaurant 233
Ban Chiang 162
Ban Wacharachai 229
Blue Elephant 161
Cabbages & Condoms
167-8
Chote Chitr 155-6
Circle of Friends 163
Face 166, **7**
Harmonique 163
Hemlock 155

Hua Raw Night Market &
Chao Phrom Day Market
229
In Love 157
Jay Fai 155
Jay So 163
Jay Tiw 245
Jep's 233
Kai Thawt Jay Kii 163
Kaiyang Boran 156
Kalapapreuk on First 167
Kaloang Home Kitchen
157-8
Khaao Chae Naang Ram 241
Khrua Aroy Aroy 163
Khrua Chom Ao 238
Khrua Khao Yai 248
Kim Leng 156-7
Kok Kaat 245
Krua Noppharat 156
Kuaytiaw Reua Tha Siam
160
Lung Lek 229
Mondee 241
Nang Loeng Market 170
Old Siam Plaza 159
Or Tor Kor Market 171,
91
Paa Lek 229
Pan 156
Phae Krung Kao 229
Phen Phrik Phet 241
Phetphaiboon Plaza 240
Phu Yai Thawngyib 238
Rachanawi Samosawn
155
River Bar Café 170
Rub Aroon 154
Ruen Mallika 166
Sanguan Sri 160
Soi Pradit Market 164-5
Somboon Seafood 162
Suan Lum Night Bazaar 165
Thip Samai 156
Thonglee 169
Victory Point 171
Wang Lang Market 154-5
Yuy Lee 170

THAI/MUSLIM
Home Cuisine Islamic
Restaurant 163
Muslim Restaurant 164
Naaz 164
Narknava 248
Roti-Mataba 156
Yusup 171

VEGETARIAN
Arroi 157
Baan Suan Pai 171
Chennai Kitchen 162-3
Komala's 168
Mashoor 163
May Kaidee 157
Ranee's Guesthouse 156
Tamarind Café 167
Vegetarian Food Centre
171-2

WESTERN
Baan Phra Arthit 156

ENTERTAINMENT &
THE ARTS
CINEMAS
Alliance Française Bangkok
190
EGV 190
Goethe Institut 190
House 190
Lido Multiplex 190
Major Cineplex 190
Paragon Cineplex 190-1
Scala Multiplex 191
SF Cinema City 191
SFV 191

CULTURAL
CENTRES
Alliance Française Bangkok
189
Goethe Institut 189
Japan Foundation 189
Neilson Hays Library
Rotunda Gallery 189
Thailand Cultural Centre 189

DINNER
THEATRE
Sala Rim Nam 189
Silom Village 189-90
Studio 9 190
Supatra River House 190

GALLERIES
100 Tonson Gallery 191
About Café/About Studio
191
Bangkok Art & Culture
Centre 191
Bangkok University Art
Gallery 191

lonelyplanet.com

INDEX

Eat Me Restaurant 191
Foreign Correspondents'
    Club of Thailand 191-2
Gallery F-stop 192
Gallery Ver 192
H Gallery 192
Jim Thompson Art Center
    192
Kathmandu Photo Gallery
    192
National Gallery 192
Numthong Gallery 192
Queen's Gallery 192
Silpakorn University
    192-3, **95**
Surapon Gallery 193
Tadu Contemporary Art 193
Tang Gallery 193
Teo+Namfah Gallery 193
Thavibu Gallery 193
Whitespace 193

KÀHTOEY CABERET
Calypso Cabaret 190
Mambo Cabaret 190

THEATRE
Bangkok Playhouse 188
National Theatre 188
Patravadi Theatre 188
Sala Chalermkrung 188-9
Siam Niramit 189
Traditional Thai Puppet
    Theatre 189

SHOPPING
ANTIQUES
Ámantee 139
House of Chao 136
L'Arcadia 138

BOOKS
Asia Books 139
B2S 139
Bookazine 139
Orchid Press 136

CAMERAS
Niks/Nava Import Export
    136
Sunny Camera 136

000 map pages
000 photographs

CLOTHING
It's Happened To Be a
    Closet 130
Marco Tailors 136

DUTY FREE
King Power 140

ELECTRICAL GOODS
Chiang Heng 136-7
Pantip Plaza 132

FOOD
Nittaya Curry Shop 130

GEMS & JEWELLERY
Johnny's Gems 131
Uthai's Gems 132

HANDICRAFTS
Charoen Chaikarnchang
    Shop 131
Nandakwang 138
Narayana Phand 135-6
Taekee Taekon 130
Tamnan Mingmuang 136
Thai Home Industries 136
Thai Nakorn 130

HEALTH SUPPLIES
Traditional Medicine Shops
    128

MALLS
Baan Silom 137
Central Chidlom 133
Central World Plaza 133
Emporium Sjhopping
    Centre 138-9
Erawan Bangkok 133
Gaysorn Plaza 133-4
Mahboonkrong (MBK) 134
Promenade Arcade 134-5
River City 137
Siam Center 135
Siam Paragon 135
Siam Sq 135
Silom Galleria 138

MARKETS
amulet market 129-30, **4**
Amphawa Floating Market
    236

Bangrak Market 113
Chatuchak Weekend
    Market 140-1, **5**
Damnoen Saduak Floating
    Market 235-6
Don Wai Market 236
Khlong Toey Market 121
Pak Khlong Market 77,
    132
Patpong Night Market 137
Phahurat market 131
Phetphaiboon Plaza 240
Pratunam Market 133
Sampeng Lane 131-2
Saphan Phut Night Bazaar
    132
Suan Lum Night Bazaar
    137
Soi Lalai Sap 137
Tha Kha Floating Market
    236
Thanon Khao San market
    130-1
Thanon Sukhumvit Market
    138
Vespa Market 141-2

THAI SILK
Jim Thompson 138

SIGHTS
BUILDINGS & STRUCTURES
Abhisek Dusit Throne
    Hall 80
Amarindra Hall 55
Baiyoke II Tower 104
Bang Kwang & Khlong
    Prem Prisons 123
Bank of Asia 113
Borombhiman Hall 55
Chakri Mahaprasat 57
Democracy Monument 73
Dusit Hall 57
Golden Mount 67-70, 75
Grand Palace 55, 64
Hualamphong Railway
    Station 83
Jim Thompson's House
    97-100, **4**, **92**
Lak Meuang 58-9, 64
October 14 Memorial 73
Old Customs House 107,
    114
Sao Ching-Cha 72, 75
Victory Monument 103-4

CAVES
Khao Bandai-It 239
Khao Luang 239

CEMETERIES
Chung Kai Allied War
    Cemetery 242-3
Kanchanaburi Allied War
    Cemetery 242

CHURCHES
Assumption Cathedral 113
Church of Santa Cruz 82
Holy Rosary Church 38, 86
Phutthaisawan (Buddhai-
    sawan) Chapel 60

FORTS
Mahakan Fort 70-1
Phra Sumen Fort 38, 74

GALLERIES
National Gallery 60
Silpakorn University Art
    Gallery 62, **95**
Thailand Creative & Design
    Center 117

MANSIONS
Kukrit Pramoj House 113
Phayathai Palace 104
Phra Nakhon Khiri 239
Vimanmek Teak Mansion
    38, 80

MUSEUMS
Ancient Cloth Museum
    81
Ban Kamthieng 116-17
Bangkok Doll Factory &
    Museum 104
Bangkokian Museum
    107, 114
Chantharakasem National
    Museum 226
Chao Sam Phraya National
    Museum 226
Children's Discovery
    Museum 123
Corrections Museum 76
Forensic Medicine Museum
    66
JEATH War Museum 243
King Prajadhipok Museum
    73-4, 75
National Museum 60

Royal Barges National
    Museum 65-6
Royal Elephant Museum 81
Thailand-Burma Railway
    Centre 242
Wang Suan Phakkat 104
WWII Museum 242

PARKS & GARDENS
Benjakiti Park 116, 121
Dusit Park 80, **5**
King Buddhalertla Naphalai
    Memorial Park 238
Lumphini Park 106-7, **5**
Rama IX Royal Park 123
Rommaninat Park 76
Sanam Luang 60-1,
    63-4, **89**
Santichaiprakan Park 74
Saranrom Royal Garden
    61, 77

STREETS & THOROUGH-FARES
Thanon Maharat 59-60
Thanon Plaeng Naam 88
Thanon Sumhumvit 116-22
Thanon Yaowarat 88

TEMPLES & SHRINES
Ao Mae Kuan Im Shrine
    237
Erawan Shrine 26, 102
Lingam Shrine 101
Phra Thii Nang
    Phutthaisawan 28
Ratchaprasong Intersection
    Shrines 102-3
Sri Gurusingh Sabha 83
Sri Mariamman Temple
    111-13
Trimurthi Shrine 103
Wat Amphawan
    Chetiyaram 238
Wat Arun 65, **4**
Wat Benchamabophit 81
Wat Bowonniwet 28, 74-5
Wat Chai Wattanaram 227
Wat Chi Prasoet 239
Wat Chong Nonsi 28
Wat Ko Kaew Sutharam
    239
Wat Lokayasutharam 227
Wat Mahathat 63, 239

Wat Mangkon Kamalawat
    83-5, 88
Wat Na Phra Mehn 229
Wat Pa Luangta Bua
    Yannasampanno 244
Wat Phai Lom 239
Wat Phanan Choeng 227
Wat Phet Samut Woraw-
    ihan 237
Wat Pho 57-8, 59, 64,
    2, 5
Wat Phra Kaew 38, 55-7,
    64, **95**
Wat Phra Mahathat 227
Wat Phra Mongkhon
    Bophit 227
Wat Phra Si Sanphet 227
Wat Ratburana 227
Wat Ratchanatda 75
Wat Saket 67-70
Wat Satthatham 237
Wat Suthat 28, 71-2, 76
Wat Suwandaram 28,
    227
Wat Tham Khao Pun 244
Wat Thammikarat 227
Wat Traimit 85
Wat Tritosathep Maha-
    worawihan 28
Wat Yai Chai Mongkhon
    227-9
Wat Yai Chom Prasat 237

THEME PARKS
Ancient City 248
Dream World 248
Siam Park City 248

UNIVERSITIES
Chulalongkorn University
    103
Silpakorn University 61-3,
    192
Thammasat University 62

ZOOS & AQUARIUMS
Dusit Zoo 81
Queen Saovabha Memorial
    Institute (Snake Farm)
    107-10
Safari World 123-6
Samphran Elephant Ground
    & Zoo 248
Samut Prakan Crocodile
    Farm & Zoo 248
Siam Ocean World 101

SLEEPING

APARTMENTS
House by the Pond 202
Siri Sathorn 202

BOUTIQUE HOTELS
Bangkok Boutique Hotel
    219
Davis 217
Dream 218
Eugenia 217-18
Ibrik Resort 203
Ma Du Zi 217
PhraNakorn Nornlen 207
S15 218
Shanghai Inn 208
Sheraton Grande Sukhum-
    vit 217
Siam@Siam 210

BUDGET HOTELS
Krung Kasem Srikung
    Hotel 208
Malaysia Hotel 215
Reorn Pae Amphawa 238
Rikka Inn 205
Roof View Place 206

BUNGALOWS
Ao Nuan Bungalows 234
Baan Ku Pu 238
Jep's Bungalows 234
Lima Coco 235
Lung Dam 234
Malibu Garden Resort 234
Palm Garden Lodge 249
Sai Kaew Beach Resort
    233-4
Samed Sand Sea 234
Samed Villa 234
Silver Sand 234
Tok 234
Tubtim Resort 234
Vongdeuan Resort 234

GUESTHOUSES
A-One Inn 211
Artists Place 213
Baan Dvara Prateep 230
Baan Hualampong 209
Baan Lotus Guest House
    230
Banchomkao 241
Bangkok Christian Guest
    House 216
Bannkunpra 230

Blue Star Guest House 246
Boworn BB 206
Chantana House 230
Lamphu House 206
New Road Guesthouse 213
Penguin House 216
Ploy Guesthouse 245
Pong Phen Guesthouse
    245-6
Prakorp's House 206
Prasuri Guest House 206
Rabieng Rimnum Guest
    House 241
River View Guest House
    208-9
Sala Thai Daily Mansion
    216
Shambara 205-6
Sugar Cane Guest House
    246
Thai House 221
Tony's Place 230
Villa Guest House 206

HOSTELS
Bangkok International
    Youth Hostel 207
HI Sukhumvit 220
Lub*D 214
Shanti Lodge 207
Sri Ayuttaya Guest House
    207
Train Inn 209
Urban Age 214

HOTELS
All Seasons 215
Amari Airport Hotel 220
Arun Residence 203
Asia Hotel 210-11
Atlanta 219
Aurum: The River Place 203
Baan Thai Sang Thian
    Samed 234
Bangkok Centre Sukhumvit
    25 220
Bangkok Marriott Resort &
    Spa 220-1
Buddy Lodge 205
Chakrabongse Villas 203
Citichic 218
Erawan House 205
Federal Hotel 219
Grand China Princess 208
Grand Inn Come Hotel 220
Grand Mercure Park Avenue
    219

INDEX

Jungle House 249
La Résidence Hotel 214
Lamphu Treehouse 205
Le Fenix 218
Le Vimarn Cottages 235
Majestic Suites 219
Miami 217
Napa Place Bed &
 Breakfast 219
New Siam Riverside 205
Niagara Hotel 214-15
Novotel Suvarnabhumi
 Airport Hote 220
Old Bangkok Inn 204
P&R Residence 213
Pathumwan House 211
Rama Gardens Hotel 220
Refill Now! 221
Reflections Rooms 221
Reno Hotel 211
River View Place Hotel 230
Rose Hotel 214
Royal Diamond 241
Royal Hotel 206-7
Saikaew Villa 234
Seven 218
Suan Luang Hotel 230
Suk 11 219-20
Sun Hotel 241
Swiss Park Hotel 216-17
Triple Two Silom 214
Viengtai Hotel 205

VIP Guest House/Golden
 House 211
Wendy House 211
We-Train International
 House 220

LUXURY HOTELS
Banyan Tree Hotel 215
Dusit Thani 213
Four Seasons Hotel
 209-10
Grand Hyatt Erawan 210
Grand Millennium
 Sukhumvit 217
Metropolitan 215
Millennium Hilton 212-13
Nai Lert Park Hotel 210
Oriental Hotel 212
Peninsula Hotel 212
Shangri-La Hotel 212
Sofitel Silom Bangkok 214
Sukhothai Hotel 215

RESORTS
Ao Prao Resort 234-5
Baan Amphawa Resort &
 Spa 238
Baan Tai Had Resort 238
Kasem Island Resort 245
Kirimaya 249
Paradee Resort & Spa
 234

Park Lodging 249
Royal River Kwai Resort &
 Spa 245
Samet Ville Resort 234
Sap Tai Cabbages &
 Condoms Resort 249
Village Farm 249

**SPORTS &
ACTIVIITES**
CYCLING
ABC Amazing Bangkok
 Cyclist Tou 265
Grasshopper Adventures
 265
Velo Thailand 265

MASSAGE
Buathip Thai Massage
 196
Rasayana Retreat 197
Ruen-Nuad Massage &
 Yoga 197
Skills Development Center
 for the Blind 197
Wat Pho Thai Traditional
 Massage school
 197-8

PILATES
Pilates Studio 198

SPAS
Banyan Tree Spa 196
Nakornthon Thai Medical
 Spa 196
Oriental Spa 196-7

TÀKRÂW
Lumphini Stadium 200, **7**
National Stadium 200

THAI BOXING
Lumphini Stadium 199, **7**
Ratchadamnoen Stadium
 199

YOGA
Absolute Yoga 198
Yoga Elements Studio 198

TOP PICKS
architecture 40
art 28
books 29
film 35
food 147, 162, 167, 170
for children 61
free Bangkok 103
music 33
shopping 134
sleeping 203
views 155, 213

000 map pages
000 photographs

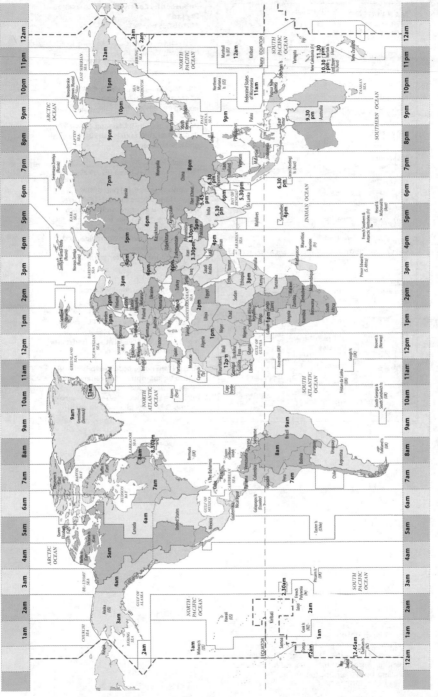

295

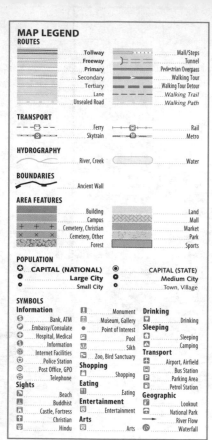

MAP LEGEND
ROUTES

	Tollway		Mall/Steps
	Freeway		Tunnel
	Primary		Pedestrian Overpass
	Secondary		Walking Tour
	Tertiary		Walking Tour Detour
	Lane		Walking Trail
	Unsealed Road		Walking Path

TRANSPORT

	Ferry		Rail
	Skytrain		Metro

HYDROGRAPHY

	River, Creek		Water

BOUNDARIES

	Ancient Wall

AREA FEATURES

	Building		Land
	Campus		Mall
	Cemetery, Christian		Market
	Cemetery, Other		Park
	Forest		Sports

POPULATION

	CAPITAL (NATIONAL)		CAPITAL (STATE)
	Large City		Medium City
	Small City		Town, Village

SYMBOLS

Information
- Bank, ATM
- Embassy/Consulate
- Hospital, Medical
- Information
- Internet Facilities
- Police Station
- Post Office, GPO
- Telephone

Sights
- Beach
- Buddhist
- Castle, Fortress
- Christian
- Hindu

- Monument
- Museum, Gallery
- Point of Interest
- Pool
- Sikh
- Zoo, Bird Sanctuary

Shopping
- Shopping

Eating
- Eating

Entertainment
- Entertainment

Arts
- Arts

Drinking
- Drinking

Sleeping
- Sleeping
- Camping

Transport
- Airport, Airfield
- Bus Station
- Parking Area
- Petrol Station

Geographic
- Lookout
- National Park
- River Flow
- Waterfall

Published by Lonely Planet Publications Pty Ltd
ABN 36 005 607 983

Australia Head Office, Locked Bag 1, Footscray, Victoria 3011,
☎ 03 8379 8000, fax 03 8379 8111, talk2us@lonelyplanet.com.au

USA 150 Linden St, Oakland, CA 94607,
☎ 510 250 6400, toll free 800 275 8555, fax 510 893 8572, info@lonelyplanet.com

UK 2nd fl, 186 City Rd, London, EC1V 2NT,
☎ 020 7106 2100, fax 020 7106 2101, go@lonelyplanet.co.uk

© Lonely Planet 2008
Photographs © as listed (p277) 2008

All rights reserved. No part of this publication may be copied, stored in a retrieval system, or transmitted in any form by any means, electronic, mechanical, recording or otherwise, except brief extracts for the purpose of review, and no part of this publication may be sold or hired, without the written permission of the publisher.

Printed by Hang Tai Printing Company.
Printed in China.

Lonely Planet and the Lonely Planet logo are trademarks of Lonely Planet and are registered in the US Patent and Trademark Office and in other countries.

Lonely Planet does not allow its name or logo to be appropriated by commercial establishments, such as retailers, restaurants or hotels. Please let us know of any misuses: www.lonelyplanet.com/ip.

Although the authors and Lonely Planet have taken all reasonable care in preparing this book, we make no warranty about the accuracy or completeness of its content and, to the maximum extent permitted, disclaim all liability arising from its use.